FAMILY BUSINESS

THIRD EDITION

Ernesto J. Poza
Thunderbird: The Garvin School of International Management

SOUTH-WESTERN
CENGAGE Learning™

Australia • Brazil • Japan • Korea • Mexico • Singapore • Spain • United Kingdom • United States

SOUTH-WESTERN
CENGAGE Learning

Family Business, Third Edition
Ernesto J. Poza

VP/Editorial Director: Jack W. Calhoun

Executive Editor: Melissa Acuna

Developmental Editor: Jennifer King

Editorial Assistant: Ruth Belanger

Marketing Manager: Clinton Kernen

Marketing Coordinator: Sara Rose

Content Project Manager: Darrell E. Frye

Media Editor: Rob Ellington

Manufacturing Buyer: Doug Wilke

Production Service: Macmillan Publishing Solutions

Sr. Art Director: Tippy McIntosh

Cover Designer: Paul Neff, Paul Neff Design

Cover Image: ©Superstock

For product information and technology assistance, contact us at
**Cengage Learning Academic Resource Center,
1-800-423-0563**

For permission to use material from this text or product, submit all requests online at
www.cengage.com/permissions
Further permissions questions can be e-mailed to **permissionrequest@cengage.com**

Library of Congress Control Number: 2008944279

Student Edition

ISBN-13: 978-0-324-59769-1

ISBN-10: 0-324-59769-X

South-Western Cengage Learning
5191 Natorp Boulevard
Mason, OH 45040
USA

Cengage Learning products are represented in Canada by Nelson Education, Ltd.

For your course and learning solutions, visit
academic.cengage.com

Purchase any of our products at your local college store or at our preferred online store **www.ichapters.com**

Printed in Canada
1 2 3 4 5 6 7 13 12 11 10 09

To Karen and Kali,
With love and recognition that creating is a family venture

TABLE OF CONTENTS

PREFACE vii

ABOUT THE AUTHOR xv

PART I THE FAMILY BUSINESS: WHAT MAKES IT UNIQUE?

chapter 1 THE NATURE, IMPORTANCE, AND UNIQUENESS
OF FAMILY BUSINESS 1

chapter 2 GREAT FAMILIES IN BUSINESS: BUILDING
TRUST AND COMMITMENT 27

chapter 3 OWNERSHIP OF AN ENTERPRISE BUILT TO LAST 49

Case 1 The Binghams and the Louisville Courier-Journal Companies 67

Case 2 SMALL FAMILY BUSINESS Power Play at the Inn 69

Case 3 The Ferré Media Group 69

Case 4 SMALL FAMILY BUSINESS "She'll Always Be My Little Sister" 77

Case 5 The Vega Food Company 78

PART II LEADERSHIP IMPERATIVES FOR THE FAMILY
AND BUSINESS: SUCCESSION AND CONTINUITY

chapter 4 SUCCESSION: CONTINUING ENTREPRENEURSHIP
AND THE NEXT GENERATION 85

chapter 5 SUCCESSION AND THE TRANSFER OF POWER 107

Case 6 Sigma Motion, Inc. 127

Case 7 SMALL FAMILY BUSINESS The Ambivalent CEO of the
Construction Company 137

Case 8 SMALL FAMILY BUSINESS Borrowing to Grow at Andrews Company 138

Case   9   SMALL FAMILY BUSINESS *Adams Funeral Home* 139

Case   10   *Fasteners for Retail (Part A)* 141

Case   11   *Ferré Media Group (Part B)*......................................156

Case   12   *The Cousins Tournament* 160

PART III BEST PRACTICES FOR THE MANAGEMENT AND GOVERNANCE OF THE FAMILY BUSINESS

chapter 6   CREATING THE STRATEGY............................. 167

chapter 7   PLANNING THE ESTATE 187

chapter 8   FINANCIAL CONSIDERATIONS AND VALUATION OF THE FAMILY BUSINESS 201

chapter 9   KEY NONFAMILY MANAGEMENT: THE VISIBLE COMMITMENT TO MANAGING THE FAMILY BUSINESS PROFESSIONALLY. 231

chapter 10   FAMILY BUSINESS GOVERNANCE: ADVISORY BOARDS AND BOARDS OF DIRECTORS............................... 247

chapter 11   FAMILY COMMUNICATION: FAMILY MEETINGS, FAMILY COUNCILS, AND FAMILY OFFICES 271

chapter 12   CHANGE, ADAPTATION AND INNOVATION: THE FUTURE OF FAMILY BUSINESS.................................... 293

chapter 13   CONTINUING THE SPIRIT OF ENTERPRISE: LESSONS FROM CENTENNIAL FAMILY COMPANIES. 325

Case   13   *PrivateCo Business Valuation Report*............................345

Case   14   *Reliance Industries (Part A)*.....................................355

Case   15   SMALL FAMILY BUSINESS *The Son-in-Law* 367

Case   16   SMALL FAMILY BUSINESS *The New MBA* 368

Case   17   SMALL FAMILY BUSINESS *Real Estate Development Partners, Inc.*..............369

Case   18   SMALL FAMILY BUSINESS *Glassking Distributor Company* 373

Case   19   *New Way Distributing* 373

Case   20   *The Reliance Group (Part B)*....................................375

INDEX............................... 379

PREFACE

Family business is a vibrant area of growing interest today among researchers, theorists, investors, policymakers, practitioners, and many others—with good cause. Recent research has demonstrated that family firms are top performers. Whether measured by the bottom line, value creation for shareholders, or their capacity to create jobs, family companies outperform their nonfamily counterparts. The turbulence brought about by global hypercompetition, too, has created an increasing awareness that speed, sustainability, flexibility, quality of product and service, brand, customer relationships, employee care, and patient capital are genuine sources of competitive advantage. These advantages are often pursued via idiosyncratic business strategies deployed by firms that are family-owned and family-controlled. Family businesses, to be sure, confront substantial challenges, but they also often possess unique advantages born out of a unique and dynamic family–business interaction.

Many of the assets that differentiate a family-owned or family-controlled business from other forms of enterprise revolve around the relationship between the family and its business, especially the guidance that family members exert as managers and as shareholders. In the aftermath of recent corporate meltdowns, business schools are engaging in a broader range of research and dialogue on governance and the role of shareholders and boards. In this same vein, the potential value of family ownership, stewardship, and control has been convincingly demonstrated in recent years. Consider the long-term leadership focus of the Washington Post Companies by Donald Graham after Katharine Graham's death. And consider the Ford family, who, during a period of turmoil at the large auto producer, continued to support William Clay Ford, Jr., as chairman of the Ford Motor Company and his quest to keep the company independent.

Alongside these very visible examples of family ownership and family leadership are hundreds of smaller, lower-profile, privately held family businesses with the same commitment to continuity from generation to generation. From the United States, Europe, Latin America, Asia, Australia, and the Middle East comes compelling evidence of the commitment of business families to building firms that last.

Few businesses of any type enjoy long, successful lives today. When the Standard and Poor's Index of 90 major U.S. companies was created in the 1920s, companies on the list stayed there for an average of 65 years. But, by 1998, a firm's expected tenure on the expanded S&P 500 list was a mere 10 years. According to Bain & Co., the average U.S. corporation now has a 14-year life expectancy!

Family businesses are extremely important to the economic well-being of the United States and the other free economies of the world. Between 80 and 95 percent of businesses in the United States and Latin America and over 80 percent of businesses in Europe and Asia remain family-owned and family-controlled. These same businesses, small and large, young and old, account for more than 50 percent of the gross domestic product of the world's most advanced economies and employ a majority of the population. It is unfortunate that the stereotype of nepotism in family businesses tends to overshadow, in the eyes of the media, academic researchers, business schools, and the government, the significant contribution these enterprises make day in and day out.

In the past 5 years alone, several top-ranked academic journals (including the *Academy of Management Journal, Organization Science, Administrative Science Quarterly,* the *Journal of Business Venturing, The Journal of Finance,* and *Entrepreneurship Theory and Practice*) have published articles exploring the unique agency costs, strategic resources, features, and issues of family businesses. Quality research in established periodical literature is sure to generate more knowledge of the exceptional challenges and advantages of family businesses, with the prospect of useful implications for practice. The fact that family business is becoming the focus of research in management, economics, law, and the behavioral sciences also bodes well for the possibility of positively influencing their current dismal survival statistics. Most family businesses (approximately 67 percent) do not survive beyond the founding generation under the control of the same owning family, and only about 12 percent make it to the third generation.

Educational programs in family business at the undergraduate and graduate business-school levels have grown tremendously in the past several years. This book captures that progress by pointing to key leadership tasks and a set of management, ownership, and family practices that can help mediate the relationship between a family and its enterprise. These practices will go a long way toward ensuring that the unique strengths and competencies of the family enterprise (for example, speed and long-term orientation)—and not its much-heralded vulnerabilities (for example, nepotism and family conflict)—retain the upper hand. Leading, managing, growing, and governing family enterprises for a global economy are tasks that increasingly require a set of skills, abilities, and practices that serve sustainability and continuity.

APPROACH

Written with next-generation family business owners, family business advisors and their educators in mind, this third edition of *Family Business* is the result of an interdisciplinary inquiry into the advantages enjoyed and the challenges faced by family businesses.

New to this third edition are:

- Revealing new statistics and research findings with significant implications for family business management.

- An expanded treatment of the truly idiosyncratic approach to strategic planning by family firms, including a recognition of the concurrent influence of individual, family, and industry cycles and the need for parallel family and business planning.

- An entirely new chapter on financial matters: Communicating through accounting, business valuation (including a valuation case exercise), responsible shareholder education, financial measures that matter, the importance of cash-flow management, the advantage created by patient family capital, and the need for liquidity options.

- More engaging decision-making cases in which the reader is asked to assume the role of the CEO or successor and make those large fact-based calls.

- A larger number of short small family business cases for the many readers who come from small to medium-sized family businesses.
- Suggested media resources.
- More comprehensive global treatment of the world of family business, taking advantage of the unique resources of the Thunderbird School of Global Management.
- And finally, a new and improved organization of the text leading to clear and actionable leadership initiatives and best practices in management and governance.

Focusing on the best practices available to family firms promotes the capacity of family members to better lead family-owned businesses into succeeding generations. The book offers advice to the next generation of service providers to family enterprises (such as consultants, attorneys, bankers, financial planners, and family therapists) and to corporate partners in the supply chain (such as managers of dealership networks in the automotive, appliance, and industrial equipment industries), who depend on family-owned businesses for distribution and sales.

It should be noted that *Family Business* is a scholarly book. Rooted in theory, research, and practice, it goes beyond traditional textbooks by not only fostering understanding of family-business theory and family dynamics but also exploring its subject with a managerial action orientation. Taking advantage of my appointment as Professor of Global Family Enterprise at the Thunderbird School of Global Management, this third edition of *Family Business* includes a larger and more diverse collection of real-life (not composite) cases and exercises from around the globe. Based on actual family-business documents, these cases and exercises disclose concepts and practices that have benefited other family businesses. Moreover, this edition of *Family Business* goes beyond basic "how-to" books by reviewing both theory and recent research, thus supporting informed and context-relevant planning and decision making.

Reading and working through this book provides an opportunity to better understand the unique opportunities and challenges faced by family businesses. These businesses are, after all, important to millions of enterprising families globally, to 85 percent of the employee population, and to the future of free economies around the world. Family businesses continue to be the primary engines of global economic activity.

It would be a disservice to the next generation to continue to dwell on the problems and stereotypes of family firms; these are already quite prevalent in the business and family-business literature. Instead, my goal is to pass on the torch of accumulated knowledge (much of it quite recent) about family firms. It is my hope that readers will take away from *Family Business* a variety of sound managerial, governance, and family practices that will increase the odds that their family-owned or family-controlled corporation will continue from generation to generation.

ORGANIZATION

Part I defines the particular characteristics of family-owned and family-controlled businesses and describes the unique challenges faced and advantages enjoyed by these companies. Part II personalizes these concepts by presenting the critical leadership tasks for both generations involved in succession and continuity efforts: the next-generation leaders, who perform the delicate task of respecting the past while advocating change and adaptation with a new vision for the company; the CEO, who builds institutions of governance, promotes shareholder loyalty, and then passes the torch to a successor; and finally, the CEO spouse or other trusted third party, who promotes trust and family unity and communication.

Part III is a collection of the family, management, and governance practices that the latest research has identified as both protecting family firms from the unique hazards they face and providing for the deployment of their unique sources of competitive advantage. These practices include planning the estate so as to ensure business agility in the next generation, planning strategically for the rejuvenation and continued growth of the business, complementing the skills of the owning family with those of capable nonfamily managers in the top-management team, using advisory boards or boards of directors to provide a benchmark and hold management accountable to shareholders, and holding frequent family meetings to facilitate communication and planning.

Part III also provides glimpses of the future of family businesses, addressing the need for change and adaptation and the leadership required. It also reflects, with the assistance of fifth- and sixth-generation CEOs, on the lessons learned by successful centennial family companies. Recognizing that competitive fitness is not limited to large, management-controlled multinationals, it also presents a strategic perspective on growth opportunities for family businesses. Its optimistic assessment of the future of family business is rooted in trends emerging from the economic developments of the early part of the 21st century.

DIVERSE CASES AND EXERCISES

Cases about family businesses are provided for each major segment of the book. The 20 carefully screened cases (some available only through the book's website at www. cengage.com/management/poza) are as diverse as family businesses themselves. They show both male and female CEOs in the process of passing the torch to female and male next-generation leaders. The businesses represented are geographically diverse, with locations in North America, Latin America, Asia, and Europe. They range in size from $15 million to $23 billion in annual revenues, and they operate in a wide variety of industries. Owning families are of diverse ethnic backgrounds. The cases are not meant to illustrate either effective or ineffective practices but rather to promote reflection, discussion, and active learning of the concepts presented in the book. Consequently, questions accompany each case to provide a framework for discussion. These questions can be found on the book's website at www.cengage.com/management/poza.

I gratefully acknowledge the support that the Fairfax Foundation and the Conway family provided in the preparation of the Fasteners for Retail cases. I am similarly indebted to the Ferré Rangel family for their candor and support in preparing the Ferré Media Group case. I would also like to thank Ray Koenig, president, Koenig Equipment for his generous support of family business case development. For permission to publish "The Cousins Tournament," I am indebted to Kelin Gersick. For reasons of privacy, others who gave consent to publish cases about their family businesses must remain anonymous. Finally, I would like to acknowledge my debt to John H. Davis and Louis B. Barnes, whose study of the Graham family raised some of the notions included in my work.

Exercise questions based on actual company documents, such as a family-business constitution, and current family business situations are provided on the book's website at www.cengage.com/management/poza. In addition to being used to launch robust class discussions, these exercises, along with the case material, can be assigned as papers, projects, or homework.

TEACHING AND LEARNING

A group of PowerPoint presentation slides accompany every chapter, providing instructors with a complete set of basic notes for lectures and providing students with a helpful set of review materials. These slides, which highlight and synthesize key concepts for greater recall, are available for download at www.cengage.com/management/poza.

An Instructor's Manual is also available to faculty who adopt *Family Business,* 3rd ed. Prepared by the book author, Ernesto Poza, it has the dual objective of reducing preparation time and making your teaching more effective. It provides comprehensive and integrated teaching support, including notes for the cases. Visit the book's website at www.cengage.com/management/poza, where you will find links for downloading resources related to this book.

ACKNOWLEDGMENTS

This third edition of *Family Business* is ultimately the expression of a community of learning in the field of family business. Back in the early 1980s, this community met often in New York City and included innovators, scholars, and practitioners, like the late Richard Beckhard, then an adjunct professor at the Sloan School of Management at MIT; the late Barbara Hollander, a family therapist; Iván Lansberg, John Ward, Elaine Kepner, Matilde Salganicoff; and family business owners George Raymond and Rod Correll. Léon Danco, the pioneering family business consultant, has also greatly influenced my work. Don Jonovic, a family-business speaker, consultant, and independent board member first got me interested in the field. I am indebted to them all. Their friendship has been constant and inspiring.

My practice, as a family-business advisor and board member, has vested this book with a unique point of view. My first consulting assignments with family-owned businesses took place in 1979. I owe a world of gratitude to those pioneers—the Grupo Alfa and the Garza family, Thetford Corporation, the Grupo Salcedo and the Salcedo and Arosemena families, and the M&M Mars division of Mars, Inc. Since then, many other family enterprises have entrusted their succession planning, strategic growth plans, leadership development, family meetings, and unique approaches to governance to our collaboration. In all cases, these family businesses have been in search of more than solutions—they have been in search of continuity and of excellence. I respect their desire for privacy and thank them all immensely for the opportunity to make a difference. Many of their stories are told anonymously throughout this book.

True innovators in academia have also shaped this book. Theodore Alfred, Scott Cowen, and Richard Osborne, at Case Western Reserve University, invited me to join the faculty, challenged me to perform as a scholar and educator, and provided me with the opportunities for research, teaching, and service that are most responsible for the contents of *Family Business,* 3rd ed. Robert Hisrich, Garvin Professor of Global Entrepreneurship at the Thunderbird School of Global Management, also provided continuing support and commitment and challenged the inquiry to assume a global reach. Angel Cabrera, Thunderbird's president, Dean Dale Davison, and Robert

Hisrich have given me the opportunity to continue doing what I love to do, this time in a truly global setting.

Michael Horvitz and the Horvitz family made the third edition of *Family Business* possible through a generous gift that established the Partnership for Family Business and the Discovery Action Research Project at Case. I also want to thank Bruce Grossman, Vice-Chairman Grupo Continental, who has been very generous in helping me launch the Center for Global Family Enterprise at Thunderbird's School of Global Management.

For reviewing various chapters of the manuscript and preparing helpful critiques, I thank Keith H. Brigham, Texas Tech University; Alan L. Carsrud, Florida International University; Jason G. Caudill, Carson-Newman College; Rebecca S. Greene, Texas Tech University; Daniel R. Hogan, Jr., Ph.D., Loyola University; Stan Mandel, Wake Forest University; Dr. JoAnne Norton, California State University, Fullerton; Alan F. Pippenger, University of Dayton; Ram Subramanian, Montclair State University.

I very much appreciate the significant contribution that my colleague Pramodita Sharma, Professor, Wilfrid Laurier University, made to Chapter 5, "Succession and the Transfer of Power." I also want to thank Tracey Messer and Reiko Kishido, doctoral students and research associates who helped with the collection and analysis of Discovery data. Tracey was also a key associate in the writing of three of the cases and one of the chapters in this edition of *Family Business*. I am indebted to Associate Professor Susan Hanlon, University of Akron, for her contributions to Chapter 1. And thank you Carol Pacelli for making the final proofing and editing process a breeze.

At Cengage, I would like to recognize the high standards and extraordinary efforts of Jennifer King, Melissa Acuna, Editor-in-Chief; Michele Rhoades, Senior Acquisitions Editor; Jennifer King, Developmental Editor; Kimberly Kanakes, Executive Marketing Manager; Nathan Anderson, Marketing Manager; Suellen Ruttkay, Marketing Coordinator; and Tippy McIntosh, Senior Art Director.

The deadlines were aggressive, and everyone did his or her part to make it all happen.

As a teacher, the contributions of fellow scholars and practitioners are always in the top of my mind. I want to particularly thank John Davis, Kelin Gersick, Iván Lansberg, and Marion McCollum. Their groundbreaking social and systemic appreciation of family businesses and their governance is evident throughout the book.

I also want to thank the following people for their thoughts, ideas, encouragement, discussions of pedagogy, and clinical and casual case conversations over the past 20 years: Clay Alderfer, Mauricio Alvarez, Joan Amat, Joseph Astrachan, Glenn Ayres, Antonio Barderas, Louis B. Barnes, Otis Baskin, Peter Baudoin, Nan-b de Gaspé Beaubien, Carmen Bianchi, David Bork, Joyce and Robert Brockhaus, Bonnie Brown, Fredda Herz Brown, Ira Bryck, Katiuska Cabrera-Suárez, Randy Carlock, Fernando Casado, Guido Corbetta, Leslie Dashew, Thomas Davidow, Philip Dawson, Fernando del Pino, Francois deVisscher, Ernest Doud, Nancy Drozdow, Ann Dugan, Barbara Dunn, Gibb Dyer, Claudio Fuchs, Miguel Gallo, Leonard Geiser, Joseph Ginsburg, Joe Goodman, Salo Grabinsky, Bruce Grossman, Wendy Handler, Lee Hausner, Ramona Heck, Frank Hoy, Thomas Hubler, Dennis Jaffe, Ema Juárez, Dirk Jungé, Carlos Kaplún, Paul Karofsky, Andrew Keyt, Kacie LaChapelle, Sam Lane, Gerald LeVan, Mark Litzsinger, Jon Martínez, Gregory McCann, Ruth McClendon, Stephen McClure, Marion McCollum, Drew Mendoza, Susana Menéndez-Resquejo, John

Messervey, Howard Muson, Richard Narva, Patricia Nelson, Sharon Nelton, Joseph Paul, Bruce Sanford, William Sauer, John Schoen, Amy Schuman, Paul Sessions, Pramodita Sharma, Michael Shulman, Marc Silverman, Jordi Solé Tristán, Ritch Sorenson, Olga Staios, Eleni Stavrou, Stephen Swartz, Albert Thomassen, Michael Trueblood, Nancy Upton, Marta Vago, Francisco Valera, José Villareal, Karen Vinton, René Werner, Mary Whiteside, Kathy Wiseman, Thomas Zanecchia, and Gary Zwick.

To my extended family—Hugo, Carmen, Hugo II, Karen, Carlos, Heidi, and the nephews and nieces—I want to say thank you for your love. And to Karen and Kali, I want to express all my love and my thanks for the sacrifices made in support of the writing of this book, for their love, and for their commitment to growth, change, and family unity.

Ernesto J. Poza
Professor of Global Family Business and Entrepreneurship
Walker Center for Global Entrepreneurship
The Thunderbird School of Global Management
1 Global Plaza
Glendale, Arizona, United States of America

ABOUT THE AUTHOR

Ernesto J. Poza (BS, Yale University; MBA/MS, Massachusetts Institute of Technology) is an internationally recognized, top-rated speaker and consultant to family-owned businesses. A leading authority in the field, he is also Professor of Global Family Business and Entrepreneurship at the Thunderbird School of Global Management. As an educator and consultant, he challenges business owners to revitalize mature businesses through strategic thinking, succession planning, and change management. His work has been featured on CNN, NBC, and NPR, as well as in *Business Week, Fortune Small Business, Family Business Magazine, Inc., Industry Week,* and *The New York Times.* Poza is on the editorial board of *Family Business Review* and writes a regular column, *Family Inc., for Business Week SmallBiz.*

In recognition of his contribution to the field of family business, the Family Firm Institute awarded him the Richard Beckhard Practice Award in 1996. His research interests are in the areas of family-business continuity, new venture creation, family-business governance, leadership of change, and family entrepreneurship. As head of E. J. Poza Associates, a consulting firm based in Scottsdale, Arizona, he has advised family-owned, family-controlled, and *Fortune 500* companies, including Huber & Co., Mars, Scripps, Grupo Alfa, Grupo Femsa, Grupo Ferré, Sherwin-Williams, Goodyear, and General Motors. He is the author of *Smart Growth: Critical Choices for Business Continuity and Prosperity* (Jossey-Bass Publishers) and *A la sombra del roble: La empresa privada familiar y su continuidad* (Editorial Universitaria).

Ernesto Poza is a founding member and Fellow of the Family Firm Institute (http://www.ffi.org). He serves on the boards of several family-controlled corporations and helps family-owned and family-controlled companies plan for continuity from generation to generation.

THE NATURE, IMPORTANCE, AND UNIQUENESS OF FAMILY BUSINESS

Entrepreneurial companies often become family-owned businesses. While the spouse of the founder may have done work on behalf of the new venture in the early stages, the real transition from an entrepreneurial to a family business typically happens when the children of the company founder join the business as employees. The business may very well continue to be an entrepreneurial company and may prefer to be known that way because the owners are concerned with the perception of nepotism and lack of professionalism often ascribed to family businesses. But once next-generation members join the ranks of employees and/or shareholders, the nature of the firm changes, as do its challenges and its unique competitive profile.

Family businesses are ubiquitous. Family-owned and family-controlled firms account for approximately 90 percent of all incorporated businesses in the United States, where approximately 17 million family firms (including sole proprietorships) operate.[1] A full one-third of all *Fortune 500* companies are family-controlled, and about 60 percent of publicly traded firms remain under family influence.[2] Many family businesses are small, but there are approximately 138 billion-dollar family firms in the United States alone, with 19 such firms operating in France, 15 in Germany, 9 each in Italy and Spain, and 5 each in Canada and Japan.[3] In the United States, family firms account for 64 percent of the gross domestic product, or approximately $6 trillion, 85 percent of private-sector employment, and about 86 percent of all jobs created in the past decade. In Germany they represent approximately 80 percent of all businesses and employ 80 percent of the working population. Family businesses are also ubiquitous in the economies of Spain and France, where they are estimated to represent approximately 80 percent of all companies and account for about 75 percent of the

---

[1]Astrachan, J., & Carey, M., Family Businesses in the United States Economy. Paper presented to the Center for the Study of Taxation, Washington, D.C., 1994. Also see Colli, A., *The History of Family Business: 1850 to 2000.* Cambridge: Cambridge University Press.

[2]Bristow, D. K., *Composition of US Stock Exchanges Firms.* Los Angeles: UCLA Directors Institute: Unpublished study, 2000.

[3]Rottenberg, D., ed., "The Oldest Family Businesses." *Family Business Magazine*, Winter 2002, p. 44.

employment. And in Italy, India, and Latin American countries the estimates sky-rocket, with 90 percent to 98 percent of all companies being family firms.

One study also found that contrary to the prevalent stereotype of family businesses as nepotistic and conflict-ridden underperformers, family firms perform better than nonfamily firms.[4] In fact, the study notes, 35 percent of the S&P 500 firms are family-controlled (with the families owning nearly 18 percent of their firms' outstanding equity), and these family-controlled firms outperformed management-controlled firms by 6.65 percent in return on assets (using either earnings before interest, tax, depreciation, and amortization [EBITDA] or net income) during the past decade. Similar results were found in terms of return on equity. Family firms were also responsible for creating an additional 10 percent in market value between 1992 and 1999, as compared with the 65 percent of the S&P firms that are management-controlled.

The evidence therefore says that U.S. firms with founding-family ownership perform better, on average, than nonfamily-owned firms. This strongly suggests that the benefits of family influence often outweigh its costs. Arguably, family businesses are the primary engine of economic growth and vitality not only in the United States but in free economies all over the world.

In Europe as a whole, family-controlled firms (with a minimum family stake of 50 percent) outperformed the Morgan Stanley Capital International Europe index by 16 percent annually from 2001 to 2006. (The study controlled for size and sector effects, and neither of these was an important driver underlying the solid out-performance of family-controlled businesses.) Another study of European family-controlled firms (this one with a minimum family stake of 10 percent and $1 billion in market capitalization) found that family companies outperformed the pan-European Dow Jones Stoxx 600 Index by 8 percent annually from the end of 1996 to the end of 2006.[5] Notice that the data all come from family-controlled but publicly traded firms. Unfortunately, no research currently compares the performance of the privately held universe because the data are unavailable to scholars.

Data from research conducted in several other countries are discussed in this chapter's section on Competitive Advantage: The Resource-Based View and summarized in Table 1.1. These give us many glimpses of the contributions of family businesses to the global economy.

Besides financial outperformance, families and families in business seem also to be a significant factor in the creation of new ventures. While the venture capital industry seems to be credited for its role, it is wealthy individuals and families in business that provide the bulk of the seed capital and early-stage funding for a large segment of the entrepreneurial population. Of the 286 million entrepreneurs worldwide who launched new ventures since the mid-1990s, only 19,000 were financed by venture capital firms, which raised only $59 billion, versus the $271 billion provided by family and friends operating as angel investors.[6]

On the down side, approximately 85 percent of all new businesses fail within their first five years of operation. Among those that survive, only 30 percent are successfully

---

[4]Anderson, R., & Reeb, D., Founding Family Ownership and Firm Performance: Evidence from the S&P 500. *The Journal of Finance, 58*(3), 2003, pp. 1301–1328.

[5]Credit Suisse, "Family Holdings Outperform Competitors: Credit Suisse Launches Family Index," press release, Zurich, January 30, 2007.

[6]Kauffman Center for Entrepreneurial Leadership & Babson College, 2002 Global Entrrepreneurship Monitor. Presented to the United Nations, April 2003.

table **1.1**	**Family Business: The Statistical Story**	
Family businesses constitute	80%–98%	of all businesses in the world's free economies.
Family businesses generate	49%	of the gross domestic product (GDP) in the United States.
Family businesses generate more than	75%	of the GDP in most other countries.
Family businesses employ	80%	of the U.S. workforce.
Family businesses employ more than	75%	of the working population around the world.
Family businesses create	86%	of all new jobs in the United States.
A total of	37%	of *Fortune 500* companies are family-controlled.
A total of	60%	of all publicly held U.S. companies are family-controlled.
Number of family-owned businesses in the United States:	17 million	
Number of U.S. family-owned businesses with annual revenues greater than $25 million:	35,000	
Family business outperformance of nonfamily businesses in the United States:	6.65% annually in return on assets (ROA)	10% in market value
Family business outperformance of nonfamily business in Europe:	8%–16% annually in return on equity (ROE), depending on the study.	
Family business outperformance of nonfamily business in Latin America (Chile):	8% annually in return on assets and return on equity.	

SOURCE: Dreux, D., Financing Family Business: Alternatives to Selling Out or Going Public. *Family Business Review*, *3*(3), 1990; Gomez-Mejía, L., Larraza-Kintana, M., & Makri, M., The Determinants of Executive Compensation in Family-Controlled Public Corporations. *Academy of Management Journal, 46*, 2003; Daily, C., & Dollinger, M., An Empirical Examination of Ownership Structure in Family and Professionally Managed Firms. *Family Business Review*, *5*(2), 1992; Beehr, T., Drexler, J., & Faulkner, S., Working in Small Family Businesses: Empirical Comparisons to Nonfamily Businesses. *Journal of Organizational Behavior, 18*, 1997; Astrachan, J., & Carey, M., Family Businesses in the U.S. Economy. Paper presented to the Center for the Study of Taxation, Washington, D.C., 1994; Oster, S., *Modern Competitive Analysis*, New York: Oxford University Press, 1999; Bristow, D. K., *Composition of US Stock Exchanges Firms*. Los Angeles: UCLA Directors Institute: Unpublished study, 2000; Anderson, R.C., & Reeb, D.M., Founding Family Ownership and Firm Performance: Evidence from the S&P 500. *The Journal of Finance, 58*(3), 2003, pp. 1301–1328. Credit Suisse, "Family Holdings Outperform Competitors" and "Credit Suisse Launches Family Index," Zurich, January 30, 2007; and Martínez, J., & Stohr, B., Family Ownership and Firm Performance: Evidence from Public Companies in Chile. Unpublished paper presented at the International Family Research Association, 2005.

transferred to the second generation of the founding-family owners. This high failure rate amounts to the squandering of a significant opportunity for job and wealth creation in many communities. Not all family businesses that are not passed down to the next generation go on to close their doors, but many do.

And the odds get worse in the transitions between the second and third generations and the third and fourth generations, when only 12 percent and 4 percent of such businesses, respectively, remain in the family. This seems to prove true the old adage "from shirtsleeves to shirtsleeves in three generations."[7]

Today, there is a widespread myth that a company is prehistoric and on the road to extinction unless it is "high tech" or has grown to be a very large, diversified multinational corporation. Ironically, this myth is often promoted by news media that are largely family-controlled; leading newspapers such as the *New York Times* (owned by the Sulzberger family), the *Washington Post* (the Graham family), and the *Wall Street Journal* (the Murdoch family) come to mind. Yet, in the presence of widespread global hypercompetition, family businesses that are niche-focused and high quality and have great customer service are thriving. You might be surprised to learn that Smucker's, Perdue Farms, Gap, Levi Strauss, L.L. Bean, Hermés (France), Zara/Inditex (Spain) Mars, Femsa/Tecate (Mexico), Bacardí, William Grant & Sons (Scotland), Osborne Wines (Spain), Fidelity Investments, Banco Popular (Puerto Rico), Timken, Reliance Industries and Modi Group (India), LG Electronics (Korea), Casio (Japan), Marriott/Ritz-Carlton, American Greetings, Hallmark, Ford Motor, Fiat (Italy), BMW (Germany), Kohler, Roca (Spain), Nordstrom, Ikea (Sweden), Metro A.G. (Germany), SC Johnson, Bigelow Tea, and Wal-Mart are all family-owned or family-controlled. And then there are thousands of smaller and less well known, but just as successful, family-owned businesses—companies that build homes and office buildings, manufacture unique products, and provide custom services; that are the backbone of most supply chains and distribution channels; and that are the retailers for much of what consumers buy.

WHAT CONSTITUTES A FAMILY BUSINESS?

What do we mean by the term *family business*? Because of the variety of firm profiles, the definition has proven more elusive than you might think.

- In a comprehensive study of family businesses, Chrisman, Chua, and Sharma found 21 different definitions of *family business* in their review of 250 research articles.[8]
- Family businesses come in many forms: sole proprietorships, partnerships, limited liability companies, S corporations, C corporations, holding companies, and even publicly traded, albeit family-controlled, companies. That is why estimates of the number of family businesses operating in the U.S. economy range between 17 million and 22 million. Worldwide, estimates of all enterprises considered to be family businesses range between 80 percent and 98 percent.

---

[7]Ward, J., *Keeping the Family Business Healthy: How to Plan for Continued Growth, Profitability and Family Leadership*, San Francisco: Jossey-Bass, 1987.

[8]Chrisman, J., Chua, J., & Sharma, P., *A Review and Annotated Bibliography of Family Business Studies*, Boston: Kluwer, 1996.

- In a large-scale study of the role of family contractual relationships within the Spanish newspaper industry, a business was considered to be a family business if the last name of the CEO and/or the editor was the same as that of the owners.[9]

- Another empirical study took the position that family firms are theoretically distinct from other closely held firms because of the influence of altruism on agency relationships (relationships between shareholders and management). The authors of this study went on to say that family firms are differentiated by both the active involvement of family in firm management and the intent of family members to retain ownership of the firm. They ultimately defined a *family business* as an enterprise in which two or more family members own 15 percent or more of the shares, family members are employed in the business, and the family intends to retain control of the firm in the future.[10]

- Another article ascribed the uniqueness of a family business to the very different influence that family has on ownership, governance, and management participation through strategic direction, direct family involvement in day-to-day operations, and/or retention of voting control.[11]

Taking into account this full range of research and analyses, this third edition of Family Business *considers family businesses to constitute the whole gamut of enterprises in which an entrepreneur or next-generation CEO and one or more family members significantly influence the firm. They influence it via their managerial or board participation, their ownership control, the strategic preferences of shareholders, and the culture and values family shareholders impart to the enterprise.*

Participation refers to the nature of the involvement of family members in the enterprise—as part of the management team, as board members, as shareholders, or as supportive members of the family foundation. *Ownership control* refers to the rights and responsibilities family members derive from significant ownership of voting shares and the governance of the agency relationship. *Strategic preferences* refers to the risk preferences and strategic direction family members set for the enterprise through their participation in top management, consulting, the board of directors, shareholder meetings, or even family councils. *Culture* is the collection of values, defined by behaviors, that become embedded in an enterprise as a result of the leadership provided by family members, past and present. Family unity and the nature of the relationship between the family and the business also define this culture.

This book, therefore, adopts an inclusive theoretical definition of a family business that focuses on the vision, intentions, and behaviors, vis-à-vis strategy, succession, and continuity of the owners. *Ownership structure aside, what differentiates family businesses from management-controlled businesses are often the intentions, values, and strategy-influencing interactions of owners who are members of the same family. The result is a unique blending of family, management, and ownership subsystems to form an idiosyncratic family business system. This family–*

---

[9]Gomez-Mejía, L., Nuñez-Nickel, M., & Gutierrez, I., The Role of Family Ties in Agency Contracts. *Academy of Management Journal, 44,* 2001, pp. 81–96.

[10]Schulze, W., Lubatkin, M., Dino, R., & Buchholtz, A., Agency Relationships in Family Firms. *Organization Science, 12*(2), 2001, pp. 99–116.

[11]Astrachan, J., Klein, S., & Smyrnios, K., The F-PEC Scale of Family Influence: A Proposal for Solving the Family Definition Problem. *Family Business Review, 15*(1), 2002, pp. 45–59.

management–ownership interaction can produce significant adaptive capacity and competitive advantage. Or it can be the source of significant vulnerability in the face of generational or competitive change. The dominant decisions in a family business, according to this inclusive theoretical definition, are "controlled by members of the same family or a small number of families in a manner that is potentially sustainable across generations of the family or families."[12]

Thus, we arrive at a working definition of a family business as a unique synthesis of the following:

1. Ownership control (15 percent or higher) by two or more members of a family or a partnership of families
2. Strategic influence by family members on the management of the firm, whether by being active in management, by continuing to shape the culture, by serving as advisors or board members, or by being active shareholders
3. Concern for family relationships
4. The dream (or possibility) of continuity across generations

The following characteristics define the essence of the distinctiveness of family firms:

1. The presence of the family
2. The overlap of family, management, and ownership, with its zero-sum (win–lose) propensities, which in the absence of growth of the firm, render family businesses particularly vulnerable during succession
3. The unique sources of competitive advantage (like a long-term investment horizon) derived from the interaction of family, management, and ownership, especially when family unity is high
4. The owner's dream of keeping the business in the family (the objective being business continuity from generation to generation)

SUCCESSION AND CONTINUITY

Family firms are unique in the extent to which succession planning assumes a key and very strategic role in the firm's life. Because competitive success, family harmony, and ownership returns are all at stake at the same time in the firm, carefully orchestrating the multiyear process represented by succession across generations of owner-managers is a priority. There are hundreds of reasons why organizations fail, but in family-owned and family-controlled companies, the most prevalent reason relates to a failure in succession planning. Whether the causal reason is incompetent or unprepared successors, unclear succession plans, a tired strategy that is unable to contain competitors, or family rivalries and bids for power, if a family business is going to survive, it has to successfully craft its succession process. Chapters 4 and 5 will treat the subject of succession quite thoroughly, but its considerable role in the uniqueness of family firms deserves early recognition in this book.

---

[12]Chua, J., Chrisman, J., & Sharma, P., Defining Family Business by Behavior. *Entrepreneurship Theory and Practice, 23*(4), 1999, pp. 19–37.

Three patterns of ineffective succession were identified in one study:[13]

1. **Conservative:** Although the parent has exited the business, the parental shadow remains, and the firm and its strategies are locked in the past.
2. **Rebellious:** In what is often an overreaction to the previous generation's control of the firm, the next generation launches a clean-slate approach to the organization. As a result, traditions, legacies, and even the business model or its "secret to success" are destroyed or discarded.
3. **Wavering:** The next generation is paralyzed by indecisiveness, unable to adapt the business to current competitive conditions; it also fails to make its mark and assume leadership effectively.

The study concludes with the reflection that the patterns were observed so frequently that many family firms will undoubtedly have to battle these syndromes in order to provide for family business continuity across generations of owners.

BUILDING FAMILY BUSINESSES THAT LAST

Without vision and leadership from members of two generations and the use of select family, management, and governance practices, the future is bleak for family-controlled enterprises. The blurring of boundaries among family membership, family management, and family ownership subjects family businesses to the potential for confusion, slow decision making, or even corporate paralysis. An inability to adapt to changes in the competitive marketplace or powerlessness to govern the relationship between the family and the business will ultimately undermine the enterprise. As a result, a family business that lacks multigenerational leadership and vision can hardly be positioned to retain the competitive advantages that made it successful in a previous, often more entrepreneurial, generation.

It takes ongoing dialogue across generations of owner-managers about their vision for the company to build a family business so that it continues. Family businesses that have been built to last recognize the tension between preserving and protecting the core of what has made the business successful on the one hand and promoting growth and adaptation to changing competitive dynamics on the other.[14] Family businesses that are confident that each generation will responsibly bring a different but complementary vision to the business have a foundation on which to build continuity.

THE SYSTEMS THEORY PERSPECTIVE

Systems theory is the theoretical approach most often used in the scholarly study of family business. It remains pervasive in the literature today. In the systems theory approach, the family firm is modeled as comprising the three overlapping, interacting,

---

[13]Miller, D., Steiner, L., Le-Breton-Miller, I., Lost in Time: Intergenerational Succession, Change and Failure in Family Business. *Journal of Business Venturing, 18*, 2003, pp. 513–531.

[14]Porras, J., & Collins, J., *Built to Last*. New York: HarperCollins, 1997. Note that while the authors do not identify the businesses that are family-owned or family-controlled, many of the enterprises chosen as exemplary are (or until recently were) family businesses.

figure **1.1** | **The Systems Theory Model of Family Business**

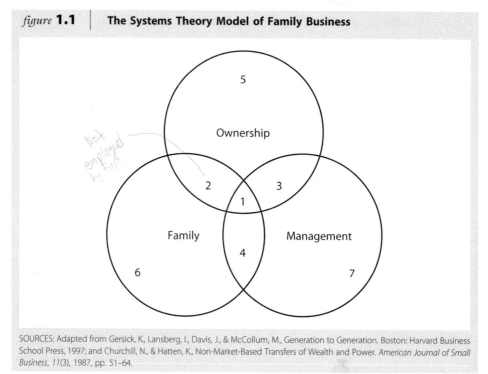

SOURCES: Adapted from Gersick, K., Lansberg, I., Davis, J., & McCollum, M., *Generation to Generation*. Boston: Harvard Business School Press, 1997; and Churchill, N., & Hatten, K., Non-Market-Based Transfers of Wealth and Power. *American Journal of Small Business*, *11*(3), 1987, pp. 51–64.

and interdependent subsystems of family, management, and ownership.[15] According to the systems theory model graphically represented in Figure 1.1, each subsystem maintains boundaries that separate it from the other subsystems and the general external environment within which the family firm operates.[16] In order for the organization to perform optimally, the subsystems must be integrated so that the entire system functions in a unified way.[17] General systems theory also suggests that to reverse the natural progression toward entropy or decline, the three subsystems and the larger family business system all have to increase their requisite variety (internal capabilities) in order to successfully cope with increasing variety in the environment.

This model suggests that a family firm is best understood and studied as a complex and dynamic social system in which integration is achieved through reciprocal adjustments among subsystems. For this reason, the family subsystem is expected to have a strong impact on the ownership and management subsystems, and vice versa. Understanding comes only when all three subsystems, with their interactions and interdependencies, are studied as one system. Emphasis in this research stream is appropriately focused on the interactions of the three subsystems and on the

[15]See Davis, P., Realizing the Potential of the Family Business. *Organizational Dynamics, 11*, Summer 1983, pp. 47–56; and Lansberg, I., Managing Human Resources in Family Firms. *Organizational Dynamics, 11*, Summer 1983, pp. 39–46.

[16]Alderfer, C., Change Processes in Organizations. In: M. Dunnette, ed., *Handbook of Industrial and Organizational Psychology*. New York: Rand, 1976.

[17]McCollum, M., Integration in the Family Firm: When the Family System Replaces Controls and Culture, *Family Business Review*, 1(4), 1988, pp. 399–417.

integration mechanisms used to determine outcomes of the larger system that provide mutual benefits to all system members.

The developmental processes of the family members and nonfamily managers in the various subsystems, along with the developmental cycle of the enterprise, for example, will also be constantly bringing change to the mix. So, from a system perspective, the family firm will be facing different systemic alignments and misalignments as the next generation joins the firm, the earlier generation ages, and the firm experiences a new period of accelerated growth resulting from product or service innovation, for instance. Interestingly though, some research has found no significant difference in many of the dynamics or practices present in first-, second-, and third-generation family firms, except that a greater number of second- and third-generation firms have engaged in succession planning than did their first-generation counterparts.[18]

Issues, priorities, and problems will be defined differently by different members of the family in business. The individual perspectives of members of the family and the firm will understandably be different because of their positions in the system. For example, a parent who is CEO and 100-percent owner of the firm (represented by position 1 in Figure 1.1) will likely view things very differently than will a family member who is not active in management and does not own any shares in the business (position 6). Similarly, a nonfamily manager (position 7) is likely to have a very different perspective as a result of her or his unique placement in the family business system.

In its more extreme forms, this phenomenon leads to categorization of family businesses based on their propensity to have a family-first, ownership-first, or management-first perspective on issues. As a result of this propensity, priority may be given to that particular subsystem over others, and even over the entire system. In other words, in its most extreme forms, this phenomenon can lead to significant suboptimization of the family–ownership–management system commonly known as a family business, which leads, theoretically, to a lower level of performance than the business is capable of achieving.

FAMILY-FIRST BUSINESSES

In family-first family businesses, employment in the business is a birthright. The stereotype of nepotism, which still dominates most people's views of family businesses, derives from this not-so-infrequent suboptimization of the family business system. Clearly, if employment is based solely on the applicant's last name, merit and other important criteria in the selection and succession processes are devalued or entirely irrelevant. Understandably, nonfamily managers with high career aspirations are often reluctant to join family businesses out of concern for their future prospects. Unless their exercise of due diligence assures them that their career ambitions will not be thwarted by a lack of family connection, high-potential nonfamily managers may choose never to join family-owned or family-controlled firms.

Because a family-first family business exists primarily for the purposes of the family, perks that transfer from the business to family members are often extensive. Financial systems may be obtuse by design, and secrecy is often paramount. After all, lack of transparency supports the ability of family members to reap rewards beyond what would be deemed reasonable under standard human resource, compensation, and

[18]Sonfield, M., Lussier, R., First-, Second-, and Third-Generation Family Firms: A Comparison. *Family Business Review*, *17*(3), September 2004, pp. 189–201.

benefit policies. Consequently, the business often becomes part of a lifestyle. The Rigas family and Adelphia Communications were ultimately prosecuted by the Securities and Exchange Commission (SEC) and other federal and state authorities as a result of a tangled web of relationships between the business and the family that were deemed to represent extensive self-dealing to the benefit of Rigas family members.

While well-managed and well-governed family businesses may have sound reasons for paying all the members of the next generation in top management equal or nearly equal salaries, family-first businesses tend to equalize compensation regardless of a family member's responsibility, results, and overall merit. Ironically, because their primary concern is family, the level of commitment of family-first businesses to the continuity of the business across generations depends on the agendas of individual family members and the levels of conflict associated with running the business. Family-first businesses are likely to choose continuity only if members of both the incumbent and the succeeding generations aspire to this goal and if the incumbent generation has sufficient resources in retirement to make this possible. In cases in which neither generation dreams of continuity or sees value in having the enterprise be a legacy for the next generation, the business will most likely be sold at the end of a generation. And even if family members aspire to perpetuate the company, family-first businesses have great difficulty in providing for continuity, since successor selection, strategic renewal, and governance of the relationship between family and business all require a strong commitment to sound business-management principles.

The absence of balance and clear boundaries between family, ownership, and management is not always resolved by putting the family first. On the contrary, business management or ownership could just as easily be favored in decision making and action taking, again to the detriment of the whole family business system.

MANAGEMENT-FIRST BUSINESSES

Management-first family businesses are likely to actively discourage family members from working in the business and/or to require work experience outside the business as a prerequisite for employment. The performance of employed family members is reviewed in the same manner as the performance of nonfamily managers, and human resource policies generally apply equally to family and nonfamily employees. Compensation is based on responsibility and performance, not on position in the family hierarchy. And the scorecard on business performance is all business; for example, the focus is on profitability, return on assets, market share, revenue growth, and return on equity. Once in the company, next-generation family members are often viewed in terms of how they will be able to manage and grow the firm—in other words, in terms of their utility and potential contribution to the business.

When family members meet socially, the conversation often turns to business subjects. Family events—even weddings and honeymoons—are sometimes arranged (as in the movie *Sabrina*), canceled, or delayed for business reasons. There is no automatic commitment to family business continuity among management-first companies because the enterprise is seen as a productive asset. As an asset, it could just as easily be folded into a larger company through a tax-free exchange of stock with a publicly traded corporation or sold through an employee stock ownership plan.

OWNERSHIP-FIRST BUSINESSES

In ownership-first family businesses, investment time horizons and perceived risk are the most significant issues. When shareholders come first, the priority is risk-adjusted economic returns or owner rents—for instance, shareholder value, EBITDA, earnings growth rates, and debt/equity and debt/asset ratios.

Ownership-first family businesses may have shorter time frames within which financial results are evaluated. Just as impatient and greedy investors on Wall Street, aided by analysts and the media, can pressure well-managed publicly traded companies into short-term thinking, family shareholders who are not active in the business, and who have little understanding of management and the time cycles involved in new strategies or new investments, can get in the way of effective operation of a family-controlled business. These family members can cause the business to lose the founding culture, which valued the role of *patient capital, or investing in the family business for the long term.*

Patient capital—one of the significant sources of competitive advantage of many family businesses—disappears at the hands of greedy shareholders. Siblings and cousins, caught in the web of high expectations for short-term returns via dividends, distributions, or the creation of shareholder value, are prone to second-guessing family members in management. Family managers, who better understand the limited capabilities of the business to deliver on the promise of high returns, are most likely managing in the long-term interest of shareholders. If family unity suffers as a result of this pressure by some family members for high returns and short time frames, a loss of will and vision may result. Family business continuity may be abandoned in favor of immediately recapturing, via sale of the company, the value created by previous generations.

BLURRED SYSTEM BOUNDARIES

Because of the complexity implicit in a system that is composed of three subsystems, each potentially with different goals and operating principles, family businesses are vulnerable to the consequences of blurred boundaries among the family, ownership, and management subsystems. Research in the social sciences—both psychology and economics, for example—suggests that emotion can lead to behaviors and actions that rational thought would seldom support. As a result, family patterns or dynamics, replete with emotional content, can easily override the logic of business management or ownership rents.

Lack of awareness on the part of company employees or family members that the particular assumptions that go into decision making are based on whether an issue is considered a family, ownership, or management issue may create incongruent policies and bad decisions. In the most extreme, but still quite common, circumstances, family rules may overtake the business. For instance, suppose a younger son insists on starting work after 10 A.M. every day, despite the requirement that, as a customer service manager, he report to work by 7 A.M. His father or aunt, to whom he reports, may choose to avoid the conflict and anxiety his tardiness provokes by ignoring it and allowing it to go on. Avoiding resolution of this disagreement out of fear or altruism only diminishes problem-solving ability; unchecked, problems can grow for years. Succession hurls many of these unsettled issues to the forefront of family business management, often at a very vulnerable time in the life of a family business.

THE ALTERNATIVE TO BLURRED SYSTEM BOUNDARIES: JOINT OPTIMIZATION

Implicit in systems theory is the capacity to jointly optimize interrelated subsystems in such a way that the larger system can be most effective and successful in the pursuit of its goals. Intuitively, reaching this state would seem akin to reaching nirvana, and it is equally as difficult. Yet thousands of family businesses, many of them featured throughout this book, achieve precisely that. They balance the goals and needs of each of the subsystems in what appears to be a masterful walk across a tightrope. Through family forums, governance bodies, strong cultures, family unity, strategic planning, fair policies, and solid managerial practices, they inspire a commitment to something larger than the self—the greater good.

Companies facilitate joint optimization of family, management, and ownership subsystems by writing policies that guide the employment of family members in the business. They further optimize the relationship by developing policies that guide the involvement of family members in nonmanagement roles—for example, board service, philanthropy, and family council leadership. As a result, some family members join the business as employees, while others become responsible shareholders and stewards of the family's resources.

In these companies, the performance of employed family members is reviewed in the same manner as that of nonfamily managers, with compensation decisions based on both level of responsibility and performance. Siblings or cousins in the same generation may, therefore, receive quite different salaries and benefits packages. Other firms engaged in joint optimization may pay a team rate, equalizing compensation in the interest of promoting overall corporate—and not just divisional or business unit—responsibility. Family members are encouraged to work outside the business first to get some experience. If they later join the family business, their development for top leadership is often a priority. When family members meet, the pendulum is allowed to swing back and forth between family and business priorities. These families realize that such a flexible and balanced approach allows them to invest in the subsystems in ways that, in the long run, benefit the larger system: the family business.

These families and firms have a commitment to family business continuity. Efforts to jointly optimize ownership, family, and management systems often indicate the family's desire to use the business to transfer important values and a proud history and at the same time to strive for continued improvement and growth. In these companies, ownership and organizational structures accommodate both the family-ownership strategy and the competitive strategy of the business.

A leading family-owned medical device distribution company, for example, developed a statement of company culture and values that displays a deep understanding of the powerful effects of joint optimization. Its culture and values statement says:

We are:

- Family-Owned, Professionally Managed. We are a family acting in the Company's best interest.

We believe in:

- Integrity: We do what we say we will do.
- No Walls: We have no barriers to communication.

- Tenacity: We have an unrelenting determination to reach objectives.
- Profitability: We are committed to performance and results.
- Improvement: We are never satisfied.
- Service: We are loyal to our customers and respect them.

THE AGENCY THEORY PERSPECTIVE

Traditionally, agency theory has argued that the natural alignment of owners and managers (the agents) in a family business decreases the need for formal supervision of agents and for elaborate governance mechanisms, thus reducing agency costs of ownership in family firms. More recently, however, agency theory has been used to support the opposite conclusion. These researchers have hypothesized that family firms have one of the more costly forms of organizational governance. They posit that the altruism of owner-managers leads to increased agency costs emanating from their inability to manage conflict among owners and between owner-managers and nonfamily managers.[19] Other researchers have concluded that when family ties exist between owners and agents, executive entrenchment (the reluctance to transfer power to others) increases and as a result, so do agency costs.[20] Other potential sources of agency costs are attributed by both sides to goal incongruity between the CEO and the rest of the family: (1) the CEO's ability to hold out, based on his or her status within the family, (2) a preference for less business risk, (3) lack of career opportunities for nonfamily agents, (4) lack of monitoring of family members' performance, (5) lack of monitoring of the firm's performance, and (6) avoidance of strategic planning because of its potential for fostering family conflict. Strategic decisions that could highlight potential conflicts of interest between a firm's shareholders and its owner-managers include decisions about diversification, rate of growth, debt intensity, investment, CEO compensation, and CEO tenure or entrenchment.

According to agency theory, a firm's board is an important mechanism for limiting managers' self-serving behavior in situations in which a firm's managers and its owners have conflicting goals. For this reason, experts on corporate governance recommend the inclusion of outsiders as lead or presiding directors on corporate boards to ensure the board's independence from top management. This recommendation is based on the belief that inside directors, by virtue of their employment with the firm, are beholden to a CEO for their careers and are therefore unlikely to monitor the CEO's actions effectively. In contrast, outside directors are expected to provide more vigilant monitoring in order to maintain their reputations and avoid liability lawsuits.

Research suggests that agency costs may be controlled or avoided through the use of certain managerial and governance practices. Some researchers recommend a mechanism that would enable a family business to monitor the performance and decision making of family executives.[21] Others believe that a set of managerial practices, as opposed to any one specific practice, will facilitate control of these unique agency costs.[22]

---

[19]Schulze et al., op. cit.

[20]Gomez-Mejía et al., op. cit.

[21]Ibid.

[22]Schulze et al., op. cit.

This third edition of *Family Business,* on the basis of the latest research, presents this latter perspective. Based on global research on family firms, the book is organized around three leadership imperatives and five best practices to manage the unique risks posed by the overlap of family, ownership, and management of the firm. Chapters 4 through 11 discuss the unique challenges and then, through an action orientation, help the reader arrive at a series of managerial and governance best practices relevant to family firms in general or to an individual family business situation.

THE STRATEGIC PERSPECTIVE: COMPETITIVE CHALLENGES FACED BY FAMILY BUSINESSES

My experience both as a scholar and as an advisor to more than 100 family-owned businesses for the past two and a half decades substantiates what business owners often perceive as posing unique challenges to their businesses. For example, many owners see shrinking product life cycles as requiring their companies to innovate more and to adapt and renew their strategies more frequently. They also perceive intense cost competition and rapid change in distribution and value chains as requiring tremendous agility and, thus, as representing serious challenges to their firms.

Family business owners are also well aware of the increasing individualism in younger generations, whose members often view extended family and legacy as if they were alien constructs. Owners are equally concerned by the media's version of who the winners are in globally competitive markets. According to the media, large multinational, publicly traded companies are the only possible winners in the increasingly competitive landscape. This bias concerns many family business owners, who fear that the next generation of owners is growing up thinking that family businesses represent the "lagging edge" and that the exciting career opportunities lie elsewhere.

On the other hand, next-generation members are often concerned about what they perceive as the entrenchment of the current-generation CEO. In an era in which life expectancy has increased significantly, fears about the CEO never relinquishing power may be difficult to dispel. And both generations worry that the growing complexity and severity of corporate, individual, and estate-tax laws may predispose owners to make tax minimization a priority, to the detriment of other important considerations, such as agility and corporate control.

It is important to note that the agency cost studies referred to here did not include a comparative nonfamily business sample. Thus, these studies highlighted possible agency costs of altruism and CEO entrenchment in family firms but failed to address the relative impact of a different set of agency costs on nonfamily firms (e.g., the increased costs of sophisticated financial and auditing systems and staff; in the United States, the costs of compliance with the Sarbanes–Oxley Act alone are estimated at over $800,000 per year for small and midsized firms). Indeed, an equally viable possibility is that the unique differences provided by family ownership and control are a source of competitive advantage and that this advantage outweighs the unique agency costs of family firms. In other words, the literature on agency costs has not yet helped to resolve the question of whether agency costs hinder family firms or whether the interaction between business and family represents a net positive for the family firm.

COMPETITIVE ADVANTAGE: THE RESOURCE-BASED VIEW

The competitive advantages inherent in family businesses are best explained by the resource-based view of organizations. From this theoretical perspective, a firm is examined for its unique, specific, complex, dynamic, and intangible resources. These resources—often referred to as "organizational competencies"—embedded in internal processes, human resources, or other intangible assets, can provide the firm with competitive advantages in certain circumstances. In a family firm, one of these resources may be overlapping owner and manager responsibilities, which can lead to advantages—such as reduced administrative costs and speedier decision making, the result of streamlined and less-costly monitoring mechanisms that are made possible by the existence of family trust. This owner-manager overlap is also credited with enabling longer time horizons for measuring company performance, which results in share-holders behaving as patient family capitalists.

Other resources unique to family firms may be customer-intense relationships, which are supported by an organizational culture committed to high quality and good customer service, and the transfer of knowledge and skills from one generation to the next, which makes it easier to sustain and even improve firm performance.[23] Owner-ship commitment (willingness to hold on and fight) over the long term, rather than shareholder apathy and capital flight (e.g., readiness to switch from IBM shares to GE shares in the portfolio), is yet another possible source of competitive advantage. The Ford, Hewlett, and Packard families have all exemplified this potentially unique resource in their ownership stance vis-à-vis CEO performance in the past decade.

The unique resources that family businesses can call on to create competitive advantage are:

- Overlapping responsibilities of owners and managers, along with smaller company size, which enable rapid speed to market.
- Concentrated ownership structure, which leads to higher overall corporate productivity and longer-term commitment to investments in people and innovation.
- A focus on customers and market niches, which results in higher returns on investment.
- The desire to protect the family name and reputation, which often translates into high product/service quality and the higher returns on investment that being a high-quality leader produces.
- The nature of the family–ownership–management interaction, family unity, and ownership commitment, which support patient capital, lower administrative costs, skills/knowledge transfer across generations, and agility in rapidly changing markets.

Family firms, for instance, may routinely be able to make decisions more quickly and may therefore take advantage of opportunities that others miss. Quick decision making is critical in business, and tight-knit families in business move fast. Clear Channel Communications grew from 16 radio stations in 1989 to more than 1200 (and

---

[23]Cabrera-Suarez, K., De Saa-Perez, P., & Garcia-Almeida, D., The Succession Process from a Resource-and-Knowledge–Based View of the Firm. *Family Business Review, 14*(1), 2001, pp. 37–47.

36 television stations) in 2006. Mark P. Mays, the founder's son, notes that when making acquisitions, they move like lightning.

In 2002, family-controlled enterprises on the S&P 500 reinvested $617.8 million, compared with a meager $79 million for their nonfamily counterparts. (Even though family-controlled enterprises represented only a third of the S&P 500, they reinvested almost 10 times as much during the recessionary year that followed the bursting of the Internet bubble and 9/11.) Family-controlled companies were also less likely to pay out dividends, with 61 percent making these payouts as compared with 77 percent of nonfamily firms.[24] This is compelling evidence of the higher propensity of family-controlled and closely held firms to invest with a long-term horizon. Research has found that the practice by family-controlled and closely held firms to continue to invest in people and technology through the ups and downs of economic cycles leads to higher company productivity. According to another study, three additional competitive advantages that the family firm enjoys are: efficiency, with lower overall administrative costs because of the owner-manager overlap; social capital, with its transfer of knowledge and relationship- and network-building benefits; and opportunistic investment, based on its speed and agility in the face of new opportunities.[25]

In a study conducted in 2003 involving a sample of 700 family businesses in Germany and France, the firms in which families had significant influence and there was considerable overlap between ownership and management roles enjoyed appreciably improved financial performance. However, when the family's representation in management far exceeded the cash-flow rights of their ownership stake, the firm's performance suffered.[26]

In Spain, the performance of 8000 large- and medium-sized family and nonfamily firms was compared based on 2002 data. Spanish family firms performed better in terms of return on equity than their nonfamily counterparts of the same size and in the same industry. Family involvement in management by itself did not prove to have a positive impact on the firm's performance.[27]

A study of six European stock exchanges, from London's FTSE to Spain's IBEX, done by Thomson Financial and reported in *Newsweek* consistently found that family firms in Europe outperformed their counterparts.[28]

In Latin America, a study of 175 firms traded in the Bolsa de Comercio de Santiago (Chile's principal stock exchange) compared the performance of 100 family firms with that of 75 nonfamily firms during the 10 years between 1994 and 2003 and found that family firms outperformed their counterparts in return on assets and return on equity (both measures of profitability). They also performed better in Tobin's Q, a proxy

---

[24]Weber, J., et al., Family, Inc., *BusinessWeek*, November 10, 2003, pp. 100–114.

[25]Carney, M., Corporate Governance and Competitive Advantage in Family-Controlled Firms. *Entrepreneurship Theory and Practice*, 29, 2005, pp. 249–266.

[26]Jaskiewicz, P., Family Influence and Performance: An Empirical Study for Germany and France, European Business School, International University Schloß Reichartshausen, Germany. Unpublished paper presented at a meeting of the International Family Enterprise Research Association, 2003.

[27]Menéndez-Requejo, S., Ownership Structure and Firm Performance: Evidence from Spanish Family Firms, University of Oviedo, Spain. Unpublished paper presented at a meeting of the International Family Enterprise Research Association, 2005.

[28]Best of the Best, *Newsweek*, April 12, 2005.

figure **1.2** | **The Relative Performance of Family Firms**

Performance of Family Firms and Nonfamily Firms

	Family-Controlled Firms	Management-Controlled Firms
Shareholder Return	15.6%	11.2%
Return on Assets	5.4%	4.1%
Revenue Growth	23.4%	10.8%
Income Growth	21.1%	12.6%
(Between 1992 and 2002, S&P 500 list)		

Performance of Family Firms Compared to Nonfamily Firms

Return on Assets (ROA) + 6.5%*

Market value* + 10%†

*In EBITDA terms, between 1992 and 1999, S&P 500 list; similar outperformance in return on equity
†Tobin's Q market value to replacement value of assets, between 1992 and 1999, S&P list.

SOURCES: Weber, J., et al., Family, Inc. *Business Week*, November 10, 2003, pp. 100–114; and Anderson, R., & Reeb, D., Founding Family Ownership and Firm Performance: Evidence from the S&P 500. *The Journal of Finance, 58*(3), June 2003, pp. 1301–1328.

measure of the creation of market value during that period. In Chile, a majority of the publicly traded firms (57 percent) were family-controlled.[29]

In the United States, it was the pioneering study by Anderson and Reeb[30] that prompted the international research discussed previously. Their study found that family-controlled firms in the S&P 500 outperformed management-controlled firms by 6.65 percent in return on assets and return on equity and created an additional 10 percent in market value between 1992 and 1999. For a comparative view of the data supporting the relative performance and unique competitive advantages of family firms, refer to Figures 1.2 and 1.3.

The ability of a particular family business to capitalize on its unique advantages depends on the quality of the interaction between business and family. It is precisely this interface that agency theorists suggest needs to be addressed with a series of managerial and governance practices that will safeguard the firm from any family-based hazards. Measuring the perceptions of different stakeholders, monitoring executive performance, and implementing a particular set of prescribed managerial and governance practices can all contribute to controlling the hypothesized costs and turning the unique features of family firms into resources that actually produce competitive advantage.

The importance of (1) jointly optimizing the ownership, management, and family subsystems, (2) controlling agency costs, and (3) ultimately exploiting the unique resources available to family businesses in order to achieve competitive advantage provides both the theoretical framework and the practical take aways contained in this book.

---

[29]Martinez, J. & Stohr, B., Family Ownership and Firm Performance: Evidence from Public Companies in Chile. Unpublished paper presented at a meeting of the International Family Enterprise Research Association, 2005.

[30]Anderson, R., & Reeb, D., op. cit.

figure **1.3** | **Competitive Advantages of Many Family Businesses on Seven Dimensions**

I. Speed to Market (Data based on firm size, not form of ownership. Family businesses, on average, are smaller.)

Market	Company Size (in sales)	Time to Bring New Product to Market
United States	>$100 million	22.6 months
	<$100 million	16.0 months
In Japan	>$100 million	19.1 months
	<$100 million	14.0 months
In Europe	>$100 million	23.4 months
	<$100 million	15.9 months

SOURCE: Boston Consulting Group, http://www.bcg.com.

II. Strategic Focus on Niches*

Market Size	Business Performance (as measured by ROI)[†]
<$50 million	28.1%
$50 to $100 million	26.8%
$100 to $250 million	24.2%
<$1 billion	10.9%

*Based on market size served, not family ownership. Family businesses more often than not compete in the relatively smaller niche markets as opposed to larger market segments)
†4-year average return on investment (ROI).

SOURCE: Clifford, D., & Cavanagh, R., *The Winning Performance: How America's High Growth Midsize Companies Succeed.* New York: Bantam, 1985.

III. Ownership Concentration and Corporate Productivity*

Stock concentration is positively correlated with

- Related diversification

- R&D expenses/employee

- Training expenses/employee

- Overall corporate productivity

*Sample composed of largely but not exclusively family-controlled companies.

SOURCE: Hill, C., & Snell, S., Effects of Ownership Structure and Control on Corporate Productivity. *Academy of Management Journal, 32*(1), 1989, pp. 25–45.

IV. Relative Quality and Return on Investment*

Relative Product Quality	Return on Investment (as measured by ROI)[†]
High	27.1%
Medium	19.8%
Low	16.8%

*Based on quality positioning, not on family ownership. Family businesses have a demonstrated capacity to compete on the basis of brand, reputation, and high relative quality, but the sample includes nonfamily firms.
†4-year average ROI.

SOURCE: Clifford, D., & Cavanagh, R., *The Winning Performance: How America's High Growth Midsize Companies Succeed.* New York: Bantam, 1985.

figure **1.3** *(Continued)*

V. Patient Capital and Long-Term Perspective

- Average tenure of 18 years for owner-managers versus 8 years for public-company CEOs is correlated with commitment to the long term and making efficient long-term investments in the family business.[*]

- Company continually optimizes the mix among family, management, employees, customers, and ownership for higher long-term profitability.[†]

[*]Daily, C., & Dollinger, M., An Empirical Examination of Ownership Structure in Family and Professionally Managed Firms. *Family Business Review, 5*(2), 1992; and James, H., Owner as Manager, Extended Horizons and the Family Firm. *International Journal of the Economics of Business, 6*(1), 1999.
[†]Adapted from Waterman, Robert H., Jr., *What America Does Right.* New York: W. W. Norton, 1994.

VI. Total Costs

	Family Businesses	Other Businesses
Lower cost of capital[*]	When the business owner controls 100% of the stock and the stock is in the hands of family shareholders enjoying family harmony, the effective cost of capital is nearly 0%. While there is an opportunity cost, cash flow from the business can be reinvested for growth without paying out high dividends or taxes or incurring high interest on debt.	Financing costs for other businesses can range from 25%–30% for venture capital to 17%–20% for mezzanine financing to the prime rate for bank financing.
Lower administrative costs[†]	According to the agency cost literature, the overlap between owner and manager or principal and agent allows family-owned businesses to enjoy lower administrative costs because of lower CEO compensation, reduced levels of supervision, and reduced investment in financial systems and controls.	

[*]deVisscher, Francois, When Shareholders Lose Their Patience. *Family Business Magazine, 11*(4), 2000.
[†]Gomez-Mejía, L., Larraza-Kintana, M., & Makri, M., The Determinants of Executive Compensation in Family-Controlled Public Corporations. *Academy of Management Journal, 46*(2), 2003, pp. 226–237.

VII. Agility and Customization Capability in Rapidly Changing Markets

- Inventory and quality costs of capital-intensive, long-run manufacturing have increased in the past decade. The greater flexibility of new manufacturing and distribution-retail-service technology (including numerical control equipment in the factory and low-cost PCs in distribution centers and retail points) makes smaller runs economically attractive. Family firms often populate this space.

- Increasing demand for customization, rapid changes in consumer preferences, and shorter product life cycles lead to rewards for opportunity-seeking owner-managers who can make decisions fast. Family firms often compete in this space, a legacy of their entrepreneurial past.

- Internet-based, value-added partnerships in the supply chain make agility possible across the value chain. An early example was the Milliken–Levi Strauss–Dillards (all family businesses) electronics data interchange supply chain agreement in the early 1980s.

SOURCE: Poza, E., Look Who's Out There on the Cutting Edge. *Family Business Magazine, 4*(1), 1993.

THE STEWARDSHIP PERSPECTIVE

This perspective claims that founding-family members view the firm as an extension of themselves and therefore view the continuing health of the enterprise as connected with their own personal well-being.

In a meeting of the fifth generation of the Blethen family, owners of The Seattle Times Company, chairman and publisher Frank Blethen spoke of the commitment from every Blethen generation that resulted in 100 years of caring leadership and stewardship of *The Seattle Times* and other newspapers in the corporate group. He emphasized the need to value the extended family over individual or branch needs and challenged individuals who accepted participation in the family clan to assume the stewardship responsibilities in order for them to be successful as individuals.

He went on to assert that understanding the individual's responsibility toward the group is essential—as is having realistic expectations of what you do and do not get from being a member of the Blethen family and The Seattle Times Company. More than money, family members inherit a responsibility to others, to stewardship, so that the enterprise they received from the earlier generation may successfully pass on to the next.

In 1980, a long strike threatened the viability of this commitment. "Frank Blethen concedes the strike was a tremendous financial hit to The Times, causing him for the first time in his life to consider the possibility of selling. Fortunately those darkest moments ultimately strengthened the family's resolve. The stewardship they feel toward the newspaper and its place in this community is too important."[31]

As stewards of the firm, family owners often place individuals on the board who have industry knowledge and who can provide objective advice and advocate for a going concern. The independence of the board is less an end in itself than a reflection of the family's commitment to avail itself of complementary skills that the family lacks, such as legal, financial, succession-planning, accounting, and international-marketing skills and knowledge. The directors are chosen to promote continued corporate health, based on their ability to provide advice that adds value. As such the board has a positive impact on the financial performance of the firm through its advice more than through its monitoring or supervisory function.

Interestingly, among S&P 500 firms, independent directors hold more than 61.2 percent of the board seats in nonfamily firms but only 43.9 percent in family firms. And the performance advantage, in terms of return on assets/return on equity (ROA/ROE) and market valuation, demonstrated by family firms between 1992 and 1999 relative to management-controlled firms[32] vanishes in the absence of an independent board providing company oversight. Even more strikingly, and consistent with agency theory, the most valuable S&P 500 firms are those in which independent directors balance board representation by family members. Firms with continued founding-family ownership and relatively few independent directors perform significantly worse than do nonfamily firms.[33]

In family firms then, whether from an agency or a stewardship perspective, independent and advisory directors remain the primary line of defense against the managerial opportunism, expropriation, and entrenchment that large, controlling

---

[31] *The Seattle Times*, Sunday, January 21, 2001.

[32] Anderson, R., & Reeb, D., op. cit.

[33] Anderson, R., & Reeb, D., op. cit.

shareholders can exercise in relation to minority shareholders, employees, and other stakeholders. From the agency perspective, they do so through their monitoring and supervisory role; from the stewardship perspective they do so through their advisory, objective, and committed stance to the ongoing concern. Independent and advisory directors can prevent excessive CEO compensation, flawed decision-making processes, stale strategic planning, and unearned perquisites, while limiting the family's undue influence through enhanced board dynamics and subcommittees of the board. Most importantly these boards can prevent an unqualified or incompetent family member from becoming the next CEO.[34]

ETHICS, SOCIAL RESPONSIBILITY, AND THE FAMILY BUSINESS

Family businesses are generally perceived as being less socially responsible because of their incentive to protect family wealth. They are also often perceived as less ethical because of their incentive to reduce tax liabilities and derive competitive advantage by whatever means possible in the often private, less-transparent world of most family businesses. But there is an opposite and quite compelling argument: that family businesses have a built-in desire to uphold the family company's image and protect the family's name and reputation. In fact, this third edition of *Family Business* makes the related argument with regard to the quality of the product/service the firm creates (see Figure 1.3, IV) by presenting the higher returns on invested capital possible when the firm is a high-quality provider. S.C. Johnson (maker of Raid, Off, Windex, and Oust) reminds us that they are a family company at the end of every company ad. They do this because of the perception (supported by their own market research) that family businesses care more about quality, care more about the environment, and can be counted on to stand behind their product/service far into the future.

Research using data drawn from *BusinessWeek* and the social performance rating given by Kinder, Ludenberg, Domini & Co., compared 261 firms—some family-controlled, others management-controlled—from the S&P 500 over a 10-year period. It found that although family businesses are no more likely to engage in positive social initiatives than are nonfamily companies, they are less likely to engage in activities that have negative social consequences. The authors conclude that the results point to the importance that image and reputation have for family businesses.[35]

FAMILY BUSINESS RESEARCH

The field of study of family enterprises goes back only to 1975, when entrepreneur, family business educator, and consultant Dr. Léon Danco published his pioneering work, *Beyond Survival: A Guide for the Business Owner and His Family.*[36] Two

---

[34]Shleifer, A., & Vishny, R., A Survey of Corporate Governance. *Journal of Finance,* 1997, pp. 737–783.

[35]Dyer, W.G., & Whetten, D.A., Family Firms and Social Responsibility: Preliminary Evidence from the S&P 500. *Entrepreneurship Theory and Practice, 30,* 2006, pp. 777–783.

[36]Danco, L., *Beyond Survival: A Guide for the Business Owner and His Family.* Cleveland: The University Press, 1975.

watershed events played key roles in turning the study of family business into a field:

1 The publication of a special issue of the journal *Organizational Dynamics* in 1983[37]

2 The launching of a specialized journal, *Family Business Review,* in 1986[38]

Still, between 1975 and the early 1990s, most of the published work on family businesses was anecdotal, rooted in the stories of consultants and observers of these mostly privately held enterprises. Only in the past decade has research begun to struggle with the definition of *family business* and to address its unique characteristics.

Notwithstanding the dearth of research on this unique form of organization, family businesses most likely constitute the earliest form of enterprise. Whenever parents— whether engaged in making a craft, cultivating the soil, or even ruling a country— welcomed members of the next generation as helping hands in the pursuit of that enterprise, a family business was born.

Today, family businesses are considered by many scholars to be on the cutting edge of corporate performance, job creation, return on investment, quality of product and service, flexibility, customization capability, and speed to market.[39] They are also well known for their vulnerability to decline after the retirement or demise of the founding entrepreneurial generation.[40] The agency cost literature has traditionally argued that when owners hire managers or agents, additional oversight and control mechanisms are required, resulting in an increase in enterprise-management costs.[41] More recent literature argues that agency costs are significant for family companies as a result of CEO entrenchment, conflict avoidance, and altruism.[42] The most recent research on family-firm performance, discussed earlier in this chapter, puts most of these competing arguments in perspective by clearly demonstrating that the benefits of the family– business interaction outweigh its costs on the basis of overall performance over extended periods.

One of the research studies we will be referring to in this third edition of *Family Business* is the Discovery Action Research on Family Business. This study was conducted in the form of "action research," with companies participating in the Partnership with Family Business at the Weatherhead School of Management, Case Western Reserve University, and in family business programs at the University of Pittsburgh and the University of St. Thomas. The action research constituted an iterative process of diagnosis, feedback, and collaboration with members of participating firms and families. The sample for this study included 868 executives and family members who had been involved over the past 11 years in 90 businesses. Specifically, the sample was made up of 303 family members in the business (68 percent of family members), 145 family members not active in the management of the business

---

[37]Burke, W.W., ed., *Organizational Dynamics.* New York: American Management Association, 1983.

[38]Lansberg, I., ed., *Family Business Review,* 1(1), 1986.

[39]See Astrachan & Carey, op. cit.; Kleiman, R., Petty, W., & Martin, J., Family Controlled Firms: An Assessment of Performance. *Family Business Annual,* 1, 1995, pp. 1–13; and Poza, E., *A la sombra del roble.* Cleveland: Editorial Universitaria, 1995.

[40]See Danco, op. cit.; Poza, E., *Smart Growth: Critical Choices for Family Business Continuity and Prosperity.* San Francisco: Jossey-Bass, 1989; and Ward, op. cit.

[41]Daily, C., & Dollinger, M., An Empirical Examination of Ownership Structure in Family and Professionally Managed Firms. *Family Business Review,* 5(2), 1992, pp. 117–136.

[42]See Schulze et al., op. cit.; and Gomez-Mejía et al., op. cit.

(32 percent of family members), and 420 nonfamily managers. Of those family-member respondents who identified their position in the family, 90 were CEOs (22 percent), 48 were spouses of CEOs (12 percent), 111 were sons (27 percent), 73 were daughters (18 percent), and 84 were "other" (21 percent). This "other" category included siblings of the CEO, sons- and daughters-in-law, nephews, and nieces.

This study's findings suggest that a positive family–business interaction is at the heart of creating unique and idiosyncratic competitive advantages in family firms. This research suggests safeguards that can prevent higher agency costs and highlights resources and capabilities borne out of the positive family–business interaction that can provide unique benefits to family firms. Both the safeguards and the sources of competitive advantage will be discussed in the chapters that follow.

How a family's influence might affect the strategic and economic decisions of a business and how these might affect the company's performance (and vice versa) is the frontier of much current research. Until recently, most business scholars ignored family businesses. This notwithstanding, most businesses globally are family businesses.

Scholars who did research family firms for the most part concluded that they were anachronisms and that because of nepotism, agency problems, and family conflict they were largely inefficient.[43,44]

Recently, three characteristics of the family form of governance have been identified as distinguishing them from other forms of organization. These were referred to by Carney[45] as parsimony, personalism, and particularism. *Parsimony* refers to the propensity of family firms to be vigilant about their financial resources, due to the fact that the family owns those resources. *Personalism* refers to the unique power resulting from the combination of ownership and control held by the same family. This concentration of power frees family firms, relative to nonfamily firms, from the need to account for their actions to other constituencies, giving them the discretion to act as they see fit. *Particularism* is the product of this concentration of power and its resulting discretion. Family businesses, scholars argue, have the *particular* ability to use idiosyncratic criteria and set goals that deviate from the typical profit-maximization concerns of nonfamily firms. And these three characteristics provide family firms with advantages in efficiency, social capital, and opportunistic investment.[46]

There has been modest diffusion of family business research and education in the past decade. According to the Family Firm Institute in Boston (see http://www.ffi.org), there are now more than 100 family business programs in the United States alone. And while most of the substantial research with lasting impact has also been produced in the past decade, its influence on the larger fields of management and organization is still minuscule. Great incentives for further research on family firms and for greater impact on managerial science by family firm studies now exist, given the well-documented higher performance of family firms relative to their nonfamily counterparts. Mainstream organizational research has ignored the unique advantages of the family business form, largely as a result of stereotyping family firms as the

---

[43]Carney, M., Corporate governance and Competitive Advantage in Family Controlled Firms. *Entrepreneurship Theory and Practice, 29,* 2005, pp. 249–265.

[44]Chrisman, J.J., Chua, J.H., & Steir, L.P., Sources and Consequences of Distinctive Familiness: An Introduction. *Entrepreneurship Theory and Practice, 29,* 2005, pp. 237–247.

[45]Carney, op. cit.

[46]Chrisman, J.J., Steir, L.P., & Chua, J.H., Personalism, Particularism and the Competitive Behaviors and advantages of Family Firms: An Introduction. *Entrepreneurship Theory and Practice, 30,* 2006, 719–729.

antithesis of professionally managed firms—nepotistic, irrational because of the family influence, secretive, and small and insignificant. Given the recently documented out-standing performance of family firms relative to management-controlled firms these assumptions would appear to be in dire need of a substantial update.[47]

SUMMARY

1 Family businesses are the primary engine of economic growth and vitality in free economies all over the world. Being unique in their attributes, they are also unique in the assets and vulnerabilities that they bring to the marketplace.

2 Family businesses constitute the whole gamut of enterprises in which an entrepreneur or next-generation CEO and one or more family members influence the firm via their par-ticipation, their ownership control, their strategic preferences, and the culture and values they impart to the enterprise.

3 Family businesses that have been built to last recognize the tension between preserving and protecting the core of what has made the business successful and promoting growth and adaptation to changing competitive dynamics.

4 The Discovery Action Research project is a longitudinal study whose findings suggest both safeguards that can prevent higher agency costs and resources and capabilities that can provide unique benefits to family firms.

5 In the systems theory approach, the family firm is modeled as comprising three over-lapping, interacting, and interdependent subsystems of family, management, and own-ership, making possible significant adaptive capacity and competitive advantage through joint optimization.

6 Agency theory has traditionally suggested that the overlap in ownership and manage-ment found in family firms is an asset.

7 More recently, agency theory has been used to argue that family firms have one of the more costly forms of organization. Increased agency costs result from the owner-managers' inability to manage conflict, executive entrenchment, lack of performance monitoring, and a prefer-ence for less business risk, among other things. A firm's board is an important mechanism for limiting managers' self-serving behavior in situations in which a firm's managers and its owners have conflicting goals.

8 The resource-based view of family businesses holds that competitive advantages result from: (1) overlapping responsibilities of owners and managers and small company size, enabling rapid speed to market; (2) focus on customers and market niches, resulting in higher returns on investment; (3) concentrated ownership structure, leading to higher corporate productivity; (4) desire to protect the family name and reputation, translating into high-quality products/services; and (5) family–ownership–management interaction, family unity, and ownership commitment, supporting patient capital, lower administrative costs, skills/knowledge transfer between generations, and agility in rapidly changing markets. A prescribed set of management and governance practices will help the firm capitalize on these resources.

9 The stewardship perspective on family firms argues that responsible ownership by any given generation is characterized by its commitment to something larger than the indi-vidual (e.g., the family clan) and by its dedication to passing a healthy firm on to the next

---

[47]See Daily & Dollinger, op. cit.; and James, H., Owner as Manager, Extended Horizons and the Family Firm. *International Journal of the Economics of Business*, 6(1), 1999.

generation. Appreciation of the legacy, advocacy for the ongoing concern, and advisors on a board that complement the family's competency set are often present in family firms with this perspective.

10 There is now compelling evidence that family firms outperform nonfamily firms. Studies have claimed that as family firms grow, their performance advantage remains in effect only if professionalization of the management of the firm has been achieved and a board that provides advice and independent oversight is present.

Great Families in Business: Building Trust and Commitment

Bob Reardon is fed up with his seven brothers and sisters. Their business had accumulated cash for an acquisition that Bob believed could "make" the company, but his siblings voted dividends for themselves instead. Reardon Supply is a $100-million-a-year manufacturer owned equally by the Reardon siblings. President since his dad retired nine years ago, Bob, 49, has done a superlative job, increasing revenues sevenfold, organizing an outside board of directors, and installing strategic planning companywide.

Although Reardon Supply is very efficient, has no debt, and is very liquid, its growth rate is slowing. Its competition (no longer local companies but national and international conglomerates) is squeezing margins, and more of its customers are going overseas. Running at capacity, it needs extensive capital expenditures to stay competitive.

All of Bob's siblings are settled in careers and lives outside Reardon Supply. Lately, some have become concerned about their general lack of liquidity and diversification, and have expressed an interest in cashing out. Others seem to resent Bob's salary, although they're very glad to have "one of their own" in charge. In particular, Bob's older sister, Nancy, believes he is overpaid. Her husband, Phil, is the president of a public company. Although Phil's company dwarfs Reardon, Reardon is more profitable, and Bob earns more than Phil.

A family council meeting is coming up soon. Once again, Bob is faced with siblings who do not want to hear that Reardon Supply's world is changing. He knows he has to do something, but what?[1]

Secrecy, lack of information, low levels of family emotional intelligence (or inability to recognize our own feelings and those of others and to manage our emotions and relationships with others), and little knowledge of the business among at least some family members all threaten commitment by the family to the continuity of a

---

[1]Poza, E., ed., Shareholders at the Crossroads. Family Firm Institute Case Study Series. *Nation's Business*, May 1991, p. 65.

family-controlled corporation. These deficits may be the result of a founding culture that supported autocratic leadership and control or a reincarnation of this culture in a later generation. Or they may arise from the family's belief in the many espoused benefits of privacy: flexibility and stealth in relation to competitors, minimization of tax liabilities, and management of expectations of relatives, nonfamily employees, and even unionized workers.

After years of the incumbent generation not communicating and editing and/or hiding financial statements, profit margins, cash flows, and market share information, the ability of younger family managers to substantively assist in the management of the enterprise, not to mention to become capable successors, is eroded. Whatever the intent of the CEO, years of requesting signatures with the all-too-familiar "Just sign here" and being secretive about financial and estate-planning information undermine the commitment of the spouse and the now-adult children to the dream of having the enterprise continue from generation to generation.

The presence of the family is the essential difference between a family business and other forms of enterprise, whether ownership shares are privately held or publicly traded but with family control. The most recent family-business literature cited in this chapter highlights the role that the family and its culture play in creating both organizational challenges and unique competitive advantages. In the past, researchers and educators in the field of business have largely ignored the family as a fundamental variable in their research and teaching. This is detrimental to both our understanding of family firms and of the management of firms in general, given that 90 percent of businesses in the United States are family businesses, employing 59 percent of the workforce and accounting for 49 percent of the country's gross domestic product.[2] To a large extent then, models and theories of management have been less robust and less generalizable than needed by management science, an eminently pragmatic discipline and field of study.[3] In fact, many widely used business-school cases in strategy, marketing, and organizational behavior like Steinberg, Inc., Zara, J Boats, and Corning, Inc. and widely read business books like *Built to Last*[4] and *Good to Great*[5] either totally ignore or only casually acknowledge the presence of an owning family.

Perhaps even more surprising is that even in the family-business literature, family members who are not active in the management of the family business are often ignored in the process of understanding or describing the business. Nevertheless, family members who do not participate in the management of the business often have significant influence on the deliberations, decisions, and long-term processes of the family-owned or family-controlled corporation.[6] And when these members' perspectives and contributions are not considered, not deemed legitimate, or

---

[2]Shanker, M., & Astrachan, J., Myths and Realities: Family Businesses' Contribution to the U.S. Economy. *Family Business Review, 9*(2), pp. 107–119.

[3]Dyer, W.G., The Family: The Missing Variable in Organizational Research. *Entrepreneurship Theory and Practice,* Summer 2003, pp. 401–416.

[4]Porras, J., & Collins, J., *Built to Last.* New York: HarperCollins, 1997.

[5]Collins, J., *Good to Great: Why Some Companies Make the Leap . . . and Others Don't.* New York: Harper Business, 2001.

[6]Heck, R., A Commentary on "Entrepreneurship in Family vs. Non-Family Firms: A Resource-Based Analysis of the Effect of Organizational Culture," by Shaker Zahara, James C. Hayton, and Carlo Salvato, *Entrepreneurship Theory and Practice, 28*(4).

underweighted, they may experience a sense of inequity.[7] This sense of injustice, whether by minority shareholders, participating members, or younger members of the family is often a cauldron for eventual family conflict.

Even owners of small family businesses seem to adopt the stereotypical assumption that significant involvement of family members is a sign of a poorly run business. But there is evidence from the 1997 National Family Business Survey, a large study of smaller family firms (with mean gross business revenues of slightly more than $1 million), that each additional family member employed (including temporary and part-time) in the business is associated with at least a small ($2,000) increase in annual revenue. Revenues also increased when family tension was reduced, when the two- or three-generation family lived together, and when family members reallocated time from sleep to the business and hired temporary help during busy times.[8]

This chapter will first address family systems theory, genograms, and family history in an effort to promote a greater understanding of a very complex subject. It will then discuss how to manage family issues in order to influence in a positive way the unique interaction between a family and a business that lies at the core of every family firm.

THE STORIES OF TWO VERY DIFFERENT FAMILY CULTURES

THE BINGHAMS AND THE LOUISVILLE COURIER-JOURNAL COMPANIES

The following stories convey how differently secrecy, open communication, family cultures, and policies guiding the interaction between a family and its business can influence the fate of a company.

On Thursday, January 9, 1986, Barry Bingham, Sr., announced that the *Louisville Courier-Journal* would be sold. The Binghams had remained unable to communicate and resolve the differences between members of the family. (If you have not already done so, please read Case 1: The Binghams and The Louisville Courier-Journal Companies for additional background information.) An agreement was reached on that fateful day with the Gannett Company, and the Bingham family members cashed out. All emerged cash-rich, but some who cared about the legacy were heartbroken.

Much had gone wrong in the Bingham family's leadership of the *Louisville Courier-Journal* and its other media properties. Absent was a visible commitment to continuity on the part of Barry Sr., the chairman and CEO. Also absent was a board with independent outsiders. Lacking too was spousal leadership by Mary Bingham as a trust catalyst (a facilitator and communications catalyst)[9]; she could have provided the glue that would have kept the Bingham family united and focused on a win–win environment. Relationships in the Bingham family appeared to be characterized by an emotional distance, which created an irreparable gulf between adults of two generations. Barry Sr. never vested full authority in Barry Jr., as evidenced by several instances of

---

[7]Stewart, A., Help One Another, Use One Another: Toward an Anthropology of Family Business. *Entrepreneurship Theory and Practice*, Summer 2003, pp. 383–396.

[8]Olson, P., et al., The Impact of the Family and the Business on Family Business Sustainability. *Journal of Business Venturing, 18*, 2003, pp. 639–666.

[9]La Chapelle, K., & Barnes, L., The Trust Catalyst in Family-Owned Businesses, *Family Business Review, 11*(1), 1998, pp. 1–17.

second-guessing his son, the president, and by his retaining voting control. By never communicating his commitment to continuity or his plans to transfer voting control to his son and by approving the sale of the company when a consensus could not be reached, he frittered away his power as a father, a CEO, and majority owner to promote continuity across generations. Continuity, at least in retrospect, would have been preferable to the observed outcomes—high capital gains and estate taxes paid by Bingham family members, an extended family that remained fractured and distant after the sale, and the loss of jobs and a community-responsive local newspaper.

The sale of the company did not, after all, bring the family together as Barry Sr. had expected. Each member of the third generation went off on her or his own. Years later, their conflict would remain unresolved. Several fourth-generation members openly regretted the decision to sell the company and the loss of identity, legacy, and opportunity that it represented for them. After all, the dream that "someday all of this would be theirs" had found fertile ground in their minds as they grew up. Many of the actions that the Binghams could have taken to reverse course and prevent the disadvantaged sale of their properties would have been in the province of family meetings. But without such a governance body, the conflict was taken to the board of directors, composed primarily of family members, which was clearly overwhelmed by the conflict and paralyzed by its membership. Board members Sallie and Eleanor had spent most of their lives away from Louisville, the family, and the family enterprise. They had pursued careers that hardly prepared them for leadership of an important media company.

In the absence of family meetings, next-generation family members lacked the education, information, give-and-take communication, and emotional intelligence that would have promoted understanding among the individual heirs. When Barry Sr. named Sallie and Eleanor to the board, he gave them influence far beyond their capacity to understand and plan for the not-too-distant succession and transfer of power. Membership in a family council (to be discussed later in this chapter as a way of managing and even preempting some sources of family conflict) could have fostered the understanding needed for such planning, through years of working together in council meetings.

THE BLETHENS AND THE SEATTLE TIMES COMPANY

In the same industry, a decade or so later, an even older media institution planned for the continuity of the business under family control, making family meetings a central governance body. In a meeting of the fifth generation of Blethens, chairman and publisher Frank Blethen spoke of the commitment of every Blethen generation, which had resulted in 100 years of caring leadership and stewardship of the *Seattle Times* and other newspapers in the corporate group. He emphasized the need to value the extended family over the individual or family branch, and he challenged individuals who participated in the family business to assume stewardship responsibilities. He asserted that, in order for them to be successful as individuals, it was essential that they understand the individual's responsibility toward the group.[10]

More than money, what Blethen family members inherit through their ownership of the Seattle Times Company is a responsibility to others and to stewardship, so that the enterprise they received from an earlier generation may be successfully passed on to

---

[10]Fancher, M., Coming Together after Strike to Rebuild Relationships, Trust. *The Seattle Times*, January 21, 2001.

the next. Documents drafted in the mid-1970s by third- and fourth-generation members committed the firm and the family to two basic goals: "To perpetuate Blethen family ownership and to maintain the dominance of The Seattle Times Newspaper." These commitments were tested in April 2000, when a protracted strike created such financial problems for the newspaper that it was on the verge of having to shut down. Frank Blethen calls the period after the strike "Back to the Future." He likens the situation at that time to the early 1980s, when his generation of family owners and senior managers started taking over the company. "He concedes the strike was a tremendous financial hit to the *Times,* causing him for the first time in his life to consider the possibility of selling. Fortunately those darkest moments ultimately strengthened the family's resolve. The stewardship they feel toward the newspaper and its place in this community is too important."[11]

So, instead of quitting in the face of serious adversity, the extended family recommitted itself to perpetuating family ownership and building a stronger *Seattle Times,* fully aware of the personal sacrifices that this decision would entail.

Members of the fourth generation were proud to report during their family council, the "Fifth Edition Family Business Meeting," that on their watch both the business and the family had become better off. In the 1990s alone, the company grew from two daily newspapers to six daily newspapers, two weekly newspapers, and two major information websites; assets grew 215 percent; and cash flow increased 33 percent. Dividends paid out by the Blethen Corporation approached $30 million—a significant accomplishment, given that only 20 years earlier no dividends were being paid. The Blethens were also proud to report that the *Seattle Times* had been a finalist for six Pulitzer prizes and had been named the 14th best newspaper in the United States, almost certainly making it the best regional newspaper in the country. At this family meeting, there was much information shared and much to be proud of. It is precisely this kind of education and information-sharing that keeps patient capital patient.

Unlike the adult Bingham children, the next generation of Blethens was being prepared for stewardship and family unity. The fifth generation was being coached in the value of subsuming individual agendas for maximum and immediate gain in order to achieve a greater long-term gain for all.

ZERO-SUM DYNAMICS AND FAMILY CULTURE

It is within the rights of ownership to focus on individual gain and to retain the right to immediate liquidity. However, multigenerational family-controlled businesses, even those with some exposure to public markets, are largely illiquid enterprises. This lack of liquidity and need for selfless interest can be a burden for family members operating in a society that tends to focus on the short term, the last quarter, the day trade. They will bear this responsibility willingly only if opportunities to acquire information, to be educated, and to engage with important family values of stewardship are plentiful. Inclusion, affection, and mutual influence across generations and between active and inactive shareholders are a must. Investing sweat equity in disseminating information to family members and encouraging multiple avenues of participation gives rise to

---

[11]Ibid.

trust, a spirit of service, and a sense that everyone is in the same boat on the same long journey.

Because of the myriad ways in which us-and-them behavior can manifest itself, multigenerational families are fertile ground for zero-sum dynamics. Zero-sum dynamics in relationships are characterized by exchanges in which one party's perceived gain is the other party's perceived loss. For example, if one branch of the family uses educational assistance for next-generation members, another branch assumes that less will be available for its children. Or, if family members in top management are to be compensated at a fair market rate, those not active in management assume that they will have to settle for lower dividends to accommodate those salaries. Even more critically, if those active in top management agree on a growth strategy, family members employed elsewhere believe that, in settling for greater reinvestment in the business, they will have to accept reduced distributions to shareholders. This us-and-them zero-sum dynamic can be triggered by any perceived difference: male–female, active–inactive, richer–poorer, better educated–less educated, older–younger, blood relative–in-law. Zero-sum dynamics become rooted in reality when the enterprise or family wealth stops growing or is in decline—that is, when the pie is not getting any larger. Members of multigenerational families that operate on the assumption that another family member's gain is their loss are fertile ground for the development of family conflict.

THE FAMILY SYSTEMS PERSPECTIVE

Family systems theory is a theory of human behavior that considers the family to be the building block of emotional life and uses systems thinking[12] to understand the complex interaction between individual members of the family unit. In the family systems literature, the family represents a group-level phenomenon—a higher-order level than that of the individual. A higher-order system, from this perspective, offers the opportunity to bring about change at that system level and to leverage changes at lower-level subsystems—that is, change in the family, whether brought about by therapeutic intervention or some other means, is more likely to bring about sustainable change in the individual members of the family. Developments in family systems thinking by Drs. Murray Bowen, Monica McGoldrick, Fredda Herz Brown, and others[13] help in the analysis of the intricate dynamics of interdependent family life.

The family systems perspective argues that the same interdependence that accrues benefits of connectedness and the satisfaction of social, physical, intellectual, and emotional needs gives rise to unmet expectations and personal distress. The emotional interdependence of families may very well have evolved to fulfill a primary mission of family life—unity in the face of the need to protect, feed, and nurture family members, particularly the next generation.[14] But that same interdependence gives rise to many conflicting needs, desires, and priorities as the family grows and ages.

---

[12]Emery, F. (ed.) *Systems Thinking*. Middlesex, England: Penguin Books, 1974.

[13]See Bowen, M., *Family Therapy in Clinical Practice*. New York: J. Aronson, 1978; Herz Brown, F., *Reweaving the Family Tapestry*. New York: W.W. Norton, 1991; and McGoldrick, M., *Genograms: Assessment and Intervention*, 2nd ed. New York: W.W. Norton, 1999.

[14]See http://www.thebowencenter.org.

While families often look to blame an individual member whenever there is trouble and tensions mount, family systems theory argues that sharing responsibility for the difficulty and its remediation is more effective than pursuing individual solutions.

The family systems perspective also argues compellingly for the tremendous influence of an individual's family of origin. The premise is that we all carry much baggage from our two or three preceding generations, and that patterns and processes set in motion during those generations still matter. Therefore, the analysis of earlier generations is essential to understanding what ails or distresses a family in the present. Bowen's theory of family systems in summary states that:

1. A family is a system.
2. Family systems transfer rules, patterns, messages, or expectations about the behavior of its members.
3. Individuals and families can still learn behaviors and establish patterns different from those transferred by messages from the family of origin.
4. Tension and distress tend to make individuals go back to patterns and behaviors learned from their family of origin, unless by purposeful self-differentiation and maturation, a different behavior is learned and used.[15]

Differentiation of self is therefore a foundational principle of family systems theory. It suggests that emotions are very old and very powerful in the context of our family history and that only to the extent that they are complemented with thought, even under conditions of stress, can individuals rise from the historic patterns. Precisely because of the difficulty implicit in self-differentiation, individuals often behave as if they were pouring their emotional selves onto others, which in family systems theory gives rise to Bowen's concept of triangulation.

Triangulation is the predictable emotional pattern among three people, with the third, the outsider, being "triangled" as a result of the emotional outpouring in the relationship between the other two family members. For example, a husband and wife, in conflict over their respective needs to control or influence the marital relationship to their satisfaction, may triangle a young son or daughter. The son or daughter, feeling the tension, acts out in some way and diffuses or distracts the couple from the original conflict and creates a new focus for family attention. The less well differentiated the people in the triangle are, the more likely it is that emotions will get the upper hand and impair family members' ability to think themselves out of the situation creatively. In large, extended families, scores of triangles exist, and according to this theory whenever two people are in conflict, a triangled person is not far away from being brought into the discussion for support or reassurance. But ultimately it is the task of the two in conflict to resolve the situation, and not through the triangled third, who is most at risk by getting in the middle, unless she or he is masterfully self-differentiated.

Bowen's theory of family systems also describes the potential for cutoffs from the family of origin, meaning unresolved emotional attachments to parents that lead to family members distancing themselves from their families of origin, sometimes only to "repeat the sins of their past"—for example, by distancing themselves from a spouse.

Family systems theory fundamentally aims to increase our understanding of family patterns and behaviors and of how these might help or hinder relationships between

---

[15]Bork, D., *Family Business, Risky Business*. New York: AMACOM, 1986.

family members and between the family and its business. By assuming a historical (three-generation minimum) perspective, it also helps clarify family messages and family values that still influence family members' actions, decisions, and attitudes in the present. By shedding some light on these and the way a family communicates, plans, and resolves or denies conflicts, it also helps business families get better at addressing the problems, challenges, and opportunities they face.

Family life and the analysis of family behavior is not the central focus of this book. But family dynamics and a family's emotional intelligence are important subjects for students of family business to understand and address. The endnotes provide great resources for readers who are inclined to study the subject further.

Family business owners, nonfamily management in family firms, and service providers to family businesses all need to better understand the complex family matters and the powerful emotional fields that have a great impact on a family-owned or family-controlled enterprise—whether the subject is management, strategy, successor selection, the location of new plants and offices, acquisitions, or the ability to adapt and compete. In the sections and chapters that follow, family, as a subject, will continue to influence the discussions of the unique challenges and opportunities of a family business. Also keep in mind that while this section has been referring to family systems, since the family is only part of the whole family-business system, the book will generally refer to the family subsystem. While in family systems theory the family is a system all to itself, it is a subsystem in the context of the higher-order system called "the family business." (See Chapters 1 and 2 for a fuller description of the family-business system perspective and the family subsystem's role in it.)

THE ROLE OF GENOGRAMS AND FAMILY MESSAGES IN HELPING US UNDERSTAND THE FAMILY SYSTEM

A genogram, a cousin of the traditional family tree, informs us not just of family names, relationships, ages, and lineal descendants, but also captures critical events (e.g., a divorce), the quality of relationships (e.g., highly conflictual or extremely close), and important messages transmitted across generations (e.g., "education and hard work are both important"). It can alert us to patterns of illness (e.g., heart attacks and alcoholism) and to the role that a second marriage and the younger heirs could play in estate and succession planning. On July 30, 2005, for example, Lachlan Murdoch resigned from News Corp., parent company of Fox News and the *New York Post*. News sources attributed the resignation to unresolved differences between Lachlan, 33, and his father, News Corp. CEO Rupert Murdoch, 74, regarding the treatment of his 3- and 2-year-old stepsisters in the estate plan. Critical incidents in family life can all be recorded in a genogram to better understand the implications of family on important family and family-business issues such as business succession, estate plans and ownership transfer, family unity, likely alliances, and likely sources of conflict.

Genograms have been widely used by family therapists, and more recently, by family-practice physicians and family-business consultants to help their clients understand the influences of their families on relationships and behavior under stressful

figure **2.1** | **Genogram Template**

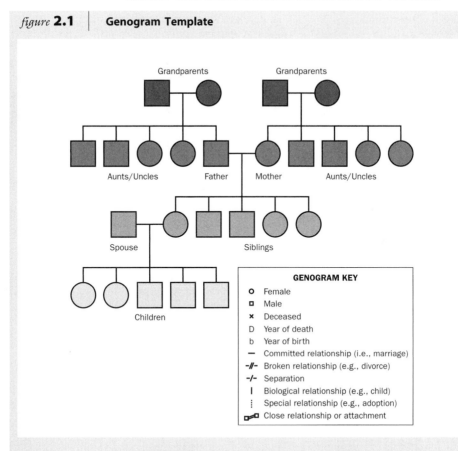

conditions. Family firms often experience significant conflict, the potential being greater than for other firms because of the overlap of family and business.[16]

To construct a genogram of your own family, follow the genogram template provided in Figure 2.1 and the key of symbols as defined in that template. Use pen and pencil or the "Draw" program that is part of Microsoft Word to draft your own genogram. (Genealogy software is also available for download and purchase and may make the task a little easier. An Internet search using the term *genogram* will guide you to other useful resources.)

Some cautionary statements to keep in mind in the process of developing your family's genogram include:

1. Doing the research for a genogram may entail sensitive conversations with some members of your family. Be careful about these conversations, and request permission from all participants before going ahead with your inquiry. Proceed only if family members have expressed permission for you to do so. If this is a class assignment, explain that to your relatives and disclose the instructor's

---

[16]Lee, M., & Rogoff, E., Research Note: Comparison of Small Businesses with Family Participation versus Small Businesses without Family Participation: An Investigation of Differences in Goals, Attitudes, and Family/Business Conflict. *Family Business Review*, 9(4), 1996, pp. 423–437.

figure **2.2** **The Family Genogram: One Example**

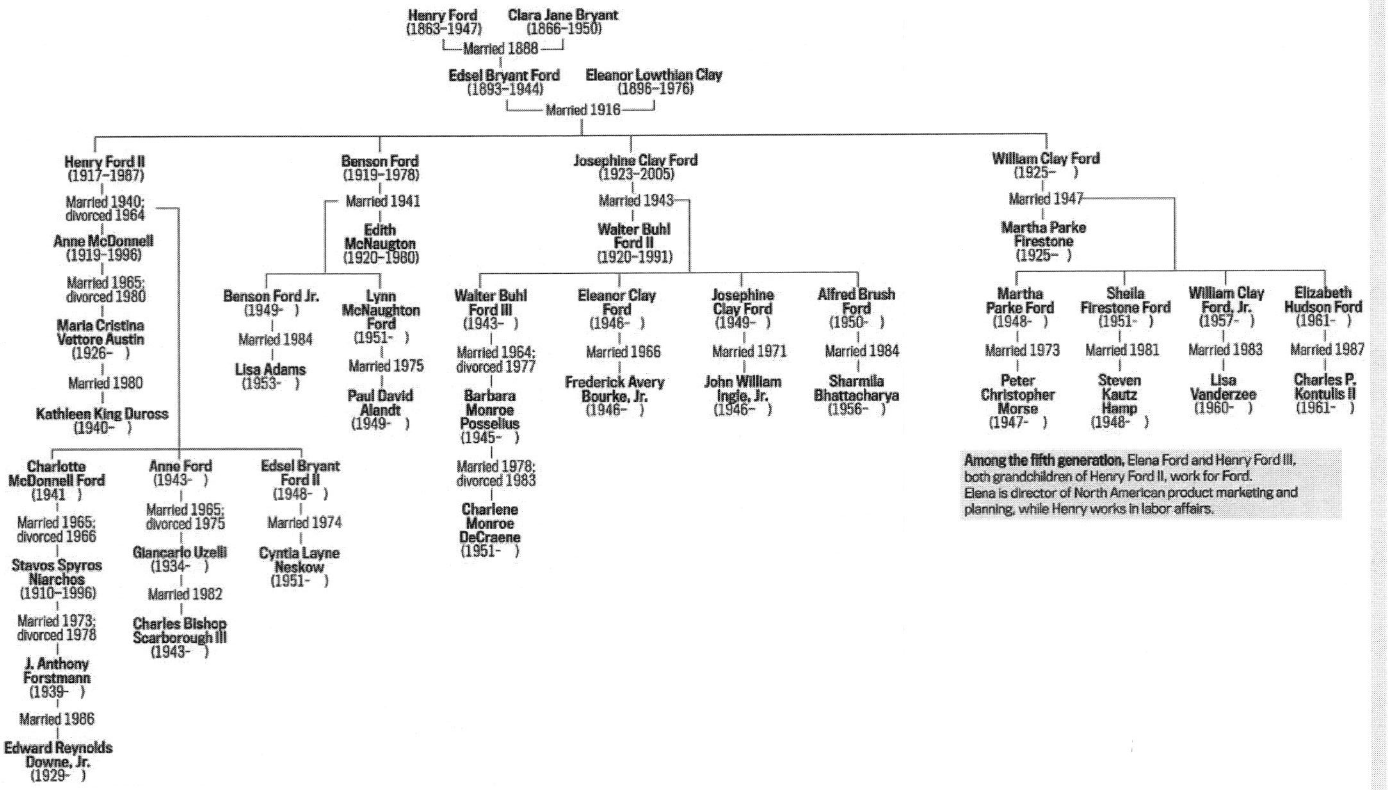
Henry Ford
(1863–1947)
Clara Jane Bryant
(1866–1950)
Married 1888
Edsel Bryant Ford
(1893–1944)
Eleanor Lowthian Clay
(1896–1976)
Married 1916
Henry Ford II
(1917–1987)
Married 1940; divorced 1964
Anne McDonnell
(1919–1996)
Married 1965; divorced 1980
Maria Cristina Vettore Austin
(1926–)
Married 1980
Kathleen King Duross
(1940–)
Charlotte McDonnell Ford
(1941)
Married 1965; divorced 1966
Stavos Spyros Niarchos
(1910–1996)
Married 1973; divorced 1978
J. Anthony Forstmann
(1939–)
Married 1986
Edward Reynolds Downe, Jr.
(1929–)
Anne Ford
(1943–)
Married 1965; divorced 1975
Giancarlo Uzelli
(1934–)
Married 1982
Charles Bishop Scarborough III
(1943–)
Edsel Bryant Ford II
(1948–)
Married 1974
Cyntia Layne Neskow
(1951–)
Benson Ford
(1919–1978)
Married 1941
Edith McNaugton
(1920–1980)
Benson Ford Jr.
(1949–)
Married 1984
Lisa Adams
(1953–)
Lynn McNaughton Ford
(1951–)
Married 1975
Paul David Alandt
(1949–)
Josephine Clay Ford
(1923–2005)
Married 1943
Walter Buhl Ford II
(1920–1991)
Walter Buhl Ford III
(1943–)
Married 1964; divorced 1977
Barbara Monroe Posselius
(1945–)
Married 1978; divorced 1983
Charlene Monroe DeCraene
(1951–)
Eleanor Clay Ford
(1946–)
Married 1966
Frederick Avery Bourke, Jr.
(1946–)
Josephine Clay Ford
(1949–)
Married 1971
John William Ingle, Jr.
(1946–)
Alfred Brush Ford
(1950–)
Married 1984
Sharmila Bhattacharya
(1956–)
William Clay Ford
(1925–)
Married 1947
Martha Parke Firestone
(1925–)
Martha Parke Ford
(1948–)
Married 1973
Peter Christopher Morse
(1947–)
Sheila Firestone Ford
(1951–)
Married 1981
Steven Kautz Hamp
(1948–)
William Clay Ford, Jr.
(1957–)
Married 1983
Lisa Vanderzee
(1960–)
Elizabeth Hudson Ford
(1961–)
Married 1987
Charles P. Kontulis II
(1961–)
Among the fifth generation, Elena Ford and Henry Ford III, both grandchildren of Henry Ford II, work for Ford.
Elena is director of North American product marketing and planning, while Henry works in labor affairs.

SOURCES: Hayes, W., Henry: A Life of Henry Ford II. Detroit: Detroit News Research, *The Detroit News*, 1990; and Ford Motor Co., Detroit: Detroit News Research, *The Detroit News, 2007.*

commitment to confidentiality. Make sure that the commitment to confidentiality is discussed in class.

2. After creating your genogram you should be equally careful about whom you discuss it with and under what conditions or principles of confidentiality.

3. Different people may have different information and different perceptions about what the genogram says and means. Be receptive to differences, and encourage open discussion of them. A difference of opinion about the nature of a relationship between two of the people diagrammed should not result in a new disruption to the family.

After drawing the genogram and recording dates, ages, and so forth, proceed in your inquiry to capture critical events and important family messages from the individuals portrayed on the genogram and list them alongside their spot on the genogram. (See the sample genogram in Figure 2.2.)

At the end of this chapter, the "Family Matters Project" will guide you further in the process of completing a genogram, an analysis of family messages, and a family history. Whether the project is assigned in class or not, I encourage you to invest your time and energy on a project like this one. Some students have launched such a project only to have other members of the family join them, eventually publishing a family history book in celebration of an important family or family-business anniversary. I have several in my personal library. They represent cherished gifts of love and hard work woven into the story of the still-living American Dream.

FAMILY EMOTIONAL INTELLIGENCE

The concept of emotional intelligence refers to the capacity for recognizing our own feelings and those of others and the ability to manage our emotions and our relationships with others.[17] Family emotional intelligence aims to improve the ability of individual family members to know their feelings in order to use them appropriately to make decisions. It also enables family members to manage their emotional life without being hijacked by patterns in their family of origin and increases empathy for others' emotions. Ultimately, emotional intelligence increases the ability to handle feelings with skill and harmony even when differences between family members exist, so that teamwork and loving family relationships can thrive.

Because of the tremendous importance of emotional intelligence in the context of business families, I have routinely used emotional competence inventories in executive-development programs for next-generation members.

Drs. Daniel Goleman and Richard Boyatzis developed a 63-item assessment that is available to universities worldwide, the Emotional Competence Inventory–University Edition (ECI-U). (See http://www. hayresourcesdirect.haygroup.com.) Coaching and mentoring based on the results of a 360-degree survey-feedback process, which measures key emotional competencies as perceived by others in the family and in the family business, can be a tremendous asset to all family members. It is particularly helpful to next-generation members, who are often starved for more-objective feedback.

---

[17]Goleman, D., *Working with Emotional Intelligence*. New York: Bantam Books, 1998.

table **2.1**	The ECI-U Model

Self-Awareness	Social Awareness
Emotional self-awareness	Empathy
Accurate self-assessment	Organizational awareness
Self-confidence	Service orientation
Self-Management	**Relationship Management**
Emotional self-control	Developing others
Trustworthiness	Inspirational leadership
Conscientiousness	Influence
Adaptability	Communication
Optimism	Change catalyst
	Achievement orientation
Initiative	Building bonds
	Teamwork and collaboration

SOURCE: Boyatzis, R., & Goleman, D., The ECI-U Model. Published and distributed by The Hay Group, http://www.haygroup.com, 2001.

The ECI-U provides feedback that is focused on the strengths and weaknesses of the individual respondent and his or her relationships to others (as viewed by other family members, coworkers in the business, managers, direct reports, suppliers, and even customers) and targets specific competencies to be developed to enhance the individual's emotional competency. This goes a long way toward enhancing a business family's emotional competence. (See Table 2.1.)

HOW FAMILIES ADD VALUE: THE FAMILY–BUSINESS INTERACTION FACTOR

In the Discovery Action Research Project on Family Business at Case Western Reserve University, several constructs emerged from the analysis of responses to the Family Survey. One of these constructs is family harmony. A family business with a high degree of family harmony tends to be more effective in planning for business continuity.[18] Such harmony exists when family members share values of accommodation and cooperation and handle conflict appropriately.

Tolerance of differences—the extent to which a family constructively tolerates differences of opinion and outlook on sensitive issues—is another construct that has proven useful in understanding family dynamics and a family's relationship to the business. It represents the quality and the nature of communication within a family. Family meetings provide the opportunity for nonactive family members to share their perspectives and/or concerns regarding the business, which are often very different from those of family members who are active in the business. Advocates maintain that the positive effects of family meetings derive from different stakeholders' talking to and

---

[18]Poza, E., Hanlon, S., & Kishida, R., Does the Family Business Interaction Factor Represent a Resource or a Cost?, *Family Business Review*, *17*(2), 2004, pp. 99–118.

gaining understanding of each other and thus being more likely to make decisions that are mutually beneficial for all parties. Stakeholders who communicate also tend to be more aware of the likely reactions to and consequences of their decisions.

In the most recent analysis of data from the study, a new composite index—Family Unity—was developed. The Family Unity index characterizes the family system and is the sum of the Family Harmony, Tolerance of Differences, and Participation and Succession scales. Based on scores on this index, firms were divided into two groups. Results of difference testing between these groups indicated that firms with significantly different scores on the Family Unity, Business Opportunity, and Family–Business Interaction indices also had significantly different Management Practices scores. The degree of family unity, how the family perceived business opportunities, and how positive the relation was between firm and family all influenced the managerial practices used and the extent of their use.

Family unity, as measured, was correlated with effective management practices, including planning activity, performance feedback, succession-planning disclosure, advisory boards, and family meetings. These findings indicate that investing in the family's health and harmony—via guidelines for employment of family members, clear standards for succession and ownership-transfer processes, and promotion of cooperation and positive relations among family members—should pay off for the firm. They further support the important role that family meetings and retreats can play in fostering business effectiveness and continuity by creating a new reality for family members.[19] The findings also point to the utility of having advisors and family members work with a principal architect of the family–ownership–management system, such as the CEO or the CEO's spouse, to address the consequences (both intended and unintended) of his or her policies and practices.[20]

The study also highlighted an idiosyncratic, inimitable, and intangible resource residing in some family businesses, which provide these companies with an opportunity for competitive advantage and superior performance. This resource for the value-creation process of a particular firm is the result of the unique interaction between the family and the business. If a firm's unique family–business interaction is not assessed and managed, or if a firm doe not recognize this interaction and invests in it as a valuable resource, its relative worth can quickly erode. The family–business interaction can even become an encumbrance to the firm, resulting in, for example, increased agency costs and a threat to its competitive advantages.

THE BENEFITS OF FAMILY MEETINGS

Beating the odds of having to deal with the zero-sum dynamics in the family environment, as discussed earlier in this chapter, is perhaps the most compelling reason for holding frequent family meetings and creating a family council. As will be discussed in Chapter 11, family councils are to shareholding families what boards are to family-controlled businesses. They represent a reliable forum for the education of family members—particularly those not active in the management of the business—about the

---

[19]Habbershon, T., & Astrachan, J., Perceptions Are Reality: How Family Meetings Lead to Collective Action. *Family Business Review, 10*(1), 1997, pp. 37–52; and Poza, E., & Messer, T., Spousal Leadership and Continuity in the Family Firm. *Family Business Review, 14*(1), 2000, pp. 25–35.

[20]Habbershon. T., & Williams, M., A Resource-Based Framework for Assessing the Strategic Advantages of Family Firms, *Family Business Review, 12*(1), 1999, pp. 1–25.

state of the business, its financial performance, its strategy, and the competitive dynamics it faces. Family councils also offer a safe haven in which to teach family members about the various rights and responsibilities that accompany being a business owner and manager. In the case of older multigenerational families, family council meetings are where important distinctions between ownership and stewardship are communicated, as at the Blethen Fifth Edition Family Business Meeting.

FAMILY UNITY AND CONTINUITY

By engaging the family in its responsibilities vis-à-vis *Face to Face* the business, family meetings often help the family become stronger. In multigenerational families that do not share in the ownership/stewardship of an enterprise, it is rare for the adult members of the extended family to remain close and actively involved. The United States is a land of nuclear families, where members of the next generation often move to far-reaching geographic locations and lead separate lives, often disconnected from the extended family. Seldom are work and love found in the same town in which the extended family is located. A family business can represent a wonderful gift to many families that still care about family.

Studies of family-controlled corporations, including the Discovery Action Research study, underscore the importance of family unity in the search for continuity.[21] Family unity is a strong predictor of (not necessarily a cause of, but highly correlated with) the successful use of a set of best managerial and family practices by family companies. Many of these best practices are discussed in this book—using boards with independent outsiders; placing nonfamily managers in key positions, in which their skills complement those of top family managers; holding frequent family meetings; and establishing a family council. Family unity is also a defining element in the relationship between the owning family and the business. Therefore, family unity affects the firm's ability to capitalize on the unique capabilities and/or resources that family members bring to the company's business model. Thus, it helps the company translate core competencies into a unique set of competitive advantages.

Family companies represent a kaleidoscope of stakeholders, many with very different perspectives on business strategy, succession plans, the need for change in the company and the nature of the change needed, innovation, growth, the managerial capability of top management, the fairness of compensation plans, and career opportunities. These perspectives are rooted in the stakeholder's role as an owner only, as an owner-manager, as a family member with no share ownership, as a member of the current or next generation, or as a key nonfamily manager. Given these diverse views, establishing principles and practices for group-level goal setting, for the review of performance in light of the established goals, and for problem solving and conflict resolution are particularly relevant.

Well-structured processes that involve family members in developing policies and setting direction can increase trust, a sense of unity, and commitment to goals (like continuity) deemed important by family members. After all, organizational behavior research has demonstrated that people support that which they helped create—and when they do, their company often performs better. When his company was the first

---

[21]Poza, E., et al., op. cit.

national family business inducted into the Family Business Hall of Fame in 1996, Fisk Johnson, president of SC Johnson: A Family Company, made the following statement:

> *We call our values "Family values . . . World class results." They are not radically different from the values you hear from major* Fortune 500 *companies, but I think we are better able to practice those values as a family-owned business. People care about making quality products, really care about the family, each other, and the success of the company. I believe this caring attitude translates into the success of the company.*[22]

Processes that involve family members in defining the nature of the desired relationship between the business and the family promote family unity and create some of the intangible assets that allow family businesses to achieve a competitive advantage.

PLANNING AND POLICY MAKING

Having family members rush into uninformed, democratic decision making is one of the biggest fears of current-generation family and business leaders when they hold a family meeting or create a family council. According to the CEO of a medium-sized, family-controlled financial services firm, "Some of my siblings and most of my nieces and nephews have no clue about what is going on in the business or what I have been doing on the estate plan. How am I going to open all of this up for their participation? All I will get is uninformed opinions and passionate second-guessing. And of course they'll want to vote on it."[23] First and foremost, family meetings should be about education and communication. Over time, they will become effective planning and policy-making bodies—that is, if the education and communication phases have been properly carried out.

Open and safe processes for sharing information among family members in family council meetings are prerequisites for effective planning and policy making by family groups. Because many family-controlled companies, for understandable reasons, decide to create a family council in order to dismantle the culture of secrecy established by the previous generation, a gradual evolution is best. Decision making should be ruled out as one of the functions of the family council. Voting should be banned, as it is not a relevant tool. The focus should be on conversations, deliberations, and policy making. The council must strive to come up with plans and policies that most family members are willing to support. Several types of policies that stand out in their usefulness to families in business are:

1. An employment policy that outlines the levels of education and experience required for employment in the business. It should be based on merit and company need, not membership in the business family.

2. A subcontractor policy that offers guidelines for arms-length transactions in an open competitive marketplace. The bidding processes should create a level playing field for relatives and nonfamily alike.

3. A board service policy that includes criteria for the selection of family members to serve on the board as at-large representatives of the owning family. The

---

[22]Personal conversation with the author, June 1996.

[23]Personal conversation with the author, June 2005.

system should provide a link between family strategy and company strategy without giving undue influence to family members.

4. A family council service policy that states the criteria for selecting family members to serve as group coordinators of the family council and other committees that may be formed. Among possible goals of other committees are a family newsletter, a family history project, and philanthropic activity.

5. A dividend policy, not to specify the amount of dividends to be paid (which is a company decision), but rather, to discuss family needs, balance them against reinvestment in the business for growth needs, and then inform management of the general sentiments of family members.

6. A liquidity policy that includes principles supporting the desired relationship between the controlling family and the company in the future and recognizing that individuals or particular family branches may have cash-flow needs. This policy usually differentiates between small transactions and the sale of large blocks of stock within the family or back to the company and references the legal documents in effect (such as buy–sell agreements).

7. A family constitution, used primarily in older and larger multigenerational family businesses. This document is a collection of the established policies and a statement of family history, family commitment, and the desired relationship between the company and the owning family. (See Chapter 11 for an excellent example of a family constitution drafted by the members of a fourth-generation family business.)

Let's now consider an example of one of the policies just described—the family employment policy.

THE FAMILY EMPLOYMENT POLICY

Families that appreciate the utility of family meetings are, sooner or later, candidates for policies spelling out family participation, particularly the form of participation closest to the heart of a family-controlled business—company employment. By the time a family company is in its second or third generation, the number of potential family candidates can be overwhelming to employment based on merit.

Family employment policies, including promotion practices, need to be written down and communicated to create greater clarity, transparency, and a sense of fair play. Employment policies speak loudly to the principle of equal opportunity. Whereas the importance of these policies to family members is obvious, family employment and promotion practices are also of great concern to nonfamily managers seeking employment in family-owned and family-controlled companies. Second-, third-, and fourth-generation family firms need highly capable nonfamily managers, who are critical to successfully running and governing a family business. Communicating anything less than equality in career opportunities to potential and current key nonfamily managers will result in losing them to more meritocratic employers.

The family employment policy shown in Figure 2.3 was drafted by 18 cousins, third-generation stakeholders in a $95-million family-owned company. The second-generation siblings, including the current CEO and chairman of the board, reviewed this draft and revised it only slightly. It was then brought to the family council for final approval.

figure **2.3** | **Employment Policy of Global Construction Corporation**

Our Family Employment Policy

Purpose: The purpose of this policy is to define the criteria, procedures, and processes that will govern how lineal descendants and/or their spouses enter and exit from the family-controlled company's employ. This employment policy is intended to remove the ambiguity that currently exists so those interested family members can shape their career paths accordingly. We believe that clear, constructive communication of this policy will contribute to the long-term success of our family and Global Construction Corporation.

Philosophy: We are a family committed to our members being responsible, productive, and capable citizens who practice the work ethic and make constructive contributions to society. We believe that for a family member to be employed in this company, there must be a legitimate job, opening, or company need, and a family member with the skills to match. It is the policy of Global Construction Corporation to search out and employ, at all levels, individuals who have managerial abilities and who show evidence of ability and initiative in previous assignments. Furthermore, the company will seek those who exhibit self-confidence and high self-esteem and who are both independent and show evidence of leading responsible lives at work and with their families.

We subscribe to the philosophy that a family member will not automatically be granted a position in the company when seeking employment. That, with the input of the human resources professional on staff, family members will be considered on a par with nonfamily candidates for employment. High-level nonfamily employees are evidence of professionalism, high standards, accountability, and commitment to business continuity. They raise the bar for family members and the company as a whole. The company will, however, strive to employ family members when appropriate opportunities arise. After all, it is in the best interest of the company to have committed ownership that understands and supports the future of the corporation.

We also believe in responsible stewardship of the family enterprise. We want to emphasize values like education, a strong work ethic, competence, independence, and commitment to the greater good of the corporation and the extended family among family members who are shareholders but choose not to be employed by the corporation.

Employment Conditions:

1. Family members must meet the same criteria for hiring as nonfamily applicants.

2. Family members are expected to meet the same level of performance required of nonfamily employees. Like nonfamily employees, they will be subject to annual performance reviews and to the same rules guiding firing decisions.

3. As a general principle, and whenever feasible, family members will be supervised by nonfamily members to ensure greater objectivity and accountability.

4. Compensation will be appropriate for the position held; this means that salary and benefits will be market-driven and based on recent salary surveys.

5. Family members must have at least 3 years of work experience and an MBA or graduate degree in a field related to our business to be considered for upper management positions. In the absence of an MBA or a graduate degree in a related field, 5 years of related and/or management experience is expected. The 3 or 5 years of experience should show evidence of high performance, increased responsibility and greater competence that has been recognized by the employer in the form of at least one promotion or high-visibility project assignment. Previous successful work experience outside of the family company is considered an important predictor of the contribution potential and fit of family members at Global.

6. Family members interested in company employment must make their interest known, by writing to the President or Chief Executive Officer and initiating the process of mutual self-selection. Family members will not be officially canvassed for particular positions or job openings, nor will openings be routinely communicated to family members. The initiative must remain with the individual interested in employment. Only after the written notification and the identification of relevant employment opportunities, will candidates fill out the application forms and submit them for appropriate consideration by the director of human resources.

Note: The name of the company has been changed to protect the business family's privacy.

GUIDELINES FOR POLICY MAKING

The following simple set of guidelines can help families that are developing family–business interaction policies:

1. Ideally, involve as many family members as are relevant to the particular policy being developed. Relevance is defined by expertise on the subject(s) to be discussed, by the need of family members to feel included, and by the potential effect of the policy on those family members. Still, it may be preferable to start small—for example, in third-generation family firms at first involve only direct descendants, not their spouses; welcome spouses at later meetings, once the group has developed a foundation for policy-making activity. Ultimately, this is a judgment call, based on many factors. (Having recently participated in a very successful first family council, attended by 35 direct descendants and their spouses, I got some firsthand evidence of effective group work by a large number of family participants, including in-laws. The decision to include spouses in this first meeting was in response to the identified goal of ensuring that second- and third-generation spouses feel they are "in the same boat" as the heirs.)

2. Look at the big picture, and formulate a mission statement or outcome goal that defines what is best for the extended family and the business. Refrain from favoring policies that repeatedly put one individual or family branch above the interests of all.

3. Focus on the future and let go of the past. Self-management (as the management literature refers to it) is critical in moving away from repetitive retelling of past incidents and instead breaking new ground that will prevent or minimize the occurrence of similar situations in the future.

4. Use experienced facilitators, who can play a significant role in helping a family business focus on the future, and benchmark your drafts of policies against those of other successful family-owned or family-controlled companies.

5. Agree on the process you will follow to develop, review, edit, redraft, approve, and ultimately enact policies with confidence that people will support them because they helped create them.

TRUSTS, LEGAL AGREEMENTS, AND PERSONAL RESPONSIBILITY

Trying to force people you don't trust to do what you want them to do over generations is doomed to failure. No matter what you write into the trust instrument, there are no ironclad guarantees that the company won't be sold. You have to get the people who can make or influence the decision to keep the company to buy into your vision.

—*John P. C. Duncan, Attorney*[24]

Plenty of evidence now exists that generation-skipping restrictive trusts, ostensibly crafted to maintain business continuity and family unity, fail miserably in preventing

---

[24]Quoted in McMenamin, B., Close Knit. *Forbes*, December 25, 2000.

next-generation members from doing with the company as they see fit. While these instruments often do protect and preserve the asset-based legacy for a time, family estrangement and asset sales will result unless a way is found to rediscover the intangible, value-based legacy of the founder and earlier generations.

Rediscovering this legacy takes time and conversation. It takes family history projects, candid discussions regarding the strategies and growth opportunities sought by the different generations, and family members acting as chief trust officers. It takes making history come alive again. At one start-up of a family council, a second-generation sibling kicked off the meeting not with the usual discussion of goals and expectations for the meeting but rather by reading a fictional letter from her deceased father. Her father supposedly wrote this letter after finding out that his widowed spouse, 5 second-generation heirs and their spouses, 18 grandchildren, and 7 of the grandchildren's spouses would be meeting together at a family council. Its purpose was to convey to all family members in attendance a sense of history, a sense of priorities, the founder's commitment to a few essential principles, and his tremendous appreciation for the job done by his three successors in the management of the business.

This family's first family council meeting was launched with a tremendous sense of history and a personal challenge to the next generation to "do the right thing" as the family and the business moved forward. No amount of legal expertise or foresight in the drafting of legal documents can match the goodwill and personal responsibility that next-generation members begin to assume when the importance and relevance of both family and enterprise are stated so eloquently. If ever there was a compelling reason for family councils in multigenerational family-controlled companies, this is it. Only the shareholders who are engaged by the founder's and successors' shared dreams and vision will choose to be stewards of the legacy. The rest will put their individual interests and agendas before anything else and will most likely exhibit all the behaviors of rich but ungrateful heirs.

CONFLICT MANAGEMENT

The success of a multigenerational family-owned company is evidence that orderly governance and resolution of problems within the family or in the family's relationship to the business were provided for before they overwhelmed the enterprise. Conflict is inevitable in families, and more so in families that live, work, and control assets together. One of the benefits of family meetings is the forum they provide for minimizing the potential for conflict and addressing the problems that confront multigenerational families. Some of the significant problems that can be addressed in family meetings include the following:

- Frustration over alienation or lack of inclusion. This source of conflict is widespread as a result of the emotional distance between family members who are active in management and those who are not and between members of the powerful current generation and those of the significantly less powerful next generation. Geographic separation and lack of frequent and consistent communication only heighten this conflict and often lead to mistrust and a propensity for zero-sum dynamics.

- Anger over the unfairness of hiring practices, promotions, family benefits, and other opportunities enjoyed by some but not by others. In many families, "fair" means "equal." But in multigenerational families, when being fair means being equal, family leaders soon run out of options. The family and, often, the company become paralyzed.

- Frustration over dividend policies and lack of liquidity. By the time a family-owned company has begun to hire its third generation of family members, the financial needs of the various branches and individuals have become incredibly diverse. A third-generation owner-manager receiving a fair market salary as a manager or corporate officer faces a very different reality from that of a cousin pursuing a medical degree and raising two children.

All of these problems must be addressed in family meetings and resolved to the best of the family's ability. Active listening is at the heart of much family meeting activity. It leads to two-way communication that addresses the sources of feelings and allows plans to be drafted or changed as necessary. Because some of these feelings are based on perceptions—things that some see and others do not—the education mission of family meetings can go a long way in creating common ground and ameliorating conflicts rooted in misinformation or misunderstandings.

I hope this chapter has created greater understanding of a family's influence on a family business. Greater understanding of this complex subject goes a long way toward promoting more creative solutions to the unique challenges posed. Chapter 11 will address in greater detail the alternatives, approaches, and possible solutions to these unique challenges. That chapter's action-learning orientation will also provide the reader with tools to enhance the value-creation process that families are responsible for in creating distinct competitive advantages for their firms.

SUMMARY

1   Secrecy, lack of information, and absence of education threaten continued commitment by family members to the continuity of a family-controlled corporation.

2   Multigenerational families, because of the myriad ways in which us-and-them behavior can manifest itself, are fertile ground for zero-sum dynamics.

3   Family systems theory makes a great contribution to the understanding of family dynamics and the influence of the family in a family business.

4   Family genograms and family histories represent a great study tool for family members in a family business.

5   Family meetings and family councils are a reliable forum for the education of family members about the business. In family meetings, family members learn about the rights and responsibilities that accompany being an owner-manager and about the important distinctions between ownership and management. They also provide a forum to minimize the potential for conflict within the family.

6   Family unity is a strong predictor of the successful use of best managerial and family practices by multigenerational family-controlled companies; the same practices that have been found to be highly correlated with family-business continuity. In this way, families are the source of intangible assets that add value to the firm's competitive capacity.

7   Policies that are especially useful to family businesses include an employment policy, a subcontractor policy, a board service policy, a family council coordinator and committee service policy, a dividend policy, a liquidity policy, and a family constitution. (See the end of Chapter 11 for a sample family constitution.)

EXERCISE | **Exercise 2-1: Family Matters Project**

Read the material on genograms in this chapter. Make appointments with several members of your family (multiple generations and branches) to interview them (in person or by phone) about your family's history. Prepare a list of questions that captures special incidents, family stories, special messages attributed to particular family members, family traditions, and values.

Be curious about what has happened in earlier generations and its impact for next-generation members of the family. Then, write your family's story, following these steps:

1. Create a genogram of your own family, displaying, at the very least, the three most recent generations and the names and ages of parents, grandparents, and great grandparents on both your mother's and your father's sides. Next to their names, list any major events or "family messages" attributed to those represented in the genogram; for example, next to Grandpa you may display his favorite saying, "Working is Living." You may also want to list the state in the United States or the country where they lived.

2. Narrate your own personal history, diary, or story in a way that you share with the reader what you know/have learned about your family history, about the relationship between family members, about the relationship between the family and the business. Also reflect on what this history has taught you about:

   • Family values: work ethic, fairness, equality, equity, caring, commitment, etc.
   • The family's hopes and aspirations through the generations
   • The role of communications and information
   • Conflicts, cutoffs, and the impact of illness, death, or divorce, etc.
   • The role of money
   • Departures from the family business, stock buy–sells between family members, succession struggles
   • Peak experiences and notable successes in the family's history
   • Family's experience with in-laws and the perspective on the family by in-laws
   • Getting along in areas such as handling differences and uncovering and solving problems
   • Commitment to legacy and family-business continuity

3. For the benefit of your family and business, what aspect of your family's history is worth preserving, and which should be left behind?

4. The paper should be five to seven (double-spaced) pages long. Your professor should make adequate provisions to ensure that this material will be handled with the utmost confidentiality.

Note: Although the suggested length of the paper is five to seven pages, be aware that some students have initiated an inquiry into the family's history with this project that has resulted in the family developing and publishing a book about the family's history. In several cases, a professional writer has been contracted to continue the work initiated by the student project. In other words, if your curiosity takes you farther, and you are amenable, do not constrain the project to the suggested length.

Ownership of an Enterprise Built to Last

The family represents a substantial and idiosyncratic contributor to what makes family firms fundamentally different from nonfamily firms. This is obvious, even if as the previous chapter points out, the family's influence has been stereotyped more often than it has been well understood by management experts and the business media. But an equally substantial influence on the family business is its ownership and control structure. This feature remains underexplored and even more misunderstood in the fields of finance, management, and family business.

In family firms, *ownership* is sometimes used interchangeably with words like *money* and *wealth*. Chapter 7 will address these and wealth transfer through estate planning. This chapter will use the term *ownership* primarily to refer to company share ownership and the corporate control exercised by shareholders.

As pointed out in Chapter 1, several studies have shown that family-controlled firms enjoy better financial performance than management-controlled firms. The evidence suggests that U.S. firms with founding-family ownership perform better, on average, than nonfamily firms.[1] An earlier study on the effects of ownership structure and control on corporate productivity among *Fortune 500* companies (35 percent of which were also family-controlled) revealed that ownership affects a firm's productivity. Concentrated ownership was found to result in higher overall corporate productivity.[2]

Notwithstanding the established influence of ownership on firm performance, it is not unusual to hear CEOs, particularly of first- and second-generation entrepreneurial and family firms, comment, if not outright brag, that they held their last shareholder meeting on the way to their favorite vacation spot. Those same CEOs later complain about the entitlement culture of next-generation members of the family and of their inability to comprehend what it takes to make the business successful.

Understanding and successfully leading the owners of the family firm—its shareholders—is an essential part of the CEO's job. This is certainly the case the minute the firm stops being owned by the single, founding entrepreneur.

---

[1]Anderson, R., & Reeb, D., Founding Family Ownership and Firm Performance: Evidence from the S&P 500. *The Journal of Finance, 58*(3), June 2003, pp. 1301–1328.

[2]Hill, C., & Snell, S., Effects of Ownership Structure and Control on Corporate Productivity. *Academy of Management Journal, 32*(1), 1989, pp. 25–56.

As second-generation family members become owners, some may work in the business, while others may not. Maintaining unity and a realistic assessment of business and career opportunities among family members and shareholders in this situation becomes very difficult. This challenge usually grows exponentially in third- and later-generation family businesses. Shareholder disagreements regarding compensation, dividends, liquidity, return on investment, business strategy, financial results, the estate plan, and management succession are often responsible for the implosion of otherwise successful family companies. This is not just a family dynamic issue, but also an ownership issue, with precedents in finance, business management, and corporate and criminal law.

If a family business is going to preserve one of its intangible yet well-documented competitive advantages—its propensity to manage with a long-term horizon—investments in the ownership subsystem are essential. That means investing in:

1. the design and execution of an appropriate ownership and control structure
2. the education, access to information, and engagement of shareholders
3. the creation of institutions that govern the interaction between the owners and the firm

Shareholders in a family firm who are not treated even more transparently and professionally than shareholders in a management-controlled *Fortune 500* company are likely to spell trouble for the advantage of patient capital. Not only may there be historical family dynamics affecting a shareholder's willingness to trust a relative's assessment of the business and its performance, but shares in a family company are usually less than liquid (thinly traded) or outright illiquid (privately held). The implication of this important difference in the ownership of a family firm is fundamental. Shareholders often depend significantly on their family business asset; much more so than shareholders who own heavily traded shares of management-controlled companies. If they are not "in the know" because they are not involved in management, this dependence turns to a heightened sense of risk. Healthy adults resist blind dependence on people or things they do not understand and trust. When it comes to financial assets, they seek to both better understand and to diversify in order to manage the risk of too many eggs in one basket. But what can a family member and shareholder in a family firm do about this dependence? In most cases, converting the family company stock into cash is either not an option ("There is no buy–sell agreement, and besides, it would be disloyal."), not an easy option (it's never been done before and not even a company valuation exists), or not a smart move, considering what may be a bright future for the company and the capital-gains tax consequences of a sale.

Nevertheless, it seems reasonable to suggest that shareholders who voluntarily choose to remain shareholders are more likely to be an asset than a liability to a firm so influenced by the power of owners. Boards can certainly assist in promoting a loyal and positive relationship between shareholders and the firm they own. But shareholder meetings represent one of the best opportunities to educate owners about their responsibilities and what the company and its management expect of shareholders. Shareholder meetings also allow for financial, business, and competitive information-sharing and communication on other issues critical to a family firm in a disciplined and proactive manner. In conjunction with an effective board and family meetings, shareholder meetings represent the best safeguard for healthy governance of the family's influence on the business and vice versa.

figure **3.1** | **Managers versus Owners**

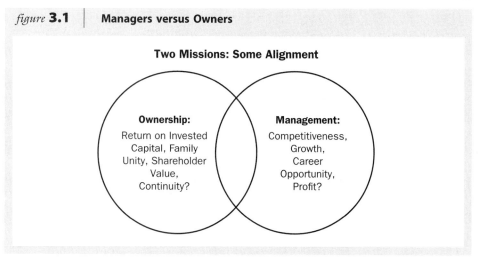

Two Missions: Some Alignment

Ownership:
Return on Invested
Capital, Family
Unity, Shareholder
Value,
Continuity?

Management:
Competitiveness,
Growth,
Career
Opportunity,
Profit?

SHAREHOLDER PRIORITIES

What are the sensible priorities of shareholders? Not the sensible priorities of managers or family members, but of shareholders. What shareholders usually want most is risk-adjusted economic returns captured in shareholder value and dividends or distributions.

Cash flow or earnings before interest, taxes, depreciation, and amortization (EBITDA), net earnings, earnings growth rates, and debt/equity and debt/asset ratios are therefore important elements of the financial scorecard of a family enterprise. Managers, on the other hand, tend to be more concerned with market share, competitors, growth, and their own compensation and career opportunities. Their scorecards often reflect this bias by focusing more on revenues, sales growth, and market-share numbers, sometimes to the detriment of profitability and healthy profit margins. But it is profit that drives both shareholder value creation and the possibility of other shareholder returns, like dividends. (See Figure 3.1 for a contrasting view of the missions of shareholders and managers.)

Family shareholders expecting to fulfill their responsibility of aligning management interests with shareholder priorities and holding management accountable need a thorough understanding of financial statements. They need to be able to make sense of what the numbers say about the firm and its competitiveness. Financial literacy is, therefore, essential knowledge for every shareholder, not just the ones active in the management of the company. Without it, the desirable alignment of management and shareholders is at risk. Without it, family-business shareholders can easily become just as indifferent or impatient, fickle, and greedy as investors on Wall Street. The latter, aided by analysts and the media, often pressure well-managed publicly traded companies into short-term thinking. Family shareholders inactive in the business, with little understanding of management and the time cycles involved in new strategies or new investments, can hamper the effective operation of a family-controlled business. They can bring about significant erosion of the founding culture, which valued the role of hard work and patient capital and understood the benefits of owner–manager alignment.

If family unity suffers as a result of this pressure by some family members for high returns and short time frames, a loss of will and vision may result. In the short to medium term, then, a family business may lose one of its precious sources of competitive advantage in relation to larger management-controlled firms. In the longer term, family-business continuity may be abandoned in favor of immediately recap-turing, via sale of the company, the value created by previous generations. (See Case 5: The Vega Food Company for an intriguing example of this dynamic and what family-firm leaders can do to arrest this development.)

How can family businesses develop committed and responsible shareholders? Let us first address the responsibilities of shareholders to the firm. We will then discuss best practices in the governance of the owner–firm relationship and the education of and communication with shareholders.

RESPONSIBILITIES OF SHAREHOLDERS TO THE COMPANY

DEFINE AND THEN DEMAND REASONABLE RETURNS ON SHAREHOLDER EQUITY OR INVESTED ASSETS

Past success has led the management of many companies to be less demanding for continued high profitability and shareholder returns. Satisficing employee goals and expectations, letting up a little on the creative and hard work of innovation, and not ruffling feathers within a supply chain or with competitors may make life easier for managers, but it is not fair to shareholders and their invested capital. Owners have to be management's conscience on this front.

David Packard once convened a meeting of the Packards and charged them with the responsibility of holding Hewlett-Packard (HP) management accountable. Aware that next-generation members of the family had not joined HP as employees, Mr. Packard challenged family members/shareholders to remain part of the winning formula for the then-thriving, global high-technology business. (HP was a family firm at the time. The Hewletts and the Packards collectively owned approximately 24 percent of the outstanding shares.) David Packard and Bill Hewlett, after retiring from management posts at HP, had together been a critical change catalyst in the 1980s, when as a result of significant successes, management seemed incapable of realizing that competition in the scientific measurement instrument field, which they had dominated, was increasing. Packard and Hewlett turned their concern into a campaign to challenge management to develop new products that would keep the company healthy. Through their oversight on the board of directors and engaging personal communications with the nonfamily CEO and key management, they participated in prompting the product-development work that ultimately led to the launching of HP's very successful printer lines and their high-profit-margin ink cartridges.

Similarly, the sixth-generation cousins of the Osborne family, shareholders of Casa Osborne/Osborne Wines in Spain, issued a management wake-up call. Ignacio Osborne said in a personal conversation with me, "What Tomas (his cousin) and I did to create the needed fundamental change was to present very early in our leadership of the company a series of alternatives to the board and described eloquently what the challenged situation of the company was. The contrast between our vision and the then unsuccessful situation set the task out for the board and the company. We also described to the board how our generation of owners thought the company had to be managed in order for it to have a future."[3] This served as a wake-up call that sig-nificantly transformed the company and its management.

---

[3]Author's personal conversation with Ignacio Osborne.

PROVIDE THE VALUES AND PRINCIPLES OF DOING BUSINESS AND ENSURE THEY REMAIN INSTILLED IN THE COMPANY

Tim Timken, sixth-generation chairman of the board of The Timken Company revealed in the research on centennial family companies discussed in Chapter 13, that he believes he has a special role as an owner and Timken family member with regard to the preservation of important company values. His role is to make sure that The Timken Company's founding values do not slip away. Because, he added, what drives the firm's continuity is its products, but, "Behind our products, there are consistent values. The Timken Company has always believed that our four values: ethics and integrity, quality, innovation, and independence are central. We have been consistent with them for over 105 years. These values go back to our founders, my great-great-grandfather, who believed passionately in them and to this day we hold those in everything that we do."[4]

The point is not that family-owned and family-controlled firms are more ethical or more value-driven than other companies, although some research seems to bear out that claim and the claim that family-controlled firms are more responsible to the community. The point is that many family-controlled firms continue to be successful by finding their bearings, their principles, in founding values. Examples abound: L. L. Bean, SC Johnson, Marriott, The Washington Post Companies, W. L. Grant & Sons (Glenfiddich), Edgepark Surgical, and until recently, Hewlett-Packard with its "HP Way." These values are passed down from generation to generation through the intimate side of the owning family. Owners who share a family history often assume the responsibility of being the moral compass for the corporation. Stewardship of the values and the legacy is clearly an ownership responsibility.

DEFINE THE OWNING FAMILY'S STRATEGY AND COMMUNICATE OWNING-FAMILY PRIORITIES

Owner values influence family priorities and vice versa. In the Timkens' case, the value of independence, of wanting to control their own destiny, rests on the premise that as a company, they know how to run the business better than anybody else does. This makes a priority of preserving a low debt/equity ratio, which restrains the amount of debt the company is willing to assume and as a result the speed at which The Timken Company can grow.

Shareholders in a family firm have a responsibility to tell management, often through the board of directors, what the family's strategy and priorities are. This principle rounds out the first responsibility of shareholders in family companies: define a target and then demand that the target shareholder return on invested capital is met. It affirms that the expectations of management go beyond the achievement of a set of financial goals. Both the economic and the noneconomic considerations of the owning family must be put on management's agenda so that a unique group of shareholders gets from top management not a one-size-fits-all set of financial results but rather outcomes tailored to these shareholders' priorities.

The family's strategy may include preferences about locations in which the firm operates, preferences regarding diversification within an enterprise or holding-company structure (since the largest asset is usually the family firm), and the owning family's desired role in the management of the firm going forward; does the family, for

---

[4]Author's personal conversation with Tim Timken.

example, want to continue the tradition of owning-managing or perhaps delegate the management to nonfamily executives in the next generation?

Family-business consultants are sometimes brought in by boards of directors and CEOs of family-owned and family-controlled companies to survey, canvass, and otherwise work with the owning families to develop such a family strategy. (The Family Business Ownership Transfer and Estate Planning Inventory found at the end of this chapter has been used for that purpose.) In its absence, boards have a difficult time holding management accountable for the things that matter to shareholders. For a board, being a compass, providing direction, and conducting satisfactory reviews of corporate behavior, business strategy, and managerial performance are next to impossible without the owning family having defined the ultimate goal.

A family-owned industrial group in Latin America with annual revenues of approximately $300 million was facing significant competitive and financial challenges. Although management, which included some family members, was devising a rescue and turnaround plan, they charged a third-generation-cousins committee with the drafting of a family constitution (a sample family constitution can be found in Chapter 11) and the creation of multiple scenarios for the desired future of the corporation, including the owning family's preferred relationship to the firm in the next generation. In their deliberations, the cousins' generation developed seven possible scenarios[5]:

Scenario 1. *The cigarette boat:* The family company reinvests, places some significant bets on new products and services, proceeds with speed, and grows the business aggressively. Profits are less important in the short run than market share and being a rule maker in the industry.

Scenario 2. *The Chinese junk:* The family company continues and is preserved. To outsiders, there is no evidence of change. Things just look a little older. To insiders, it is obvious that while the legacy has been preserved, the company has been modernized and professionalized. Profits are maximized in the short and medium term.

Scenario 3. *The toy boat:* The family company is a hobby of sorts, a source of pride and entertainment for its shareholders. It preserves family members' place in society and continues to give them access to important political and social networks. Profits are important only to the extent that they serve the above purpose.

Scenario 4. *The family bank:* The family company finances the activities of shareholders in a variety of profit-making and nonprofit organizations. Dividends, family benefits, and other perks make family members' lives of financial independence possible. Profits are needed in the short term to provide the dividends and distributions that will fund family members' obligations.

Scenario 5. *The company in auction:* The family company is getting itself ready for a sale to the highest bidder. Making the company look pretty financially is of the essence in the short term.

Scenario 6. *The company in controlled liquidation:* The family company is selling assets—entire business units, product lines, famous brands, technology, real estate, and equipment—as market opportunities arise that maximize their value.

---

[5]See Magretta, J., Governing the Family-Owned Enterprise: An Interview with Finland's Kristen Ahlstrom. *Harvard Business Review*, January/February 1998, pp. 112–123, which inspired some of these scenarios.

Scenario 7. *The Chapter 11 company:* The family company seeks protection from creditors while it reorganizes itself in the interest of reemerging as a more capable competitor.

After a lengthy and often impassioned discussion of the various scenarios, the committee decided that only one scenario was truly desirable. The family company had to choose to become a cigarette boat, scenario 1. This meant carrying out the difficult work of slimming down the company to remake it into a more nimble enterprise. The overall business would emerge smaller, more focused in its distinctive competitive advantages, and more agile. The committee considered that both vision and business strategy had been lacking and that the extensive diversification in the past decade had eroded all discipline with regard to competing on the basis of established core competencies or relative strengths. The cousins recognized that in the post-NAFTA (North American Free Trade Agreement) globally hypercompetitive world, it was better to be focused and best in class in a few products and services than to be able to say that "we do everything, from A to Z." Wisely, they also figured that the determination of which business units could readily become cigarette boats and which would play the role of family bank, would require thorough analysis of the business.

Without a successful turnaround, the above deliberations are nothing short of idle conversation with management jargon included. But while the final score is not yet in, this and other shareholder input to the board and top management as to the owning family's strategy proved invaluable in the ongoing efforts to provide for a turnaround and family firm continuity.

EFFECTIVE GOVERNANCE OF THE SHAREHOLDER–FIRM RELATIONSHIP

In Chapter 1 we referred to the systemic overlap between the family, ownership, and management subsystems that make up a family enterprise as the potential source of invisible crossovers that endow a family company with the ability to enjoy unique, idiosyncratic, and hard-to-replicate competitive advantages. Some literature refers to this source of competitive advantage as "familiness." In this book we largely refer to it as a positive owner–family–business interaction in recognition of the contribution that each of the subsystems makes to the overall unique capabilities enjoyed by family firms.

But just as the interaction between ownership, family, and management is the source of what may constitute a competitive advantage, it is simultaneously the source of the biggest challenge faced by family firms: the effective governance of the shareholder–firm relationship. (Not unlike business leaders who are confronted with the fact that a personal quality that represents a strength in their leadership profile also poses their biggest weakness or developmental challenge under certain other circumstances.)

THE ROLE OF THE BOARD

Evidence from the study discussed earlier in this chapter comparing and contrasting the performance of family-controlled companies with that of management-controlled firms, acknowledges the superior performance of family firms.[6] But a follow-up study

---

[6]Anderson, R., & Reeb, D., Board Composition: Balancing Family Influence in S&P 500 Firms. *Administrative Science Quarterly, 49,* 2004, pp. 209–237.

made the superior performance in shareholder value contingent on the composition of the board of the company in question. In other words, this follow-up research found that consistent with agency theory, the higher-performing firms were those in which representation on the board is balanced between independent directors and family members. In fact, family firms with relatively few independent directors performed significantly worse than the average nonfamily firm in the sample.[7] And since smaller family firms tend to be under less public scrutiny than larger firms, the presence of independent directors and independent advisors on a board probably plays an even larger role in minimizing the potential agency costs of the ownership–family–management relation. However, the study also found that a moderate presence of family members on the board provides substantial benefits to the firm, so the addition of independent members and advisors is not meant to exclude continuing family participation on the board.

At Casa Osborne, Ignacio Osborne, reflecting on the need to add an independent perspective to the board and one more informed with timely customer preferences, observed: "It used to be that the taste of Osborne family members, sophisticated as it was, determined the taste of our products and defined what quality in wines meant. Not anymore. Now we conduct market research, do focus groups, pay attention to trends and changing consumer tastes." He added: "One of the successes we had is we went very quickly. A new business plan for the company was drafted, discussed by the board until we reached some consensus for the future of the company. It was just business and company (not family) and then we managed the communication with the rest of the shareholders to let them know what we were trying to do and why."[8]

The role of the board is prominent in the governance of the relationship between a family and its business when the owner–family–business interaction is preserved as a positive-sum dynamic. Because of the board's importance, next-generation leaders of family companies frequently undertake a critical review of any restructuring effort involving their board. They all come back to the idea that a lot of communication and education, beyond what is deemed traditional board work and strategic planning processes, is necessary because of the family's legacy on the board. The family's identity remains attached to the company's, so if the company is going to change in order to adapt and grow, the composition of the board has to change. Ignacio Osborne confessed that "in the span of two years, I took 12 years out of the average age of our board."

THE ROLE OF SHAREHOLDER MEETINGS, FAMILY MEETINGS, AND MEETINGS OF THE FAMILY COUNCIL

As already acknowledged, the board is not the only institution with significant influence on the effective governance of the owner–firm relationship. Most of the absolutely essential communication, education, and sharing of financial and strategic information discussed here takes place in regularly scheduled shareholder meetings, family meetings, and meetings of the family council. This keeps the shareholders involved and fulfills the legal requirement to recognize the rights of minority shareholders. In family firms in which the extended family is large and the ownership

---

[7]Ibid.

[8]Author's personal conversation with Ignacio Osborne.

structure has not been pruned—as in the case of a fourth-generation firm with 6 branches and 64 family members who are shareholders—representative family councils may be a vehicle for educating and informing family shareholders. These representative councils or committees of the council, sometimes referred to as "asset boards," can also provide the board with input regarding the family strategy and develop policies regarding family participation in the firm. In the case that heirs' or next-generation members' stock is held in trust, similar activities are carried out in regularly scheduled meetings of the trustees.

So, the effectively governed shareholder–firm relationship goes something like this: A new shared vision emerges in response to customers' needs. This reenergized vision drives the strategic-regeneration process. Family management and family shareholders are both a part of that process. Family shareholders are kept in the information loop even if they do not work in the company or regularly attend family meetings. Shareholder meetings play an important role in educating and informing the controlling family members. The family council and family meetings extensively acknowledge the family strategy, and these bodies' deliberations are linked to the family's board agenda through at-large representation of the family on a board that is complemented by representation by independent board members. By effectively governing the shareholder–firm relation, the unique agency costs of family firms (like CEO entrenchment and conflicts between the interests of majority and minority shareholders sometimes evidenced in CEO compensation and benefits vs. dividends disputes) do not outstrip the value of the invisible crossovers and competitive advantages created in earlier generations. By keeping the overlap between ownership and management healthy, competitive advantages can be exploited and the traditional agency costs faced by nonfamily firms (the costs of separating management from ownership and having managers as agents of the owners) are mitigated.

Chapters 10 and 11 in Part III, Best Practices, discuss in more detail the functions of boards, shareholder meetings, and family meetings and also ways to make them more effective in governing the owner–family–business interaction. So let us now proceed to the absolute prerequisite of responsible ownership—education of and communication with shareholders.

INFORMATION, COMMUNICATION, AND EDUCATION: SHAREHOLDERS

In order to successfully carry out their responsibilities, owners need to know what those responsibilities are and how to exercise them. That is why the education of and continuing communication with shareholders is essential to the healthy continuity of a family firm.

The ability to read and understand a financial statement with a high degree of comprehension is a must for shareholders. Of course, those statements first need to be provided on a frequent and timely basis, and ideally—as do the financial statements from Berkshire Hathaway discussed later in this chapter—include plenty of top management narrative and discussion of the meaning of the most important facts contained in the report. Financial statements that aim to educate and inform, without assuming the presence of an advanced degree in management, are essential to family-firm shareholders in carrying out their responsibilities as owners. Certainly, it should be the responsibility of these same owners to do their part to become financially literate through their own study and careful and disciplined participation in shareholder meetings designed for the purpose of educating and informing. Top management, whether family or not, plays a key role in this education and information and should participate in some part of the shareholder meeting. Board members who may be asked to provide a bridging function between owners and managers and who should already be financially astute, can attend portions of the shareholder meeting and meet with particular shareholders to perform this educational and financial coaching role outside of board meetings. An outside advisor—perhaps an accountant, a lawyer, and/or a financial planner—can also play a significant role in this education. Shareholders can reach accurate conclusions about what the financial information means and the managerial actions it should prompt only with study, perspective from the experience of others, and information about competitors and others in the industry. As part of their financial literacy, owners should also be able to understand the capital structure of the firm, know debt levels in relation to owners' equity, and therefore be able gauge their ability to operate independently or be subject to the influence of banks and other sources of capital in how they run their business.

The appropriate measures of profitability in a particular industry, plus measures of return on invested assets, return on shareholders' equity, return on sales, and the growth trajectory of these over time are essential to have and understand. How a particular company's results stack up against those of competitors and others in the industry is the ultimate arbiter of whether the firm is winning or losing in the hyper-competitive marketplace, and therefore whether the owners need to issue a wake-up call to management, replace management, or make different capital allocation decisions going forward. Holding these numbers close to the vest (whether the vest of the founding CEO, of family members who hold key jobs in management, or of nonfamily CEOs or key managers who prefer not to be held accountable by the other shareholders) undermines the fundamental advantage that so many family firms enjoy—a long-term horizon on their investment decisions.

José Pinedo at El Caballo, in Seville, Spain, considers the education of family shareholders to be the biggest contribution he has made to his family in business. Through board meetings and hundreds of informal conversations with shareholders over several years, he says: "My family now knows the difference between family and business, realizes the value of management and professionalization. My family now understands, in depth, what a company is. Now we talk about dividends and the way we have that discussion is totally different from five years ago. Besides the board meetings and the hundred of informal conversations, we established a new holding company structure four years ago and began to have meetings where the financial information is very transparent to all shareholders."[9]

Trust is not an article of faith among adults. As adults, trust comes from information, reliability and predictability, accessibility, shared goals, emotional bonds, a sense of fairness, and transparency. These generate confidence in understanding the people and the situation the company is in. Success and meeting performance goals tend to enhance trust; the absence of these often gives rise to mistrust. Frequent updates about financial matters and the state of the business promote trust. Goal alignment and family

---

[9]Author's personal conversation with José Pinedo.

unity (being in it together, as partners) make trusting easier since these lead to similar interpretations of this information. In their absence, the same information can lead different people to very different conclusions.

Shareholders who are not sufficiently informed and involved can become suspicious and concerned. They can feel that the playing field is not even and that they are being taken advantage of by shareholders who work in the business. Of course, this sense of disparity is often exacerbated by the fact that those working in the business are receiving salaries and other compensation. And as an attorney I know likes to say, on a day-to-day basis, ownership return is measured by take-home pay. This represents a kernel of wisdom, because the illiquidity of family businesses makes their value hard to keep track of, and the dividends paid out are often minuscule to nonexistent.

Shareholders not active as employees in the business then harbor concerns about excessive executive compensation and benefits—the new expensive company car and the country club membership. Over time, these same shareholders become less willing to invest in business expansion, preferring profit distributions through a dividend, bonus, and/or board fee. When these shareholders become frustrated enough, they may consider filing a lawsuit against the company and the active or majority shareholders claiming they have been treated unfairly. Or they may sue the board and company officers for self-dealing or mismanagement. Newspapers, magazines, and television are filled with stories like these.

Information regarding the estate plan also needs to be shared with family shareholders. Chapter 7 will go into this subject in much more detail, but it bears stating here that communication about matters of the estate must not stop at the estate planning attorney's or tax accountant's door. This information also needs to be discussed with the CEO's spouse, next-generation members, other family shareholders, and even trusted key nonfamily managers. Family meetings and meetings of the family council are the perfect forum for such education and information-sharing.

OWNERSHIP STRUCTURE: DESIGN AND EXECUTE IT

Many family businesses begin as entrepreneurial firms that exploit the advantages of speed and agility, being able to turn on a dime. When faced with competition from a large multinational company that needs 16 levels of approval for a new product, system, or approach to the market, family businesses consistently win. Unfortunately, a number of these entrepreneurial companies discover the costs of losing this advantage when they continue in later generations of the owning family. Ownership-transfer policies motivated by a desire to love and treat all heirs equally or expectations of equality by family members are likely to promote an impasse, to the detriment of continued agility and competitiveness.

Leaders of enterprises find that distributing voting shares equally among shareholders often erodes a next-generation owner-manager's ability to lead. Successors need to manage the business with ample capacity to lead. Stock ownership by complicated trusts can also be a problem. Unless ownership and management have been sufficiently differentiated through the presence of nonfamily managers with a great amount of influence in the top management team, trustees, too, can second-guess a firm's management into paralysis.

Unlike ownership, the authority to lead is earned rather than inherited. However, transferring ownership without an eye toward corporate control makes it more difficult to acquire the authority to lead.

OWNERSHIP STRUCTURE AND CLASSES OF STOCK

An unavoidable consequence of successfully transferring a family-owned company in which there are both active and inactive shareholders is that the ever-expanding number of owners naturally makes it more difficult for family members active in the business to manage effectively. As a result, a particular generation's ownership structure is not appropriate for the next. Ownership structures do not transfer well across generations.

One approach to this challenge is to redesign the capital or ownership structure of the company by recapitalizing its stock. For example, recapitalizing the common stock into two classes (voting and nonvoting) allows the senior generation to divide the estate equally among heirs in terms of value, but differently in terms of corporate control.

Phantom stock can also be created to provide incentives for key nonfamily management to behave like owners. Phantom stock mirrors the value of regular company stock but does not dilute the family's actual ownership and has no voting rights. It can also represent a very effective retirement vehicle for important nonfamily members of the top management team, again without the risk of losing the control inherent to regular voting stock.

BUY–SELL AGREEMENTS

Buy–sell agreements are contractual arrangements between shareholders and the company. They are typically used by family business owners to facilitate an orderly exchange of stock in the corporation for cash.

The most obvious benefit of a buy–sell agreement is that it allows some family members to remain patient shareholders while providing liquidity to family members with other interests or goals. In this way, families can prune the corporate family tree across generations. A buy–sell agreement is often the primary vehicle through which family shareholders can realize value from their highly illiquid and unmarketable wealth—company stock. The ability to sell their stock and achieve liquidity, even if unexercised, often pleases previously dissatisfied shareholders. Most recommit, retain their shares, and engage in a renewed and revitalized spirit of enterprise ownership with the rest of the family.

Although most buy–sell agreements are written so that only death or discord triggers their use, some are created to provide liquidity windows for family members in general. Dissident shareholders, for instance, may be mollified by an annual redemption program funded by annual contributions from cash flow or retained earnings earmarked for this shareholder redemption fund or pool. This would apply only in the case of privately held, family-owned companies. (In some cases, a family holding-company structure would allow shareholders of family-controlled but publicly traded firms to establish a similar arrangement.) The redemption fund is typically constrained by risk-management limits. The debt/capital ratio of the firm, for instance, cannot exceed a safe limit determined by the board and still have stock redeemed that year.

IN CLOSING

CEOs of family firms have to address the issue of corporate control and shareholder liquidity, because as Jim Collins says in *Good to Great*,[10] *who* is on the bus is ultimately very important. In family businesses, *who* is on the shareholder bus is extremely important to the long-run commitment and the patient capital required.

Ray Koenig is the CEO of a third- to fourth-generation Deere farm implement distributor that has $102 million in annual revenues. Koenig Equipment is in the centennial firms research sample discussed in Chapter 13. Koenig has changed the corporation's code of regulations to allow only family members active in the business to own company shares. This, he says, will have the two-pronged benefit of providing retirement funds for members of the third generation (who will be selling their stock) and an orderly transfer of control to next-generation members who are active in the business.

SUMMARY

1 Family-controlled firms outperform management-controlled firms in return on invested assets and value creation for shareholders. But this performance advantage disappears in the absence of independent board member oversight complementing family board members' commitment on the board.

2 Leaders of family firms seldom make a priority of actively leading the shareholder group.

3 Investments in the ownership subsystem of a family firm protect the positive owner–family–management interaction deemed responsible for keeping family capital patient. In its absence, the long-term investment horizon that provides family firms with a competitive advantage disappears.

4 Governance of the shareholder–firm relationship is essential. The tools for governing that relationship are the board, shareholder meetings, and family meetings.

5 Ownership structures do not transfer well across generations. They need to be analyzed, redesigned, and executed in response to the growth in the number of shareholders and the increasing diversity of shareholder goals.

6 Providing shareholder liquidity through dividends, buy–sell agreements, and redemption funds is essential to preserving concentrated ownership and family control as a source of competitive advantage.

---

[10]Collins, J., *Good to Great: Why Some Companies Make the Leap ... and Others Don't.* New York: HarperBusiness, 2001.

APPENDIX

Warren E. Buffett and Berkshire Hathaway do an outstanding job of educating their shareholders through their annual reports. Through a set of principles, established in Berkshire Hathaway's Owner's Manual, efforts are also made to align minority shareholders with the values and principles that the controlling shareholders believe have led to Berkshire Hathaway's success. A copy of this Owner's Manual can be seen at http://www.berkshirehathaway.com/owners.html. Although only the "Owner's Manual," first published in 1996 and reissued in 1999, are available, Warren Buffett and Charlie Munger, Berkshire's vice-chairman, both make extraordinary efforts to submit to shareholders a narrated and very eloquent discussion of the financial results of the firm through an annual letter to shareholders. This is a much more comprehensive letter to shareholders than most companies produce to accompany their annual reports. The attempt is clearly to educate shareholders and engage them in a dialogue that informs and aligns their interests with those of the controlling shareholders. The hope is that by offering this Owner's Manual and referring to the annual letter to shareholders (available at http://www.berkshirehathaway.com), students of family business will aim to be equally forthcoming and eloquent in their education of and communication with their own family-business shareholders, whether active or inactive in the business, majority or minority shareholders, young or old, male or female.

EXERCISE 3-1 | **Ownership Transfer and Estate Planning Inventory**

The following Family Business Ownership Transfer and Estate Planning Inventory has been used in a variety of family business situations.[1] It has often been assigned as prework and then analyzed by a third-party consultant in preparation for a family council or family business retreat. The survey has consistently promoted candid conversations about what the owning family wants and what its priorities are regarding the estate and the transfer of ownership in a family business. Anonymity is essential to promoting a high level of candor about what is typically a very hard subject for family members to discuss. Having multiple generations and multiple branches (including in-laws) of the family participate in discussions of the results at the same time can be a very effective way to promote communication. Using a third-party facilitator is sometimes advisable, depending on the family's history and communication skills. The inventory, as presented here, assumes that a family business is being transferred from a second (G2) to a third (G3) generation, hence the G2 and G3 designations in questions 6, 7, and 8. These questions could just as easily read G1 and G2 or G3 and G4, as the case may be.

Invite your students to complete the survey as a check on their particular priorities.

The Family Business Ownership Transfer and Estate Planning Inventory
Individual responses will be kept confidential. Feedback will be in aggregate scores. It will take 10 minutes to fill out.

1. What should be our family's primary motivation for estate and continuity planning? (Please select only one.)
   a. To increase inheritance for the next generation(s)
   b. To reduce estate taxes
   c. To provide continuity for the family-owned enterprise
   d. To make charitable contributions
   e. To preserve jobs and remain a source of employment for the many families that depend on the business for their livelihood
   f. To increase shareholder value today
   g. To increase long-term shareholder value
   h. Other

2. Which statement most closely reflects your views regarding estate and continuity planning? (Please select only one.)
   a. I feel no particular responsibility to conserve assets for the next generation(s) and would prefer to spend the assets during my lifetime.
   b. I feel no particular responsibility to conserve assets for the next generation(s); however, I am happy to have whatever is left pass on to them upon my death.
   c. I feel no particular responsibility to conserve assets for the next generation(s); however, I feel responsible for the continuity of the family-owned business.
   d. I feel no particular responsibility to conserve assets for the next generation(s); however, I intend to plan the estate in a manner that will maximize their inheritance.
   e. I feel a responsibility to conserve assets for the next generation(s) and to do what is possible to promote continuity of the business from generation to generation.
   f. Other

---

[1] Adapted from Jonovic, D., *Family Philosophy Questionnaire*, Cleveland: Family Business Management Services, 2000; and Fithian, S., *The Legacy Questionnaire*, Quincy, MA: The Legacy Companies, 1998.

3. Regarding the investment objectives of shareholders, which of the following are most important to you? (Select only one in each paired choice, a or b.)

   a. To build value for future generations
   b. To maximize value for current owners

   a. To reinvest profits for maximum growth
   b. To maximize distributions to owners for increased liquidity

   a. To focus more on growth than on minimizing risk
   b. To focus more on minimizing risk than on growth

   a. To use leverage (debt) to fund growth
   b. To use current cash flow to fund growth

4. What total return-on-equity or return-on-investment objective do you have in mind?

   a. 10 percent
   b. 15 percent
   c. 20 percent
   d. Other

5. Regarding returns on your investment, which would you prefer?

   a. Growth in equity appreciation, or value of the business
   b. Dividends, distributions, or cash payouts

6. G2 family members may be concerned that next-generation members lack the skills to manage the assets they inherit. Which statement most closely reflects G2's view? (Please select only one.)

   a. G2 believes the next generation does not possess the necessary skills to manage the wealth and ownership responsibilities involved and does not feel a responsibility to help it acquire these skills or coach them in the interim.
   b. G2 believes the next generation does not possess the necessary skills to manage the wealth and the ownership responsibilities involved and does feel a responsibility to help it acquire these skills or coach next-generation members in the interim.
   c. G2 believes the next generation does possess the necessary skills to manage the wealth and the ownership responsibilities involved, but G2 still prefers to pass assets on through a trust or through some other vehicle that requires professional management.
   d. G2 believes the next generation does possess the necessary skills to manage the wealth involved but not necessarily the ownership responsibilities involved in a family-owned business.
   e. G2 believes the next generation does possess the necessary skills to manage the wealth and the company ownership responsibilities involved, and G2 feels comfortable that the next generation will manage its wealth and ownership responsibilities effectively.
   f. G2 is unsure about the skills and interest of the next generation to manage the assets and to be a responsible owner of a family-owned business.

Please discuss any skills or qualities that the next generation could benefit from having in terms of being seen as more ready and qualified for the management of wealth and/or family business ownership.

   (In questions 7 and 8, we are interested in both G2's and G3's perspectives and their assessment of how the other generation perceives the issues.)

7. Warren Buffet says "Parents should leave children enough money so that they would feel they could do anything, but not so much that they could do nothing." Which statement more closely reflects G2's perspective? (Please select only one.)

   a. G2 agrees with Warren Buffett.
   b. Regardless of their needs, parents should always leave the maximum inheritance to their children.
   c. Parents should leave their children the minimum inheritance required to meet the children's individual lifestyle needs.
   d. When the inheritance is in family company stock, parents should make family-business continuity priority number one.
   e. If the inheritance is in family company stock, parents should make sure that equal distribution is priority number one.
   f. When the inheritance is in family company stock, parents should make sure that a fair distribution meets the continuity needs of the business, the inheritance preferences of the parents, and the financial needs of the children.

   If you selected statement f, rank the three issues in order of priority:

   _____ continuity of the business
   _____ inheritance preferences of the parents
   _____ financial needs of the next generation

8. Which statement more closely reflects G3's perspective? (Please select only one.)

   a. Parents should always leave the maximum inheritance to their children.
   b. Parents should leave their children the minimum inheritance required to meet the children's individual lifestyle needs.
   c. When the inheritance is in family company stock, parents should make family-business continuity priority number one.
   d. When the inheritance is in family company stock, parents should make sure that equal distribution is priority number one.
   e. When the inheritance is in family company stock, parents should make sure that a fair distribution meets the continuity needs of the business, the inheritance preferences of the parents, and the financial needs of the children.

   If you selected statement e, rank the three issues in order of priority:

   _____ continuity of the business
   _____ inheritance preferences of the parents
   _____ financial needs of the next generation

9. Have next-generation members been able to learn sufficiently about the business?

   _____ Yes   _____ No

   Please explain your answer.

10. Do next-generation members have the opportunity to influence the planning for the future ownership of the business?

   _____ Yes   _____ No

   Please explain your answer.

THE BINGHAMS AND THE LOUISVILLE COURIER-JOURNAL COMPANIES

On January 9, 1986, Barry Bingham, Sr., chairman of the *Courier-Journal* and *Louisville Times,* abruptly decided that the Bingham family, which had owned the newspapers for nearly 70 years, would sell the business. Barry Sr., about to turn 80, hoped that his decision would bring a measure of family peace. Instead, it brought further blaming, family discord, chaos, and agony.[1]

In 1918, Judge Bingham, Barry Sr.'s father, had bought a majority interest in the *Courier-Journal* and the *Louisville Times,* Kentucky's preeminent newspapers, for $1 million. When Judge Bingham died in 1937, Barry Sr. was 32 and actively involved in the family business, which by then included a radio station and a printing company in addition to the newspapers.

The business grew as the Louisville postwar economy prospered. Barry Sr. married Mary Caperton and had five children: Worth, Barry Jr., Sallie, Eleanor, and Jonathan. Jonathan, the youngest, died at the age of 22, when he was electrocuted stringing wires for an outdoor party. Just two years later, Worth, the eldest, who had seemed destined by his charm, smarts, and primogeniture to be the successor, died in a bizarre car accident: A surfboard sticking out of his car's window hit a parked car; as it broke, it ricocheted and decapitated Worth.

Barry Jr., a year younger than Worth, had always been more interested in the radio business than in the print media, but he agreed to serve as president of the Louisville Courier-Journal Companies in the early 1970s. Sallie, who was five years younger than Barry, had set out on a career as a fiction writer in New York City. She had some success, getting some of her early works published. She returned to Louisville in 1977, after suffering several major setbacks in her writing career. Eleanor, eight years younger than Sallie, had worked professionally on a series of video documentaries, some financed by the dividends of her *Courier-Journal* stock. But her work never landed her the network job she had hoped for, so in 1978 she also returned home from California to work at WHAS, the company radio station. Barry Jr. and his sisters had never been close. In fact, they had barely seen each other in more than 20 years because the difference in their ages and early careers had taken them in separate directions.

Soon after Sallie and Eleanor returned, Barry Sr. named them to the company's board of directors. They would have both voice and vote in matters of the enterprise.

---

[1] Jones, A., "The Fall of the House of Bingham," New York Times, January 19, 1986; and Jones, A., "The Binghams After the Fall," New York Times, December 21, 1986.

Barry Jr.'s perspective on what happened then reads like a classic tale of sibling rivalry and backroom politics. According to Barry, his sisters knew little about the business. Barry, on the other hand, had been working in the family business for almost 20 years and running it for a decade. But the fact that they did not understand the business did not keep them from second-guessing his every move through memos, through letters to the editor and op-ed pieces published in the company newspapers, and through persistent questioning of Barry Jr. during board meetings. Even his mother, Mary, on more than one occasion expressed on the editorial page, without warning, opinions contrary to Barry Jr.'s. In a rather familiar pattern for the Bingham family, Barry Jr. would learn about these opinions by reading the paper or stopping by the employee bulletin board, where sometimes surprising memos from other members of the family would be posted.

To the outside world the family appeared rife with conflict. Seemingly, it was capable of communicating about what ailed it and its businesses only in print, never face to face. In the early 1980s, as broadcast news and other channels of information gained favor, the demand for newspapers slumped. Evening newspapers in particular— the Bingham's other newspaper, the *Louisville Times* was an evening daily—began to close their doors. Both the family and the business had problems to address and no way to address them.

The board became paralyzed by the sibling dynamics. Finally, Barry Jr. gave Barry Sr. an ultimatum: Either Sallie and Eleanor had to leave the board or he would resign as president of the enterprises. Eleanor resigned. Sallie, however, would not, and when she was not reelected by her own family, the war began. Sallie fired the first shot by announcing to the family that she wanted to sell all of her interests in the companies. Lehman Brothers valued Sallie's shares at between $22 million and $26.3 million, but her own appraiser valued her holdings at $80 million. Despite the huge gap, negotiations began. Sallie ultimately lowered her asking price to $32 million, but Barry Jr. would never agree to anything higher than $26.3 million, and the negotiations stalled. In the meantime, Eleanor decided that she, too, wanted to sell or swap her newspaper shares for WHAS (the radio station) shares. In a final attempt to pressure his children into a compromise, Barry Sr. issued an edict, nicknamed the 13th commandment, that if Barry Jr. and Eleanor could not come to an agreement, the companies would be sold.

Soon thereafter, Barry Sr. issued a memo announcing that the company would be sold. Barry Jr. saw the memo posted at the employees' bulletin board. At the age of 80, Barry Sr. still controlled 95 percent of the stock through a voting trust, so the decision to sell was clearly his to make.

Unable to communicate and resolve their differences, family members cashed out. All emerged cash-rich, but those who cared about the legacy were heartbroken. The newspapers had won eight Pulitzer prizes and were bastions of quality journalism in the South. Barry Jr. called a companywide meeting after the announcement to express his disagreement with his father's decision to sell the company and to tell employees how much their collective past meant to him. Employees wept as Barry Jr. spoke; they knew this speech marked the end of an era.

The Bingham papers were taken over by the Gannett Company, which proceeded to close down the evening newspaper, reduce personnel by a third, and cut news staff by 10 percent. Advertising and circulation for the morning paper increased, as did profits. The *Louisville Courier-Journal* had an impressive financial turnaround. But editorial standards changed, and Pulitzer prizes proved elusive.

SMALL FAMILY BUSINESS | CASE 2

POWER PLAY AT THE INN

Fronting on the Pacific Ocean, the Inn at the Wharf boasts 410 guest rooms and suites, two dining rooms, a lobby bar, and the lively Gull's Nest nightclub. The inn's annual revenues are $15 million.

Robert May, 57, purchased and remodeled the inn in 1970. His wife Katherine, although not now active in the business, has assisted in decorating and menu design. They have three children: Jake, 35; Amy, 30; and Andy, 24.

Three years ago, Jake and his wife Elaine, wanting to settle down from their life as rock musicians and start a family, were welcomed back. Jake manages the Gull's Nest. Elaine, a stabilizing force for Jake, especially during the stress of on-the-road tours, is interested in using her art skills at the inn.

Business degree in hand, Amy took over office management five years ago, including computer operations, for the inn. She and her husband, who is not involved at the inn, have a son.

Andy will soon receive his degree in hotel and restaurant management and expects to work at the inn upon graduation.

Today, Robert arrived home looking haggard. Questioning him, Katherine soon discovered that Amy had come into Robert's office and burst into tears. Jake had been through her office with an old buddy who represented a computer company and informed Amy that he was considering purchasing a new computer system for the inn. "And besides that, Dad, I'm pregnant again. Can I handle my job and two children?"

Robert called Jake to his office and inquired about the computer decision. Much to Robert's surprise, Jake pulled out his wallet and presented a new business card: "Jacob May, General Manager, Inn at the Wharf."

What should Robert do now?

This case study of a family-business dilemma is part of a series by the Family Firm Institute edited by Ernesto J. Poza. The cases are real, but identities have been changed to protect the privacy of the individuals involved. Reprinted with permission from The Family Firm Institute, Inc. All rights reserved.

THE FERRÉ MEDIA GROUP | CASE 3

This is a very successful family corporation. *El Nuevo Día* enjoys the highest circulation of any newspaper in Puerto Rico, and the three-year-old *Primera Hora* is the fastest growing daily. Combined, they dominate the market for news and advertising on the island. Our family name has the highest recognition factor in all of Puerto Rico, according to a recent survey. But as we move the enterprise to members of the next generation, how do we nurture a culture of cooperation and communication vs. sibling and branch rivalries as the extended family grows? How do we integrate their spouses into what they are doing, to what they are working so hard to build? For that matter, what should we be doing to prepare the generation after that for stewardship and the continuity of this family enterprise?

—*Antonio Luis Ferré, Chairman, Grupo Ferré Rangel*

These were the questions that Antonio Luis Ferré, chairman of the Grupo Ferré Rangel, was asking himself as he pondered the next phase of the multiyear succession process he had been leading since 1993. At stake were a media and publishing empire and a family that was an icon in Puerto Rico. *El Nuevo Día* and the Ferré family were among the most trusted institutions in the country, and the paper's editorials and news coverage calmed or roiled political life on the island. Its investigations made or broke administrations and governors. Five next-generation members were either already successfully running business units or in leadership positions in the editorial departments of the newspapers or in the holding company. The Grupo Ferré Rangel consisted of publishing and other media, printing, recycling, real estate, a family venture capital fund, and, until 2002, a controlling stake in Puerto Rican Cement, a New York Stock Exchange (NYSE)–listed company with $250 million in annual revenues.[1]

AN ENTERPRISING FAMILY TRADITION

Antonio Luis Ferré's grandfather founded Puerto Rican Cement in 1944. Luis A. Ferré, his successor and Antonio's father, had earned an engineering degree from MIT before joining the growing company, into which he eventually brought his sons. Antonio joined Puerto Rican Cement in 1955, after graduating from Amherst College. He received his MBA from the Harvard Business School in 1957. At Puerto Rican Cement, he worked first in production and labor relations, later becoming general manager and eventually president of the company. But by the mid-1960s, amid tension and sibling rivalry, Antonio and his brothers agreed to divide up the companies and their shares rather than risk further family disharmony.

In 1968, Luis A. Ferré was elected governor of Puerto Rico. That same year, Antonio paid his father $400,000 for the struggling small newspaper *El Día*, located in the southern city of Ponce. Antonio nurtured the dream of turning *El Día* into the largest and most influential newspaper in Puerto Rico. He preferred the news business to the cement business because of its involvement in politics and the world of words and ideas, as well as its deep roots in the community. He nevertheless continued serving as president of Puerto Rican Cement. He led this firm as it became the first Latin American company to be listed on the NYSE, and eventually he became its chairman.

Antonio moved operations of the small *El Día* to the capital city of San Juan, and on May 18, 1970, he published the first edition of *El Nuevo Día* (ENDI). As its name implied, the new daily would be different, modern, and dynamic. It would have a fresh new tabloid look and display its agility with independent and informative news coverage.

---

[1]Puerto Rican Cement agreed to be acquired by CEMEX, the multinational cement company headquartered in Monterrey, Mexico, on June 12, 2002, for approximately $180 million and the assumption of all outstanding debt.

ENDI's first editorial, entitled "What We Believe," declared that the publisher did not wish to just create one more newspaper, one more business, but rather, he wished to express the aspirations of a people. The editorial stated, "We want to be a manifestation of the new Puerto Rico and the new Puerto Rican." The editorial went on to assert that as a public trust, the pages of *El Nuevo Día* would always be open to those who, with respect for the reader and Puerto Rico's well-being, wanted to express their thoughts and opinions to others. *El Nuevo Día,* the editorial further declared, would fight crime and corruption and bring to light the social ills that beset the people of Puerto Rico so that, as citizens, they might better understand the social problems they confronted. This first edition consisted of 32 pages, and the printing was outsourced. Competition at the time consisted of two very successful large-circulation Spanish-language newspapers—*El Mundo* and *El Imparcial*—and an English-language newspaper, the *San Juan Star.*

Only 2½ years after its founding, *El Nuevo Día* had become an important editorial voice. Its circulation grew from 40,000 to about 120,000 over the next 5 years, as its competitors folded. *El Mundo* and *El Imparcial,* newspapers with afternoon editions, got into financial trouble, and *El Imparcial* ceased publication. In the mid-1970s, when ENDI covered and investigated corruption in the ranks of the police on the western part of the island, it was denounced as irresponsible and sensationalist. Sued in federal district court by the police department, *El Nuevo Día* confronted the first of what would be a series of attacks on its journalistic independence. The continuing coverage of corruption and abuses and excesses by the executive and legislative branches of the government would forge a stronger character and a new journalistic image for the paper. Its growth accelerated, and by 1978 the new daily had surpassed the circulation of its largest rival, *El Mundo,* and had become the largest print advertising medium in Puerto Rico. By the mid-1980s, daily circulation had grown to about 180,000, and by 1990 circulation had surpassed 200,000 copies.

In 1995, when *El Nuevo Día* celebrated its 25th anniversary, its honors included being among the top 10 Spanish–Portuguese language newspapers in Latin America; being ranked among the top 45 dailies, by circulation, in the United States; and being a source of employment for close to 1000 dedicated people. During the celebration ceremonies, Carlos Cabrera, one of the newspaper's mailroom employees, remembered how in the mid-1980s, after a fire broke out in the old press building, he and others had joined in fighting the blaze before the firemen arrived. After the fire was controlled, Antonio Luis Ferré came and personally thanked him for his efforts. Cabrera remembered saying to his colleagues, "An owner like him is very hard to find. That is why everybody wants to work here—they know it is a great company." Cabrera went on to highlight the strong culture of cooperation and caring that the founder had built. (Figure A shows the mission statement of *El Nuevo Día.*)

El Nuevo Día had grown to an average of 206 pages an issue, with a circulation of approximately 230,000 issues daily and 245,000 issues on Sunday. New sections and features kept the product young and fresh. It held a 70 percent share of the advertising market and was now being printed in color. Diversification was being pursued, and a series of companies—some related to publishing, others not—had been founded. By the late 1990s, the Grupo Ferré Rangel consisted of two newspapers, including ENDI and the young *Primera Hora;* El Día Directo, a telemarketing company; Virtual, Inc., an Internet portal and electronic version of *El Nuevo Día;* Pronatura, a recycling company; Advanced Graphics Printing; City View Plaza, a real estate development *figure* **A** | **The Mission Statement of El Nuevo Día**

Our Mission
El Nuevo Día is a family enterprise, a leader in the communications industry, committed to excellence on behalf of its customers. As a communications medium, with editorial independence, we keep citizens informed, serve as a free forum of ideas, and disseminate democratic and cultural values with the intent of promoting a fairer society.

Our Creed
Integrity, Respect, and Humility
Customer Service
Excellence
Leadership
Profitability
Spirit of Enterprise
Open Communications
Teamwork
Socially Responsible and Community Responsive

figure **B** | **Grupo Ferré Rangel Companies**

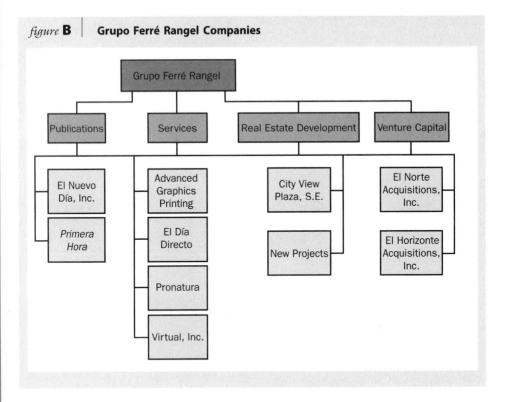

company; and a family venture capital company (that included El Norte Acquisitions, Inc., and El Horizonte Acquisitions, Inc.). Antonio Luis Ferré and his five sons and daughters all worked in the company, holding key positions with profit-and-loss responsibility in the businesses and editorial responsibilities in the newspapers. (Figure B provides a chart showing the companies under family control.)

THE FERRÉ RANGEL FAMILY

The Ferré Rangel family represents the fourth generation of a long line of business and civic leaders, and entrepreneurs. The first-generation business was a foundry. As the business grew, it added paper and cement to the mix. Over the generations, the company expanded to Florida, Panama, and Cuba and then lost some of those businesses to political and economic changes. In the 1960s, the third-generation leader, Luis A. Ferré entered politics and became the governor of Puerto Rico. Soon thereafter, the family company confronted a financial crisis that led to the restructuring of the company. Some of the businesses, now owned by individual third-generation family branches, survived while others did not. It was then that one of Luis A. Ferré's sons, Antonio L. Ferré became the CEO of Ferré-family-controlled but NYSE-listed Puerto Rican Cement, sold to Cemex in 2002.

Antonio Luis Ferré married Luisa Rangel in 1964. She was the daughter of a successful bank president who, in 1960, had migrated to Puerto Rico from Cuba. Antonio considered his marriage to be his most important and best decision. Luisa, he says, influenced him tremendously through her counsel; she placed great emphasis on keeping the family informed and nurturing the participation of the children in the family and the business. Luisa held a variety of positions within *El Nuevo Día* over the years, including book review editor; more recently, she led the Ferré Rangel family foundation. She was also on the board of directors of *El Nuevo Día* and the Grupo Ferré Rangel, the holding company. As of 2005, their five children—María Luisa, 41; Luis Alberto and his twin brother Antonio Luis (Toño), 39; María Eugenia (Mañu), 38; and Loren, 35—were all married and had children of their own (see Figure C).

Antonio and Luisa believed that the succession process began before the beginning. In other words, the way they brought up and educated their children had much bearing on the family's ability to both attract to and retain in the enterprise the very capable members of the next generation. They lived by the maxim "Plenty of love, equally distributed." They paid attention to the unique needs and potential of each individual child as he or she grew. They communicated frequently with each of them. The women in the family maintained that tradition into adulthood, calling each other daily, while the men reputedly had less frequent contact with each other and the female family members. All next-generation family members considered themselves ambitious and equally capable. They were encouraged not to harbor rivalries but rather to enjoy things as a group.

At an early age, the Ferré Rangel children were told that their only inheritance would be their education. The rest was up to them, and therefore seeking excellence and doing things well would be important to their futures. As they grew into adulthood, they had the advantage of good schools, summer educational experiences, and the careful selection of colleges and graduate schools. Their involvement in the business began while they were still in college, but their jobs in the company after graduation emphasized a ground-up approach. They all worked in lower-level jobs, whether as writers, researchers, reporters, or administrators, and generally reported to nonfamily managers. They were mentored and received feedback on their performance, both from their direct supervisors and from their parents, who oversaw their development. The adult siblings considered it critical that they agree on business goals, since they could all conceivably want to be president of the company.

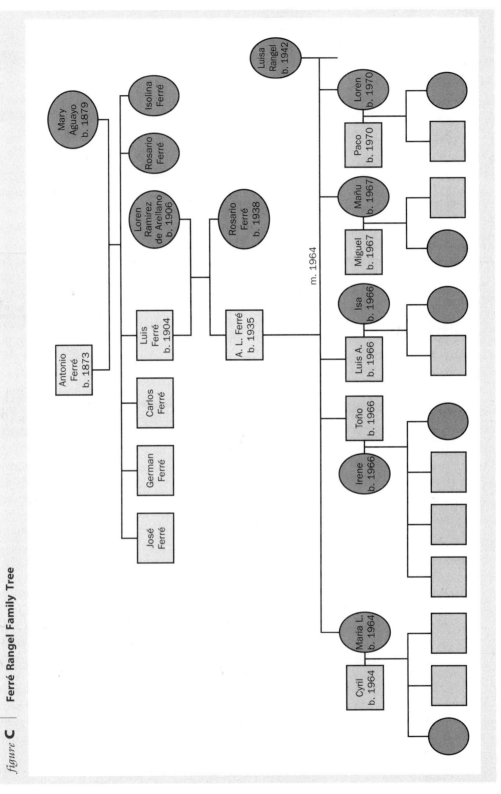

figure **C** | **Ferré Rangel Family Tree**

Antonio Luis Ferré, ENDI's founder, had been president and editor-publisher for 25 years. As he began to transfer his power, he insisted that the next generation pay attention to the details. Antonio felt that the newspaper business lived and died by those details and, over the long term, by its reputation for responsible citizenship and journalistic independence. He considered himself a very good role model for the next generation on this issue. He believed that the best way to lead was by example: "Luisa and I are good role models of a strong work ethic, compassion and love towards others, integrity and Christian values, respect for others and their ideas, steadfastness, and a good marriage."

Antonio L. Ferré in collaboration with fourth-generation members of the family continued to grow the company by, among other things launching the new paper *Primera Hora* in 1998 and a Spanish language newspaper in Orlando in 2003.

FAMILY COUNCIL MEETINGS

In 1993, the Ferré Rangel family began to meet regularly as a family to discuss family and business issues. Collectively, over the next several years, they developed a family constitution, a document that guided their succession-planning discussions. In it, they established guidelines for the involvement of family members and the eventual transition across generations. The family constitution included a statement of family values; criteria for employing family members and restricting the employment of in-laws; behavioral expectations of next-generation members involved in the company; principles regarding the relations between family and nonfamily managers; guidelines for decision making, including Antonio's tie-breaking role during the next five to seven years; policies for the performance reviews of next-generation members; and a commitment to the professional management of the family-owned enterprise by both family members and key nonfamily executives.

Family council meetings, which were held monthly, were given top priority in the busy schedules of all the owner-managers. These half-day meetings included discussions about the business, investments, the succession process, conflicts between the siblings or between family and nonfamily managers, relationships between family members, and stress management. Any emerging conflicts were addressed. Discussion of individual aspirations was encouraged. According to one in-law, family dynamics improved as a result of the meetings: "I am a lot more confident and optimistic since these family meetings started and the brothers and sisters started communicating more and more regularly. It takes time to express and listen to other opinions and understand the different perspectives. Without it, and without accommodating others' ideas, all you are doing is competing."

Family unity was given the utmost priority in these meetings, and through much communication, listening, and compromising, trust was built. These family-only meetings became the family council.

In 1995, the first family weekend retreat was held. It included the spouses of next-generation members. Spouses were briefed on the state of the business (financial results, strategy of the various business units, and new developments) with the intention of leveling the playing field for all participants. Later in the retreat, the family reflected on its legacy and recommitted to several core values that it wanted to pass on to the next generation. Subsequently, the family developed a mission statement for its principal holding, *El Nuevo Día*, and for the Ferré Rangel family. The family mission *figure* **D** | **Visions for the Grupo Ferré Rangel, as Stated at Family Retreats**

Grupo Ferré Rangel Vision 2000 (Developed in 1997)

We continue to let larger, more highly capitalized media and communications firms experiment with the new technology. By lagging somewhat in the adoption process, we will be knowledgeable of the latest advances while remaining flexible and more able to capitalize on unique growth opportunities. All new growth opportunities have enjoyed profit margins equal to or better than those obtained by our benchmark company, El Nuevo Día. We are being increasingly more strategic in our thinking, which has led to new business units in advertising, communications, entertainment, and information. We have captured the core competence of the newspaper—content (knowledge and information)—and made it available via a variety of media or channels of distribution that we also own.

Grupo Ferré Rangel Vision 2005 (Developed in 1997)

El Nuevo Día dominates the advertising market with a 30 percent market share of the total market and 70 percent of the printed media market. Its reporting is leading edge, using the latest technology to give customers the best and most readable information. Perspective, analysis, and research/investigation are as much a part of the daily newspaper as is reporting. We have maintained net profit levels of 15 percent, thereby protecting our financial and, most importantly, our journalistic independence. Our Internet site is considered the primary source of information on Puerto Rico by U.S. companies and others interested in doing business on the island. Our structure is that of business units with different strategic profiles, all reporting to the holding company—the Grupo Ferré Rangel. We realized that running the collection of businesses as an ownership team was impractical, and the holding company allowed us to clearly delineate responsibilities and hold key family and nonfamily managers accountable while nurturing family unity.

As a family, we have been able to advance a series of communication and information technologies through businesses that are as essential to the infrastructure of the Puerto Rico of tomorrow as Puerto Rican Cement was essential to the infrastructure of Puerto Rico's past growth and development.

statement acknowledged the important role of spouses in a supportive role vis-à-vis the family members who worked in the family enterprise. Several spouses had demanding careers of their own in other fields.

Over the next several years, these annual retreats continued to update spouses on the family enterprise, promote analysis and discussion of family business cases with relevance to the family's current situation, nurture candid discussion about the unique skills and career aspirations of various next-generation members, and review the dynamic vision for the family and the firm (see Figure D). Preliminary designs for the holding company, which was to become the Grupo Ferré Rangel, were also drafted at these meetings.

As he prepared himself for a family retreat, Antonio recalled,

I had set 2004 as the target date for the transition because I wanted us to plan and be disciplined about doing what we needed to do to be ready. But I started noticing some impatience with the process, a certain rush to the presidency, that I found quite troubling. I wanted to be able to remain as a mentor and advisor to the leaders of the next generation and not feel pushed out.

What is Antonio Luis Ferré struggling with? Since he is personally committed to the orderly transfer of power to the next generation in five years, what should he be giving priority attention to now as the incumbent CEO? And what does he need to do next to ensure continuation of the spirit of enterprise and Ferré Media Group's history of innovation?.

This case was prepared by Professor Ernesto J. Poza as the basis for a class discussion rather than to illustrate the effective or ineffective handling of a family-business management situation. For permission to publish this case, grateful acknowledgment is made to Antonio Luis Ferré, chairman, and María Luisa Ferré Rangel, president, Grupo Ferré Rangel.

SMALL FAMILY BUSINESS | CASE **4**

"SHE'LL ALWAYS BE MY LITTLE SISTER"

Martin Schmidt is the second-generation owner and manager of a construction company that builds office towers. He is in his late 50s and recently became concerned about his daughter, Dorothy, and her increasing desire to join the family business. Marty's middle child, Robert, has been with Schmidt Works for four years and is widely viewed as Marty's likely successor. Marty's other child, his oldest son, moved far from home after a falling-out with his father. Marty's wife is not involved in the business.

Marty admits that Dorothy is well prepared for a career with Schmidt Works. She has studied at Ivy League schools, has worked successfully in a multinational conglomerate, and holds an MBA. When Marty was asked about his reservations about Dorothy's joining the firm, he replied: "I'm scared to bring her into the company. I know she's qualified, but I just can't see my Dotty leading and giving orders. She's a good girl, and I know that no one in this business will listen to her."

Bobby shares his father's opinion that Schmidt Works is not "the right place for Dotty." He says: "I don't see her working in this industry—it's physically exhausting work. I'm afraid she'll fail, and she isn't able to handle failure. She'll always be my little sister—I'll never get over that. I just want to protect her, and I don't have time to hold her hand. Her insistence on joining the business is beginning to irritate me."

Dorothy says: "I've always wanted to be in the business, and as a family member, I should be allowed to join. My only problem is getting my father and brother to take me seriously. If I present some expert's idea, they listen, but my opinion is usually overlooked and not discussed. I feel frustrated and a little hopeless about even things I'm confident about."

What should Dorothy do in this situation? And what should Martin's next step be?

This case study of a family-business dilemma is part of a series by the Family Firm Institute edited by Ernesto J. Poza. The cases are real, but identities have been changed to protect the privacy of the individuals involved. Reprinted with permission from The Family Firm Institute, Inc. All rights reserved.

THE VEGA FOOD COMPANY

In February 1997, Francisco Valle, Jr., president of Industrias La Vega, organized the first family council meeting in the owning family's history to address problems he was having with his youngest sister, Mari, a shareholder in the company. He felt that the problems were not of his making and were interfering with his management of the company. Francisco, 45, had worked closely with his father, Francisco Sr., since 1976 and had become president of the company in March 1994, when his 72-year-old father was killed in an automobile accident. Industrias La Vega was a Spanish meat-processing business that produced hams, sausages, and other delicacies for domestic and export markets. The $104.8-million-a-year business was demanding, of course, but Francisco Jr. felt most challenged by the family conflicts that often overwhelmed him.

The ownership structure of Industrias La Vega had been updated just months before the tragic accident involving Francisco Sr. At the request of Francisco Jr., who was concerned about the possible loss of control of the enterprise he had comanaged with his father for years, Francisco Sr. and his attorneys had created two classes of stock. The voting A shares did not pay dividends. The nonvoting but dividend-bearing B shares had a par value 10 times higher than that of the A shares.

Except for brief stints, none of the Valle daughters had worked in the business prior to their father's death. Ana, the second eldest daughter, was an artist, and she had been instrumental in designing the image and logo of a new premium product line. Working alongside her father, she had created the look for the Gold Label line of meats and cold cuts, Francisco Jr. had not been particularly enthusiastic about this new line.

Mari, 27, the youngest of the Valle siblings, was concerned about her future and the security of her own young family after her father's death. She worried about how her interests as a shareholder would be protected. She had trusted her father completely, but she was not sure she had the same faith in Francisco Jr.

She did admit to being a little more optimistic now that Francisco was making an effort to get closer to the lower-level employees and be more of a leader in the company. As it turned out, Francisco was his father's successor not only in the company, but also in politics. His father had won a Senate seat in the last elections before his tragic accident. Francisco campaigned for and won the seat, and served what would have been his father's term. Mari and his four other sisters chided Francisco about being so effective in his political campaigning and yet unable to instill a team spirit among the company's employees. He was, in fact, still spending 3 to 4 days a week on political endeavors.

The farmers and cattle ranchers of whom Francisco Sr. had been a lifelong customer trusted him. As a major customer for their products, he had had much influence with them. His successful run for the Senate at the age of 72 was evidence of the degree of this influence, even outside business circles. In the food-processing industry, good relations with the government represented an asset for the Valle family, from which both generations derived competitive advantage.

THE VALLE FAMILY

The Valle family was wealthy by the standards of the small town in which they had most of their production facilities. Francisco Valle, Sr., was a self-made entrepreneur. He married Isabel in 1947 and had five daughters and a son (see Figure E). In 1997, Valle family members included Isabel, 71, Francisco Sr.'s widow; Rosa, 47; Francisco Jr., 45; Ana, 42; María, 38; Tere, 33; and Mari, 27. Of these, only Francisco Jr. and Tere worked in management positions at the family company, and Tere had joined only three years earlier.

Relations between family members were warm, particularly among the women, though several next-generation members had created very different lives for themselves. Rosa and María lived overseas but visited Isabel two or three times a year. The only son, Francisco Jr., had studied agribusiness overseas and then returned to run the family business.

In a traditional display of primogeniture, Francisco seemed preordained to be the successor to his father. He took his responsibilities toward his mother and sisters seriously, although they all complained a little about not being involved enough, not being kept sufficiently informed, and not being treated the same way Francisco was treated by the company. Francisco received a reasonable CEO salary, bonus, and benefits package. But the sisters' dividends were nowhere close to his take-home pay, and Francisco, with his expensive tastes, seemed to flaunt the difference. A palatial home, luxury car, helicopter, boat, and assorted other "toys" all seemed essential to Francisco in his executive post. A couple of the sisters were divorced and had additional financial responsibilities toward their own children. Even Isabel lived in a more modest house and drove a less expensive car than Francisco did.

Family members characterized themselves as being "hermetically sealed," meaning that they were not great communicators. This was particularly true on the subject of money; the few conversations about finances that took place were one on one and had the quality of family gossip. Tere remembers one of her sisters saying, "Is it true that you receive 1 percent of the company's profits and Francisco gets 10 percent? That is robbery!" Francisco was often the target of the gossip, but mostly he ignored it, except for telling himself and his advisors, "After all, I have been the one working the business for more than 20 years now."

There was plenty of evidence of love, caring, and tenderness in the family. There was less evidence of respect for titles, organizational structure, hard work, reporting relationships, institutions, and formality of any kind. The family seemed ill-equipped for financial responsibility. In the past, dividends had been distributed infrequently. Individual family members' needs were brought to the attention of Francisco Sr., who usually granted requests, as a generous father would. For Mari, the youngest daughter, who grew up surrounded by evidence of the family's wealth, and for other siblings who needed money for new houses or trips, asking was often akin to receiving.

FAMILY COUNCIL MEETING, FEBRUARY 1997

Francisco took the initiative in sponsoring this first family council meeting. It followed a day-long shareholders' meeting, at which financial information and the state of the

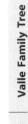

figure **E** | **Valle Family Tree**

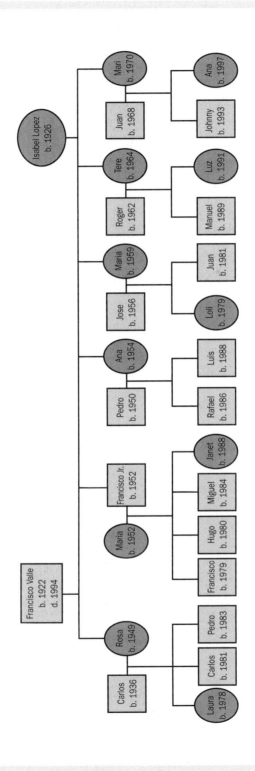

table **A**	Financial Results for Industrias La Vega, 1992–1999							
	1992	**1993**	**1994**	**1995**	**1996**	**1997**	**1998**	**1999**
Sales	42.5	51.7	57.4	69.4	84.1	104.8	112.6	109.7
Cost of sales	32.1	36.6	41.1	52.6	62.6	78.2	79.6	74.9
Gross margin	10.4	15.1	16.3	16.8	21.5	26.6	33.0	34.8
Administration expenses	5.6	10.2	11.9	13.3	19.6	18.8	22.4	22.7
Interest expenses	0.0	0.0	0.0	0.0	0.0	3.1	4.4	5.6
Net profit	4.8	4.9	4.4	3.5	1.9	4.7	6.2	6.5

business were discussed with shareholders. The news for shareholders was not great. Although company sales had continued to increase, profits had plummeted in the past couple of years, and dividend distributions had been cut (Table A).

With Tere's help, Francisco had interviewed and selected the family-business advisor who facilitated the family council meeting. The consultant had conducted a private meeting with every member of the family. A few days prior to the meeting, Mari told the family business consultant,

> It is important that each of us know what we have, what we don't, and what we can and cannot do as shareholders. We have to speak clearly about these things. Right now, bringing up the subject is taboo. We need more transparency in all of this. We need to recognize that we are all siblings here.

Tere observed, in her meeting with the advisor,

> The reason for these meetings is that we need Industrias La Vega to continue as a family business. In order for that to happen, Francisco needs to be supervised. There has to be more balance between Francisco and the sisters. Those inside the company have to live by corporate rules, manage with transparency, and meet the needs of the inactive shareholders. There has been too much centralization by Francisco. Financial information about the company has to be sent out regularly and explained in such a way that all shareholders understand it. Without this education, there will be no sense of justice. But don't get me wrong; we love each other a lot. We have grown in family unity. My mother is a very strong woman and a very steadying influence.

Isabel expressed her own expectations of the meeting this way:

> In the interests of the family and the business, everything has to come out well defined and organized. Things have to be clear for everybody, after some discussion and reflection, so that there is no second-guessing later.

The meeting started with the setting of meeting goals and behavioral norms for constructive problem solving and conflict resolution. Feedback from the conversations with the family-business consultant was provided for family members to discuss, clarify, and then use to build an agenda that responded to the identified needs, problems, and opportunities. Selected as the two top-priority items on the agenda were: (1) the lack of clarity and organization in the ownership structure, estate plan, and financial reporting mechanisms for shareholders, and (2) the lack of a well-organized family forum and board of directors. Board meetings existed only on paper, and only family members were on the board. Although a mini–family-business presentation made by the consultant early in the meeting may have influenced the selection of topics, both Tere and Francisco had attended a family-business course for next-generation members and had been convinced of the need for both of these governance bodies. Obviously, their opinions had significant influence in the larger shareholder group. Other topics selected for discussion included the need to define the responsibilities of shareholders toward the business and of managers toward shareholders, the need to define the rules guiding relations between members of the family acting as suppliers or subcontractors to the company, and the third-generation scholarship fund.

By the end of this first family council meeting, an action plan had been drafted that directed various family members to review the ownership structure and the possession of stock certificates, retain a valuation expert to perform a company valuation, review and account for the family benefits that individual members had been granted in order to make appropriate decisions regarding family benefits in the next shareholder meeting, and continue to schedule open conversations about what shareholders wanted from the business—things such as higher dividends, more reinvestment for long-term growth, and liquidity of shareholdings via buy–sell agreements. An agreement was reached among family members that the company hierarchy would be respected, and any information required by shareholders regarding the company and its finances would be directed to Francisco, the president, and not to accounting department personnel. Francisco, in return, agreed to respond to such requests in a timely manner. Shareholders also reached agreements regarding the other expectations they had of management and what management could rightfully expect of shareholders.

Finally, a discussion of family-business boards produced a consensus on the desirability of a board with independent outsiders and a list of board responsibilities. These responsibilities were to promote the continuity of the business, review the strategy of the business, review and approve financial reports and budgets, review the compensation of key executives, and provide oversight on large capital investment decisions. The criteria for selecting board members were to be developed by a task force made up of Francisco, Tere, and Rosa. The selection of independent board members themselves and the holding of the first board meeting were deemed to be the responsibilities of Francisco, though shareholders wanted to be consulted.

FAMILY COUNCIL MEETING, SEPTEMBER 1997

The next family council meeting was held in September 1997. This meeting addressed three new topics: (1) the family foundation (a study of its various projects in the past 5 years had been done), (2) college scholarships for members of the third generation, and (3) the possibility of selling a couple of parcels of company farmland. The bulk of the meeting was focused on following up on the action plans drafted at the February meeting. While there had been much progress on many fronts, shareholder information, company valuation, and liquidity concerns had not been addressed by the time this second meeting was held. And a new board of directors or advisory board had not been assembled.

MARI BRINGS IN THE ATTORNEYS

The semiannual family council meeting was scheduled to take place in May 1998. Mari felt sick, and checked herself into a hospital for observation. This precluded her from attending the meeting. Instead, she sent two attorneys whom she and her husband had retained to put pressure on Francisco for fuller disclosure of corporate financial information. The family council meeting was canceled after a brief conversation with the attorneys to determine the nature of their involvement.

Francisco was very upset and quite worried that if the company's accounting and financial records were scrutinized, they would be found lacking and this would create more chaos and family disharmony and possibly even result in legal ramifications. The business, as a result of a very strong entrepreneurial culture and unsophisticated financial and administrative systems, had very unsophisticated accounting procedures. Francisco Sr. had never been very concerned about establishing such systems. Now, the responsibility for historical reconstruction of financial information had fallen on Francisco Jr. He said,

That was the reason that I could not be any clearer with shareholders about the books than I was. I was not hiding anything; they had the same information I had available to me. But I knew how shrewd those two attorneys that Mari hired were, and I was very worried for the family and the business's reputation.

In the aftermath of the family council meeting, Francisco stayed very close to his mother, Isabel, and consulted her often on what to do. But, of course, all of this was very hard on her, as she did not want this to be the legacy of her very successful late husband. Francisco respected Isabel's wisdom and her ability to influence her daughters. Mari had hired the lawyers, but most of her sisters were secretly rooting for her. They too wanted to better understand what they considered to be rightfully theirs. Isabel talked to her daughters on many occasions during that period about the importance of preserving the family and about the need to give Francisco time to run the company, get things in shape, and show them what he could do. But her arguments did not dissuade Mari, who continued her inquiry through her attorneys.

About this time, company and family attorneys finally unraveled the details of the estate plan. It was determined that upon Francisco Sr.'s death, Francisco Jr. held 50 percent of the voting A shares and 20 percent of the nonvoting dividend-bearing B shares. Each of his five sisters owned 15 percent of the B shares, and Isabel retained 5 percent of the B shares and the remaining 50 percent of the voting shares. Voting control, therefore, rested in the hands of the founder's surviving spouse and Francisco Jr., the successor president.

Hurt and disillusioned by Mari's actions, Francisco began the process of negotiating with Mari and her attorneys for a buyout of her shares. On the advice of her mother-in-law, an influential banker, Mari asked for $10 million, but she was offered $4 million. During the last round of negotiations, Francisco, concerned about the future of both the family and the business, agreed to $6 million on an installment basis—a price he considered exorbitant but worth the peace of mind and the ability to move on, both of which he so desperately wanted. Mari agreed to this offer, and sold all of her shares to Francisco, who, as a result, now owned 35 percent of the B shares.

FAMILY COUNCIL AND SHAREHOLDERS' MEETINGS, OCTOBER 1999

Family council meetings were not held for over a year, while the wrangling and negotiations were going on. In October 1999, family members held their next family council and shareholders' meetings. (Mari, who was no longer a shareholder, decided not to attend either meeting.) The agenda for the 1-day shareholders' meeting and the

table **B**	Dividends for Industrias La Vega, 1995–1999	
1995		$181,000
1996		$322,000
1997		$639,000
1998		$1,256,000
1999		$1,488,000

additional day for the family council meeting included discussion of a draft of a shareholder buy–sell agreement, discussion of the new dividend-distribution policy, and discussion of a draft of a family constitution. The family constitution included an emergency contingency plan naming Tere, the one sister active in management, as the successor if something should happen to Francisco.

THE PRUNED FAMILY TREE GROWS

All this upheaval and animosity did have several positive side effects. Francisco dedicated himself fully to the business. He fired several members of the top-management team who were hurting his efforts to professionalize the business, replacing them with competent key managers. Concurrently, he began to successfully execute a growth strategy that had been in the planning stages for several years. In 1998, revenues and net profit rose to $112.6 and $6.2 million, respectively. Then, in 1999, when revenues went down slightly, to $109.7 million, net profit rose to $6.5 million (see Table B). Starting in 1998, dividends increased significantly, which gained Francisco much respect with shareholders.

Francisco retained a financial consultant as the CFO and, to his delight, found that this CFO knew as much about business as he did about finance and was a great general manager. Francisco now had key nonfamily managers whose skills complemented those that he and Tere brought to the corporation. Together, they turned things around dramatically and increased company profitability.

While Mari achieved her goal of liquidity and personal oversight over her own inheritance, the other family members recommitted themselves to the business and stayed involved. The work of the family foundation continued. The foundation was successful in getting a highway named in memory of Francisco Sr., and all the family members got together to honor and celebrate the family's proud past. The increased participation by the Valle sisters in committees, task forces, the family council, shareholders' meetings, and the family foundation led to a greater sense of transparency and ownership. As they walked to a shareholders' meeting in the spring of 2000, Ana reflected on the changes:

> *A long time ago, my father gave one of my siblings $650,000 to buy a house. Francisco has been adjusting distributions to equalize us all with that gift. After that, we will receive our dividends based on our ownership stake and company profitability. Dividends have increased. We receive company information. We exert a great effort to be fair. We've come a long way.*

This case was prepared by Professor Ernesto J. Poza as the basis for class discussion rather than to illustrate the effective or ineffective handling of a family-business management situation. For permission to publish this case, grateful acknowledgment is made to the chairman and the executive vice president of the company. Note that while the case is factually and historically accurate, the names have been changed to protect the privacy of the family.

CHAPTER 4

SUCCESSION: CONTINUING ENTREPRENEURSHIP AND THE NEXT GENERATION

President Toshitaka Kongo is the 50th-generation family business leader of Kongo Gumi, while his 51-year-old son, Masakzu Kongo, waits in the wings for his turn at the helm of the world's oldest Osaka-based family firm that specializes in building and repairing religious temples.

Mark Brooke and his brother Massimo Brooke, who represent the 15th-generation family members, jointly head John Brooke & Sons, a United Kingdom–based firm established in 1541. Originally a manufacturer of fabrics for military personnel, under Mark's leadership the company has changed its focus to development of an entrepreneurial park.

Craigie Zildjian and her sister Debbie Zildjian, who represent the 14th-generation family members, jointly head the Zildjian Cymbal Company, the well-known cymbal smiths of Massachusetts, U.S.A.

As indicated by these examples culled from the *Family Business Magazine's*[1] list of the 100 oldest family firms of the world, despite the doom and gloom represented by the often-quoted statistics that a third of family firms do not make it to the second generation,[2] there are many examples of successful multigenerational firms.

In Italy, third-generation Agnellis now control Fiat. In France, the Peugeot heirs work at the company, serve on its board, and control the company. In Germany, second-generation Quandt family members own 46 percent of BMW shares. In Japan, the Toyoda family still has much influence on Toyota through potential successor Akio Toyoda, the youngest member of its board. And in the United States, fourth-generation Ford chairman William Clay Ford serves alongside a nonfamily CEO, Alan Mulally. Note that all of these examples come from a highly capital-intensive industry,

---

[1]N.B. This chapter was written in collaboration with Professor Pramodita Sharma, John Molson School of Business, Concordia University, Canada. See http://www.familybusinessmagazine.com/oldworld.html.

[2]See Ward, J., *Keeping the Family Business Healthy.* San Francisco: Jossey-Bass, 1987.

requiring multiple sources of external capital. During the past decade, the auto industry has also had to deal with intense competition and global consolidation.

In other industries, too, family successors are taking over in record numbers. Third-generation Blake Nordstrom became president of the elegant retail chain and James Hagedorn, whose family controls much of Scotts, became the lawn-care company's chief executive. At Fidelity Investments, the largest mutual fund company, Abigail Johnson was named president of investment management operations and may succeed her father, Edward C. Johnson III, as chairperson. In the food industry, Jim Perdue, a member of the third generation, has become chairman of Perdue Farms, succeeding Frank Perdue, and John Tyson has taken over the running of Tyson Foods from the largest shareholder, his father Don. Still, no trend is a trend if it does not have exceptions. Leon Gorman, grandson of the founder of L.L. Bean, has stepped down as president and chief executive officer and found a successor outside the family, for the first time in the company's history. Gorman's three sons chose not to work at L.L. Bean, but the family is careful to point out that the new CEO worked at the company for 18 years before this promotion and shares the company's core values and traditions, which presumably came from founder Leon Bean and his descendants. Perhaps, as Ford Motor Company has done in previous generations, L.L. Bean will skip this generation but remain on the lookout for capable members of the next generation who want the challenge of running the family business. At Anheuser-Busch, August Busch IV led the $12 billion corporation for the past 2 years. The company agreed to be acquired by InBev in 2008. August A. Busch III had first turned over the roles of president and chief executive officer to Patrick Stokes, a 59-year-old loyal employee, a few years ago. As an interim CEO, Stokes, Anheuser-Busch's first nonfamily chief executive in 140 years, was expected to provide the next-generation member with both mentoring and additional preparation time.

The founder and his or her spouse clearly play a significant foundational role in building a family firm that is worthy of and able to transfer to the next generation. However, the role of the next generation is at least as critical in ensuring the longevity of family firms.[3] Without interested and able next-generation family members in owner-manager or responsible shareholder roles, these firms will not survive as family firms beyond the founding generation. While it is certainly not imperative that the leadership of family firms be passed on to the next generation of family members, as succession should not be confused with success,[4] research has convincingly shown that in the presence of able and trustworthy successors, family firms are well positioned to outperform their nonfamily counterparts.[5]

In deciding whether or not next-generation family members should be involved in the family firms, keep in mind that there needs to be a good fit between the abilities and interests of these family members and the needs of the business at its current stage of development. It cannot be assumed that the interests, strengths, and abilities of the next generation are identical to those of the current generation of leaders, or that the attributes required to launch a business are the same as those required to grow or manage it. Thus, it is imperative to conduct a careful evaluation of the business needs and the family members'

---

[3]See Handler, W.C., The Succession Experience of the Next Generation. *Family Business Review*, 5(3), 1992, pp. 283–307.

[4]Kaye, K., When the Family Business Is a Sickness. *Family Business Review*, 9(4), 1996, pp. 347–368.

[5]Anderson, R.C., & Reeb, D.M., Founding-Family Ownership and Firm Performance: Evidence from the S&P 500. *Journal of Finance*, 58(3), 2003, pp. 1301–1328.

abilities and interests to ensure simultaneous success of the business and career satisfaction of family members in this business.

Given the long tenures of careers in family firms and the significant influence a leader has on all aspects of a firm, it is imperative to clearly understand: (1) the fundamental nature of the task of next-generation leaders in family firms—the rewards and challenges, and how their task is different from the founders'; (2) the fit between the needs of the firm and the attributes and interests of next-generation family members; and (3) strategies that can be used to prepare the next-generation leaders for an effective stint at the helm of a family firm. This chapter provides an up-to-date state of knowledge on each of these important topics to enable you to make an informed decision about whether to join your family business, and if you do, how to best prepare for a career in it that will simultaneously provide for long-term career satisfaction and high performance on both family and business dimensions.[6]

IS THE NEXT GENERATION GOOD ENOUGH TO RUN THE BUSINESS?

Before her death, Katharine Graham proclaimed that, notwithstanding the fact that many of the large newspapers had become management-controlled, family control was still the name of the game for most of the high-quality newspapers, like the *Washington Post*, the *New York Times*, and the *Wall Street Journal*. Her son, Don Graham, whom she chose to succeed her as CEO and publisher, had had a lengthy developmental journey. Don served his country in Vietnam and then returned to the United States to work a beat in Washington, D.C., as a policeman, not a reporter. A couple of years later, he joined the *Washington Post* and began to amass experience in the news and media industries with a variety of assignments at the *Post* and a business education from Harvard Business School.

Empirical deduction from a systematic review of succession experiences has led me to the following conclusions:

1. Many next-generation members of business-owning families want to lead and are ready to work hard and make the sacrifices necessary to be responsible leaders. Determining whether this is true of the next generation in your own family is key. Evidence can be found in work hours, flexibility, adaptability, willingness to serve, commitment to a mission larger than themselves, education, respect for what has made the business successful so far, and overall discipline in both thought and action.

2. The multiyear succession process of many next-generation executives has included a number of challenging assignments, particularly those for which outcomes are measured in profit or loss and are clearly attributable to the successor. Early in their development, these next-generation executives usually worked outside the family business, where results are more objectively and exclusively attributable to performance, unbiased by family influences. After they joined the family enterprise, assignments generally included profit-center and general-management responsibilities that replicate the often-conflicting demands on the chief executive, who is ultimately responsible for profit or loss

---

[6]See Sharma, P., An Overview of the Field of Family Business Studies: Current Status and Directions for the Future. *Family Business Review, 17*(1), 2004, pp. 1–36.

and the creation of shareholder value. Given the flexibility of the financial software now available, even small, single-unit family businesses can create successor accountability for profit or loss. Information on results—the bottom line—and the discipline created by this accountability determine readiness and capability far more effectively than bloodline does.

In larger companies, these early assignments were often far from company headquarters. In the case of multinational businesses, many early experiences happened abroad. For example, after running his own Fort Worth real estate empire, Ross Perot, Jr., worked in the London office of Perot Systems before succeeding his father as Perot Systems chief executive.[7]

3. Through solid performance and interpersonal skills, next-generation members have earned the respect of nonfamily employees, suppliers, customers, and other family members, often shareholders, whom they will serve and lead.

4. In most cases, the successor-development process included much education—college, industry-sponsored programs, and business schools. MBAs helped many successors gain both the skills and the confidence they needed to steer a responsible professional or middle-management career into top management echelons. Unfortunately, MBA programs do not usually address ownership and the unique role that it plays in the leadership of family-led companies. Programs acknowledge trading and perhaps investment, but seldom patient long-term ownership. Graduating students often head to Wall Street and consulting firms, which seldom advise on the owner-manager relationship from a long-term perspective. However, ownership education is increasingly becoming available at leading business schools through entrepreneurial and family-business curricula.

5. Coaches and mentors, both inside and outside the family, have been an important feature of the developmental journey. Gina Gallo, of Gallo Wines, credits both Julio Gallo, her grandfather, and Marcello Monticelli, a 35-year Gallo veteran, with being her mentors. A third-generation family member, she has assumed primary responsibility as winemaker and marketer for the Gallo of Sonoma line of premium wines. She is attempting to do one of the hardest things in business—reposition a brand identified with low price and fair quality to a much higher-value price point. Marketers had suggested that Gallo launch the wines under a different name precisely because of the image problem, but a sense of pride in the family and the name decided the issue for Gina.[8]

6. The process of deciding whether the potential successor was right for the job, for the company, and for the company's strategic needs took many years. Sometimes, it included an assessment by an outside professional, such as a psychologist, who coached the successor through evaluations by peers, supervisors, subordinates, customers, suppliers at work, and relatives at home. The Goleman–Boyatzis Emotional Competencies Inventory, a 360-degree assessment tool, focuses on 52 behaviors linked to executive success. (See http://www.hayresourcesdirect.hay-group.com.) After taking this inventory, participants receive feedback and coaching as appropriate. Successor candidates who have experienced this process and been accountable for profit and loss know themselves and their strengths and

---

[7]Ward, L., Passing the Perot Torch. *Dallas Morning News,* March 29, 2000, p. 1H.

[8]McLean, B., Growing Up Gallo. *Fortune Magazine,* August 14, 2000, p. 211.

figure **4.1** | **A Profile of Successful Successors**

Successful Next-Generation Leaders Share These Characteristics:

- They know the business well; ideally, they like or even love the nature of the business.
- They know themselves and their strengths and weaknesses, having had the necessary outside experience and education.
- They want to lead and serve.
- They are guided responsibly by the previous generation, by advisors, and by a board of outside directors.
- They have good relationships and the ability to accommodate others, especially if part of a successor team (siblings, in-laws, or cousins).
- They can count on competent nonfamily managers in the top-management team to complement their own skills.
- They have controlling ownership or can lead, through allies, as if they do.
- They have earned the respect of nonfamily employees, suppliers, customers, and other family members.
- Their skills and abilities fit the strategic needs of the business.
- They respect the past, and focus their energies on the future of the business and the family.

SOURCE: Adapted from Davis, J., Successor Development. Presented at the International Family Enterprise Institute meeting in Montreal, 1998.

weaknesses well (see Figure 4.1). Such a degree of self-awareness is often hard for next-generation members to achieve because of the large shadow cast by their family predecessors.

7. A board of directors—or a committee of that board made up primarily of independent outsiders—performed the final review of successor performance and the fit between the candidate and company strategy. These directors also offered advice on the timing of the succession. In companies that created advisory (nonstatutory) boards composed of independent outsiders, in lieu of having independent outsiders on their board of directors, these boards provided a forum for many discussions about selecting and anointing the CEO successor. Throughout the several years over which the succession process occurred, board members, individually and collectively, were very active in the assessment, the facilitation of difficult conversations, the review of pertinent information, and the ultimate appointment of the successor.

Including a committee of outside directors or an advisory board not only ensures more thorough and objective data gathering, analysis, and decision making, but also suggests to other candidates, nonfamily executives, and both family and nonfamily shareholders the independent and objective nature of the decision. Shareholder support of the decision is always important, but it is especially so in publicly traded family-controlled firms.

REWARDS AND CHALLENGES FOR LATTER-GENERATION FAMILY MEMBERS

Working in a business with one's family name on the door presents wonderful rewards and inherent challenges. One index of success for a family firm is whether it can attract and retain high-caliber family members and nonfamily employees who commit to achieving organizational objectives. Given the limited labor pool of family members and their critical role in family firms should they choose to pursue their careers within it, it is extremely important to achieve a good fit between their talents and interests and the opportunities in the firm. To assess whether a family firm provides careers for junior members of the family that will afford sustainable benefit to the firm and the individual, a good starting point is to understand the rewards and challenges these firms provide for the members of a family.

REWARDS

Business has often been a part of the developmental environment for junior-generation family members. This is an outcome of the often blurred boundaries between family and business in family firms. Research on occupational choices[9] provides ample evidence of the significant influence of parents' occupations on their children. Juniors often engage in occupations closely related to those of their parents, as these lie within their comfort zones.

Unknown to them or the senior generation, children absorb a lot of business-related information during their formative years. Their formal first workday at the family firm is really not their first at all. Their learning curve is not steep because knowledge has been transferred to them without formal efforts, endowing them with precious stocks of accumulated knowledge about the business, its employees, and external stake-holders. Over at least several years, the successful business has developed processes and strategies to overcome the liabilities of newness that affect entrepreneurial companies; it has retained a stable set of customers, and created a reputation that has enabled it to survive and grow. Professors Dierickx and Cool[10] have best illustrated the importance of this phenomenon, what they refer to as time compression diseconomies, by the following dialogue between a British Lord and his American visitor:

AMERICAN VISITOR: "How come you got such a gorgeous lawn?"

BRITISH LORD: "Well, the quality of soil is, I dare say, of the utmost importance."

AMERICAN VISITOR: "No problem."

BRITISH LORD: "Furthermore, one does need the finest quality seed and fertilizers."

AMERICAN VISITOR: "Big deal."

BRITISH LORD: "Of course, daily watering and weekly mowing are jolly important."

AMERICAN VISITOR: "No sweat, just leave it to me! That's it? No kidding?!"

BRITISH LORD: "There is nothing to it old boy; just keep it up for five centuries."

Research has shown the critical role of reputation in building and sustaining a business as people are much more likely to buy products from companies they know and trust.[11]

---

[9]For example, Barling, J., *Employment, Stress, and Family Functioning,* New York: Wiley, 1990.

[10]Dierickx, I., & Cool, K. Asset Stock Accumulation and Sustainability of Competitive Advantage. *Management Science, 35*(12), 1989, pp. 1504–1514.

[11]Aldrich, H. *Organizations Evolving.* London: Sage, 1999.

Suppliers prefer long-established relationships, and other service providers, such as bankers, know the company well. Anyone starting a career afresh can easily relate to the significant advantage of those who are starting out in an established firm that has been in their family for a few generations or even a few years. Add to this the comfort of knowing that the probability of being fired from this firm is much lower than for their compatriots seeking jobs in companies unknown to them, of reporting to bosses whom they have never met before, or of starting a venture from scratch and the "advantaged" start the junior generation gets in their family firms begins to crystallize, to say nothing about the social and economic benefits that are part and parcel of pursuing a career in family firms.

CHALLENGES

But not all is rosy for the junior-generation leaders. Careers are long and obligations deep-rooted in many family firms. And primogeniture (where the eldest son is expected to take over the business) or coparcenary (equal division of the CEO's job among siblings) may prevail.[12] Both pose difficult challenges for the entering generation, the family, and the business. Even if next-generation members are capable and interested in pursuing careers in their family firms, norms like these may set incapable or uninterested juniors on the road to a long, unsatisfactory or plateaued[13] career in their firms. Alternatively these norms can exclude the more capable family members because of fears of engaging in incongruent hierarchies,[14] in which there is a mismatch in their positions within the business and their perceived seniority levels in the family.

If the business is under the tutelage of the founding generation, the characteristics of the entrepreneur, such as the high need for autonomy, independence, and achievement,[15] that enabled the business to be successful in the first place can prove challenging when the junior generation tries to build a career in the family firm. The shadow of the founder[16] generally looms large on these firms as his or her success projects a larger-than-life aura. Whereas the founder was instrumental in laying the ground rules for the firm and establishing its culture, the juniors are positioned to play the game with preestablished rules, while finding ways to make their mark and rejuvenate and gain legitimacy in the business.

Questions linger about whether the kids are good enough to run the business or possess the passion and talents of the founding generation. Unlike in nonfamily firms, those in charge have extensive information on those entering the firm, which may prevent them from viewing the younger generation as capable professionals. Behaviors in the children's younger years may hinder the parent's ability to view them as professionals. When following a legend, the junior generation needs to effectively manage various stakeholders while driving from the backseat or being under constant watch when in the driver's seat. In the first few years, there is a continuous tension to prove

---

[12]Chau, T.T., Approaches to Succession in East Asian Business Organizations. *Family Business Review*, 5(2), 1991, pp. 24–30.

[13]Malone, S.C., & Jenster, P.V., The Problem of Plateaued Owner Manager. *Family Business Review*, 5(1), 1992, pp. 21–41.

[14]Barnes, L. B., Incongruent Hierarchies: Daughters and Younger Sons As Company CEOs. *Family Business Review*, 1(1), 1988, pp. 9–21.

[15]For example, Hornaday, J., & Aboud, J., Characteristics of Successful Entrepreneurs. *Personnel Psychology*, Summer 1971, pp. 141–153.

[16]For example, Davis, P. S., & Harveston, P.D., In the Founder's Shadow: Conflict in the Family Firm. *Family Business Review*, 12(4), 1999, pp. 311–324.

that their claim to their position in the business is legitimate and based on their interests and abilities, rather than being a reward for being born with the right family name.

As industries, businesses, and humans[17] go through their life cycles, the talents and structures needed for sustained competitive advantage change over time. Here the 4-by-100 relay race is an apt analogy.[18] The successful running of a relay race requires careful planning of the sequencing of the runners and their timing and baton-passing technique. While the best starter should run the first leg, poor baton passers should occupy the first or last positions. The final runner needs the most competitive disposition. Thus, strategic sequencing may help to win the race, as different characteristics and strengths of the first, second, third, and last runner can be used effectively.

Even when the junior generation possesses the talents and ideas that can launch the firm to new levels of success, the combined influence of the natural human tendency to resist change and the success brought forth by the previous generation makes it difficult to appreciate the need for change and the unique talents of the juniors. Moreover, the human tendency to value current possessions more dearly than those that might be acquired in the future[19] further escalates the commitment to the status quo. Labeled as the "endowment effect," this propensity for possessiveness for an object and the perception of its value has been found to increase with the duration of ownership and the costs incurred over time.[20] Eager to maintain the status quo, those in the inner circle of the current leader, who are generally of the same age group, consciously or subconsciously resist attempts to change, as a generational conspiracy[21] of sorts is experienced by the junior generation eager to make its mark on the business.

Thus, a concerted effort needs to be made to ensure that there is a fit between the interests and abilities of the next generation and the opportunities in the family business. A mechanism for the development and training of these family members for leadership positions needs to be provided. And an objective evaluation system needs to be established as a base from which to launch a rewarding career and the continued success of the family firm.

NEXT-GENERATION ATTRIBUTES, INTERESTS, AND ABILITIES: INGREDIENTS FOR RESPONSIBLE LEADERSHIP

Given the impact of the family on business and vice versa, responsible leadership of family firms requires skills and talents that would enable building a profitable firm while simultaneously ensuring good family relationships. As depicted in Figure 4.2, positive performance on family dimensions ensures high cumulative emotional capital, while

---

[17]Examples, Greiner, L. E., Evolution and Revolution as Organizations Grow. *Harvard Business Review,* May-June 1998, pp. 55–67; and Levinson, D., *Seasons of a Man's Life.* New York: Knopf, 1978.

[18]Dyck, B., Mauws, M., Starke, F.A., & Miske, G.A. Passing the Baton: The Importance of Sequence, Timing, Technique, and Communication in Executive Succession. *Journal of Business Venturing, 17,* 2002, pp. 143–162.

[19]Kahneman, D., Knetsch, J. L., & Thaler, R. H., Experimental Tests of the Endowment Effect and the Coase Theorem. *Journal of Political Economy, 98*(6), 1990, pp. 1325–1348.

[20]Knetsch, J. L., The Endowment Effect and Evidence of Nonreversible Indifference Curves. *American Economic Review 79,* 1989, pp. 1277–1284.

[21]See Lansberg, I. S., The Succession Conspiracy. *Family Business Review, 1*(2), 1988, pp. 119–143.

figure **4.2** | **Performance of Family Firms**

		Family Dimension	
		Positive	**Negative**
	Positive	**I** ***Warm Hearts*** ***Deep Pockets*** High Emotional and Financial Capital	**II** ***Pained Hearts*** ***Deep Pockets*** High Financial but Low Emotional Capital
Business Dimension	**Negative**	**III** ***Warm Hearts*** ***Empty Pockets*** High Emotional but Low Financial Capital	**IV** ***Pained Hearts*** ***Empty Pockets*** Low Financial and Emotional Capital

SOURCE: Sharma, P., An Overview of the Field of Family Business Studies: Current Status and Directions for the Future. *Family Business Review, 17*(1), 2004, pp. 1–36.

good business performance enables building of a firm's financial capital. Sustainable family firms enjoy high cumulative stocks of both emotional and financial capital. As firms go through different stages in family and business life, from time to time they may slip into cell II or III. Based on the accumulated stocks and strategies used, those that last for a long time rebound back to cell I, but a move toward cell IV foretells failure for the family firm.

DESIRABLE NEXT-GENERATION ATTRIBUTES

Research directed to understanding the desirable attributes for successors[22] suggests that integrity and commitment to business are the two considered most important by the senior generation of leaders of family firms. The ability of those in the junior generation to garner the respect of employees is ranked a close third. Of course, competence is an important factor in selecting a successor, as evidenced by the fact that decision-making and interpersonal skills were ranked fourth and fifth. However, it seems that it is more important that family-business successors be capable of making decisions that are in the best interest of their family and the business, while gaining the respect and trust of family members and employees. Competence without integrity or commitment does not make the senior generation confident about transferring the leadership of the business to juniors. No matter how qualified the juniors are in other respects, if they cannot be trusted to make decisions that are in the best interest of the business and the family, they are not considered ready to lead family firms.

---

[22]Chrisman, J. H., Chua, J. J., & Sharma, P., Important Attributes of Successors in Family Businesses: An Exploratory Study. *Family Business Review, 11*(1), 1998, pp. 19–34.

The next generation's skills in marketing, sales, finance, strategic planning, and technical aspects were considered moderately important. Even educational level and experience in business or the firm itself was regarded as only moderately important. Also revealing was the fact that gender, age, birth order, or being from the founders' bloodline were considered only minimally important. Given the general perception that family firms blindly follow family norms with respect to such demographic factors, this finding bodes well for the longevity of family firms, as it indicates a move toward making choices of leaders based on their good intentions, interests, abilities, and relationships rather than on birth order, gender, and/or related family norms. The above findings are based on a study of over 500 owners of midsized Canadian family firms; however, replication of this study in India[23] confirmed similar perceptions of family-business leaders with respect to desirable successor attributes.

NEXT-GENERATION INTERESTS

A question that needs reflection and clear resolution for next-generation family members seeking to pursue a career in the family firm is "What are their motivating factors?" or "What is the basis of their commitment?" Researchers studying commitment in family firms[24] distinguish between four motivating factors that compel the next generation toward a pursuit of careers in the family firm. The reasons for the next generation's decision to join the family firm can vary, as is evident in the following statements made by four family-firm successors.[25]

TIM: I'm one of the luckiest guys to come out of the University because I haven't been slotted into a specific job. We have an item that we manufacture from scratch, we warehouse it, we wholesale it, and we retail it. I see the business from every angle and I'm involved in it from every angle. It's kind of neat to be able to do that. . . . I love being part of my family business.

POLLY: I felt touched; I felt needed, but I felt uncertain that this [moving to the family business] was a good move. . . . He [my father] said that the most important thing right now is for you as a Stillman to be visible here because your sister is out. . . . [W]e need another family member here. And so with that kind of plea I had no choice in my mind. I couldn't let the family down. So I dropped everything I was doing and. . . . I just went the next day and started working.

ROB: At that point we really didn't know what her [Rob's wife's] involvement was from a shareholders' standpoint. And what we found out was she was heavily involved to the point where it dwarfed what we were doing personally and all of a sudden it did change our perspective. . . . It sort of changed our outlook on it (their family business). . . . that is when we decided we cannot pass this up.

---

[23]Sharma, P., & Rao, S.A., Successor Attributes in Indian and Canadian Family Firms: A Comparative Study. *Family Business Review*, 13(4): 2000, pp. 313–330.

[24]Sharma, P., & Irving, G., Four Bases of Family Business Successor Commitment: Antecedents and Consequences. *Entrepreneurship Theory and Practice*, 29(1), 2005, pp. 13–33.

[25]Handler, W.C., Managing the Family Firm Succession Process: The Next Generation Family Member's Experience. Unpublished doctoral dissertation, Boston University, 1989; and Sharma, P. Determinants of the Satisfaction of the Primary Stakeholders with the Succession Process in Family Firms. Unpublished doctoral dissertation, University of Calgary, 1997.

BOB: I was always afraid of change (working outside of family business). I'll stick it out. . . . I really think, in a way, being so cowardly, I've really been lucky I've done as well as I have so far. . . . It could have been a lot worse.

Tim joined the business because it offered the variety of tasks and job satisfaction that he desired and valued and he has a strong belief in and acceptance of the organization's goals, combined with a desire to contribute to these goals and confidence in his ability to do so. In essence, he *wants to* pursue such a career and is excited by related possibilities. This basis of commitment has been referred to as "affective commitment."

Polly, on the other hand, had made a decision to work elsewhere until her father indicated that she was needed in the family business. Because of her father's request, she felt obligated to join the family firm. In essence, she is trying to foster and maintain good relationships within the family and is compelled by a feeling that she *ought to* join the family business. Such commitment is referred to as "normative commitment."

Rob and his wife decided to pursue careers in his in-laws' firm only after realizing the extent of their ownership stake in the business, their perceived value of this stake, and the related opportunity cost of not pursuing careers with the firm. Thus, their motivators are based on their perceptions of substantial opportunity costs and threatened loss of investments or value if they do not pursue a career in the family firm. "Calculative commitment" drives such next-generation family members, as they feel they *have to* pursue such a career.

Finally, Bob's decision to pursue a career in his family firm was based on his perceived dependence on the firm as a safe haven and his lack of confidence in his ability to pursue a career outside this firm. The underlying mind-set driving his decisions is a *need to* pursue such a career.

Although all four of these next-generation family members decided to join their family businesses, thereby exhibiting the identical behavior, the bases or compelling reasons for their behavior differed considerably. It is quite possible that their subsequent behaviors in relation to the family business will vary too, having implications for their effectiveness and for firm performance. Those like Tim, who are propelled by their desire to contribute to the business and are confident in their abilities, are likely to be the best performers.

At the other extreme are next-generation members such as Bob, with high perceived dependence on the family firms, who suffer from feelings of insecurity and low self-efficacy. Although not yet proven empirically, it is expected that such family members are the least likely to be progressive and to enjoy a productive career in their family firms. The likes of Polly and Rob are expected to be selective in their efforts because they would be guided by their motivation either to keep the senior generation satisfied or to ensure that their individual wealth is being protected and enhanced. Either of these cases does not suggest efforts and outcomes that reflect the best interests of the family business. Next-generation members and their family firms would be well served if they understood what is really attracting them to spend their lives and careers in the business. If the motivator is any other than affective commitment, honest reflection and candid dialogue are needed. Finding alternative ways to appease the obligations toward senior family members, enhancing the ownership interests of the juniors through education and family communication, or finding ways to further the juniors' abilities and confidence would be appropriate. Thoughtful planning of next generations' careers in the family business can be most beneficial, and is the topic we next explore.

CRAFTING THE NEXT-GENERATION CAREER PLAN

The overlap of family relations, business management, and ownership in family firms requires that junior-generation family members be competent in the dimensions of ownership, management, and leadership of familial relations. Given the challenging nature of this task and the opportunity to start preparation early in life, the socialization of juniors would best be started in early childhood.

SMART MONEY MANAGEMENT

To ensure that the next generation is ready to handle their ownership duties with regard to money effectively, training can start from the time they are old enough to get pocket money and open a bank account. A good way to develop a sense of financial responsibility among very young next-generation members is to provide them with their own expense account, based on quarterly or semiannual budgeting—and no possibility of additional deposits in the case of overspending.

Chapter 5 describes a business owner who held one-on-one business education sessions with the next generation during family vacations and gave his children their own checking accounts for school and life expenses after determining, with their input, an appropriate budget. Actions such as these reduce the propensity of parents to use money to control their children as they grow. They also help children assume personal responsibility for financial matters early in life.

Families following prudent money-management practices encourage the rule of thumb that we refer to as $3 + 3 + 3 + 1 = 10$—that is, every \$10 earned (or received by a young child) should be split into four parts: three of which are consumed, three reinvested in the individual's development such as learning new skills, three saved for future needs, and one shared with those in need (philanthropic causes). Those socialized with this training are better positioned to use this smart money-management strategy in their business.

A strong work ethic is the most influential counterbalance to any experiences with the advantages of wealth. But in addition to a work ethic, young next-generation members need an understanding that the family's estate requires stewardship in order to be preserved and grown for subsequent generations. Through family meetings, special education for the young heirs, and/or early experiences in financial manage-ment, the children will begin to realize that the company is not simply a source of cash for them but is, instead, a responsibility requiring stewardship. Heirs who approach an operating company with a checkbook mentality certainly increase the probability that the business and the family will both be destroyed. In fact, experienced business owners argue that the risk of business failure rises exponentially with the development of a sense of entitlement and aspirations of liquidity.

MANAGERIAL WORTHINESS

Next-generation leaders need to overcome the general perception by family, nonfamily employees, and outsiders that their position in the business is a product of their birth in the owning family rather than being based on their abilities. Business experience both in and outside the family firm comes in handy to develop different types of skills, grow as well-rounded individuals, and build confidence and self-efficacy. Some families make it imperative for juniors to work outside the business for a specific number of years before joining the family business. Others value experience within the family firm more than experience with other firms. Similarly, the value assigned to educational attain-ment varies from one family firm to another. While some families attribute great value to achieving a particular type or level of educational training, others value mentoring and on-the-job training more. Successful families have been found to use a large variety of techniques to prepare the next generation effectively.

The overall objective on this dimension is to ensure that the next-generation leaders are well prepared to handle the managerial responsibilities of their business. Effective planning starts with understanding the needs of the business and the type of preparation that would enable the development of competence and confidence, while simultaneously ensuring that the junior generation gains legitimacy in the eyes of internal and external stakeholders. The incumbent leaders of the senior generation can help by articulating and establishing the norms[26] and clarifying the preparatory goals that the next generation must achieve to signal their readiness for a career in family firms. For their part, juniors who are interested in pursuing a career in their family firms must seek clarification of these requirements and plan their preparatory phase of life accordingly.

When young next-generation members come to work in the business, their compensation needs to be market-based. Using compensation to communicate love, to respond to personal needs, to communicate equality, or even to engender a sense of sacrifice on behalf of the corporation is not helpful. Along with market-based compensation should come performance reviews, which help to assess results against goals. Treating next-generation members in the same way as nonfamily employees reinforces a merit rather than an entitlement culture. Most importantly, performance reviews provide next-generation members with developmental feedback at a time in their careers when it is most useful.

Results of the Discovery study indicate that performance reviews are least often done with members of the owning family.[27] The reasons are easy to understand: A family member is not the person best qualified to do a performance review of another family member, and key nonfamily managers are hesitant to hold next-generation members of the family to high standards because, after all, they may someday end up working for those family members. Yet next-generation members are seriously handicapped when their careers proceed in a performance-feedback vacuum. Senior nonfamily executives who enjoy much security in the company and are personally confident and independent are ideal candidates for carrying out this task, even if they are not the direct supervisors of the family members. In this case, the supervisor, the senior nonfamily manager, and the next-generation member all meet to review performance and to establish a new set of goals for the next relevant period.

FAMILY RELATIONS

Effective performance in the family firm requires management of relationships with family members who are actively involved in the business as well with as those who are not. The seeds for effective intergenerational and intragenerational relationships are sown from the early years in an individual's life. The parent–child relationship and its growth into an adult–adult relationship is enhanced by the laying of clear ground rules for children,[28] integrity in relationships, and role modeling of behaviors deemed desirable in the next generation.

---

[26]Frishkoff, P. Rules for Entry into the Family Business. *Succession Solutions,* Winter, 1997.

[27]Poza, E. J., Alfred, T., & Maheshwari, A., Stakeholder Perceptions of Culture and Management Practices in Family and Family Firms—A Preliminary Report. *Family Business Review, 10*(2), 1997, pp. 135–155.

[28]Kaye, K., *Family Rules: Raising Responsible Children.* Lincoln, NE: iUniverse, 2005.

Sibling relations[29] are largely the result of how parents handle their relations with multiple children. The overall objective is to develop sibling relations that are close but not enmeshed, separate and differentiated but not isolated, and to provide intellectual and emotional stimulation without destructive rivalry. In the early childhood years, most children seek the time, attention, and affection of their parents. When multiple siblings are involved, each uses strategies (unconsciously, in most instances) to optimize their share of these precious resources. Parents can help enhance these relationships by ensuring that they minimize intersibling comparisons on attributes that are unchangeable, such as color of eyes, height, etc. Encouraging each child to appreciate and celebrate the strengths of the other and to help each other to further develop their unique strengths is also useful. As grown-ups, siblings can work toward improving these relationships by understanding that the source of rivalries often lies in competition for parental love and the limited time and energy that parents had on any given day.

Another important index of the success of a family firm on familial dimensions is the caliber of talent attracted and retained through marriage.[30] A measure of parents' success is how well they have prepared the next generation's competitive advantage as compared with their cohorts, and the value added to opportunities made available to the next generation. One individual joining a family through marriage or long-term relations with a family member has the potential to influence about a hundred years of a family's family and business life.

Research suggests that parents have two windows of opportunity to enhance the long-term success of the family through choices of mates made by the next generation—before children reach puberty and then after they choose their spouses for themselves. Before puberty, parents can help raise the standards and sights of their children, make them aware of the difference between substance and packaging, and help to remove narrow prejudices and blinders while developing respect for diverse qualities in humans. Once an in-law selection has been made, the senior generation can render support and enhance relationships by working with the strengths of the new family member and being accepting of him or her. The advice from the senior to the junior generation before they commit to marriage and the raising of children is to ask whether this is the person who the junior generation member would consider raising children with and thereby letting them influence the values of the extended family and its next generation.

SIBLING AND COUSIN TEAMS

Cases in which a team of siblings or cousins assumes power, through an "office of the president" or an "executive committee," represent only a small minority of all CEO successions. In cases in which no individual team leader is chosen, the concern is that the choice may represent not the CEO-parent's informed decision as architect of the firm's continuity but, rather, his or her inability to decide. Making such an important decision tugs at the heart of any father or mother. While most chief executives in family businesses are also parents, clearly they need to wear their CEO hat when confronting this decision.

The family leader may love everybody equally, but the CEO is compelled by administrative tradition and current management practice to choose one individual from among many loved ones. Sometimes, next-generation members collude in this

---

[29]Friedman, S.D., Sibling Relationships and Intergenerational Succession in Family Firms. *Family Business Review,* 4(1), 1991, pp. 3–20.

[30]Kaye, K., Mate Selection and Family Business Success. *Family Business Review,* 12(2), 1999, pp. 107–115.

dynamic. Rather than be denied the top spot, next-generation members may suggest structures that minimize the differences among them. Assisting in making this emotionally charged decision is another way in which a board can help the chief executive with the process of making a decision about succession.

As an experiment, one smart, successful, and well-intentioned CEO created an office of the president. The three third-generation members' abilities, contributions, and capacity to work together were tested under this structure for about three years. Two siblings ran independent divisions and the other was the chief financial officer, but all three were part of the office of the president. Notwithstanding the significant attention given to developing and facilitating the concept, the office of the president did not, in the end, significantly help the three siblings manage their interdependence successfully. The CEO, on the advice of his board and with the support of all but one next-generation member, decided to appoint a single successor CEO of the corporation. Currently, all three siblings are board members, and five independent outsiders ensure review and accountability at the holding-company level.

NEXT-GENERATION PERSONALITIES

As they grow up, siblings often adopt very different but complementary personalities; one son may be great at marketing, while a daughter may excel in operations or finance. Such differences present unique opportunities for staffing a growing business. On the other hand, these differences may constitute grounds for much disagreement and conflict. The past is perhaps the greatest forecaster of the future, so evidence of collaboration rather than competition among a group of siblings is the best predictor of their capacity to work together as a team.

When it comes to teams that include cousins or in-laws, the differences are often even more pronounced, because these next-generation members grew up with different parents, who influenced their development differently. Parenting the next-generation members of one team, for example, were one brother who liked to spend his money and live well, another brother who was frugal, and a sister who was extremely religious and charitable.

INTERDEPENDENCE OF TEAM MEMBERS

Interdependence, or coordinated independence, is a central issue for sibling and cousin teams, and a very difficult one to manage. It is at the root of most disagreements between and across generations. The best way to minimize the difficulties that may arise is to design an organizational structure that establishes very different roles for the different members of the next generation. For example, one sibling might be assigned to run the London office, another to run operations, and the other to run the sales division. This was the approach chosen by Samuel Curtis Johnson III at SC Johnson. Of course, he also built a board at the holding-company level, through which all four sons and daughters, plus three independent outsiders, could meet and work through the unavoidable issues of interdependence, such as capital-allocation decisions.

Only rarely do sibling and cousin teams in family businesses share an office (as in the concept of the office of the president) or split the positions of CEO and COO between them. More often, they function as a top-management team. In other words, several members of the family, whether in marketing, finance, or general management of a division, report to one chief executive officer. This is the case at the Gallo and the Mondavi wineries. It is also true of the Estée Lauder Companies, where Aerin Lauder, the granddaughter of the founder of the cosmetics giant, has joined with members of the previous generation and cousins in a team effort. Clearly, family members were chosen based on their skills and how those skills complement each other, with some members working in marketing, others in operations, and still others in the international arena.

After a CEO has taken great care to create different posts, with clearly differentiated roles, what else can be done to avoid second-guessing, working at cross-purposes, sending multiple signals to employees, and general wear and tear on family relationships? Some guidelines for managing interdependence are:

1. Establish common goals.
2. Reflect those different roles in an established organizational chart.
3. Develop procedures that reduce wear and tear on the relationship. For instance, establish a process for role negotiations between parties, a process for team building, and a code of conduct or list of ground rules to be observed by all parties.
4. Establish forums for discussing relationships and sharing feelings on an ongoing basis so that bad feelings are not allowed to fester and multiply unchecked. Disciplined communication in regularly scheduled meetings during which the participants address the question "How are we doing?" and not just "What are we doing?" makes a huge difference in the success of sibling and cousin teams.
5. Transfer ownership with full recognition that the next-generation CEO needs to have not only the job and the title but also the ability to lead, whether alone or with true allies, as if she or he had 51 percent of the voting stock. Anything less could easily create paralysis and deprive the new leader of the ability to be nimble and agile, a competitive advantage of many entrepreneurial and family-owned businesses.

The fact that so many family-owned and family-controlled businesses today are enjoying successful transfers of power to next-generation members may be a direct result of more-sophisticated use of management practices such as performance reviews, and governance practices such as reliance on boards of directors, advisory boards, and family councils. All of these practices assist the CEO in ensuring that succession is not about nepotism and privilege but rather about demonstrated capabilities and accountable execution of managerial and/or ownership responsibilities by the next generation.

A VISION FOR THE COMPANY: TAKING IT TO THE NEXT LEVEL

Each generation has the responsibility of bringing to the business their own vision for the future of the business.

—Samuel Curtis Johnson III, former Chairman, SC Johnson: A Family Company[31]

Compared to their predecessors, younger members of a business family are often more inclined to accept new technologies and more likely to assume the risks that go along

---

[31]Personal conversation with the author, June 1996.

with promoting growth of the business. If their chosen profession is management, next-generation members are likely to want to engage in strategic planning, to redesign information and financial systems, and to pursue digital strategies or e-commerce opportunities. How can the skills and visions of the next generation be most usefully tapped by the family enterprise?

The business reason for welcoming the next generation's ideas is that their complementary skills and perspectives are precisely what a family business often needs in its struggle to update itself in order to grow and continue to create value for its customers. When the fourth-generation members of Sidney Printing Works in Cincinnati joined the family company, they provided the necessary skills for the business to become a strong contender in the new era. In this case, the two generations were fundamentally in agreement on their vision for company growth—a situation that does not happen all that often. While continuing to use traditional methods to print labels, signs, maps, and product literature, Sidney Printing Works, with the aid of its fourth-generation family members, now assists customers with web materials, helps them submit designs digitally for production in multiple media, and customizes and archives those designs for multiple end uses. Ultimately, a new business unit called SpringDot, Inc., was created, acknowledging this innovative use of next-generation skills.[32]

Comcast provides another example in which a vision of company growth was supported by two generations, but on a much larger scale. In 2002, Ralph Roberts helped his son Brian snag the cable business from AT&T, and Brian became the CEO of Comcast, the number-one cable company in the United States, serving 22 million homes. Even with concessions made to AT&T management, the Roberts family gained control, and Brian has had the opportunity of a lifetime to make his father's and his vision a reality. Certainly, it is not always this easy.

DISAGREEMENTS: HAVING THE DIFFICULT CONVERSATIONS

My father forced me to think and to present my ideas in a forceful way because he said no to everything. He took the position of devil's advocate. And everything I brought in for approval—to buy a hotel, build a hotel, grow a hotel business, to change the strategies—he'd say no.

—*J. W. Marriott, Jr., CEO and Chairman of the Board, Marriott International*[33]

If there is a disagreement worth having in a family-controlled company, it is a disagreement about the vision and future direction for the firm. Implicit in conversations about strategy across generations is the tension between fully appreciating and respecting what has made the business successful so far and fully accepting that, given the accelerated rate of change in today's global marketplace, the firm will be overtaken by the competition and eventually driven to extinction unless it is willing to adapt.

Consider the experience of a family company I will call Madco Industries. Madco found itself in a strategic dilemma. The CEO's son, who was vice president of finance, was convinced that Madco, a regional distributor of high-priced industrial equipment,

---

[32]Sulkes, S., Old-Fashioned Business of Printing Meets Dot-Com World at SpringDot. *The Cincinnati Post*, August 29, 2000.

[33]Gregersen, H., & Black, S., J.W. Marriott, Jr., on Growing the Legacy. *Academy of Management Executive*, *16*(2), 2002, pp. 33–39.

could grow and prosper if it complemented its existing operations with the creation of a new channel of distribution via the Internet. His father, the CEO, was equally convinced that doing so would be a bad idea on two counts. First, it would set up a competitive situation between the new company and the existing one and, potentially, between father and son. Second, it could damage relationships with distributors in other parts of the country with whom, in the absence of competition, relationships were cordial and competitive dynamics gentlemanly.

The situation first came to my attention when the son and potential successor called with the news that he was leaving the firm. After obtaining his MBA and then returning to the family firm, he had implemented a new financial information and control system. Since that assignment was now done and he wanted to have a little entrepreneurship in his life, the idea of starting a Web-enabled company appealed to him. He described how he had suggested the new digital strategy to the CEO and how the latter had quickly dismissed it, with the words "over my dead body." The son could not refrain from responding to this ultimatum, so he said, "If we don't do it, somebody else will, and then somebody outside our family will be eating our lunch." So, I suggested that he have his father give me a call to arrange a meeting for the three of us.

At the beginning of the meeting, father and son could hardly speak to each other, even with my assistance. Emotions were running high. By the end of the afternoon, though, we had crafted what seemed like a reasonable plan. The potential successor would write a business plan for his new idea, price shares in the new company on the basis of the seed capital required, and get a 20-minute slot on the agenda of the next meeting of the eight distributors from around the country. This meeting was held every year in the hometown of one of the distributors. That year, it was Madco's turn to host, and the meeting was scheduled to take place in two months. Because the eight distributors had assigned territories and competed not with each other but with others throughout the country, this meeting provided a forum for learning and candid conversation. The potential successor would thus get his opportunity to present the business plan and see whether the other distributors considered it a viable idea and would buy shares in the new venture. The CEO closed our extended lunch meeting by telling his son, "If you manage to sell as little as one share in the project, I am in too."

While this plan represented quite a challenge to the young man, it seemed like a reasonable turn of events. The potential successor might get an opportunity to be an entrepreneur. In the meantime, his decision to leave the family business was at least delayed. His father felt strongly that the only way he would consider changing his mind was if the idea passed the marketplace test, especially among people he respected and with whom he had a relationship he wished to protect.

At the group meeting, the son successfully sold several shares in the new business venture. The e-commerce company was launched as a collaborative venture between several of the distributors, and the son became the new venture's president. About a year and a half after its successful launch, the publisher of a trade publication in their industry made an offer to acquire the new company. On the basis of that offer, it appeared that the successor had managed to create more shareholder value in 18 months than the CEO had created in a whole generation. Very impressed with the offer, and cognizant that it could take another lifetime to achieve such returns if they did not accept the transaction, the son and his partners, including his CEO father, decided to sell.

While the new venture did not remain in the family company's fold for long, it represented great growth and creation of shareholder value for the company and a tremendous learning opportunity for the successor. He is again looking for entrepreneurial opportunities and is a little better financed this time around.

In conflict-averse families, parents often attempt to squelch sibling rivalry or intergenerational conflict. They seek to alleviate conflict because they feel anxious about the expression of differences or aggression by the now-adult children. In these families, next-generation members remain dependent on parents to resolve their differences well into adulthood. Controlling parents join in creating an unhealthy equilibrium, a dismal dance in which next-generation members operate primarily out of their dependency and powerlessness—the exact opposite of the entrepreneurial and enterprising behavior desired in next-generation business leaders.

RESPECTING THE PAST AND FOCUSING ON THE FUTURE

The tension across generations around the issues of growth and innovation is neither new nor exclusively a product of new technology or the e-commerce revolution. Many years ago, as a young chemist working in the company's lab, Samuel Curtis Johnson III, now-deceased chairman of SC Johnson: A Family Company, tried to convince his father that he had the formula for a breakthrough product, an insecticide. Reports are that several attempts at convincing his father of the soundness of the idea were rebuffed with a simple "Remember, son, we are a wax company." Samuel Curtis continued to perform his assigned job faithfully at the lab and carry out his "skunk works" project on the side. He also continued to bring up his idea and advocate its merits in subsequent meetings with his father, only to receive the same admonition. Finally, young Samuel Curtis reportedly added a tiny amount of wax as an inert ingredient to his formulation for the insecticide. When he once again took the new product, now part of the wax family of products, to his father, it received the go-ahead; after all, the insecticide was now wax-based.

A fourth-generation member of the family insists that it was not the adding of wax that changed the father's mind but rather the young chemist's persistence and continued hard work on the new product formula. Whatever the reason for the change of heart, S.C. Johnson II finally became convinced that the idea was sound and that the product did not stray too far from the company's established strengths and core competencies. What is undeniable is that, during the third generation of family leadership, the company grew from $60 million in annual revenues to $4 billion. And, according to company sources, much of the growth and the lion's share of profits came from the new product lines related to insect control, with brand names like Raid and Off! Is it any wonder that S.C. Johnson III advocates allowing each generation to bring his or her own vision to the business?

SOME FINAL RULES OF THE ROAD FOR NEXT-GENERATION LEADERS

Analysis of the age data from the Discovery Action Research Project shows a compelling pattern in the respondents' answers. Those 51 years of age and older and those 30 and younger were routinely more positive about the family, the family business, and its management practices than were respondents in the 31-to-50 age bracket. The research included parents, sons, daughters, nieces, and nephews. This finding is similar to that of

Davis and Tagiuri, who suggest in their work on the influence of life stage on father–son work relationships that the most harmonious relationship occurs when the father is in his 50s and the son is between 23 and 33.[34] The Discovery findings are consistent with, and may help explain, the increased harmony across generations at that stage.

Davis and Tagiuri also suggest that when the father is in his 60s and the son is between 34 and 40, the work relationship is rather problematic. Discovery study findings, too, would suggest a more difficult relationship, based on the perceptual gap between the relatively less positive 31-to-50-year-old and the 51+ CEO. Both studies clearly imply that the next-generation leader should expect difficult conversations, especially those about strategy, to become more problematic as she or he reaches the mid-30s and 40s and the CEO advances to his or her 60s. It is essential, therefore, to create forums for continuing the dialogue and maintaining the relationship—regularly scheduled meetings, fishing/hunting trips, joint vacations, etc. CEOs' initiatives at building institutions of governance are also very important. Boards of directors with independent outsiders, nonfamily managers in top management positions, family meetings, and family councils all create more balanced and rational discourse on subjects that may carry emotional content.

Research by Colette Dumas found that while sons develop their sense of identity by separating from their father and "proving their mettle," daughters do so through continued affiliation with their father as mentor.[35] This difference means that a next-generation daughter or niece could easily display continued caring for the previous-generation CEO and the enterprise, be more interdependent than a son or nephew, and still be quite capable of leading the enterprise. Although style is clearly not the critical criterion for the success of next-generation leaders, there is an unfortunate tendency to view a daughter's less confrontational style as a weakness in relation to the challenges of leadership. If the next-generation leader is not the eldest male of his generation, this creates special challenges that should be met with caution. Incongruent hierarchies exist in the family and the business when the individual's position within the family is different from his or her position within the business.[36] Incongruent hierarchies have made succession a more difficult process for many deserving next-generation leaders.

Regardless of gender, next-generation leaders have to understand that their mission is to lead, concurrently, the business, the family, and the shareholders. They must recognize that different perceptions about what is and what needs to be are rooted not necessarily in personalities and politics, but in the fact that nonfamily managers, family members not active in the business, and other shareholders may have different needs and goals than family members actively participating in the business.

Like it or not, change is in the job description of next-generation leaders. How effectively and rapidly that change is pursued, how well articulated the need for change is, how much next-generation leaders respect the past, and how clear the vision remains after the change will make all the difference.

The essence of the next-generation leader's mission is to appreciate all that has made the business and the family successful and harmonious thus far and to simultaneously

---

[34]Davis, J.A., & Tagiuri, R. The Influence of Life-Stage on Father-Son Work Relationships in Family Companies. *Family Business Review*, 2(1), 1989, pp. 47–76.

[35]Dumas, C., Preparing the New CEO: Managing the Father-Daughter Succession Process in Family Businesses. *Family Business Review*, 3(2), 1990, pp. 169–181.

[36]Barnes, L. B., *Organizational Transitions for Individuals, Families and Work Groups.* Englewood Cliffs, NJ: Prentice-Hall, 1991.

focus on adapting and changing the family–management–ownership system to meet the new competitive environment and opportunities. In this way, continuing success and continuity across generations can be assured.

SUMMARY

1 Members of the next generation of family business owners are taking over from their predecessors in record numbers and are willing to make the sacrifices necessary to be responsible leaders.

2 Early in their career development, many next-generation members work outside the family business, where results are more objectively and exclusively attributable to their personal performance, unbiased by family influences.

3 The right fit between a next-generation member's capabilities and the firm's needs is essential. Crafting development plans and career paths that support the discovery process with regard to mutual fit in a feedback-rich environment is also critical. The process of deciding whether the potential successor is right for the job, for the company, and for the company's strategic needs involves years of experience and assessment.

4 Next-generation members are rewarded for joining the family business through the career opportunities they enjoy relative to the challenge faced by other career launchers whose families do not own firms. Another immediate reward is the speedier learning curve that results from the transfer of knowledge taking place over years of membership in the family in business.

5 The shadow of the founder, incongruent hierarchies between family and firm, and questions about next-generation members' capabilities (rooted in much more data than is ever available on a nonfamily candidate for a similar position) all represent challenges to next-generation leaders.

6 Resistance to change and the frequent imperative to rejuvenate the family firm often challenges next-generation members to perform the difficult and demanding role of change agents.

7 Ownership education is becoming increasingly important in the successor-development process.

8 Coaches and mentors, both inside and outside the family, are an important feature of the developmental journey.

9 A board of directors, a committee of that board made up primarily of independent outsiders, or an advisory board can be extremely helpful in the appointment of a successor.

10 Heirs to the family business must learn early in their lives that they will earn a position in the business rather than inherit it. They should also learn to manage their own money at an early age.

11 When a team of siblings or cousins is chosen for the leadership position, the CEO must establish common goals, carefully create different posts with clearly differentiated roles, reflect those roles in an organizational chart, develop processes that support teamwork and disciplined communication, and transfer ownership with full recognition that the next-generation CEO needs to have the ability to lead.

12 Next-generation members have to prove themselves capable of managing the firm, managing the money (shareholder value and returns), and managing the family relationship. Running the business successfully is not sufficient.

SUCCESSION AND THE TRANSFER OF POWER

CEOs of family businesses have a mandate to drive the success of their businesses—that is, first and foremost, CEOs have the responsibility of keeping the family company competitive. Without the commitment to optimize potential every day in every way, any enterprise is likely to wither. But are family-business CEOs fulfilling the longer-term mandate of institutionalizing the enterprise, of building great companies that will thrive from generation to generation?

THE CEO AS ARCHITECT OF GOVERNANCE

Blurred system boundaries, as discussed in Chapters 1 and 2, present the strongest case for the need to build institutions to govern the relationships between family, ownership, and the management of the business. If family rules become business rules, or vice versa, conflict is avoided; however, problem-solving ability is diminished, and agency costs are incurred. And if this pattern continues for too long, no amount of succession planning can ensure the continuity of the business for the next generation.

Unfortunately, the critical and urgent need to build institutions of governance is often lost on the CEO. In a study conducted by the Partnership for Family Business at the Weatherhead School of Management, Case Western Reserve University, the most statistically siginificant finding was that CEOs of family businesses perceive both the business and the family much more favorably than do the rest of the family and nonfamily managers.[1] The findings further indicate that CEO-parents perceive the business in a significantly more positive light than do other family members along the dimensions of business planning, succession planning, communication, growth orientation, career opportunities, and the effectiveness of their boards. In the absence of dissatisfaction with the status quo, they may be the last to recognize the importance of engaging in still one other leadership responsibility—creating the institutions that will effectively govern the family–business relationship in their absence.

These same owner-managers are more satisfied than are the rest of the family and nonfamily managers with how the employment of family members and their participation in the business are being handled. CEOs believe that there is clarity and understanding among family members of succession requirements and the manner in

---

[1] Poza, E., Hanlon, S., & Kishida, R., Does the Family-Business Interaction Represent a Resource or a Cost? *Family Business Review, 17*(2), pp. 99–118.

which the estate and business ownership will be transferred across generations. CEO-parents also perceive the relationships among family members more positively than do other family members and feel to a greater degree that the expression of differences is encouraged. CEO-parents are significantly more positive in their assessment of the extent to which younger-generation managers in the business are listened to and their ideas considered. These findings indicate that older-generation managers may well be unaware of the concerns harbored by other members of the firm and the family—or perhaps they just appreciate them with a perspective unavailable to the rest of the (usually younger) family members and nonfamily managers.

It is not surprising that the more positive perceptions held by CEOs apply not only to the firm but also to family-related subjects. This highly congruent finding suggests that any efforts to improve the business by advisors on the board or by consultants to family businesses will face resistance from the CEO on two interrelated fronts—family and firm—both of which are relevant to continuity planning.

These are not surprising findings, given the tremendous autonomy of CEOs of family-owned businesses and how little feedback these CEOs generally receive on their performance from either family members or key nonfamily managers. The power implicit in being the top manager, principal owner, and head or partner of the family limits and changes the nature of the information provided to the CEO-parent.

CEOs are also significantly more certain that the length of time he or she will continue in this role is understood. This finding supports the observation that many more CEOs *think* about retiring or changing their responsibilities than *act* on it. Few actually make announcements or behave in a way that commits them to a transfer of power within a specified period of time.

On all of the dimensions measured, CEO-parents have a more positive perception than do younger members of the family, particularly those 41 to 50 years old who are working in the business. CEOs' perceptions may be skewed by their own success, and the CEOs may have difficulty seeing problems in what they have created and continue to manage. Or they may be in a life stage at which the problem-solving efforts in which others continue to engage assume a less important role than making peace with one's dream and one's family. Either way, inattention to the needs perceived by younger members of the family, the CEO's spouse, and/or key nonfamily management for increased communication, planning, and disciplined action can preordain a heretofore very successful CEO to fail the final test of greatness. CEOs have to lead the timely transfer of power to the next generation while in full command of their abilities and in full control of the corporation.

Recognizing the existence and magnitude of the differences between CEO owner-managers and the rest of the family and nonfamily managers in the business is an important step in having a CEO confront the brutal facts of the firm's and the family's current situation. Results of the study mentioned above consistently reinforce the central role of the CEO and parent as architect of the systems, culture, and practices of both firm and family. Thus, a CEO's positive bias may implicitly depreciate others' views, resulting in a decreased ability to detect important problems. It may also threaten the retention of key nonfamily managers and members of the next generation of owner-managers, and thus thwart the adaptation and very survival of the business.

It may be that simply because CEOs know more about what is in place and what is planned, they perceive things more positively than do those who lack that knowledge and are dissatisfied with not knowing. Another, perhaps more important, implication is that they are much more satisfied with what they have created than are others key to the business. They are also much less likely to experience sufficient dissatisfaction with the status quo to want to change anything, even if it is in the best interests of family-business continuity. This lack of motivation by the CEO may thwart efforts to promote the readiness of the next generation and to build the institutions necessary to govern the relationship between the family and the business in the future.

What kinds of governing institutions do CEOs need to build? Research on best practices indicates that a board of directors/advisory board, a family council, a family assembly, an annual shareholders' meeting, and a management team that includes a number of top-notch nonfamily managers can all play a role in improving the family–management–shareholder interaction. (These institutions of family business governance will be thoroughly discussed in the chapters that follow, so no additional detail will be provided here.) Only after constructing an infrastructure founded on these governing institutions can the CEO-architect confidently proceed with his or her plan to transfer power to the next generation.

THE TRANSFER OF POWER

Chief executives preparing to transfer power do not, single-handedly, have to make succession happen. They may not even have to be among those working hard to make it happen. But, to be sure, they have to be the architects of the transition and then know when to get out of the way, letting the engineers, contractors, and tradespeople (advisors, staff, and next-generation members) take over. Several studies, however, show evidence that CEOs in family-controlled companies are prone to long tenures and even entrenchment. By not making way for the torchbearers of the future, these CEOs tend to seriously weaken the company's ability to continue across generations.[2]

Transferring power in any setting is never easy. Its successful, smooth transitions are one of the reasons General Electric is so admired. GE develops general management thoroughly and broadly. And periodically (though not very often), it supports the orderly transfer of power to the next-generation manager, as Jack Welch did in 2001.

For many, the drive for power is as much a life force as the needs to achieve and to be loved. In the family business, transfer of power is further complicated by the demands of family relationships and the sheer potency of ownership. In other words, transfer of power in the family business is not just a matter of passing the management on to the next generation, as at GE, but it is also a matter of passing on the family leadership and the ownership control. Many stories of failed successions in privately held and family-controlled companies reflect the difficulty of doing all three of these things within a reasonable period of time. The Bingham dynasty of Louisville, Kentucky, ended in 1986. Barry Bingham, Jr., had been appointed president of the *Louisville Courier-Journal* years earlier, but in the mid-1980s his father, Barry Bingham, Sr., still retained majority control, voted his daughters onto the board of directors, and eventually decided to sell the company, all without consulting Barry Jr.

In other cases, some of which I have personally observed in my work as a family-business advisor, significant ownership stakes have been passed on to the next

---

[2]See Sonnenfeld, J. A., & Spence, P. L., The Parting Patriarch of a Family Firm. *Family Business Review*, 2(4), 1989, pp. 355–375; Gomez-Mejía, L., Nuñez-Nickel, M., & Gutierrez, I., The Role of Family Ties in Agency Contracts. *Academy of Management Journal*, 44, 2001, pp. 81–96; and Poza, E., *Smart Growth: Critical Choices for Family Business Continuity and Prosperity*, San Francisco: Jossey-Bass, 1989.

generation but without passing on any real voting power or control. Motivated by a desire to minimize the effect of estate-tax laws that threaten the continuity of the business, transfers often begin early. But the preparation of next-generation members for responsible ownership and stewardship is delayed or overlooked. This often means that controlling ownership (a majority of the voting stock) and top-management posts stay in the hands of the previous generation longer than necessary, making a mockery of the presumed transfer of power.[3]

These out-of-phase transfers of management and ownership create extremely difficult leadership challenges for new CEOs. This is especially true when succession is triggered by the unexpected illness or sudden death of the CEO-parent.

You will find no advocacy of early transfer of ownership in these pages. The intent is to promote understanding that the transfer of power needs to be uniquely designed for each family and business in such a way that family leadership, ownership control, and company management are all part of the transfer. Congruency in the transfer of power, as represented by management post, family leadership capability, and ownership shares, is at the heart of an effective transition across generations of owner-managers.

THE CEO AS ARCHITECT OF SUCCESSION AND CONTINUITY

CEOs who have crafted a winning succession in a business do not necessarily fit the profile of a hero, as depicted by the larger-than-life charismatic characters in a Hollywood movie. Instead, most are modest, substantive entrepreneurs or serious professionals (usually in second-, third-, or fourth-generation firms) with a mission. They are hard-working plow horses, not show horses. They care more about doing the right thing for the company and its continuity than about promoting their own egos or agendas. In this sense, they are very similar to successful chief executives of well-known publicly traded companies, the so-called Level 5 leaders.[4]

CEOs of family businesses are building companies to last, so they cannot afford to become narcissistic, spotlight-hungry performers. These owner-managers are stewards of a legacy that has a life of its own, with a value beyond that of the individual CEO. Recognition that the business is not bound to the life span of its current leader leads many CEOs to once again assume the role of architect, as they confront succession and continuity. Architects realize that, for their vision to become a reality, they must enlist the right people and then execute the right strategies to ensure both sustainability and continuity. The "right people," by the way, usually have to be in the top-management team and among the governors of the shareholder group; they may be complemented by board members and outside advisors.

Samuel Curtis Johnson III, deceased fourth-generation chief executive of SC Johnson: A Family Company, arrived rather easily at the realization that he had to be the architect of the transition. Herbert Fisk Johnson, second-generation president of SC Johnson, died suddenly in 1928, without leaving a will. The battle that ensued between siblings ultimately gave 60–40 majority control to Herbert Fisk Johnson, Jr. (Samuel Curtis's father). Samuel Curtis still remembers the 10 long years that it took

---

[3]Barnes, L. B., *The Precista Tools Case*. Boston: Harvard University Publishing Clearinghouse, 1988.

[4]Collins, J., *Good to Great: Why Some Companies Make the Leap . . . and Others Don't*. New York: Harper Collins, 2001.

his father to settle his grandfather's estate. Consequently, his father vowed not to do that to his son, and Samuel Curtis, in turn, vowed not to do it to his sons and daughters either.[5]

Assuming the responsibilities of the chief architect, he assembled a continuity-construction project team for the $5 billion, 100 percent family-owned enterprise. Team members included not only his capable heirs but also key nonfamily managers, one of whom served as bridging president for several years while the next generation of Johnsons got ready to succeed Samuel Curtis. Independent outsiders on the board and a small cadre of family, estate, and family-business consultants assisted the project team. Over a span of more than 10 years, Johnson family members planned with these key nonfamily professionals the building of a unique structure for the Johnson family and the SC Johnson company, much as Frank Lloyd Wright and his team had designed a unique headquarters for the company in Racine, Wisconsin, in the late 1930s.

The continuity planning consisted of many meetings and conversations, much soul-searching and reflection, a variety of developmental assignments for next-generation members, the appointment of interim nonfamily presidents, and the reenactment of a trip that Herbert Fisk Johnson, Jr., had made to Brazil in the 1930s to study carnauba wax. This trip was sponsored in the interest of reclaiming the legacy and sharpening the vision for next-generation members.

Wills, shareholder agreements, an organizational structure that gave each sibling a division to run, and ownership stakes that gave each sibling controlling interest in his or her own division were all part of the plan. Also, an ownership board was created, consisting of all four siblings and three external advisors (in case conflicts should arise). What is traditionally considered soft, a family culture, with all its subtleties and nuances, was coupled with the business equivalents of structural beams and a knowledge of physics.

MINICASE

Kathy Gardarian founded Qualis International in Orange County, California, in 1988 to sell and distribute packing products to retailers like Home Depot. After graduating college, her son Leo, 23, joined the firm in 1990. At the time, Qualis needed a logistics-and-distribution system to support its rapid growth. Unlike many same-gender entrepreneur/next generation teams (father–son or mother–daughter), who often have more difficult and competitive relationships, Kathy trusted Leo fully to perform the challenging task. "We have always been best friends," Kathy says of her son. And according to Kathy, having a male manager in what is a male-dominated industry is a real asset. Over the past 18 years, Qualis has grown, now having four distribution centers around the country and doing about $28 million in business annually. Kathy remains the sole owner, but Leo was recently made president and is on track to have ownership transferred to him. Do you think there is any basis to the anecdotal evidence that cross-gender succession is easier and more likely to succeed? Why or why not?

SOURCE: Adapted from Jaffe, D., & Herz Brown, F., When Succession Crosses Genders. *Family Business Magazine*, 15(2), Spring 2004, pp. 46–47.

---

[5]Barboza, D., At Johnson Wax, a Family Hands Down Its Heirloom. *New York Times*, August 22, 1999, p. B1.

Once the right people were in place, the strategies for the various divisions were working, and the institutions for governing the relationship between the business and the family were built, Samuel Curtis Johnson III decided it was time to retire. He was 72, and he knew he could not run the company forever.[6]

CEO EXIT STYLES AND THE TRANSFER OF POWER

This section draws heavily on research done by Jeffrey Sonnenfeld and P. L. Spence, as reported in their 1989 article in *Family Business Review*.[7] In fact, the first four departure styles discussed in this section—monarch, general, ambassador, and governor—are the products of their research. Observation and direct involvement in over 100 succession and continuity processes over the past 25 years have led me to adapt Sonnenfeld and Spence's original typology to include two additional CEO exit types: the inventor and the transition czar. These six most common CEO exit types are described below.

THE MONARCH

Kings and queens rule for life; they have no retirement provision in the law. They have no expectation of early departure to compensate them for years and years of presiding over wars, calming social unrest, and leading very visible and demanding sociopolitical lives. Because succession cannot take place while the monarch is alive, many Greek and Roman tragedies and several of Shakespeare's better-known works feature palace revolts and death by poisoning. Monarchs rightly operate on the assumption that they will die with their crowns on.

Many business owners rule as if guided by the same principle. Years after the generally accepted retirement age of 65, they still show up daily at work to read the mail, to make or receive a few calls, and to reverse or second-guess decisions made by next-generation or key nonfamily managers over the past 24 hours. Effectively, they rule the company during a three- to four-hour workday.

Monarchs hire and fire a whole series of aspiring general managers, presidents, and chief operating officers. The better these are, the sooner they go, because monarchs do not imagine that anyone could ever replace them. In this context, Dr. Franz Huebel, CEO of Precista Tools, comes to mind. With Huebel hiring and firing four different bridging presidents in the span of five years and resisting the participation of next-generation members in top management, succession came only after Huebel had a fatal heart attack.[8]

Monarchs in business do not talk about succession, nor do they set a date for departure or a deadline for change in responsibility. They genuinely seem to believe that illness and death are things that happen only to others—those poor souls who never ran their own empire. Monarch types are prevalent among business owners because having lifelong control over their own lives, careers, and companies, as well as the lives and livelihoods of their employees, leads them to be the last to accept that

---

[6]Ibid.

[7]Sonnenfeld & Spence, op. cit.

[8]Barnes, op. cit.

time is no longer on their side and what lies ahead may more easily be measured in months than in years.

They refuse to talk about letting go, even to their closest advisors. As a result, succession planning never takes place, responsibility that would help to develop the next generation of managers is never delegated downward, and information is closely controlled through the assistance of a loyal accountant or CFO. Consequently, the secret ingredients of the company's success are never fully revealed.

If a monarch rules the family business, chaos will likely follow his or her death. In the vacuum created upon the monarch's departure, greed and a thousand hidden agendas will flourish, destroying in months what took a whole lifetime—or even several generations—to create.[9] The daughters, sons, nieces, nephews, and in-laws of a monarch had best be prepared for conflict, political turmoil, and loss of both individual self-worth and company net worth. A coup d'état seldom works in a family business. Advisors or service providers to royalty find out, sooner or later, that there is no timely way to help a business monarch when succession and continuity are the goal. In the business world, there are no moats large enough, no technology slow enough, and no competition genteel enough to allow sufficient time for mourning and recoronation to take place.

The General

Unlike monarchs, generals partly retire in a display of self-discipline, per the rules of the military. But these chief executives leave office reluctantly and plot a return. Generals wait patiently, hoping that the younger officer or popularly elected leader will demonstrate his or her sheer inadequacy. When that happens, they return triumphantly to right the wrongs and rescue the unit that lesser people could not save. Today's general lives six months out of the year in Florida, California, or Arizona but plays golf with a cell phone on standby, hoping for the call suggesting that Junior has just made the biggest blunder of his life. Why? Because it is precisely that piece of news that will bring the general back into service, making his or her heart beat strongly and passionately again. He or she flies back to town, reappears in the office, and retakes control, as if never having missed a day of work.

Generals live for the day when they will be called back into service to right the wrongs, real or not, committed by next-generation managers. (Unfortunately, the wrongs are sometimes fabricated by a group of loyalists; they may be key nonfamily managers who never had much use for the young scion, or they may be siblings and cousins who are still jealous about not having been chosen for the leadership position.) Since businesses are hardly ever problem-free or steadily successful, odds are that the general, much like the monarch, will continue to rule, undermining the capacity of anyone else in the organization to succeed at the helm.

If a general runs the family business, other officers and enlisted personnel need to know that their new responsibilities and authority will be only part-time, because the general will be back soon to take full-time possession of all available power. Heirs to a general should learn to enjoy the times when they are in control of the business, because the feeling will be short-lived. Willingness to drop a new information systems project, advocacy of a human resource issue, or a new strategic plan as soon as the

---

[9]Danco, L., *Beyond Survival: A Guide for the Business Owner and His Family*, Cleveland: University Press, 1977.

general reports back to duty is a must. Advisors and consultants to the part-time regime should build or maintain bridges with the general. Otherwise, their consulting project will be considered useless and too expensive the minute she or he returns to the company.

THE AMBASSADOR

Most family business owners take on the role of either a monarch or a general when they exit their business. Fewer owners become ambassadors.[10] Ambassadors exit the business by delegating most of the operating responsibilities to next-generation members and/or key nonfamily managers but hold on to their diplomatic or representational duties on behalf of the corporation. In the fast-food industry, both Dave Thomas, founder of Wendy's International, and Colonel Harlan Sanders, Thomas's one-time mentor at Kentucky Fried Chicken, chose this path. They became marketing spokespersons—the personas, or public images—for their businesses and, through ads and personal appearances, reinforced the power of the brand that they embodied. In both cases, business operations were delegated to key nonfamily members of the top-management team.

George Soros of Soros Fund Management is becoming an ambassador, as he turns to writing a book and leading his charitable foundations. At the same time, he is making room for his son Robert, the eldest of five children and the only one to join the family business. Robert's preparation in the financial industry occurred outside the family company. He worked for several investment firms and banks between 1986 and 1994, when he joined the Soros Fund.[11]

Ambassadors make room for top-notch nonfamily managers and next-generation members. They allow others to learn the business first-hand and to eventually take over responsibility for running the enterprise. The CEOs prone to become ambassadors include those who enjoy people, like to travel, and have always entertained the idea of living several months of the year in a city that is also a key market, such as London, Paris, or New York. CEOs who discover another calling in philanthropy or public service (say, the Salvation Army, the Jewish-American Committee, or the U.S. Senate) are candidates for this exit type as well. Ambassadors make good board members for a few years after their exit as CEOs.

Ambassadors should proceed slowly with their exit, making sure that the next-generation and/or key nonfamily managers are indeed capable and ready to take over day-to-day operations. An ambassador who rushes to the exit may have no option but to return, as would a general, to fix the problems of the corporation. The heirs of an ambassador-type CEO are lucky indeed. They merely need to prepare themselves thoroughly and avoid competing with the CEO for visibility outside the business. Advisors to this type of CEO should build bridges with key nonfamily management and the next generation because, without such relationships, they are likely to be replaced by a younger and less expensive service provider.

---

[10]Sonnenfeld & Spence, op. cit.

[11]Zuckerman, G., & Calian, S., George Soros Alters His Style, Making a Role for Son Robert. *Wall Street Journal*, June 16, 2000, p. C1.

THE GOVERNOR

It is an unfortunate fact of family business that fewer than 5 percent of all family business owners exit after having set a deadline for the transfer of power.[12] In the interest of a smooth succession and continuity of the business, Jack Welch, the largest individual shareholder at General Electric, left his post that way, after naming Jeff Immelt to replace him. GE is one of the best-managed companies in the world. Perhaps more than any other company, GE enjoys a competitive advantage derived from a core competence known as management expertise. Its management—more than its products, technology, marketing, or financial prowess—is what gives GE an edge. Few public or private management-controlled companies have CEO succession take place in such an orderly fashion that the company's sustainability or continuity is not threatened.

Governors set a departure date and announce it publicly, thus committing themselves to the goal of transferring power within an established time frame. By making the date public, they lend a sense of urgency to planning for the inevitable transition and enlist other key management personnel, employees, suppliers, and customers in the process. As chairman and CEO of *El Nuevo Día* and the Grupo Ferré-Rangel (a newspaper, media, and industrial conglomerate in Puerto Rico), Antonio L. Ferré did just that. During the eight-year period following the announcement of his departure date, family members both inside and outside the business and key nonfamily managers worked feverishly and tenaciously to accomplish a smooth succession that would ensure sustainability and continuity for the enterprise.[13]

THE INVENTOR

Jack Bares, CEO emeritus of Milbar Corporation and current CEO of Meritool, a hand-tool product-development company, is a great example of another CEO exit type: the inventor. More than anything else, Jack had always enjoyed developing hand tools for new applications. So when Jack, his daughter, the board, and other heirs decided that they were ready for succession, Jack started an engineering and product-development company. Milbar was purchased by Jack's daughter in a clear demonstration of her commitment to the enterprise and its continuity. While she succeeded him at Milbar, the inventor moved across the street to continue developing new tools, his life's work.[14]

The *inventor* designation is really a metaphor for an exiting CEO who takes on a satisfying key position in another enterprise. The inventor could just as easily be called the marketer, the private investor, or the tinkerer. Frank Mars, who ran Mars Inc. for many years, transferred power to sons Forrest and John Mars and created a small gourmet chocolate company. He named the new enterprise and its products Ethel M as a gesture of love for his wife and built a whimsical "chocolate factory" that I and thousands of tourists in Las Vegas have visited to learn about chocolate and the making of premium chocolate confections.

Inventors are creative people. Once they have built systems and institutions that will help the next generation lead successfully, they are usually ready to pursue their next dream. Heirs to inventors are very fortunate. They can request coaching and negotiate for advice on an as-needed basis. It helps to schedule breakfasts, lunches, or "wisdom meetings" with the CEO on a regular basis. Advisors and service providers to an

---

[12]Sonnenfeld & Spence, op. cit.

[13]Author's personal communication with Antonio L. Ferré, October 2002.

[14]Author's personal communication with Jack Bares, March 2000.

inventor should build bridges to the next generation but be aware that successors will more than likely want to choose their own advisors.

THE TRANSITION CZAR

Because it is very difficult to do so, very few CEOs choose to exit by becoming the lead agent in the multiyear transition known as succession. However, transition czars can add significant value to succession across generations, particularly when family companies are complex and multinational and owning families are large and multigenerational.

CEOs may choose the role of transition czar out of a desire to consult during the managerial and political processes that a complicated transition requires. While some CEOs enjoy being an ambassador for the company, others prefer being the shuttle diplomat, or the "Henry Kissinger," of the company and its shareholders.

Samuel Curtis Johnson III, retired CEO of SC Johnson, took on this responsibility as much to ensure a successful succession as to begin his process of transitioning out of the CEO role. In this role, he both coached the next generation and supported their development in unique and differentiated ways. Eventually, as a skilled architect would, he crafted a succession and continuity plan that structurally divided the business in such a way that the siblings in the next generation would remain united in friendship.[15]

Transition czars need to be aware of the difficulties inherent in being at the center of changing what they created. It often helps to seek outside advice from both a board and family-business consultants. It is difficult leadership work.

Transition czars often carry out the succession and continuity responsibility with significant assistance from the CEO spouse. This team effort allows the CEO to concentrate on codifying the institutional memory of both the business and the family (through a family constitution, for instance) and building the institutions that will ensure effective family-business governance (like boards and family councils). Meanwhile, the CEO spouse works to create trust and family unity in such a way that visions about the firm's future are further understood and agreed upon and the unique and complementary contributions of different family members and key nonfamily managers are better appreciated. (See Figure 5.1.) The role of the CEO spouse is discussed further next in this chapter.

---

figure **5.1** | **Leadership Imperatives for the Current Generation as It Transfers Power**

- The CEO and CEO spouse: As coarchitects of family-business continuity, communicate their vision and commitment to continuity.

- Help build institutions that will help the next generation govern the business–family relationship.

- Exercise a trust-catalyst function in family communications and planning activity leading to a family strategy and a succession plan.

- Make a priority of the development of the next generation—from sons and daughters to CEOs and key management.

- Help the next generation owner-managers build bridges with important stakeholders: other family shareholders, key nonfamily management, employees, suppliers, customers, local government, etc., and then depart.

---

[15]Barboza, op. cit.

Heirs to a transition czar need to be patient and very self-aware in their relationships with the CEO. Whether the person they are relating to is in the CEO role or the parent or relative role makes a huge difference in how they should act. Keeping the right "hats" on the right people is particularly tricky but also particularly worthwhile for an heir to a transition czar.

Transition czars realize the risks posed by a power vacuum, and provide active leadership of the entire succession process with family members, key nonfamily managers, customers, and suppliers.

PROMOTING TRUST AMONG FAMILY MEMBERS IN THE PROCESS OF TRANSFERRING POWER

CEO spouses play a key, if often invisible, role in most family-controlled corporations. They are in the background of most stories of successful (e.g., Reliance Industries, Case 14 in this book), stressful (e.g., *New York Times*), and troubled (e.g., Wang Laboratories) generational transitions.[16]

Family-business research has largely ignored the role of the CEO spouse. With regard to the tragic tale of the *Louisville Courier-Journal* (discussed in Chapter 2), owned by the Bingham family, the *New York Times* stated, "In the drama there is no single villain, nor a hero or healer who might have bridged the gulf of distrust and anger."[17] Although the writer does not refer exclusively to Mary Bingham, the CEO spouse, her role in the family's tragedy is woven throughout this and various other reports about the end of the Bingham dynasty. The multiple levels on which CEOs influence succession planning and the ensuing dilemmas have been acknowledged by CEOs themselves, their advisors, and scholars. But people other than the incumbent CEO also significantly influence leadership succession and continuity in the family firm.

The CEO spouse, in particular, is an important actor in both of these processes. The media and the more scholarly literature seldom address or acknowledge the roles and perspectives of CEO spouses. Yet some studies have identified CEO spouses as being central to succession and continuity processes in family-controlled companies.[18] Also evidence shows that female CEO spouses, because of their longer life expectancy, are often called on to provide interim to full CEO leadership of the corporation and the family–business relationship before a full transfer of power to the next generation ever takes place. Their active engagement in the multiyear succession process is therefore a must.

THE UNIQUE ROLES OF THE CEO SPOUSE

The CEO spouse often has a unique role as steward of the family legacy, facilitator of communication, and touchstone of emotional intelligence in family relations. CEO spouses often play a determining role in successful generational transitions, but not without facing tensions and dilemmas.

---

[16]See, for example, Barboza, D., op. cit.; Wells, M., Are Dynasties Dying? *Forbes*, March 6, 2000, pp. 126–131; and Cohen, D., The Fall of the House of Wang. *Business Month*, February 1990, pp. 23–31.

[17]Jones, A., The Fall of the Bingham Dynasty. *New York Times*, January 19, 1986, p. 1.

[18]See Poza, E., & Messer, T., Spousal Leadership and Continuity in the Family Firm. *Family Business Review*, 14(1), 2001, pp. 25–35; and LaChapelle, K., & Barnes, L., The Trust Catalyst in Family-Owned Businesses. *Family Business Review*, 11(1), 1998, pp. 1–17.

The findings discussed here are the direct result of structured conversations with CEO spouses.[19] These conversations revealed the central, yet often invisible, part that CEO spouses play in the generational transition process. Over and over again, in seldom-recognized ways, these spouses assume a key role in initiatives to improve the relationship between the family and the managers of the business and to further orderly governance of the ownership system.

The discrepancy between the spouse's degree of influence and his or her degree of visibility to the firm and its ownership group were illustrated by my conversation with one CEO spouse. This spouse complained about the small and rather unimportant role she played in her family's business. Then, a few minutes later, she told me that she was the reason her brother and her son were now working for the firm. Significantly, company employees credited her brother with increasing profits through disciplined inventory management. And they credited her son, who had worked outside the family business after earning an MBA degree, with building a financial infrastructure that enabled better management of operating costs. This CEO spouse neither recognized nor was recognized for her significant impact on the business and its capacity for continuity.

The research team interviewed CEO spouses to learn more about their role as a coarchitect of succession and continuity. The interview questions focused on the spouse's contributions to the business as a parent and as a partner, as well as his or her role as a coarchitect of the unique relationship between family and business.[20]

The study found that spouses assume different leadership functions, depending on their relationship with the CEO, their knowledge of and interest in the business, and their commitment to a vision that includes continuity of family participation in the business. Three other factors influence the role adopted by a spouse in a family-controlled business: (1) the perception of need, described by spouses as dependent mostly on the quality of the relationship between the CEO and next-generation member(s); (2) the spouse's ability to perform the needed leadership role; and (3) the availability of others to perform communication-promoting and trust-enabling functions. The study found some traditional spousal types but also found many CEO spouses comfortably assuming multiple leadership roles as needs changed.

Regardless of the role played, CEO spouses repeatedly described themselves and other spouses as:

- Being stewards of the family legacy.
- Keeping "family" in the family business.
- Instilling a sense of purpose, responsibility, and community in family members.
- Embodying a spirit of cooperation and unconditional support.[21]

---

[19]Ibid.

[20]Poza, E., Alfred, T., & Maheshwari, A., Stakeholder Perceptions of Culture and Management Practices in Family and Family Firms. *Family Business Review*, 10(2), 1997, pp. 135–156.

[21]I wish to thank the student research team that conducted the inquiry process with CEO spouses. The team members from the Partnership for Family Business Program at Case Western Reserve University were Gina Burk, Kim Hastings, Betty Moon, Karen Magill, and Susan Spector. [Some of the material in this chapter was first published in an article by Ernesto J. Poza and Tracey E. Messer in *Family Business Review*, 14(1), March 2001.]

ROLE TYPES OF THE CEO SPOUSE AND THE TRANSFER OF POWER

Interview data from the sample of CEO spouses were analyzed in the context of the original research question: What unique contributions do CEO spouses make to the family-owned business? Six leadership or role types emerged: (1) business partner, (2) chief trust officer, (3) senior advisor/keeper of family values, (4) free agent, (5) jealous spouse, and (6) "interim CEO" spouse.

THE BUSINESS PARTNER

Some spouses are critical to the business, whether through their financial investment in it or because of their professional, technical, or administrative skills. Some of these spouses begin as business partners during the start-up and early stages of company development and then move on to a different role. Others remain active business partners. Among those who move to a different role later in life, their presence and determination in those early days is the subject of family anecdotes and family pride.

One business partner started a new division in a business run by the fourth-generation CEO. She told us, "My husband had wanted me to join the company for a long time. The custom decorative hardware business I started within the company has grown to where many women are working at home and earning an extra $1,000 a month for their families. We need to have opportunities like this in our economy."

The business partner's advice is often sought, both on and off the job. He or she shows up regularly for work and is responsible for a variety of projects. Business partners may be the lineal descendants of the owning family and have effectively employed the CEO spouse to run their inherited business. Or they may be large shareholders (e.g., 50-percent owners) and therefore act as a full partner of the CEO.

The economic advantages of having two highly committed owner-managers working side by side can include a more flexible and lower-cost management structure. Such benefits seldom come without complications, however. One business partner acknowledged the unique challenges of working side by side when she said, "You want to be sure what role you want to play. Do you want to play marriage or business partnership, or both? For me, it is difficult to do both."

Accounting, finance, and human resource managers were common functional roles for CEO spouses. Sometimes the spouse is the accountant or CFO, depending on his or her skills and the size and complexity of the business. Sometimes the spouse is the family's financial officer and overseer of the family's wealth: "Financial planning, I am very much in the middle of that. Because that, in a sense, is the other side of the business that has nothing to do with what the company manufactures. It has more to do with managing family affairs, and I am very much involved in that."

Although the advantage of having a trusted family member in these functional roles is evident, the spouse's adoption of these roles may enable a culture of secrecy to persist in the family business. Having problems or difficulties relating to company finances, relations with customers, or employee relations handled privately by one of the business's most trusted members—the CEO's spouse—enables secrets to remain "in the family." Another drawback is that the spouse may take credit for things done by other employees and thus have a negative impact on the culture of the organization.

THE CHIEF TRUST OFFICER

Some CEO spouses see their major contribution to the family-owned business as providing the glue that keeps everyone united through the predictable challenges faced by families who work together. These spouses, known as chief trust officers, act as healers, mediators, facilitators, and communication conduits for their families. They are the fence-menders in business and family relationships. Individuals performing this role are sometimes referred to as trust catalysts.[22] The following statements from CEO spouses illustrate this role:

- "You've heard the term *pillow talk?* I listen to my husband, I listen to my daughter, I listen to my son, and I put it all together."
- "I am the peacekeeper, the troubleshooter, and fence-mender."
- "I bring intuition, insight, discernment. I am the spiritual captain, the nurturer of love, respect, and honor. I also bring an ability to see things in context."
- "What I bring to this process is creativity and a kind of glue. I bring a staying quality that rides through rough or smooth times, consistent and dogged. I also bring an ability to keep an eye on a distant spot, rather than focusing on pieces. It's about focusing. If you can do that even in the squabble of the short term, then you can keep your balance."

These spouses often remind family members of the need for balance between work and family. They may also take responsibility for family initiatives, like creating a family council, writing the family's history, hosting weekly or monthly family gatherings, being the contact person for facilitators of semiannual family retreats, and planning family vacations and multigenerational celebrations. Sometimes polar opposites of their business-first CEO spouses, chief trust officers try to balance family and business by advocating a family-first agenda.

Chief trust officers often have a unique appreciation of the interpersonal and developmental challenges in family-business continuity. Their capacity to understand and articulate various stakeholders' points of view frequently enables them to broaden the dialogue from an exclusive focus on facts to a wider view, encompassing both facts and feelings, so that better decisions can be made. These spouses are often effective at putting succession planning and transition to retirement on the CEO's agenda.

THE SENIOR ADVISOR/KEEPER OF FAMILY VALUES

Although akin to the chief trust officer, the senior advisor is more than a relationship problem-solver; he or she helps the children grow up with a sense of the business, its history, and its customers. Also known as the keeper of family values, the senior advisor instills a sense of what the business stands for and what it means to the family. While nurturing a love for the business among family members, senior advisors often have no visible role in the business. Their independence and lack of visible influence over business issues enhance the respect they command in matters of great importance to the family and the business.

These spouses are deans of the intangible crossovers between family and business. Katharine Graham, former CEO and chairperson of the *Washington Post,* attributed to these crossovers much of the commitment to quality shown by family-owned

---

[22]LaChapelle & Barnes, op. cit.

newspapers. She said, "I don't think it's an accident that the newspapers best known for quality in this country—the *New York Times,* the *Wall Street Journal,* the *Los Angeles Times,* the *Boston Globe,* the *Washington Post,* and outstanding papers in Dallas, Sacramento, California, St. Petersburg, Florida, and elsewhere—are, or were until recently, family controlled. It seems that certain attributes essential to quality are more easily provided by families than by public companies."[23]

In addition to a commitment to quality, senior advisors may bring an antidote to the CEO's propensity to create a culture of secrecy, with its corresponding sense of loneliness. One senior advisor believes that the role she plays is that of an anti-isolation agent in continuity efforts in the family business: "When you live in a relatively small town and you know people who have a family business, they don't talk about [it]. So you are very isolated. You might think you are the only person having a certain kind of problem. No one is ever going to tell you you are not unique."

Senior advisors often promote family values that advocate family-business continuity. One spouse told us, "In the end, it isn't dad's business. The business belongs to the children. And if the business continues, it will belong to the grandchildren. So what I can do for the business is love them all." This same spouse added, "A family business is an extension of your family. It is an extension of your love, your trust and respect. You can't separate them."

Some CEO spouses recognize that they are role models for the next generation, the builders of new legacies—legacies the preceding generation may not have considered important. One senior advisor–type spouse in a third- to fourth-generation business stated it this way: "In a very male-oriented culture in the business, it's good if there are roles there for women to follow because of me. There are now more than male role models. Three out of our four grandchildren are girls; this new legacy is important."

Senior advisors are keenly aware that for the family legacy to remain vibrant and alive, it has to change and adapt itself to the present and the future. After all, "The business that my husband runs isn't the business that his father ran, and the same will be true for the next generation."

These spouses often have active lives as community leaders, volunteers, grandparents, and bearers of the legacy for multigenerational family-owned businesses. As free agents, they are available to fulfill other roles (e.g., chief trust officer or even business partner) should the business and/or the family urgently need their contributions.

Despite the wide-ranging influence they have, senior advisors often are not interested in controlling the business or in gaining recognition or appreciation for the role they play. They know, as do others close to the action, that in the areas of love for the business and the family, commitment to legacy, and intangible crossovers (e.g., love in the family evidencing itself in the quality of products), these spouses are masters.

THE FREE AGENT

The free agent is often very aware of both family and business matters, having perhaps served the family-owned business in some capacity earlier in life. But this spouse chooses to develop an identity separate from the CEO and the family business: "My role is being me, not the wife and not the mother. I believe it is very important for a

---

[23]Graham, K., Journalistic Family Values. *Wall Street Journal,* March 20, 2000, p. 18.

spouse to maintain a separate sense of self. I feel so sad when I see a woman who feels so lost when her husband dies because he was her whole life. A woman can't be the most helpful and supportive she can be if she does not have some understanding of who she is separately."

Free agents often believe that there is no need for them to be any more involved with the business or the family than they are because other people are satisfactorily performing the role of chief trust officer or trust-facilitator:

> *Paul never had a peer discussion with his dad about the real estate development business he had started. That is why when we went on vacation, about twice a year, at 4:00 p.m. every day, Paul would have a session with the kids. When they were young, it was with cookies and milk, then pop, then beer and wine. Paul would talk to them about the business, about different memories, where the grandparents came from and similar topics. It was a fun family meeting. It was an important foundation of respect. No one else's father talked to them about the business. Another thing that Paul did was to sit down with the kids at the beginning of the school year and discuss what they [thought] their expenses [would] be. Then Paul would write them a check, and they had to manage it. Paul wondered sometimes if the kids ever got extra money from me. Never did we give them extra. They had to manage the money and they did. You have to trust them. Parents tend to hold money as control. I think Paul thought of it because his father never did it with him.*

Free agents are usually available for consultation and advice during particularly trying or challenging times in the life of the family and the business. But, in general, these spouses thrive on their marginality vis-à-vis the business. One spouse confided, "She [my daughter] is now the CEO, her brother reports to her on some things but also runs his own division, [and] it is entirely up to the two of them to make it work. Other than being supportive of her, I have nothing to do with the management of the business." Another free agent recognized that for succession and continuity to go smoothly, both she and the CEO had to leave their roles: "Our job is to teach them to walk and then walk away. We both must walk away."

Free agents are the polar opposites of jealous spouses, with their constant reactiveness to the business. One free agent told the researchers, "Claire, who I met in one of the sessions, is jealous of her husband. It's her family's business, but the husband is running it. So she, and others like her, is constantly involved in intermediating. If they had a life of their own, ..."

THE JEALOUS SPOUSE

Many entrepreneurs and family business owners, particularly those who are first or second generation, have a mistress-like relationship with their business. The family has to compete with the business for the CEO's recognition, affection, financial resources, and time. In this context, many spouses experience jealousy; competition with the business for time and affection is a prominent theme in their lives.

Jealous spouses feel that the CEO loves the business so much that it has become her or his first priority. Jealousy of a spouse's commitment to her or his work is not limited to spouses of family business owners. Spouses of attorneys, doctors, executives in public companies, and others in extremely demanding professions can all suffer the same fate. Yet in family-owned businesses, the overlap of family and business makes the jealous spouse a particularly hearty type. Reflecting on her role over the years in the family business, one spouse said, "I am the political pawn. . . . I was an only child and often events connected to me, such as school events, graduation, and my wedding, were used as opportunities to cement relationships with important family shareholders." Today, she is the spouse of a third-generation CEO, and the pattern continues.

On the other hand, jealous spouses may provide the motivation for greater delegation and professionalization of the business so that its success and survival depend less on the superhuman efforts of the CEO.

THE "INTERIM CEO" SPOUSE

While not one of the role types discovered in the preceding study (none of the spouses in the sample had been called on to perform as interim CEO), female CEO spouses (because of their longer life expectancy) are often called on to provide either interim or full leadership of the corporation and the family–business relationship before a full transfer of power to the next generation takes place. The high incidence of succession processes that are complicated by the death or incapacitation of the founding entrepreneur, before the full transfer of power has taken place calls for the active engagement of CEO spouses (of either gender) in the multiyear succession process.

Installing spouses as interim CEOs can, under some circumstances, constitute a very adaptive response to the goal of keeping the family business under the founding family's control across generations while not subjecting the firm to unmotivated, untested, or incompetent leadership.

Reasons why a CEO spouse may be a fitting new CEO or bridging CEO:

- Potential successors are too young or are not quite ready to become the CEO, and a motivated surviving owner represents both a role model and a provider of substantive mentoring in their developmental process.

- No successors are yet qualified to carry out the chosen strategy—for example, a business plan to significantly expand the company to serve a global rather than a regional marketplace.

- Key nonfamily employees are deemed not capable of the key leadership role or of performing to the standards of an owner-manager

- The owning family recognizes that the business needs leadership that will focus on the future, not the past, and therefore leaving things on autopilot is not an option.

I have argued in the preceding chapters that the family–business interaction factor represents a tremendous source of value in the creation of inimitable competitive advantages. If that is the case, a compelling argument could easily be made for the advantage of a person who embodies that family–business overlap—that is, a family member in the CEO role. The decision about whether a CEO spouse is a good succession alternative then is contingent on the particular needs and opportunities that the business faces, the skills that are present or absent in younger family members, and the capabilities of available or recruitable key nonfamily managers. For these reasons, it makes sense to cast a wide net in the selection of the best successor CEO, whether a family member or not.

IMPLICATIONS OF CEO EXIT STYLES AND CEO SPOUSE ROLES FOR SUCCESSION AND THE TRANSFER OF POWER

What do CEO behaviors say about their most likely exit type? What do the CEO's spouse and children and key nonfamily managers think is likely to be the CEO's departure style?

Monarchs and generals are the worst enemies of succession. They deny the facts and they stonewall, refusing to engage key nonfamily managers and the next generation in building readiness for sustainability and continuity across generations. Little preparation can take place and little hope maintained when so many questions remain unanswered: Will the family keep or sell the business? Will family or nonfamily members run it? Will they run it successfully or right into the ground?

Monarchs and generals may be the reason why the average tenure of CEOs in family-owned businesses is more than double that of CEOs in management-controlled companies (18 vs. 8 years).[24] However, it can be argued that the difference in tenure is due to the tendency of senior executives in publicly owned firms to think more about retiring wealthy at 40 or 50 and less about legacy, while family-business CEOs consider the long-term interests of shareholders to be paramount.

Clearly, management theory and research on best practices do not support short CEO tenures or quarterly scorecards that distort the concept of shareholder value. Nor do family business theory and practice particularly encourage extremely long CEO tenures (30 to 40 years, for example), which may represent CEO entrenchment. A monarch or general is not likely to be working for the long-term sustainability and continuity of the business. Nor is he or she likely to be concerned about the hidden costs of such long tenure to the business, to next-generation members, and to family health and harmony.

Monarchs and generals must seriously consider changing their ways or face destroying what is often their most important creation. If change is out of the question, appointing a bridging president and an effective board of directors or advisory board with independent outsiders may help ameliorate the negative impact of these exit types on succession and continuity.

Ambassadors, governors, inventors, and transition czars all allow for a generational transition to be planned and eventually executed. They also provide for time to realistically assess the company's unique situation and evaluate successors' capabilities and developmental needs. Ultimately, the CEO is the architect not only of the unique business he or she created but also of the most appropriate structure for succession and continuity.

The CEO spouse, on the other hand, has a great opportunity to lead by building trust in the family-business system. In many instances these spouses have engineered outcome-changing feats in the processes of succession and continuity. (Examples of this remarkable influence can be found in both Case 5: The Vega Food Company and Case 14: Reliance Industries.) However, spouses are not the only individuals who can perform these roles. Family-business literature and my own experiences and research

---

[24]Daily, C., & Dollinger, M., An Empirical Examination of Ownership Structure in Family and Professionally Managed Firms. *Family Business Review*, 5(2), 1992, pp. 117–136.

include examples of others performing these functions, including the CEO, an uncle or aunt, a consultant, and a minister, priest, or rabbi who is close to the family.

Still, CEO spouses tend to feel a special calling with regard to their trust-building role and to have a self-awareness about the type of individual who can perform the role successfully.

Also, changes may occur in the CEO spouse's role type across her or his own life cycle as well as across the life cycles of the CEO, the family, and the business. Sometimes CEO spouses who were once business partners migrated to the role of chief trust officer or free agent. No single cause has been found for these shifts, which sometimes simply reflect changing needs. At other times, the shifts were the result of personal development phases or just the personal preference of the CEO spouse. Whatever the cause, CEO spouses were clearly aware of changing roles over time.

Whether CEO spouses are in formal or informal positions, recognized or unrecognized for their contributions, they often adopt a role in preserving and strengthening family unity and the feasibility of family-business continuity.

CEO spouses, along with the CEOs, were coarchitects of family unity, family communication, and business practices. The CEO spouses found ways to make contributions they felt were important—even when standing on the margin of the business. Marginality need not result in invisibility, provided the overall family-business agenda stresses love, legacy, and continuity over power. Theirs is an important leadership role.

SUMMARY

1 CEOs of family businesses perceive both the business and the family much more favorably than do the rest of the family and nonfamily managers.

2 To ensure both the long-term ability to govern the family–business relationship and the promotion of continuity, CEOs must enlist competent people both in the top-management team and as the governors of the shareholder group; these individuals can be complemented by board members and outside advisors.

3 The six most common CEO exit types are the (1) monarch, (2) general, (3) ambassador, (4) governor, (5) inventor, and (6) transition czar.

4 CEOs who want their companies to continue to be successful beyond their lifetimes allow for a generational transition to be planned and eventually executed. They also provide for time to realistically assess the company's unique situation and evaluate successors' capabilities and developmental needs.

5 The CEO spouse plays unique roles in the family business, including steward of the family legacy, facilitator of communication, touchstone of emotional intelligence in family relations, and coarchitect of successful generational transitions.

6 CEO spouses often play a critical role as interim CEOs because of the unexpected death or illness of the CEO. This is especially true for female CEO spouses, given their longer life expectancy.

7 The six role types of the CEO spouse are (1) business partner, (2) chief trust officer, (3) senior advisor/keeper of family values, (4) free agent, (5) jealous spouse, and (6) interim CEO.

8 Shifts may occur in the CEO spouse's role type across her or his own life cycle as well as across the life cycles of the CEO, the family, and the business.

9 As architects of institutions for the governance of the family–business relationship, successful CEOs implement the following best practices:

   a. Pursue strategic growth by building on the firm's core competencies (Chapter 6).

   b. Plan the estate with business agility, not just tax minimization, in mind (Chapter 7).

   c. Leverage the family's skills and abilities by hiring capable and dedicated nonfamily managers for leadership roles (Chapter 9).

   d. Welcome the review of outside board members who continuously raise the bar for the owner-manager (Chapter 10).

   e. Promote communication and accommodation among family members through frequent family meetings or an ongoing family council (Chapter 11).

SIGMA MOTION, INC.

After founding Sigma Motion and overseeing its growth for the past 25 years, Ron Burton was planning to pass the reins over to his two sons, Bob and Michael. Sigma Motion was well positioned in the market and on its way to planning for family-business succession; the company had a board of advisors, a strategic plan, and next-generation members who had been active in the management of the business. The question in everyone's mind was, "When will the torch be passed, and how?" Ron Burton was now 70, and both sons were in their 30s. The youngest, Michael, wrote this letter to the CEO soon after returning from a European sales trip.

March 30, 2001

Mr. Ron Burton, CEO/Chairman

Sigma Motion, Inc.

4950 E. 49th St.

Pittsburgh, PA 15201

Dear Ron,

It saddens me to be writing you this letter because my love for this business grew out of our shared excitement and vision for Sigma. Without getting into great detail, I feel that it would be in the best interest of the business for me to redirect my efforts elsewhere. At points over the past several months I considered the possibility of staying and fighting for the leadership position of the company, but I have now realized that a battle of that sort would do more damage than just simply leaving the company.

My commitments to customers, reps, trade shows, and training extend through May 24. The scheduled travel with reps will be completed May 8. My experience with John, whom I recommend as my replacement, tells me that he will rise to this occasion and will carry the Sigma Motion flag proudly. He will certainly need your support as he works with manufacturing.

I have not talked about my plans to leave the business with anyone. I will let you choose the appropriate time to share the news. While I realize that this will certainly disrupt the operation internally and throughout the market, it is my feeling that my departure at this time rather than years from now will minimize the effects. Please let me know what I can do to ensure that this is a smooth transition. I expect that you will not share this letter with anyone.

Sincerely,

Michael Burton

Vice President, Sales & Marketing

Research associates Charlie Braun, Jeff Chaney, Chris Hetz, and Todd Silverman assisted in the preparation of this case, under the supervision of Professor Ernesto Poza, to provide a basis for class discussion rather than to illustrate either effective or ineffective handling of a family-business situation. Note that while the case is factually and historically accurate, the names have been changed to protect the privacy of the family. For permission to publish this case, grateful acknowledgment is made to the chairman of the company.

THE EARLY YEARS

Ron Burton became interested in sales and distribution while growing up, watching his father run a wholesale automotive parts distributorship. After high school, he attended college and then returned to Pittsburgh to work at an auto dealership. His hopes were to someday run his own business, as his father did. Ron spent 2 years at that dealership. He left when he realized that there was little chance of buying out the current owner. His next stop was his father's business, which he felt could be expanded significantly. When his father refused to agree to his growth plans, Ron, with his father's encouragement, became a manufacturing representative. He decided this was not a bad way to get closer to his dream of someday working for himself.

For the next 10 years, he represented a variety of product lines for several industrial products manufacturers. At the time he started his business, he had little money, a strong work ethic, a great deal of credit, and a lot of ideas. By 1967, Ron Burton was one of the top salespeople in the country for Erie Products Corporation.

Two years later, Erie Products was sold, and Ron founded The Screw Supply Company, a distributorship for Erie Products. He soon realized that he could add more value by getting into the final stages of manufacturing. In 1970, he added "end machining" capabilities to his company.

His close relationship with Erie Products enabled Ron and his organization to acquire expertise in the field of linear motion, which is responsible for producing movement along one dimension. Products that accomplish such motion include conveyor belts and "screws," which are actually rods with threads that fix the dimension of the movement and a nut that travels back and forth along the threaded rod; Ron focused on the screw technology.

In 1975, he decided to expand product offerings into Acme screws. Adopting a new company name, Sigma Motion, Inc., he trademarked product names and began to add manufacturing capabilities. In 1978, a new division was established to tap the jack/worm gear screw market. Jacks produce vertical movement, lifting or lowering platforms.

The company continued to grow throughout the late 1970s and early 1980s, with Ron at the helm. Sales came from a wide variety of sources, but the focus was always on precision motion and superior engineering. In 1982, the company secured orders from television networks for satellite dish actuators—the first of a number of television network contracts. When "the best" was needed, Ron wanted customers to know that Sigma Motion was the answer.

Throughout the 1980s, Sigma Motion continued to expand its product line. Gradually, previously contracted operations were brought in-house in order to ensure quality and to respond more quickly to customer needs for prototypes and quick delivery.

By 1987, the company had 55 employees and two physical locations. Over the next 10 years, great change took place in the organization. Bob Burton, Ron's eldest son, joined the company in 1989 and began work at the gear division in the manufacturing department. That same year, the company opened another manufacturing facility. In 1994, the company again expanded, opening a West Coast manufacturing facility.

This growth came at a price, and by 1994 the company was in serious financial trouble. The gear company acquisition never generated the synergies that Ron had hoped for, and the debt assumed for the acquisition of expensive gear-grinding equipment became a serious burden to the company. An old friend agreed to invest in the company and helped save the business.

By 1997, the company was back on its feet again and had consolidated operations in a 120,000-square-foot facility located in Pittsburgh, Pennsylvania. This was also the year that Michael, Ron's younger son, joined the company in the sales department. The movement to centralize brought with it a change in the organizational structure. Bob, who was operations manager at the gear division, became vice president of manufacturing and operations for all of Sigma Motion, Inc. The two plant managers who were running the Acme and Ball screw facilities both left the organization and were replaced internally by promoting group managers.

To help propel Sigma Motion into the 21st century, Ron Burton put together a professional top-management team, developed a strategic plan, and launched an advisory board.

PRODUCT LINES

Sigma Motion produced four distinct product lines, all based on linear motion. The company's focus turned to expanding these existing product lines and increasing sales within each, as opposed to developing entirely new products. One of the initiatives was to develop metric versions of existing product lines, thereby opening up the large European and Asian markets.

Each of the products was positioned at the high end of the segment, with heavy emphasis on quality and precision. The company's products competed primarily with hydraulic and/or pneumatic systems, as well as other manufacturers' screw-based systems. In general, the advantage of a screw system over hydraulic or pneumatic solutions is that the drive motor can be much smaller, and one motor can drive multiple screws much more easily.

Sigma Motion products were used by the medical, airline, timber, transportation, and communications industries. They also constituted component parts for innumerable types of manufacturing and machine-tool equipment. Descriptions of its four product lines follow.

> *Acme screws:* Acme screws are very similar to the nuts and bolts available in hardware stores. Sigma Motion focused on applications in which very precise positioning is required, such as in the device that adjusts an electric car seat (Figure F).
>
> *Ball screws:* Ball screws differ from Acme screws in both the shape of the groove in the screw and the fact that the nut rides on ball bearings (Figure G). The advantages of this type of screw over Acme screws are a much longer life and exponentially less friction and heat (i.e., less energy loss and heat distortion). A typical application for a ball screw would be in the wing flaps of an airplane.
>
> *Jacks/worm gear screws:* These days, the most promising product line at Sigma Motion is a jack. Rotational motion from a drive motor is translated 90 degrees through an interlocking gear to a rotating screw; the translation gear is called "worm gear" (Figure H). Uses for this unique jack design include leveling tables, airport jetways, and raising Billy Joel and his band out of a pit and up through the bottom of the custom-made concert stage. Sigma Motion has one of the best-designed jacks on the market and has introduced a 5-year guarantee on the product, something that had been unheard of in the industry.

figure **F** | **Acme Screws**

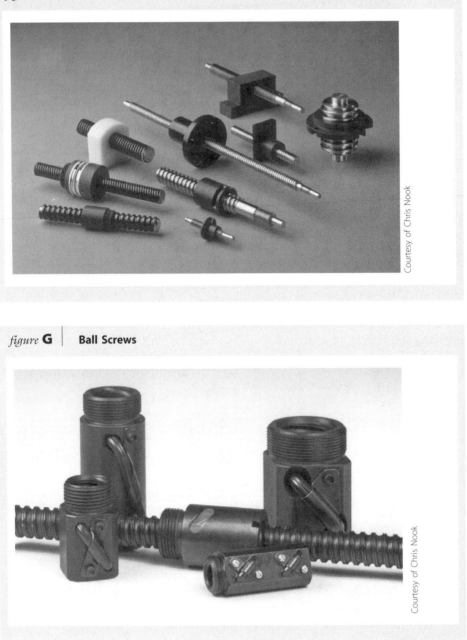

Courtesy of Chris Nook

figure **G** | **Ball Screws**

Courtesy of Chris Nook

Linear bearings and shafting: The closest thing that Sigma Motion had to a commodity product was their line of linear bearings and shafting, which are cylindrical rods of steel on which sleeves full of ball bearings move back and forth (Figure I).

figure **H** | **Ball Screw Jack (Left) and Machine Screw Jack (Right)**

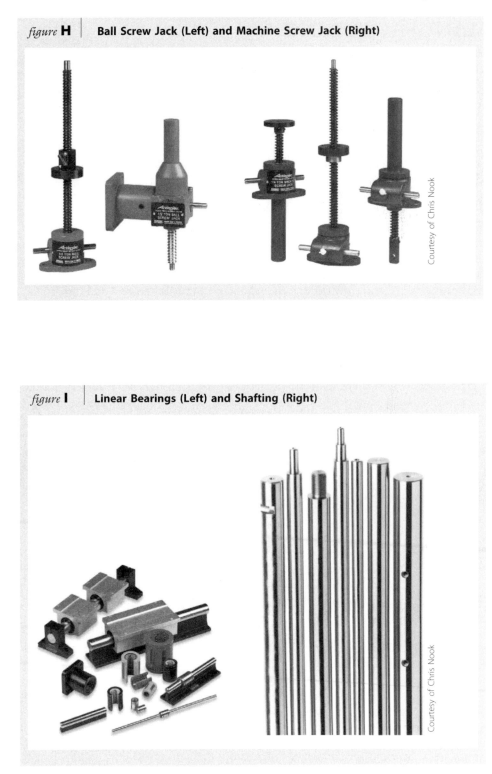

Courtesy of Chris Nook

figure **I** | **Linear Bearings (Left) and Shafting (Right)**

Courtesy of Chris Nook

MANUFACTURING

Sigma Motion's mission statement is as follows:

> *Sigma Motion's mission is to be an innovative and responsive organization whose linear motion products are engineered, manufactured, and delivered to meet or exceed our customers' specifications and expectations.*

Manufacturing was central to the success of Sigma Motion. Since the company's reputation was built on quality and precision, the company had taken the road of continuously upgrading its manufacturing equipment and demanding more and more from its suppliers.

Sigma Motion bought raw steel, bearings, and roughly cast housings and worm gears for jacks. Then the company took over the process and did everything from engineering components and complete systems to machining the dies necessary to form grooves in the bar and using computer-aided machines to finish the housings and gears. Sigma Motion controlled anywhere from 70 to 90 percent of the manufacturing process, more than any of its competitors. Although this resulted in significant overhead costs, the company felt that the advantages in quality control and turnaround time were worth the price. Sigma Motion could provide a customer a prototype product within 2 weeks of the request, a feat unmatched by any of its competitors.

One particular technology that set Sigma apart from some of its competitors was its expertise in "rolling," or cold-forming, grooves onto a bar to make the screws. In cold-forming, the rolling dies (cylindrical shapes about 16 inches in diameter with the mirror groove cut in them) actually displace the steel through brute force from the round rod shape into a grooved screw. The result is a very strong, very precise grooved rod with minimal waste—in one pass through the equipment. The machinery required to do this is very specialized, and Sigma Motion owns the largest rolling machine in the world, which can roll bars up to 15 inches in diameter.

Sigma Motion had also been improving its internal documentation for processes and procedures. Some customers had requested that Sigma Motion become ISO 9001–certified, so the company began work on certification in 1998.

SALES AND DISTRIBUTION

Sigma Motion sold through six in-house sales representatives. They were employees of Sigma Motion and serviced corporate accounts with which they had developed relationships over time. They sold Sigma Motion's products in addition to other related manufactured goods.

Michael, who was vice president of sales, wanted to gradually move away from the manufacturer-representative channel because of customers' perceptions that these reps add a questionable amount of value to Sigma's products. Still, some of the manufacturer reps derived 25 percent of their total commissions from Sigma. Sigma Motion also solicited direct sales from manufacturers that needed linear-motion solutions. This was a growing part of the business and included customers such as the U.S. government and some automotive component suppliers.

Sigma Motion also worked with a number of large manufacturing distributors. Although most products were highly customized, there were a few standard products in the lineup. The company had both a paper and an Internet catalog.

When Michael joined the company in 1997, one of the first things he did was buy a few of the competitors' jacks and have the engineers take them apart. Compared to Sigma's, the competitors' products used inferior materials across the board and also had design weaknesses. It took some time to come up with a way to exploit this favorable difference; ultimately, the company began drafting a 5-year guarantee. In the fourth quarter of 1999, most company advertising was focused on the 5-year guarantee.

CORE COMPETENCY AND COMPETITIVE ADVANTAGES

Sigma Motion's core competency was designing and manufacturing linear-motion components and linear-motion systems, which were used in a wide range of applications in which straight-line, controlled movement was required. Sigma Motion had several key competitive advantages that allowed it to excel in its core business:

1. **Small size:** The fact that Sigma Motion was a small company (approximately $20 million in annual revenues) gave it the ability to rapidly adjust to changing market conditions and changing customer needs. Its primary competitor was a company with over $100 million in annual revenues.

2. **Customization:** Sigma Motion was unique in that it controlled 90 percent of the processes required to bring its products to market. In conjunction with its small size, the vertical integration gave Sigma the ability to customize or change a product quickly to meet a customer's need.

3. **Strong applications-engineering team:** Sigma Motion's strong engineering team gave it a competitive advantage in two areas: (1) It helped the company accomplish its mission of introducing new and innovative products in the linear-motion marketplace. (2) It gave Sigma the ability to answer tough technical questions much more quickly than the competition could, and this translated into increased sales.

4. **High quality:** Sigma Motion was perceived by its customers as the "Rolls Royce" of linear-motion products. The company's products consistently out-lasted those of the competition. The company offered a 5-year warranty on some of its products because of this competitive advantage.

5. **Depth of product line:** Sigma Motion had a product portfolio that covered all linear-motion products and most sizes. Many of its competitors could compete only in the small sizes or the large sizes, while Sigma Motion owned equipment that allowed it to manufacture both, giving Sigma an advantage when taking on complicated and integrated products.

6. **Management team:** Ron Burton had put in place a senior-management team that was extremely competent and forward-thinking. Evidence of this forward-thinking was found in the financial control systems that had been implemented and the company's Internet strategy.

FINANCE

Financially speaking, Sigma Motion had its share of ups and downs. Over the course of 30 years, it nearly went out of business entirely because of the lack of financial controls. At the time of this writing, Sigma Motion, a C corporation, has about $20 million in annual revenues and enjoys a healthy net profit margin after tax. As a manufacturing company with approximately 10,000 products, Sigma Motion has invested heavily in assets, including equipment, inventory, and accounts receivable.

"Flash Reports" send red flags concerning overtime, waste/scrap, and other month-to-date numbers to help management keep its finger on the pulse of the operation. Other reports on daily shipments and orders are posted in the employee lunchroom for all to see.

The following financial goals were part of the company's strategic plan:

1. Achieve 10 percent growth in volume each year for the next 5 years.
2. Install an electronic labor-collecting barcode system. This will save time running payroll for 160 employees and will provide valuable management information by allocating each employee's time by job function every day.
3. Implement a shop-floor reporting system that will tie into an Enterprise Resource Planning (ERP) program accounting for all costs, direct and indirect, and measure variances against standards in time, setup, overhead, efficiency, scrap, etc.
4. Develop product-line–specific income statements, using activity-based costing.
5. Become debt-free. Ron Burton wanted to turn the company over to his sons with zero debt.

Ron Burton wanted to make sure that the business was endowed with the capacity to continue to grow and succeed, regardless of the decisions his two sons would ultimately make about running the business. Both Bob and Michael were well known by the advisory board members and were considered capable successors, even though they were both still growing into leadership positions.

FAMILY, OWNERSHIP, AND MANAGEMENT

FAMILY

The Burton family consists of Ron Burton, age 70; his wife, Mary; Bob, age 34; and Michael, age 32. The Burtons all live in the Pittsburgh area. Family gatherings are fairly regular for holidays, birthdays, and family weddings. In addition to the more formal events, they see each other informally at least once a month.

Mary married Ron in 1966, and shortly afterward she married Sigma Motion. Mary said, "Sigma Motion is Ron's baby, life, and livelihood, all in one. I don't think he'll ever retire completely."

On the whole, communication was good between family members, although the spouses were generally spared conversations regarding the business. Even during Sigma Motion's darkest hour several years ago, Ron did not tell outside family members about the financial problems. However, one spouse recently complained, "I wish I knew what my husband does all day and what kinds of problems or issues the business is facing."

In the absence of formal family meetings to discuss the business, everyone seemed to confide in Mary. Ron would discuss issues regarding their sons, and each son or daughter-in-law confided in Mary when sibling rivalry reared its head at the office.

Mary's job as a mediator, listener, and sounding board was an informal one, and she was more than happy to play this role.

OWNERSHIP

Ron Burton had lived in the Pittsburgh area for a long time and was a well-known civic leader. His connections outside the linear-motion industry enabled him to tap other CEOs to serve on the company's advisory board. This commitment to community, family, and friends was obvious to all and influenced the culture at Sigma Motion. Ron began working on his advisory board in 1998. The board was launched and chartered with overseeing the financial, strategic, and management succession issues of the company. He had gifted a large number of nonvoting shares to each of his children over the years; the rest of the nonvoting and all voting stock belonged to him.

MANAGEMENT

From the Burton family, only Ron, Bob, and Michael were involved in the business. Ron was the CEO and chairman, Bob was the vice president of operations, and Michael was the vice president of sales. Ron had placed the two sons in separate functional areas on purpose, to best use their unique skills in ways that added value to the company. Michael and Bob generally worked well together, but each frustrated the other at times. Mary was often called on to facilitate and to mediate the differences between the two siblings.

In addition to the family members in management, there were a number of key nonfamily managers, including Chuck Briscoe, president; June Goldberg, chief financial officer; Jim Collins, marketing manager; and Ron Bates, chief engineer.

The nonfamily managers' perspective was that Sigma Motion was one company that was all business. June Goldberg said, "Even though Sigma Motion is a small family business, Mr. Burton runs it as if it were a large corporation." But other nonfamily managers talked about the Burtons owning the place: "Sometimes things are done simply because the owners said so." Last year, though, Ron Burton started to delegate more and more of the responsibility to his management team. While still the ultimate decision maker on some things, he passed day-to-day decision-making authority to his management team. Rarely did he overturn top-management decisions made in his absence.

The outside managers were at Sigma Motion because they wanted to be. June Goldberg left the *Fortune 500* culture because she "wanted something different in her everyday work life." Jim Collins said, "I wanted to make a difference in a smaller organization as opposed to being a cog in the wheel of a larger organization." They felt strongly about the close-knit family culture. They also preferred the flexibility afforded by Sigma Motion. Employees at all levels were willing to offer their assistance, even when a task was outside their area of responsibility. It was this culture, and the competitive compensation given to nonfamily managers, that had enabled Sigma Motion to retain such managers.

Bob, the eldest son, had 8 years of experience on the operations side of things. He knew how to operate every piece of equipment in the company and did an excellent job relating to the employees. However, key managers had some concerns regarding Bob's lack of engineering education and outside experience. Nonfamily managers

| *figure* **J** | **Top-Management Team at Sigma Motion** |

Ron Burton, CEO
Chuck Briscoe, President
Bob Burton, Vice President of Operations
June Goldberg, Chief Financial Officer
Jim Collins, Marketing Manager
Ron Bates, Chief Engineer
Michael Burton, Vice President of Sales
Tom Hubler, Quality Control Manager

thought it would be very helpful for Bob to have an engineering degree or a technical background—some considered it necessary. Bob had shown both maturity and business acumen in the past. In January 1999, Ron Burton offered Bob the job of president, with Briscoe remaining as a senior consultant. Bob calmly declined the offer, stating that he did not think that he was ready, nor did he think the company could afford to hire another top-level manager to replace him as vice president of operations.

Michael had no more formal technical training than Bob did. And he had not spent time on the manufacturing floor as his brother had. Michael did receive his MBA from Case Western Reserve University and had worked outside the family business for 3 years. He had had investment banking and asset-based lending positions with an important regional commercial bank. When he joined the business at a high level—vice president of sales—many in management, including his brother Bob, had difficulty accepting him initially. Over time, he seemed to have garnered much respect.

The company did use titles (see Figure J), but Ron Burton did not care much about formal organizational charts or exact job descriptions; he had always focused on getting results. As long as goals were being met, he thought, the rest took care of itself. The organization included no formal compensation packages. The lack of red tape seemed to lead to a gentler form of politics and a much closer working relationship among coworkers, according to managers. This culture, the career opportunities, and the competitive compensation were credited with the retention of key nonfamily managers.

Both Michael and Bob reported to Chuck Briscoe, the nonfamily president. Occasionally, Briscoe was left out of the loop when one of the sons would go straight to Ron Burton with ideas, issues, or problems. Briscoe served as a bridging president, between the two generations of Burtons. In March 2000, Ron began to develop the first strategic plan for Sigma Motion. Late that year, the team completed the strategic plan, which highlighted the core competencies of the company and stated an overall objective of becoming a $50 million company by 2009.

SUCCESSION PLANNING

Sigma Motion did not have a succession plan in place. Since both sons had increased their responsibility in the business, Ron had decided to charge ahead with some estate-planning work. Transfer or sale of the shares that he currently held had not been planned, although it had been discussed with Mary, Bob, and Michael. Verbal

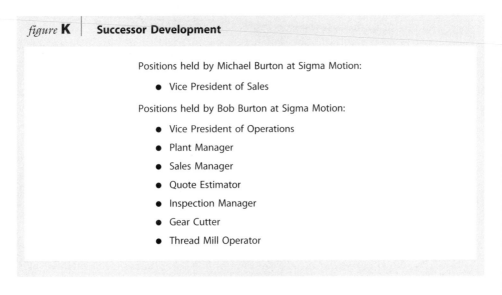

figure **K** | **Successor Development**

Positions held by Michael Burton at Sigma Motion:

- Vice President of Sales

Positions held by Bob Burton at Sigma Motion:

- Vice President of Operations
- Plant Manager
- Sales Manager
- Quote Estimator
- Inspection Manager
- Gear Cutter
- Thread Mill Operator

agreements existed, and the parties involved had made assumptions. Ron's plans included transferring the voting shares equally to his two sons.

Ron Burton did not want to pick a single next-generation CEO of Sigma Motion. He felt that Bob and Michael would be able to run the company as a sibling team. Bob, with a background in operations, and Michael, with a background in finance and sales, complemented each other and could make a great team (Figure K). But Michael and Bob were not as confident that it would all work out. They felt that they were always competing with each other for voice, for influence, for the limelight. Their goals also appeared to be quite different. Luckily, their roles were also different, and therefore day-to-day conflict was minimized. Still, when it came to leadership style, business strategy, and the company's financial structure and risk propensity, they had very different perceptions of what the future ought to look like.

Sigma Motion had an excellent customer base, a solid balance sheet, and some talented outside management on the team. Succession was inevitable, despite the fact that Ron would never completely "retire" from the business. Given Michael's apparent decision to leave, how could Ron Burton fulfill his dream of having both sons work as a sibling team at Sigma Motion?

SMALL FAMILY BUSINESS   CASE   **7**

THE AMBIVALENT CEO OF THE CONSTRUCTION COMPANY

Dick Symanski, 55, owns a construction company in the Northeast. Despite the slowed economy in his part of the country, Dick has been able to maintain his company's substantial profitability as a result of selective bidding, minimal debt, and other good management techniques.

Even though his business is very successful, Dick is completely at a loss over what to do about two sons in the business. Alan and Harry, both in their mid-30s, have each begun to press their father for an opportunity to lead the company. But Dick has taken no action, and his sons have begun to believe that he has no appreciation for their contribution to the success of the company. The sons also see Dick as passive and indecisive, qualities they resent.

While Alan and Harry have both demonstrated solid technical expertise over the years, their management skills have not been tested. Dick is just not sure what their leadership capabilities are. But more than that, they are the children from his first marriage—to a woman whose alcohol abuse left scars on Dick and his entire family.

Dick is happily remarried, and children from the second marriage are beginning to push for roles in the company. Dick is afraid that giving Alan and Harry stronger roles will result in anxiety in his new family. But he's just as sure that not doing so will escalate the tension between Dick and his older sons as well as reopen wounds from the first marriage.

Dick regrets his inability to act—it reminds him of his frustration with his own father, who seemed equally indecisive when Dick worked for him in another business. Dick wants to please everyone and avoid a further split in the family.

Part of a case series by the Family Firm Institute edited by Ernesto J. Poza. The cases are real, but identities have been changed to protect the privacy of the individuals involved. Reprinted with permission from The Family Firm Institute, Inc. All rights reserved.

SMALL FAMILY BUSINESS | CASE **8**

BORROWING TO GROW AT ANDREWS COMPANY

Revenues and gross profit for the Andrews Co., a $25-million-a-year manufacturing firm, have been lower this year than in the past two. John Kemper, a loan officer for First Commercial Bank, has worked with the Andrews account for many years. Yesterday, Michael Andrews, the senior member of the family management team, met with Kemper to discuss a loan for expanding manufacturing facilities and an increase in the current line of credit. Kemper asked Michael about his long-range plans for the business and was given a sketchy 2-year financial projection. When Kemper asked about management's capability to reverse the declining gross profit trends, Michael confidently pointed out that he had brought all of his four children into management positions and had given them each the title of vice president.

Kemper knows the two oldest children fairly well. The oldest, a daughter, while very bright, has always given her husband and children first priority. The second, a son, seems uncommitted to managing anything except the amount of beer he consumes at a local tavern.

Earlier today, Kemper called Michael to tell him that while the bank is going to continue its current loans, it is unwilling to grant additional credit at this time. Michael became enraged and threatened to move his entire banking business to a competitor,

Second National Bank. After fuming for several hours, he has called a meeting of the family management team to consider alternatives.

SMALL FAMILY BUSINESS | CASE **9**

ADAMS FUNERAL HOME

Adams Funeral Homes turned 132 years old in 2006. It is owned and operated by two generations, the third and fourth, of the Adams family. Richard Adams, current president, hired Dr. Fred White, a retired professor from State University, as a Special Assistant to the President in 2004. Dr. White, who worked 15 to 20 hours a week at the funeral home, is now Charles Adams's special assistant. Charlie is Rick's nephew and potential fourth-generation successor. Charlie's father, Robert (equal owner with Rick) is also active in managing the family business and considers his son well qualified to be the successor. Rick's son, who previously worked in the business, is currently active in politics and does not see himself as a successor to the business. An executive-team meeting is scheduled to address the issue of succession. Charlie and Robert have done the preparations necessary to support the selection of Charlie as the next-generation leader of the family business and to name him president soon thereafter. What should Rick do? What would be appropriate next steps? If this were not a family business, what would you recommend be done at Adams Funeral Homes?

Adams Funeral Homes, originally known as Thomas W. Adams Funeral Home had grown successfully through the 1960s from one to three locations. In the 1970s, a turning point, the firm could have really flourished with the growth in Macon, Georgia, and the surrounding communities. But the Adams family failed to capitalize on those opportunities. Then in 1980, Paul Adams (former President and 51% owner) passed away and his family decided to claim his stock in entirety from the funeral home, for about a million dollars. This transaction absorbed any capital that could have then been used for further expansion.

Fourth-generation member Charles Adams attended Georgia State University and graduated in 1999. He then went to mortuary school for a year and joined the family business full-time in August 2001. Ever since he was 11 or 12 years old, he had been regularly helping in the business. In fact, Charlie remembers working alongside his grandfather when he was only 7. Upon graduation, and perhaps the result of his Catholic background and undergraduate studies in philosophy and religion, Charlie sought a profession that, in his words, "made a difference in people's lives." Having known the funeral home business intimately, he felt aligned with the business's mission and purpose. He joined Adams as a funeral service intern and worked his way from the bottom up: embalming, coordinating funeral services, helping out with arrangements, and the like.

His reflections on the strengths and weaknesses of Adams Funeral Homes when he joined the family firm in 2001 are the following: On the plus side, Adams was customer-focused, clear on its mission of serving grieving families and acknowledging that especially when facing the death of a loved one, the family is always right. On the negative side, Charlie remembers, the business was not being led.

Joseph Adams, Charles's uncle had died in 1997. Soon thereafter a nonfamily manager became the company's general manager. Top management during this period seemed to have little respect for several of the associates. The business office in particular seemed to be in chaos; too many people without the right skills. The needed financial, human resource, and general-management skills were nowhere to be found. The financial results of the business were terrible, and personnel problems were snowballing into serious threats to the business. It was obvious to everybody, Charlie says, that the business needed to change and to do so in a hurry.

On January 2, 2002, the General Manager was fired. His contract had to be bought out at a high cost. Adams Funeral Homes annual revenues were approximately 9 million at the time. Luckily the CFO (who was part of the old administration) stayed with the firm. A human resource and general business manager who had been hired in late 2001, the CFO had previously worked for Coca-Cola, and was seen as a needed infusion of professionalism into the business. She undertook the functions of human resources, finance, purchasing, and information technology and helped the business to track its costs and receivables to maximize profits.

More recently, another family shareholder, one of Charlie's uncles, died. A buy–sell agreement was in force. (The buy–sell regulates the transfer of shares to inactive shareholders.) The shares in the hands of his uncle's widow converted to nonvoting shares upon his uncle's death. A company buyout of those shares is currently being negotiated. The cost associated with the buyout will constrain Adams's ability to finance promising growth initiatives.

Regular weekly meetings of the family management team were established during the past year and a new marketing plan is being developed. Charlie believes that the family needs to again get excited about its business and its prospects. He wants to grow the business. But he is also well aware that any changes will have to build on, not take away from, the tremendous reputation and brand that has been built over three generations. Focus groups of past clients and competitor clients are helping to identify Adams's continuing strengths as a top service provider and flag issues for improvement.

Charlie adds, "While we are pursuing these new marketing initiatives, we know who we are and how we do business. Word of mouth and community involvement are also paramount to us. And in any efforts to improve and grow we know that we cannot be focused on the bottom line only, if we are going to do well in the long term. This business requires a sense of calling, it is a great ministry."

QUESTIONS:

1. Should Charlie be chosen as the next president of Adams Funeral Homes? Why or why not? Should this happen in the meeting scheduled for the following Thursday?

2. What process should be used to arrive at a plan and a final decision?

3. What actions or steps should be included in that plan?

4. Should nonfamily managers be considered for the job? Why or why not?
5. What should be done on the ownership front to support a financially viable transfer and a smooth succession without paying unnecessarily high estate and transfer taxes?

FASTENERS FOR RETAIL (PART A)

CASE **10**

In December 1999, Gerry Conway faced the toughest decision of his 37 years as an entrepreneur. Something had to be done about the long-term future of Fasteners for Retail (FFr), the business he had founded in 1962. The company had been extremely successful, with sales doubling every 5 years since the 1980s, and the market for the company's point-of-purchase display products was still growing. Within the past 2 years, the company had begun to expand from an enormously successful catalog company into a full-service provider to global retail chains.

With no dominant players in FFr's niche, Conway saw nothing but opportunity ahead. Still, he was concerned. The company had been debt-free from the start, but feeding its continuing growth would require an infusion of cash. At 69, Conway felt that this was more risk than he wanted to assume. An even more pressing concern was his son and heir apparent's recent announcement that he did not want to become FFr's next president and instead planned to leave the company. None of his other children were interested in becoming part of the leadership team. Conway mused,

> I am a good entrepreneur, but I am not managerial in nature and I don't like that part of the business. I have a good manager here in Don Kimmel [the nonfamily company president]. It is time to move on. Until a year ago, I couldn't decide what to do because I was ambivalent, but now I have reached a point where I want to make a transition.

This decision would affect the future of his family, his business, and its 95 employees. Should he sell the company, appoint a nonfamily CEO, or persuade another family member to come into the business?

THE FOUNDER

Gerry Conway was the classic American entrepreneur—visionary, charismatic, driven, impatient, and independent. Born in Cleveland in 1931, Conway was the ninth of 13 children. His love of the retail environment, his strong independence, and his deep appreciation of people stemmed from his childhood experiences:

> With a little exaggeration, I can say that I've been in retail for 60 years. My Dad managed approximately 200 food stores, and my first jobs were as a stock boy and butcher's assistant. At home, we'd talk about business over the dinner table. With

11 sons and 2 daughters in the family, it was a lively conversation. I already had the entrepreneurial itch, and, from the grocery experience and from having a news-paper delivery route, I learned how to get along with people.

After college, Conway and his wife, Marty, returned to Cleveland. He began working for an industrial firm and quickly learned that, while sales attracted him, working in a large corporation did not. Conway's next job was with a smaller firm:

I started selling display lithography for a small printer. When that company went belly up, I founded Gerald A. Conway & Associates and became a display-printing broker. I was 31 years old, had $600 in the bank and a wife and six kids counting on me. For the first five years, I had one goal—survival. Even after we were established, the company was a central part of my life.

Conway was an extremely personable man. He made friends and networked with ease. One day, a colleague suggested that he sell the plastic parts that retailers use to display signs (called display and merchandising accessories) as part of his printing broker business. The advantage of selling accessories was that he could sell the same product to many companies simultaneously, which was not possible in display printing, for which each printing job was customized. An early product idea was the Arrowhead fastener, which was designed to hold coupons and signs on store shelves (Figure L). It was a best seller from the start. For the next decade, Gerald A. Conway & Associates was a printing broker and a supplier of display accessories.

During this time, Conway struggled with alcohol:

In 1970, alcohol was becoming a problem, but through a self-help program I chose sobriety and regained focus in my life. The following year, my first year sober, my income shot up by about 35 percent—a direct correlation. So, anyway, that was a significant event in the business and for my family.

THE POINT-OF-PURCHASE INDUSTRY

In the mid-1970s, Gerald Conway & Associates was renamed Fasteners for Retail (FFr) to acknowledge its exclusive focus on display accessories and fasteners within the point-of-purchase (P-O-P) industry.

The P-O-P products include the signs, displays, devices, and structures that are used to merchandise services or products in retail stores. The P-O-P industry was estimated to be a $13.1 billion sector, based on 1997 industry figures (Table C). FFr's segment was estimated to be approximately $600 million. While the broader P-O-P market was expected to grow at 4 percent annually, FFr and its competitors experienced much higher growth rates. FFr, for example, had grown 19.6 percent annually since 1984.

The accessory hardware segment (FFr's niche) was highly fragmented. No single supplier had more than 10 percent of the subsupplier market, and many competed in only a few product categories. FFr was the largest company in this niche, with a market share of approximately 7.5 percent. The company's major product offerings included shelf and nonshelf channel sign holders, display hooks, display construction, and custom products. FFr also offered shelf systems, ceiling display systems, product strips, hang taps, literature holders, and other accessories. Several key contractors manufac-tured these products for FFr, but no single manufacturer had unique or proprietary capabilities.

figure **L** | **Arrowhead Fasteners**

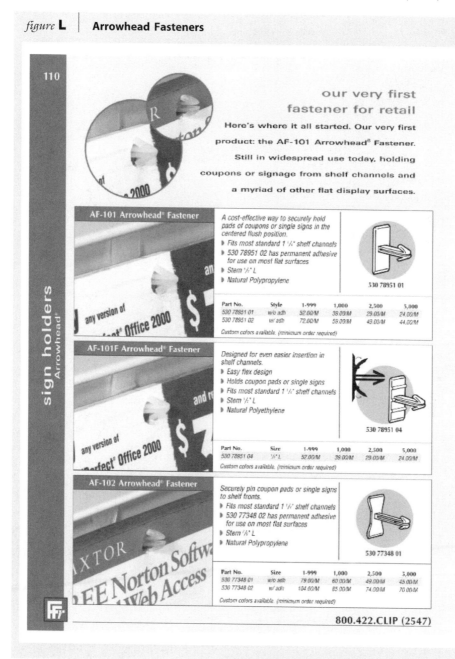

FASTENERS FOR RETAIL (FFr): VALUE ADDED FROM THE START

FFr distinguished itself from its competitors in several important ways. The company offered a broad and innovative product line, free samples, quick turnaround on orders, and a liberal sales return policy.

table C	P-O-P Industry Trends

P-O-P products are displays, signs, structures, and devices that are used to identify, advertise, and/or merchandise an outlet, service, or product and that serve as aids to retailing.

2002	$15.5 billion
1997	$13.1 billion
1996	$12.7 billion
1995	$12.0 billion
1994	$11.1 billion

- Almost three-quarters of customer purchase decisions are made in-store, at the point of purchase.
- Product proliferation is on the rise.

Supermarket Assortments:

| 1992 | 13,067 SKUs |
| 2001 | 30,580 SKUs |

SOURCES: Point of Purchase Advertising Institute; POPAI Consumer Buying Habits Study; and Food Marketing Institute.

FFr Products

The willingness to emphasize new products became a defining characteristic of the business. While the company's early expansion began with imported Swedish design accessories, the product line grew because of Conway's creativity and dissatisfaction with the status quo.

Successful design accessories are functional, fit a specific space, and are inexpensive. New products were developed from scratch, acquired, or adapted from other industries. Conway excelled in all aspects of product development—imagining how new products could meet customer needs and seeing how existing products could be used in or improved for the P-O-P market. Two products in particular, the Shipflat literature holder (Figure M) and SuperGrip sign holders (Figure N), were critical to FFr's success in the early 1980s. (The complete FFr online catalog can be found at http://www.ffr.com.)

Shipflat Literature Holder

At a trade show, Citibank challenged FFr to make a better literature holder. At the time, literature holders were made from rigid plastic. Only four holders could be shipped per box, and they frequently broke in transit. After a year of effort, FFr successfully designed attractive and durable literature holders that were unique in that they shipped flat and were set up at the point of use, eliminating breakage and reducing inventory space and shipping cost. Citibank had exclusive rights to the Shipflat for several years, and it placed the Shipflat at the core of its credit card program. Working with Citibank enhanced FFr's credibility and raised its visibility in the market; Citibank recognized the company as an "Outstanding Merchant" for its product and customer service. The Shipflat became FFr's first proprietary product in the literature holder category and was well received by auto clubs, insurance companies, and pharmaceutical firms, among others. Within 2 years, the Shipflat became FFr's top seller.

figure **M** | **Shipflat Literature Holders**

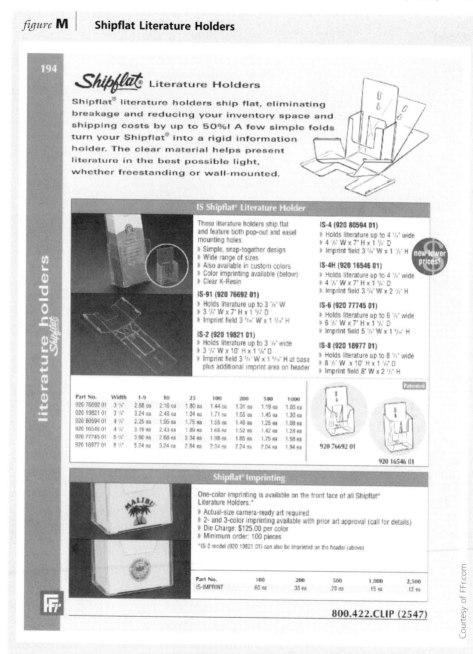

SuperGrip Sign Holders

In the early 1980s, a new product began appearing in the accessory market. FFr recognized this product's superior holding ability—it was able to hold paper signs in place more securely than existing technology. It represented a threat to FFr's product line, so the company tracked down the patent and began trying to develop its own version of the clip. At almost the same time, the clip's Canadian inventor, unhappy

figure **N** | **SuperGrip Sign Holders**

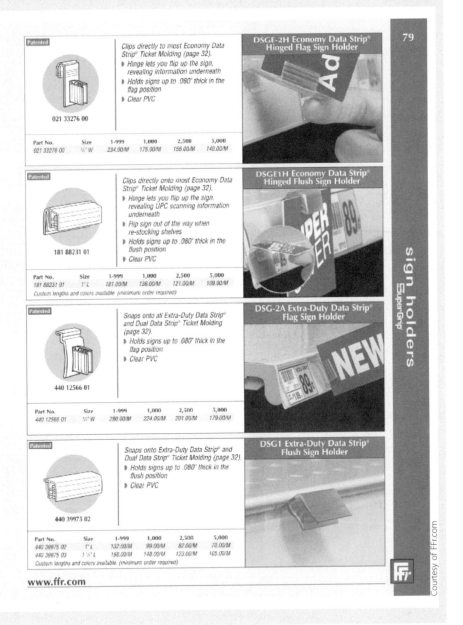

with his distributor, negotiated with FFr to distribute the product. FFr began distributing the clip and eventually purchased the patent with its Canadian partner. FFr renamed the clip and applied the technology to its existing products, thus expanding the product line. SuperGrip products were very successful with both retailers and consumer goods companies and, at one point, accounted for almost 20 percent of sales.

For years, FFr's marketing thrust was proprietary products. More recent efforts focused on developing an increasing number of custom products, designed to meet specific customer needs. New products were introduced as they were designed, without concern for cannibalizing sales of existing products. FFr encouraged the development of both custom and proprietary products, promoting internal competition.

FFr typically offered customers more than 100 new products every year. New product ideas came from FFr personnel, from customers, and from the acquisition of new product concepts. New-product development statistics were impressive. In a niche known for commodity products, FFr had almost 75 patents and patents pending. Patented products accounted for 20 percent of all products offered and represented a significant competitive advantage. On average, products that had been developed in the past 5 years accounted for 30 percent of sales. FFr valued and actively protected its designs.

SERVICE

FFr's products and superior service separated it from its competition. Independent audits repeatedly found that customers rated FFr's customer service as superior. An early hire recalled,

> When I began working here, we weren't quite sure who we were or what market we were in, so we looked around at other organizations and emulated what was best about them. Through that process, we became leaders. Following Gerry's lead, we never took things for granted. As a family-owned company, we were able to respond quickly to opportunities and customer needs.

While its competitors maintained limited inventories and dictated shipment terms to customers, FFr offered a complete line of products, kept a well-stocked inventory, bagged products to meet the customer's specifications, and shipped products as requested. Other vendors offered better prices but poorer service. FFr came to dominate its market by offering both service and selection:

> We created our competitors. After a few years, they looked at us and said, "We can do that too." We had a broad product line and did custom work; others began adopting those programs. Our success in branding is evident from the wide-scale copycatting of our colors, style, and product line.

FFr was both a direct sales and a marketing sales company. It relied on its sales force, direct mail catalog, trade media advertising, trade shows, and sample department to promote its products. The company's unique product catalog, the FFR Yellow Pages, set a new standard for the industry and helped establish FFr as a "first-look supplier" within the industry. The sales organization consisted of a direct sales force, international distributors, a customer service group, and a telemarketing staff.

FFr CULTURE

From its first hire on, FFr was a company whose employees, from designer to warehouseman, focused on customer satisfaction (Table D). As a 16-year veteran recalled,

> Gerry had the ability to hire people who would work independently, but in a common direction and for a common goal. He was fortunate to have surrounded

---

table **D** | **FFr's Statement of Values**

Fasteners for Retail
Welcome to FFr!
On behalf of all the employees at FFr, I welcome you to the FFr team and our thriving organization. We realize you may have put significant time and effort into your decision to join FFr, and we are pleased you have made a commitment to further your career with us. It's important we work together to fulfill both your professional goals and our overall company goals.

Since 1962, FFr has been recognized as a leader in custom and stock merchandising systems and accessories, as well as in providing outstanding customer service. We are very proud of this recognition, as well as our long-term customer and employee relationships.

To this end, the following Statement of Values guides our daily operations:

- Commit ourselves to excellence in creativity, quality, and service.

- Treat our customers and each other with respect.

- Seek opportunities for continuous improvement, with our goal being 100 percent customer satisfaction.

- Focus on developing and maintaining customers for life by maximizing the value we provide.

- Work as a team to support each other and achieve our goals.

We realize our continued success rests solely on our ability to recruit and retain the best people, like you.

Again, welcome to FFr. I wish you every success in your career with us.

Sincerely,
Donald F. Kimmel
President & COO

---

himself with people who had the sense of urgency and good work ethic to make things happen. This was true even of outsourced services. . . . Employees of our service center treated our clients as if they [the service center employees] were actually FFr.

FFr's customer-first focus extended to the company newsletter, which told tales of employees going above and beyond expectations to deliver superior customer service. It offered hints for achieving customer satisfaction, solicited new product ideas, and reported on product development. The newsletter also filled a more traditional communication role, introducing new hires and announcing promotions, company anniversaries, and birthdays.

Maintaining profit margins was also part of the FFr culture. President Don Kimmel recalled,

When I arrived, the focus on margins was so strong that I occasionally had to take a hammer to break it a bit. We would rather lose an order, if we couldn't beat the hell out of a supplier to get the margin we wanted, than deviate from our margins.

FFr GROWTH IN THE 1980s

FFr grew at a consistent and steady pace. In 1980, the company had five employees and sales of $3 million. Business began to boom in the early 1980s as a result of an expanding product line and a larger sales force. FFr grew steadily, adding employees in accounting, customer service, product design, and marketing. Company offices were moved to accommodate additional warehouse and distribution functions. Paul, one of Conway's sons, observed,

> *Dad managed the business like a football halfback, scanning the horizon looking for an opening and then heading for it. He was never afraid to explore new business possibilities and was always looking for opportunities.*

This opportunistic philosophy supported FFr's growth. The business was always profitable, there was no debt, and the company never got tied up in long-term commitments. Production and most warehousing were subcontracted, and office space was leased. The company made quick decisions, and arrangements with vendors were frequently based on handshakes.

The flip side of FFr's opportunism and speed was that it lacked a business plan and strategic discipline. When Conway came across an interesting idea, he wanted to implement it. Company lore had it that when Conway sat next to a consultant on an airplane, the consultant would be on site the following week to redesign something. This approach led to some important innovations and prevented the company from becoming stagnant, but it also created a sense of confusion and the feeling that priorities were constantly changing.

To keep the company growing, Conway realized that he needed to hire a president with managerial expertise. Although he understood the value of management, he was an entrepreneur, not a traditional manager. The company went through several presidents. FFr, for a time, was a company with an organizational chart but not a lot of organization. That changed in the late 1990s.

FFr GROWTH IN THE 1990S AND BEYOND

In the early 1990s, Conway and his wife, Marty, joined Case Western Reserve University's Partnership for Family Business. Through the program and conversation with other business owners, Conway began to see the need for different points of view regarding the business, and he decided to establish an advisory board:

> *One of the things that sprang from the family business program was that we set up a board of advisors. The board consisted of four independent current and former company CEOs. It included my brother and my son, Stuart, who ran his own non-profit organization. Preparing for these meetings was a great discipline. The Board challenged me through a review process and an implied evaluation of my performance. These men had all managed their own businesses. From their advice, I learned that entrepreneurship alone isn't enough to generate continued growth. Management and systems become essential once a business reaches a sales volume of $10+ million or has 50+ employees.*

These advisors helped the family better understand nonfamily management's needs and helped nonfamily managers appreciate the unique aspects of family firms. Most significantly, the board encouraged Conway to professionalize the staff and to build internal controls and an infrastructure (Figure O). The board had no statutory power but did provide good advice and served as a valuable sounding board.

After several unsuccessful hires, Conway named Don Kimmel as president. Kimmel was the perfect foil to Conway's creative vision and energy. He introduced a financial system and an organizational structure to complement the creative design and sales energy that had propelled the company for many years. Kimmel's strengths as a

figure **O** | **Organizational Chart of FFr, 1999**

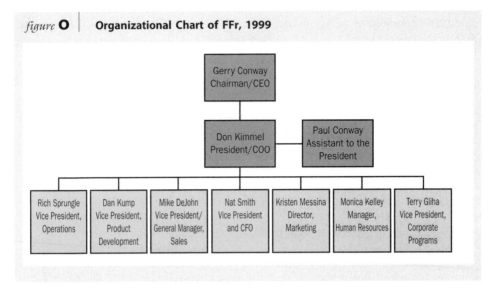

manager allowed Conway to shift out of the daily management role and focus on sales and product design, his strengths.

Under Kimmel's leadership and with the support of the advisory board, FFr began a rigorous strategic-planning process in 1997. An internal analysis recommended that the company upgrade its management talent, consolidate its sales organization, and focus on selling to the major retail chains. These chains were rapidly expanding and represented a potential $600 million market. The needs of these retailers were different from those of FFr's traditional customers, so FFr created a chain program selling division and made other internal changes to address those needs. The company expanded its engineering, design, and in-house sales team to meet customer expectations. FFr revisited its previously inviolate margins and adjusted them to be price-competitive. It began sharing cost and margin information with its suppliers, partnering with them to meet customer needs for design and price. The company made its first significant sale to Wal-Mart in 1998. A few years later, program sales to retailers accounted for over 20 percent of sales.

FAMILY INVOLVEMENT

Family involvement began in the 1970s, when the Conway children earned extra money by putting adhesive on the backs of Arrowhead fasteners. They had all done odd jobs for FFr, but of the seven children only three worked in the business as adults (Figure P).

Initially, the children did not see joining FFr as a career option. During their formative years, the company was pretty much a one-man operation. In the words of one son, "There was nothing to join." As the company grew, several of the children began to consider joining the firm.

Kevin, the eldest, joined in the early 1980s and became an outstanding salesman. Kevin had Gerry's gift for sales and was frequently on the road, visiting customers and

figure **P** | **Conway Family Tree**

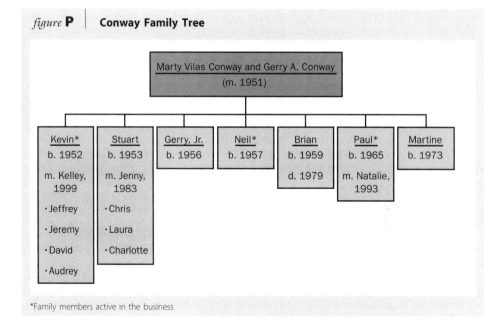

*Family members active in the business

closing on orders. Kevin worked at FFr for many years until health problems prompted him to resign.

From an early age, the youngest son, Paul, planned to join FFr. At his father's urging, he began his work career with another employer. It was only after he had been successful there that he joined FFr in 1988; his first job was in the marketing department.

Neil, the fourth son, worked in the warehouse. Neil was diagnosed with schizophrenia during his first year of college, and the structure of part-time employment in the warehouse worked well for him and for the company. As a result of the positive work experience with Neil, FFr hired other workers with neurobiological disorders.

It was not until the early 1990s that Gerry Conway began to focus on succession. His attention was driven by the company's success, his sons' active presence in FFr, and participation in the family-business program. Through the program, the Conways were introduced to the components of a well-executed succession process, including strategic planning, communication and accommodation among family members through family meetings, estate planning for business agility, leveraging family skills with those of nonfamily managers, using outside board members as advisors, and promoting the development of the next generation.

Family meetings were a high point for Gerry's wife, Marty:

> *From the family business program, we learned about family meetings. We had an outside facilitator at the first meeting, and it was marvelous—he had experiential learning games for us to play and different ways to communicate. By the third meeting, different family members were taking responsibility for planning activities for the meetings. The focus for the meetings shifted to the business of family from family business. Everyone in the family looked forward to the family meetings. They*

were a chance for us all to be together as a family. We talked about business and caught up with each other as family.

The family meetings were important to Gerry as well:

Before we had family meetings, I kept pretty much everything to myself. I was not that open. One of the things I learned was the importance of communication. At the first meeting, there was a critical point where I had to remind my family that while this was a family business, I had to make the final operating decisions.

As adults, all seven next-generation members of the Conway family got along well and respected each other and each other's life and career choices. They also respected FFr—"the house that Gerry had built"—and the family values that Marty continued to nurture. Their sense of family unity was balanced by an appreciation for individual differences.

As part of their estate planning, Gerry and Marty created a trust and transferred the majority of their FFr shares to their children. However, Gerry retained voting rights. Family meetings began around this time and proved to be a useful way for the new owners, particularly those not active in managing the business, to learn more about the business and the estate.

ESTATE PLANNING

One of the goals of the Conways' estate plan was to transfer a substantial amount of the value of FFr to their children during their lifetime so as to avoid estate taxes, but to do so without relinquishing control of the company. Gerry and Marty knew that by transferring sizable value while they were alive they would avoid the 55 percent estate tax—not only on the value transferred but also on the future growth of the value transferred. In order to transfer value without relinquishing control, the company's stock was split into voting and nonvoting shares. Nonvoting shares were used for gifting purposes.

In addition, the Conways used a grantor-retained annuity trust (GRAT) for each child. In other words, the nonvoting shares were transferred into a trust for each child, and the trusts required that Gerry and Marty, as grantors, receive an annuity (income stream) from the trusts for a period of years. The per-share value of the shares transferred was reduced by the present value of the annuity interest Gerry and Marty retained, meaning that they could give more shares away.

After a period of years, the GRATs terminated in accordance with the trust provisions. Children who were over 30 took their shares outright; the shares belonging to those who were not over 30 remained in successor trusts. In order to provide liquidity in the event of the untimely death of a shareholder, the Conways and their children entered into shareholders' agreements for the voting and nonvoting shares. They funded the cross-purchase obligations in the agreements with life insurance policies, held in an insurance trust.

SUCCESSION: KEVIN'S AND PAUL'S STORIES

While Kevin was the first child to join FFr, he was never a candidate for CEO. Like so many excellent salesmen, he did not like managerial activities. As the company grew, his interest in it waned, in part because he disliked the increased number of systems that were implemented to support the company's growth.

Paul Conway joined FFr a few years after Kevin did. Paul's earliest memories were of working for FFr. When he was 8 years old, he had put adhesive tape on the backs of 10,000 Arrowhead fasteners and had earned enough money to buy his first bicycle. An entrepreneur was born. Over the next 10 years, he and his friends continued to put adhesive on the backs of fasteners each time they needed spending money.

Paul began seriously imagining his future with FFr while he was in high school. He worked at FFr during college vacations and then joined another business after college graduation to gain additional work experience. After only 1 year, FFr's nonfamily marketing manager encouraged Paul and Gerry to negotiate Paul's entry into the company. Paul began work as a marketing assistant and sales representative and rotated through FFr's business units. Paul had clear ideas about how he wanted to be perceived:

> *I admired my Dad's knack for success and was happy to be with him in the business. Still, I wanted to make sure that I was not the typical SOB [son of boss]. I didn't want to take advantage of my family relationship or have people perceive that I was, even though I knew that some people would, no matter what I did.*

Paul became the international sales manager and built FFr's international business while also maintaining a position in the marketing department. After 7 years, he became the marketing manager. Two years after that promotion, Paul was asked to become the assistant to the president, Don Kimmel. The timing of the offer was significant. FFr's rapid expansion had left Don without time for long-range planning. Adding Paul to the executive suite provided needed support and allowed Paul to learn the business from a different vantage point:

> *I reached the Peter Principle as Marketing Manager. I didn't have formal training and the position was getting a little unwieldy for me. I just didn't have the tools, and Don needed help with management. Either I was going to use this new role as a launching pad or I was going to figure out that I didn't want to work at FFr anymore and would move on to something else.*

For the first time in his career at FFr, Paul was working directly with his father on a regular basis. With greater access to management's decisions, he came to a realization about his future with FFr:

> *I didn't like my Dad's management style. I'd always tell him about it, and we'd talk it through. We argued at times, but our arguments were always short-lived. It was as healthy an element of communication within our family as I had. But regardless of that, the disagreements were part of why the experience grew sour. I started to think about the reality of working in a larger corporation. When the business was smaller and a little more family-oriented, it was more enjoyable to me.*

Paul worked for over a year to clarify his goals, first to understand what leading FFr would mean and then to explore other career opportunities. In his view, Gerry was able to manage the business because he had grown with it. Paul felt that he was less equipped than his Dad to manage the large and growing business (Table E). Members of the advisory board felt that Paul could learn the job if he wanted to, and that having

| *table* **E** | **Annual Revenues for FFr, 1994–2001** |

Year	Net Sales ($ millions)
1994	18
1995	23
1996	29
1997	33
1998	41
1999	47
2000	52
2001	62

an experienced management team in place would give him time to learn. One board member recalled:

> At the beginning of the succession process, Paul was really the only son who was actively involved in the company. I thought that Paul would become president and believed that he had the capability to do the job well.
>
> At one point, Paul said that he didn't want to be in the position of making some of the tough decisions. Now that is being very honest, but I think he was looking at the responsibilities and the pressures of being the CEO as being more than they needed to be. Gerry was a loner in the way he ran his business. Paul may not have realized that he could do the job differently—probably in a more decentralized and collaborative way. I kept wondering if there was something I might have done with respect to Paul that would have made him feel more comfortable in the potential role.

Gerry's brother, FFr board member Bill Conway, suggested that Paul give himself more time in the business before he made a decision about becoming CEO. Paul thought about his choices for about a year and ultimately decided that he wanted to leave the company and become a teacher. The decision to leave FFr was not easy:

> I felt like I was the last of the Mohicans—the last possible guy to run the company. When I decided that I didn't want to do it, I felt guilty. . . . My Dad deserved a lot of credit. He really wanted to pass the business along to one of his children. After I said that I didn't want to stay in the business, he said "ok," and then we met as a family to discuss the implications.

SUCCESSION: MARTY'S POINT OF VIEW

Marty Conway was one of Gerry's chief advisors. While Gerry was the obvious leader of the company, it was Marty who signed the checks and kept an eye on corporate finances. She had a public role at company functions and was a people booster. She played a more significant role behind the scenes, supporting Gerry as he considered important business changes, such as handing over the administrative reins or making personnel changes. Both family members and outsiders described Marty as the glue that worked behind the scenes to hold the family together through the predictable challenges that families who work together face. She summed up Paul's role at FFr as follows:

> When Paul would come over, Gerry and Paul would talk business all the time, which used to drive me crazy. But that was just part of their life together. The only person I

really talked to about the business in terms of succession was Paul. When Paul was young, he said, "Someday, I am going to grow up and I am going to run the company."

After he graduated from college he went to work. . . . Gerry's advice to all of them had been if you want to join the company, you have got to go out in the real world first. Paul worked very hard for an insurance company and won salesman of the year during his first year. At that point, FFr was just starting to grow. I said, "If you really want to get involved in this company, now is the time." So Gerry took him in then.

SUCCESSION: GERRY'S DILEMMA

Gerry Conway was a passionate entrepreneur, a business builder. During the early part of his career, he traveled extensively, meeting customers and serving as chief salesman, marketer, and innovator for the company. Whether he was on the road or in the office, his presence was felt throughout the organization.

Conway's life had been organized around his family and his company. For almost four decades, home and work were the center of his life—his passion and his zeal. He had always thought of them as being joined. Suddenly, that didn't seem possible any more:

Kevin was out of the picture. Stuart had, long ago, decided that he didn't want to work in the business. Paul recently had decided he didn't want the responsibility. None of the other kids were interested. At the same time, I felt frustrated every day as I tried to handle this big company. I thought it was time to move on.

Then, his thoughts shifted to his personal situation, and he said to himself,

Oh my God, what am I going to do with the rest of my life? I hadn't done a tremendous amount of planning on the retirement side. I had done some, but the demands of running a business didn't leave a lot of time.

As Conway contemplated the future of FFr, his management team put the finishing touches on the company's new strategic plan. The plan made a strong and well-supported case for making a significant capital investment to develop fulfillment capabilities, to consider manufacturing selected items, to expand sales internationally, and to increase the product line through strategic acquisitions.

Conway intuitively knew that the time for the business to aggressively explore these growth opportunities had arrived. Funding the plan would take all the cash out of the business and would also require outside financing. A combined advisory board and family council meeting was scheduled for the following week. It was time for Conway to decide what action to take.

Research associate Tracey Eira Messer prepared this case under the supervision of Professor Ernesto J. Poza as the basis for class discussion rather than to illustrate the effective or ineffective handling of an administrative situation. For permission to publish this case, grateful acknowledgment is made to Gerald Conway, chairman emeritus of Fasteners for Retail.

FERRÉ MEDIA GROUP (PART B)

> *Our success with continuity in this generation comes from learning from the failure of the second and third generation transitions. My father really set out to do it differently and he approached it very conscientiously, with a lot of discipline, having learned in his generation that a group of entrepreneurially prone individuals without a coherent structure can get into a lot of trouble.*

—*María L. Ferré, fourth-generation president of the Grupo Ferré Rangel*

María Luisa credits her father and her mother, Luisa Rangel, with promoting strong family unity coupled with unusual support for individual differences in this fourth generation. Perhaps because of the journalistic culture that runs in the family, the opinions of the individual children, however different, were constantly sought and appreciated as they grew up. María L. Ferré adds: "Our success in continuing the entrepreneurial spirit is a result of five professionals who know they complement, they need each other, to be successful. We respect each other and our differences. The siblings have selected me to lead them. So the major distinction between us and the previous generation is the sense of confidence that comes from knowing that we now have a coherent structure to govern the relation between people who are naturally entrepreneurial in nature."

The fourth generation, true to its legacy, is also quite entrepreneurial. Aware of their make-up, fourth-generation siblings have dedicated themselves to building a coherent structure that won't stifle entrepreneurship but that will effectively govern the relationships between them.

THE NEXT GENERATION

Between 1997 and 2002, every member of the next generation grew into a position of significant responsibility. Antonio's son Toño joined Puerto Rican Cement. He worked in production and then management and eventually became the fourth-generation president of the company. He reported to a key nonfamily executive, Luis Nazario, then CEO of the company.

Daughter Loren played a key role in the development of City View Plaza, a real estate development that appealed to her artistic and design capabilities. She later became the marketing manager who helped launch *Primera Hora*. María Eugenia became president of *El Nuevo Día*, the flagship newspaper, which is a major employer, an asset-intensive company, and a public trust. The paper requires both visible leadership in the community and administrative acumen in the company—a perfect fit for María Eugenia's capabilities. Luis Alberto became the paper's editor. He changed much of the editorial style and substance, while retaining the respect and loyalty of the independent souls in the newsroom. As president of the holding company, María Luisa led the Grupo in its strategic renewal.

Next-generation members continued their education and leadership-development work in academic and seminar settings, but their true education was occurring not in the classroom but in the workplace. They were getting feedback from the work itself, their direct supervisors, and Antonio Luis Ferré. He regularly scheduled meetings with top family managers and acted as their mentor and senior advisor.

Along with developmental opportunities, the new roles of next-generation owner-managers brought visibility and profit-and-loss implications, both of which increased the amount of work they had to do. There was little time for anything other than work. Workdays were long and arduous. The balance between work and family life was being threatened. According to some, family communications and, thus, investments in family relationships and family unity suffered during this period. Luisa acted as the chief trust officer, keeping the family side on the agenda. She provided help to keep the family together at a time when the speed and intensity of developments appeared likely to throw them into chaos. Some next-generation members helped her in this role.

NONFAMILY MANAGEMENT: THE EXTENDED BUSINESS FAMILY

During this final stage of the multiyear succession-and-continuity process, the family appeared less united in the eyes of key nonfamily managers. Family members had to come to grips with the fact that differences of opinion or priorities among Ferré Rangel family members were providing opportunities for these nonfamily managers to take sides. Still, family members had much confidence in the level of professionalism of these managers.

A family council meeting produced an action plan to address the gaps in communication and to improve the family's relationships with key nonfamily managers during the entire succession-transition period. The frequency of family and nonfamily management meetings was increased. Periodically, key nonfamily managers were invited to attend the family council meeting. Bridges were built to clarify the succession process and its direction for all involved, thereby reducing stress and unnecessary wear and tear on an important part of the fabric of the enterprise.

World-class professional managers had a long history in the Grupo. They had always held responsible positions in Puerto Rican Cement, whose latest CEO, Miguel Nazario, was not a family member. Various entrepreneurs had helped Antonio Luis Ferré launch *El Nuevo Día*. For instance, Carlos Castañeda had had editorial responsibilities at the Associated Press and *Visión* and had been the Latin American editor for *Life* magazine before setting the framework and editorial style for the first edition. Antonio Arias, Fernando Sánchez, and Adolfo Comas Bacardí were all experienced top managers who joined the firm and remained with it for the rest of their careers. The Grupo provided advancement opportunities and compensated managers with market-based pay and benefits plans. It also had a history of involving nonfamily managers in top-level decision making and in setting the direction of the company. However, the entry of five next-generation members within a 7-year time frame and the talk of succession were casting a shadow over future career prospects for nonfamily employees.

But as the strategic-planning process moved into high gear, the holding-company structure permitted the promotion of nonfamily managers to the presidency of several business units. Carlos Nido, who assumed the presidency of Virtual, Inc., and Luis González, who moved to the holding company as vice president of corporate sales and marketing, saw their responsibilities increase immediately. Nonfamily managers then began to believe that the succession process could be a real win–win opportunity for the extended business family.

CORPORATE STRATEGY MEETING, FEBRUARY 1999

María Luisa became president of the Grupo Ferré Rangel in late 1998. A year earlier, some next-generation members had observed that there was a significant gap between the planning in which they participated at family council meetings and their ability to then make and execute decisions. Key nonfamily managers, it turned out, had similar difficulties; there was clearly a disconnect between planning the work and working the plan. One of María Luisa's first highly visible acts of leadership of the newly structured holding company was to sponsor a series of strategic-planning sessions. With the assistance of a corporate-strategy consultant, she sponsored a series of education and planning meetings that focused the strategy of each of the business units, clarified the roles of the Grupo and central services, and created a stronger culture of accountability. María Luisa reflected on the reason for the renewed strategic planning effort at the holding-company level: "We need to guide these various communications companies to the future. I do not believe we can direct all of this as a team, without growth. Growing is very important."

Strategic planning was not new to the company. In fact, while the tremendous success of *El Nuevo Día* might have led many corporate leaders to rest on their laurels, Antonio Luis Ferré was not one of those. He had sponsored strategic reviews since the 1980s. In the 1990s, both as a continuation of this discipline and as an extension of it in order to accommodate the entry of the next generation into the business, he had created a new ventures unit, RANFE (Rangel Ferré). RANFE was charged with giving serious consideration to the appropriate diversification of the company as the next generation of owner-managers took over.

The FCC was in the process of changing regulations affecting the ownership of multiple media companies within particular markets. Given the increased competition already available via cable TV systems and the Internet, the FCC was moving toward allowing the same company to own multiple media channels serving a market. This presented additional growth opportunities, as well as increased financial risk; most of the new media were capital-intensive. Which would produce the desired growth, while maintaining profitability—market specialization (concentrating further in the Puerto Rican market with new media) or market diversification (investing in growth opportunities in new markets)?

Primera Hora was a successful example of growth through market specialization. Management saw a need for the product in the local market; researched the product in the United Kingdom, Costa Rica, and Chile; and hired talented top management to help lead the effort. Working with a key nonfamily circulation manager, Hector Olave, and supported by the Grupo's strategic 5-year plan, Loren Ferré had managed to grow daily circulation to 120,000 in just 3 years. The much older competitor in that niche, *El Vocero*, had a circulation of 155,000.

There were concerns about stress, and yet the enterprises were humming with new energy. Next-generation members were rediscovering what they loved about the company and beginning to understand what unique contributions they could make to the Grupo. Next-generation members were also called on to act as ambassadors on behalf of *El Nuevo Día* and the Ferré Rangel family. The journalistic independence of the flagship newspaper was once again being attacked.

EL NUEVO DÍA VERSUS THE GOVERNMENT

Directing its always independent journalistic voice at the incumbent governor of Puerto Rico and his administration, *El Nuevo Día* had published a series of articles that revealed incompetence, corruption, self-dealing, and undue process. The governor and his administration responded swiftly; they mounted a campaign to discredit *El Nuevo Día,* pulled all government advertising (from tax notices to bond-issue announcements) from the paper, and failed to issue the environmental permits needed to operate the Puerto Rican Cement plants. The government was attempting to shut down the Grupo Ferré Rangel just as the Nixon administration had attempted to silence *The Washington Post* in its investigations of Watergate and the Pentagon Papers.

El Nuevo Día filed suit in federal court to stop the unjust and excessive use of governmental powers. This landmark first amendment rights case was settled out of court in Washington, D.C., in late 2000, but only after exacting a heavy price from the flagship newspaper (circulation dropped by 30,000 during this period) and the cement company. The family did come together and emerged triumphant, with renewed strength of character and commitment to its mission, its legacy, and the journalistic independence of its newspapers. The next generation now understood firsthand that the newspaper business sometimes requires financial and personal sacrifices to uphold the public good and preserve the freedom of the press.

MARÍA LUISA FERRÉ FACES NEW CHALLENGES

The organizational structure of the group had changed with the creation of the Grupo Ferré Rangel as a holding company. Business units were more clearly separated from *El Nuevo Día,* and the presidents of the respective units had more authority in the new structure. A strategy, strategy-implementation plan, and budget were developed for each business unit. The presidents of individual business unit reported to María Luisa, chairman of the board and president of the holding company. The 14-person board of the holding company was composed of 7 Ferré Rangel family members: 5 key executives from the various companies and 2 independent outsiders, a professor and former industry association president and a general manager of a smaller family-owned corporation. Several next-generation members were now concerned that this board of directors was not holding management accountable to any significant extent. According to the siblings, the large number of family members and key executives on this board made it a great developmental vehicle, but one prone to rubber-stamping.

Next-generation members believed that, as a result of the 5-year developmental stretch, they had all found their niches and their unique ways of contributing to the business. But they still harbored concerns about their ability to make the big decisions as siblings and co-owners, without the tie-breaking role of Antonio.

Spouses of the next-generation heirs, the in-laws, seemed to be getting pulled into taking sides over the amount of work and the pressures of public service and public-relations activities. The estate plan was developed with the advice of an estate-tax attorney. Several classes of stock were created, and voting stock was to be held only by family members who were active in the management of the company. Any next-generation member choosing to leave the company would immediately have their stock revert to nonvoting stock and be redeemed over a period of time.

All of the power and responsibility were transferred to the next generation. But who would have the final word in, say, a $1 million investment in a new press, when significant investment was also required in Virtual, Inc.? Who would decide whether to diversify the business and what steps to take in this direction? And what about the 12 grandchildren, ages 2 to 14, who might one day want to be involved with the Grupo Ferré Rangel? Who would decide which of the grandchildren met the criteria for employment at the Grupo? It was September 2005, and María Luisa Ferré was pondering these and other questions.

What does María Luisa Ferré need to do next? What advice would you give her on leading her sibling owner-manager team forward on all of these fronts?

THE COUSINS TOURNAMENT

CASE **12**

At the Blanchard family's 1993 New Year's Eve party, Al Blanchard talks for the first time about retiring as president of Grandview Industries. Al, 67, is standing on the back porch of his rambling Southern California home, sharing brandy and cigars with his younger brother, Morris, with whom he has worked for 27 years. "I only want to do this for one more year, Morris," he confides. "I've had enough." "Then he asks: "Do you want to run the company, or should we turn it over to one of the kids?"

Morris has been asking himself the same question for several months. It has not been easy being in his older brother's shadow for so many years. However, Morris suffered a heart attack in 1989, and he, too, is looking forward to more leisure, and devoting more time to the small travel business in which he is an investor. Always a realist, Morris knows it is too late for him to take over a $200 million company with 2,000 employees. "I would be willing to manage things for a short time if you want to leave right away," Morris tells his older brother. "But I think we need to turn things over to one of the boys."

Al and Morris's father, George Blanchard, founded Grandview Industries with a partner in 1934. The original company, called Grandview Electric, made small motors for windshield wipers and other automobile components. Under Al's leadership, the company has grown into a diversified manufacturer of a variety of electrical systems for vehicles and small aircraft, with five divisions in California as well as distribution outlets abroad.

George Blanchard and his wife, Molly, had five children—including two daughters, Sarah and Germaine, and a third son, Arnold—but only Al and Morris have had careers in the business. Al joined Grandview before his brother and was quickly viewed as his father's natural successor. A hefty, former high school football player, he was not as dynamic as his father, but he was solid and hard-working, with a certain inner toughness and affability. Morris, five years younger, was a wiry bundle of energy, always filled with new ideas and schemes for reorganizing divisions, creating alliances with suppliers, and taking Grandview Industries into new markets. Morris never got along with his father and that may be one reason his career took him to the far reaches of the company. He lived abroad for years, developing new customers in Europe. Privately, Morris often expressed impatience and frustration with Al's conservative leadership, but never publicly. Fortunately—or perhaps by George Blanchard's design—their separate responsibilities kept them apart.

In more recent years, the two brothers had developed a greater appreciation of each other's contributions and roles; they had drawn closer. Morris is now at headquarters, as vice president of marketing, and he and Al meet almost every day to discuss company policy. Although Al respects his brother's opinions, he remains the undisputed leader. His fraternal affection for Morris does not mean he believes in shared decision making.

Their New Year's Eve conversation has stirred up a lot of buried feelings. George Blanchard died at age 73, a year after his wife, Molly. The founder left equal amounts of Grandview stock to their five offspring. By then, Al was already running the company. Besides Morris, the only other family member with a position in the business was Sam Chafee, Sarah's husband.

A staunch Methodist family, the Blanchards were a model of togetherness and public respectability. Sister Sarah, a voluble personality, now 61, was for a time a local talk show host. But by and large the family kept a low profile in the affluent community.

The only real threat to family harmony occurred in 1977 when Sarah's husband, Sam Chafee, angrily left the company. An accountant by training, Sam was the company controller, but he had larger ambitions and claimed that Al and Morris were sidetracking his career. Al used his contacts to help Sam get another job, and tried to smooth over Sarah's ruffled feelings, but the incident strained her relationship with her brothers.

Al saw himself as the custodian of the family's wealth. He wanted to keep stockholders committed to the family legacy, but at a distance from operations—a delicate balancing act. George Blanchard gave his oldest son one piece of advice that he has never forgotten: "You will keep the family happy," he said, "if you keep putting dividends in their pockets. As long as you support their lifestyles, you will be the best executive in the world. Begin to lose money, and you will become an ignoramus overnight."

Grandview's gradual expansion reflected Al's determination to protect dividends. Nevertheless, the company grew steadily, tripling total sales during the 1960s and 1970s. Al had brought four outsiders onto the board, which originally consisted of all five siblings and the company's primary banker, now retired. In the early 1980s, he restructured the company, taking it public but keeping family control by creating classes of stock and a holding company. The strategy was a financial success, fueling further expansion while continuing to provide a good income to family members. Each of the five siblings retained equal voting control of the holding company, in keeping with the wishes of the parents. Family stockholders were comfortable and had few complaints. No one raised questions about what would happen if Al were no longer around.

Meanwhile, the family was growing rapidly, with many early marriages in the third generation and already eight children in the fourth. By 1990, there were six third-generation members in the business. Al and Morris each have two sons in management. Germaine and Arnold each have one, but both are young and in junior roles. Sam and Sarah's two sons and daughter have made careers elsewhere, as their parents urged them to do after Sam's bitter experience.

At a subsequent engagement party for Sarah's daughter in the spring of 1993, Al announces his decision to retire to the family, gathered on the patio of the Chafees' beachfront home. There are expressions of good wishes and a little kidding about Al's age. But Al's brief remarks have stirred up anxieties about the future. His brother Arnold argues that Al should stay on as CEO for another 8 or 10 years, since things at the company are going so well. Germaine jokes about calling her lawyer and selling her stock before morning.

The following weeks are filled with anxious phone conversations between family members. If Al has had any kind of plan for succession in mind, he has never divulged it to other family members, including Morris.

Al reflects on his relationships with each of his siblings, and how he has managed this complex family over the years. He asks Morris whether he thinks they should have a family meeting or form a family council. Morris feels the two of them should manage the succession choice themselves. "We don't want a lot of extraneous factors brought in," he says. "There are only a few people who might be chosen anyway. Why open it up to the fantasies of our sisters about their sons and daughters?"

Al is tempted to go along, but he feels the cat is too far out of the bag to resolve the issue unilaterally. Instead, he decides to create a succession committee to lay out a process for selecting the next CEO and determine the timing of the transition. Seeing that Al has made up his mind, Morris suggests that Peter Franklin be asked to serve as chairman. Peter, the owner of a large freight shipping company, has been a friend of Morris's since college and was the first nonfamily member added to the Grandview board in 1980.

Peter agrees to serve. He has great respect for both Al and Morris as businessmen. He also knows that Al is tired and the company has been slowing down as a result. He thinks Grandview is in excellent condition and ready to make a major jump in size, diversification, and market reach. For those reasons, the choice of successor will be critical.

Al and Morris agree that the committee should have two other nonfamily board members besides Peter. Al argues that the family appointees ought to be members of the next generation not working in the business. Morris argues that because both of his children have jobs at Grandview that would cut out his branch. In the end the brothers appoint Sarah's younger son, Andy, and Morris's daughter, Mary.

The committee is formed, but Peter is already having second thoughts about serving as chairman. All the Blanchard siblings take a passionate interest in their father's legacy and, he realizes, each will push for his or her offspring. He also knows Grandview is way behind in preparing the next generation for leadership. There is no succession plan, and Peter wonders why. Is it Al's personality, or Morris's? Or do both fear that talking about issues might dredge up bitter feelings and cause a rift in the family?

Faced with what is shaping up as a thankless task, Peter nevertheless begins formulating a mental scorecard of the leading candidates' strengths and weaknesses. Of the cousins working in the business, he figures, two stand out as contenders for the top job.

1. Al's oldest son, Joe, who at 42 is also the oldest member of the third generation. Trained as an engineer, Joe has worked in production for most of his career at Grandview. But in recent years he has become more of a manager. Quiet, calm, and thoughtful like his father, Joe led the company's efforts to introduce team methods of work under its TQM [total quality management] program. His greatest plus is that he gets along well with all branches of the family. He is well liked and steady; he has performed well in every sector he has managed. But he is not regarded as charismatic or a strategic thinker.

2. Morris's oldest son, Bill, 41, is a trouble-shooter who enjoys his reputation as a hard-nosed manager. A business school graduate, Bill is performance-focused and demanding. His father brought him to Europe to turn around one of Grandview's subsidiaries there, and he did an outstanding job of reorganizing the business and cutting payroll. Bill is also the only cousin in the business with significant international experience, which Peter knows will be important in developing the company's future markets. He has made money for Grandview in businesses that looked marginal to family stockholders. But his abrasive style is not appreciated by his cousins—especially Joe. A few have confided to Peter that they would be uncomfortable trusting their assets to Bill.

The other cousins in the company are either too young to be considered or have not yet demonstrated exceptional ability. Only Mary, 32, Morris's daughter, appears to have the talent for a leadership position. Mary is a chemist and metallurgist who holds a middle-management position in R&D. Although bright and exceptionally good at her job, Mary has never expressed any ambition to do anything beyond research. In any case, women in the family have always been subtly excluded from management. It is the company's loss, Peter feels, but he sees no indication that the family is yet ready to accept a woman as CEO.

As he runs down his list, Peter realizes that the cousin he admires most is not on it. Edward Chafee, 40, Sam and Sarah's oldest son, isn't in the company. By leveraging the stock he had received as a young man, Ed has built a very successful electronic hardware business in Silicon Valley. Starting out as a computer whiz, he has in recent years shown a flair for deal making as well as for motivating his employees. Ed was the youngest president ever of the State Manufacturers' Association; he has even been mentioned in Inc. magazine's "Young Presidents to Watch" column. As far as Peter can tell, he is also popular with his cousins, although he does not socialize with them very often.

Al and Morris, however, are clearly not considering Edward. When Peter accepted the job as committee chair, Morris had said: "We have several children who have been working hard and doing a fine job in the company. Help us pick the right one." Peter has to keep reminding himself that his friends are not only business owners, they are fathers.

At the first meeting of the succession committee, the members agree there is no one individual who stands out as the obvious choice, and that all the cousins now working in the company can use more experience in general management.

Following this discussion, the tension in the room rises when Peter Franklin reports: "Al and Morris have come to the same conclusion about the readiness of any of the potential candidates. But Al does not want to continue as president after the end of the year. Therefore, Morris has agreed to take over the CEO role for an interim period, until a successor has been chosen and is ready."

The silence that follows is deafening. Andy Chafee, Sarah and Sam's son, argues that the business will do better if Al hangs on longer. The issue is debated, but no clear consensus emerges. Finally, Morris's daughter, Mary, speaks up: "None of you trust my father. You believe he will interfere in this process in the interest of my brother, Bill. I don't want my father to take on this job either. His heart is not strong enough, and he should be resting instead. But I resent your assumptions about him. He would have been better for the company than Uncle Al all along. We should be glad to have him."

Now there is another embarrassed silence, followed by many statements of support for Morris. But a long-festering issue is now on the table. The committee goes home with a lot that is troubling to think about.

At the next meetings of the committee, the members cannot agree on a process, let alone a list of candidates. Meanwhile, pressures from other family members are beginning to build. Peter reads a letter from Sarah, in which she writes: "I am pleased that the family has persuaded you to chair such an important committee. Having someone not in the family run this committee is the only way we can have objective decisions. I would like to add one other point: There are many members of the younger group who might be the best choice to head this company, who are not in the company now. Are they disqualified? Some of them were discouraged from making a career in the company before. I would like to see them have a chance."

Peter has already gotten an earful on the same issue from Al and Morris's other sister, Germaine, a friend. "If you could convince Edward to give up his business or bring it into the company," she says, "he's clearly the best of the bunch. But I don't think you could offer him enough to do it. Once you've been a success as your own boss, why would you want to work for the family?"

A short time later, Peter talks with Ed Chafee at a YPO [Young Presidents Organization] lunch in San Cupertino. Ed is curious about how the committee is progressing and, when Peter makes a few oblique references to Ed's own career, he suddenly says: "If you're considering inviting me into this tournament, I think you don't know my family. Al is a nice man; he is truly interested in keeping the family together and finding the best successor. But Morris is out to accomplish his own agenda—which is getting Bill into the president's office."

Peter likes Ed's directness. "All right," he says, "let's leave Morris out of this for a minute. What do you want? What's your agenda?"

"I like my own business," Ed replies. "We've grown to $25 million this year. The future looks good. We have some deals pending that could help us sustain growth for several years to come. It would take a very generous salary, freedom to run Grandview my way, and some financial buyout of my own company for me to take this job."

"Let's be clear," Peter says. "Nobody is offering you a job. We're talking about whether you are interested in becoming a candidate." Then, after a pause, Peter says: "I understand your position, but you are only presenting one side. You are successful, but your company will never be anything but small potatoes compared with Grandview. With strong management and strategic leadership, Grandview can become a major player on an international scale. The facilities are modern and highly productive, there is a good mix of mature and young products, and the balance sheet is in excellent shape. Are you ambitious enough for that opportunity?"

"You make an interesting case," Ed says, smiling. "Captain of my own yacht or the family's hireling on an ocean liner. I honestly don't know. Let's keep talking about it."

What Ed does not share with Peter is his feeling—which has been popping into his head lately—of how much it would mean to his mother, Sarah, if he became the next leader of Grandview.

The following week, Peter has lunch with Al. "I need more guidance from you," Peter says. He tells Al that he feels trapped by conflicting loyalties and responsibilities. "For example, do you want the committee to consider only family members inside the company?"

"My friend," Al replies, "I see that my sisters have been talking to you about their boys. Let me put your mind at ease. There is no solution that will please all of this family. The five of us have kept all our eggs in one basket, the way our parents wanted it to be, for a long time now. I thought it would be relatively simple to continue that for another generation. Morris still thinks so—probably because he thinks that the eggs will fall gently into the hands of his own son. But I'm not so sure. I don't know what's the best choice for the business. My son Joe has solid potential. Morris's boy, Bill, is stronger in some areas, weaker in others. Both of them are dedicated to this company and deserve to be rewarded for that commitment. That's where you come in. Do the right thing for the business. I will try to make it fly with the family."

Peter is beginning to appreciate what a strong-willed and complicated group the Blanchards really are. On the ride home, he reminds himself that Grandview Industries is not a small operation. Hundreds of employees depend on its continued vitality. What everyone needs now is a process that the whole family will support, leading ultimately to the choice of the best possible leader for the company's future. Is that a reachable goal?

When the committee reconvenes, Peter immediately lays it on the line. "We cannot continue to just discuss issues as we have been," he warns. "We have a deadline for a plan: two months. We have to focus on resolving three issues by the end of our next meeting." The three issues to be decided are (1) What should be the process for choosing the next president? Does the committee's present composition ensure maximum acceptance and support of whatever plan is proposed? Should the committee be changed or a new one created? Should Al and Morris be involved? (2) Does the interim CEO plan, with Morris serving until a new leader is chosen, make sense? Or will it only exacerbate tensions between the siblings? (3) Should Ed Chafee be considered? Or should only cousins who have experience in the company be considered?

Gersick, K. E., The Cousins Tournament. *Family Business*, Winter 1995. Reprinted with the permission of the author.

CREATING THE STRATEGY

> I don't think it's an accident that the newspapers best known for quality in this country ... are, or were until recently, family controlled. It seems that certain attributes essential to quality are more easily provided by families than by public companies. These are the qualities that I think are most important: First, deep roots. Families offer longevity—and thus a knowledge of, and commitment to, the local community that's hard to get from professional managers who come and go .... Second, a perspective that extends beyond the next quarter's earnings per share .... Finally, family ownership provides the independence that is sometimes required to withstand governmental pressure and preserve freedom of the press.
>
> *—Katharine Graham, Late Chairman of the Washington Post Company[1]*

Strategic planning is done differently in family-controlled corporations, where both management and the family shareholder group must be engaged in thinking about the future. The family shareholder group needs to establish its own goals and define the nature of its desired relationship with the business. If family members intend to continue to own the business in the next generation, will they manage it themselves, or would they prefer to have professional nonfamily managers run it for them? Family and business planning occur in parallel, creating a new, more inspired and idiosyncratic family-business strategy.[2]

Given their unique role in the strategic planning of family-controlled companies, family shareholders must be careful not to usurp top management's responsibility for thinking strategically on behalf of the business. In addition, the ownership group of any company must not lose sight of its primary objective—creating value for its customers. Only in this way can a business create value for itself. This ongoing process of creating customer value will generally result in healthy profit margins and cash flows, which will then lead to an increase in shareholder value.

While it may sound simple, value creation for the customer in a constantly changing competitive environment is difficult for an organization that for the most part prefers to maintain the status quo. And most organizations, whether family-controlled or not, engage in some resistance to change. From a strategic perspective, family-owned enterprises are most susceptible to accelerated decline and failure because of their heavy reliance on an individual entrepreneur or next-generation CEO. Founders often display a natural disdain for organizational architecture, such as establishing systems,

---

[1]Graham, K., Journalistic Family Values, *Wall Street Journal*, March 20, 2000, p. A18.

[2]Carlock, R. & Ward, J., *Strategic Planning for the Family Business*. New York: Palgrave, 2001.

professional managerial practices, and governance mechanisms. And next-generation leaders may also exhibit this disdain for managerial discipline as they engage in the strategic regeneration and growth of the business. After all, professional managerial practices have bureaucratic roots, and the desire to flee from the bureaucracy of a publicly owned global behemoth is frequently the reason for an entrepreneur starting his or her own company.

When multiple members of a family become active in management and/or engaged as shareholders in thinking about the future of the enterprise, disagreements often arise, and paralysis may set in. The varying perspectives of active and inactive shareholders increase the likelihood of conflict. And conflict makes strategic planning a task likely to be avoided.

The speed and agility that once gave a competitive advantage to the family business are often sacrificed across generations. The timeliness with which decisions are made and executed suffers tremendously, robbing a firm of its ability to turn on a dime.

Time lags are likely to be created as the business grows from being run by an entrepreneur (who knew that the cash from a potential sale would either stay in the customer's pocket or move to his or her pocket) to being run by the family or management. The firm may rely on management meetings and six sigma process improvement objectives to achieve quality and may have to hold family meetings to educate shareholders on business strategy, finance, estate planning, and estate-tax implications (Figure 6.1).

The time lags can be significant, especially when the shareholder ranks change to an ownership-first orientation from a customer-first orientation. This tendency among family-owned companies to focus internally is perhaps the strongest rationale for engaging in strategic planning. Strategic thinking represents a breath of fresh air in

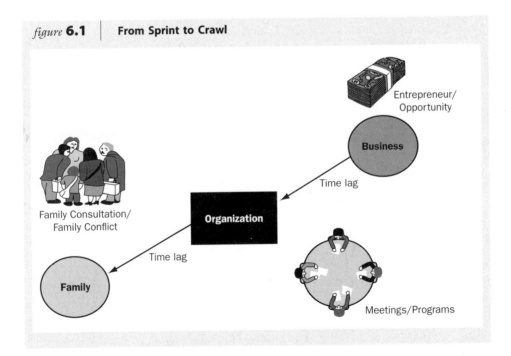

figure **6.1** | **From Sprint to Crawl**

what could otherwise be a vacuum, inhabited by owners and managers oblivious to changes in the competitive environment.

STRATEGIC PLANNING 101 AND THE FAMILY BUSINESS

Perhaps the most influential work ever in strategic planning, *Competitive Advantage*, by Michael Porter, was published in 1980.[3] More than 25 years later, his work is still profoundly relevant. It is particularly so for family businesses, which often populate the middle to downstream portions of a supply chain. In these positions, competitive advantage is dictated as much by capabilities as by the dynamics embedded in the industry in which they compete. Porter's work suggested that competitive intensity is a function of five forces: (1) the threat of new entrants, (2) the bargaining power of buyers, (3) the threat of substitute products, (4) the bargaining power of suppliers, and (5) the rivalry that exists among existing firms as a result of the first four forces and the number and relative power of competitors, industry growth, high fixed costs, lack of differentiation or high switching costs and high barriers to exit.

Picture the domestic airline industry as you read the list of contributors to rivalry, the fifth force. But even in that dreadful situation, there are effective competitors like Southwest, JetBlue, and, among the legacy carriers, Continental. So the right strategy and its execution matters.

The threat of new entrants, the first force, is conditioned by capital requirements for entry, product differentiation (including through patents and proprietary technology), the economies of scale available to firms in that industry, the costs incurred in switching providers, the access to distribution channels by the new entrants, and any other cost disadvantages resulting from location, government subsidies, access to raw materials, and learning-curve effects.

Porter suggests that the bargaining power of buyers, the second of the five forces in his model, also influences the capacity to create competitive advantage. If the buyer purchases large volumes compared to the seller's sales, if the buyer purchases are a significant portion of the buyer's total costs, and if the products bought are undifferentiated, the buyer faces low switching costs. The buyer is well ahead particularly if the product is not critical to the quality of the buyer's products. Picture the U.S. auto industry in its relationship to thousands of family-owned suppliers. Nevertheless, many small- to mid-sized family-owned parts suppliers, metal stampers, and plastic injection molders, for example, have successfully grown their revenues and profits under these conditions through high-quality, high-service, partner-like product development relationships and proprietary technology.

Substitute products, the third force, is conditioned on technological breakthroughs, the degree to which the technology in the product is proprietary or widely accessible, and its costs.

The model argues that the fourth force, supplier bargaining power is also critical. Suppliers have power when there are few suppliers who are not facing the threat of substitute products, the customer is not an important one to the supplier but the supplier product is an important input for the buyer, the supplier product is differentiated, or the supplier poses the threat of forward integration.

---

[3]Porter, M., *Competitive Advantage*. Boston: Harvard Business School Press, 1980.

Depending on the impact of the five forces on your firm's industry, Porter argues, there are three generic strategies available for competitive advantage: cost leadership (Dell is a good example), differentiation (the family-controlled Research in Motion's Blackberry is an example), and focus, a customized hybrid of cost and differentiation approaches for a particular niche or market segment (family-controlled Marriott Hotels, with their broad spectrum of branded properties from Ritz-Carlton to Fairfield Inns, is a lucid example).

While industry dynamics are all-important to the competitive dynamics underlying the playing field for a particular firm, business owners and managers are always looking for what they can do to improve their own lot, regardless of what that lot currently is. Over time, strategic planning moved from Porter's Five Force model to more action-oriented and strategy-implementation-focused approaches. One of these was the development of a tool that achieved widespread diffusion: the analysis of relative strengths, weaknesses, opportunities, and threats (SWOT).

As practiced by one of the pioneers of that era, Ram Charan, the analysis would begin by looking at the business and its environment and asking these questions: What are the most critical changes in the business's environment that have occurred in the past few years? What additional critical changes do you foresee affecting the business in the next few years? What are the implications of these changes for the mission of the business, and which represent threats and which opportunities?

Then the strategy, or direction in which management is taking the firm, would be identified (ideally in about 1000 words). This preliminary strategy would be evaluated and its implications for the industry (including possible reactions by competitors) explored. Then the planning group would engage in competitor analysis by asking the following questions: Who are the major competitors, accounting for 60 to 80 percent of the market share? What is the basis of competition—quality, customer service, delivery speed, cost, or something else? And how does this company stack up against each one of its major competitors on each of the factors that make up the basis of competition? A matrix chart (Table 6.1) would then be developed to summarize the relative competitiveness of the firm. The relative strengths and weaknesses would be discussed and how the company would meet its objectives by using company strengths and exploiting competitor weaknesses would be mapped out as part of strategy development.

Finally, all this analysis would be summarized in a marketing-strategy-and-implementation plan that outlines a financial plan with the allocation of resources, changes needed in the organization, and a disciplined execution plan with action steps, people responsible for the action to be taken, and follow-up or completion dates.

While eminently practical, some of these later developments in the strategic planning field led a number of practitioners to gloss over the painstaking and time-consuming work of setting a direction, carving it in stone, communicating it, and repeating the message over and over again. Critics argued that the net result of all the new analysis and implementation-planning methods was that CEOs were now relieved of going out to employees, to suppliers, and to customers, and obsessively talking about the essence: "This is what we stand for and this is how we wish to conduct business" until everyone understood it and was committed to being different from the competition. After all, being different is what strategy is all about. In the absence of being different, the only basis of competition is cost.

More-recent developments in strategic planning include a positive approach. According to this approach, the secret to successful strategy is to build on strengths,

| table **6.1** | **Basis of Competition SWOT Analysis** |

Product Line: [Basis of Competition]

Competitors	Market Share, percent	Quality +/–/0	Ease of Use +/–/0	Speed +/–/0
A (Own firm)				
B (Other competitors)				
C				
D				
E				
F				
Total Market	100 percent			

This table uses quality, ease of use, and delivery speed as examples of the basis of competition in the industry. Firms get a plus sign (+) if they compete favorably (are strong) on that basis relative to the other competitors, a (–) if they are weak relative to the competition, and a (0) if they are neutral, that is, if that factor did not represent a strength or a weakness relative to the competition.

core competencies, and sources of value uniquely available to a particular company. Because, as previously outlined in this book, the core competitive advantage of a family business lies in its unique ownership form and the unique sources of value this creates, it is this more recent approach to being different that will be treated more thoroughly in the sections that follow.

Being creatively different is at the heart of the success of a family business, and strategy matters. Strategic planning requires a new level of communication among family members, between the family and management and between management and the board. It also requires ample financial and market information. And in a family business, strategy requires building on the different perspectives and the predictable disagreements across generations, generations who in their love and respect for each other attempt to reconcile the wisdom of the past with the much-needed focus on the future.

THE ZERO-SUM FAMILY DYNAMIC AND STRATEGIC PLANNING

Besides the critically important business function of strategic planning for family-controlled companies, by promoting much-needed communication among shareholders, it also performs a key family function. Engaging in conversations about the corporation's plans for the future creates a predisposition to open additional channels of communication, thereby counteracting the natural propensity for secrecy found particularly among first- and second-generation firms. It also helps define the individual as part of an interdependent network—the extended family—in a way that today's society, with its preference for rugged individualism, seldom does. Few things are as damaging to the long-term survival of family-controlled firms as secrecy and "me-ism" among those who hold shares in the corporation. A zero-sum dynamic exists within a family business when there is no business growth; golden opportunities for some stakeholders are linked to lost opportunities for others, resulting in no net gain at the level of the extended family. The zero-sum dynamic is a precursor to business failure and disharmony in the family.

In the absence of growth, zero-sum dynamics becomes a corrosive influence, often overriding the goodwill and best intentions of even the healthiest of families. In a declining business, family conflicts can easily get the upper hand. Any centralization of power carried out to address the decline represents a gain of control by some and a reduction in participation by others. This often leads to the erosion of individual responsibility and the desire to blame others. The vicious cycle continues as the goal becomes protecting individual interests or minimizing personal risk as opposed to growing the business or maximizing its gains. When this happens, promising alternatives for growth may be rejected as competition and in-fighting for resources—and for right or might—spread.

In the business, employee morale suffers and turnover increases. In the family, conflict may reach crisis proportions.[4] A study of small private companies showed that these businesses are much more susceptible to the effects of decline than are larger publicly traded corporations.[5] It seems that the greater momentum and larger pool of accumulated resources, human and financial, act as buffers against an environment that threatens a firm's survival. In plain language, evidence shows that when the pie is not getting larger, family shareholders often begin to fight over the size of their slices.

Strategic planning, with its natural bias toward growth, serves a family-controlled company well, because growth is the source of new jobs, increased wealth, developmental opportunities, influence, and greater family unity. Growth, as described here, is not a goal in itself, but rather it is the outcome of thinking strategically about the future. In other words, efforts to create value for customers also create wealth and career opportunities for shareholders.

After almost 100 years of operation, the McIlhenny Company, makers of the peppery Tabasco Sauce, formulated a strategic plan for growth. Accustomed to receiving substantial dividends from operations, shareholders had become concerned about the dilution of dividends as the next generation grew to 90 members. Leaders of this family-owned company decided that the risk of unhealthy conflict among family members dictated that the company grow in order to avoid the zero-sum family dynamic. New products were created and product lines extended, even though in the short term this meant that shareholder dividends would be even lower in order to reinvest in the business and gun the engines of growth. But as a result of shareholder commitment to the growth strategy, the Tabasco label now graces not just the little bottle of red hot sauce, but bottles of a variety of chili sauces and ready-to-add spicy mixes for Cajun-style home cooking.

---

[4]Poza, E., *Smart Growth: Critical Choices for Family Business Continuity.* San Francisco: Jossey-Bass, 1989; Cleveland: University Publishers, 1997.

[5]Cameron, K., Whetten, D., & Kim, M., Organizational Dysfunctions and Decline. *Academy of Management Journal, 30*(1), 1987, pp. 126–138.

CREATING VALUE WITH UNIQUE BUSINESS MODELS

The term *business model* was first popularized during the Internet bubble era. It was then dismissed by many as part of what did not work about that era. Still, every business has a business model—what has made the business successful so far—whether explicit or not. They capture the firm's underlying logic (how the pieces fit together) and its strategy for creating and capturing value in its supply chain. Business models matter because they help make explicit the assumptions of cause-and-effect relationships in business success. They provide the language for conversations on strategy— how our firm is different from the competition and how we can translate that into creating value in unique ways for our customers. Successful businesses create and capture significant value by doing things that differentiate them from the competition.

Firms wanting to pass on the knowledge of what has worked so far for the business to the next generation and those knowing that they have to change the recipe some in order to remain successful for another generation need to make this knowledge explicit and engage owners and managers in adapting it to the current realities of the firm.

How do family-controlled enterprises create value for their customers and capture that value in a path to greater profitability? Speed and agility have already been mentioned as competitive advantages often inherent in entrepreneurial and small, privately held companies with first-generation leadership. The result of unique organizational capabilities, speed allows the business to stay close to the customer, whether through personal or digitally enabled relationships, and to detect when the customer needs change. Dell, the owner-managed computer and digital services company, is well known for its speed. Michael Dell has been the architect of a company that not only makes customized computers quickly through its innovative choice board on the Internet but also accelerates cash flow and asset turns by collecting on the sale before the company even orders the necessary raw materials and assembles the computer. Family-controlled Research in Motion, well-known for its very successful Blackberry handheld device, has also moved quickly and nimbly among giants in the wireless and telecommunications industries.

The seven primary sources of value on which family companies can build competitive advantage are: (1) financial resources, such as cash and securities; (2) physical assets, such as plants and equipment; (3) the product (sometimes protected by patents) and its price and performance; (4) brand equity, which is the market's perception of a distinction in quality or reputation, a perception created over time; (5) organizational capabilities, which are the competencies residing in employees and unique organizational architectures; (6) customer–supplier integration (once called "distribution and logistics"), which includes new ways of getting the product or service to the customer in any form, at any time, and in any place[6]; and (7) a positive family–business relationship, the source of patient family capital. Combining these seven sources of value in various ways, as if different pieces in a custom-assembled puzzle, will give rise to a unique business model, one that is rooted in the core competencies of the business and can create value for both the owners and the customers. (See Figure 6.2 for a graphic representation of this model.) Competitive advantages created by real assets (such as

---

[6]Boulton, R., Libert, B., & Samek, S., *Cracking the Value Code*. New York: HarperCollins, 2000.

figure **6.2** | **Sources of Value Creation: The Family-Business Specific Mix**

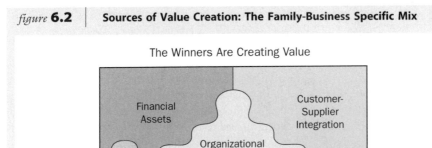

financial resources and equipment) can be copied or cloned and are often temporary and transient. Competitive advantages created by intangible assets (people, their knowledge and skills, company values, patient family capital, and other organizational capabilities) are often more defensible and longer-lasting. The clear tendency then is for family businesses to create a business model that relies more heavily on the sources of value on the right half of the puzzle.

FINANCIAL RESOURCES

Traditionally, family-owned companies have bemoaned the fact that they are at a disadvantage when competing with global publicly traded corporations. The financial and physical assets of public companies dwarf those of all but the largest family-owned companies—like Mars, Inc., with over $30 billion in annual revenues and more than 60,000 employees after its purchase of the Wm. Wrigley Jr. Company in 2008. Unlike Mars, many family-controlled companies have addressed this perceived disadvantage by going public, while retaining voting control by the family. The Washington Post Company is a case in point; in its quest to grow in editorial influence and business reach, it went public in 1971.

Financial constraints are clearly a barrier to the healthy growth of family-owned businesses.[7] Unless the business regularly avails itself of the financial markets by issuing debt and equity (or the company is in the insurance or banking business, both of which are great cash generators), financial assets are not likely to be a source of value for a unique business model.

The beauty of creating value for customers, shareholders, and employees through a unique business model is that it helps the business stand out from competition in the marketplace. A unique model that has the capacity to deliver value (a capacity that the business models of many of the dot-coms operating in the spring of 2000 did not have)

---

[7]See, for example, Gallo, M.A., & Sveen, J., Internationalizing the Family Business, *Family Business Review*, 4 (2), Summer 1991, pp. 181–190.

will likely provide a level of differentiation and sustainable competitive advantage that cookie-cutter strategies or financial resouurce–intensive strategies cannot provide.

PHYSICAL ASSETS

Physical assets are seldom major contributors to value creation. The advantages implicit in the "big get bigger" folklore have been wildly exaggerated. The ratios of sales to physical assets of two global behemoths, Microsoft and U.S. Steel, provide a little perspective on the subject. Microsoft's ratio is 12.26, while U.S. Steel's is only 1.96, as a result of its oversized investment in plant and equipment.[8] Which company has greater cash flows and has created more shareholder value? In June 2008, after a severe multiyear decline in the value of technology stocks and multiyear global appreciation in steel producers because of the infrastructure demand from China and India, Microsoft's market capitalization was still $266 billion, more than 13 times greater than that of U.S. Steel. Of course, successful competition in the steel industry requires significant assets. But, as mini-mills and other innovators in the industry have shown, these assets need not always be in the quantities held by larger, integrated steel producers.

Most family-controlled enterprises today are better served by explicitly choosing *not* to base value creation on physical assets, recognizing both their own fiscally conservative profile and the potential financial danger that such assets represent. As technology, market requirements, and customer needs and wants change, physical assets have a tremendous ability to become liabilities.

THE PRODUCT: ITS PRICE AND PERFORMANCE

The product itself—sometimes protected by patents—and its price and performance can be sources of value creation. Although these sources of value are often associated with technology firms, engineers, inventors, and tinkerers have created many of today's mainstream businesses in low-tech environments. Honey-Baked Hams of Cincinnati, Ohio, for example, owes much of its current success to the fact that its founder's invention, a spiral-cutting machine, was repeatedly rejected by large meat processors. Desperate, but not prone to giving up easily, founder George Kurz decided to take advantage of patent protection on the machine to establish a ham-retailing operation. Instead of building a manufacturing operation to produce ham-cutting equipment, he built a retail empire.

Over three generations, owner-managers turned what began as a product performance advantage (with the design for the slicing machine sketched on the back of a paper napkin) into a brand-equity advantage. Customers value the difference that the spiral cut produces in the ham's taste and are willing to pay a premium for it.[9]

BRAND EQUITY

Brand equity is a well-known source of value for family-controlled companies. Casual-clothing manufacturers (e.g., Levi Strauss), hotel chains (e.g., Marriott), and brewing companies (e.g., Corona's Modelo) all have it, as do many fashion houses (e.g., Ralph

---

[8]Davis, S., & Meyer, C., *Future Wealth*. Boston: Harvard Business School Press, 2000.
[9]Author's personal conversation with George Kurz, June 2001.

Lauren and Hermès), fragrance producers (e.g., Estée Lauder and Carolina Herrera), and wine and spirits companies (e.g., Cakebread and Bacardi).

The Washington Post Company is a family-controlled company that enjoys significant brand equity. The brand equity of this diversified media organization results largely from a commitment to quality journalism and independent thinking, forged during a turbulent period in the 1970s when the company decided to publish both the Pentagon Papers and stories about the Watergate scandal. In her later years, Katharine Graham devoted much of her time to public speaking and writing that enhanced the Post's brand equity. During this time, she relied on her son, Don Graham, third-generation publisher and CEO, to run the company with a team of nonfamily managers.

The Post's nonvoting B stock is publicly traded. Voting control, however, rests in the A stock owned by Don Graham and his three siblings. The Post had approximately 19,000 employees, annual revenues of $4.2 billion, and profits of $289 million in 2007. In addition to publishing the *Washington Post*, the company owns *Newsweek* magazine, six network-affiliated TV stations, a cable network with more than 600,000 subscribers, education-related businesses (e.g., Kaplan), and interests in other media-related companies.[10]

ORGANIZATIONAL CAPABILITIES

Often, brand equity was built over many years through unique values and organizational capabilities. What values and organizational capabilities are responsible for most of the value creation of family-controlled companies? Fisk Johnson, president of SC Johnson: A Family Company, has said that it is the people—who care about the customer and each other—who make his company customer-oriented, flexible, and fast. When asked the meaning of the company theme "Family values ... World class results," he said that it means "replacing chlorofluorocarbons or CFCs from aerosol products much earlier than the competition and government regulations would have had us do, because we knew our customers cared about the environment and we did too." Without a hint of boasting in his voice, he added, "And we took CFC out of our entire product line in five working days, unheard of in our industry." This speed and nimbleness are the result of an organizational capability built on several generations of skilled people who care about their customers and the integrity of their products.[11]

In addition to values, unique organizational capabilities also include internal processes in administration or manufacturing—for example, processes that streamline the flow of information, resources, or parts within the firm. Companies with unique organizational capabilities are capable of differentiating themselves and creating value in ways that others find difficult to replicate, whether through enterprise-management systems, electronically enabled product-development teams, or the simpler but equally significant interdisciplinary project teams and multi-skilled manufacturing, service, and procurement or supply teams.

---

[10]Hoover's Company Profile, http://www.hoover.com, and Fidelity Investments research data, July 2005.

[11]Author's personal conversation with Fisk Johnson, June 1996.

CUSTOMER–SUPPLIER INTEGRATION

Because of the significant influence of PCs and the Internet on sourcing and logistics, the traditional distribution system has changed dramatically, and so have the relationships and relative power of firms across the entire value-added chain. During the 1990s, many family-owned distribution and retail companies feared for their survival as their suppliers developed a web presence and threatened to take out the "middlemen." Consolidators, with Wall Street financing, bought out many of these family-owned businesses that feared for their future. While the fears proved greatly exaggerated, profit margins, ways of doing business, and the relative power of firms in their respective distribution chains were forever changed.

The firms that survived know a thing or two about sustainable competitive advantage. Yet they must continually ask themselves: To what extent do we need to deploy a digital strategy that will enhance our relationship with suppliers, customers, and our customers' customers? The changes that the Internet has wrought on the value-added chain in almost every industry—notwithstanding the demise of a significant number of dot-coms—have only begun to be discernible. Just as the Internet did not totally replace television, radio, and newspapers, new customer–supplier integration networks will not totally eradicate more traditional distribution channels and relationships. But it is certain that the Internet and its applications have eroded, and will continue to erode, some of the value of traditional approaches, thereby making it harder to create value for customers without somehow adding digital service capacity to the mix.

At Madco, a distribution company with $26 million in annual revenues, two generations of owner-managers argued for months about whether to engage in digitally enabled distribution. While the father/CEO wanted nothing to do with a strategy that could possibly cannibalize their existing business, the son/vice president of information technology was confident that, if Madco did not move into the digital arena, another firm, perhaps from outside their industry, would come in and serve that customer need.

THE NATURE OF THE FAMILY–BUSINESS RELATIONSHIP

The nature of the interaction between the business and the family constitutes a unique competency and source of value in family-owned and family-controlled businesses. When this interaction is characterized by family unity and forward-thinking by family members, companies are more likely to engage in managerial and governance practices that control agency costs and bank on unique resources that produce idiosyncratic organizational capabilities.

To better understand this issue, researchers in the Discovery Action Research study asked the following questions: To what extent may family unity and the unique interaction between the family and the business be measured? and To what extent is the interaction associated with the behavior of the firm?[12] Results of this study indicated that firms with significantly different scores on the family unity index, business

---

[12]Poza, E., Johnson, S., & Alfred, T., Changing the Family Business Through Action Research. *Family Business Review*, 11(4), 1998, pp. 311–323.

opportunity index, and family–business interaction variable also had significantly different scores on the management and governance practices index.

Family unity was found to correlate positively with effective management and governance practices, including strategic planning activity, performance feedback, succession planning disclosure, advisory boards, and family meetings. These findings seem to indicate that investing in the family's health and harmony—by establishing guidelines for family participation in the business and the employment of family members, setting clear standards and processes for succession and ownership transfer, and nurturing ways of promoting cooperation and positive relations among family members—pays off for the firm.[13] They further support the idea that family meetings, retreats, and councils can play important roles in promoting the effectiveness and continuity of a family business by creating among family members a new reality characterized by goodwill, team problem-solving, and recognition of business opportunities.[14]

Since laws of economics and competitive dynamics apply equally to family-controlled companies and management-controlled corporations, any competitive advantages gained by family businesses must be the result of strategic thinking and a commitment to uniquely creating value for the customer. The aura of a "family effect" does not suspend the demands of a constantly changing competitive environment.[15] But the results of the Discovery study suggest that family unity and effective family–business interaction make certain practices and strategies more likely and sustainable. For example, study results indicate that steps taken to promote family unity also make strategic planning processes more likely. The study results also suggest the converse—that one of the unique goals of family-owned companies, family unity, is more likely to be achieved by running the business like a business, using the latest management and governance practices, including strategic planning.

And strategic-planning processes have already been linked in several family-business studies to family-business continuity.[16]

THE LIFECYCLE OF THE FIRM, THE FAMILY, AND THE NEED FOR PARALLEL STRATEGIC PLANNING

Because of the unique nature of the relationship between the family and the business in a family business and the substantial contribution to a unique set of competitive advantages derived from this relationship, strategic planning in a family firm relies on a parallel process. That is, it requires both the shareholders (family owners) and the management (often a team of owner-managers and nonfamily managers) to think about, plan, and execute strategy in tandem. It is to the benefit of the family business, and not just to the family, to acknowledge the wishes of the owners in its

---

[13]Habbershon, T., & Astrachan, J., Perceptions Are Reality: How Family Meetings Lead to Collective Action, *Family Business Review, 10*(1), 1997, pp. 37–52.

[14]de Visscher, F., When Shareholders Lose Their Patience. *Family Business Magazine, 11*(4), Autumn 2000, pp. 9–12.

[15]See Poza, op. cit.; and Ward, J., *Keeping the Family Business Healthy.* San Francisco: Jossey-Bass, 1987.

[16]Litz, R., & Kleysen, R., Your Old Men Shall Dream Dreams, Your Young Men Shall See Visions: Toward a Theory of Family Firm Innovation with Help from the Brubeck Family. *Family Business Review, 14*(4), 2001, pp. 335–351.

strategic-planning activity and to expect in return enough shareholder commitment for family capital to behave patiently, allowing for tax-effcient transfers of this capital and a long-term perspective on the strategy of the business.

Both the systems theory and resource-based perspectives of family business, as discussed in Chapter 1, argue for a better alternative to the family-first or business-first approach to family business. They suggest that approaches that jointly optimize the family–business interaction are far superior. These approaches give rise to unique resources that allow the family firm to enjoy distinct competitive advantages while controlling or "governing" issues and challenges (like undue family influence in management decisions) uniquely confronting them.

The first challenge to joint optimization of a family and business is posed by the potential for being out-of-sync in terms of time and life cycle, as discussed below.

The statistics on the long-term survival of family-owned businesses are alarming. Entrepreneurial firms have a dismal record with respect to preserving the spirit of innovation that motivated their founding and propelled them through their early years. In fact, only about 30 percent of these firms survive under the same owning family beyond the first generation. Only about 12 percent survive to the third generation, and only 4 percent survive to the fourth.[17]

Beyond the exciting and exhausting start-up phase and the subsequent growth phase lies organizational maturity. At the mature stage, the business represents a complex set of stakeholders: the banks that have financed the growth, the family members who have worked in the firm since high school or college, the key nonfamily managers who have contributed substantially to the business's success, other family members with financial and/or emotional interests in the enterprise, other investors, lower-level employees, and the government. As discussed at the beginning of this book, each of these stakeholders has a different perspective on the enterprise and feels entitled, for different reasons, to certain benefits or returns. Banks want timely debt repayment, profitable new lines of credit, and no surprises. Family members often seek shareholder value creation and high returns on equity, along with employment opportunities. For key nonfamily managers, market-based compensation, career opportunities, and high regard by the owners are essential. Like politicians who run election campaigns according to poll results, leaders of family-controlled enterprises, overwhelmed by the complexity of the stakeholder base, may lose the vision that was so much a part of the young organization. This absence of vision often sets the stage for decline (Figure 6.3).

Add to this the CEO/entrepreneur's well-deserved feeling of satisfaction at having finally achieved success, wealth, and influence; maturity of the business brings great risk of protracted decline, leading to the eventual sale or death of the enterprise. But is this total overlap between the life cycle of a founder and his/her firm really necessary? More to the point, does the firm have to die when its founder retires, falls ill, or dies?

What happens to the family business when we acknowledge its own life cycle as related to but separate from the life cycles of the individual CEO, the industry, the shareholders, and the family? Randy Carlock, then a professor at the University of St. Thomas and a former business owner himself, captured the complexity in the diagram shown in Figure 6.4, that he used in co-teaching the MBA-level family-business management course with his associate Thomas Hubler.

---

[17]Ward, J., *Keeping the Family Business Healthy: How to Plan for Continued Growth, Profitability and Family Leadership.* San Francisco: Jossey-Bass, 1987.

figure **6.3** | **Stages of Business Development**

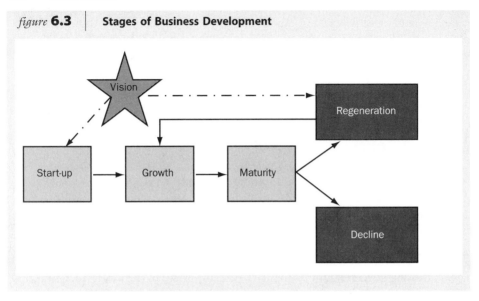

The complexity can easily be overwhelming. Because of family life cycles, what one generation of the family sees as a priority may not be what the next generation perceives as being fundamental. Because of the ownership life cycle, what one branch considers fair may not be what another branch is advocating. Because of the firm's life cycle, what the firm needs in order to remain competitive (reinvestment) may very well not be what shareholders (ownership lifecycle) had in mind when several of them committed to a significant investment outside the firm in a family real estate partnership. For that matter, what the industry in general is experiencing (contraction and consolidation) may be requiring a batten-down-the-hatches strategic orientation for the next few years just as the next generation joins the business full of optimism and looking for growth and opportunity.

Leading-edge practitioners, best-in-class family businesses globally, and scholarly research all point to some promising approaches to this real, not overly dramatized, complexity of the family firm. The most promising of the options is parallel strategic-planning activity by the top management team and the family council or family assembly (see Chapters 3, 10, and 11 for more detail on these bodies) mediated and finally ratified by a company's board of directors.

It usually begins with candid conversations among family-business shareholders in the safe environment of a family council. Over a series of meetings, shareholders develop a family vision that encompasses the desired relations, going forward, between the family and its business. Shareholders may also reaffirm their commitment to continued family control of the business from generation to generation, or not. Perhaps they commit only to one more generation, letting each generation tackle this choice anew. Next, shareholders discuss and develop policies that respond to questions about requirements that family members need to meet before they are hired into the business, their desire to have it continue as a family business that is professionally managed, their expectations on returns on family capital (for example, mimum 15 percent return on investment) and their willingness to reinvest in the business for continued growth.

figure **6.4** | **Life Cycle Stages Influencing Family-Business Strategy**

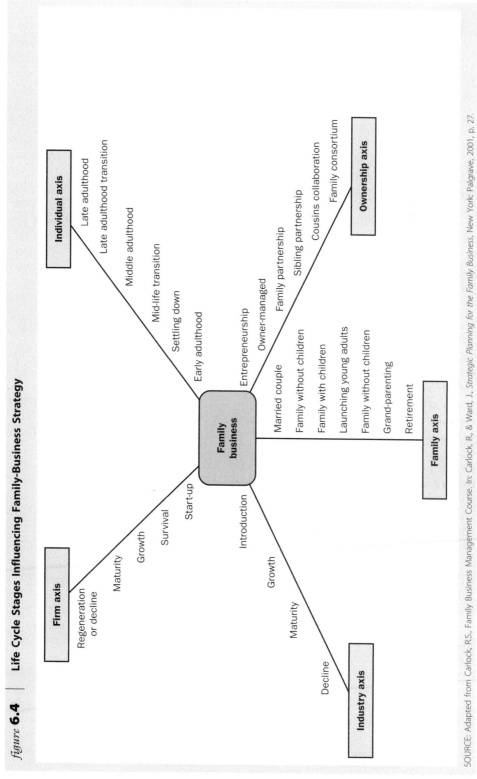

SOURCE: Adapted from Carlock, R.S., Family Business Management Course. In: Carlock, R., & Ward, J., *Strategic Planning for the Family Business*, New York: Palgrave, 2001, p. 27.

Simultaneously, more-formal strategic-planning processes are taking place in the management ranks. These analyze the competition, the firms's strengths and weaknesses in relation to competitors, changes and trends in the industry, and the firm's supply chain, resulting in a summary strategy statement that flags unique challenges and opportunities. And the culmination of this work is the identification of a set of strategic actions requiring human, organizational, and financial resources.

The dual-path trajectory of the parallel strategic-planning process then intersects. In a strategic-planning session of the board of directors, where family shareholder interests as well as purely business interests are represented (via key family and perhaps nonfamily managers and independent members of the board), strategic choices are made, and the business model of the family business is updated.

Perhaps it goes without saying that the "purely business interests" referred to in the previous paragraph are really the business customers' interests. Family and nonfamily managers alike have to lead the family business in ways that create value for the customer and enable it to capture the value created via profitable operation of the business. In other words, in this parallel strategic-planning process, the CEO, family-business leaders, and board members are the advocates of customers' changing interests, tastes, and priorities. By advocating those interests fervently, they make it possible for shareholders to trust the promise of long-term shareholder value creation.

THE CUSTOMER-ORIENTED COMPANY

The enterprise that creates value for its employees and shareholders (the family) first creates value for its customers. This family business has come to understand that, in today's economy, being successful requires providing customers with the service or product they want in any form, at any time, and in any place. In order to accomplish this, the customer-oriented company relies heavily on unique organizational capabilities and core competencies that have translated into competitive advantage precisely because they respond to what customers value.

Many owners of family-controlled companies eloquently discuss what they consider to be their traditional core competencies: quality products/services, skilled employees, and speed and agility. What is largely missing from both the strategic-planning literature and the conventional wisdom of practicing owner-managers is an analysis of whether these competencies add value from the customer's perspective.

What matters to customer-oriented companies is the outcome from the perspective of the customer who is using their product or service. Only if customers see value in what a particular organizational capability does for them can that capability turn into a competitive advantage for the firm (see Table 6.1). Because customer needs are constantly changing, strategic planning may require a reevaluation of these competencies as family-owned and family-controlled companies move from one generation to the next. An organizational realignment may even be needed to pursue value creation from a customer's perspective.

The practical implication of Figure 6.5 for the often internally focused world of the entrepreneur and business owner is that an individual capability or set of capabilities may become unimportant to customers when, for example, lower prices from competitors override qualitative considerations such as delivery speed, product or service quality, proprietary technology, customer service, brand equity, and customization capacity. Alternatively, what are thought to be core competencies may be more fiction than fact. For example, the company may have made a premium-quality product once

figure **6.5** | **Turning Core Competencies into Competitive Advantages**

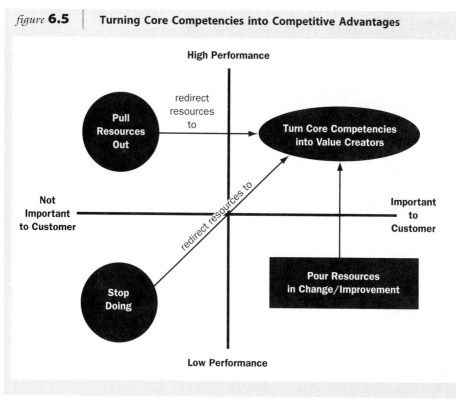

upon a time, but today's product may not be considered superior by customers who also purchase from competitors.

The result of both of these dynamics in a globally competitive marketplace is that business owners have to continuously ask themselves two questions: (1) Is the product or service we are providing still important to the customer? (2) Is what we are producing or supplying still performing at a superior level? Based on the answers to these questions, resources may need to be moved out of some areas and into others to ensure that the current set of core competencies truly results in competitive advantage. Ultimately, only those capabilities valued by the customer provide the family firm with opportunities for gaining differentiation and competitive advantage. And to the extent that the core-competency-turned-competitive-advantage is a resource rooted in the unique family–business interaction, it may be difficult for others to replicate.

STRATEGIC PLANNING AND DISCIPLINED EXECUTION

Strategy planning in a family business is not a grand analytical exercise. It is more like playing improvisational jazz, guided by the lead musician's vision for the piece. But the vision, the direction, is anything but experimental. Strategy making is guided by the owner's vision for the future and a legacy derived from the firm's competencies, both of which insulate the process from chaos and loss of control.

MINICASE

The veteran jazz musician Dave Brubeck and his wife, Iola, have five sons and one daughter. Four of the sons have chosen to pursue musical careers. Dave insisted that the children take piano lessons while they were young so that they would acquire musical competency, but he had no interest in their launching musical careers. Although they usually work as independent musicians, Dave and his four sons have collaborated on several musical projects, including the 1974 album *Two Generations of Brubeck* and the 1997 album *In Their Own Sweet Way*. In their collaborations, family members tend to welcome exploration and discovery.[18] Dave's oldest son, Darius, commented, "Even though the music is deeply familiar, almost subconsciously so for me, rehearsals take a long time because we all contribute ideas—anything is worth a try—and because Dave keeps astonishing me with the depth and breadth of his creativity. There is probably overall more humor and risk taking. In two words: It's fun."[19]

[18]Litz & Kleysen, op. cit.
[19]Gloyd, R., Notes from the Producer, from the Telarc recording *In Their Own Sweet Way*, CD-83355.

Among those who contribute to "strategy jam" sessions in a family business may be family members with controlling ownership and key nonfamily managers. Contributors may also include directors of the board or advisory board members who review the strategy developed by management and controlling family members. Crafting a strategy from the accumulated wisdom of the current generation of owners and managers, the dreams and aspirations of the next generation, and the timeless wisdom of loyalty to one's customers leads to innovation and healthy growth for the business across generations.

General systems theory suggests that as environments become more turbulent or fast-changing, the challenge for businesses is to build the requisite ability to deal with variety.[20] As an increasing number of new and unpredictable events occur, companies either develop the ability to deal with that variety or fail to respond appropriately and thus fail to thrive in the new environment. Although the Royal Dutch/Shell Group is not a family-controlled company, it provides a good example of the ability to meet new challenges because it did what seemed at the time to be impossible: It thrived during the oil crisis of the 1970s. Its approach to strategic planning was rooted in creating multiple scenarios of competitive conditions in the world marketplace. In effect, Shell's top management bet on "preparedness," as the military calls it, discussing many alternative scenarios rather than focusing on the most likely scenario and then building a strategy to fit it. Shell used the strategic-planning process not as an exercise in predictability, but as a way to increase the skills of top management in dealing with variety.

Despite Shell's success, not many companies have increased their agility by adding the requisite ability to deal with variety through strategic-planning efforts. After all, developing a budget to support the chosen strategy is the next step, and budgets require some degree of certainty and predictability. Indeed, in many corporations,

[20]Miller, J., Living Systems: Basic Concepts, *Behavioral Science*, *10*(3), July, 1965, pp. 193–237.

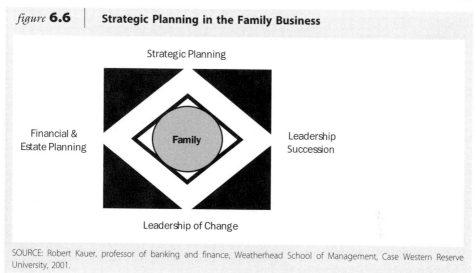

figure **6.6** | **Strategic Planning in the Family Business**

SOURCE: Robert Kauer, professor of banking and finance, Weatherhead School of Management, Case Western Reserve University, 2001.

predictability in the face of changes or variances are what budgets and strategic plans are all about.

For CEOs of family-controlled companies, one of the essential aspects of preparedness is succession and continuity planning. They will lead the succession process only once in their lifetimes, and they must prepare for it through sound strategic thinking. Succession is not an event. Rather, it is a series of new and unpredictable experiences having to do with the management of the business, the leadership of shareholders, and the promotion of long-term family trust and unity (Figure 6.6). Shell Oil bet on preparedness in the face of unpredictable events by investing in increasing top management's mastery of variety and unpredictability. By doing so, it gave its top management and operating systems the skills necessary to improvise, to be nimble, and to win what has become for all businesses an increasingly unpredictable competitive war for customers. Family-controlled companies must emphasize preparedness in their strategic planning—or be prepared to fail.

THE UNIQUE VISION OF FAMILY-CONTROLLED COMPANIES

A unique vision and business model are needed to lead an enterprise to competitive fitness. However, after 25 years as an observer and advisor to family-controlled companies around the world, I believe that it is possible to list a set of preferred strategies used by family-controlled companies to create value for customers in differentiated ways. The list that follows is not meant to be a shortcut to creating a unique and creative strategy or an enticement to use cookie-cutter strategies. Developing strategy is hard work. Strategy is about making choices, and choosing to be different. Companies, particularly the often less well-capitalized family companies, cannot afford to be all things to all people.

What this list is meant to reinforce is the idea that, however fragile family-controlled companies may appear in a fast-changing competitive environment seemingly dominated by global behemoths, regenerating and growing the enterprise in the interest of continuity is neither easy nor quick, but it is eminently doable. Family-controlled companies have turned the following competencies into value creators for their customers and, thus, into competitive advantages for their firms:

- Rapid speed to market
- Flexibility and nimbleness in response to customers and competitors
- Strategic focus on proprietary products and specialty niches that afford more protected profits
- Concentrated ownership structure that provides more patient capital and commitment to the long term, enabling the company to build brand equity, promote customer loyalty, and sponsor continued reinvestment in family unity and unique organizational capabilities
- Lower total costs derived from reduced agency costs—for example, in administration, supervision, and financial controls
- High quality of product and/or service that builds brand equity, reputation, and higher profitability
- Capacity for customization

Creating something different that has value for the customer is at the heart of achieving competitive advantage. Family-owned and family-controlled firms frequently rely on the set of competencies just discussed to gain competitive advantage. Clearly, for a family business, strategic planning that focuses on organizational capabilities rooted in intangible assets, including values, family unity, and the nature of the family–business interaction, plays a critical role in developing a unique, hard-to-replicate strategy and business model.

SUMMARY

1 The primary objective of strategic planning in any company is to create value for its customers. Only in this way can it create value for itself.

2 Time lags can be significant, especially when an ownership-first orientation replaces a customer-first orientation.

3 The zero-sum dynamic is a precursor to business failure and disharmony among family-business members. In the absence of growth, family businesses become very vulnerable during the succession process.

4 A steep decline at the end of a successful product line run or the end of a generation's leadership can be the result of the small size of a family business, its propensity for zero-sum family dynamics, limited access to financial assets, and/or the paralysis of business operations.

5 Strategic planning increases owners' and managers' awareness of changes in the competitive environment and promotes much-needed communication among shareholders. With its natural bias toward growth, strategic planning is a great antidote to the challenges of the late maturity and decline stages.

6 The seven primary sources of value for family businesses, giving rise to a unique business model for each family business, are (1) financial resources, (2) physical assets, (3) the product, (4) brand equity, (5) organization capabilities, (6) customer–supplier integration, and (7) the family–business relationship.

7 Competencies that create value for customers and firms include rapid speed to market, flexibility in response to customers and competitors, strategic focus on proprietary products and specialty niches, concentrated ownership structure, reduced agency costs, high quality of product and/or service, and capacity for customization.

Planning
the Estate

Reliance Industries is a conglomerate earning $15 billion in annual revenues (and the subject of Reliance Industries and the Ambani Family case on page 355). Dhirubhai Ambani, its founder, died at the age of 69 without a will. His two sons, Anil and Mukesh, faced succession with a large measure of sibling rivalry and almost brought the business down. Thanks largely to a timely and influential intervention by Kokilaben, their mother, the siblings negotiated an agreement that split the company in two.

Estate planning is a family-business owner's favorite target of procrastination. Planning the estate has the potential to save a business-owning family hundreds of thousands (or millions) of dollars and to allow for continuity of the business, both of which are important to most entrepreneurs and business owners. Still, carrying out the planning is seldom deemed urgent enough to be made a priority. The absence of estate planning puts at risk what has taken a generation or two to build, often doing irreparable damage to the business and to family relationships.

Given the importance of the subject, why is estate and ownership transfer planning often avoided, delayed, or done without comprehensive outside professional help? When it is finally done, why is it often done without consulting those most affected by the plan and its implications?

While time pressures, the cost of professional advisors, and aversion to insurance products and agents are often blamed, irrational optimism is more fundamentally responsible for the failure to plan one's estate. The likelihood of illness and the inevitability of death loom large late in an owner's life. Not wanting to discuss illness and death—and their implications for the family and the business—is an understandable reason to procrastinate. Woody Allen once quipped that he didn't mind dying; he just didn't want to be there when it happened.

Loss of control is another reason people delay planning. Research on entrepreneurs and successful CEOs has found that they have a wide locus of control, which few look forward to giving up. Letting go of the very control that has been a source of advantage, success, autonomy, and personal freedom is not a simple matter. In addition, although successful business builders seem to have no trouble focusing on things they know well, they are quite averse to committing time and energy to a subject with which they are completely unfamiliar. And as if these inherent sources of resistance were not enough, many CEOs fear family conflict. They may be concerned that this kind of planning will require such difficult conversations among family members that open warfare will erupt among them. Some may worry that the outcomes of these difficult discussions will be too uncertain and/or unpleasant to carry out.

A family business is often a family's principal asset or at least a significant portion of a family's net worth. The 1997 American Family Business Survey found a majority of respondents saying that approximately 60 percent of the family's wealth was locked up in the business. One-fifth of all respondents said that 80 percent of the family's wealth was in the business.[1] The most recent survey (2007) found that 71 percent of all family-business owners were very optimistic about the future. Their optimism appears well-founded, as revenues rose 74.4 percent between 2004 and 2007. And many reported growing more quickly (27.1 percent) than their competitors. (Only 15.4 percent reported growing more slowly.)[2]

Because of the importance of the business to the family's economic well-being, the owner's estate plan must treat the business as an ongoing concern and not just a collection of assets. The continued successful management of the business is a priority both for the business to survive and for economic returns to the owning family to continue. Thus, planning for the estate and ownership constitutes a strategic decision. The timely transfer of equity down a generation represents not only a tax-saving transfer of financial resources but could also represent the step necessary to keep the business in the family. This chapter is primarily written with the U.S. estate-tax law provisions in mind. Fortunately, most countries in Europe and a fair number in Asia and Latin America have already abandoned estate taxes on the premise that they discourage capital formation and capital flows, hurt the economy, and are an unfair form of taxation on assets previously taxed.

THE FAMILY-BUSINESS OBITUARY

A family-owned company in Ohio manufactured auto parts. New technologies and the need for precision mold making made it a very capital-intensive business. The family consisted of the parents and five children, only two of whom were active in the business. The company was successful and represented about 75 percent of the parents' net worth. The parents owned 95 percent of the shares in the business. The remaining 5 percent was owned by the lawyer who had originally incorporated the business and took shares in lieu of his customary fee.

Mom and Dad's lifelong intention was for the business to stay in the family. They had not done any planning toward this end because they were both young (53) and had still not decided which of their active children would eventually be the one to run the company. They had standard "me-to-you and you-to me" wills, with the remainder going equally to the kids. The company owned a $9 million key man life insurance policy on the father and CEO. The company had no working board of directors.

On a skiing vacation both parents and one of the inactive (married) daughters were killed in a freak accident. The life insurance and a majority of the nonequity assets were used to pay the estate taxes. What the four surviving children effectively inherited was an interest in the company of almost 20 percent each, with the interest of the deceased sister going to her children.

---

[1] Arthur Andersen/Mass Mutual Family Business Survey, 1997.

[2] Mass Mutual/Kennesaw State/Family Firm Institute, American Family Business Survey, 2007.

table **7.1**	Estate-Tax Exemptions	
Year(s)	**Unified Credit**	
2006–2008	$2.0 million	
2009	$3.5 million	
2010	Unlimited. Zero estate tax during 2010 only.	

Four years after the tragic accident, the company went out of business. Other than the money taken out as salaries by those who had previously been active in the business, the heirs got nothing. First there was a fight between the two active children over who should be CEO. Then, although family meetings were being held on a regular basis, these were never about helping the company succeed but rather about how the five families, since they were equal owners, could get money out of the business. And money they took. Eventually the company was sued—by the 5 percent stockholder—over self-dealing and corporate waste. The husband of the deceased sister convinced the other two inactive siblings to join with him and vote the two active siblings out of a job. One of the active siblings then sued the company for wrongful termination.

Total chaos in the business and conflict in the family occurred because of so little planning. The parents knew what they wanted, but they never put a plan in place to make it happen. This family had created millions in wealth over a generation and then lost it all in 4 years.

ESTATE TAXES

On June 7, 2001, President George W. Bush signed into law the Economic Growth and Tax Relief Reconciliation Act, which changed federal gift and estate-tax provisions. This act is likely to be changed again in the near future, as there have been nearly 100 tax-code changes affecting gift and estate taxes in the past 20 years. In any case, it currently has a sunset provision that makes it applicable only through December 31, 2010. In 2010, and that year only (as of this writing, anyway), there will be no estate-tax liability, and therefore business owners will have the freedom to transfer ownership at death without regard for estate-tax consequences to heirs or to the continuity of the family business. Between now and then, federal estate-tax rates will fall gradually. In 2007, the maximum estate-tax rate fell to 45 percent. The 45 percent estate-tax rate is also effective in 2008 and 2009 and then will vanish in 2010.

The unified credit exemption—which, in 2002–2003, was increased to $1 million, will grow to $3.5 million by 2009 (Table 7.1). This means that, by 2009, a married couple could transfer up to $7 million of their estate free of estate taxes.

State inheritance taxes are another factor that family-business owners must consider in estate planning. Until the 2001 law was passed, 100 percent of state inheritance tax liabilities, up to a certain limit, could be credited against federal taxes. Starting in 2005, inheritance taxes paid at the state level were allowed only as a deduction and not as a credit. This change, which is not widely known, meant that some estates faced an increase rather than a decrease in their total tax liability (combined federal and state estate taxes). Because the specific implications for individual firms and families vary by state and by the size and particulars of the estate, there is no substitute for consulting professional advisors who know the details of the situation.

THE ESTATE PLAN

Business owners who plan their estate with only tax minimization in mind get what they deserve—a reduced tax bill and a business that will not continue across generations.
Lèon Danco, first family business consultant in the world.

The very progressive and substantial nature of the estate tax has driven many family-business owners to focus on tax minimization as the essential element of their estate planning. Certainly, the estate plan needs to ensure sufficient liquidity so that, upon the death of the current generation, the estate taxes and any outstanding debts can be paid without selling or unfavorably mortgaging the business, or selling its assets at distressed prices. Estate taxes are generally due within 9 months after the owner's death. Because equity in a closely held family business is both highly illiquid and unmarketable,[3] and because the U.S. Treasury expects the tax bill to be paid in cash and on time, high estate-tax liabilities pose a significant threat to family businesses whose owners have procrastinated.

Given the complexity of the tax laws and the tendency of business owners to be pressed for time and prone to maintaining control and secrecy, it is no wonder that tax reduction is the primary subject addressed in estate planning. This limited focus in the estate plan represents a risky but frequent turn of events for family businesses facing generational transitions. And it is estimated that 40.3 percent of family businesses will change leadership across generations in the next 10 years.[4]

Many owners consider their estate planning completed when they have selected some transfer-of-wealth approach with their accountant or tax attorney. They fail to address other important aspects of generational transfers, including the following:

- Financial and retirement needs of the CEO and the CEO spouse
- Strategic needs of the business versus financial needs of the estate
- Ownership successor development
- Relationships among family members
- Day-to-day management of the business
- Corporate governance and voting control in the next generation
- Next-generation expectations for the business
- Needs and dreams of individual heirs
- Stewardship capacity of next-generation members as either owners or managers
- Willingness of family members not active in the management of the firm to be loyal shareholders and represent patient family capital
- Economic value of the business to family members who do not participate as employees of the enterprise
- Liquidity needs of inactive or minority shareholders
- Retention of nonfamily top managers and their continued commitment to the enterprise

Estate plans must also consider the possible need for restructuring of corporate forms and assets in order to maximize wealth retention for heirs and for charitable

---

[3]Author's personal conversation with Philip Dawson, June 2002.
[4]Op. cit., Mass Mutual/Kennesaw State/Family Firm Institute, American Family Business Survey, 2007.

giving, if the owner is philanthropically inclined. Some corporate forms and estate-planning techniques will be reviewed later in this chapter.

Because of the appreciation in the value of shareholder equity over time, estate taxes make a compelling argument for an earlier rather than a later transfer of accumulated value to heirs. Over 10 years, a rather modest 6 percent annual growth rate (including inflation) in the value of a family business produces an asset with almost double (1.8 times) its former taxable value. Similarly, a business growing at a healthy, but not extraordinary, 12 percent rate will triple in value in a decade. The dilemma is that, during those 10 years over which the value of the estate is growing, the current generation is probably well served by retaining voting control. That way, the current generation can provide oversight ("nose in, fingers out") while learning more about the next generation—how they perform when tested by competition, recession, periods of fast growth, union negotiations, and in some cases even challenges to their leadership by other family members.

A successful entrepreneur in the product-identification industry efficiently transferred his Pacific Northwest firm to one son precisely as it was about to grow significantly in revenues, profits, and value. He pursued this transfer of ownership with tremendous expediency, convinced that his son had tested positively for his ability to lead the company. He was concerned that gift and estate taxes would make the accomplishment of his dream much harder in a couple of years. So he commissioned a third-party business valuation, gifted almost all of his stock (freezing the value of his estate before equity growth wreaked havoc on it), and paid the appropriate gift taxes, all at the age of 54. He kept the company building and other properties as income-producing assets (leased at market rates to what was now his son's company) and then proceeded to start work in a nearby office suite turned laboratory. He had a new product he wanted to develop and a new business he wanted to grow—he set out to be an entrepreneur all over again. Seldom are transfers of equity ownership, income sources, and control as straightforward as this one was.

An estate plan that encompasses a family business has to address the appropriate allocation of income sources to the founder, his or her spouse, and nonactive family shareholders, as well as the inheritance or beneficial equity interest of the heirs. It also has to address financial control of the corporation via buy–sell agreements, the transfer of voting and nonvoting stock, and the allocation of stock to the appropriately qualified heirs (and, in some cases, employees).

As discussed in previous chapters, family-business leaders wear many hats—those of parent, spouse, CEO, chairman of the board, principal shareholder, and philanthropist, to name just a few. Succession and continuity planning is the most intellectually and emotionally challenging facet of balancing these multiple hats.

PRESERVING SPEED AND AGILITY

Speed and agility are a must for ongoing concerns. Jack Welch, during his tenure as CEO of General Electric, established as a primary mission getting the multi-billion-dollar, multi-million-employee conglomerate to behave like a much smaller firm. He championed organizational innovations like the Work-Out, six sigma processes, and a high-performance culture to make speed and agility core features of GE.

Many family businesses begin as entrepreneurial firms that exploit the speed-and-agility advantage. These companies are capable of turning on a dime. When faced with competition from a large multinational company that needs multiple levels of approval for a new product, system, or approach to the market, family businesses consistently win. Unfortunately, a number of these entrepreneurial companies discover the costs of losing this speed-and-agility advantage. The departure of the CEO/entrepreneur may create a power vacuum, leading to inaction or paralysis. Or a cumbersome trust arrangement or consensus-dependent copresidency, often referred to as an office of the president, may leave a company unable to make strategic or operating decisions promptly.

Ownership-transfer policies motivated by a desire to love and treat all heirs equally or expectations of equality by family members are likely to promote an impasse, much to the detriment of continued competitiveness.

GIVING SUCCESSORS THE CAPACITY TO LEAD

Leaders of enterprises find that distributing voting shares equally among shareholders often erodes the leader's ability to lead. Stock ownership by complicated trusts can also be a problem, unless ownership and management have been sufficiently differentiated through the presence of nonfamily managers with influence in the top team, boards of directors that include independent outsiders, and employment policies that spell out the prerequisites for family members working in the business. By about age 40 or so, even the more patient successors begin to chafe at not having sufficient voting stock in a business that they have presumably shown they can run effectively on a day-to-day basis. To successors in this situation, it seldom matters whether the stock was purchased or received as a gift from the current-generation CEO.

Unlike ownership, authority is earned rather than inherited. However, transferring ownership without an eye toward corporate control makes it more difficult for the new owner to acquire the authority to lead, which has to be earned slowly and in the trenches. As discussed in earlier chapters, next-generation leaders need to be able to lead, whether through direct control or through the creation of alliances, as if they had 51 percent of the vote.[5]

Consider the following short history of a family-business consulting assignment. A 48-year-old president (but not CEO or controlling owner) of a heavy-equipment refurbishing company was at his wit's end. He had tried to talk with his father about succession and about his getting the authority to truly lead the business. He had already run the business in 6-month increments while his father wintered in Florida. The father, who was 70 years old at the time, did not consider his son ready to run the business yet and would not transfer any voting stock. As is often the case, both parties had sound arguments for their position, but the son's inability to get full authority to lead, with management and ownership structure support, resulted in his deciding to retire early. He moved with his spouse and kids to their favorite vacation spot in the Caribbean. And Dad, who was not having as much fun in semiretirement as he had hoped, went back to work full-time. The continuity of this business was now in jeopardy.

Withholding the authority to lead—either by not transferring voting stock at the appropriate time or by requiring that a variety of next-generation shareholders with equal amounts of stock reach a consensus on important decisions—is likely to limit the life span of the corporation to that of the current-generation CEO. Another possibility is a veto by an upset minority. (A perfect example of this conundrum, is the Bingham family, owners of the *Louisville Courier-Journal*, in its decision to sell the family

---

[5]Author's personal conversation with John Davis, June 2001.

business, as discussed in Chapter 2.) Neither the business nor the family is well served in either case.

CORPORATE STRUCTURES AND CLASSES OF STOCK

As a business passes to succeeding generations, the ever-expanding number of owners makes it naturally more difficult for family members active in the business to efficiently manage it. This is an unavoidable consequence of having a family-owned company in which there are both active and inactive shareholders. Both the health of the company and family relationships may suffer if this potentially explosive issue is not addressed.

One technique that is frequently used is to rearrange the governance structure of the company by recapitalizing its stock. For example, recapitalizing the common stock into two classes (voting and nonvoting) allows the senior generation to divide the estate equally among their heirs in terms of value, but differently in terms of corporate control. Then inheritors of nonvoting stock can be given a way to make their inheritance liquid through buy–sell provisions. This effective method of using corporate governance to deal with active and inactive next-generation inheritors is available to any form of business, both C corporations and S corporations. If the family-business assets are owned by a limited liability company (LLC) or a family limited partnership (FLP), variations on this method can be used to achieve the same result.

Another stock-governance technique used successfully to transfer ownership down a generation is preferred stock recapitalization. This technique is available to both C corporations and family limited partnerships in which significant growth is expected. The value of the senior generation's ownership is frozen, and all succeeding growth in the value of the enterprise is realized by the heirs.

BUY–SELL AGREEMENTS

Buy–sell agreements are contractual arrangements between shareholders and the company. They are typically used by family-business owners to facilitate an orderly exchange of stock in the corporation for cash. To prevent the stock from ending up in unfriendly hands—or even the hands of friendly in-laws—such agreements typically include a provision that the stock will be first tendered to the company or to family members through a right of first refusal.

The most obvious benefit of a buy–sell agreement is that it allows some family members to remain patient shareholders while providing liquidity to family members with other interests or goals. In this way, families can prune the corporate family tree across generations. A buy–sell agreement is often the primary vehicle through which family shareholders can realize value from their highly illiquid and unmarketable wealth—company stock. The ability to sell, whether exercised or not, often makes the difference between feeling fortunate to be able to participate in a family enterprise and feeling enslaved and controlled by it.

While most buy–sell agreements are written so that only death or discord triggers their use, some are created to provide liquidity windows for younger family members. A 30-year-old facing the prospect of purchasing her or his first home, for instance, could convert shares to cash at a predetermined value.

VALUATION OF THE BUSINES

Determining the value of a business is as much art as science. A business valuation is rendered in a report written by a qualified appraiser for a variety of purposes, including

---

table **7.2** | **Valuation Approaches**

Accounting Approach

- Book value

Market Approaches

- Multiple of equity

- Multiple of earnings

- Multiple of sales

- Comparison with publicly owned or privately held companies in the same industry to determine at what multiple of total adjusted earnings (EBITDA), cash flow, and/or return on adjusted invested capital they have traded, adjusted for real estate and other assets.

Income Approaches

- Net present value of future benefits

- Net present value of cash flows or capitalization of earning capacity

- Net present value of expected dividends

Cost Approach

- Appraisal of tangible and intangible assets (particularly suited to appraising the value of holding companies)

---

business succession, estate and tax planning, litigation, and the exercise of buy–sell agreements. The outcome of any valuation is frequently influenced by the purpose of the valuation. For example, tax valuations tend to be more conservative than valuations for the purposes of a sale or public offering. When stocks are closely owned, values will in general be lower. Minority blocks of stock especially will have a discounted value, reflecting their lack of marketability. Lack of marketability and illiquidity discounts will be about 20 percent for majority blocks; 35 to 45 percent discounts are common for minority interests. On the purchase side, a premium of up to 30 percent is often applied for controlling shares. Conversely, smaller size and lack of managerial depth often result in a discount of about 15 percent when the benchmark firms used in market approaches to valuation are publicly traded. Although tax-law changes have made valuations more market-sensitive and less dependent on arbitrary formulas, deep discounts are allowed in recognition of the lack of marketability of family-owned firms. Table 7.2 shows several approaches to valuation. Keep in mind that just as the purpose of the valuation influences the determination of value, it also influences the valuation method used.

Other considerations in arriving at a final valuation include past transactions involving the company and the nature of shareholders' agreements. While shareholders in a family business often agree on a valuation formula, it is important to note that formulas that do not follow one of the approaches listed in Table 7.2 and/or are not regularly reviewed and updated have been successfully challenged by the IRS.

Finally, agreeing to and implementing a valuation method while the senior generation is still involved can go a long way toward continued family harmony when later redemptions occur.

Trusts

Trust designations constitute an alphabet soup of names, including GST, GRAT, and IDGT (intentionally-defective grantor trust). The real challenge with trusts is ensuring that the right one is used—the one that fulfills the intentions and needs of the owning family.

Trusts are a double-edged sword. In the past, many trusts—particularly the generation-skipping trust (GST)—were used to gain a tax advantage. But the control retained by the gifting generation generally created such difficulties, both for next-generation members and trustees and for the generation of grandchildren, that appreciating the transfer as a gift was the last thing on anybody's mind. Although they comprise only a small subset of the trusts available, GRAT and IDGT are discussed below because they are considered by tax attorneys and estate-tax specialists to be particularly beneficial in today's business environment. Both have been upheld thus far by the tax courts and so do not represent uncharted or untested legal territory. However, history has shown that the IRS likes to challenge clever estate-planning methods, so always check with tax advisors before choosing a trust as a means of reducing estate taxes.

GRANTOR-RETAINED ANNUITY TRUST

A grantor-retained annuity trust, or GRAT, allows you to transfer property to heirs without incurring a gift tax or using up the lifetime unified credit allowance. The annuity formula used to repay the grantor of the trust is IRS-approved. Let's assume that an S corporation (which can now have different classes of common stock) recapitalizes, splitting its stock into 10 percent voting and 90 percent nonvoting shares. The grantor transfers the nonvoting stock to the GRAT, and the GRAT pays the grantor an annuity from cash flow for a fixed term. Shorter-term GRATs (which may be layered over the years) reduce both the risk of poor business performance during the term of the trust and the risk of the grantor's dying before the end of the term. Death by the grantor prior to the end of the annuity would result in the property's being included in the grantor's taxable estate. Under the GRAT, the heirs then receive the remainder of the trust when the annuity is fully paid off.

INTENTIONALLY-DEFECTIVE GRANTOR TRUST

The intentionally-defective grantor trust, or IDGT, enables you to transfer nonvoting stock to heirs without gift or estate-tax liability. Using this type of trust, an S corporation might recapitalize the corporation so that 10 percent of its stock represented voting shares and the other 90 percent represented nonvoting shares. The grantor would then fund the trust with a gift of 10 percent of the sale price, or value, and sell the nonvoting stock to the trust. (Why 10 percent? Mortgages provide a precedent for transferring property on the basis of a 10 percent downpayment.) The trust would pay the grantor with an installment note pledging the stock as collateral; the grantor would not have to pay income tax on the interest received on the note but would assume an income-tax liability on the income from the trust. To fit the particular needs of the grantor and heirs, the terms of the note can be varied, including the number of years it will be held and the exclusion/inclusion of prepayment penalties.

Equity and Nonfamily Employees

Most family businesses prefer not to grant shares of stock to nonfamily members, even if they are key executives. Those nonfamily employees who do hold stock in a family business suffer the same plight as family shareholders. The stock is illiquid and unmarketable. So, unless the family plans to sell the business, these shares constitute little more than a provision for retirement and seldom provide the incentive that the grantors aspire to create.

A few businesses have developed phantom stock plans with the aim of creating performance-based cash incentives for key management without actually distributing company stock. Under such plans, company stock is valued periodically, and the phantom stock reflects any shareholder value created. Whenever title to the phantom stock vests—whether it is annually or several years in the future—the company redeems the stock from the key nonfamily employees.

EMPLOYEE STOCK OWNERSHIP PLANS

The outright sale of a family-owned company may result in capital gain, income, gift, and/or estate taxes, depending on how the sale is structured. In general, traditional sales, whether to family members or to people outside the family, are not tax-efficient; they give rise to a capital-gains tax liability that reduces the net after tax wealth that can be passed on to the next generation. On the other hand, next generation members may not be interested in or capable of running the business. Because of the illiquid and unmarketable nature of family-business stock, family members may realize more current value from an outright sale of the business than from a transfer of ownership within the family, even with the significant tax liability.

Employee stock ownership plans, or ESOPs, represent a tax-advantaged exit strategy for some family-business owners who want to create liquidity, diversify their portfolio of assets, and/or reward employees for years of hard work. The financing costs of this kind of transaction are generally low, as a result of government policy that encourages ESOPs through incentives in the form of tax breaks to banks, which are then able to pass along their reduced lending costs to the ESOP companies. As the ESOP company repays the loan, employees' accounts are credited with shares. ESOPs are akin to a qualified retirement plan for employees, with individual employee accounts invested in company stock. If the family is willing to put at least 30 percent of the company's equity into the ESOP, then there are also further tax incentives to the family. ESOPs require frequent appraisals of the company's value, as well as maintenance and oversight of the individual accounts within the plan. Consequently, annual administrative costs can be high. Under certain conditions, ESOP members must also be given the right to vote their shares.

PITFALLS TO AVOID IN ESTATE AND OWNERSHIP TRANSFER PLANNING

The mistakes that business owners should make every effort to avoid in estate and ownership transfer planning are summarized below.

- *Procrastinating in planning the estate and ignoring the inevitability of the owner's eventual death.* The emotional barriers to estate planning and ownership transfer are formidable. However, it is ultimately the responsibility of business owners to lead their families and their businesses into the future by actively planning for the continuity of their businesses and the harmony and financial security of their families. Early planning—so that there is sufficient time to test the plan and its assumptions—should be every family-business owner's goal. It does not make sense to leave the final decisions regarding the family business to the IRS or to consensus-seeking next-generation members when the owner has dedicated a lifetime to building that business.

- *Single-mindedly pursuing tax minimization to the detriment of the continuity of the business.* Business owners who doggedly pursue tax minimization in estate planning often get what they planned for—a lower tax bill and a business that will not survive beyond their generation. It is important to remember that the family-business legacy is about much more than money; it is about a work ethic, a customer orientation, product/service quality, integrity, freedom, continuity, family harmony, and charitably giving to the communities in which the family business has lived.[6]

- *Failing to use estate planning as an opportunity to teach the next generation and to pass on a legacy, not just financial assets.* Greed may step into the vacuum created when goodwill and love are not articulated and acted on by the business leader. Family meetings should be held to discuss family principles and philosophies. Through personal storytelling and the use of communication media, the family's history, the company's culture, and the business's successful strategy can be captured and passed along to the next generation.

- *Failure to make business continuity the cornerstone of the planning.* Senior family members must recognize that the survival of the business is the most important result of the planning. It is the business that provides jobs and financial support for the generations to come, and if the business fails then so has the planning. Family and company decisions should be made with this in mind.

- *Confusing fairness with love and a desire to treat all heirs equally.* Parents are expected—and want—to love their children equally. But individual children have different needs. Throughout their children's lives, parents learn that loving equally does not mean treating equally. The estate and ownership transfer plan needs to reflect this reality. Equality in ownership and/or managerial responsibility often leads to paralysis of business operations and undermines the speed-and-agility advantage naturally enjoyed by most family-owned businesses. Establishing the continuity of the business as the primary goal in estate planning will almost always create the best result for the family as a whole.

- *Failing to communicate and consult with heirs in order to understand what individual family members most value, desire, and need.* People tend to better support that which they have helped to create. Communication and consultation will make the people affected by estate-planning decisions more willing and better able to carry out the spirit, as well as the legal text, of the plan. To be effective in achieving goals beyond tax minimization, estate plans need to be tailored to the unique needs, values, and goals of the heirs and the business. If the difficult conversations are held early and often enough, the changes and accommodations necessary to include those things individual family members most value and want can be built into a flexible model of estate and ownership transfer planning, one that is acceptable to many different individuals and the company.

---

[6]Danco, L., & Nager, R., The Ten Most Common Mistakes in Estate Planning. *Family Business Magazine*, Spring 1993, p. 36.

- *Insufficiently preparing successors and/or failing to acknowledge the specific strengths and weaknesses of next-generation members.* Wishful thinking about the capabilities of successors or, in the name of consensus, giving an angry minority veto power over what next-generation leaders consider to be in the best interest of the family and the business is a recipe for disaster. Expecting immediate readiness from successors rather than instituting a multiyear learning and testing period is equally foolish. Accountability for profit and loss on the business side and the capacity to lead the company and its family shareholders are abilities developed only over time. Differentiating the economic value of the stock from the controlling interest is an effective tool for estate planning. Another important tool is differentiating the forms of participation by family members in the business by developing policies that establish different prerequisites for working in top management, becoming a lower-level employee, and qualifying for board service (see Chapter 2).

- *Failing to submit the estate and ownership transfer plan to a professional advisor or board of directors for review.* Professional advice on estate planning and ownership transfer is not an area in which family-business owners should be thrifty. Advice from top-notch professionals on gift and estate-tax laws can result in millions of dollars in savings. More importantly, such advice often allows heirs to receive more personal value for the money, family unity to be preserved, and the business to continue, either under family control or under new management and ownership. Advisory or statutory boards can also do much to provide oversight of the multiyear planning process, and they can be invaluable in the event of the untimely death of the company leader. Because tax codes are changing constantly, both professional advisors and a board that includes outsiders can be helpful in staying on top of the changes and promoting periodic reviews that update estate and ownership transfer plans to reflect current realities.

THE ROLE OF THE BOARD OF DIRECTORS

In July 2007, the 70-year-old owner of a $65 million construction materials company died unexpectedly. He had been, up until that point, in relatively good health. Two years earlier, this owner had initiated an advisory board with independent outsiders. His death, while a great tragedy to the family, did not become a tragedy for the business. The advisory board had, in its oversight capacity over the 2-year period, made the owner accountable for progress in the leadership development of the next generation, and both a son and a daughter were being groomed for general management through jobs with profit-and-loss responsibilities. The board had also repeatedly put on its meeting agenda the subject of estate planning and ownership transfer and had held conversations with the owner's professional advisors to ensure follow-through. And the spouse and co-owner of the company had attended the advisory board meetings and had championed its work with the tax and estate-planning consultants.

Board members had also facilitated discussions with the potential successors and other members of the family. The board asked probing questions to help family members develop a sense of the goals, principles, and philosophies that should guide the development of the estate plan. In so doing, they improved the probability that the decisions made would be fair and create value and that family relationships would be maintained or improved. In the absence of a board, this owner might have procrastinated, as most owners do, and this company too could have faced a forced sale or liquidation.

Statutory boards of directors have a certain leverage with owners in regard to topics (such as estate and ownership-transfer planning) that are prone to evoke denial, fear, and procrastination on the part of the owners. A board composed of family members is generally not much help in getting an owner to do what is so much more easily avoided. Therefore, a family business capable of assembling a board, whether statutory or advisory, that includes independent outsiders is much more likely to successfully plan the estate and ownership transfer in a timely manner.

Individual members of family-business boards are often selected on the basis of their abilities as street-smart peers; that is, they are business owners who have already been where this company's CEO is headed. By design, then, many of the advisors and directors have already had the succession experience and may have a network of resources they can recommend to the CEO for assistance in planning the estate and implementing the transfer of ownership.

SUMMARY

1 Business owners often delay estate planning for the following reasons:
   - They do not want to discuss their death and its implications for the family and the business.
   - They do not want to give up control of the business.
   - They are trying to avoid potential family conflicts.

2 Federal and state gift and estate taxes in the U.S. are progressive, expensive, and capable of decimating a family business whose primary asset is illiquid and unmarketable company stock. Implications of tax laws for individual families and businesses are best addressed in consultation with professional advisors.

3 An estate plan must address the appropriate allocation of income sources to the founder, his or her spouse, and nonactive family members, as well as the inheritance of the heirs. It must also address corporate control issues.

4 The speed and agility that help family businesses gain competitive advantages in the marketplace must not be hampered by an inability to make decisions promptly, whether caused by a cumbersome trust arrangement, a consensus-dependent copresidency, or the desire to treat all heirs equally.

5 Withholding the authority to lead—either by not transferring voting stock at the appropriate time or by requiring that important decisions be based on a consensus of next-generation shareholders with equal amounts of stock—is likely to limit the life span of the corporation to that of the current-generation CEO.

6 Recapitalizing common stock into two classes (voting and nonvoting) allows the senior generation to divide the estate equally among the heirs in terms of value, but differently in terms of corporate governance. In preferred stock recapitalizations, the value of ownership by the senior generation is frozen, and all succeeding growth in the value of the enterprise is realized by the heirs.

7 A buy–sell agreement is often the primary vehicle for family shareholders to have their highly illiquid and unmarketable wealth—the company stock—realize its value.

8 Valuation approaches include the accounting approach (book value); market approaches (multiple of equity, multiple of earnings, multiple of sales, comparison of companies within the same industry); income approaches (net present value of future benefits, net present

value of cash flows or capitalization of earning capacity, net present value of expected dividends); and cost approach (appraisal of tangible and intangible assets).

9 Two types of trusts particularly beneficial to family businesses in today's environment are the grantor-retained annuity trust (GRAT) and the intentional defective grantor trust (IDGT).

10 Employee stock ownership plans (ESOPs) represent a tax-advantaged exit strategy for family-business owners who want to create liquidity, diversify their portfolio of assets, and/ or reward employees for years of hard work.

11 Professional advisors and a board of directors that includes independent outsiders can help a family business successfully plan the estate and ownership transfer in a timely manner.

FINANCIAL CONSIDERATIONS AND VALUATION OF THE FAMILY BUSINESS

Family businesses are the backbone[i] of the global economy. From the neighborhood mom-and-pop grocery store to the large privately held multinational corporations, such as Cargill, their shared intent to remain significantly family-owned classifies these businesses as family businesses. Recent research on private companies and publicly held family-controlled businesses leaves no doubt that family businesses have a tremendous impact on the local economies in which they operate. The recent "FBN survey: Families' Importance to economies" conducted by the Family Business Network surveyed eight European countries and found that despite globalization, most businesses are still controlled by a family. They found that family businesses are predominantly in the manufacturing, construction, wholesale/retail, and property sectors, and on average, provide at least one in three jobs in their local economies.[1]

Another study, based on the *BusinessWeek 1000* firms, validated the large number of family firms in the economy and also found that companies with founding family control reported:

- Higher profit margins
- Faster growth rates
- Higher sales/cash flow per employee
- More stable earnings
- And more capital reinvested in the firm[2]

These research studies and previously mentioned ones, validate what family-business owners have known for years: Owning a family business can be a win–win situation for the family in terms of business and personal financial success. Family-controlled businesses are a viable organizational structure and add significant value to the economy.

N.B. This chapter was written by Dr. Mary Daugherty, Professor of Finance, University of St. Thomas, Minneapolis, and family-business shareholder.

[1] www.fbn-i.org

[2] McConaughy, D., Founding Family-Controlled Corporations: An Agency-Theoretic Analysis of Corporate Ownership and its Impact upon Performance, Operating Efficiency and Capital Structure. Doctoral dissertation, University of Cincinnati, 1994.

In this chapter we will look at some of the key financial metrics as they apply to family firms. After evaluating the financial statements, we will turn to the topic of cash flow. Cash is indeed king, and family businesses tend to hoard it. We will evaluate the importance of cash in analyzing the current status of the company and its ability to forecast growth going forward. We will end with a detailed discussion of valuation because, after all, everyone wants to know what their company is worth.

OVERCOMING THE ACCOUNTING LANGUAGE BARRIER

Businesspeople communicate using accounting terms. As with any field there is a technical language of business that can intimidate family members who don't have a business background. The accounting language must be mastered by family-business owners who wish to be effective shareholders.

All the talk about earnings before interest and tax (EBIT), earnings before interest, tax, depreciation, and amortization (EBITDA), discount rates, return on assets, return on equity, profits, and cash flow is important to understand. When you understand the language you can then use this information to determine what adds value to your business. Ultimately, all business owners want to enhance the value of their business. As the value increases, the business, the shareholders, and all the stakeholders (employees, their families, and the communities the business serves) enjoy new opportunities for financial rewards.

As students of family-business organizations we need to understand some basic financial measures that play a role in measuring the success of the family business. If we want our family business to be a strong contributor to the economy, and in the process add value to shareholders, we need to know what business actions add value over the long term. Some financial tools to add value are generic to all businesses. Other metrics provide a unique perspective that well-oiled family businesses can use to increase the long-term value of their business.

FINANCIAL MEASURES THAT MATTER

Beyond the competitive forces and strategic goals discussed elsewhere in this book, the basics that every business owner needs to know include understanding the financial statements of the company—the balance sheet and the income statement. Analyzing the financial statements of the company will help the owner assess the financial strengths and weaknesses of the business. In addition, just as in our personal lives, we need a very clear understanding of our cash position. It is very important to understand how the business generates and uses cash. Ultimately we want to put all this information together to ascertain the future prospects for the business. It is the future prospects that provide the value that the company is worth today.

THE BALANCE SHEET

The balance sheet for ABC Family Business, Inc. is shown in Table 8.1. The balance sheet shows the financial picture for ABC, Inc. as of December 31, 2006, 2007, and 2008. The balance sheet lists the assets of the business, all the goods and property owned by the company, and any uncollected amounts due ("accounts receivable") to the company from others. The liability section includes all the debts and amounts owed ("payables") to outside parties. The equity section represents the shareholders'

table **8.1**	Balance Sheet for ABC Family Business, Inc.		
	2006	**2007**	**2008**
		in millions of dollars	
Assets			
Cash	14.33	17.23	19.91
Accounts receivable	14.31	15.17	16.08
Inventory	13.64	14.46	15.33
Total current assets	42.28	46.86	51.32
Fixed assets	44.00	51.00	59.00
Less accumulated depreciation	8.20	13.30	19.20
Net fixed assets	35.80	37.70	39.80
Total assets	78.08	84.56	91.12
Liabilities			
Accounts payable	6.20	6.57	6.97
Total current liabilities	6.20	6.57	6.97
Long-term debt	0.00	0.00	0.00
Equity			
Common stock	30.00	30.00	30.00
Retained earnings	41.88	47.99	54.15
Total equity	71.88	77.99	84.15
Total liabilities and equity	78.08	84.56	91.12
Net Working Capital (NWC) and CAPEX			
NWC	36.08	40.29	44.35
Change in NWC	4.41	4.20	4.07
CAPEX	6.00	7.00	8.00

ownership interest in the company—that is, what the company's assets would be worth after all claims upon those assets are paid. Equity includes the initial investment in stock made by the owners and the additional investment in the company made by the owners—that is, retained earnings. Simply put, ABC holds assets to generate sales. ABC paid for those assets by using either debt or equity. The only reason ABC should hold an asset is to generate profits for the company.

ABC holds cash, accounts receivables, and inventories as short-term assets. Short-term assets are cash and anything that can be converted to cash within 1 year. Based on the most recent year, 2008, ABC currently is extending $16.08 million in credit to customers that ABC expects to collect on within the next year, most likely within the next few months, depending on the credit terms. ABC also is holding $15.33 million in inventory that will be sold within 1 year. Under fixed assets, ABC has net property, plant and equipment on the books at a historical value of $39.8 million. This represents the capital equipment, assets not intended for sale that are used to manufacture, display, store, and transport the company's products and house its employees. The generally accepted way to report fixed assets is cost minus the depreciation accumulated through the date of the balance sheet.

Depreciation arises because the Internal Revenue Service requires companies to write off the expense of the fixed asset over its estimated useful life. So even though the business paid for the equipment at the time of purchase, it can only be written off (i.e., expensed) each year on the income statement by the percentage of use based on its economic life. On the balance sheet, net property, plant, and equipment consist of the cost of the various assets less the depreciation accumulated. The accumulated depreciation is the total depreciation over the life of all the assets of the business except land. Land is not a depreciating asset, and indeed, many family businesses own substantial real estate listed on their balance sheet at cost. Therefore, the real estate is often understated on the balance sheet and has provided options for generating cash or creating holding companies for many families in the past decade.

On the liabilities side of the balance sheet, ABC owes $6.97 million to creditors from whom it has bought goods or services. This current liability will need to be paid within 1 year, depending on the credit terms. ABC does not hold any long-term debt—that is, debt due beyond 1 year of the balance-sheet date. If the company did hold debt, it would need to be paid back based on the specific terms of the contract when the debt was originally issued. Any details of debt-repayment obligations can be found in the company's footnotes to the financial statements.

ABC shareholders own $84.15 million in equity. It is ABC's net worth, or its assets after subtracting all the liabilities. The $30 million listed as common stock is the investment in equity capital provided by the owners of the firm. The retained earnings of $54.15 million are the accumulated profits the company earned and has reinvested—that is, "retains" in the company. These are internally generated funds that are reinvested in additional assets to fund the growth of the business. It is *not* the same as cash, although some of it may be held as a cash asset. Retained earnings increase, or decrease if there is a net loss, each year by the amount of income earned or lost, less dividends declared to shareholders. Therefore, the more the company pays in dividends, the less it has of its own profits to reinvest in the business. The less the company pays in dividends, the more the company has to reinvest in the business. Ultimately, total equity is the owner's net ownership position in the company. If the company reinvests profits over time, any profits made from the reinvestment that are not distributed to the owner will be reflected in an increased total equity value. The owner benefits either way.

The ABC balance sheet lists three other items, addressing the question: How much money is the business currently spending to create growth and ensure future profits? NWC is the net working capital, the difference between total current assets and total current liabilities. Since current liabilities represent debts due within 1 year, a positive NWC represents the amount of current assets left if all current debts are paid. With $44.35 million in working capital in 2008, ABC easily met its obligation to suppliers while being well positioned to meet obligations, expand volume, and take advantage of opportunities as they arise in the business. The change in NWC indicates the additional investment in working capital from 1 year to the next. For 2008, ABC reported a change of $4.07 million, indicating increased investment in short-term assets.

The final line item is CAPEX, capital expenditures. This is the additional investment in long-term—fixed—assets, year over year. ABC has invested an additional $8.0 million in fixed assets in 2008. Year-to-year increases in working capital and capital expenditures are a positive sign of a company's investment in future growth. Typically companies require assets to support growth in sales. The company invests in assets with the goal of providing a better return to shareholders over what the shareholder could earn on their own from the dividend distribution. Shareholders should prefer that the company keep the money for reinvestment if the company can earn more than the shareholder can earn from other investments with similar risk characteristics. But this assumes that the liquidity needs of the owners have been met or can be met by other means.

THE INCOME STATEMENT

The income statement (Table 8.2) measures how well the company used its assets to generate income in any given year. Specifically, an income statement matches the revenues earned from selling goods or services against all the costs and outlays incurred to operate the company. The difference is the net income (or net loss) for the year. The income statement shows the record of a company's operating results for the year and serves as a guide in anticipating how the company may do in the future. For ABC Family Business, Inc. sales in 2008 were $107.19 million. This was offset by the cost of goods sold of $69.67 million—the costs the company incurred to purchase and/or produce the products made available for sale. ABC reported $37.52 million in gross profit, which is the actual profit from sales after recognizing product costs.

The next expense is $21.44 million in selling, general, and administrative (SG&A) expenses. These expenses are grouped separately from cost of goods sold to allow analysis of other expenses related to selling the product. When we subtract SG&A expenses from gross profit, we obtain earning before interest, taxes, depreciation, and

table **8.2** | **ABC Family Business, Inc. Income Statement**

	2006	2007	2008
	in millions of dollars		
Sales	95.40	101.12	107.19
Cost of Goods Sold (COGS)	62.01	65.73	69.67
Gross profit	33.39	35.39	37.52
Selling, general, administrative	19.08	20.22	21.44
EBITDA	14.31	15.17	16.08
Depreciation	4.40	5.10	5.90
EBIT	9.91	10.07	10.18
Interest expense	0.00	0.00	0.00
EBT	9.91	10.07	10.18
Income taxes (tax rate, 39.4%)	3.90	3.97	4.01
Net income	6.01	6.10	6.17

amortization (EBITDA). EBITDA is a widely used measure of operating performance. It is a good indicator of the company's ability to pay its debt, and it allows a view of operating performance that is not influenced by the capital structure of the firm (the financing decision) or the effect of different measures of depreciation.

Depreciation expense for ABC in 2008 was $5.9 million, leaving the company with earnings before interest and taxes (EBIT), of $10.18 million. EBIT is also referred to as operating income, the income available after subtracting all operating expenses from sales. Depreciation is considered an operating expense on the income statement because it is the write-off for the economic life of the assets held in that particular year. Interest expense is reported as $0.0 because ABC has no long-term debt reflected on the balance sheet. This left ABC with earnings before taxes (EBT) of $10.18 million. When we apply a tax rate of 39.4 percent the company ends up with net income of $6.17 million.

FINANCIAL STATEMENT ANALYSIS

The bottom line is that ABC Family Business, Inc. reported earnings of $6.17 million on sales of $107.19 million. So what does this mean? We must analyze the data from the income statement and the balance sheet to answer this question. The analysis involves calculating financial ratios as shown for ABC Family Business, Inc. and the industry in Table 8.3. Ratio analysis standardizes the data to facilitate comparisons with the company to itself over time and with competitors. The ratios highlight the company's strengths and help identify areas in which management can make improvements.

Days sales outstanding is accounts receivable divided by average sales per day. It reflects the average number of days it takes after making the sale to receive the cash from the sale. The more time it takes to convert accounts receivable to cash, the more it costs the company in extended financing to the customer. ABC collects on sales too slowly (54.75 days versus 43 days for the industry). The industry earns the cash 12 days sooner. ABC needs to evaluate not only its credit policy—that is, maybe its credit terms are too lenient—but also the creditworthiness of its customers. The slow payment time may also lead to receivables that never get paid.

Fixed-asset turnover is sales divided by net fixed assets. The turnover tells us how well fixed assets are being used to generate sales. It is also referred to as fixed-asset

table **8.3**	ABC Family Business, Inc. <u>Key Ratios</u>			
	2006	**2007**	**2008**	**Industry Data**
Days sales outstanding	54.75	54.75	54.75	43.00
Fixed-asset turnover	2.66	2.68	2.69	2.40
Total-asset turnover	1.22	1.20	1.18	1.80
Inventory turnover	6.99	6.99	6.99	7.5
Debt ratio	7.94%	7.77%	7.65%	20.00%
Gross margin	35.00%	35.00%	35.00%	35.00%
Profit margin	6.30%	6.03%	5.75%	5.60%

utilization rate. Businesses try to hold the right amount of fixed assets to support growth in sales. The trick is to plan to have enough fixed assets to provide the necessary resources for production without having those fixed assets be underutilized. We can observe how idle fixed assets hurt profitability by simply looking at the automobile industry. Automobile manufacturers specializing in trucks and SUVs were sitting with significant idle capacity in 2008, which was causing them to report record losses. The lack of sales, combined with the heavy costs of unused assets, was taking a toll on the industry's profitability. It is difficult to downsize to meet less demand when you have significant fixed costs tied up in equipment. Fortunately for ABC, this is not their situation. The company is reporting a steady fixed-asset turnover over time, and it is higher than the industry.

Total-asset turnover is sales divided by total assets. It tells us how effectively all the assets of the company are being used to generate sales. The only reason to hold assets is to generate sales. This is a problem area for ABC. Their total-asset turnover is significantly lower than the industry and has been steadily declining over the past 3 years. We have shown that they are doing a good job of utilizing their fixed assets so the problem is in the current assets—that is, receivables, inventory, and cash levels. As we already have shown, the company carries receivables for too long. This is forcing the company's total-asset turnover to be low. In addition, the company should look at the inventory turnover. ABC is selling its level of inventory about seven times per year and the industry is selling a bit better, at 7.5 times a year. This indicates that ABC is carrying its inventory for longer than its competitors. The company should evaluate whether they can meet the same level of sales with less inventory on hand. Inventory management is a very important consideration, because although inventory costs money to hold, inventory that is not in stock costs money in lost sales. For example, a company like Best Buy has to manage its inventory very closely to make sure it meets customer demand without overstocking.

The debt ratio is calculated as total debt (long-term debt plus current liabilities) divided by total assets. ABC does not have any long-term debt, but it does carry short-term debt in the form of accounts payable. ABC's suppliers provide short-term financing for almost 8 percent of the assets of the company. The rest of the assets are financed by equity—that is, the owners of the firm. All assets are funded either through debt or equity. In the case of ABC, similar to many other privately held companies, most of the assets are funded through equity. The debt level is significantly lower than the industry, which finances 20 percent of its assets through debt.

Gross margin and profit margin examine the profitability of the company. Ultimately, the owners want to know how much of sales actually translate to profits for the owners. Gross margin is calculated as gross profit divided by sales. ABC earns 35 cents on every dollar in sales. This is the same gross margin as the industry, which indicates that the industry as a whole has similar input costs. Profit margin is calculated as net income divided by sales. ABC earns 5.75 cents on every dollar in sales. This is a higher profit margin than the industry, although it has been trending down for the past 3 years. The company needs to pay increased attention to their cost structure—SG&A expenses in this case—to try to control costs. The other option is to increase sales. Increasing sales may be difficult for ABC to do when the company already has very lenient credit terms as compared with its competitors.

THE DUPONT APPROACH TO RETURN ON EQUITY (ROE)

The DuPont method for calculating ROE (Table 8.4) breaks down like this:

$$\text{ROE} = \frac{\text{Net Income}}{\text{Revenue}} \times \frac{\text{Revenue}}{\text{Assets}} \times \frac{\text{Assets}}{\text{Equity}}$$

or

$$\text{Pre-Tax Profit Margin} \times \text{Asset Turnover} \times \text{Capital Structure}$$

The DuPont method focuses on: (1) expense control through the profit margin, (2) asset utilization through the total-asset turnover, and (3) debt utilization through the equity multiplier. ABC is experiencing declining profit margins and poor asset utilization, which causes its return on assets to be significantly lower than the industry as a whole. In contrast, Wal-Mart has a fairly low profit margin but more than makes up for it by having a high asset turnover. The equity multiplier measures the amount that equity is multiplied—that is, enhanced—by the use of leverage—that is, debt. This leverage effect encourages companies to use debt financing. When a new investment provides a return greater than the cost of the financing, it benefits the owners. If the owners can use capital provided by debt holders, the owners can make the difference in return over and above what set rate needs to be returned to debt holders. If the company can successfully use debt to grow the firm, the return to shareholders will be enhanced. The return on the invested money raised through debt must be greater than the cost of the debt to add value to the firm. In the case of ABC, their lack of debt financing further hurt their ROE.

The DuPont method is an excellent way to quickly assess the financial strength of a company. A company that has high profitability and high asset utilization but low debt may have the same ROE as a company with a very high level of debt and very low profitability. The DuPont method allows the analyst to see what is driving return and make a judgment call on the financial strength of the company. Although many family businesses hesitate to use debt, debt financing is an excellent tool to enhance return to the shareholder. Of course, the debt must be managed. But if the company can handle the risk, especially companies with reliable earnings streams, debt is a viable tool to fund growth and enhance shareholder value.

Table 8.5 shows the impact of higher interest expense offset by lower equity. If a company uses more debt financing, the return on assets (ROA) is lowered because the interest payments lower net income. But the use of debt also lowers equity, so debt financing increases ROE. Even though there is less net income, the income that is available is divided among fewer equity owners, so the net effect is an increase in the shareholder's return. Clearly, debt financing can enhance returns for shareholders. But debt financing

table **8.4**	DuPont Method Breakdown of ABC's ROE			
	2006	**2007**	**2008**	**Industry**
Profit margin	6.30%	6.03%	5.75%	6.00%
Times total-asset turnover	1.22	1.20	1.18	1.80
Equals return on assets	7.69%	7.22%	6.77%	10.80%
Times equity multiplier	1.09	1.08	1.08	1.25
Equals ROE	8.35%	7.82%	7.33%	13.50%

table **8.5**	The Impact of Higher Interest Expense	
Net income	$100	
Total assets	$1,000	Return on assets = 100/1000 = 10%
Total equity	$500	Return on equity = 100/500 = 20%
Assume the company buys back $100 in equity by taking on debt:		
Interest	$10	
Net income	$90	
Total assets	$1,000	Return on assets = 90/1000 = 9%
Total equity	$400	Return on equity = 90/400 = 22.5%

adds risk to the company and ROE does not explicitly consider risk. ROE ignores the total amount of capital used and concentrates solely on the equity investment.

EFFECT OF IMPROVING DAYS SALES OUTSTANDING (DSO)

The analysis of the financial statements of ABC, Inc. showed problems with asset utilization, particularly short-term assets. ABC, Inc. needs to look for ways to improve their use of assets. Table 8.6 shows the impact of a better credit policy on the ROA and the ROE for ABC Family Business, Inc. By enacting a credit policy that matches the industry ABC, Inc. would be able to increase both measures of return. The cash that was tied up in accounts receivable could be put to more productive uses. In this scenario, we assumed the cash was used to buy back stock. The other drag on return for ABC is the large cash position. If we had further assumed that the company would use some of the excess cash to buy back stock or distribute cash to shareholders, this would show a similar positive

table **8.6**	What Is the Average Level of Sales per Day for ABC, Inc.?	
Sales/day =$ 107.19 million/365 = $293,671 sales per day		
If we assume that reducing the DSO to the industry average of 43 days does not have a negative impact on sales, what is the cash savings?		
Old accounts receivable = $293,671 * 54.75=	$16.08 million	
New accounts receivable = $293,671 * 43 =	$12.63 million	
Cash available = $3.45 million		
If we further assume the additional cash is used to repurchase stock, what is the effect on ROA and ROE? (use DuPont equation to show specific changes)		
Old total assets = $91.12 million	ROA = Profit margin times total-asset turnover	
New total assets = $87.67 million (91.12 − 3.45)	Therefore, new ROA = 5.75% × (107.19/ 87.67) = 7.0%	
Old equity = $84.15	ROE = ROA times equity multiplier (debt/ equity)	
New equity = $80.70	Therefore, new ROE = 7.0% × (87.67/80.70) = 7.6%	

affect on the ROA and the ROE. As can be seen from this example, the DuPont analysis is an excellent tool to identify areas for improvement in financial performance.

FAMILY BUSINESS ACCOUNTING—IS IT REALLY DIFFERENT?

ABC Family Business, Inc. is a fairly typical family firm. It enjoys a high cash position and a low level of debt. ABC is carrying approximately 17 percent of sales in the form of cash. This is a very high cash position. If we assume that the average cash position held by ABC's competitors is approximately 5 percent of sales, then ABC is carrying over $14.5 million in excess cash (107.19 × 5% = 5.36 million. 19.91 – 5.36 = ~$14.5 million). Unless there is a specific reason ABC is carrying excess cash—for example, for a planned acquisition—this $14.5 million is a drain on earnings, as it is not being used to generate sales. The company could use this excess cash to pay distributions to shareholders, to buy back stock for liquidity or estate-planning needs, or purchase productive—that is, revenue-generating—assets. ABC is already holding excess dollars in receivables and inventory, as previously discussed. Both of these asset accounts are currently hurting ABC's asset-utilization ratios by tying up cash in unproductive uses.

ABC, like many other family businesses, currently carries no debt. This means that the family is providing all the financing for growth. We saw earlier, using the DuPont equation to calculate ROE, that debt financing can enhance returns. In Table 8.7 we have a new balance sheet for ABC that reflects a change in capital structure for the company. The recast balance sheet now shows that the assets are 37 percent debt-financed, with the remaining 63 percent being financed through equity.

The income statement now must reflect the interest cost associated with the new long-term debt (Table 8.8).

The key ratios have also been recalculated to reflect the new capital structure for ABC Family Business, Inc. (Table 8.9).

The new capital structure causes ABC, Inc. to "multiply" the ROE to reflect the benefit to the shareholder of funding additional growth through debt. Table 8.10 shows the improved financial position based on the addition of debt in the capital structure.

As you can see, ABC has successfully improved its return on equity from 7.33 percent to 9.13 percent in 2008 by funding some of its growth opportunities with debt rather than owner's equity.

WHAT IS YOUR BUSINESS WORTH?

Having just evaluated the company's current financial position, we can use these data to evaluate the value of the firm going forward. Businesspeople operate in a world of financial accountability and value every day. Every business owner, regardless of whether he or she ever intends to sell the business, wants to know "How much is my business worth?" This is one financial yardstick that everyone understands. For privately owned business families, this yardstick is not readily available. Unlike the publicly owned company that lists a price that each share is worth in the marketplace every day, the value of a private company is much harder to ascertain. There is a whole field of study, and many profitable business valuation firms, that look specifically at the issue of valuing companies that have no public market. If your family business needs a valuation for a specific purpose, such as a sale or transfer of stock, you should hire a professional appraiser. When hiring an appraiser it is recommended that you consult the

table **8.7**	ABC Family Business, Inc. Balance Sheet		
	2006	**2007**	**2008**
		in millions of dollars	
Assets			
Cash	11.91	13.59	15.07
Accounts receivable	14.31	15.17	16.08
Inventory	13.64	14.46	15.33
Total current assets	39.86	43.22	46.47
Fixed assets	44.00	51.00	59.00
Less: accumulated depreciation	8.20	13.30	19.20
Net fixed assets	35.80	37.70	39.80
Total assets	75.66	80.92	86.27
Liabilities			
Accounts payable	6.20	6.57	6.97
Total current liabilities	6.20	6.57	6.97
Long-term debt	25.00	25.00	25.00
Equity			
Common stock	5.00	5.00	5.00
Retained earnings	39.46	44.35	49.31
Total equity	44.46	49.35	54.31
Total liabilities and equity	75.66	80.92	86.27
NWC and CAPEX			
NWC	33.66	36.65	39.51
Change in NWC	3.19	2.99	2.86
CAPEX	6.00	7.00	8.00

professional organizations listed in Table 8.11. These organizations credential valuation specialists. But all business owners should understand the basics of valuation so they can determine what adds and subtracts from their company's value in their day-to-day management of the business. The following discussion on valuation is designed to help the business owner understand the valuation process and what exactly drives value in the family business.

BUSINESS VALUATION

Business valuation is the art of estimating the economic value of an owner's interest in a business. Ultimately, the value is an opinion guided by sound judgment. There are many variables that enter into a valuation, and clever financial analysts can come up

table 8.8 | **ABC Family Business, Inc. Income Statement**

	2006	2007	2008
		in millions of dollars	
Sales	95.40	101.12	107.19
COGS	62.01	65.73	69.67
Gross profit	33.39	35.39	37.52
Operating expenses	19.08	20.22	21.44
EBITDA	14.31	15.17	16.08
Depreciation	4.40	5.10	5.90
EBIT	9.91	10.07	10.18
Interest expense	2.00	2.00	2.00
EBT	7.91	8.07	8.18
Income taxes	3.12	3.18	3.22
Net income	4.79	4.89	4.96

table 8.9 | **ABC Family Business, Inc. Key Ratios**

	2006	2007	2008	Industry Data
Days sales outstanding	54.75	54.75	54.75	43
Fixed-asset turnover	2.66	2.68	2.69	2.4
Total-asset turnover	1.26	1.25	1.24	1.8
Inventory turnover	6.99	6.99	6.99	7.5
Debt ratio	33.04%	30.89%	28.98%	20.00%
Gross margin	35.00%	35.00%	35.00%	35.00%
Profit margin	5.02%	4.84%	4.62%	5.60%
Times interest earned	3.40	3.44	3.48	3.50

table 8.10 | **DuPont Breakdown of ROE**

	Base	2006	2007	2008
Profit margin	5.18%	5.02%	4.84%	4.62%
Times total-asset turnover	1.28	1.26	1.25	1.24
Equals return on assets	6.62%	6.34%	6.04%	5.74%
Times equity multiplier	1.78	1.70	1.64	1.59
Equals ROE	11.76%	10.78%	9.91%	9.13%

table **8.11**	**Who Does Private Business Valuations?**
Look for credentials from these professional organizations:
American Society of Appraisers (ASA)
Institute of Business Appraisers (IBA)
National Association of Certified Valuation Analysts (NACVA)
American Institute of Certified Public Accountants (AICPA)
Chartered Financial Analysts (CFA)

with any value the owner wants to see. It is the process of the valuation itself that yields the best opinions, not the manipulation of assumptions to get to a predisposed number. Because the process is an art and not a science, it is very important that the business owner know the assumptions and be able to track how any change in an assumption can change the value of the business.

UNDERLYING FACTORS IMPACTING VALUE

There are six underlying factors that ensure the valuation is being done to suit the needs of your family business: fair market value, going-concern perspective, highest and best use, future prospects, substitutions, and objectivity.

By far the most discussed factor in private valuations is the Fair Market Value definition based on IRS Revenue Ruling 59-60, as defined in Figure 8.1. This definition is widely used by professional business appraisers in approaching valuation. Fair market value implies the value should be based on a free-market decision. It is easier to understand fair market value by identifying examples of transactions that do *not* qualify as fair market value. If a transaction is not in cash, if payment is deferred, if the transaction is between two family members, if the offering period was very short, if one of the parties was experiencing potential bankruptcy—any of these situations would disqualify the transaction as reflecting fair market value.

In addition to considering fair market value, the business-valuation professional must evaluate the company as a going concern—that is, the value as an ongoing operating business. If the business exists to produce widgets, then the company should be valued as a widget manufacturer, not as a sum of the different pieces of equipment and inventory that could be sold. And what if part of the building used to produce

figure **8.1**	**Fair Market Value—IRS Revenue Ruling 59–60**

"Fair Market Value is the price at which the property would change hands between a willing buyer and a willing seller when the buyer is not under any compulsion to buy and the seller is not under any compulsion to sell, both parties having reasonable knowledge of relevant facts. Court decisions frequently state in addition that the hypothetical buyer and seller are assumed to be able, as well as willing, to trade and to be well informed about the property and concerning the market for such property."

widgets is rented out for occasional meeting events? The company must be valued based on its highest and best use. If the best use of the building is to produce widgets, then that is the use for which the asset—the building—should be considered, not the value of the building from a landlord's perspective. The value is based on using the assets of the business to generate the highest economic value for the business.

The key to a sound valuation judgment is to evaluate the future prospects of the business. After all, it is the future prospects that cause a buyer to want to own the company going forward. What has happened in the past can indicate strong management, accounting controls, and good products but all that can change quickly. The past is history, what we want to value is what the future prospects of the company are worth to us today. If I simply look at the past performance I may completely miss the fact that the product is obsolete (e.g., typewriters), or the management team has left or retired (e.g., Bill Gates), and the company may be facing a much different competitive landscape than the one they dominated. A related factor is substitute or alternative products. AT&T dominated the landline phone market for decades, but with the proliferation of cell phones and PDAs, the landline phone market is vastly different.

The final factor that impacts value is objectivity. It has already been stated that any clever valuation expert can come up with a predetermined value by simply manipulating the various assumptions that are used to calculate a value. But to truly reflect sound valuation principles, the valuation must be objective. The valuation analyst must use only supportable data to come up with a value. This means that the valuation analyst must be careful not to be swayed by irrational exuberance. We all know what can happen, just look at the dot-com valuations of 2001, or the summer of 2008 valuations for any stocks related to oil and energy production. Family-business owners, emotionally and financially tied to their businesses, can easily buy into the mindset that their business deserves a high value without being able to substantiate this claim with supportable data. The private-business-valuation analyst must be able to differentiate between realistic future economic prospects and overzealous anticipation.

OTHER FACTORS IMPACTING THE VALUATION

There are four key factors analysts review in determining an appropriate valuation for the business: growth, profitability, management, and risk. Growth is impacted by the overall economic and financial market outlook as well as the specific industry environment. Data on the economy and financial markets is readily available from sources such as the Department of Commerce and Standard & Poors. The industry data is available from various sources as well, including the S&P Industry Outlook, trade journals, and trade association research specific to the industry. The final influence—the growth factor—is company specific and is a result of the analyst's assessment of the other three key factors. The profitability of the company in terms of net income and cash flow, the strength of the management team and the specific risks of the company all play a role in the final valuation. The valuation analyst reviews the nature and history of the business, the general economic and industry outlook, the financial condition of the firm as reflected in its financial statements, and the ability of the company to generate cash and make cash distributions. The specific risks of the business are assessed by evaluating the relative size of the business, the position of the company in the industry, the sustainability of earnings, the sustainability of the product in terms of substitutes or technological obsolescence, the breadth of the customer base, the diversity of products by type and geographic footprint, and the degree of financial leverage. A $100 million widget manufacturer that has three large customers representing 80 percent of their business and 40 percent debt is worth less than a $100 million custom widget manufacturer with no customer representing more than 5 percent of annual sales and no debt. Though this example may seem obvious, it is the responsibility of the valuation analyst to come up with measurable metrics to justify the appropriate valuation in each case.

ADJUSTMENTS FOR FAMILY ACCOUNTING

Non-operating adjustments segregate items not required for the ongoing operation of the business. One could argue that the high level of cash that many family businesses hold is a non-operating adjustment. Typical discretionary adjustments faced by family businesses are salary distortions (pay either significantly higher or lower than the industry) and perks such as club memberships for family members or personal secretaries who handle planning of personal events. These operational adjustments should be reflected on the income statement in compensation changes so that the valuation analyst can determine sustainable future cash flows without these distortions. Other discretionary items include assets such as a corporate jet, which, if not for family use, would not be financially justifiable for business. On the balance sheet the valuation analyst needs to separate operating assets from non-operating assets, or family perks, to determine the value of the operating business.

How does the valuation analyst determine that these distortions exist? The first step is to facilitate a comparison between the subject company and other businesses in the same industry. Outliers in terms of assets, liabilities, income, or expenses should be scrutinized to determine whether it is a result of "family accounting." Interviews must be held with the CEO, CFO, and other top management in the company. If this does not include family members, then family members should also be interviewed. The valuation analyst needs to develop a "clean" base year that can be used to develop projections for the company going forward. If distortions are reflected in the base year of the financial statements, the projections and the valuation itself will be inaccurate.

Once we review the company's historical performance, segregate any non-operating assets and liabilities, and account for adjustments based on "family accounting issues," we are ready to conduct a valuation.

VALUATION METHODS

To determine ABC, Inc.'s operating business value, we first must determine the company's enterprise value. Enterprise value represents the value attributable to the entire operating entity, prior to considering the company's specific capital structure. It is the value of the equity capital plus the outstanding debt of the company offset by the amount of cash the company holds. Enterprise value considers the fact that an acquirer of the business acquires the whole business, including the outstanding debt of the company. This is offset by the fact that the acquirer also receives the acquired company's cash. The cash effectively lowers the cost of acquiring the company. Two companies may have the same market capitalization but have very different enterprise values. Enterprise value is considered the economic value of a company.

There are three common valuation approaches that we will consider to determine the enterprise value for ABC Family Business, Inc. All three are typically used by professional appraisers to determine a value for a going-concern privately held business.

The first is the discounted cash flow method. This method produces an estimate of current value based on future prospects for the company. This method provides the user the most flexibility in terms of assumptions, but this also is one of the method's greatest shortcomings—too many estimates can complicate the process and/or lead to manipulations in the data. The second approach is the guideline-public-company method, in which ABC, Inc. is compared to publicly traded companies that have similar business profiles. ABC's value will be determined by analyzing the price at which publicly traded companies have traded relative to sales and EBITDA. The advantage of this approach is that there tends to be plenty of data available and the comparison companies have "known" market values. The disadvantage of this approach is that it is difficult to find a company with similar operating and financial characteristics as the private company being valued. In addition, there are a large set of trading multiples that may be used, and the results will vary. The final approach is the guideline-transaction method, which establishes a value based on recent business sales of entire companies or divisions of companies. The advantage of this approach is that the value is based on an actual sale of a business and there is a more accurate size and business-risk comparison available. The disadvantage is that the data are not always publicly available and may reflect distortions that are not readily obvious to the outside observer—that is, an analyst may not be able to determine whether the transaction was at fair market value.

First Approach: Discounted Cash Flow

The discounted-cash-flow approach converts the company's estimated future cash flow into a value for the company by applying a discount rate. The discount rate reflects the risk that the projected cash flows are not actually realized in the future. This approach requires estimates of the future cash flows of the company, the timing of those future cash flows, and an appropriate return that "covers" the risk of being wrong on the estimates. Let's look at each of these estimates separately.

ESTIMATING FUTURE CASH FLOWS

To estimate future cash flows, we need to start with the current financial statements. Table 8.12 shows the Income Statement and Balance Sheet for ABC Family Business, Inc., for the past 3 years along with estimates for the next 2. The first step of the process is to develop realistic assumptions regarding ABC's future cash-flow-generating ability. These estimates were developed by a careful analysis of the growth prospects for the company incorporating the industry outlook, the capital markets outlook, and company-specific factors, including management projections and independent judgment by the valuation analyst. The more thorough the analysis of the current and future prospects, the more confidence the analyst can have in the many assumptions required to develop the forecast. The most important aspect of forecasting the future is to have very accurate current data that can be used as a base year. Therefore, any adjustments for family accounting and nonrecurring events, such as a settlement on a lawsuit, should be made prior to forecasting future estimates. We want to forecast based only on operating events that are part of the ongoing operations of the company. For our purposes we will assume that the base year, 2008, is an accurate reflection of the financial statements of ABC Family Business, Inc.

The financial statements reflect the accounting profits and historical value of the assets and liabilities. Our forecasts for 2009 and 2010 are structured to reflect our best *table* **8.12** | **ABC Family Business, Inc. Balance Sheet and Income Statement (in millions)**

	Base	2006	2007	2008	2009F	2010F
	\multicolumn{6}{c|}{in millions of dollars}					
Assets						
Cash	11.16	14.33	17.23	19.91	26.39	28.53
Accounts receivable	13.50	14.31	15.17	16.08	11.36	12.04
Inventory	12.87	13.64	14.46	15.33	16.25	17.22
Total current assets	37.53	42.28	46.86	51.32	54.00	57.80
Fixed assets	38.00	44.00	51.00	59.00	65.00	71.00
Less: accumulated depreciation	3.80	8.20	13.30	19.20	25.70	32.80
Net fixed assets	34.20	35.80	37.70	39.80	39.30	38.20
Total assets	71.73	78.08	84.56	91.12	93.30	96.00
Liabilities						
Accounts payable	5.85	6.20	6.57	6.97	7.39	7.83
Total current liabilities	5.85	6.20	6.57	6.97	7.39	7.83
Long-term debt	0.00	0.00	0.00	0.00	0.00	0.00
Equity						
Common stock	30.00	30.00	30.00	30.00	30.00	30.00
Retained earnings	35.88	41.88	47.99	54.15	55.91	58.17
Total equity	65.88	71.88	77.99	84.15	85.91	88.17
Total liabilities and equity	71.73	78.08	84.56	91.12	93.30	96.00
Balance	0.00	0.00	0.00	0.00	0.00	0.00
NWC and CAPEX						
NWC	31.68	36.08	40.29	44.35	46.61	49.97
Change in NWC		4.41	4.20	4.07	2.26	3.36
CAPEX		6.00	7.00	8.00	6.00	6.00

(Continued)

	Base	2006	2007	2008	2009F	2010F
Sales	90.00	95.40	101.12	107.19	113.62	120.44
COGS	58.50	62.01	65.73	69.67	73.85	78.29
Gross profit	31.50	33.39	35.39	37.52	39.77	42.15
Operating expenses	18.00	19.08	20.22	21.44	22.72	24.09
EBITDA	13.50	14.31	15.17	16.08	17.04	18.07
Depreciation	3.80	4.40	5.10	5.90	6.50	7.10
EBIT	9.70	9.91	10.07	10.18	10.54	10.97
Interest expense	0.00	0.00	0.00	0.00	0.00	0.00
EBT	9.70	9.91	10.07	10.18	10.54	10.97
Income taxes	3.82	3.90	3.97	4.01	4.15	4.32
Net income	5.88	6.01	6.10	6.17	6.39	6.65

estimate of the financial picture for ABC going forward. As mentioned earlier, EBITDA is the measure of operating profit for the company—how much operating income a company can produce—so it is this number that is used as the measure of expected income. But EBITDA is different from cash flow. EBITDA tells us what the firm generated in operating cash flows but does not consider the additional investment required for funding future growth. Firms need to support sales with assets. We need to consider the additional investment in assets to accurately reflect the value of the business. Free cash flow takes this into consideration by calculating cash flow *after* taking into account reinvestment requirements to support growth. Table 8.13 shows the free cash flow for ABC Family Business, Inc. for 2009–2010. Free cash flow is the

table 8.13 | Free Cash Flow

	2009, Expected	2010, Expected
EBIT	10.54	10.97
Depreciation	6.50	7.10
EBITDA	17.04	18.07
Less: NWC investment	2.26	3.36
Less: capital expenditures	6.00	6.00
Debt-free cash flow	8.78	8.71

cash flow available after the company funds additional investment in short-term assets—that is, net working capital—and long-term assets—that is, capital expenditures.

As discussed earlier, net working capital investment is the additional investment in short-term assets such as inventory. If a company is expanding a product line, they need to increase the inventory of that product line so that it is available for sale. Some portion of that additional investment in inventory is likely to be bought on credit so that the difference—that is, additional inventory less additional accounts payable—is the net working capital investment. Notice that we are not interested in the absolute number for working capital. We are only interested in determining the change in net working capital from one period to the next. It is the change in net working capital that represents a use of cash. If we are holding the same level of inventory year after year, the actual physical inventory will change (inventory turnover) but the additional cash investment in the inventory will not change. Free cash flow is interested only in measuring the additional sources or uses of cash that are not captured in EBITDA. In the case of ABC, Inc. we are forecasting an additional investment of $4.01 and $4.02 in net working capital for 2009 and 2010, respectively.

Capital expenditures are the additional investment in long-term assets such as equipment. If a company is expanding a product line, often it needs to invest not only in inventory but also in equipment that is used to make that inventory "ready" for sale. For example, if a food company is adding a new line of ketchup it will need an additional investment in inventory of tomatoes, vinegar, and spices (short-term inventory assets), but it may also need to make an additional investment in a mixing machine and a packaging machine. These machines are long-term assets and are therefore considered capital expenditures. So unless a company has idle assets, any future growth forecasts must be supported with short- and long-term assets, hence net working capital investment *and* capital expenditures. Again, in the case of ABC, Inc., we are forecasting an additional investment of $6 million in capital expenditures for 2009 and 2010.

Is it possible to have positive EBITDA and negative free cash flow? Definitely. Does this cause a drop in value of the company? Not necessarily.

It takes money to make money. It is imperative that management and shareholders understand what percent of future profits will be needed to fund continued growth for the business. A firm must plan for growth and provide the appropriate assets to make the growth happen. It is very common for a fast-growing company to have negative free cash flow in the building years, and then (hopefully) be rewarded with very-fast-growing free cash flow in later years, when the investment in growth pays off. Many companies manage their growth over time so that the investment in future cash flows is funded by the growth in EBITDA. For family businesses, it requires family buy-in to fund business growth. For example, consider a company like Gander Mountain, which went public in 2004. This company was in a growth mode at the time. The rapid growth this company was managing required big infusions of capital for real estate, store fixtures, construction, and myriad other costs. The company had gotten a large chunk of its capital from the deep pockets of the family. After evaluating other options to raise money, the Erickson family decided to spin off Gander Mountain and take it public. This allowed the company to raise the money it needed for future investment in working capital and capital expenditures while allowing family members the option of raising cash rather than continuing to invest it.

TIMING FUTURE CASH FLOWS

Identifying free cash flow into the future cannot be done indefinitely. Indeed, companies cannot grow at a fast pace indefinitely. All companies face a mature phase in their business, and at that point the company no longer needs large additional investments in net working capital and capital expenditures. This stage of a company life cycle allows for a terminal value to capture a constant cash-flow level in the future. The challenge for the analyst is to identify when the mature phase begins. The further out the analyst forecasts terminal value, the more challenging the year-to-year forecasts become. But the offset is that a terminal value that is forecasted within a few years carries a very high weight in the calculation of the value of the company. Ultimately, the value of a company is only as precise as the assumptions that went into the calculation. Yet, the advantage of the discounted-cash-flow method is the ability to create a sensitivity table that shows how much the value can change depending on the assumptions used. In our example, ABC, Inc.'s terminal value represents the value of the cash flow and business beyond the forecast period ending in 2010. By assuming that the long-term growth rate will be a constant 3 percent, similar to the growth rate of the economy, beyond year 2010, with all capital expenditures offset by depreciation, we can apply the 3 percent growth rate to the 2010 free cash flow. This gives us a free-cash-flow number of $8.97 million. That free-cash-flow number must be discounted by our discount rate minus the long-term growth rate—that is, the growth offsets the risk—to give us a terminal value of $33.23 million in year 2010. Basically, we are making the assumption that $33.23 million represents the value of the cash flow and hence the business value of ABC, Inc. beyond the forecast period ending in 2010.

ESTIMATING APPROPRIATE RETURN

By far the most controversial assumption in the discounted-cash-flow method is estimating an appropriate return that "covers" the risk. The discount rate is based on the risk of the company achieving the forecast results and the return required by investors for bearing this risk as holders of the equity securities. If a company is bought today for $1 million, then $1 million is the value based on the buyer's view of what the future cash flows of the company are worth to her in today's dollars. She has effectively discounted back the future cash flows by her required return based on her perception of the risk. She believed $1 million was an appropriate price to pay for the future cash flows of the company. The only way to find the present value—that is, what the company is worth today—is to assign a required return to the future cash flows that is reflected in the price today. A required rate of return, unfortunately, is not a universally agreed-upon number. There are many different approaches to determining the appropriate return. There are also many finance terms used to describe this discounting. In addition to referring to the discount rate as our "appropriate return," the discount rate is also often referred to as the "cost of capital," "the required return for the company," or the "hurdle rate."

So how do we begin to figure out the appropriate return? The intuitive approach suggests that we evaluate what a reasonable investor would expect as a return given the risks of the company's business and industry. The return an investor will require is driven by the risk of a company's line of business and, because of the repayment requirements on debt and the tax effect of interest, its use of debt. Required returns vary widely across industries and companies. Some lines of business are clearly riskier than others; it is less risky to sell basic food products than it is to sell high-end luxury goods. It is also much riskier to invest in businesses that use a large amount of debt financing—that is, airlines. I like to think of the appropriate return as the rate that addresses the question of "How wrong can I be?" regarding my estimates of the future cash flows. The more likely it is that I could be wrong, the riskier the cash-flow stream and therefore the higher this appropriate rate should be to pay for that risk.

From a family-business perspective, the appropriate return is affected by three factors: shareholders' perception of risk, liquidity concerns, and the shareholder effect. Just like any investor, if family shareholders perceive a high amount of risk with their investment, they will demand a higher return. So to minimize the cost of equity, management must convince shareholders that they can manage the company well. Shareholders need to understand the business strategy and believe that management can execute that strategy. This requires management, the board, and the family all to work together to understand the goals of the business and the goals of the family. A related issue is liquidity. In the public markets the shareholders can get instant liquidity by simply selling shares in the open market. But family shareholders typically do not have that option. The less liquid the investment, the higher must be the required return on the investment. Failure to provide for shareholders' liquidity needs coupled with shaky shareholder commitment weakens the core competitive advantage of family firms—patient capital. The final consideration regarding the appropriate return is the shareholder—that is, family—effect. If the family business has a cohesive and committed shareholder group that understands and believes in the company strategy for growth, the company will benefit from more patient capital. In this case patient capital provides a competitive advantage.

A more systematic approach to measuring an appropriate return is to create a discount rate that is inferred from the rate that is being earned on other investments. The book *Stocks, Bonds, Bills and Inflation* by R.G. Ibbotson and R. A. Sinquefield[3] provides historical data on stock returns over the past 70 years. The book provides data for various asset classes and company size. This is the standard reference used by financial experts to begin to develop an appropriate rate of return that should be required on a specific investment. This reference includes historical data on both equity and debt that can be used to "build" a discount rate—a weighted average of the cost of debt and equity, that is, the capital, for the firm. The cost of debt is the interest rate a company must pay on new loans, such as a new bond issue. It reflects the long-term cost of debt financing for the company as determined by the bond markets. Since interest expense is tax-deductible for corporations, the cost of debt is adjusted to an after-tax cost of debt. The equity capital is a more challenging process. It is the cost of equity that is built up to reflect the risk characteristics of the privately held company.

The public markets rely on the capital-asset pricing model (CAPM) to determine a market-driven discount rate for equity. Basically this involves starting with the basic premise that an investor requires at a minimum a return equal to the 10-year Treasury bond, a pseudo-risk-free rate. Then the market assesses an additional return based on the volatility of that individual stock against the market return—that is, beta. If the stock's return over time has been more volatile than the market it will have a beta greater than 1. If the stock's return over time is less volatile than the market it will have a beta less than 1. This beta is then multiplied by the equity risk premium—the rate

---

[3]Ibbotson, R.G., & Sinquefield, R.A., *Stocks, Bonds, Bills and Inflation: Historical Returns (1926–1987)*. Charlottesville, VA: Research Foundation of the Institute of Chartered Financial Analysts, 1989.

figure **8.2** | **ABC Family Business, Inc. Build-up Method to Calculate Discount Rate**

Composed of two elements:

Risk-free rate

Risk premium(s)

Build-up model for cost of equity:

Risk-free rate (RFR) = 5%

+ Equity risk premium (ERP) = 7%

+ Small-size premium = 8% (small firm riskier than large firm)

+ Industry and company risk premium = 10%

= Expected return on equity

investors require over the risk-free rate—to compensate them for the additional risk of investing in the equity market. This approach is acceptable for publicly traded companies with a measurable beta, but privately held companies do not have betas.

Elements of the CAPM can be used to develop an appropriate rate of return for privately held businesses. In the case of ABC Family Business, Inc. the assumptions regarding the build-up of the discount rate are shown in Figure 8.2. Using the risk free rate and an equity risk premium as the minimum return, a private business investor can refer to the Ibbotson and Sinquefield data to develop additional return criteria. The first add-on should be a size premium. The historic data show that small companies have provided higher returns but represent higher risk. An appropriate small-size premium, in this case 8 percent, is added as a risk measure. The second add-on is a qualitative premium based on the company and industry risk factors relative to a portfolio of similar but publicly traded equity securities. ABC requires a qualitative premium of 11 percent to compensate investors for the unique risks that ABC possesses relative to the publicly held companies in its industry. These premiums added together represent a 30 percent cost of equity for ABC Family Business, Inc. The investor can then compare the company's calculated cost of equity to the medians of publicly traded companies in its industry as defined by Ibbotson's cost of capital. Of course, valuation analysts also use their own database and years of experience to determine the reasonableness of the discount rate. Based on all known comparison, the cost of equity of 30 percent for ABC, Inc. is appropriate.

After a cost of debt and a cost of equity are determined, we can compute the appropriate discount rate to apply to the future cash flows. In the case of ABC Family Business, Inc. the company uses only equity financing. The cost of debt and the weight of debt in the capital structure is zero. Therefore, the appropriate discount rate for this company is 30 percent.

DISCOUNTED-CASH-FLOW VALUE

Table 8.14 shows the current value of ABC Family Business, Inc. based on our assumptions for future cash flows, a terminal value, and a discount rate. Notice that each year's cash flow is discounted back to today's date. Hence, the second-year cash *table* **8.14** | **Net Present Value of ABC Family Business, Inc.**

Discount rate	30%			
Constant growth rate	3%			
Net present value		2008	2009, Forecast	2010, Forecast	2011, Forecast
---	---	---	---	---	---
Free cash flow			8.78	8.71	8.97
Terminal value				33.23	
Sum			8.78	41.95	
Number of periods Discounted			1	2	
Discounted values			6.75	24.82	
Net present value	**31.57**				

table **8.15** | **Net Present Value Sensitivity to Discount Rate**

Discount rate	25%			
Constant growth rate	3%			
Net Present Value		2008	2009, Forecast	2010, Forecast	2011, Forecast
---	---	---	---	---	---
Free cash flow			8.78	8.71	8.97
Terminal value				40.79	
Sum			8.78	49.50	
Number of periods Discounted			1.00	2.00	
Discounted values			7.02	31.68	
Net present value	**38.70**				
Discount rate	35%			
Constant growth rate	3%			
Net present value		2008	2009F	2010F	2011F
Free cash flow			8.78	8.71	8.97
Terminal value				28.04	
Sum			8.78	36.75	
Number of periods Discounted			1.00	2.00	
Discounted values			6.50	20.17	
Net present value	**26.67**				

flow plus the terminal value in year 2, which reflects all the future cash flows as a perpetuity, are discounted back at the discount rate of 30 percent for two periods. A 2-year forecast was used based on the assumption that ABC is entering its mature phase and will have a 3 percent long-term growth rate, similar to the growth rate of the economy, beyond year 2010. (For an explanation of terminal value and the 2-year time frame for the valuation, see the "Timing Future Cash Flows" section, above).

Table 8.15 shows the sensitivity of the firm's value to a change in the discount rate. In order to test the sensitivity of changes in the discount rate we calculated the

table **8.16**	Equity and Per-Share Value of ABC Family Business, Inc.

Net present value	26.67
Add cash	19.91
Remove debt	0.00
Total equity value	46.58
Number of shares	1000000
= Value per share	**$46.58**

indicated enterprise value based on discount rates of 25 percent and 35 percent. The enterprise value based on these changes ranged from $26.67 to $38.70. A higher discount rate—that is, higher risk—results in a lower valuation, while a lower discount rate results in a higher valuation. If the discount rate used is too high, the value of the company will be underestimated. If the discount rate used is too low, the value of the company will be overstated.

Table 8.16 calculates the value of the equity rather than the value of the firm. We start with the value of the firm, add back the cash as it belongs to the shareholders, and take out the debt, as it is an obligation of the shareholders as owners to get the total equity value of the firm. By dividing this number by the number of shares outstanding, we get a per share value of the firm.

GUIDELINE PUBLIC COMPANY METHOD

This market approach to valuation compares the values of select publicly traded companies to those of their privately held counterparts. The analyst applies valuation multiples derived from the guideline companies to the financial data of the subject company to get a value. The challenge is to find companies that are comparable based on size, business mix, capital structure, and profit growth potential. Often, the comparable companies are more diversified in their business interests, so the analyst must make adjustments by business line. Equally important, the analyst must consider the current status of the overall public equity markets. The financial markets can be extremely volatile. For example, the values of financial companies were substantially lower mid-year 2008 versus mid-year 2007. The comparable data must match by date of the input data.

Table 8.17 shows the financial data comparisons for ABC versus comparable public companies. The companies operate in the same industry with similar Standard Industrial Classification (SIC) codes and business descriptions. ABC, Inc. is not an exact match, the comparable companies as a whole have more sales, carry more assets, and use less working capital, but they are sufficiently similar to merit comparison.

table **8.17**	ABC Family Business, Inc. vs. Comparable Public Companies

Financial Data (in millions of dollars)			
	Sales	Total Assets	Net Working Capital	NWC/Sales
Industry mean	145	100	32	22.07%
ABC Family Business, Inc.	107	91	44	41.38%

Table 8.18 outlines the historical and forecasted sales growth rates for ABC, Inc. relative to the mean growth rates of the public companies in its industry. ABC has been growing 20 percent faster than its peers over the past 12 months, and it is projected that they will continue to outpace their peers over the next 12. During the past 5 years ABC's compound annual growth has exceeded its competitors. Companies experiencing higher growth rates tend to be valued higher in the marketplace, as evidenced by higher valuation multiples.

ABC has significantly higher profitability, as evidenced by the higher EBITDA margins (Table 8.19) than its peers over the past 12 months, the past 5 years, and according to the next 12-month forecast. In general, companies with higher margins tend to be valued higher in the marketplace. The higher-margined businesses are assessed higher valuation multiples.

The enterprise valuation multiples of sales and EBITDA for the industry peers are listed in Table 8.20. These multiples are calculated as of the valuation date, as well as for each of the preceding five and three fiscal year ends for all the companies in the industry peer group. By reviewing multiples over a number of years we can see the change in values as reflected by market changes over time. The bull market of the past few years came to an abrupt end in 2008. This development will certainly be reflected in the multiples investors are willing to pay for sales and profits. These are the multiples for the industry, but it is important to remember that ABC, Inc. has a faster growth rate in sales than its peers and is more profitable.

table 8.18 | ABC's Sales Growth Rate

	Next 12 Months	Past 12 Months	5-Year Compound Annual Growth Rate
Industry mean	5.00%	5.00%	4.30%
ABC Family Business, Inc.	6.00%	6.00%	4.77%

table 8.19 | EBITDA Margins: ABC Family Business, Inc. vs. Industry

	Next 12 Months	Past 12 Months	5-Period Margin
Industry mean	9.50%	11.50%	10.50%
ABC Family Business, Inc.	15.00%	15.00%	16.00%

table 8.20 | Enterprise Valuation (EV) Multiples of Industry Peers

	EV/Sales Multiples			
	Next 12 Months	Past 12 Months	3-Period Mean	5-Period Mean
Industry mean	0.30	0.38	0.40	0.37
		EV/EBITDA Multiples		
Industry mean	3.0	4.0	4.2	3.4

table **8.21**	Enterprise Value (EV) Based on Sales and EBITDA, ABC Family Business, Inc.

EV/Sales Multiples	Next 12 Months	5-Period Mean
	0.30×	0.37×
Sales over next 12 months, $113.62	$34.08	$42.04
Sales over past 12 months, $107.19	$32.16	$39.66
EV/EBITDA Multiples	**Next 12 Months**	**5 Period Mean**
	3.0×	3.4×
EBITDA over next 12 months, $17.04	$51.12	$57.94
EBITDA over past 12 months, $16.08	$48.24	$54.67

Just looking at the 5-period mean and the next 12 months and applying the multiples forecasted over that period to sales and EBITDA for ABC, Inc. gives us the values in Table 8.21. In this case, it was appropriate to use the most recent and 1-year forecasted sales and EBITDA data, as the company exhibits a fairly consistent growth in sales and profitability. If the company being valued exhibited a more erratic growth pattern, or the company had experienced unusually low or high sales and earnings in recent years, it would be more appropriate to use longer-term averages. In addition, although market values dropped significantly in 2008, it seems appropriate to use multiples based on the next 12 months to reflect the current situation, but then offset that with a longer-term average. Over time the market does experience some reversion to the mean, so a historically low multiple for the next 12 months should be countered by the longer-term higher average. Given the range of values calculated based on these multiples, ABC Family Business, Inc.'s indicated enterprise value is between $32.16 and $57.94. Recognizing that ABC, Inc. has stronger growth and profitability than its peers, it seems reasonable to assume a value in the mid to high end of this range.

GUIDELINE TRANSACTION METHOD

The guideline transaction method, also referred to as the "merger and acquisition method," evaluates past sales of companies or divisions to determine appropriate valuation multiples for the comparison company. Ideally, guideline transactions are in the same industry as the company being analyzed. If that is not possible companies with similar investment characteristics in terms of products, growth, cyclicality, or asset size are considered. The valuation multiples are very sensitive to merger and acquisition activity. Figure 8.3 shows the EBITDA multiples by transaction size from 2004 through 2007. ABC Family Business, Inc. falls in the small transaction range, $25 million to $50 million. The multiple has ranged from 4.9 times EBITDA in 2002 to as high as 9.2 times EBITDA in 2005. The trend is headed lower for 2008–2009. Table 8.22 applies this multiple range to EBITDA for the most recent and forecasted 12 months to calculate a range of values. Based on the multiples and acknowledging that the trend is moving down, a reasonable range of indicated enterprise value is $78.79 to $156.77. This range is significantly higher than the range based on comparisons to the industry's publicly traded companies. I would be hesitant to put too much faith in the values derived from transactions, as this market changed significantly during 2008. If

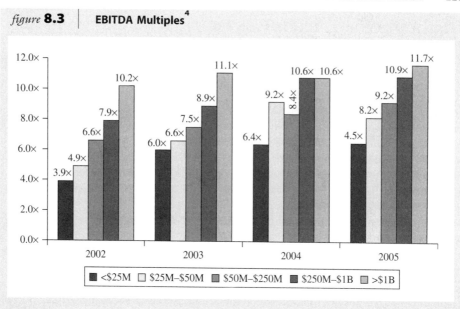

figure **8.3** | **EBITDA Multiples**[4]

Legend: ■ <$25M □ $25M–$50M ■ $50M–$250M ■ $250M–$1B ▨ >$1B

table **8.22** | **Enterprise Value Based on EBITDA Multiples**

EV/EBITDA Multiples	Low for Past 4 Years	High for Past 4 Years
	4.9×	9.2×
EBITDA over next 12 months, $17.04	$83.49	$156.77
EBITDA over past 12 months, $16.08	$78.79	$147.93

we consider that the average EBITDA multiple for this industry at 3.5 times is lower than the average for all transactions, we should consider a more reasonable value range of $56.28 (3.5 times EBITDA over the past 12 months) to $78.79.

ESTIMATE OF ENTERPRISE VALUE

Based on the three methods of valuation, the range of values for ABC Family Business, Inc. is as follows:

Discounted Cash Flow Method	$26.67 million to $38.70 million
Guideline Public Company Method	$32.16 million to $57.94 million
Guideline Transaction Method	$56.28 million to $78.79 million

The range is quite wide, which is common in a decelerating economic growth environment as observed in 2008. The increased market volatility and uncertainty surrounding future cash flows produces a wider valuation range. The analyst must assess the economic, market, industry, and company-specific situations to build a case for what value within the range is appropriate. I would argue that ABC, Inc. should be valued toward the high end of the range because of the company's higher margins versus the industry and the potential for credit improvement.

---

[4]Sample Appraisal Report. Minneapolis: Chartwell Capital Solutions, 2008.

DISCOUNTS FOR LACK OF CONTROL AND MINORITY POSITION

The value of a privately held company is subject to discounts for lack of control and lack of marketability. Controlling owners have decision-making authority that minority holders do not have. For example, controlling owners can increase compensation, reduce the dividend payout, alter the use of the company's assets, and make decisions about capital structure. In other words, controlling owners can make all of the firm's business decisions. Let us assume that an equivalent firm with similar characteristics—same size, same industry segment, same markets, etc.—was just acquired. The buyer paid a 30 percent premium over the pre-announcement share price of $1.00, so the buyer paid $1.30 per share for the company. The minority discount for this company is equal to $1 - (1.00/1.30)$. Therefore, the minority shares are worth 77 percent of the controlling shares.

So what are the levels of value? The controlling interest is the value an investor is willing to pay to acquire more than 50 percent of a company's stock. The typical premium paid to the controlling owner is 25 to 50 percent. There is an acquisition value that is even higher than the controlling value. That higher acquisition value is reserved for the types of acquisitions that enhance the strategic positioning of the company or add synergies that cannot be replicated by any other buyer. The next level of value below controlling value is referred to as "marketable minority." This level of value represents the perceived value of equity interests that are freely traded without any restrictions. This is the value that is attached to publicly traded stocks. Presumably, most investors in publicly traded stocks are minority owners; they own only a small number of shares versus the total number of shares outstanding for a public company. Yet there is a liquid, active market for most publicly held stocks, so they are certainly marketable. The lowest level of value is the nonmarketable minority position. This is the level at which noncontrolling equity interests in private companies are valued. Not only are many family-business owners minority owners—that is, they own less than 50 percent of the shares of their family business—but they also are not able to sell their stock to anyone outside the family. *Marketability* is defined as the ability to convert the business interest into cash quickly, with minimum transaction and administrative costs, and with a high degree of certainty as to the amount of net proceeds. All else being equal, an interest in a privately held company is worth less than an interest in a publicly traded company because no established market exists. This situation requires the stock to be discounted for lack of marketability. The levels of value and the associated premium or discount is shown in Figure 8.4.

Minority and marketability discounts normally are multiplicative rather than additive. Therefore, the discounts are sequential. If the starting point is control value, then the minority discount needs to be subtracted. That leaves us with a marketable minority value that is then discounted for lack of marketability. The resulting value is the per-share value of the non-marketable minority shares. Let's assume that ABC Family Business, Inc. is worth a control value of $46.58 per Table 8.18. The fully discounted value of ABC becomes:

$46.58 Control Value
  13.97 Less: Minority interest discount ($.3 \times 46.58$)
= 32.60 Marketable minority value
  13.04 Less: Lack of marketability discount ($.4 \times 32.60$)
= $19.55 Value of nonmarketable minority shares

figure **8.4** | **Company Values When Discounts and Premiums Are Applied**[5]

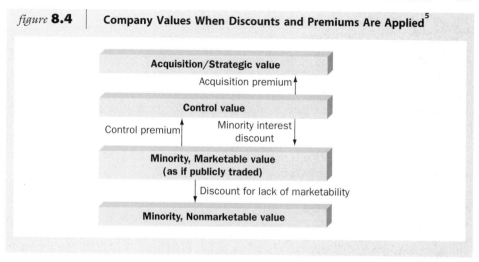

A minority shareholder in ABC Family Business, Inc. holds stock worth $19.55 per share.

NONFINANCIAL RETURNS AND COSTS NOT CAPTURED BY BUSINESS VALUATION

Make no mistake about it, the financial education of family shareholders represented by traditional financial metrics and periodic business valuations, is a significant contributor to transparency, trust among shareholders, and, therefore, the health of the patient capital advantage of family businesses.

But beyond owner discretionary expenses (e.g., golf club membership, luxury car, or one-time expenses of some form or other) there are other nonfinancial private benefits to family-business shareholders. These may include investments in brands or ventures that convey a high reputation for the family (e.g., in support of the arts, community philanthropy, medical research), a long-range internationalization project undertaken to enhance future opportunities for the next generation, investments that diversify the family's wealth as contained in the family company that reduce risk but do not readily create value (versus distributions or dividends from the business being used to create a diversified portfolio of stocks and bonds).

The nonfinancial returns, let's call them emotional returns, are often as real to business-owning families as the financial returns are. They are just not captured in the traditional business valuation or appraisal process. These returns may be positive, as the list above suggests or negative, as when family conflicts make family-business leaders wonder whether keeping the business in the family is worth it.

A total-value formula has been developed by family-business scholars Astrachan and Jaskiewicz[6] that suggests taking the nonfinancial returns into consideration in the following manner:

---

[5]Astrachan, J., & Jaskiewicz, P., Emotional Returns and Emotional Costs in Privately Held Family Businesses: Advancing Traditional Business Valuation. *Family Business Review*, 21(2), 2008, pp. 139–149.
[6]Mergerstat Review

Total Value = Financial Value + Emotional Value, or,

TV = DCF + DFPB + (ER − EC)

where TV = total value of the business to the owner, including its financial value (FV = the value of the discounted cash flows [DCF] and the value of the discounted financial private benefits [DFPB], benefits not usually available to employees or holders of shares in publicly traded companies, plus the net value of all the emotional returns [ER] realized and emotional costs [EC] incurred by the business-owning family).

Because emotions play a significant role in financial decisions, this nontraditional perspective may complement and help further our understanding of strategic decision making in privately held family businesses.

SUMMARY

1 It is the owner's responsibility to understand the financial position of the company. The example of the ABC Family Business, Inc. used in this chapter highlights the important information contained in the financial statements.

2 Company financial statements do not have to be complex. A CFO can consolidate the financial statements to make them easier to understand.

3 Shareholders have a responsibility to ask for time at shareholder meetings to discuss the financial statements and the cash needs of the business.

4 Responsible shareholders should also spend time evaluating the company's strategy for growth and evaluate the options to finance growth.

5 There are many resources available to help owners learn more about their companies and industry financial metrics. Owners can subscribe to industry trade journals, gather reading materials on financial-statement analysis, make use of websites that provide basic finance and accounting tutorials, attend community courses, or hire financial educators to help the shareholders become more knowledgeable owners.

6 Business valuations are extremely valuable to families in private businesses. They measure and inform family shareholders of progress toward goals and can facilitate pruning the family tree without conflict by making buy–sells among family shareholders possible.

7 A family shareholder group who is more knowledgeable about the financial position of the company and who understands how value can be added to the business provides yet another competitive advantage for the family business.

8 Beyond the financial returns, families in private businesses often derive noneconomic benefits from family-business ownership. The total value of a business to its shareholding family is a combination of the financial value and the emotional value of the enterprise to the family. Strategic decisions, like whether to sell or grow the family business, are more likely a function of the total value of the business to its shareholders than the financial value alone.

KEY NONFAMILY MANAGEMENT: THE VISIBLE COMMITMENT TO MANAGING THE FAMILY BUSINESS PROFESSIONALLY

> [*The Washington Post*] is family-oriented—and that makes me nervous as I look around me at other family businesses and what becomes of them. I also see what replaces them when they go downhill. I am trying hard to get strong, able managers around me in an effort to combine the advantages of both.
>
> —*Katharine Graham, late Chairman of the* Washington Post Companies, *in a 1976 letter to a friend*[1]

The literature on family businesses is overwhelmingly focused on issues of concern to the owning families: family relationships, successor development, estate planning, succession, and wealth transfer. There has been little discussion of—and few data on—the most productive ways to manage relationships between family and nonfamily managers. Yet family businesses of any significant size depend on the quality and effectiveness of nonfamily managers to ensure their continued success and growth. In a survey of owners of successful family businesses that were 200 years old or older, the *Financial Times* of London asked respondents what enabled their companies to continue across so many generations. Beyond quality of product and/or service, business owners credited their firms' continuity to a strong sense of family history, the ability to exclude incompetent family members, and a willingness to employ nonfamily executives whose unique set of skills added value. Their willingness to employ nonfamily executives also more readily enabled these firms to establish hiring practices that were considered fair yet raised the standard for the position. It made it possible to hire only

The author wishes to express his appreciation to Theodore Alfred, with whom he first collaborated on the Discovery research project on family business. This research was first in its field in highlighting the different perspectives of nonfamily managers in family-owned companies.

---

[1]Nelton, S., Lessons from Katharine Graham, *Family Business Magazine*, Autumn 2001, p. 12.

qualified family managers. Survey respondents said that, by doing so, these firms both ensured business health and maintained family control.

THE PERSPECTIVE OF NONFAMILY MANAGERS

The Discovery Action Research Project on family business found that nonfamily managers tended to regard their firms positively; in fact, most would like to see the companies continue as family businesses.[2] Despite the positive attitude, the study identified several problems in the relationships between owners and nonfamily managers. Specifically, the researchers found significant differences between the two groups' perceptions of the efficacy of management and governance practices. Differences also existed in perceptions of the capacity of the firms for innovation and change. And the study revealed some anxiety on the part of nonfamily managers concerning the qualifications of potential successors and the ambiguity of their own positions in the company. To enhance their understanding of questionnaire responses, the researchers personally interviewed key nonfamily managers in the firms participating in the study. The views of one highly regarded nonfamily executive were typical: "I really love working for these people," he told the research team, "but I need more structure. It's nice to be treated like family, but I'd like to know more about where my job begins and ends and how I'm doing."

While both nonfamily and family managers expressed overall positive feelings about their firms, nonfamily managers were generally less positive about management practices and succession issues. Many "love the firm, but. . . ." The differences uncovered in the study represent important challenges, offering significant opportunities for owner-managers to improve the motivation and performance of their top employees. That is the subject of a number of suggestions and actionable recommendations later in this chapter.

A DELICATE BALANCE

Research by W. Gibb Dyer, Jr., of Brigham Young University identified serious dilemmas that confront owners of family businesses in their dual roles as family members, on the one hand, and managers, on the other.[3] Balancing the sometimes competing demands of family and business is a challenge for nonfamily managers, too. "Owners have given me much responsibility," one nonfamily manager told the researchers. "Now the delicate balance is between performance in what they hired me to do and keeping the chemistry going with the family."

Obviously, task competence is central to the role of nonfamily managers. Some of the nonfamily managers surveyed were in charge of strategic planning, sales, finance, marketing, manufacturing, or human resources. Some were bridging presidents, who had taken over operations from the older generation until the younger generation was ready to lead. Clearly, key nonfamily managers are expected to keep up to date with professional management practices and be solid contributors in executive, functional, and project areas. Staying current and competent is the best antidote to concerns that

---

[2]Poza, E., Alfred, T., & Maheshwari, A., Stakeholder Perceptions of Culture and Management Practices in Family and Family Firms. *Family Business Review*, 10(2), 1997, pp. 135–156.

[3]Dyer, W.G., *The Entrepreneurial Experience*. San Francisco: Jossey-Bass, 1992.

figure **9.1** | **Primary Business Concerns of the Nonfamily Manager**

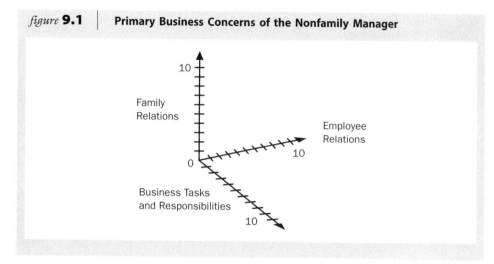

nepotism may have an influence on career opportunities. The complexity of getting the job done, however, is compounded in a family firm by the need to skillfully manage relationships with family members. One nonfamily manager expressed a common conflict:

> *The third generation of owner-managers is in the wings, and my affiliation is with the second generation. In less than 10 years, I may have to let go, if the second generation retires or lessens its role. You see, I am having to "discipline," or be the bad guy, by supervising two of the next-generation family members. And what if I end up having to work for them? I would still need to work; I have two young kids.*

Accepting the fact that his or her job includes responsibilities beyond those associated with the position is essential for the nonfamily employee. Management literature has argued over the years that both task orientation and employee relations orientation are important elements of leadership.[4] In the case of family businesses, nonfamily managers would be well served by behaving as if success requires special attention to tasks, employee relations, and relations with family members (Figure 9.1). Nonfamily managers need to encourage family members to give their comments and feedback directly to other family members, without using the nonfamily employee as the messenger. When family members talk to nonfamily managers about other family members they invite an "us-and-them" struggle and put nonfamily managers in a precarious position.

CONCERNS ABOUT MANAGEMENT AND GOVERNANCE PRACTICES

The ratings provided by nonfamily managers on the performance feedback, succession planning, career opportunity, and advisory board scales in the study[5] were quite different from those of family members in the business. No significant differences were

---

[4]Hersey, P., & Blanchard, K., *Management of Organizational Behavior: Utilizing Human Resources.* 5th ed., Englewood Cliffs, NJ: Prentice-Hall, 1988.

[5]Poza et al., op. cit.

found between the two groups in the business planning, communication climate, and growth orientation scales.

CEOs saw their firms as more innovative than did nonfamily managers. As a group, nonfamily managers tended to be less satisfied with innovation and product development, and they were consistently less satisfied than CEOs with management practices and systems.

With regard to values and planning assumptions, family members were more likely than nonfamily managers to agree with the statement "People in this organization know what we stand for and how we wish to conduct the business." This difference raises interesting questions about how family members in management convey their business values and philosophies to employees. When these are transmitted primarily through the family, nonfamily managers and employees may be left out of the loop. This fairly normal "lack of transparency" by family management also raises a question about the extent to which family management routinely engages nonfamily employees, even key nonfamily management, in strategic initiatives.

Planning for the future is a key management activity. Yet it seems that nonfamily managers are often left behind in this important journey. The nonfamily managers in the Discovery study reported being less involved in "planning the work and working the plan" than were the family managers. As one key nonfamily executive told the research team, "I know more about Bob's grandchildren than I do about where we are headed as a business."

This sense among nonfamily managers may be based on comparisons with previous jobs in other corporations, in which they felt that they had a greater role in planning and leading. Alternatively, it may be the result of their perception that they are being kept in the dark regarding succession. Or they may have been left out of the loop in some important business-planning activities.

Concerns about Succession

Next-generation and other family members were relatively more confident than nonfamily managers that the business would stay in the family. The two groups also differed in the degree to which they believed that the successor to the present leader would be a member of the owning family, with nonfamily managers much more certain that the next CEO would be a family member. So, somewhat counterintuitively, while nonfamily managers were less certain that the company would remain a family company, they were much more convinced that the next CEO would be a family member. And a significant difference existed on the extent to which nonfamily managers and family members agreed with the statement "The successor CEO here will be the best of possible candidates regardless of family relationships." Perhaps not surprisingly, family members were more positive than were nonfamily managers that this would be the case.

These findings present a challenge for CEOs of family companies: How can they motivate top-flight executives who realize that the top leadership positions are likely to go to family members who may be less qualified than they are? Some nonfamily managers nurture unrealistic expectations about their future role in the company until the next generation has actually moved into key positions. For this reason, CEOs have to be aware of the thin line between unrealistic expectations and demotivation, and they must find ways to prevent their best nonfamily managers from crossing it.

CAREER OPPORTUNITIES FOR NONFAMILY MANAGERS

I want the next generation of leaders to see Marriott International as being the best at what it does. . . . We're not trying to develop the company and sell our family interest on the open market. We're trying to maintain our long-term family commitment, since whatever wealth our family has is totally caught up in this business. We've devoted our lives to it; I've devoted a lifetime to it; and I hope my kids will. . . . At the same time you watch [other associates] grow and see them develop at work; you see someone enter Marriott as a bellman and become a senior vice president. The opportunity to provide people with that sort of growth experience is very special, special indeed. . . . The foundation of Marriott's success for 75 years has been our enduring belief that our associates are our greatest assets . . . and a focus on growth.

—*J. W. Marriott, Jr., Chairman and CEO, Marriott International*[6]

Family-business research shows that career opportunities are unique resources that family companies can turn into a competitive advantage.[7] Career opportunities for family members and nonfamily managers are important assets in promoting business continuity. Confidence that future career opportunities will be available to them is important for nonfamily managers, but such confidence is not always easy to maintain in a family business. After all, stories of nepotism in family businesses abound. And the reality is that in many family-owned and family-controlled companies there is a preference for—if not a commitment to—continued family management.

Can both family and nonfamily managers enjoy the prospect of career opportunities in the future? For the health of the business, they must. Otherwise, instead of counting the best and brightest nonfamily employees among its resources, the company incurs the costs associated with high turnover, low morale, the inability to recruit top-notch managers, and the inability to set benchmarks for family managers. A merit-based and professionally run family-business culture is essential. And the surest way to provide career opportunities to family and nonfamily managers is to promote continued business growth.

COMPENSATION AND BENEFITS

Nonfamily managers are generally less satisfied than family managers with their compensation and benefits. Respondents in this study were asked the extent to which they agreed or disagreed with the statement "Nonfamily managers are compensated fairly and equitably here." On a scale of 1 (disagree) to 5 (agree), CEOs averaged 4.45, the rest of the family 4.36, and nonfamily managers 3.78. This difference is significant, since there is only one chance in a thousand that the difference is purely random. Complaints from nonfamily managers in the study sometimes involved comparisons of the family business with public companies:

- "Owners only look at sales and profitability here. Other corporations would have more criteria against which to evaluate you."

---

[6]Gregersen, H., & Black, S., J.W. Marriott, Jr., on Growing the Legacy. *Academy of Management Executive, 16*(2), 2002, pp. 33–39.

[7]Poza, E., Hanlon, S., & Kishida, R., Does the Family–Business Interaction Factor Represent a Resource or a Cost? *Family Business Review, 17*(2), 2004, pp. 99–118.

- "Bonuses are said to be performance-based, but we have very loose goals. In fact, goal-setting is nonexistent, which means that the bonus is subjective."
- "Career paths to senior positions are not equally available to nonfamily managers."
- "I miss the benefits from a large company, especially vacation policy. We get very little vacation. Owners work very hard, but they also enjoy very flexible schedules—we don't."[8]

Although executive pay varies from industry to industry, nonfamily managers generally seem to be paid less than their counterparts in public corporations. A study comparing compensation policies and practices in large family businesses and publicly held firms found that the average salary in management-controlled (publicly held) firms was 15.4 to 29.5 percent more than the average salary reported for owner-controlled firms.[9] This study indicated no differences in economic performance between these two types of businesses and therefore attributed the pay differential to the agency costs of running a business when management and shareholders are different entities. In other words, family businesses enjoy lower labor/employee compensation costs but it appears that this is particularly to the detriment of nonfamily employees (although there is some evidence that family-member CEO salaries are also generally lower than they are for CEOs of management-controlled companies).

Although nonfamily managers tended to be less satisfied than family members with their financial compensation, several nonfamily managers in the Discovery study nevertheless highlighted the nonmonetary rewards and advantages of working for a family-owned business. As one person put it, "The family feeling and accessibility to the top are definite pluses of working in a family business."

Vacation policies were an issue in at least one firm, in which nonfamily managers saw family members as enjoying more leisure time than they did. Although nonfamily managers acknowledged that owners work very hard, they pointed out that owners also tend to have flexible schedules, something that nonfamily managers craved. Several research projects have studied the attractiveness of this flexibility to women family members who join a family business.[10]

Unlike larger publicly held companies, which usually have organizational charts and job descriptions that define who does what, entrepreneurial and smaller family businesses often manage their staffs to maximize flexibility and avoid the very costly redundancy of people. For nonfamily managers, this may mean assuming responsibility and taking the initiative and then having to move out of the way when the owner gets involved. On the bright side, the active and flexible role of many family-business owners allows employees to see that the owners "work feverishly at making things right, so you know why things are important to them."

Some nonfamily managers described relationships in their firms as relaxed, unstructured, and informal. Others reported that they avoided a lot of social contact with family leaders. One of them noted, "I keep my distance. I'm their friend, but I'm not their friend." Another nonfamily manager described the fine line he walked in his company:

---

[8]Poza et al., op. cit.

[9]Werner, S., & Tosi, H., Other People's Money: The Effects of Ownership on Compensation, Strategy and Managerial Pay. *Academy of Management Journal*, 38(6), 1995, pp. 1672–1691.

[10]Cole, P., Women in Family Business. *Family Business Review 10*(4), pp. 353–371, 1997.

Sometimes I take an interest in the company that is even larger than the owners', which helps with the chemistry. But then I need to [be able to] let go at the drop of a hat, too. Good chemistry in this case means that I have a common background with the owners, common values. The two owners and I are regular guys, of middle-class origin, with no pretensions. We are about the same age and of similar work ethic; we all work hard, are industrious, and have high energy.[11]

PERFORMANCE FEEDBACK

Nonfamily managers rate their firms' practices consistently higher than did family managers in only one important category. Nonfamily managers, especially those 51 years old or older, were more satisfied with the performance feedback they received.

Owner-managers who were 51 years old or older were more satisfied with their performance feedback than were 31- to 50-year-old owner-managers. It is possible that older owner-managers get feedback from boards of directors and do not really crave it anyway. The fact that younger family managers reported relatively less satisfaction with performance feedback is significant. While not surprising, this finding points to what may be the Achilles heel of successor development in family companies: CEO-parents provide the next generation with little or no feedback on their performance because they find it difficult to stop wearing the "parent hat."

Nonfamily managers, who often serve as mentors, may limit their negative feedback to younger family members because of the risks inherent in providing such feedback. As one respondent noted, "[I] could be working for them in a few years." The result of the disinclination to provide even "constructive criticism" is that potential successors are deprived of feedback, and on-the-job learning opportunities are squandered during the most critical development period.[12]

EXTENDING THE FAMILY CULTURE TO NONFAMILY MANAGERS

Despite the need of many family firms to maintain a culture that maximizes the loyalty and performance of nonfamily managers, for too long these managers have been taken for granted by owner-managers (and ignored by family-business researchers). Nonfamily managers often feel like outsiders. For this reason, owners must make a diligent effort to demonstrate to them how much their contributions are valued.

Greater openness by CEOs to the perceptions and views of others would clearly be helpful. In addition, CEOs need to close the gap that exists between them and both nonfamily and family managers in the perception of their firms' management practices and ability to handle future challenges. A CEO must take action not to imperil the continuity of the firm by being out of phase with its developmental needs; potential for improvement on this front is enormous. An ongoing dialogue with top managers may well uncover differing assumptions regarding the firm's future. Boards with independent members seem to be a natural mechanism for aiding CEOs in this discovery process, since outside directors are more neutral observers of the agendas of both family and nonfamily managers. If CEOs are willing to listen, active boards and

---

[11]Poza et al., op. cit.

[12]Handler, B., Succession in Family Business: A Review of the Research. *Family Business Review*, 7(2), 1994, pp. 133–157.

succession-planning committees that involve nonfamily managers and high-influence outsiders can make a distinct contribution to a positive succession process and business continuity. They can also increase the commitment and enhance the performance of nonfamily managers.

MOTIVATING AND RETAINING NONFAMILY MANAGERS

How can owner-managers motivate top executives who realize that the firm's prime leadership positions are likely to go to family members? How can family companies retain such executives, who could go to another company where they could likely earn more and have a more clearly structured job in which achievement itself was a key motivator? How can family-business leaders motivate nonfamily managers without allowing them to participate in setting the direction for the business? How can owner-managers ensure the loyalty of nonfamily employees in the absence of equity participation?

Many owner-managers, blinded by their own success, have difficulty seeing problems in the company's practices and procedures, which they have developed and for which they are primarily responsible. Researchers have found that owners' pride in what has made the business successful so far sometimes creates a barrier to change. This often causes a damaging disengagement from key nonfamily managers and next-generation family managers because of the absence of common ground. Nonfamily and next-generation family managers charged with bringing about changes and assuming leadership of continuous improvement opportunities lack the support they need to be successful. Increased self-awareness of this propensity to deny the facts on the part of CEOs can result in significant contributions to future growth for both the family and the business.[13]

It may be up to a nonfamily manager, an independent board member, or an outside advisor to issue the wake-up call. Given the CEO's role as the primary architect of the firm, a CEO's belief in the validity of the firm's business practices may, implicitly at least, depreciate others' views. Lack of motivation on the part of top management to detect problems can threaten the effectiveness or the very survival of the business. Given the significant differences in perceptions of owner-managers and nonfamily managers, taking action to identify and assess problems could allow the CEO to learn enough about the company's current situation to make more appropriate decisions about the company's future. Nonfamily managers and outside advisors play a critical role in facing the facts to ensure business continuity, so creating an environment that promotes their retention and continued commitment are essential (Figure 9.2).

A NONFAMILY MANAGER AS A BRIDGING PRESIDENT OR CEO

Family businesses, especially during the first two generations, are reluctant to hire a nonfamily CEO. One reason may be the culture of independence and deep sense of personal/family identity—which frequently survives across generations—embedded in many entrepreneurial companies. In other family businesses, family members subscribe to a business model that considers a family company superior, both in its character and

---

[13]Poza et al., op. cit.

figure **9.2** | **Ways to Create a Beneficial Environment for Nonfamily Managers**

- Build family/nonfamily management teams that provide complementary skills at the top and set benchmarks for running the family business professionally. Doing so also sends a clear signal to nonfamily managers that career opportunities are available.

- Discuss career advancement opportunities for nonfamily managers—and how the succession process may affect these opportunities—with candor. This is essential and is greatly appreciated by key nonfamily managers. The change and discontinuity that the prospect of succession represents are great stressors and demotivators of ambitious nonfamily employees.

- Involve nonfamily managers in business planning and succession planning. Soliciting their participation in discussions of the strategic direction of the business gives them a much greater sense of inclusion and more focused motivation.

- Offer compensation and benefit plans that are benchmarked to others in the industry, the profession, and the community. Adopting fair pay plans will diminish the risk of losing key contributors. Equity ownership—or, more likely a phantom stock plan that parallels value creation in the common stock and rewards performance over the longer term—is a great motivator.

- Use performance measures—scorecards—to build motivation. Top management derives much motivation from the feedback the job itself provides. Revenues, profit margins, market share, and other financial information all provide significant motivation.

- Hold meetings periodically between key nonfamily managers and shareholders to promote mutual understanding and respect for the different roles and contributions of each.

- Educate the entire family, whether active or inactive in the company, about business and management in order to create common ground between family and nonfamily managers. For example, a quasi-MBA curriculum for the family could be part of family-business meetings (see Chapter 11).

- Survey nonfamily employees periodically to assess the work climate and determine whether the relationship between management and ownership is healthy or requires attention. Effective nonfamily managers must have high levels of maturity and self-confidence, as well as the ability to self-manage; they must not only perform the task they were hired to do but also nurture their relationships with multiple generations of owners and owner-managers.

- Emphasize nonfamily employees' contributions to the family business. American Greetings, for example, watches its internal communications and press releases to ensure that the balance between family and nonfamily is right. Making nonfamily employees part of a successful family in business builds a culture in which people truly are a competitive resource.

- Treat family members like employees when they are at work. Call them by their professional names, require that they follow employee policies and rules, and expect just as much from them as you would from any competent nonfamily manager.

- Use advisory boards or boards of directors with independent outsiders. Such boards help nonfamily managers to feel confident that the family company is being run professionally and objectively, with merit—not blood—as the major determinant of success.

- Develop a family constitution that spells out policy on family employment and family-business relations. This will increase the perception of fairness and mutuality and also reduce the chances of inappropriate family interference in management. (See the sample family constitution in the Exercise section of Chapter 11.)

- Hire high-caliber key nonfamily managers to be bridging presidents or full-term CEOs of the corporation and business mentors of the family shareholders. A nonfamily CEO can serve as a bridge across a generation of owners, as the family-controlled Ford, Marriott, Scripps, and L.L. Bean companies all demonstrate.

organizational climate and in its ability to deploy unique competitive advantages. (We have argued that very point in Chapters 1 and 6.) Still others perceive ownership and management to be one and the same, deeming their separation inconceivable. Some—notwithstanding the evidence from Ford Motor Company, Corning, and hundreds of smaller family firms that have entrusted the CEO job to an outsider for an interim period or for an entire generation—consider the appointment of a nonfamily CEO an irreversible decision, a slippery slope leading to corporate bureaucracy. Although a review of the research and literature, as we have done in previous chapters, would partially support all of the above considerations, there are also compelling reasons for actively considering a key nonfamily manager as a bridging CEO.

Realistically, at least under some circumstances, a nonfamily CEO would constitute a very adaptive response to the goal of keeping the family business under the founding family's control across generations while not subjecting the firm to incompetent, unmotivated, or simply not the best available leadership for a chosen business strategy. (See, for example, Case 10: Fasteners for Retail for an examination of some of these issues.) The following are possible reasons why a family enterprise should consider a nonfamily CEO:

- The outgoing family CEO is not capable of leading a succession process and/or choosing among the children he/she loves equally.
- No successors are qualified to carry out the chosen strategy—for example, a business plan to significantly expand the company to serve a global rather than a regional marketplace.
- Potential successors are too young or are not quite ready for the job, and a world-class outsider could represent both a role model and a provider of substantive mentoring during their developmental process.
- The owning family recognizes that the business needs leadership that will focus on the future, not the past.
- The business needs dramatic change. Internal candidates, especially members of the owning family, are too wedded to a particular product, location, or way of doing business that is now under heavy competitive attack and incapable of producing a profit.
- The owning family sees the need for change but desires to keep the business under family control; thus, they prefer a transformational nonfamily CEO to an outright sale of the company.

The E.W. Scripps Company, the multimedia concern, acquired Shopzilla, the comparison shopping Internet company. Shopzilla was founded in 1996 by two Wharton School students as a class project and had only recently achieved profitability. Kenneth Lowe, the nonfamily chief executive officer and architect of this move also successfully argued for Scripps' push in the past decade into a variety of new media (like the Food Network, Home and Garden TV, and Shop at Home). This significant strategic shift into new media has produced handsome financial results and rewarded Scripps shareholders with better returns than those achievable through newspaper publishing only.[14] In fact, E.W. Scripps split itself into two separate companies—E.W. Scripps Publishing and Scripps Networks Interactive, Inc.—on July 1, 2008, reflecting

---

[14]Hallinan, J., So Far, Scripps Has Bet Right on New Media. *Wall Street Journal,* June 10, 2005, p. C1.

management's commitment to making better capital-allocation decisions going forward while simultaneously increasing shareholder value by differentiating two very distinct businesses in the eyes of investors and financial analysts.

The decision to go outside the family for the chief executive position is always a difficult but immensely important one. It goes without saying that no one family has all the varied skills required for success in today's hypercompetitive world or a monopoly on leadership ability. But on the other hand, I have argued in the preceding chapters that the family–business interaction represents a tremendous source of value in the creation of competitive advantages. If that is the case, a compelling argument could easily be made for the advantage of a person that embodies that family–business overlap—that is, a family member in the CEO role. Whether to go outside the family or not, then, should be a decision contingent on the particular needs and opportunities that the business faces, the family's preferences, and certainly the skills that are present or absent in family-member candidates. For these reasons, there is no question that it makes sense to cast a wide net in the selection of the best successor CEO, whether family member or not.

John Marriott, 47 years old and one of Bill Marriott's four children, is currently vice-chairman of Marriott International's board of directors. He is also CEO of JWM Family Enterprises, L.P., a private partnership that develops and owns hotels. Marriott International is a $13 billion in annual revenues business ($18 billion if you include the revenues from Host Hotels, a REIT [real estate investment trust] that owns many hotel properties, run by Bill's brother Richard). Bill Marriott, who is now 75, is chairman of Marriott International. But while ownership succession has gone along family lines, management succession has welcomed a key nonfamily manager. William Shaw, a long-time Marriott employee and until recently its President and COO, will become the company's new nonfamily CEO.[15]

Essential to the success of a nonfamily CEO is building credibility with the multiple stakeholder groups (shareholders, employees, customers, supply-chain partners, industry leaders, etc.). A nonfamily CEO expected to bring about change needs to proceed with a sense of urgency but slowly enough to also incorporate traditional values and established core competencies of the family business into the plans. This CEO has to communicate extensively and help shape a consensus on the board and among shareholders regarding the new business plans. The outside CEO also has to provide detailed and timely financial and operating information to all shareholders and eventually groom his or her own successor, sometimes a next-generation family owner-manager.

The worst that could happen with hiring a nonfamily CEO, generally speaking, is that he or she proves not to meet the requirements of the job. In that case, it is always easier to fire an incompetent outsider than it is to fire a daughter, son, nephew, sibling, or cousin.

Perhaps the most encouraging finding of the research on nonfamily managers in family business is that so many have positive views of their firms and their futures. And most are managing change in anticipation of new opportunities and a new, improved family firm. Most key nonfamily managers are not there on day one, but over time their understanding of the uniqueness of a family business grows and so does their appreciation for this form of enterprise. (See Figure 9.3 for an inspirational letter from a

---

[15]Binkley, C., As Succession Looms, Marriott Ponders Keeping Job in Family. *Wall Street Journal*, May 19, 2005, p. A1; Hoover's and Edgar Online data on Marriott International, Inc., per October 3, 2008, search report.

figure **9.3** | **Nonfamily CEO Letter to the Business Owning Family**

January 29, 2004

Dear Joe and family,

As the fifth year of my tenure as CEO draws to an end and the company celebrates its 40th anniversary, I thought this would be a perfect time to reflect on what I have come to realize about the extraordinary nature of working in a family company. When I first arrived at the Jones Corporation, I knew this was a place in which I could flourish. Jones Corp. had everything that was important to me at the time, a great product with a niche market, a strong balance sheet, and an excellent work environment. I could capitalize on these foundation elements and make the owners wealthy. However, after 5 years, I've come to realize how shortsighted I was. Working for Joe Sr. has given me a chance to learn about true leadership, not of a business, but of a family business.

I must admit, when young, inexperienced, and, as he now says so himself, somewhat overconfident, Joe Jr. came into the business followed closely by his younger sister and brother, I thought I was seeing the beginning of the end. It seemed as though providing jobs to three untrained, inexperienced young family members would distract us from what the business could become. The immediate, intruding family conflicts that followed their arrival reinforced my concerns. I became convinced they were an immense liability and I anticipated difficult times ahead. Then Joe Sr. started the family meetings with all of the outside shareholders with the predictable outcome, it seemed to me, to provide a forum for several family shareholders who have never worked for Jones Corp. to get involved in management of the company. If I had my concerns before, I knew we were now on a path that would divert us from the true potential of the company and render us mediocre.

Not long afterward, when Joe Sr. and Joe Jr. began to have confrontations over the direction of the company, there were many nights I told my wife how difficult it was to be in a situation in which the family issues seemed to be overtaking our attention to this wonderful business opportunity. As you now know, my goal at the time was to keep my head down and stay out of what I perceived to be family squabbles. In fact, there were many times I wished your conflicts had been kept totally separate from the management team and me.

Now, 5 years later, I see this family business in a totally different light. I realize that the tension between Joe Sr. and Joe Jr. wasn't just a family conflict, but was a struggle to forge the very best strategy that our company could pursue for the long-term health of the organization, integrating the family and shareholder groups. I realize that the conflicts during management meetings weren't family discussions that needed to be separate from the business, but were discussions that needed to play out between two important managers in the business whose family identities are as much a part of the Jones Corp. fabric as is our niche market, balance sheet, and work environment. In fact, because of the conflict that you so openly had in our strategic planning sessions and your willingness to invite management into the dialogue, I believe we have a future company that is a much stronger company than the one I had envisioned for you when I joined; one that will be strong for another generation with involved family shareholders who are part of the solution.

While I initially viewed your children as a liability, I've now come to appreciate their fierce loyalty to the success of the organization and have enjoyed watching all three in different circumstances serve as ambassadors to the organization, using the family name as a competitive advantage, winning contracts with customers and negotiating with vendors. I have also shifted from thinking of the outside family shareholder group as a potential hindrance to continuity, and I now see them as the key to continuity of the business.

Joe, there was a time when I wished you would provide protection from your family for all of us nonfamily employees. I now realize it wasn't protection we needed, it was inclusion in the family, just as you included your family in the business. I think you have provided an excellent example of the kind of inclusion we needed; you mixed us together to create long-term business solutions and did not protect either from the other. As a consequence, when I first came, I joined a company, and now I have joined a family company.

I wish the entire family continued success and I look forward to the many ways we will work as a team.

Regards,

Stephen Mason Reges

CEO

SOURCE: McClure, S., & Eckrich, C., *Working for a Family Business: A Non-Employee's Guide to Success*. Family Business Advisor Series. Atlanta: Family Enterprise Publishers, 2004, pp. 73–74.

nonfamily CEO to the family that owns the business. This letter may very well set the standard for the desired relationship between the owning family and a nonfamily CEO of the family business.)

OUTSIDE ADVISORS: THE FAMILY-BUSINESS CONSULTANT

Like many other companies, family businesses frequently rely on consultants and professional service providers to perform tasks that management either prefers not to do or considers itself unqualified or less qualified to do. Outside advisors often complement the skill sets brought into the family firm by nonfamily management. Because of the particular needs of private or family-controlled corporate entities, estate planners, insurance specialists, estate-tax attorneys, and even psychologists join the ranks of the "usual suspects"—strategy, human resource, accounting, and information technology consultants. And because of the unique nature of the family–management–ownership system, professionals that are denominated family-business consultants are preferable. They are now available to family-owned and family-controlled corporations. The profession, a highly interdisciplinary one, draws practitioners from different disciplines and professions: law, psychology, management, finance, and academia. The Family Firm Institute, a professional association that represents this new field currently lists over 1200 members worldwide. It has an annual conference, publishes a refereed journal—*The Family Business Review*—and provides both skills to new entrants and continuing education to long-term members (see http://www.ffi.org).

What does a family-business consultant do? First, much like key nonfamily management, family-business consultants can provide subject-matter expertise and an objective detachment from the family in business that adds value in a variety of ways. Family-business consultants often work with family enterprises to address management and ownership issues, including the transfer of management responsibilities and ownership (stock and control) to the next generation in a sound and tax-efficient manner. Succession and succession planning are experienced once in a CEO's lifetime. These are often handled with the help of a family-business consultant because never having performed this task means that the CEO is not an expert, while experienced family-business consultants may have faced this complex multiyear process dozens if not hundreds of times.

Sometimes, family-business consultants are brought in to help the owning family address family issues, maybe even emotional ones, that are blocking or delaying required plans and actions; for example, when a buy–sell agreement between family shareholders developed by the corporate attorney has remained unsigned and unexecuted for 3 or 4 years. Other tasks that family-business consultants are called to perform may include a strategic review or planning process, a review of compensation plans that cover siblings or cousins with very different responsibilities, sibling rivalries in the top-management team, the launching of a new board of directors or advisory board with independent outsiders in it, and the creation of a family council, the body (see Chapter 11) that acts as a board for family matters.

If you think of all the subjects covered in the list above, it becomes obvious that one of the requirements of a family-business consultant is that she or he have a holistic perspective that synthesizes the sometimes conflicting needs of ownership, family, and business management. A complementary requirement of top-notch family-business consultants, then, is that as a result of their professional code of ethics[16] and sufficient integrity and self-awareness, they refer to the appropriate "specialists" work that they are not qualified to perform—whether the required specialty is in estate planning, psychiatry, corporate law, insurance, or finance.

Why not use the professional service providers already on board—the company accountant and lawyer—to perform these tasks when they have the advantage of already knowing the business and the family? Largely because of what constitutes a primary value-adding function of the family-business consultant—his or her being new to the system, not part of an established order. And because family-business consultants make the whole family–ownership–management system their client, rather than the CEO or a branch of the family or the individual legal client (as is established by legal code for attorneys who have to perform so as to not risk engaging in conflicts of interest between parties). Finally, because the complex family–ownership–management system is trying to change, the fresh and objective perspective brought by the family-business consultant makes tasks that are impossible for others to perform doable.

Family-business consultants, like other professional advisors, deserve careful scrutiny in the selection process. Gather information, check references, find out how long they have been doing this work and how many companies they have already assisted in similar processes. Have several members of management and the ownership group interview the prospective advisors, inquire about their professional fees and any referral fees they may collect on the basis of the project or the sale of products, be explicit about outcomes expected, and have them put all of this in writing.

Keep in mind that if family-business consultants do not work out, they can be replaced. But if they do, they can remove barriers, promote momentum, and provide the discipline for continued action required by multiyear processes such as succession and the transfer of power. While the company's board can perform some of these tasks (see Chapter 10), they can often be of greater assistance in these when teamed up with competent outside family-business advisors.

SUMMARY

1 The Discovery Research study found that nonfamily managers tended to regard their firms positively.

2 For nonfamily managers, the complexity of getting the job done is compounded by the need to skillfully manage relationships with family members.

3 When business values and philosophies are transmitted primarily through the family, nonfamily managers may be left out of the loop. Steps must be taken to overcome this barrier to nonfamily management's full commitment and contribution.

4 Career opportunities for both family and nonfamily managers are unique resources that family companies can turn into a competitive advantage. Promoting continued business growth is essential to creating this win–win dynamic for both next-generation family managers and nonfamily managers.

5 Nonfamily managers responding to the Discovery study were significantly less satisfied than family managers with the equity of their compensation.

---

[16]See the Family Firm Institute's code of ethics for family business consultants, developed by its Body of Knowledge Committee and available at http://www.ffi.org.

6 Nonfamily managers serving as mentors may limit the negative feedback they give to younger family members because of the risks inherent in providing such feedback. This promotes a developmental handicap for next-generation leaders.

7 Nonfamily presidents and CEOs can perform a unique service in the interest of family-business continuity. Interim and bridging nonfamily CEOs can focus on the future and have their knowledge and capabilities launch a new strategy or a painful but required change in the organization basis or as a bridge across a generation that lacks the interest or the capabilities to lead the corporation to the next, their focus on the future and established knowledge and capabilities may uniquely fit a new strategy or painful but required change in the organization.

8 Family-business consultants represent a new branch of professional service providers who take a holistic approach to the unique challenges that family businesses face. Working together with nonfamily management and outside advisors, they can help a family business formulate a plan that serves the business well while promoting family unity.

FAMILY BUSINESS GOVERNANCE: ADVISORY BOARDS AND BOARDS OF DIRECTORS

Wemco, Inc., sold an estimated $85 million worth of neckties, largely due to the skills of its board of directors. Sound like an unusual role for a board? Well, conflicts between two brothers had resulted in the loss of business from its two major accounts, May Department Stores and Rich's Department Stores. The brothers could not agree on anything, until they agreed on appointing a board of directors that would help them get the business off dead center and perhaps even help them resolve some of their family conflicts. They appointed 12 directors, 8 of them independent outsiders. The board proceeded to take a very active role in reorganizing the company around well-defined areas of responsibility. The brothers and other key managers with product-line and functional responsibilities had their own areas now and were individually accountable, not just to the president, but also to the board. The board put strategy and strategy review at the top of its meeting agendas and ultimately helped the company turn itself around and focus outside, on its customers, not inside on turf and family conflict.[1]

Governance is a complicated subject when it comes to family businesses because of the sometimes-competing agendas of family, ownership, and business management. *Governance,* as it is used in this book, refers to the ability to optimally discipline and control the nature of the relationship between family members, shareholders, and managers in such a way that the enterprise prospers and the family promotes and protects its unity— as much for the family's sake as for the company's, given that family unity represents a source of value that can be translated into competitive advantage.[2] Public equity markets—through their capacity to create a market for corporate control—discipline management and make it accountable to a company's shareholders. The absence of these markets' influence prevents this disciplining function in family firms; after all,

---

[1]Poole, C., Family Ties. *Forbes,* April 26, 1993, pp. 124–126.

[2]Poza, E., Hanlon, S., & Kishida, R., Does the Family Business Interaction Factor Represent a Resource or a Cost? *Family Business Review, 2004, 17*(2), pp. 99–118.

figure **10.1**   **Governance Structure of Family-Owned, Family-Controlled Business**

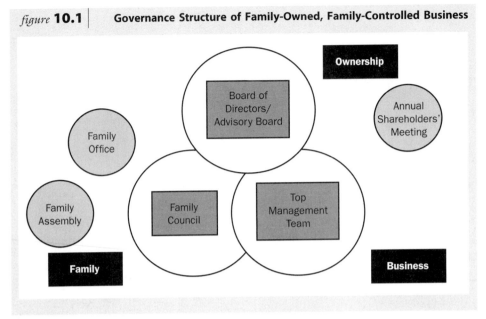

even those that are publicly traded, by definition have an overriding measure of family control.

But governance in a family firm can be fostered through different classes of voting and nonvoting stock, as discussed in Chapter 8. And it can be promoted by appropriate contributions from boards of directors, advisory boards, family councils, family assemblies, family offices, annual shareholders' meetings, and top-management teams (see Figure 10.1). Given family companies' propensity for blurring boundaries between family and business, these institutions can provide essential help in governing the all-important family–owner–management relationship. The current CEO can hardly leave a finer legacy and contribution to family-business continuity than the creation of an effective governance structure.

THE BOARD OF DIRECTORS

The primary responsibilities of a board of directors include the following:

- Review the financial status of the firm
- Deliberate on the strategy of the company
- Look out for the interests of shareholders
- Promote and protect the unity and long-term commitment of the owning family
- Mitigate potential conflicts between shareholders, including majority and minority shareholders
- Ensure the ethical management of the business and the application of adequate internal controls
- Be a respectful critic of management by asking insightful questions
- Review the performance of and hold the CEO and top management accountable for performance and good shareholder returns

- Provide advice to the CEO on acquisitions, divestitures, performance of key executives, executive compensation, human resource issues, growth opportunities, risk management, financing growth, liquidity, etc.
- Bring a fresh, outsider perspective to issues
- Assist in the recruitment, selection (sometimes through a Nominating Committee of the Board), and election of new board members
- Assist in the objective planning and managing of the multiyear succession and continuity process

Unlike many of the other governance bodies depicted in Figure 10.1, the board of directors is a legal entity, usually prescribed in the articles of incorporation. This status gives the board unique rights and responsibilities, such as reviewing the performance of the CEO and conceivably initiating his or her termination—although this would be highly unusual in the world of family-owned companies. These rights and responsibilities expose directors to a larger sphere of liability, which may require the company to provide directors with liability insurance and, in light of the rash of corporate fraud and evidence of self-dealing by corporate management, may discourage some peer CEOs from serving as independent outsiders on a board. For this and other reasons, many family-owned businesses prefer to restrict membership on the board of directors to family members and use an advisory board as a complement to the board of directors. But advisory boards are truly different from boards of directors.

— Most boards of directors emphasize their monitoring of management responsibility, with their mission guided by the implications of agency theory (discussed in Chapter 1). The emphasis on monitoring is reflected on most boards in the publicly traded and management-controlled universe of companies and some of the larger family-controlled but publicly traded companies. When it comes to small to mid sized family firms, particularly if they are privately held, boards are more likely to emphasize an advisory and value-adding responsibility; their mission is guided more by the implications of stewardship theory (also discussed in Chapter 1) than the concerns raised by agency theory. This stands to reason, since there is evidence that family-owned and family-controlled firms experience lower agency costs and fewer agency risks.[3]

Given the incentives built into family ownership and family control (i.e., significant asset allocation to one asset class, the family firm) a fairly compelling argument can be made that owners will caringly and vigilantly exercise oversight. In other words, we assume that when unity exists the combined family–ownership–management system can be trusted to monitor the enterprise. As a result, advisory boards, with a primary mission to add value through advice and counsel, not monitoring, are often quite effective. Note though, in the absence of family unity, or if the agendas of majority and minority shareholders or different branches of the family begin to diverge, as is often the case in later generations, advisory boards are less capable of the degree of influence required to carry out much-needed monitoring and oversight.[4] These boards serve at the request of the often all-powerful family CEO and have no statutory power to monitor the corporation on behalf of its shareholders.

---

[3]Chrisman, J., Chua, J. and Litz, R., Comparing the Agency Costs of Family and Non-Family Firms: Conceptual Issues and Exploratory Evidence, *Entrepreneurship Theory and Practice*, Summer 2004, pp. 335–354.

[4]Westphal, J., Collaboration in the board-room: Behavioral and Performance Consequences of CEO-Board Social Ties, *Academy of Management Journal, 42*, 1999, pp. 7–24.

THE BOARD OF DIRECTORS AND THE FINANCIAL PERFORMANCE OF THE FIRM

The financial performance of corporations has never been conclusively proven to be related to the presence of independent outsiders on the governing board. Dalton et al., in a meta-analysis of academic research, concluded that there is little evidence of a systematic relationship between governance structure and performance.[5] This was true until groundbreaking research on board composition in family-controlled firms in the S&P 500 found that, consistent with agency theory, companies in which independent directors balanced the influence of founding families on the board performed better and created greater shareholder value. On the other hand, firms that retained founding-family ownership (and relatively few independent directors served on the board) performed significantly worse than nonfamily or management-controlled firms.[6] The findings of this research follow earlier findings that seemed to point to effective governance requiring active, caring oversight[7] in addition to independence. In fact, the significantly higher performance of family firms (in terms of EBITDA and shareholder value) as compared with nonfamily firms in the S&P (cited in Chapter 1) seems to be totally conditioned on the presence on the board of independent directors balancing the caring vigilance of founding-family members. Return on assets, measured by Tobin's Q, was higher for family firms with greater board independence (75 percent of them with independent directors) versus family firms with insider-dominated boards (25 percent with independent directors).[8] Thus, it would appear that at least for the larger, and usually older, family firms in the S&P list, the caring and vigilant oversight provided by family members on the board is eventually undermined by the different incentives for majority and minority shareholders. And in the absence of shareholder unity, agency costs are incurred. Without independent outsider oversight, large shareholders such as family members seem more prone to engage in self-dealing that benefits them over minority shareholders. In this study, independent directors were found to hold a majority of board seats in nonfamily firms but less than half of the board seats in family firms. This same study found that because affiliate directors (i.e., lawyers, bankers, or accountants with a preexisting relationship with the firm) assume a greater proportion of total board seats, the performance of the family firm deteriorates. Affiliate directors do not seem to bring to board deliberations the same high level of contention, diversity of perspective, and healthy influence that independent directors bring. Similarly, when family control of the board exceeded that of independent directors, the firm's performance was significantly poorer, and when family control was less than that of independent directors, company performance was better.[9]

---

[5]Dalton, D., Daily, C., Ellstrand, A., and Johnson J., Board Composition, Leadership Structure, and Financial Performance: Meta-Analytic Reviews and Research Agenda, *Strategic Management Journal, 19,* 1998, pp. 269–291.

[6]Anderson, R. and Reeb, D., Board Composition: Balancing Family Influence in S&P 500 Firms, *Administrative Science Quarterly, 49,* 2004, pp. 209–237.

[7]See Zajac, E., and Westphal, J., Director Reputation, CEO-Board Power, and the Dynamics of Board Interlocks, *Administrative Science Quarterly, 41,* 1996, pp. 64–91; and Chatterjee, S., Board Composition: Active, Independent Oversight is not Enough, unpublished research paper, 2005.

[8]Anderson & Reeb, op. cit.

[9]Ibid.

Because of the unavailability of public records on privately held companies, studies have not been done on the extent to which this applies to the majority–minority relationship often found between working and inactive family members or between branches of the same family in these firms. At this point we can only speculate that the rationale for the findings above, given the incentives present, may very well apply to majority–minority shareholder relations in smaller, private family companies. In fact, given that smaller private firms receive less scrutiny (from analysts, bankers, government, and the media), independent directors potentially play an even more important role in reducing agency conflicts in these companies.

MINICASE | Company Ethics and Balancing Board Composition: The Case of Adelphia Communications Corp.

Adelphia Communication's Chairman and CEO, John Rigas, resigned on May 15, 2002, after 52 years at the helm of the sixth-largest cable system operator in the United States. The following day, his son Timothy Rigas, resigned as the company's chief financial officer. Both subsequently also resigned from the board as a crisis engulfed the company and rumors abounded about its eventual need to file for bankruptcy and to carry out asset sales to ensure its survival. John Rigas, 77, was facing an investigation by the Securities and Exchange Commission (SEC); 18 shareholder lawsuits that alleged different forms of fraud, self-dealing, and lack of disclosure; and an 80 percent drop in the value of the stock when it reopened after being halted from trading in the NASDAQ.

Adelphia's troubles began on March 27, 2002, when it disclosed that the Rigas family had used company assets as collateral for about $3 billion in off-balance-sheet loans to a family-run partnership that had purchased Adelphia stock. Soon thereafter nonfamily investors appeared to be pushing the company into a break-up. In 2002, the Rigas family owned about 20 percent of Adelphia's outstanding stock but had 60 percent voting control. The single largest individual shareholder was not a Rigas family member, but Leonard Tow, the chairman of Citizens Communications, a cable operator from whom Adelphia had acquired Century Communications in 1999.[10]

In 1999, with cable-system valuations at historic highs of 20 to 22 times annual cash flow, Adelphia Communications seemed like a likely target. Any transaction would have represented a financial bonanza for the Rigas family; they had acquired many of the cable systems they now operated at much lower values. But instead of selling, the Rigas family acquired additional cable systems representing about 3 million subscribers, nearly doubling the company's size in 1 year. In 2002, Adelphia Communications had about 6 billion subscribers and close to $4 billion in annual revenues.

The company, founded by John Rigas in 1952 with a compelling vision and $300 to acquire the first cable system, grew tremendously throughout the 1980s and 1990s. Highly leveraged acquisitions were the source of much of the growth. "John, like a lot of entrepreneurs, has a huge capacity for risk," says Charles Updegraff, Jr., chief executive officer of Citizens Trust Co.

---

[10]Farrell, M., *Multichannel News*, May 23, 2002.

and a boyhood friend of the Rigas family.[11] But John Rigas was not about to become a target of the consolidation in the industry. His own opinion was that "If it wasn't for the children—they've had a lot of experience, they do the job exceptionally well, they know the business and they're committed—then I would probably have been a candidate [to sell] and do what others did."[12]

John Rigas dreamed of continuity. He expected next-generation family members to participate in both ownership and management of the firm. The son of Greek immigrants, John founded Adelphia with his brother Gus. The company's name is derived from the Greek word "delphi" meaning brother. Three of John Rigas's sons worked at Adelphia—Timothy, a Wharton graduate, joined in 1979 and eventually became the CFO; Michael joined in 1981; and James, the only married son, joined in 1986. John, Timothy, Michael, James, and Peter Venetis, John Rigas's son-in-law, were all on the board of directors. Four outside directors made up the rest of the nine-person board. Independent directors were a minority and, according to company records, exercised little influence.

The company exhibited a strong family culture in other ways. Headquartered in Coudersport, Pennsylvania, town–company relationships were the source of legends. The Rigas family extended its family reach to cover employees and their family members requiring special medical attention and financial assistance in times of need. They also demonstrated significant altruism toward Coudersport; the Rigas family insisted on keeping the company's headquarters there, instead of moving it to a larger metropolis, helped fund the local hospital, plowed the roads, and refurbished buildings and public spaces to enhance the town's image. This caring attitude toward employees and the community was reciprocated with a special loyalty. An employee, for instance, bailed John Rigas out of defaulting on a $25,000 loan he used to acquire another cable operator in the 1960s by loaning him money from her inheritance.[13]

Auditors, forensic accountants, and investors ultimately discovered evidence of company payments to fund Rigas family interests: a golf course, cash advances to the Rigas family-controlled Buffalo Sabres hockey team, and to family members who faced margin calls on their investments in Adelphia stock. Adelphia also guaranteed Rigas family loans, all to the surprise of the four outside directors on Adelphia's board of directors, who along with the five family members on the board had oversight and management responsibility for the company.

In April 2005, both John and Tim Rigas were convicted in federal court of a variety of counts of fraud, self-dealing, and looting, and were sent to a federal penitentiary to serve their sentences. John and Tim Rigas were sentenced in June to 15 and 20 years in prison, respectively.

[11]Frank, R., The Wall Street Journal, May 26, 2002.
[12]Farrell, M., Multichannel News, May 20, 2002.
[13]Frank, R., op. cit.

THE FAMILY-BUSINESS ADVISORY BOARD

Establishing an advisory board with independent outsiders, instead of just relying on an internal board of directors, represents a very healthy development for many family-owned businesses. This change tends to have a positive influence on managerial accountability and succession-and-continuity planning in the firm. If, as the company grows or moves from one generation to the next, adding independent outsiders to the board of directors becomes more feasible, the advisory board can be folded into the board of directors. Table 10.1 summarizes some important points about advisory boards made by experienced outside board members during a business-school program on the subject of family-business boards.

Notwithstanding the significant differences between the propensity of boards of directors to monitor versus that of advisory boards to advise, throughout the rest of this chapter, the terms *board* and *family-business board* will be used to refer to both boards of directors and advisory boards. This is in the interest of efficiency and clarity and in recognition that for most family firms a caring and vigilant board, whether advisory or statutory, represents sound practice. In the material that follows, unless the discussion specifically distinguishes between a board of directors and an advisory board, all subsequent references to family-business boards should be understood to apply to both.

Boards versus Independent Advisors/Consultants

Advice to the CEO of a family-controlled company can come in a variety of ways. Many smaller family-owned businesses that do not have a board of directors with outsiders and have not convened an advisory board claim that individual advisors—attorneys, accountants, financial planners, business consultants, psychologists—bring enough fresh, independent perspectives to the firm. Although individual advisors are generally great contributors to the managerial expertise, strategic planning, and business activities of family-owned firms, many differences exist between fee-for-service advisors and independent outsiders serving on family-business boards.

The first issue is one of independence, which is at the heart of the concern over the propriety of accounting firms' auditing and certifying the financial statements of companies for which they also perform lucrative consulting assignments. Individual service providers generally cannot offer a family business the same capacity for independent thinking and respectful disagreement that outside board members can. Another issue is that of commitment and continuity over the long term. With the exception of some attorneys and accountants who become part of the extended family, most consultants perform their work within the limited time frame (perhaps 12 to 36 months) of a project. A major difference between independent board members and outside consultants is the board members' commitment to a longer-term relationship with the company and its principals.

Clearly, consultants and other professional service providers offer substantial benefits to family companies. But compelling reasons exist for creating a board so that independent outsiders commit over a long period to understanding, influencing, and adding value to the firm. Their unique perspective on what the CEO and other key managers are thinking and doing is invaluable to the family business.

table **10.1** | **Suggestions from a Panel of Experts on Advisory Boards**

Reasons for Having an Advisory Board

- It's lonely at the top.
- Outsiders with a commitment to the company can add perspective, problem-solving ability, expertise, strategic thinking, and a network of contacts that complement those of an able CEO and top-management team.
- Different visions of the future between generations and predictable differences between family members who are active in management and those who are not can be positively influenced by the facilitating, moderating, cajoling, and professionalism of a board.

Conditions Necessary for an Advisory Board to Be Effective

- CEO/family must be willing to share information (e.g., financial information, business plan).
- The CEO must make board members feel welcome, be willing to involve them in the business, be honest with them, and expect them to be loyal critics, not a rubber-stamp board.
- The CEO and board members must do their homework—they must be prepared for meetings and be available for follow-up action and ongoing coaching.

What an Advisory Board Can Do for a Family Business

- Assist in planning for the future
- Provide help with objective financial analysis, its review, and its implications
- Assist with strategy and product/service development
- Help the CEO establish and review goals (but not set or dictate goals themselves)
- Suggest ideas on how to make processes, relationships, etc., better
- Assist in networking with other CEOs and partnering with and benchmarking against other companies
- Help in choosing a successor
- Hold CEOs, successors, and top management accountable

Meeting Schedules and Agendas

- Typically, meetings are scheduled quarterly. The board is convened more frequently during growth or conflict.
- The focus is on planning for the future, not rehashing the past.
- Factual history and financial information are provided in materials prepared for the meeting; they are not rehashed in long discussions or presentations and so play a minimal part in the agenda.

Advisory Board Members

- Members are independent outsiders—people with whom the CEO feels comfortable and who will be supportive of but not necessarily agree with the CEO. CEOs should not include on the advisory board those whom they are already paying for professional services (e.g., their own accountants or attorneys). A minimum of three to four outside professionals/businesspeople will provide a diversity of opinion and experience and enrich deliberation.
- Suggestions for finding good advisors include networking through professionals and organizations, using relationships established with businesspeople in other situations, and framing a brief statement of the type of person being sought as a board member.
- Board members should have experience in managing, hiring, and firing; have acuity with finances; have a sense of human-resource management; be ethical; and be passionate

| _table_ **10.1** | **Suggestions from a Panel of Experts on Advisory Boards** (Continued) |

about wanting to make a difference. The first person engaged (when a board is being established for the first time) is critical, as she or he sets the standard for recruiting others. This individual should have experience on for-profit company advisory boards.

- Family members, especially potential successors, may be invited to attend meetings; however, they should not automatically be members of the board. This eliminates family politics and allows family members to be excused during sensitive parts of meetings.

- Term limits should be clearly established and have staggered end dates. However, the terms of those making a significant contribution to the business should be renewed.

- Compensation for board members will depend on the size of the business. Generally, a retainer fee, along with a per-meeting fee, is recommended.

SOURCE: Panel conversation during family company program at Case Western Reserve University, March 2001. Participants were William Litzler, CEO and outside board member; Richard Osborne, professor and outside board member; Ernesto Poza, professor, consultant, and outside board member; and Norton Rose, former vice president of human resources for Progressive Insurance, consultant, and outside board member.

MEMBERS OF THE FAMILY-BUSINESS BOARD

The board of a for-profit enterprise is meant to be a working board. Unlike its not-for-profit equivalent, it does not exist to facilitate fund-raising activities and so does not require representation from an exhaustive group of stakeholders who have the capacity to be potential donors. Because the mission of a family-business board is to work with and advise the CEO—not represent constituencies—it is better kept small. Most group dynamics research argues that board size be limited to five to nine members in order to have it remain a "working" board. The majority of those members should be independent outsiders, such as peer CEOs, business-school professors, and/or professional service providers who derive no revenues from their relationship with the company except through board service fees. Ideally, the individuals chosen should not be friends of the family, as friends tend to turn the board into a rubber-stamp board, devoid of independent and respectful but challenging thinking.

It is also important that no manager, except the CEO, be a member. A CEO and four outsiders, for example, would comprise an ideal small-company board. In larger, multigenerational family companies, it is often a good idea to include a couple of at-large representatives of the family as board members. In this case, the board could have seven or even nine members. Although the CFO, the vice president of marketing, and potential successors might be asked to attend some meetings or segments of meetings to make presentations to the board, they should not be full members. Indeed, successors should not become full members until their succession is imminent and development of their knowledge of board matters has become a priority.

Invited guests also can bring relevant information to the board and report on matters before it. But the idea is to maximize the independent, objective, and fresh perspectives that the CEO receives from board members, not to promote inclusion in order to make people feel good. If inclusion ends up limiting the contributions of board members (because they are uncomfortable discussing an employee's performance or plans affecting that employee in his or her presence), then it works in opposition to the primary purpose of a board.

RECRUITMENT AND SELECTION

When family members other than the CEO are being selected to serve on the board, as is recommended in the case of large multigenerational firms, it is important that a broad net be cast across family branches to cull the best candidates. An effective way to be selective without creating additional issues of fairness for extended families is to have a clearly written policy on board-member selection, which specifies criteria for selection and a process deemed reasonable by a majority of the family. Crafting such a policy, as well as a family employment policy, is often the responsibility of a family council (discussed later in this chapter).

The best candidates for the board of a family-controlled business are successful peers—CEOs of other private or closely held firms and key functional heads—for example, CFOs and VPs of Marketing, or business-unit managers from an S&P 500 company. These are all people who can assist in positioning your company for the future. The fact that they have been in the leadership role, hired and fired, assumed risk, struggled with changing marketplace realities, and still delivered more profits than losses uniquely qualifies them for board duty. An additional consideration should be their ability to work on a team with a diverse group of other successful individuals. Unlike the influence they enjoyed in their own businesses, their ability to add value as a board member will be highly contingent on their effectiveness in a collegial environment. And, of course, their commitment to the enterprise and its mission is essential.

MINICASE | J. M. Smucker and an Independent Board[14]

Richard and Tim Smucker, who run the now 111-year-old J. M. Smucker Co. (SJM), defy conventional wisdom. They share leadership of their family-controlled but publicly traded company as co-CEOs, an arrangement that rarely works elsewhere in corporate America. Their family, with five fifth-generation Smuckers now rising in the management ranks, avoids the squabbles that mark most business dynasties. And they seem likely to pass on an outfit that will be bigger and better-run than the already top-performing outfit they inherited from their father, the late longtime CEO Paul Smucker.

But the Smuckers face some challenges. They have tripled sales in the past 3 years by buying up iconic, but underdeveloped, brands such as Crisco, Jif, and Pillsbury baking mixes, and they now need to integrate them into the Smucker Company. Their stock, at about $48 a share, is off some $6 from its highs in 2005. And they plan to expand the $2-billion-a-year company even more aggressively, promising some 8 percent growth yearly, half through purchases of big-name brands. All that spells big change at the nation's leading maker of jelly, peanut butter, and cooking oil.

Chairman Tim, 64, and President and CFO Richard, 60, say their family—and perhaps surprisingly, their faith—will carry them through. They recently sat down with *BusinessWeek* Chicago Bureau Manager Joseph Weber. Edited excerpts from their conversation follow:

Q: You break a lot of rules: No. 1, it's rare that co-CEO arrangements work. No. 2, when a family business gets into the fourth generation and beyond, oftentimes the family interests diverge and the business goes away. How is it you're able to keep things together?

---

[14]Business Week Online, Co-CEOs at J. M. Smucker, October 4, 2004.

Richard: A family-business consultant and friend of ours, Leon Danco, said to be successful in going from one generation to the next he has found three things that families seem to have. No. 1 is that they have a strong independent board of directors, second is they have a shared religious belief—whatever that happens to be, whatever religion they practice—and third is they have a strong matriarch in the family. And I would say we've had all three of those basically in each generation.

Q: Explain those.

Richard: If you have an independent board, it shows that you're willing to listen, and you're taking in a broader view of the world, rather than what you might see if it were just family involved. Second, it's the shared values. Shared religious belief really gives you shared values .... It's how you treat people. It's how you treat your customers. It's demanding responsibility, personal responsibility, which translates into business responsibility, ethics—your personal ethics determine your business ethics. And ethics has a very key role. It's one of our basic beliefs. And then the strong matriarch in the family, she'll probably salve disputes within the family and keep the family together.

SOURCE: BW Online, October 4, 2004.

Referrals of candidates may come from other CEOs, business associates, advisors, lawyers, accountants, consultants, bankers, and university professors, particularly those involved in entrepreneurial and family-business programs in business schools. Networking through business seminars and university programs can prove very helpful. Selection of the first board candidate is critical; therefore, the standards to be met by this first recruit should be high. This individual's reputation, competence, and willingness to serve on the board will play a significant role in the company's ability to attract other highly qualified candidates. Ideal board members do not serve in pursuit of wealth or glory; they already have both. Good candidates value the company of equally successful peers and the service they can provide to CEOs and their companies. After all, most high-potential candidates are at a stage in life when giving back to the industry and the community is of paramount importance.

Board duty is not exclusively an intellectual exercise. Board members will likely be called on to assist during difficult times and to make difficult choices. This is particularly true if they are going to be involved in succession and continuity planning. In that case, CEOs who have been through the process themselves make excellent board candidates. One of the truisms of owner-manager succession is that it happens only once in a lifetime, which means that most CEOs have very limited experience on which to draw. And sometimes the experience of a later-generation CEO with his or her own predecessor is not one that he or she particularly wants to emulate. While that experience may cause the current CEO to empathize with the next-generation successor, it likely will not guide the CEO in his or her own process of letting go and transferring power. Somebody who has recently gone through the succession process, on the other hand, can be of tremendous value as a mentor, coach, and confidant.

Criteria must be developed that respond to the company's mission for its board, which will depend on the situation the company is facing when the board is assembled.

---

table 10.2 | Criteria for Board Member Selection

General Expectations

- They ask challenging questions that open up the business to an outside perspective and help it adapt to changes sooner; given the high rate of change in the company's competitive, technological, social, and regulatory environment. They also insist on thorough and convincing answers to their challenging questions.
- They hold top management accountable; everyone, especially a "lonely at the top" President/CEO can benefit from periodic reviews and feedback.
- They have ample related experience; risk-taking peers who have been through it before can help guide the CEO. Whether the "it" is seeking capital, strategic planning, growing the business, gaining market share, developing key managers, or succession.
- They bring with them a network of contacts that can help locate talent, financial resources, and new business opportunities.
- They are management professionals. A board is part of the corporate signaling process on professionalism, commitment to the long run and part of developing a great reputation.

Expectations of board members as contributors to the leadership of the company:

- Integrity. This is the core principle on which any leadership activity, including board service, is built. Being capable of acknowledging the brutal facts of the company's current situation is at the heart of board leadership. Acting as a corporate conscience on ethical behavior, while recognizing multiple stakeholder interests is also essential.
- Courage. Effective boards invite confrontation and debate. It is not personal. Effective advisors on the board offer different perspectives and challenge current or popular views.
- Team player. Advisors need to be able to engage in confrontation, collaborative exploration, and complementary value-adding deliberations (from their different skill sets). They also need to give the CEO and key management feedback frequently.

Thus, a company seeking geographic expansion of its market base may want to have on its board the president of a business unit or vice president of global marketing of a *Fortune 500* company. Functional managers—vice presidents of sales, human resources, strategic planning, and engineering, as well as chief financial officers—can be excellent candidates for board service and make special contributions to meeting a company's unique needs. (See Table 10.2 for a list of expectations to share with potential board members during the recruitment process.)

Staggering terms of board members is a good idea, as is implementing a term length of 3 to 5 years. Such a system enables the CEO to bring new, fresh perspectives to the board and at the same time relieve board members who have already contributed most of their thoughts and rich experiences. The board members who continue to reinvent themselves and show a unique ability to continue to contribute from an accumulated base of intimate knowledge of the company can always be retained beyond their specified term. This system provides the best of both worlds—it allows the CEO to easily make the transition to new directors or advisors, and it permits board members to be offered another term if their contributions continue to be significant.

It is wise to pay attention to the complementarity of potential board members' skills. Having a cross section of board members with a variety of skills, experiences, and capabilities will help to ensure that, as the board responds to the special needs of the business, the CEO receives advice from people who have demonstrated good business judgment in the past.

table **10.2**	**Criteria for Board Member Selection** (*Continued*)

- Execution. Although raw intelligence and analytical ability can be a great asset to an advisory board, only those who have executed ideas understand what it takes to make great ideas grow and bear fruit.
- A champion in the development of people—helping others succeed. Advisors need to be able to facilitate the achievements of others. They must have the capacity to get people to improve their results in the pursuit of goals.
- Persistent and proactive. An effective advisor has to follow up, take action, and make things happen, even between board meetings, in serving the mission of the board. An advisor's proactive stance on a variety of issues and activities will ultimately have an impact on the competitiveness, effectiveness, and long-term performance of the company.
- Focused on the future. Rehashing the past may promote learning from experience, but the primary responsibility of advisors on the board is to assist in creating a more effective future. The bulk of a board's agenda should focus on planning and strategizing, not on reviewing history. One implication of this—the company has a responsibility to provide financial and operational information to advisors by mail in advance of the meeting so that a minimal amount of board meeting time is spent on financial and operational reporting and review.

Expectations of board members at the task or activity level:

- Review the financial status and future prospects of the corporation.
- Assist in securing financing and launching marketing initiatives.
- Review and collaborate on business strategy, including growth opportunities.
- Promote objective dialogue on growth, financing, and ownership structures.
- Assist in networking with other CEOs, partnering with and benchmarking against other CEOs.
- Assist in career planning and professional development of key management.
- May assist, if asked by the President/CEO, in reviewing and making recommendations regarding key managers' incentive and compensation.

SOURCE: Adapted from Bennis, W., & Goldsmith, J., Learning to Lead: A workbook on becoming a leader, 3rd ed. New York: Basic Books, 2003.

MINICASE

A small specialty-apparel company contacted the family-business center of a local university for assistance in launching an advisory board. A faculty member guided the business in assembling an information book on the company and the owning family to be used to brief prospective board members. This book also contained a mission statement for the board and a succinct job description for board members. In this job description, the company CEO communicated his expectations of board candidates, should they agree to serve. The first recruit was a high-profile third-generation owner of a local supermarket chain with an excellent reputation. Once he joined the board, getting four additional outsiders to say yes to board service proved relatively easy.

During the first meeting of the advisory board, the mission statement drafted for the board was reviewed, rewritten with independent board member input, and finalized.

Expectations that the second-generation CEO and third-generation president had of board members were discussed. Also discussed at this first meeting were board members' expectations of full disclosure, access to people and information, and periodic reviews of the CEO, the president, and board performance.

COMPENSATION AND MOTIVATION

When it comes to the question of whether to provide compensation to board members, the answer is yes. Attractive compensation is important not because board members need the money but because the money signifies a firm expectation of contribution and willingness on the part of a CEO to listen to and be influenced by a group of peers who are forward-thinking and well prepared for board meetings. Board members are expected to engage in follow-up conversations and meetings with various members of the firm and/or owning family after the formal board meeting. It seems only fair that such important responsibilities not depend on volunteerism on the part of generous businesspeople.

Because of the value that board members can add through activities beyond attendance at official board meetings, their compensation often has two components: a per-diem fee for attendance at meetings and an annual retainer. Standard total compensation for board service ranges from $8,000 annually per board member (in the case of advisory boards in small family-owned businesses) to about $60,000 in cash and stock options (in larger family-controlled but publicly traded companies). Inflation and changes in the marketplace, among other factors, may affect the appropriate amounts. Thus, to be sure that the offer conveys the firm's commitment to the board and high expectations for its members, it is best to consult the marketplace before making an offer. Trade association guides, annual reports of publicly traded firms in comparable industries, and family-business centers in business schools and local universities can all offer guidance on this subject. A quick rule of thumb that many CEOs have found useful to determine board-member compensation is to divide their own salary by 220 (approximately 220 working days in a year), divide that figure by 2 (since board meetings usually last half a day or less), and then multiply by 4 (the number of board meetings in a year). Whatever the amount turns out to be, pay approximately half of it on an annual retainer basis, to communicate the importance of always being available to the firm, even between board meetings, and the other half as a per diem for board-meeting attendance.

More important than their compensation, of course, is board members' continued motivation. Unless the CEO allows the independent outsiders to influence the company with their advice, these board members are likely to exercise their ultimate act of independence and leave the board. Top-notch board members are in demand; they go where their ideas will be listened to and where their contributions will make a difference.

THE BOARD'S ROLE IN SETTING COMPANY STRATEGY

The contribution of the outside directors of Cadbury Schweppes was to ask the right questions. These questions were sometimes uncomfortable, like whether parts of the business should be sold to put more resources behind those that were to be retained, and they were not questions we would necessarily have raised from within the business. It was up to the executives to provide the answers, but from this board dialogue between insiders and outsiders a bolder and ultimately more successful strategy was hammered out than had we not had the benefit of that external view of the firm and its prospects.

—Sir Adrian Cadbury, Chairman of Cadbury Schweppes[15]

The nonfamily chairman of the board of a family-owned company contacted a family-business consultant with an assignment. Over the past several years, the board of directors had been unable to assist the family company in setting direction because the board lacked a clear sense of what the family strategy was. In other words, board members were at a loss about what the family shareholders wanted of the company. They also did not know what the family wanted its relationship to the company to be in the future and whether continued family control was desirable. The board of directors had just been restructured to add several additional outsiders, and the first nonfamily chairman of the board had been named. Board members believed that the time was right to collect data on shareholders' priorities. The consultant inquired about a variety of possible scenarios, goals, and financial return expectations before asking share-holders to select and prioritize their choices. Aided by surveys and private conversations with shareholders, the consultant summarized the results of the inquiry and reported to shareholders at a family retreat. The results were discussed, checked for accuracy, and validated with all family members present. Conversations among shareholders were then facilitated, and a third-generation/fourth-generation vision for the family enterprise was drafted. A proposed direction for the company—which shareholders were willing to support—was presented to the board immediately following the family retreat. The chairman of the board and board members made it a point to express their gratitude to family members for having provided information that would be critical in allowing them to fulfill their responsibilities as directors of the company.

Clearly, outside board members are essential to the strategy-making process in family businesses. However, appointing outsiders to the board means sharing the responsibility for the direction of the business with people beyond the family and the top-management team. It means sharing the CEO's dreams. It also means letting outsiders see the company's financial records and get personally acquainted with the members of the next generation, the shareholders, and their dreams. While this may be somewhat uncomfortable for family executives, the board needs to have access to the data and the people involved if it is to help the company plan for the future.

Top management in family firms, not unlike executives of management-controlled companies, are generally quite occupied with the daily running of the business. Strategy is often considered important but not urgent. As a result, the company's strategy is in default mode. Periodic adaptations are made as opportunities emerge, but not very often. On the other hand, family businesses that retain their entrepreneurial tradition make strategy on a daily basis. But the strategy remains locked in the heads of the CEO and a couple of coconspirators. The board provides a reminder that a disciplined, ongoing approach to strategic planning is needed. It also offers the means to make the plan more substantive, more clear, and more easily communicated to the troops. Questioning and respectful contentiousness on the part of a working board are a source of much wisdom.

---

[15]Cadbury, A., *Family Firms and Their Governance: Creating Tomorrow's Company from Today's.* London: Egon Zehnder International, 2000.

Chapter 6 reviewed strategic planning in family companies. The unique advantages enjoyed by family-owned or family-controlled businesses were discussed. It is hard to generalize on the subjects of strategy and competitive advantage, given the population of very different firms with very different products competing in very different markets and market niches. But an important competency that leads to competitive advantage in many entrepreneurial and family companies is agility in meeting customer needs. Retaining this competency across generations is not always easy. In fact, management experts have argued that computers, sophisticated information and financial systems, process reengineering, and six sigma efforts, have turned management attention inward. As a result, these managerial innovations have conspired against a customer orientation.[16] In family companies, this increasing bureaucratization—which may require that employees attend more meetings, be involved in more programs, and have less real-time contact with customers—may be accompanied by a family dynamic that slows decision making. This same family dynamic may lead to a pattern of shelving unresolved issues so as to avoid the conflict and anxiety they produce. Boards can play a critical role in breaking through the logjam and helping family companies retain their competitive fitness.

THE BOARD'S ROLE IN ADAPTATION OVER GENERATIONS

The job of the board is all about creating momentum, movement, improvement and direction. If the board is not taking the company purposefully into the future, who is? It is because of the failure of boards to create tomorrow's company out of today's that so many famous names in industry continue to disappear.

—*Sir John Harvey-Jones, Former CEO and Chairman, Imperial Chemical Industries*[17]

Customer-oriented businesses are always changing, always adapting to customer-induced changes in competitive dynamics. These businesses recognize the need to change in order to remain competitive. Families, by their very nature, are about stability, consistency, enduring values, love, and caring, all of which support individual development and family harmony. They tend to focus on legacy and continuity, not change. As a result, family companies often have difficulty dealing with conflict rooted in different visions of the future. And yet, quite naturally, the visions of two generations are likely to be very different. Some owning families seek out psychologists and family therapists in the hope of resolving conflict. Others decide to gun the engines of growth so that conflicts may be seen more dispassionately in the context of a company growing in resources and opportunities. Still other families decide to talk and talk and talk across generations, aided by their boards and advisors, until a new direction can be supported by all of the generations involved.

Adaptation is not easy. If it were, the expected tenure of S&P 500 companies would not be a mere 10 years. Nor would 80 percent of all family-owned businesses have failed to survive 60 years of operation (from 1924 to 1984).[18] The conflict between the old and the new in a family business is more often than not a personal conflict between a parent and his or her child. It cannot get any less objective than that;

---

[16]Drucker, P., Drucker on Management. *Forbes Magazine*, November 11, 1999.

[17]Harvey-Jones, J., *Reflections on Leadership*. New York: HarperCollins, 1988.

[18]Foster, R., & Kaplan, S., *Creative Destruction*. New York: Currency/Doubleday, 2001; and Ward, J., *Keeping the Family Business Healthy*. San Francisco: Jossey-Bass, 1987, p. 2.

nothing is thicker than blood. This creates an opportunity for board members to mediate, facilitate, cajole, illuminate, provoke, and ultimately get the two generations to jointly create something they both can support. After all, it takes two generations to supply the two critical ingredients for sound adaptation in a family business: (1) the wisdom to know what has worked in the past and what has made the company successful thus far and (2) the passion to seize today's opportunities, embrace change, and thrive in the decades ahead.

The Board's Role in Succession and Continuity Planning

> A formal board was introduced in the Cadbury family business on the death of one of the two brothers who ran the firm from 1861 to 1899. My grandfather recognized that the next generation of family had to be brought into the management of the firm and that a stable structure for the future direction and control of the firm had to be put in place. A board structure of this kind was less dependent on individuals than the previous partnership and it had the authority to decide on such questions as succession and the entry of family members into the firm. The board's authority stemmed from its being formally organized with a clear statement of its responsibilities and from its collegiate nature. The decisions of the board were not those of an individual but those of a team. . . . Although it was more of a management committee than a board of directors in the modern sense, that did not detract from the importance of this move. It brought order into the running of the business, it ensured that issues were dealt with and not shelved and it provided for the future continuity of the business.
>
> *—Sir Adrian Cadbury, Chairman of Cadbury Schweppes*[19]

A hospitality company with $150 million in annual revenues owns and operates several restaurant and hotel concepts. It has been working on its succession process for approximately 5 years. Although the firm is still chaired by the second-generation former owner-manager, it is now being managed and operated by his three sons, who already own a significant portion of the company stock. The owner-managers meet periodically with a family-business consultant and have initiated a family council to air and address issues pertaining to the family. This firm and its owners are not short of advisors and consultants, yet they depend heavily on the board when it comes to succession planning.

In fact, while all the other consulting is going on, the issue of how the company is going to be managed—whether by a single owner-manager and CEO to whom his siblings report or by a sibling team operating as an office of the president—is being deliberated by the board. Several recommendations have been made by the consultant, and the board has agreed to an experimental period (not called that, of course) during which all three siblings, running two separate business units and the corporate finance function, will operate as a top team and report directly to the board. The board has a contingency plan, though. It knows that if the sibling-team concept does not work, a traditional CEO can be installed. Months of conversations with the siblings, other key nonfamily managers, key customers, partners on some of the properties, and the chairman (Dad) have given the board the information it needs to be able to choose the best candidate.

---

[19]Cadbury, op. cit.

For a parent, the anguish of having to pick one, and just one, of his children to lead the family company is hard to imagine. It is avoidance of this extremely difficult decision that motivates many CEO-parents, who deeply doubt the viability of a sibling partnership, to turn the succession question over to the board. Regardless of how compelling the arguments are in favor of a particular successor, choosing one child over another for that top job is absolute torture for the CEO-parent and his or her spouse.

While a board of directors may have to rely on many others for the facts, it can always count on its independent outsiders to review the facts and render objective opinions and recommendations. And a board is in the unique position of being able to enhance the perceived quality and fairness of the succession decision by taking responsibility away from family members. This third-party stamp of approval significantly increases receptivity to the new company boss on the part of both key nonfamily management and family members.

One other critical perspective that a board of directors can bring to these deliberations is questioning the implicit assumption held by many families in business that only continuity with family members as owners and managers, or maybe even in an ownership role exclusively, is most advisable. Continuity in the hands of the founding family is not the only badge of honor or indication of success. By pushing back on the family's assumption of what constitutes success—the ultimate goal—more effective strategic decisions will be made on behalf of both the family and the company.

FURTHER RESEARCH INTO THE IMPACT OF BOARDS ON FAMILY-OWNED BUSINESSES

Data from the Discovery Action Research study suggest that the existence of a board deemed effective by respondents—along with other managerial practices such as performance feedback, succession planning, growth orientation, and business planning—was significantly correlated with positive communication processes in the firm.[20] Family-business owners who had boards with two or more outsiders acknowledged that these boards had contributed to the effective management of their firms. The following benefits of having outsiders on the board were mentioned most often:

1. They provide unbiased objective views.
2. They bring a fresher and broader perspective to issues of concern to the firm.
3. They bring with them a network of contacts.
4. They make top managers accountable for their actions.[21]

THE IMPACT OF SARBANES–OXLEY ON THE FAMILY BUSINESS AND ITS BOARD

As a result of a growing incidence of corporate fraud detected, the U.S. Congress passed and President George W. Bush signed into law the Sarbanes–Oxley Act of 2002 on July 30, 2002. Sarbanes–Oxley represented the culmination of some of the largest bankruptcies of publicly traded companies, the widespread suspicion that the financial

---

[20]Poza, E., Alfred, T., & Maheshwari, A., Stakeholder Perceptions of Culture and Management Practices in Family and Family Firms. *Family Business Review*, 10(2), 1997, pp. 135–155.

[21]Schwartz, M., & Barnes, L., Outside Boards and Family Businesses: Another Look. *Family Business Review*, 4(3), 1991, pp. 269–285.

statements of many other companies may have been tampered with, and the closing of Arthur Andersen. The SEC has the ultimate responsibility of interpreting the act and implementing the rules that determine compliance.

By holding corporate directors and key company executives ultimately accountable for the accuracy of the financial reports of their companies, the intent of Sarbanes–Oxley was to restore confidence in Wall Street and the U.S. capital markets. Nevertheless, the act has been controversial. The cost and time-intensity of compliance have proven to be quite high. A study by Financial Executives International puts the costs of complying with Section 404 of Sarbanes–Oxley at $824,000 for companies with annual revenues under $100 million.[22] This represents compliance costs approximating 1 percent of revenues and likely 15 to 20 percent of net profits for smaller publicly traded companies. These are costs that will further shrink the operating margins of companies that can ill afford it. The work, usually done by an outside auditing firm in conjunction with the company's CFO or controller also requires a company's CEO and CFO to annually certify to the SEC that the company's system of internal financial reporting and controls is in good working order.

The act has repeatedly been cited as the reason why fewer young companies are now going public. It has also been the rationale for many previously publicly traded companies going private. Cox Communications, a high-profile family-controlled cable company based in the Atlanta area, decided to go private, according to news reports, in part because of Sarbanes–Oxley. Cablevision Systems, the sixth-largest cable operator in the country, controlled by the Dolan family, also took steps to go private with an offer from the Dolans valued at $7.9 billion. The family believed that regardless of regulatory oversight, the market was undervaluing cable stocks.[23]

To the extent that Sarbanes–Oxley does not directly apply to family-owned and privately held companies, the assumption has been that it is of no consequence to these companies or their boards. Nevertheless, there is growing anecdotal evidence that banks, for instance, are in some cases expecting of their clients the same level of transparency and compliance mandated by Sarbanes–Oxley. In the absence of formal compliance, a functioning audit committee of the board or evidence of best practices in internal controls, bank clients may be forced to assume higher lending rates and fees on their corporate borrowing. Private equity investors, now more attractive to these firms because of the reluctance to do an initial public offering (IPO), are similarly increasing their review and oversight. Finally, because state laws are often highly intertwined with federal laws affecting corporations, states may soon be expecting more from all companies incorporating in the state.

Suppliers too, that depend on family businesses for the distribution or retailing of their products are deemed to be raising the bar on the financial reporting standards of their downstream partners. And if the family business is a strategic supplier to the government, you can count on higher standards going forward.

Boards of directors have no choice but to raise the bar themselves on financial transparency, timeliness, accuracy, and internal controls. Although there will be some costs, new software packages and systems derived from the compliance work done for the larger publicly traded firms will undoubtedly be available soon at much more

---

[22]FEI Survey on SOX Section 404 Implementation, Florham Park, NJ: Financial Executives International, March 2005, pp. 1–6. See http://www.fei.org.

[23]Grant, P., Dolans Seek Buyout of Cablevision. *Wall Street Journal*, June 20, 2005, p.A3.

reasonable prices. Since the work of the board so often depends on a high degree of openness and trust between board members, the CEO, and top management, a beneficial ripple effect of Sarbanes–Oxley for the family firm may very well be increased trust in the leadership ranks based on increased availability of highly reliable data.

THE FAMILY COUNCIL

The family council is a governance body that focuses on family matters. It is to the family what the board of directors is to the business. Family councils primarily promote communication, provide a safe harbor for the resolution of family conflicts, and support the education of next-generation family members about family dynamics and ownership issues.

Family councils frequently develop family-participation policies and deal with issues of liquidity, diversification of the estate, and estate planning. The business/ownership education of family members not active in the management of the business is also an important agenda item for family councils. This body is responsible for ensuring that the noneconomic goals and values of the family are articulated (sometimes via a family constitution or family charter) and given the attention they deserve within the family-business environment. Family councils seldom vote on issues but instead develop policies to guide decisions made by other governance bodies, such as the board and the annual shareholders' meeting.

A family council is often the vehicle for family philanthropy and the creation of family offices to oversee trusts and other financial matters of the owning family. Because it gives family members a voice in the business, a family council relieves some of the pressure to appoint only family members to the board. Indeed, family councils often select one or two at-large members to sit on the board of directors or advisory board in order to represent the family's interest in board deliberations. (A more comprehensive treatment of family councils can be found in Chapters 3 and 11.)

BOUNDARIES BETWEEN THE BOARD AND THE FAMILY COUNCIL

Family-owned businesses tend to have boards that are all family. Family-controlled but publicly traded businesses often remain true to this tradition, although they may allow an attorney and a couple of outsiders to serve alongside family members. For the most part, these boards remain slow to welcome independent outsiders. As a result, keeping a healthy balance between family and business remains a challenge for most family companies. An exception to the rule is evident at Cargill, the largest private corporation in the world that is 85 percent owned by the Cargill-MacMillan family. The family controls only 6 of the board's 17 seats.[24]

As they become multigenerational enterprises, family companies with a tradition of family membership on the board face another challenge: Family members expect that they will automatically become board members because of their family and ownership status. Although it is true that families are well served by at-large representation by family members, overwhelming the board with family influences is seldom in either the short- or the long-term interests of the company, the shareholders, or even the family. A line has to be drawn between family membership and board duty. Family councils

---

[24]Hoover's Online, Company Profiles, Cargill, 2005. See http://www.hoovers.com.

derive some of their ability to contribute significantly to family-controlled companies precisely by helping families draw this line and establish a system of governance that both differentiates and integrates family and business agendas. When it is perceived as an entitlement, family membership on the board, unrestrained by the input of family councils or independent outsiders, often leads to a dysfunctional board, paralyzed by the immensity and intensity of family dynamics. As illustrated by the situation at the *Louisville Courier-Journal* (see Case 1: The Binghams and the Louisville Courier-Journal Companies), when family members know very little about the business's strategy and finances, their service on the board does little to further the effective functioning of the board as a body of ultimate review and accountability.

Family councils, in the absence of boards with independent outsiders, present their own set of problems. Over time, there appears to be a propensity for family members who are not active in the business to become more aggressive in their second-guessing of company management. In the absence of outside board members with high status and good reputations, family members who do not truly understand the difference between owning and professionally running a family company may conspire to meddle inappropriately in business matters. It is as if the existence of a family council empowers shareholders to give voice to issues and concerns that lie beyond their level of understanding of company functioning.

Figure 10.2 illustrates the boundaries that should exist between family councils and boards of directors or advisory boards. Although family councils and boards have different missions, they are also well served by some degree of integration. For example, having two members of the family council serve as at-large representatives of the family on the board will help to ensure that family strategy and family preferences are appropriately considered by the board.

If a company is family-owned or family-controlled, it stands to reason that the family's agenda will, and should, play a part in deliberations on dividend policy, liquidity arrangements, transfer of ownership and control, and even the decision to recommit to continuity or to sell. The real challenge is paying attention to both the family and the business, thereby jointly optimizing the family-business system. The

figure **10.2** | **Boards and Family Councils: How They Work Together**

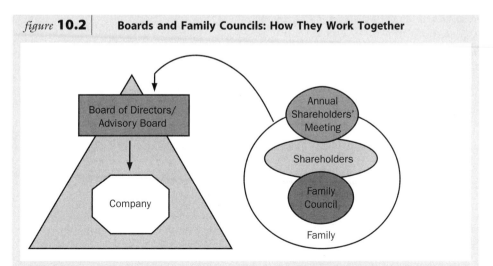

SOURCE: Adapted from Davis, J., Board of Directors of the Family Firm. Notes 9-800-025, March 28, 2001, Harvard Business School.

owning family of the hospitality company mentioned earlier in this chapter drafted a norm, or ground rule, for their family-council deliberations that speaks to this issue. In an effort to do well by both family and business, they wrote on easel paper during their first family council meeting, "We will allow the pendulum to swing back and forth between family and business priorities." Family councils will be discussed further in Chapter 11.

THE FAMILY ASSEMBLY

Because of its size, not all members of a large multigenerational family can work together as members of a family council. As a result, larger families sometimes create an annual family assembly to operate in conjunction with the family council. Family assemblies are another vehicle for education, communication, and the renewal of family bonds. They create participation opportunities for all family members at least once a year. The smaller group that makes up the family council can work on behalf of the assembly during its two or three meetings per year and then report on its progress during the annual family assembly.

THE ANNUAL SHAREHOLDERS' MEETING

The annual shareholders' meeting both meets the legal requirements of corporate law and presents an opportunity for review of management and company financial performance. During this meeting, family members exercise their responsibilities as shareholders and are informed of company's performance, returns on shareholders' equity, and dividends to be distributed. The board of directors is elected at this meeting. Shareholders may vote on other matters on the agenda, including the selection of auditors, changes to the articles of incorporation, and dividend policy. Only shareholders may attend, not extended family members or spouses who are not legal holders of stock. The shareholders' meeting usually takes place only once a year. However, special meetings may be called to address important and time-sensitive issues.

THE FAMILY OFFICE

A growing number of second- and later-generation family firms are creating family offices to assist shareholders in their owner duties and responsibilities. Although the services offered vary depending on the company, family offices can shoulder primary responsibility for joint family investments, family philanthropy, family private equity and venture capital investments, tax and legal advice to shareholders, tax-return preparation, the filing of required legal documents on behalf of the shareholder, shareholder education, the planning and execution of family-council meetings, shareholder meetings and family assemblies, and administration of shared assets or properties—for example, a family vacation property, farm, or ranch.

With roots in Rockefeller's Room 56 (so named because the family office operated out of Rockefeller Plaza's suite 56) and in the family office at Cargill, the largest private corporation in the world, many much smaller family firms today rely on their own family office or a shared-service family office, a multifamily office. The latter, usually housed in the family office of a larger family firm, represents a way to outsource the administration of a family office, with its corresponding cost savings.

Family offices assist shareholders with the responsibilities born out of their owner-ship relation to the company, and in so doing they often help make the owner–company relationship a more positive and disciplined one. (See a more detailed discussion of family offices and their functions in Chapter 11.)

THE TOP-MANAGEMENT TEAM

Family and nonfamily members of the top-management team play a key role in the overall governance of a family-controlled corporation. A top-management team that includes nonfamily managers with skills that complement those of the owning family prominently communicates the family firm's commitment to professional management and business continuity.

Key nonfamily managers help set high standards for work ethic, accountability, dedication, and expertise. These competent managers raise the bar for family owner-managers and, in doing so, send a clear message to shareholders who are not active in management. Including skilled nonfamily executives in top management will likely reduce or eliminate second-guessing by these shareholders and ensure that issues requiring deliberation and decision making stay where they belong—whether with the family, in family councils and family assemblies; with the owners, in shareholder meetings and board meetings; or with the top-management team, in day-to-day business operations. (See Figure 10.3 for a diagram of the various governance mechanisms and their interrelationship.)

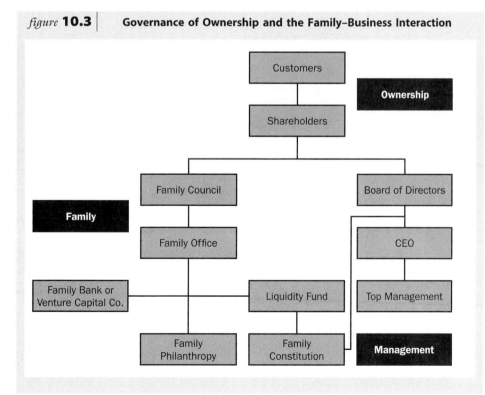

figure **10.3** | **Governance of Ownership and the Family–Business Interaction**

SUMMARY

1 Governance can be provided for through classes of voting and nonvoting stock. It can be enhanced by appropriate contributions from boards of directors, advisory boards, family councils, family assemblies, annual shareholders' meetings, family offices, and top-management teams.

2 The primary responsibilities of a board of directors include reviewing the financial status of the firm, deliberating on company strategy, looking out for shareholders' interests, ensuring the ethical management of the business, being a respectful critic of management, reviewing CEO performance and holding top management accountable, advising the CEO on substantive subjects, monitoring and mediating to reduce conflict between shareholders with divergent interests, bringing a fresh perspective to issues, and assisting in the succession and continuity process.

3 Independent directors perform a particularly valuable function for family firms, where their dominant role on boards has been shown to significantly improve the financial performance of the firm.

4 Unlike an advisory board, a board of directors is a legal entity.

5 An advisory board, which consists of independent outsiders, is often used to complement a board of directors.

6 The first recruit to a company's board is critical; his or her reputation, competence, and willingness to serve on the board will play a significant role in the ability to attract other highly qualified candidates.

7 A family council is a governance body that focuses on family matters, frequently developing family-participation policies and dealing with liquidity issues and estate planning.

8 A family assembly creates participation opportunities for all members of larger multi-generational families at least once a year.

9 At the annual shareholders' meeting, the board of directors is elected. Also, family members exercise their responsibilities as shareholders and are informed of company performance, returns on shareholders' equity, and dividends to be distributed.

10 Key nonfamily managers in the top-management team help set high standards for work ethic, accountability, dedication, and expertise. By doing so they too help govern the family–business relationship in a family company.

FAMILY
COMMUNICATION:
FAMILY MEETINGS,
FAMILY COUNCILS,
AND FAMILY OFFICES

The three Dorsett brothers are barely speaking to each other. "Phone for you" is about all they have to say.

It hasn't always been like this. For more than 30 years, Tom, Harry, and Bob Dorsett have run the successful manufacturing business founded by their father. For most of that time, they have gotten along rather well. They've had their differences and arguments, but important decisions were thrashed out until a consensus was reached.

Each brother has two children in the business. Tom's oldest son manages the plant, Harry's oldest daughter keeps the books, and Bob's oldest son is a rising outside salesman. The younger children are learning the ropes in lower-level positions.

The problem? Compensation. Each brother feels that his own children are underpaid and that some of his nieces and nephews are overpaid. After violent arguments, the Dorsett brothers just quit talking while each continued to smolder.

The six younger-generation cousins are still on speaking terms, however. Despite the differences that exist among them, they manage to get along with one another. They range in age from 41 down to 25.

The business is in a slump but not yet in danger. Because the brothers aren't talking, important business decisions are being postponed. The family is stuck. What can be done?[1]

FAMILY MEETINGS

If a company is family-owned or family-controlled, it stands to reason that the family's agenda will, and should, play a part in deliberations on family employee compensation, dividend policy, liquidity arrangements, transfer of ownership and control, and even

---

[1] Poza, E., ed., Family Firm Institute Case Study Series, *Nation's Business*, May 1991, p. 65.

table **11.1**	Family Meetings

- Are an opportunity to update family members not active in the business about the state of the business: financial results, management, strategy, and the competitive dynamics of the industry
- Are an opportunity for good communication
- Educate family members about the difference between ownership, management, and family membership
- Engage family members in responsible ownership
- Update family members on the estate plan and educate them on the management of inherited wealth
- Allow for policy making, e.g., family employment policy, ownership transfers, etc.
- Are a time for problem-solving and conflict resolution
- Provide a forum for celebration and introspection
- Are a safe harbor for planning the family's future involvement in the business

the decision to recommit to continuity or to sell. The real challenge is creating an optimal balance of ownership, family, and management that fosters a positive family–business interaction through family communication and governance of the family–business system. Family meetings constitute the best forum for achieving and maintaining this optimal balance. (Table 11.1 defines and lists family meeting tasks.)

This third edition of *Family Business* is filled with examples of owning families' efforts to get the ownership–family–management balance right using family meetings and family councils. If you want detailed accounts of family meetings and family councils in operation, all you have to do is read the cases of the Ferré Media Group, Vega Foods, Fasteners for Retail, New Way Distributing, or the Real Estate Development Partners. These are companies from a variety of industries, operating in a variety of cultures, and ranging in annual revenues from $30 million to $400 million. Brief cases from other family companies engaging in family meetings—many smaller and some larger than these—are also found in the pages that follow. These cases all represent a unique opportunity to look through a keyhole at the real-life experiences of families wrestling with achieving the right balance; one that will promote family unity and a continuing spirit of enterprise. I hope that their stories represent more than a voyeuristic adventure through the life of wealthy and enterprising families; that instead these richly narrated "real and live" cases are an inspiration to you in your efforts to create a tailored step-by-step approach to improving communication and fostering family unity.

Family meetings may educate family members about the rationale for a merit-based compensation system—one that differentiates pay levels between cousins on the basis of their different responsibilities and levels of performance. Family meetings can also educate family members on estate and estate-tax issues and guide next-generation members in the management of inherited wealth. They may also allow for policy making on issues such as: (1) family member participation in the business, whether through employment, consulting, subcontracting, board service, or the conduct of family philanthropy; (2) family strategy vis-à-vis the business, determining the desired balance between the family and the business and between growth/reinvestment and higher dividends/current returns; (3) liquidity for individuals or branches of the family who would like to diversify their assets using buy–sell agreements between shareholders; and (4) the rationale for having

table 11.2	Benefits of Family Meetings

- Understanding the family values and traditions that underlie the business and the family's commitment to the business across generations of owners.
- Appreciating more deeply the history of the family and its role in the business and in the successful competitive strategy pursued over the years.
- Understanding the estate plan, ownership-transfer plans, estate-tax liability, and the need for corporate control and agility.
- Defining, over time, the nature of family-member participation in the business. This is especially important for next-generation members who choose not to work full-time in the business but want to contribute to it in some meaningful way. Opportunities for participation—in family philanthropy, community service, and industry and trade association leadership—may be identified that add value to the enterprise and support the family's role in society.
- Providing support to family members. Family meetings can be a significant reference and support group—for example, by financially supporting the education of next-generation members and providing emotional backing to family members with special needs.
- Providing ongoing family problem-solving and conflict-resolution mechanisms. These mechanisms allow families to constructively address feelings of alienation and anger over perceived favoritism or unequal distribution of money, love, influence, or opportunity.
- Creating a transparent succession plan and continuity process.
- Reviewing the returns on the family's investment in the business and legitimizing any concerns that shareholders may have about the management of the firm.
- Making the priorities and preferences of family members known to the board of directors, which has the ultimate responsibility to mesh or at least align family priorities with the priorities and strategic imperatives of the business.
- Professionalizing the business by inviting key nonfamily managers to attend family meetings as resources, teachers, and mentors. By their very skills and abilities, these nonfamily managers convey to shareholders the tremendous value that professional management adds to the family-controlled corporation.

different classes of stock in the interest of corporate control, company agility, and the family's economic well-being. Table 11.2 summarizes the benefits of family meetings.

The very existence of ongoing family meetings or a family council as a forum for family members reduces the likelihood that family concerns will be ignored or inappropriately exported to a board of directors or a top-management team, as occurred in the Bingham family. Attendance at these meetings represents a deposit in the family's emotional bank account—an investment in increasing trust and reducing the family's propensity to become a zero-sum entity.

One multistore retailer ($8 million in annual revenues) started holding family meetings after years of not having done so, except in a most informal way around the holidays and other family gatherings. Planning succession to a third—the cousins'—generation was now on the top-management team's radar. The team was composed of four siblings and a couple of key nonfamily managers. But while succession discussions were one of the espoused reasons for beginning regularly scheduled family meetings, it was a loss of trust that drove the decision. Some members of the family were concerned about possible financial irregularities in one of the business units and wanted to address and resolve this issue. Heated discussions were sometimes part of these meetings, but the two generations ultimately agreed to put in place a better financial reporting and control system.

As a result of their deliberations, they also entered into a legally binding agreement as to the consequences of being found responsible for any fraudulent activity in their respective business units. Trust had been damaged; the already-discussed zero-sum propensities were about to take over family dynamics and the family–business relationship. This group was wise enough to use family meetings to prevent irreparable damage to the family and the family business. It would be naive to suggest that things went back to the way they were prior to this incident; they did not. But the family did address and resolve this issue in a way that made it possible for family members to have unity in the extended family and to share responsibility for the family firm.

Renewing the family's commitment to the business, a natural outgrowth of family meetings, also builds a stronger business. As discussed in earlier chapters, it represents an investment in an ownership group that appreciates the competitive advantage created by patient family capital, improving the chances that shareholders will support the firm's being managed for the long run.[2] Loyal shareholders who are patient capitalists in a family business can provide the company with a unique ability to deploy longer-term strategies, allowing the business to enjoy sustainable competitive advantages that public or management-dominated firms can ill afford.

Notwithstanding all the significant benefits discussed above, family meetings are not a universal solution for what ails families in business. It depends on the family and the unique developmental history of the family in business. The best way to determine whether holding family meetings is an appropriate practice for a family in business is to ask questions such as: Why have a family meeting? and What would be better as a result of holding a family meeting? Because a compelling reason or goal is central to the success of family meetings, Table 11.3 explains a goal-oriented approach to developing a family meeting agenda. In the absence of a compelling reason to hold a family meeting and to continue to meet, it is very unlikely that a family will invest the time and emotional energy needed to make the meetings successful and the family in business better for it.

In addition to the requirement that a family meeting respond to a well-defined set of needs and expectations and lead to an agenda that is largely goal-based, there are some other precautions to keep in mind.

1. Family meetings are not a good time to bring together relatives who are not speaking to each other. In other words, while family cutoffs (the severing of the

---

table 11.3 | Goal-Oriented Family Meetings

List the reasons you want to hold a meeting, such as to address

- Ownership issues such as dividends, family strategy, a shareholder meeting, and the estate plan
- Family issues such as preserving family unity and policy making on family member employment
- Management issues such as the financial results of the business, compensation of family members, and updates on company strategy and succession planning

Prioritize the issues for discussion.

What are the expectations? What would end up better as a result of holding the family meeting?

---

[2]Miller, D. & Lebreton-Miller, I., *Managing for the Long Run: Lessons in Competitive Advantage from Great Family Businesses.* Boston: Harvard Business School Press, 2005.

communication and relationship between two or more family members) or serious conflict may suggest to some family members that a family meeting is needed, highly and deep-seated emotional difficulties are better addressed in contexts such as family therapy than they are in family meetings. Therefore, hold your first family meeting precisely when it may appear to have no urgency to it, when everybody is getting along well. It is true that family meetings can successfully address differences and conflicts between family members, but usually not early in the process and not when the conflict is intense or deep-seated.

2. Ideally, every member of the family, including spouses (the in-laws) and children would participate. But best practices from experienced family firms suggest that it is often best to initiate the process with a developmental perspective—start with a smaller group that perhaps includes only blood relatives, and as experience and confidence builds up, involve a wider circle of family members. Spouses for instance, may initially be involved only in the information update and family/social segments of the meeting. In the case of a family meeting being held at a resort or retreat center, spouses and children would be "in residence," but would attend only those parts of the meeting.

3. Regarding children, many families have established a policy of involving only children who are older than 13 or 16 years of age in their family meetings, preferring to have a parallel gathering with fun and educational activities for those under that age.

Table 11.4 addresses a series of additional how-to's aimed at assisting the reader in his or her preparation of the meeting and the meeting agenda.

table **11.4**	**Family Meeting and Family Council How-to's**

- Decide who you are going to invite.
- Decide where you will hold the meeting, away from the office.
- Decide about the use of a facilitator and other professionals (such as a tax attorney) as resources for the discussions.
- Have the facilitator do a "reconnaissance" to build the agenda.
- Develop a structured and tailored agenda before the meeting.
- Start by developing a set of ground rules or code of conduct.
- Include communication exercises, family-business cases, and educational modules,
- Schedule time for relaxation and family fun.
- Decide on topics and issues to be covered:
  - State of the business
  - Development of a family mission statement
  - Development of family policies with regard to issues such as employment
  - Identification of policies or legal documents needed: estate, ownership transfer, buy–sell agreements
  - Management succession
  - Development of next generation
  - Estate planning
  - Family strategy and business strategic planning
  - Family communication

As family meetings and family councils develop their own experience and mature, their ability to address more conflictual issues increases. Therefore, while they should not be started during periods of conflict or when the needs of the family in the business are urgent—as, for example, when a decision to sell or continue the business under family control presents itself—over the long run, family meetings are an excellent vehicle for addressing issues that are hard to manage otherwise. These may include frustration over lack of inclusion in family and/or business matters; anger over the unfairness of hiring practices, compensation, promotions, family benefits, and other opportunities enjoyed by some but not by others; and frustration over dividend policies and lack of liquidity.

Frustration over different levels of inclusion is widespread as a result of the emotional distance between family members who are active in management and those who are not. But unmet inclusion needs could also come from the family side, as when geographic separation makes it easier for some members to remain involved than for others living in far-flung locations. Anger over different outcomes and economic benefits from the family business are also very common and are often the subject of many family meetings. And unmet expectations regarding dividends and liquidity are prevalent. Family meetings can greatly assist in clarifying what constitutes realistic expectations and in being the catalyst for developing policies and procedures—such as business valuation, buy–sell agreements, and dividend policies—that meet family needs and business capabilities.

All of these problems are addressed and resolved to the best of the family's ability by families with experience in family meetings. Because some of the problems are based on feelings rooted in different perceptions, the educational mission of family meetings can go a long way in creating common ground and ameliorating conflicts rooted in misinformation, misunderstandings, or budding ill-will.[3]

THE USE OF FACILITATORS AND ADVISORS

Family-business and organization-development consultants, along with psychologists and family therapists, can provide facilitation skills that make family meetings much more effective and constructive. Group-development and team-building consultants can also provide this facilitation and relevant group-process skills. In addition to the group-process and communication skills, a thorough acquaintance with family businesses is a plus. A consultant performing family-meeting facilitation who understands the idiosyncrasies of families in business and the uniqueness of the family enterprise is a better family-meeting facilitator.

Although there are documented examples of families in business who assume the family-meeting facilitator responsibilities themselves, usually by assigning the role to a family member with this knowledge and skill set, the use of outsiders is very advantageous. Much like the value-added contribution from independent outsiders serving on the board of a family-owned or family-controlled company, an outside facilitator has a tremendous advantage when it comes to objectivity and the perception by family members that they are a neutral third party with no axe to grind or side to take. For

---

[3]Habbershon, T. & Astrachan, J., Perceptions Are Reality: How Family Meetings Lead to Collective Action, *Family Business Review, 10* (1), 1997, pp. 37–52.

that reason, many families in business choose a nonfamily member to perform the professional facilitation of their family meetings. Some families use a facilitator for the launching of a family council or of new, more formal, family meetings. Then, after having several of their meetings and achieving a sense of proficiency on the subject of the unique requirements of family-meeting facilitation, they proceed to "in-source" this delicate work to a family member.

Whatever route is taken, the fact remains that the facilitation of family meetings is quite a complex and nuanced task. And the consequences of performing the function poorly often have lasting consequences in the family group and its relation to the family firm. Therefore, family-meeting facilitators, like other professional advisors, deserve careful scrutiny during the selection process. Gather information, check references, and find out how long they have been doing this work and how many families they have already assisted in similar processes. Have several members of the family group interview the prospective facilitator and inquire about his or her professional fees. Professionals doing this work on the expectation of referral fees or commissions they may collect on the basis of the sale of products are better avoided. Be explicit about the outcomes expected and have the facilitator put all of this in writing.

Family-meeting facilitators can remove barriers, promote momentum, and provide the discipline for continued action required for multiyear processes such as succession, ownership transfer, and continuity.

The family-meeting facilitator often begins the engagement by doing an assessment or reconnaissance of the family in question. Individual or couples interviews and surveys are often used in this process. On the basis of those findings, the facilitator then collaborates with a couple of family members on drafting an agenda for the meeting.[4] The rest of the facilitator's responsibility resides in providing the family with communications tools, group-process-awareness skills, and teamwork skills in the meeting itself. As a result of what an able facilitator does during the meeting, issues can be addressed, problems resolved, policies written, and plans formulated without unnecessarily rehashing the past or engaging in unproductive conflict. Naturally, the facilitator often also plays a role in providing follow-up to the meeting itself in an effort to make family meetings an ongoing process and not just an event. For readers interested in family-meeting facilitation and consulting to family firms, Small Family Business Case 17: Real Estate Development Partners, Inc. provides insights into the nature of family-meeting facilitation. Two publications that may prove useful are those by Hilburt-Davis and Dyer and Bork.[5] Group-facilitation-skills seminars are offered at many colleges and universities. The Family Firm Institute (see http://www.ffi.org) runs seminars that acquaint professionals with family-business consulting and family-meeting facilitation.

Other advisors may also play a significant role in the effectiveness of family meetings. Estate-tax attorneys and financial planners, for instance, may be very helpful in family meetings whose agenda includes education and discussion of the estate plan and/or ownership-transfer plans. Key nonfamily management in the business may also add value to these meetings by attending portions of the meeting dedicated to, for

---

[4]Poza, E., Johnson, S., & Alfred, T., Changing the Family Business through Action Research, *Family Business Review*, *11*(4), 1998, pp. 311–323.

[5]Hilburt-Davis, J., &, Dyer, W.G., Jr., *Consulting to Family Businesses: A Practical Guide to Contracting, Assessment, and Implementation*. San Francisco: Jossey-Bass/Pfeiffer, 2003; and Bork, D., et al., *Working with Family Businesses: A Guide for Professionals*. San Francisco: Jossey-Bass, 1996.

example, the review of the financial performance of the firm. A key nonfamily CFO could inform and educate family shareholders by attending part of the family meeting and both presenting and analyzing the firm's financial results. Similarly a vice president of marketing or sales could do an update on the competitive situation of the firm in order for family members to have a more comprehensive and realistic perspective of the business that the family controls before embarking on a discussion of family matters. In situations in which multiple advisors, guests, and facilitators are present, attention needs to be paid to the ability of the family-meeting facilitator and the other advisors to work together as a team to serve the best interests of the family. Unlike the facilitator, the advisors' and guests' attendance of the meeting should be limited to the time when their agenda item is being addressed with family members.

THE FAMILY COUNCIL

The family council represents an institutionalized form of periodically holding family meetings. The primary advantage of this more formal format for family meetings is the disciplined approach to the scheduling and holding of these meetings, even when they appear not to be needed. The family council is a governance body that focuses on family matters. It is to the family what the board of directors is to the business. Family councils primarily promote communication, provide a safe harbor for the resolution of family conflicts, and support the education of next-generation family members about family dynamics and ownership issues.

A bra manufacturer owned by two families partnering in business was facing succession to the next generation. It decided to start a family council that brought members of the two families together. A consultant was hired to be the facilitator for these meetings. The consultant soon realized that these two families first had to begin to have family meetings with their respective families and only then use the family council as the more representative and coordinating body to plan for an eventual succession. The families met separately but in parallel and discussed individual family strategy and visions for their future involvement in the business; the family council was ultimately used to create a win–win plan in the buy–sell transaction between these two families. Ultimately, these meetings pruned the two-family tree to a single family's ownership and management of the business in the next generation.

Family councils frequently develop family-participation policies and deal with issues of liquidity, diversification of the estate, and estate planning. The business/ownership education of family members not active in the management of the business is also an important agenda item for family councils. This body is responsible for ensuring that the noneconomic goals and values of the family are articulated (sometimes via a family constitution or family charter; see the end of this chapter for the sample constitution of the Kropps family). It is also an advocate for giving these noneconomic goals the attention they deserve in the context of the owning family's strategy. Family councils seldom vote on issues, but instead develop policies to guide decisions made by other governance bodies, such as the board and the annual shareholders' meeting.

A family council may be the vehicle for carrying out the family's philanthropic initiatives. Or it may oversee the creation of a family office to oversee trusts and other financial matters of the owning family. Because it gives family members, whether they are active in the management of the business or not, an ongoing voice in the business, a family council relieves some of the pressure to appoint all family members to the board. Indeed, family councils often select one or two at-large members to sit on the board of directors or advisory board in order to represent the family's interest in board deliberations.

An important caution may be appropriate here. Family councils, in the absence of boards with independent outsiders, have been known to present their own set of problems. Over time, some owning families have experienced a propensity for family members who are not active in the business to become more aggressive in their second-guessing of company management. In the absence of a board with truly independent outsiders, family members who do not fully understand the difference between owning and running a family company may conspire to meddle inappropriately in the management of the business. A family council may empower shareholders to give voice to issues and concerns that are truly of a managerial, not a family, nature and that lie beyond nonactive family members' level of understanding of company functioning. CEO leadership—assuming that the CEO is a family member and member of the family council—is therefore essential in keeping responsibility and authority where it belongs. Gerry Conway, retired chairman and CEO of Fasteners for Retail (which at that time had $48 million in annual revenues), for example, considers the ground rule he set in his family's first family council meeting to have made all the difference. As he told me: "At the first meeting, there was a critical point where I had to remind my family that while this was a family business, I had to make the final operating decisions." While the comment may have reflected some natural anxiety at opening up for discussion subjects that had previously been entirely up to him to decide in his role of founding entrepreneur, it also served notice that the management of the company was not the purview of the newly formed family council.

OWNERSHIP AND FAMILY POLICY MAKING

First and foremost, family meetings should be about education and communication. Over time, if the education and communication tasks have been properly carried out, family meetings will become effective planning and policy-making bodies.

Open and safe processes for sharing information among family members in family meetings are prerequisites for effective planning and policy making by family groups. Because many family-controlled companies, for understandable reasons, decide to have family meetings to dismantle the culture of secrecy established by the previous generation, a slow, developmental process is best. Decisions regarding management and even most ownership issues are not the function of a family meeting or family council. Most decisions having to do with ownership and management of the firm will be made in other forums: the board, the top management team, the annual shareholder meeting. The role of the family meeting then is to inform, guide, and govern the relationship between an owning family and the firm. The focus of the agendas should be on improving communication, educating, promoting open deliberations, and policy making. Family meetings and family councils must strive to discuss plans and policies that, even if not everybody's favorites, most family members are willing to support. One particularly appropriate plan to discuss in a family meeting (although not necessarily develop, since this is an issue for which business management should lead the agenda) is a succession plan guided by the three leadership imperatives and five best practices covered in this book. The succession plan developed by the two Cook brothers (see the end of Chapter 12, where the entire plan is reprinted) was released just prior to the first of a series of semiannual family meetings to be held by the Cook family. The two brothers used this first family meeting, held in a quiet retreat in northern Michigan, as their platform to communicate to shareholders the plans the two siblings shared for the future of Vue Systems, the family company with $9 million in annual revenues. Estate plans also represent a very appropriate type of plan for discussion by an owning family in their family meeting.

Several types of policies related to ownership and the family's relationship to the firm that stand out in their usefulness to families in business include

1. An employment policy that outlines the prerequisites for employment in the business. Education, experience, and the expectations the company has of family members seeking full-time employment in the firm are spelled out. Employment opportunity should be based on merit and company need, not having the right last name.

2. A subcontractor policy that offers guidelines for arms-length transactions in an open competitive marketplace. The contractor-selection process should represent a level playing field for both relatives and nonfamily.

3. A board-service policy that includes criteria for the selection of family members to serve as at-large representatives of the owning family on the board. The system should provide a link between family strategy and company strategy without giving undue influence to family members.

4. A family strategy statement in which the family's goals—required input for effective board leadership, as discussed in earlier chapters—is laid out. The family strategy could include

    a. A dividend policy, not to specify the amount of dividends to be paid (which is a company decision), but rather to discuss family needs; to balance those needs against reinvestment in the business for growth needs; and to inform the board and management of the general sentiments of family members.

    b. A liquidity policy that includes principles supporting the desired relationship between the controlling family and the company in the future. This policy recognizes that individuals or particular family branches may have cash-flow needs or may prefer to allocate their capital to alternative uses. This policy usually differentiates between small transactions and the sale of large blocks of stock within the family or back to the company and references the legal documents in effect (such as buy–sell agreements).

5. A family constitution. This document usually includes a family mission statement, a listing of family values that are important to the family enterprise and that the earlier generation wishes to pass on to the next, a collection of the policies listed under point 4 above (employment, liquidity, etc.), a list of governance bodies and their function and a statement of family history, family commitment, and the desired relationship between the company and the owning family going forward.

THE FAMILY CONSTITUTION

To govern the relationship between shareholders, family members, and managers, some family-owned and family-controlled companies write family constitutions. The family constitution, or family charter, makes explicit some of the principles and guidelines that shareholders will follow in their relations with each other, other family members, and company managers. While family constitutions are more prevalent in larger multigenerational families in business, they represent an important asset to family unity and the culture of patient family capital starting with second-generation family firms. The primary rationale for a family constitution is the realization that no amount of legal expertise or foresight in the drafting of legal documents can match the goodwill and personal responsibility that family members, both active and inactive in the management of the firm, begin to assume when the difference between family, ownership, and the management of the enterprise are understood as a result of family meetings. If ever there was a compelling reason for family meetings and family councils in multigenerational family-controlled companies, this is it: the development of a family constitution. Only the shareholders/family members who are engaged by the founder's and successors' shared dreams and vision will choose to be stewards of the legacy. The rest will put their individual interests and agendas before anything else and will most likely exhibit the behaviors of rich, greedy, and ungrateful heirs.

The family constitution usually has no legal bearing on the issues covered and instead refers to the appropriate legal documents, including articles of incorporation, buy–sell agreements, and so on, that support the family's intentions and goodwill as set out in its family constitution. The principal articles contained in family constitutions are

I. The family's vision and the nature of its commitment to the firm and its continuity.

II. The family values that have successfully guided the firm in its relations with customers, employees, suppliers, partners, competitors, and the community.

III. The desired behavior of the family toward the firm and its management—what the desired behavior of family members who are employed in the firm is and what family members need to be aware of in order to protect the company's and the family's reputation. This article guides family members in its owner–firm visibility, the use of the family name, and relations with the government and the media.

IV. Employment policy. The requirements family members need to meet in order to be considered for employment. This is often segmented into requirements for employment in management posts, requirements for temporary employment, and requirements for lower-level positions. This policy may also spell out whether in-laws qualify for employment or are prohibited from becoming company employees. A policy guiding the use of any relatives as contractors may also be included. The family-member compensation policy may also be included here. How family members' performance on the job will be reviewed and how decisions affecting their salaries and career opportunities will be made is discussed.

V. Next-generation family-member development. This policy sets out the commitment and procedures guiding the education and professional development of next-generation members employed by the firm. It sometimes also defines developmental plans for family members outside the firm, for example, through the use of family trusts to support college and graduate education of family members.

VI. Ownership policy. Stock ownership, classes of stock, and ownership transfer policies are defined. Business-valuation processes are often spelled out. Buy–sell agreements in existence are discussed. Voting and shareholder representation on the board and other entities may be acknowledged. Legal documents governing transactions of any kind are listed and their authority recognized.

VII. Family bank and/or family venture capital fund. Special funds allocated to sponsor the development of new ventures or new initiatives by members of the family are discussed and the overall terms of use of these funds discussed.

VIII. Dividends and family benefits policy. This chapter educates and guides shareholders on the expectations for returns on invested capital. It discloses reinvestment requirements and the use of reinvestment funds. It may also, if the family has agreed to it, set a ratio of reinvestment to distribution of shareholder returns. Policies related to risk and risk management, including debt-to-capital ratios may also be discussed here.

IX. Liquidity policy. This article discusses business valuation, buy–sell agreements in force, redemption funds, if any, and their use.

X. The board of directors or advisory board. Its standing, authority, and relation to management, shareholders, and other entities is discussed. Its primary functions and operating procedures are disclosed.

XI. Family meetings and/or a family council. Its primary functions and relation to the board and shareholder meetings is discussed. Membership and its standing and operating procedures are discussed.

XII. Shareholder meetings. Their role is discussed, as is their authority and legal standing. Their relation to the board and the family council is also discussed.

If a family office has already been created (discussion of the family office and its function follows), the constitution would also list and define the role of a family office and its relationship to shareholders, the family council, the board, and management of the family firm.

This list may already seem too long and elaborate for most small and medium-sized family firms in the first or second generation of owner-management. The intent was to be comprehensive but not to discourage the use of this very useful tool by multi-generational family firms with a vision of continuity. To help simplify the task, a sample constitution, that of the Kropps family, can be found at the end of this chapter. But a caution is appropriate. The value of a family constitution comes from its development more than from the final written product. Just like General and later President Eisenhower once said: "In preparing for battle I have always found that plans are useless, but planning is indispensable." I hope that by creating a clear picture of a family constitution, and including a sample constitution, the reader will engage the family in planning, discussing, and writing the document. Over several family meetings family members can develop a family constitution that captures their dreams, their spirit of enterprise, and their commitment to the continuity of the family business.

THE FAMILY OFFICE

Paradoxically, the less important some established family benefits are, the more trouble they can cause. I was once involved in a dispute in a family firm over the produce from a vegetable garden. The family home, factory and garden were all on the same site and the garden was cultivated for the benefit of those members of the family who lived on the spot. When this apparently modest benefit came to be costed out, it was clear that it was a totally uneconomic way of keeping some members of the family in fresh fruit and vegetables, quite apart from the development value tied up in food production. Any change in the traditional arrangement was, however, seen by those who benefited from it as an attack on the established order and the beginning of the end of the family firm. Eventually, the fate of the vegetable plot was satisfactorily settled. But the sooner a family firm regularizes the relationships between the family and the firm, the less time will have to be spent on matters of allocation between them, which can create trouble out of all proportion to their economic significance.

—Sir Adrian Cadbury, Chairman of Cadbury Schweppes[6]

Larger multigenerational business families often have a family office, whose duties are primarily to provide and organize a series of services for family shareholders. These services include providing legal and financial assistance with estate and tax issues; managing the investment portfolios of the family; providing information of relevance to shareholders, sometimes by producing a newsletter; and fairly and equitably distributing family or shareholder benefits, such as education funds from family trusts or foundations and even time at the family ranch or Florida beachfront property.

Nothing is as frustrating to nonfamily management in the business (or to family shareholders expecting firm and timely responses to their inquiries) as to engage in repeated phone calls regarding, for example, the availability of the Florida condo or the New York apartment for a particular holiday weekend. A simple request from a relative, part of the family subsystem, easily becomes an ordeal for a nonfamily administrator overwhelmed by the family ramifications of granting or not granting that request to the exclusion of another family member's request. Some boundary-setting function can be performed by a family office under these conditions. Rather than making a family issue a business issue, the family office officer appropriately addresses a family request. Without the fear or guilt often experienced by a business manager, especially if the family has developed guidelines for the allocation of these resources or family benefits, the matter is more efficiently and effectively resolved.

Ernest Doud has identified four stages in the evolution of family business and wealth.[7] In stage one, virtually all of the family's invested capital is committed to a highly entrepreneurial business. In this stage, there is no need for a family office; family benefits are small to nonexistent and the entrepreneur-owner and the business are often one and the same. In stage two, the family is often professionalizing the business, and nonbusiness assets are being added to the family's investment portfolio. At this stage, typically, the management of nonbusiness assets still falls on the individual owner. During stage three, the family, having professionalized the management of the business, often begins to professionalize the management of its nonbusiness investments, which now constitute a substantial portion of the family's wealth. Depending on the size and nature of nonbusiness assets, some family office functions, either from service providers or a multifamily office, may begin to make sense at this stage. The family office could assist the family with its wealth and govern the relationship between the family, the business, and its nonbusiness investments. By stage three, some business and nonbusiness assets have already been transferred to the next generation. Family meetings are being held to assist in educating heirs on wealth management and their

---

[6]Cadbury, A., *Family Firms and Their Governance: Creating Tomorrow's Company from Today's*. London: Egon Zehnder International, 2000.

[7]Doud, E., *The Evolution of Family Business and Wealth*. Redondo Beach: Doud, Hausner, Vistar, 2003.

responsibilities as shareholders or trustees; the family office assists in the development of the agenda and meeting logistics. Also at this stage, the family may have established a foundation to carry out its philanthropic goals. Because both liquidity and access to capital for growth purposes may be central concerns, the business family sometimes executes an initial public offering (IPO) and takes the company public at this stage. In stage four, the family may no longer own the operating business that was the original source of its wealth. As a financial family, it has likely professionalized the management of its investments. For these families, asset management, wealth preservation, and wise wealth utilization become the new family business. In stage four, the family office indeed is the family business.

Like family councils, family offices enhance a family's ability to govern the relationship between the family and the company, enabling more professional management of the firm and fairer and more timely handling of shareholder and family issues and requests. A family office may function as a full-time organized arm of the family council, helping the council execute the policies and guidelines it has developed.

Families with smaller businesses (companies doing less than $100 million in annual revenues and usually in stage one or two) seldom see the need for a family office, though family members may avail themselves of similar services through advisors to the business. These advisors are often willing to also provide personal professional services.

Some larger families in business (often in stages three and four, as discussed above) have in the past decade or so also begun to make it possible for families owning smaller businesses to outsource family office functions to their family office operations for a fee. A number of large family offices now operate as multifamily offices. The services they provide the large-business-owning family can be retained by the smaller-business-owning family for a fee; usually a 1.5 to 2 percent of assets under management.

WILL IT BE THIS?

Crawford Hill, one of the young Bancroft family members, owners until 2007 of Dow Jones & Co., publisher of *The Wall Street Journal*, sent this e-mail to Bancroft family members several weeks before the vote for the $60-per-share offer by the Murdochs of News Corp:

> With all due respect, it is time for a reality check. What is missing from this discussion about Dow Jones and the Bancrofts is a sense of historical perspective and evolution. ... What most of you do not know however is that the very same Jessie B. Cox that is mentioned at every turn as "family matriarch" and to whom many of us owe "the legacy" forced her incredibly talented husband, William C. Cox, top student at Milton and Harvard luminary, to retire prematurely from Dow Jones at age 40 so he could be full time in the social swirl of Cohasset. He was a star at the company!
>
> As to promoting legacy, neither she nor her daughter Jane, my mom, ever spoke of the legacy of Dow Jones, much less the possibility of actually working there or what it meant to be a steward of the business. There was no effort at promoting legacy, or educating the next generation, whatsoever. ... We talked about everything under the sun ... but never Dow Jones. ... We never had, by the way, conversations that Sulzbergers, Grahams and, yes, Murdochs, had every day!
>
> There has absolutely never existed any kind of family-wide/cross-branch culture of teaching what it means to be an active, engaged owner and more crucially, a family director.

Source: The Wall Street Journal, July 27, 2007, p. B12.

OR THIS?

LIKE FATHER, LIKE SON: If investors feel British Sky Broadcasting Group PLC Chief Executive James Murdoch is spending too heavily, they just have to look at his father, Rupert. Just like the News Corp chairman has done many times before, James is taking steps that incur short-term losses in pursuit of a longer-term strategy, in this case spending about $1.33 billion to expand into broadband Internet and telephony.

The company's strategy is seen as crucial as competition intensifies among cable, satellite and telecommunications providers to offer consumers what the industry calls a "triple play," a bundled package of television, broadband and telephone services.

While James's actions are drawing scrutiny—he said the move would lower profits by about $760 million over three years—the Murdoch family is more than willing to make long-term strategic bets, sometimes to the disappointment of investors.

Source: Financial Times, London, October 22, 2005, p.16.

Or as a second generation aspiring successor told me recently in a family business seminar I was leading in Madrid: "How I would love to have a forum where we grow, we develop good, knowledgeable, responsible and loyal shareholders!" Family meetings and family councils can make all the difference in the world for business-owning families. And in the author's experience, just a little bit of it goes a long way.

SUMMARY

1 Family meetings and family councils are a reliable forum for the education of family members about the business. In family meetings, family members learn about the rights and responsibilities that accompany being an owner-manager and about the important distinctions between ownership, management, and family membership. They also provide a forum to minimize the potential for conflict within the family.

2 Family meetings are largely about education and communication, not decision making. Policies guiding the family's relationship to ownership and management can be developed in family meetings. Some of these policies are employment, evaluation, compensation, and liquidity.

3 Family meetings are best when they appreciate the past but focus on the future. This is one of the reasons why developing and following a detailed agenda is so important. Rehashing the past *ad infinitum* seldom helps a family in business create the kind of relationship with the family business it wants in the future.

4 Family meetings or family councils should not be started when the family is in serious conflict or there has been a relationship cutoff (the severing of the communication and relationship between two or more family members). The best time to initiate this best practice is when its need is not obvious and a meeting not urgent.

5 Family meetings are a significant contributor to the unique resource that family firms enjoy: family unity. Family unity and commitment can be the source of strategies—such as managing for the long run—that differentiate family firms from other forms of enterprise and endow them with unique competitive advantages.

6 Family-meeting facilitators, with their third-party neutrality and objectivity, are a wise investment in the effectiveness of family meetings.

7 A family council is a governance body that focuses on family matters, frequently developing family-participation policies and dealing with liquidity issues and estate planning.

8 In the absence of an effective board, family councils and family meetings can embolden shareholders to exercise their power beyond what is best for the management of the family enterprise. Second-guessing management decisions and reversing strategic initiatives have sometimes been the result. The relationship between the family council and the board of directors, therefore, needs to be clearly established and the relative authority delineated to prevent an imbalance in the ownership–management–family interaction that could have a negative impact on the firm.

9 A family constitution is a collection of family policies guiding the family–ownership–management relationship. It represents a great investment in governing the relationship between ownership management and family membership.

10 A family office's primary duties are to provide and organize a series of services for family shareholders, including legal and financial assistance with estate and tax issues; management of the investment portfolios of the family; providing information of relevance to shareholders through meetings, e-mails, and newsletters; and fairly and equitably making family or shareholder benefits available to family members.

CHAPTER RESOURCE: Sample Family Constitution

To govern the relationship between shareholders and managers, some family-owned and family-controlled companies write family constitutions. The family constitution makes explicit some of the principles and guidelines that shareholders will follow in their relations with each other and company management. The following example of a family constitution is from a well-known family-owned corporation. Because the shareholders prefer anonymity, the company and family names are fictitious and the document's content has been slightly edited.

The Kropps Family Constitution

1 Introduction

1.1 **Objective** This Family Constitution has been established to serve as a reference point for relationships between family members and the business during the next 10 to 15 years, a period in which we foresee the change from the second to the third generation taking place. We, the members of the Kropps Family, recognize our common bonds and assume the responsibility for carrying on the legacy, through the Kropps Companies, into the next generation.

1.2 **Mission** In its introduction and development, it is necessary to bear in mind that the Family Constitution

- Clarifies what the Family Business wants to be and thus outlines the form and content of the main points of the relationships between the business and the family.
- Highlights ways of increasing unity and commitment, which are essential components of the family enterprise.
- Can never be contrary to what is stated in the laws governing the corporation or in the company bylaws.

1.3 **Approval and Modification of the Family Constitution** The Family Council is the competent body for the approval and, when necessary, the modification of the present Constitution.

2 Guiding Principles of the Family Constitution

2.1 **About the Founders** This company was founded by Albert and Gerald Kropps.
The company has gradually developed and grown to its current size and competitive strength, not only due to its founders' efforts and their founding principles, but just as

significantly because of the continued dedication, overwhelming professionalism, and sound judgment of the successors, the second generation.

As members of the second generation, some of whom manage this company, we want to leave written documentation for the members of the third generation of the principles that have guided the conduct of these founders and their day-to-day work and example, because they have served as an ever-present reference point in our business dealings.

2.2 **Values to Be Passed On** In the same way, we members of the second generation wish to pass on other values that form the basis of the work done during these years.

2.2.1 Work ethic and a sense of responsibility. These are the best vehicles for the continuation of the entrepreneurial idea of the founders.

2.2.2 Understanding, unity, harmony, and a bond among the shareholders. These have played fundamental roles in the continuity of the company.

2.2.3 Stewardship. As stockholders, we must always keep in mind the consequences that our actions may have for the Company, the rest of the shareholders, and our family's reputation.

2.2.4 Ethical conduct. As evidenced by discretion, honesty, and high-mindedness, it works in favor of the common good.

2.2.5 Dedication and commitment to the attainment of company objectives.

2.2.6 Confidence in the governing bodies of the company, including the people who today carry out the managerial responsibilities and those who may do so in the future.

2.2.7 Love and concern for family and the family enterprise. As a result of his/her ownership role, the family shareholder or board member should not enjoy any special treatment in his/her professional career within the businesses of the Group by the mere fact that he/she is a member of the family. In this sense, family members who are active in management will have the same rights and responsibilities that the rest of the nonfamily employees have (salary, working days, promotions, vacations, etc.).

2.3 **Other Values** The members of the second generation dedicate themselves to ensuring that the following values become gradually known and appreciated by the third generation.

2.3.1 A balance between dedication to work and dedication to family, in order that, over time, unity and an appropriate commitment of service to the company may be maintained.

2.3.2 The hope to form part of an important, socially responsible business that should be permanently able to compete advantageously. A family member's motivation should be found in the opportunity offered to him/her to be able to collaborate and contribute to the growth and continuity of the family business.

2.3.3 An understanding of the obligations and responsibilities of the shareholders of a family business, among which stand out the need to seek out the best for the company and to collaborate positively for the good of the other shareholders.

2.3.4 An understanding that participation as a shareholder of the family business is a privilege bequeathed by our ancestors, and as part of our legacy, we must use the capital responsibly to increase it, insofar as it is possible, and to pass it on to the following generation.

2.3.5 The hope to pass on to future generations a company that stands out in its field.

2.3.6 A commitment to search for solutions for liquidity and peaceful separation (in agreement with the established procedures) with shareholders who don't want to continue participating in the business or who don't share the aforementioned values.

3 The Type of Company We Want to Be

3.1 **A business in which the families,** as represented on the Family Council and the Board of Directors, *retain controlling ownership.*

3.2 **A company that is among the leaders in its field** and among the best in the industry.

3.3 **A business that is a leader in technology,** deeply committed to obtaining the lowest costs available, and with a strong network in the value-added chain in which it operates.

3.4 **A business that continues, from generation to generation, to be "A Family-Run Business,"** with members of the families on the Board of Directors and on the Executive Team. Because of this,

- Job positions cannot be indiscriminately offered to any family member.
- Family members working in the business should do so in leadership positions. Such positions, in order to be executed successfully, demand a person with a vision of unity, the ability to lead people, and advanced technical skills.
- Within the bounds of respect for personal freedom, the development of family members toward positions of company leadership is deemed a priority.

3.5 **A business with an organizational structure designed to offer both family and nonfamily managers exciting career opportunities and the ability to act with autonomy,** supported by the latest in professional management.

4 What Can Be Expected from Our Family Business

4.1 **Growth in the size of operations,** notwithstanding existing competition and the evolution of markets.

4.2 **Growth in the value of the estate,** increased shareholder value, by aiming for higher profitability and growth than the average in the industry. This will be accomplished via the following strategic commitments from top management:

- Gaining client loyalty by offering them the best product and/or service value available.
- Developing new products and services.
- Entering promising new segments and markets and abandoning those that are less so.
- Achieving the lowest costs by economies of scale, integration, and continuing vigilance against bureaucracy.
- Procuring and developing subsidiaries and joint ventures.
- Making acquisitions that ramp up the organic growth represented by the above approaches.

4.3 **Growth that is balanced,** without taking undue risks and engaging in speculation.

4.4 **Growth financed primarily out of internal cash flows.** Only in extreme cases, owing to developments in the global markets, should the company rely on external debt and public offerings.

4.5 **A market-sensitive dividend policy** that respects the company's needs for continued reinvestment.

4.6 **Extensive information provided to shareholders** about the status of the business and its markets.

4.7 **First among equals for a top management job whenever a family member is deemed apt and capable** by the President or Board of Directors for a top-management position that he/she desires. A qualified family member will be preferred for the job over a similarly qualified nonfamily candidate.

4.8 **Professional advice on ownership transfer and succession,** so that the behavior and actions of individuals do not create problems for the whole.

5 Working in the Family Business: Family Employment Policy

It is important that family members be informed of the unique responsibilities and challenges of employment in The Kropps Companies. They should be advised that in most cases they will be held to a higher standard of conduct and performance than other employees. We support an internship program to introduce future generations to the company.

5.1 General Conditions

5.1.1 Family members must meet the same criteria for hire/fire as nonfamily applicants.

5.1.2 Family members are subject to the same performance review as nonfamily members.

5.1.3 Compensation for family members will be at "fair market value" for the position held, the same as for nonfamily members.

5.1.4 Family members may be eligible for career-launching internships before age 30. This temporary employment will be limited to any one unit of employment not exceeding 12 months. Family members may be encouraged to participate in internship programs with other companies with which The Kropps Companies could reciprocate.

5.1.5 No family member will be employed in a permanent internship or entry-level position; an entry-level position is defined as one requiring no previous experience or training outside The Kropps Companies.

5.1.6 Family members seeking permanent employment must have at least 5 years' work experience outside The Kropps Companies. One of those jobs must have been at least 3 years with the same employer, during which time there must have been at least two promotions or similar evidence of rising levels of performance, competence, responsibility, and trust. It is our view that if a family member is not a valued employee elsewhere first, it is likely that that family member will be neither happy nor productive at The Kropps Companies.

5.1.7 Graduate degrees in management, engineering, and other disciplines related to the knowledge base that is essential to the success of The Kropps Companies are encouraged. A family career-development committee will be responsible for interviewing, coaching, and guiding interested family members to the Human Resources Department and other appropriate company representatives, where the ultimate employment decisions will be made.

6 Ownership of the Family Business

6.1 **Ownership of the Shares** Members of the family should retain ownership of the shares.

6.2 **Recommendations for the Owners** While maintaining the most profound respect for their freedom and individual needs and aspirations, the owners should

· Always consider the repercussions that decisions about passing on shares through estate planning will have on the business and the rest of the owners. In this sense, the desirable course of action would be always to look for ways that would most clearly facilitate the unity of the family business and the commitment of the shareholders to its continuity.

· In the most prudent fashion, make it possible for capable members of the third generation to attend, as informed and responsible shareholders, the Annual Shareholders' Meeting.

6.3 Shareholder Liquidity In order to facilitate liquidity for the shareholders, the company will do everything in its power to pay dividends and also endow a Liquidity Fund. The object of the Fund will be to provide a buyer (namely, the family business) for the shares. The intent is to guarantee liquidity in small quantities, following the spirit of the statutes and the Family Constitution.

Liquidity bylaw's key points

- *The maximum amount* offered for purchase yearly will be up to 1 percent of the total shares of the company, depending on the funds available.
- *The value of the family business* will be calculated annually, in agreement with a formula proposed by valuation experts and approved by the Board of Directors. In the aforementioned formula, the different values of the totality of the shares, whether majority or minority, must be kept in mind. The values determined by the valuation process will be made known to the shareholders.
- *Purchase-sale:* In the situation in which a shareholder would want to sell and other shareholders would want to buy at a value higher than that offered by the Fund, or in the case that the Fund may not be able to buy, the Board of Directors will authorize the purchase-sale in accordance with what has been indicated in the Buy–Sell Agreement.

7 Governing Bodies

In a family business that has the intent to strengthen the participation of the shareholders in the knowledge of the business, there are two types of governing bodies

- Those responsible for the management of the company—that is to say, those established in the bylaws, the Annual Shareholders' Meeting, and the Board of Directors. Others may be established by the Board of Directors and the Management Team, as necessary.
- The Family Council, responsible for shareholder education, communication, and developing and implementing the Family Constitution.

7.1 Annual Shareholders' Meeting During the regular Annual Shareholders' Meeting, extensive information will be offered with the purpose of enabling the shareholders to be very familiar with the family business. Family members agree to refrain from using this information indiscriminately, given its confidential nature.

7.2 The Board of Directors The Board of Directors is the highest governing body of the company after the Annual Shareholders' Meeting. The Executive Team is supervised and held accountable by the Board of Directors.

The functions of the Board, detailed in the corresponding bylaw, include

- Reviewing and approving the business's strategy
- Reviewing the financial performance of the company and holding top management accountable for such performance.
- Ensuring the ethical conduct of management and the corporation.
- Promoting the development of the managerial resources of the company.

7.3 Rules and Regulations for Board of Directors' Operations

- The election of board members is regulated by state laws and company statutes.
- Terms of service of family members on the board should not exceed three 3-year periods, encouraging the rotation to other family members most qualified to serve.
- There will always be a minimum of three high-influence independent outsiders serving on the Board of Directors.

- There can be consultants and advisors to the Board of Directors. These consultants will be independent, renowned professionals who can offer insightful information on relevant topics.
- Meetings should take place on a quarterly basis and be scheduled at least 1 year in advance.

7.4 **Family Council** The main purpose of the Family Council is to foster a strong understanding of the business, the family, and the relationship between business and family among the family members/shareholders. Its responsibilities include

- Informing and educating the family about the business.
- Facilitating the relationships of the families with the business.
- Educating the families about the legacy, disseminating the contents of the Family Constitution, and keeping it a living document.
- Proposing to all family members those changes in the Family Constitution that, based on their judgment, can help foster a greater understanding among the family members/stockholders and better relationships between owners and managers of the company.

The Family Council is made up of two members of each of the four branches in the second generation. Representative members are selected by the branches. One family member serving on the Board of Directors will also serve on the Family Council and represent a point of linkage between these two governing bodies. Total membership of the Family Council in the second generation will therefore be limited to nine. Family Council meetings will be facilitated by an outside expert on family business.

7.5 **Next-Generation Committee** We want to encourage family participation in the company. We want to raise future generations with a sense of responsibility and commitment and not a sense of entitlement. Because next-generation members may become voting shareholders, company employees, and/or board members, their participation in appropriate family and enterprise activities in advance of this development is essential. The Next-Generation Committee will include nine family members chosen by the Family Council. Membership will rotate throughout the next generation. Its primary functions will include

- Defining and guiding the educational and family business involvement opportunities for future-generation members.
- Encouraging a sense of voice and stewardship by providing feedback and ideas to earlier generations about matters affecting family–business relationships.

This Next-Generation Committee will meet on a quarterly basis and in coordination with the Family Council and the Board of Directors.

The members of the Next-Generation Committee will receive information about the state of the business in a way that promotes their education and understanding of the company.

7.6 **Family Assembly** The Family Assembly, made up of all the blood members and their spouses, will meet once a year with the purpose of

- Promoting greater knowledge and understanding of each other.
- Promoting greater knowledge and understanding of the business.
- Having fun and promoting extended family bonds.

CHAPTER 12

CHANGE, ADAPTATION AND INNOVATION: THE FUTURE OF FAMILY BUSINESS

The goal of continuity challenges owners and managers to achieve change while maintaining enough stability to keep the enterprise successful in the short term. The quest for continuity requires that the enterprise adapt, through vision and strategy, to the changing competitive dynamics that will predominate in the next generation. At the same time, there must be a deep understanding and acknowledgment of what has made the enterprise successful so far. Since different generations may have opposing views about the best strategy, achieving continuity poses a challenge to intergenerational collaboration and accommodation. Resolving the dilemma posed by a tradition of success versus the need for innovation, requires evolution, not revolution, across the multiyear succession process.

Different generations have different leadership tasks when it comes to continuity. The founding generation builds an enterprise from next to nothing and makes every effort to ensure its survival. Building on the foundation created, the next generation must grow the enterprise by rejuvenating and changing it or else face organizational decline precisely when the family is growing, a recipe for family conflict and tragedy. The third and fourth generations are often called on to again adapt the firm to changes in its competitive environment. In addition, they must be active stewards of the enterprise and the owning family's legacy, before the family's collective memory dissipates. In essence, then, next-generation leaders have to be both leaders of change and growth and stewards of culture and values.

CONTINUITY AND CULTURE

The research on organizational culture suggests that businesses that enjoy a high level of performance over the long run have a strong culture that fits the strategy of the

---

I would like to dedicate this chapter to the loving memory of Richard Beckhard, my teacher at MIT–Sloan School of Management and lifelong advisor and friend, who dedicated himself to coaching and mentoring the next generation. Many of the ideas on managing change that are discussed in this chapter were his creation. Further utilization of this material by next-generation members of family businesses will serve as a tribute to his wisdom and caring and become part of his great legacy.

business. The Marriott Corporation, for instance, has a culture that makes customer satisfaction a priority, and it educates new associates about this culture. Marriott is intimately familiar with the connections that exist among employee satisfaction, systems and structures that allow employees to actively care for customers, and the quality of service provided to guests.

Culture is a collection of beliefs, values, and ground rules that shapes and significantly influences how individuals, groups, and the company as a whole behave or operate when confronted with choices, decisions, opportunities, and threats. Company cultures are often composed of unique values that define the nature of the company's commitment to its major stakeholders: customers, shareholders, employees, suppliers, and the communities in which the business operates. Families also enjoy cultures of their own—that is, a set of beliefs, values, and principles that signficantly influence how its individual members behave. And certainly the culture of a business-owning family significantly influences the culture of the organization we call a family business. But having previously examined the family in Chapters 2 and 11, we will focus our discussion here on the culture of the family business and its influence on the business's ability to adapt and change.

SC Johnson launched an advertising campaign that highlighted the inherent strengths and advantages of being family-owned and family-operated. Its Chicago-based advertising firm, Foote, Cone & Belding, found in its research that family ownership was a tremendous asset to a business. According to the research, Americans prefer products and services from family-owned companies over those from publicly held corporations. More than 80 percent of the people surveyed believed that family companies make products they can trust, in contrast to 43 percent for publicly traded companies. Many perceived family-company products as being of higher quality. Sam Johnson, the now-deceased third-generation patriarch who grew the enterprise from $171 million in annual sales to four divisions with combined sales of $6 billion, once said, "A great family business, no matter its size, has to be more than a financial investment. To survive long term, it has to be a social positive for the employees, a benefit for the community, a passion for future generations of the family, and committed to earning the goodwill of the consumer every day."[1]

CHANGING THE CULTURE

The research on organizational culture suggests that the culture needs to be flexible—adaptive and agile in the face of change. That is, having a strong culture is not sufficient for the long-term effectiveness of a firm. Many companies with strong cultures that fit their strategies have come to realize that the very strength of the culture poses challenges to its adaptation to changing competitive environments.

In 1987, Bill Hewlett and David Packard led what they considered to be a revolution at HP, the company then controlled by the Hewlett and Packard families. Having retired from the management of the firm, they believed the company was simply resting on its laurels. Back in 1987, Hewlett-Packard primarily produced scientific measurement devices, such as oscilloscopes. It was enjoying very healthy profit margins, but, according to its founders, it was not focusing as it should on emerging

---

[1] http://www.scjohnson.com.

competition from Asia in its product lines. Hewlett-Packard needed to return to the "HP Way" in innovation and new product development in order to grow out of its overreliance on measurement systems. The result of this owner-issued wake-up call was the launching of the company's hugely successful printing and imaging business. The architects of the company's renowned strong culture were able to remold it, creating flexibility and a capacity for adaptation. Owner-managers and active owners who hold management accountable are in a unique position to help their companies remain successful over the long haul.

Leaders who have assumed responsibility for making change happen, in order to build a company that lasts, believe that leadership of this kind requires the following:

1. Challenging the status quo by asking fundamental questions and collecting external data, including customer, competitive, social, or demographic data. Leaders need to create dissatisfaction with the status quo.

2. Having an external (customer/competition) perspective. The desire for this type of perspective led IBM to tap as its new CEO Lou Gerstner, who had been running American Express, a major customer of IBM. IBM clearly was in need of fundamental change when he assumed the company's leadership. None of the key managers who had been with IBM for many years seemed capable of leading the change effort with the dispassionate drive that Gerstner demonstrated. This finding has implications for what may constitute appropriate early developmental career opportunities for next-generation members who will be called on to rejuvenate their family-owned businesses. Early experiences working in sales or in industries that represent current or potential customers can be a valuable asset. If the family business is in the food production or distribution industry, for example, a career stint with a supermarket or restaurant chain may represent a particularly valuable developmental opportunity.

3. Having the capacity to forge a new direction—to articulate a vision of where the company should be headed—that is rooted in meeting customer needs and creating value for customers.

4. Being able to generate a sense of urgency. After all, need and speed are friends of change. Jack Welch, reflecting on his fundamental reshaping of GE during the 1990s, said, "If I could begin the fundamental change effort at GE again today, based on what I have learned in the last decade, I would insist on greater speed. I would accelerate the change process and avoid a lot of the resistance, confusion and loss of motivation that was part of a slower process."[2]

The leader of the evolution needs to build the "case for change," the reasons why the company's only option is to change. By setting a deadline for the change to occur, one that is rooted in preserving the loyalty of customers, he or she establishes a sense of urgency. The leader also needs to communicate the customer-based vision and strategies to the entire organization, to repeat the message often, and to engage the rest of the organization in effective ways of determining how the change will be carried out. Cultural change takes time, but the leader must act with speed.

---

[2]Slater, R., *The New GE: How Jack Welch Revived an American Institution.* Homewood, IL: Business One Irwin, 1993, p. 261.

NEW LEADERS OF THE EVOLUTION

For the successor charged with becoming the leader of the evolution, few character-istics are as practical and influential as self-awareness and self-management. To fulfill their responsibilities and roles well, leaders often depend on words, on having a voice that compels others to act. Young leaders who have been charged with changing the firm's culture soon realize that they are the primary instruments of the change—that the nature of their relationships with others and the outcomes resulting from those relationships are very much dependent on their own actions and behaviors. Leaders of change also recognize that they will eventually be judged by whether their words and actions are consistent; that is, "Does she walk the talk?" Clearly, self-awareness and self-management are critical skills for a young leader.

As a "mere mortal," the successor charged with a company's evolution has to realize that while ownership provided the founder with power and experiential wisdom, the successor does not inherit this authority to lead. Shares of stock transfer across gen-erations, but the authority to lead has to be earned by each successive generation. It is more important to recognize that, over the generations, employees move from a dependent and loyal follower model to a more knowledgeable and mutually respon-sible partner model. And pulling employees toward the desired future is preferable to pushing them to achieve.

New leaders charged with evolution across generations face many traps (Table 12.1). The most notable is usually self-inflicted: assuming that the transfer of power implicit in being anointed as the successor confers on the successor the authority to lead. But such authority can only be earned, slowly, by demonstrating competence, caring, and con-sistency and maintaining contact and communication.

Deciding what constitutes effective leadership is very much a judgment call. Too little too slowly can be just as ineffective as too much too quickly. How is a new leader to know? Self-awareness can be developed in some MBA programs and a variety of leadership-development centers. Periodically requesting more objective and indepen-dent readings of different situations by others—a mentor, a consultant, members of the board, or members of the family council—can also be of help. Above all, successors need to avoid becoming isolated by the hard work new leadership requires. They need

---

table 12.1 | Common Traps for the New Leader

- Assuming that succession to a new management and ownership position vests the leader with the authority to lead. Authority is earned, not inherited.
- Becoming isolated from important others in the family and in the business. Staying in contact is important, even during conflict.
- Being distracted by key managers or other significant players in the family organization who have their own agendas.
- Having to always have the answer to any problem. It is a myth that "real leaders" know how to solve any and all problems.
- Keeping the existing management team too long. Fresh perspectives are necessary for the continuity of any business.
- Attempting too much too soon or too little too slowly.
- Being overly cautious or overly rebellious, depending on the new leader's historical relationship with the previous CEO-parent (or other relative).

to continue to communicate with trusted others to ensure that their early judgment calls are as wise as is humanly possible.

THE RAW MATERIALS OF A NEW CULTURE

The materials with which the architect of a new culture works are financial and information systems, organizational structure, compensation, and, on the family front, the family constitution. (See Chapter 11 for more on family constitutions and a sample document.) Culture in the organization begins to change, however slowly, when a leader changes the information people receive, alters the way they get paid and what they get paid for, rearranges job responsibilities and reporting relationships, and adapts the mechanisms for coordination and accountability. By educating and informing both active and inactive family members and engaging them in developing a picture of their desired future relationship with the business, the leader can build shareholder loyalty and a culture of stewardship.

For any of these change initiatives to proceed, the architect must first earn the right to lead in a new direction; that is, the new leader must earn the respect of key non-family managers and family shareholders who are not active in management. The successor has to lead both the business and the family. This means that the new leader has to build a set of alliances, both in the business and in the family, that will allow her or him to begin to transform the "small things" that make all the difference in the overarching goal of making the changes needed for family-business continuity. Unfortunately, many of the small things are important to people who feel much more comfortable with the status quo than with the prospect of change—and those people are in the majority. So, what can a new leader do? Table 12.2 presents a formula for change, which many successors find helpful in understanding how to approach the change process.[3]

This change formula has proven quite useful to leaders whose mission includes bringing about the adaptation and rejuvenation needed for continuity. It guides leaders in determining the actions and steps that will yield the greatest return on energy and resources invested. The formula shows that change is a multiplicative function consisting of the product of three variables: dissatisfaction with the status quo, a vision of the desired future, and practical first steps to take to achieve the goal of change. Because it is a multiplicative function, if any one of these three elements is missing or

table **12.2** | **The Change Formula**

$$C = D \times V \times FS >> RC$$

where

    C = Change

    D = Dissatisfaction with the status quo, making a clear case for change

    V = Vision of the desired future, providing a clear sense of direction

    FS = First steps in getting from "here to there," clearly outlining what must be done first

    RC = Natural resistance to change

---

[3]Beckhard, R. & Harris, R. *Organizational Transitions: Managing Complex Change.* Reading, MA: Addison Wesley, 1987.

has a value approaching zero, there will be no momentum for change. Hence, even if a clear vision and thorough knowledge of feasible practical steps are present, nothing will happen in the absence of sufficient dissatisfaction with the status quo. This simple diagnostic can help a leader prioritize activities in order to get employees' energy focused in productive and profitable ways.

The CEO of a highly visible family-controlled consumer company was extremely dissatisfied with the performance of his company over the past several years. He had tried, through the employee newsletter, management briefings, companywide state-of-the-business meetings, and meetings with the union leadership, to convince others of a need for concern, but to no avail. Frustrated at his inability to convey the sense of urgency that he and other key managers felt, he finally came to the conclusion that employees believed management would cry wolf so as to get ever higher levels of productivity from the workforce. Aware that he could not drive the company where he thought it needed to go in the face of foreign competition, the CEO set about increasing dissatisfaction with the status quo. According to his assessment, it was the low level of this variable that most deflated the momentum for change and improvement. He decided to try something quite unconventional: He began to make some of the company's analyses of its competitive situation available to local media. These media were always interested in company news because the firm was a large employer in the community.

The CEO was amazed at what a significant difference this approach made in increasing dissatisfaction with the status quo among employees and thereby increasing their readiness for change. Newspaper reports were being circulated and TV news stories retold in locker rooms, cafeterias, staff meetings, and union hall meetings. In the span of a couple of months, the CEO had achieved what had eluded him for a couple of years—the capacity to create a credible sense of urgency so that employees would join with him and top managers in changing and improving the business from the top down and from the bottom up.

Interestingly enough, family-member shareholders not active in management, many of whom lived in the community, also displayed heightened concern about the state of the business. After all, employees who ran into them were asking them about the difficulties and their opinions on the prospects for improvement. This made the family much more ready to support the CEO's decisions (including approving capital investments in productivity-enhancing technology) than they had been prior to his decision to increase dissatisfaction with the status quo by being more forthcoming with the media.

THREE STATES OF EVOLUTION

Figure 12.1 shows the three states involved in the change process: the present state, representing the current situation of the family and the business; the transition state, in which most of the change activities take place; and the future state, representing the direction in which the leader wants the organization to head. Let's begin with the future state, since, as Casey Stengel, former manager of the New York Yankees, once said, "If you don't know where you are going, you may end up somewhere else."

THE FUTURE STATE

Defining the future state of a business is equivalent to putting stakes in the ground around a set of results or changes expected in a 1-, 2-, or 3-year period. The developer needs to bear in mind both the vision and the core mission of the enterprise and the

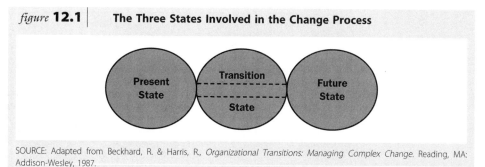

figure **12.1** | **The Three States Involved in the Change Process**

SOURCE: Adapted from Beckhard, R. & Harris, R., *Organizational Transitions: Managing Complex Change*. Reading, MA: Addison-Wesley, 1987.

owning family. Unlike a vision, which is usually somewhat abstract and longer range, the scenario for the future state should be precisely defined in financial, operational, and behavioral terms. It is best to write one scenario for the business and another for the family. New leaders should write the desired future-state scenario as if that day had already arrived, describing the accomplishments and results that should be observable. For example, the business scenario could begin, "On November 1, 2012, Premier Corporation signed the papers acquiring a resort in Florida. At the same time, it announced third-quarter results showing a revenue increase of 15 percent on comparable properties and a profit increase of 18 percent over the same period last year." The scenario should be as concrete as possible and should be a totally honest reflection of what the new leader wants for his or her future and the future of the family and business. The seven questions outlined in Table 12.3 should be considered in creating a future-state scenario. The bulleted items are suggested answers, included to provoke thoughtful consideration of the many aspects of the questions.

Compiling and discussing answers to the questions in Table 12.3 in order to develop a shared definition of the desired future state is an ideal task for a family meeting or family retreat. Later, key nonfamily managers should also be involved in the process, particularly as it relates to questions 1 through 5. Building bridges between family shareholders' and nonfamily managers' views of the future of the corporation is essential. If the company has a board with independent outsiders, board members should be provided with these answers and engaged in a discussion of both the questions and the answers. Board members will be glad to get this direction from the owner-manager, shareholders, and key nonfamily managers, and it will make them better able to serve the company and its shareholders.

An advantage of having a precise definition of the future state is that it provides information to those not involved in the drafting of the statement and improves their ability to understand how they will fit into that future. Uncertainty about and misperceptions of the implications of change on a person's future role are major sources of resistance. In addition, beginning the process with a definition of the future state allows management to take advantage of people's tendency to be more optimistic about their engagement in future opportunities than about their ability to fix current problems. Positive prospects, then, provide a positive tension. By pulling the organization and the family toward something desirable, the leader provides the fuel for the engine of change, particularly if there is a sharp contrast between the desired future state and the present state.

table **12.3** | **Creating a Future-State Scenario**

1. What would I like to see as the core family business 3 years* from now?
   - Owning/operating existing businesses?
   - Owning/operating existing and additional like businesses?
   - Managing new ventures in related industries?
   - Owning/managing assets outside the industry (i.e., diversification)?
   - Other? Please explain.

2. How would I like the management structure of the business to look?
   - Similar to the current structure?
   - Sibling partnership?
   - Family CEO?
   - Outside CEO?
   - Other? Please explain.

3. What would I like to see as the governance structure?
   - A board with a mixture of independent outsiders and family members?
   - A board with a majority of outside directors?
   - A board with a majority of family directors?
   - An active family council that meets at least twice a year?
   - An annual shareholders' meeting, with extensive discussion of financial statements and other matters of shareholder interest?
   - A family office to manage the family's investments and provide shareholder services?
   - A combination of the above? Please explain.
   - Other? Please explain.

4. What do I want my own involvement in the business to be?
   - No role in the business—a successful life and career outside the family business?
   - Active shareholder and steward with a successful career outside the family business?
   - CEO?
   - Owner-manager running one of the business units?
   - Owner-manager working at the main office (e.g., CFO or VP New Ventures)?
   - Board member?
   - Other? Please explain.

5. What are my expectations for financial returns?
   - Dividends and distributions? (Specify percent or amount.)
   - Capital appreciation through the creation of long-term shareholder value?
   - Financial resources for my children?

6. How do I want my relationship with other members of the extended family to be?
   - Characterized more by collaboration than by competition?
   - One in which we all actively care for each other and are there for each other?
   - As positive as possible, given the usual differences of opinion and disagreements about the business?
   - Not too time consuming—I really want to give priority to my nuclear family?
   - One in which we all share the responsibility for upholding and updating the legacy via a family constitution or new policies (so that, for instance, next-generation girls can have the same opportunity the boys have had to eventually manage the corporation)?

7. How do I want our family to give back to the community at large?
   - Through philanthropy?
   - Through community involvement?
   - Through government service or politics?
   - Through education?

The selection of a 3-year time frame is arbitrary; pick the time frame most appropriate to your own situation.

THE PRESENT STATE

The present state is where any dissatisfaction with the status quo must be found—and then promoted in the interest of continuity and perpetuation. Assessing the current situation is the key task of a leader trying to facilitate an evolution to a new, more appropriate structure for the family and the business. The leadership defines the need for change in terms of the present state. Many of the forces requiring change originate outside the business itself—competition, new technology, changes in consumer tastes, and so on. Other forces of change may be more internally driven, such as when a next-generation leader perceives the opportunity to turn a business that has relied primarily on its technical expertise into a more market-driven one or when a next-generation leader, after having been promoted to the presidency of the family business, experiences little increase in her ability to make decisions because of the presence of a CEO who will not let go.

Some of the need for change may also originate in the family. A younger daughter who has become president of the company, for instance, may be uncomfortably straddling two very different worlds. In the business, where she has been formally recognized as the president, she is at the top level of the hierarchy. In the family, where she is still "Daddy's little girl," the culture fails to reinforce her capacity to lead by not giving her appropriate power and influence.

Acknowledging differences and reaching accommodation on key issues are often necessary before a family and its business can mobilize for action and change. How can a leader tap that potential energy? The use of external consultants or "high-influence friends"[4]—whether board members, associates in the industry, or professionals available through educational venues like the Young Presidents Organization (YPO), The Executive Committee (TEC), or a business school or university—often helps in this process. Employee, customer, and family surveys can also provide feedback to promote action planning by the family and management group. Educational sessions with top managers to sense the state of the organization, "open-ear" meetings with different sections of the organization, and educational sessions with family members to sense the state of the relationship between the family and the business can also help.

Finally, assessment of the present state has to include an evaluation of readiness for the particular change that is being contemplated. It is essential to identify the key subsystems—departments or divisions of the company, branches of the family, individual top managers, or shareholders/family members—that will either have a bearing on the change or be affected by it. Two factors are most relevant in the overall assessment of their readiness for changes that will begin to drive the company from its present to its future state: (1) their enthusiasm and support for the proposed changes and (2) their power or capability (available human resources, funds, and family or organizational influence) to support or block the proposed changes.

The Raymond Corporation, at one point a medium-sized, family-controlled materials-handling business, acquired a privately held company that had a technology it needed to add to its product line. After performing a readiness assessment in preparation for the integration of the two companies, Raymond opted not to consolidate the companies at the same site by moving personnel halfway across the country, as had been previously decided. Instead, it created a project-management organization and made the president of the

---

[4]Barnes, L., Incongruent Hierarchies: Daughters and Younger Sons as Company CEOs, *Family Business Review*, 1(1), 1988, pp. 9–21.

acquired company its leader. The readiness assessment had exposed both the tremendous value of the individual contributors (the programmers) and their low readiness for such a dramatic move (their capability to walk out). The project-management structure allowed for the gradual transfer of the technology and the eventual consolidation of key technology transfer agents, who moved a couple of years later.

THE TRANSITION STATE

The work done during the transition period is quite different from the work associated with defining the desired future state and assessing the present state. It consists primarily of forming action plans, with unique temporary structures and systems to allow for follow-up and control of the process.

Having decided what needs to be changed, the leader now must decide where to begin the process:

- *With top management?* Should the leader begin by changing the makeup of the top-management team, the roles of the individual members, the way the team operates, or the strategies it pursues?

- *With family?* Should the leader begin by convening the family, making more information available to its members, educating family members not active in the business about business matters, creating a family council, or developing policies to guide the desired relationship between the family and the business?

- *With ownership?* Should the leader begin by restructuring ownership, changing the distribution of voting and nonvoting stock, educating others about the estate plan, developing or updating buy–sell agreements, or renegotiating existing dividend or distribution expectations?

- *With the systems that are most ready?* Should the leader begin with the individuals, departments, or groups of people most ready for the change—whether through their alignment with the desired future or out of dissatisfaction with the status quo—in order to create some early wins and develop momentum?

- *With new teams, units, or governance bodies?* Should the leader leverage the initial phase of the change process by taking advantage of the lack of history of new bodies—like a third-generation (G3) team, a strategic planning committee, a committee of the family council, or a newly formed advisory board?

- *With temporary project teams?* Should the leader create project teams with a limited lifespan in order to implement change? (As in the project-management organization created by George Raymond in order to successfully merge an acquired company.)

- *With the best practices for family-business continuity?* Should the leader focus his or her attention on one or a combination of the governance and management best practices discussed throughout this book?

CONTINUITY AND FAMILY–MANAGEMENT–OWNERSHIP STRUCTURES

The purpose of the transition state is to get family (F), management (M), ownership (O), and the relationship among the three from the present state to the desired future state (Figure 12.2). The idea is to consider each subsystem both individually and in relation to

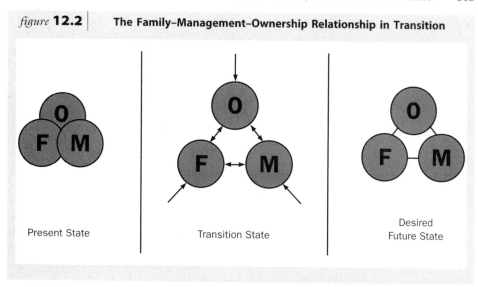

figure **12.2** | **The Family–Management–Ownership Relationship in Transition**

Present State

Transition State

Desired
Future State

the others: Do the criteria for family members to be considered for management positions in the company need to be updated? Does the family need to go out of its way to support a younger next-generation member for leadership in the company, despite a history of using primogeniture as the determinant of future company leaders? On the management front, does the company need to initiate a strategic thinking and planning process that "guns the engines" of growth? Does it need to hire new talent that better complements the skills brought by the next-generation leader, further professionalizes management, and gives the new leader confidence from having his or her own hire? And on the ownership front, does a buy–sell agreement need to be drafted? Do dividend policies need to be changed to support reinvestment in growth? Do vehicles for financing the execution of an estate plan need to be identified and insurance policies purchased? And how is all of this going to be coordinated and kept moving forward—through the use of temporary project teams or one of the new or existing governance bodies?

ORGANIZATION DEVELOPMENT APPROACHES TO CHANGE

Individual Consultation by the Family-Business Advisor with the CEO and the Successor Candidate or Candidates

Individual consultation with the CEO often is focused on helping the CEO let go of his or her leadership position and facilitating the transfer of power that is embedded in longstanding customer, supplier, and employee relationships. It may also involve the creation of structures and processes that would govern the relationship between the family and the business in the vacuum created by the incumbent leader's absence.

The ability of next-generation members of family firms to lead the organization must be accompanied by an ability to lead family members in subordinate management positions and those who make up the shareholder group. Many heirs resist this as a prerequisite to success in their leadership role. They would rather just run the business and be judged by the financial outcomes. But there is ample evidence that active leadership of these additional stakeholders is essential for success (as discussed in Chapter 11). As a result, besides overcoming the natural resistance by successors to assume more and not less responsibility, individual consultation may be directed at their taking initiatives through the family council to promote the engagement of other family members in committees, community relations, family philanthropy, and board service.

Dyadic Consultation with the CEO and Successor or Successors

The task here is often to help establish a timeline for the transfer of power while acknowledging that succession is best conceived of as a process rather than an event. Organization-development consultation may facilitate a renegotiation of goals and roles as the succession process develops and the transfer of power becomes more imminent. Also appropriate may be third-party coaching and oversight of the successor-in-development that instills accountability after the transfer of power to the new CEO.

Group Consultation with the Family or Shareholder Group

Interventions with the family or shareholder group often help them develop policies that guide the relationship between a business and its owning family and aim to jointly optimize all three subsystems: the family, shareholder group, and management.

Shareholder loyalty and patient capital are very important to family businesses, and yet there is a natural tendency for suboptimal differentiation between owner and manager roles. A family-participation policy may be part of a document, sometimes called the "family charter" or "family constitution," created by family firms primarily to regulate the relationship between the owner and management subsystems before a possible leadership vacuum engulfs the family business in the transition across generations.

Intergroup Consultation with the Family and Nonfamily Management

Change and development approaches for the organization here aim primarily to increase the stability of the firm and the family by having professional managers assume increased responsibility during leadership succession in the family firm. By raising awareness and promoting understanding of the critical role of nonfamily management in the growth and professionalization of the family firm, during a potentially turbulent period, intergroup interventions increase stability. This intergroup work may also clarify the standards to which managers are held and raise the standards for family members in the business. Recognition of the different but complementary contributions owners and managers make to the enterprise increases.

Bridging interventions between owners and key managers can enhance ownership oversight of management so that managers are held accountable for corporate performance and the pursuit of shareholder interests. Intergroup interventions with owners and key managers can also symbolically support the transfer of power to the next generation and reassure investors (family members) that the enterprise is in good hands, even if the successor CEO is still in the process of acquiring the full authority to lead.

DEVELOPMENT OF INTERPERSONAL SKILLS IN THE NEXT GENERATION

The development of interpersonal skills in the next generation is often the subject of consultation on leadership succession. After all, in order to succeed, successors need to earn the respect not just of employees and customers but of other family members, often shareholders, who may be older or for a variety of other reasons higher in the family hierarchy. The incongruence between the family's and the organization's hierarchy, the newness of the job, and the nature of the parent–child relationship all pose a unique set of challenges for effective leadership by successors.

DESIGNING AND FACILITATING WHOLE-FAMILY FORUMS AND APPRECIATIVE-INQUIRY PROCESSES

Large multigenerational families sometimes use a family forum called a "family assembly," which is created to operate parallel to the family council. Family assemblies include spouses and children, and are another vehicle for education of the extended family, communication, and the renewal of family bonds. The role of a family-business consultant facilitating this forum is that of educator, neutral third party, and shuttle diplomat when appropriate. Family assemblies create participation opportunities for all family members at least once a year, often scheduled to coincide with the annual shareholders' meeting. The smaller group of members who make up the family council can work on behalf of the assembly during its two or three meetings per year and then report on its progress during the annual family assembly.

Appreciative inquiry[5] also holds great potential as a method that enhances whole-family meeting deliberations and the healthy establishment of boundaries in the family–ownership–management system. In an environment where the quality of relationships in the family is more likely to be strained as the result of the complex set of demands imposed by multiple roles, its positive bias provides a sound alternative to the traditional deficit or problem-focused models of change. I have found appreciative-inquiry processes particularly useful during precarious circumstances that put survival of the family business at risk and as part of a developmental process for family councils and family assemblies that had recently confronted significant conflict or significant loss in the family or the enterprise.

Examples of appreciative-inquiry topics explored by several family council and family assembly retreats have included the following:

- "Family shareholders are operating with full information and enjoying full voice."
- "This is a trusting and loving family enjoying enlightened leadership and the gift of a wealth- and job-creating enterprise."
- "The sale of the business realizes shareholder value through liquidity and creates a positive-sum dynamic for the extended family."

---

[5]Barrett, F.J. & Cooperrider, D.L. Generative Metaphor Intervention: A New Approach for Working with Systems Divided by Conflict and Caught in Defensive Perception. In: Cooperrider, D.L., Sorensen, Jr., P.F., Yaeger, T.F., & Whitney, D., eds. *Appreciative Inquiry: An Emerging Direction for Organization Development.* Champaign IL: Stipes Publishing, 2001.

The search for a brighter future among extended family members can create a foundation for significant improvement in a family business. In conjunction with a review of leadership succession, competitive and strategic considerations, and the governance of the family–business relationship, it constitutes a holistic and respectful approach to increasing the effectiveness of the complex organization called a family business.

COMMITMENT PLANNING

A simple organization-development method has been quite useful to leaders of change in diagnosing the nature of existing commitment and then gaining the commitment required for evolution of the complex family-business system. The absence of such a commitment constitutes some form of resistance, passive or active, to change.

Commitment planning consists of identifying all key individuals in both the organization and the family and then asking the following questions:

1. Based on where he or she stands today, what is this key individual likely to do about the planned change? Block it? Let it happen? Help it happen? Make it happen?

2. In order for the process to be successful, where does the leader of the evolution need this key individual to be with regard to the planned change? Will it occur even if he or she is blocking it? Or does this person need to let it happen, help it happen, or make it happen?

3. What can the leader do to move this key individual from where he or she currently stands to where he or she must be in order for the planned change to be successful?

It is important to remember that, in many cases, all the leader needs from others in the organization or the family is neutrality, or to just let the change happen. While the leader of the evolution would clearly prefer to have everybody trying to make it happen, this is neither realistic nor necessary. Certainly, some key individuals may need to be prepared to let, help, or make some planned changes take place—for instance, changes in dividend policy may need the support of a majority of shareholders, and major changes in the makeup of the top-management team may need at least a "let it happen" kind of support from the retiring or transitioning chairman and CEO of the corporation.

INSTITUTIONALIZING THE CHANGE

Change has often been defined as comprising an unfreezing stage, a "making the changes" stage, and, finally, a refreezing stage. Because evolution is often so difficult to bring about, the last thing any leader wants is retrenchment, or a sliding back to the "old ways" as soon as the planned change effort is completed.

In order to be effective, then, the changes implemented during a period of evolution need to be consolidated and institutionalized in such a way that what was envisioned as the desired future state becomes accepted as the present state. The most reliable tools available for this task are organizational structures, ownership structures, compensation, dividend policies, family involvement and employment policies, a family constitution, education, financial information, and information systems serving management and shareholders. Research and practice (as discussed in Chapters 10 and 11) have identified two governance bodies that are uniquely qualified to institutionalize the evolutionary process and provide continued governance of the family–business relationship: (1) frequent family meetings, or an ongoing family council, and (2) a board—statutory or advisory—with independent outsiders.

Leaders of change should use these tools thoughtfully but freely and in an ongoing fashion to ensure that the enthusiasm that went into the evolutionary process does not vanish after the campaign is over. Consistency as well as competency is required in bringing about change and adaptation.

THE FUTURE: CAN THE FAMILY BUSINESS COMPETE AND THRIVE?

In 1998, the Follett Corporation faced the bleak prospect of disintermediation in the industry it had dominated until the advent of the Internet. Follett was 125 years old and moving to a fourth generation of family leadership. Ranked among *Forbes* magazine's 200 largest privately held firms, it consisted of 640 brick-and-mortar college bookstores and strong brand equity, founded on a solid franchise with colleges and schools that preferred to have someone else manage and operate their bookstores.

Follett had enjoyed 45 continuous years of sales growth. It distributed primarily college, high school, and elementary school textbooks; audiovisual materials; teaching aids for educators; and systems and services for libraries through wholesale and retail channels. It serviced its 640 locations out of one main distribution center and its corporate headquarters in the Midwest. In the late 1990s, new entrants in the industry, which perhaps had visions of becoming the Amazon.com of the textbook market, were challenging the company. While lacking Follett's expertise, gained through years of experience and customer orientation, they were backed by money from the public market and venture capitalists who subscribed to the e-commerce vision. With no need to show a profit, and with every incentive to grow market share to support their stratospheric market valuations, they discounted textbooks by as much as 50 percent. The excessive optimism about new technologies and the Internet had not yet peaked, as it would in March 2000 with new all-time highs for NASDAQ stocks.

"The Internet has literally shaken and totally transformed the vision and strategy at Follett," said Mark Litzsinger, the fourth-generation family member elected chairman of Follett Corporation in 2001. "The immediate worry was the possibility of being disintermediated in the distribution process—in other words, that our suppliers could go direct to our customers, students, teachers, librarians and school districts without any need for us."[6]

Follett was one of the first companies to establish a "clicks and bricks" strategy. Faced with a challenge, it launched eFollett.com to complement the reach it had already established through its 640 stores. This web presence allowed Follett to sell business to business, business to consumer, and business to education. But to get there, it had to approve a significant investment in new technologies. The problem was that this multimillion-dollar expenditure, a sizable single investment without precedent in the history of the company, had not even been budgeted—such was the speed with which change had arrived.

The board took up the request of the next-generation members of management, who wanted to be proactive in the face of accelerated change in their industry. It had to

---

[6]Author's personal conversation with Mark Litzsinger, September 2001.

consider the risks associated with the initiative, as well as those associated with not acting promptly. It had to ensure that shareholder, and not just management, interests were being addressed. Family shareholders had to confirm a strategic consensus and commitment to the strategy before the company could move ahead.

Quick approval by the board of directors led to rapid implementation of the e-commerce initiative. In short order, Follett had the premier college bookstore website, where students and teachers could order all their textbooks, reading materials, and logo wear.

AGILITY IN THE FACE OF CHANGE

It often takes a bold vision, crafted out of a sense of urgency by the next generation, to spur rapid action toward change. The next generation is often most sensitive to the need for change immediately after assuming leadership from the previous generation. Aware that the competitive environment does not hold back out of respect for the hard work done by a previous generation of owner-managers, next-generation leaders take the baton and run. Follett Corporation was a winner precisely because it appreciated the competitive strengths that had led to its success while, at the same time, attending to the need for change posed by new competitive conditions. Confronted with the challenges presented by e-commerce, Follett did not choose to sell out, turning a successful company into an investment vehicle for the owning family. Nor did it abandon its "bricks" in favor of the Internet. Instead, when faced with competition from web-based companies, it intelligently added "clicks" to its channel strategy and thus retained control of its market.

The unique and sustainable competitive advantages family businesses often enjoy can serve them well in competition against larger and often better-capitalized management-controlled firms. Their speed and flexibility, long-term strategies, strategic focus on somewhat protected niches, customer orientation, frugality, and patient capital in the presence of practices that safeguard trust and family unity constitute advantages that are not easy to replicate.

The dot-coms that made headlines in the late 1990s were pursuing strategies that were intensely digital. But as a result of all the cash generated by investors with an appetite for digital companies, they were more focused on raising equity capital than on satisfying customer needs. Given the abundance of readily available investment capital, a focus on creating value for customers seemed archaic and irrelevant.

Of course, the enthusiasm for tech upstarts did not suspend the laws of economics for long. Other competitive advantages rooted in unique (non-Internet) organizational capabilities soon demonstrated their capacity to make a difference. As a result, many family businesses—even those at the crossroads between generations, which often are mature and/or declining businesses—got an opportunity to reinvent themselves and set out on a new growth path for the next generation. Some of these companies, like Follett, consolidated their traditional strengths and then rejuvenated the company by reengineering the processes that help them integrate their suppliers and their customers with the business. By implementing new digital strategies, they added value through channels such as e-commerce.

Other family businesses (like Cemex, which is discussed later in this chapter), invested in people and organizational capabilities so as to consolidate their relationships with their customers and reinforce their high level of service and customer-support orientation. By taking unique steps, leaders of these businesses guided their companies

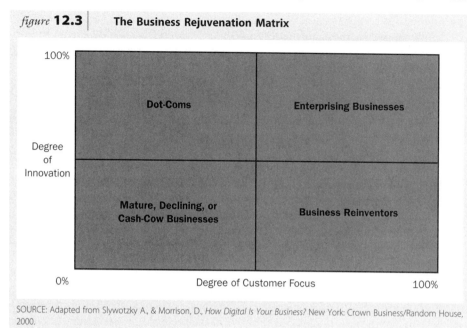

figure **12.3** | **The Business Rejuvenation Matrix**

SOURCE: Adapted from Slywotzky A., & Morrison, D., *How Digital Is Your Business?* New York: Crown Business/Random House, 2000.

to the lower right-hand and upper right-hand quadrants in the matrix shown in Figure 12.3, thereby reinvigorating their business and improving its competitive fitness through value creation for customers.

COMPETITION AND VALUE CREATION

As discussed in Chapter 6, family-owned corporations can create competitive advantage by adopting a unique combination of seven sources of value—physical assets, financial resources, product price/performance, brand equity, organizational capabilities, customer–supplier integration, and the family–business relationship.

The capacity of family businesses to deploy a unique combination of assets or competencies in order to gain a competitive advantage is rooted in the unique profile of a family-controlled company. Positive interactions between the owning family and the business make certain strategies and managerial practices more likely, less costly, and easier to implement and sustain over time than they would be in larger, nonfamily companies. When this positive, unique family–business interaction contributes to patient capital and innovative strategies and supports continued customer focus, the enterprising family ends up with a business that is built to last.

TAPPING THE NEXT GENERATION

Over the generations, younger family members have tended to be more fascinated by and more inclined to accept new technologies than have their older relatives. Members of business families are no exception. If their chosen profession is management, next-generation members are much more likely to want to engage in strategic planning, to redesign information/financial systems, and to pursue new products and e-commerce opportunities. Do next-generation members have to migrate from the family business to a *Fortune 500* company in order to pursue their dreams, or can their skills and visions be usefully tapped by the family enterprise?

The business reasons for welcoming the next-generation's ideas is that their complementary skills and perspectives are precisely what the family business often needs as it struggles to update itself to continue to create value for its customers. Sidney Printing Works in Cincinnati, Ohio, is a case in point. Instead of dashing off to work for or start their own online company, fourth-generation family members joined the family company and provided the firm with the skills it needed to become a strong contender in the new competitive reality. In addition to printing labels, signs, maps, and product literature, Sidney Printing Works could now assist customers with web materials, help them submit designs digitally for production in multiple media, and customize and archive those designs for multiple end uses. An acknowledgment of the value of the innovations contributed by the fourth generation was the creation of a new business unit called SpringDot, Inc.[7]

Indeed, if there is a disagreement worth having in a family-controlled company, it is the disagreement about vision and future direction for the firm. Implicit in the difficulty of conversing about this issue across generations is the tension between fully appreciating and respecting what has made the business successful so far and fully accepting that change is unavoidable. Leaders must recognize that unless the firm is willing to create the variety required to thrive in the presence of accelerating change, it will be overtaken by the competition and eventually driven to extinction. The Follett Corporation board of directors, for example, realized that this was the issue at stake.

Of course the disagreement could conceivably become more a battle of egos or power than a legitimate difference of opinion regarding the best strategy for the continued success of the family firm. Keeping the disagreement "on task" is therefore of the utmost importance. A recent disagreement between a father and a son at Cablevision Systems has brought a lot of consternation to family members and non-family shareholders in the family-controlled firm. Cablevision, based in Bethpage, New York, has annual revenues of $5 billion and employs about 20,000 people. Besides offering cable service to approximately 3 million customers in and around New York City, it owns Madison Square Garden, the New York Knicks, Radio City Music Hall, and Rainbow Media, a cable network unit known for its Bravo, Classic Movie, and Independent Film channels. But the issue that took center stage at Cablevision in January 2005, was a disagreement in the boardroom between Charles Dolan, 73, chairman of Cablevision, and his son James, 45, president of the company, over Voom, their satellite operation. Voom had lost $661 million in 2004 alone and James wanted to prevent continued red ink by selling the satellite assets. The board agreed, but Charles did not. He considered the prospects in satellite much brighter than in cable. The tension between these two leaders remains and has made other corporate initiatives difficult and relations with shareholders a nightmare.

But this tension is not new, and it is not exclusively a product of e-commerce or new media. As discussed in Chapter 5, when Samuel Curtis Johnson III was a young chemist working in the company's lab, he tried to convince his father, Herbert Fisk Johnson, that he had the formula for a breakthrough product—an insecticide. His idea was rebuffed on several occasions, because of Herbert Fisk Johnson's belief that the company should stick to the wax business. After several more attempts to convince his

---

[7]Callison, J., A Family Looks to the Future, *The Cincinnati Enquirer,* June 13, 2001.

father of the invention's value—and not oblivious to the oft-repeated words of his father, "Remember, son, we are a wax company"—young Samuel Curtis reportedly added a tiny amount of wax as an inert ingredient to his formulation for the insecticide. This time he received the go-ahead for his now wax-based product. SC Johnson: A Family Company grew from $171 million in annual revenues to $6 billion, with the lion's share of the profits and much of the capital to reinvest in growth, coming from the new insecticide products Raid and Off!

THRIVING THROUGH COMPETITION

Competition today is all about procuring and deploying new products and new product/service combinations in new supply-chain channels, including the Internet. Businesses are effectively creating new arrangements and new links in the value chain daily. Almost two decades ago, glimpses of this development could be gleaned from an influential article in the *Harvard Business Review*, which reported on three family-controlled companies that operated on a high-trust model supported by detailed procurement and inventory replenishment policies. These family businesses—Milliken, Levi Strauss, and Dillard's—agreed to update and coordinate their processes in order to increase the value-adding capacity of the entire chain. The electronic coordination was handled through an electronic data interchange, or EDI, system.[8]

Faced with increased competition and smaller margins, the companies wanted to reduce overall inventories and inventories of obsolete items and their associated costs, increase inventory turnovers, and still have products available for customers. The idea was to have Dillard's immediately and automatically update the number of stock-keeping units, or SKUs, in the chain. Information about the purchase of a pair of Levi Strauss blue jeans in any Dillard's store would be recorded at the cash register and then sent via the EDI network to Levi Strauss and Milliken, which would proceed, based on agreed-upon replenishment policies, to manufacture additional jeans and fabric for jean production, respectively.

Cemex, a family-controlled company founded in 1906 in Hidalgo, Mexico, is the largest cement company in the United States and one of the top three producers of cement worldwide. It has reengineered internal and customer relations processes through CEMEXNET. This digital network, coupled with the new workforce skills needed to make it work and a new logistics infrastructure with smaller decentralized plants, have enabled the company to reduce the time needed to deliver cement in traffic-congested Mexico City from 3 hours to 20 minutes, on average.[9] Because its customers, usually general contractors, face tremendous unpredictability in their work schedules from sources they cannot control—for example, environmental and work-place regulation by the government, weather conditions, union requirements, and traffic congestion—they appreciate the reliability and shorter lead times that Cemex can offer them. Decreased delivery times allow contractors to place an order for cement only when they need it and still not leave crews idle, thereby reducing their costs. For its trouble, Cemex is rewarded with a higher selling price for its cement and ready-to-mix concrete and returns on investment that are double the industry average.

---

[8]Abernathy, F., Dunlop, J., Hammond, J., & Weil, D., *A Stitch in Time*. New York: Oxford University Press, 1999.

[9]Slywotzky, A. & Morrison, D., *How Digital Is Your Business?* New York: Crown Business/Random House, 2000.

Because this organizational capability is now embedded in Cemex, the company has been able to acquire competitors throughout the world and quickly realize gains from implementing a digital strategy that allows these plants to achieve better returns. Cemex manufactures and distributes cement in 30 countries and sells cement in 60 others; worldwide sales reached 21.7 billion during the fiscal year that ended June 30, 2008. If an asset-intensive, low-margin business with slow growth rates and a highly cyclical market demand can do it, other family-controlled companies can as well.

ORGANIC COMPETENCIES AND THE BUSINESS'S FUTURE

Family-owned companies seldom enjoy a comparative advantage over their publicly traded counterparts with regard to physical and financial assets. A source of value that family firms have more traditionally commanded is a unique set of organizational capabilities—people, skills, and systems—that, in combination, may produce higher-quality products/services, quicker response times, deeper relationships with customers and suppliers, more agile customization, and lower total costs.

Innovating through new digital technologies is another strategy that may open new arrangements within the value chain, such as that developed by Milliken, Levi Strauss, and Dillard's. Family companies can restructure channel dynamics, take on strategic partners in the value chain, and get closer to the end customer in this way.

Product/service performance and reputation also have been a differentiating feature of many family companies. Over time, a product's or service's performance creates brand equity, which has been effectively deployed by family businesses, including such well-known companies as Marriott, Kohler, Hallmark, Cargill, *The Wall Street Journal,* Nordstrom, and *The New York Times* in the United States, and Hermés, Roca, Deusto, Osborne Wines, *El Nuevo Día,* Grupo Femsa, Harrod's, W.L. Grant (makers of Glenfiddich), Toyota, and BMW in other countries.

Sony (which is not a family company) provides a great example of the importance of brand equity to a company's growth and continued competitiveness. To his board members' consternation, on one of his first trips to the United States Akio Morita, representing the Sony Corporation, turned down an order from Bulova Watch Company's purchasing agent because the agent insisted that the transistor radios be branded Bulova. Although the board advised him to take the order, Morita instead committed to several smaller sales of products that would be branded Sony. At the time, Sony was an unknown brand in the United States—but its name would not remain unknown for long. Years later, Morita celebrated this decision as his best one during his long and successful career at Sony.

Most intangible assets, such as brand equity, caring and skilled employees, and committed ownership, are difficult to replicate. Thus, they offer family companies a greater probability of sustainability over time. (See Table 12.4 for a list of potential organic competencies.) But nothing lasts forever, so the top management of family companies, with the assistance of the board of directors or advisory board, should review company strategy annually to ensure that changes in the firm's competitive environment are not rendering organic competencies useless in customers' eyes. Only the competencies valued by customers can provide the family firm with competitive advantages.

table **12.4**	Potential Organic Competencies of a Family Company

- Unique or idiosyncratic organizational capabilities: people, skills, and systems
- Customer–supplier integration: relationships and systems
- Product/service price and performance
- Brand equity: reputation
- Concentrated ownership structure
- Family unity and business opportunity

table **12.5**	Focusing on Intergenerational Growth

- How can innovation be exploited to offer a greater value to customers, create a better-functioning organization for employees, and generate better returns for shareholders?
- What in the nature of the family–business interaction may represent a unique core competence that can be turned into a competitive advantage?
- What will be the company's next unique, differentiated value proposition for the customer?
- What can the next-generation leadership do to convince top management and/or the board of directors to financially support this unique, differentiated value proposition?

"INTERPRENEURSHIP": INTERGENERATIONAL GROWTH IN ENTREPRENEURIAL FAMILIES

Intergenerational entrepreneurial activity, or interpreneurship, was the subject of my first book on family business. *Smart Growth: Critical Choices for Family Business Continuity* (first edition, Jossey-Bass, 1989) argued that interpreneurship keeps the family-controlled company young and provides entrepreneurial opportunities for next-generation members.[10] Interpreneurship is often driven by new products, product-line extensions, new markets for existing products, exports, joint ventures, or strategic alliances with other members of the value chain.

Intergenerational growth through entrepreneurial activity improves the odds that the family enterprise will continue across generations. But as in the Cablevision story discussed above, disagreements about vision often make this kind of growth a difficult proposition. Answering the questions in Table 12.5 can help a next-generation leader determine the family business's potential for intergenerational growth and his or her role in it.

Growth for its own sake, without a unique strategy to support the growth effort, is to be avoided. Putting a product that creates little value for customers on the Internet or in another new distribution channel only glorifies an undifferentiated product; it does nothing to improve its competitive fitness. Just such an approach led to the tragic fate of many online businesses. Toys and groceries are commodities; the Internet has not changed that. A growth opportunity needs to be supported by competitive and economic factors that combine to create the most value for customers. Only then will family-business shareholders be able to share in the value-creation process by enjoying greater returns on their invested patient family capital.

---

[10]Poza, E., *Smart Growth, Critical Choices for Family Business Continuity.* Cleveland, OH: University Publishers, 1997.

GLOBAL OPPORTUNITIES

The future holds many growth opportunities in other parts of the world. Succession to the next generation can be a catalyst for the family business to go global. I have experienced it many times with my students at the Thunderbird School of Global Management—smart, capable, and wordly graduates, who see their major contribution to the family business in their generation as taking the business global. The phenomenon is not universal, it requires next-generation members who have this vision (something easier to find among Thunderbird students, given the school's stellar reputation in international management) a family member either sharing or at least willing to support this global vision for the enterprise, and of course a set of new competencies and capabilities. Recent research is divided on the issue. While one study found later generation family business less committed to internationalization,[11] another found that both commitment to and the extent of internationalization was positively influenced by succession to the next generation.[12]

Family companies have often been reluctant to grow internationally because of a conservative approach to fiscal management and a propensity for risk avoidance. Family enterprises have found that business risk was more easily managed by diversifying domestically than by going overseas. If the family business had an established reputation in the local market, and access to skilled nonfamily managers well versed in other industries, diversification in the well-known local market was a lower-risk growth option.

As local economies have opened up to global trade, opportunities for domestic diversification no longer seem as compelling. In Chile, for instance, the fast-tracked opening of the local economy to global trade in the 1980s produced significant restructuring of the country's economy. Many family companies closed down, unable to compete with global competitors. Other companies that either already enjoyed advantages or that began to pursue comparative competitive advantages thrived. A similar process took place in Mexico in the 1990s, with widely diversified "grupos" selling entire companies or divisions to foreign competitors while at the same time redeploying assets to businesses that continued to enjoy comparative advantages after the North American Free Trade Agreement went into effect.

Among U.S. family companies, the large size of domestic markets and a tendency toward risk avoidance have traditionally conspired against overseas growth, except by very large and professionally managed companies like Mars, Cargill, and Ford. Other companies have grown comfortable with global expansion by seeking alliances with family companies in foreign countries. Partners in these new ventures may be families they have known for years in a more unstructured, personal context. Consider the case of Simpson Investments, of Seattle, Washington. After being friends with a business family in Chile and doing some pilot tree-farm projects with them over the years, the family decided to partner with the Chileans in a $100 million pulp-mill operation in southern Chile.

While expanding overseas has become a more compelling opportunity for many family companies in the past decade, the management of risk will continue to be important. For the family businesses that do decide to enter the global marketplace,

---

[11]Okoroafo, S.C., Internationalization of Family Businesses: Evidence from Northwest Ohio, USA, *Family Business Review, 12*(2), 1999, pp. 147–158.

[12]Fernández, Z. & Nieto, M.J., Internationalization Strategy of Small and Medium-Sized Family Businesses: Some Influential Factors, *Family Business Review, 18*(1), 2005, pp. 77–89.

here are some suggestions. First, it is wise to abandon the myth that the company can remotely exercise managerial control through sophisticated financial information and control systems. When it comes to foreign operations, there really is no substitute for being there. Different reporting practices, cultures, competitive dynamics, compensation and incentive policies, and even general business practices render management through detection of financial variances useless. Identifying such discrepancies often amounts to too little too late.

Second, when growing globally is the strategy, networking through travel is a sound practice. Meeting with business, business-school, and government leaders, as well as the leaders of the competition, provides much intelligence on the appropriate adaptation of strategies for the local market. SC Johnson, for instance, has a board of directors with independent outsiders in most of the countries in which it operates. The company recruits smart, well-networked business, academic, and social leaders, who help it revise and customize its strategies and practices, infusing them with local content. Members of the Johnson family and top nonfamily managers travel often to various business locations, managing the risk of distance by adding some personal proximity to their global management portfolio.

POSITIVE-SUM DYNAMICS THROUGH FAMILY AND ENTERPRISE LEADERSHIP

Family companies moving between generations are particularly vulnerable to zero-sum dynamics. In the absence of growth or the perception of future business opportunities, there is a great propensity among family members to see winning only in terms of defeating someone else. In family companies, of course, that someone else is often a relative—the next-generation successor who patiently awaits his or her turn to lead, the branch of the family that has no members on the management team of the enterprise, the impractical cousin who is an incurable romantic. If the enterprise is growing, there is no reason why a gain for one person or family branch has to come at the expense of another. However, in the absence of growth, both the perception of opportunity and family harmony are likely to suffer.

Family unity and business opportunity are good predictors of the use of the best managerial and governance practices discussed in this book. The three leadership imperatives and five best practices covered in this book also provide the framework for the sample succession plan provided as a resource at the end of this chapter. These practices, in turn, are good predictors of family unity and the family's perception of growth opportunities. The achievement of this virtuous cycle is important for family-controlled corporations.

Given the accelerating speed of change, next-generation members are an important asset in the adaptation of the family business to new competitive conditions. They can also help to create loyalty and goodwill, rooted in opportunity, among shareholders and family members. With respect to the outside competitive environment, they have to be leaders of change, promoting dissatisfaction with the status quo and communicating a vision of a better future. In dealing with shareholders and family, these next-generation leaders have to accommodate the growing diversity of preferences of wealthier family members and inspire shareholder loyalty.

Next-generation leaders need to understand, firsthand, the value to the extended family of helping the business family achieve its noneconomic goals. These leaders must craft their own approach to meeting both economic and noneconomic family goals. It is a huge assignment, but one that many next-generation members experience as their calling—the very personal and unique way they can create value for the family business and make a difference.

Finally, let me give you a glimpse of the lessons from the centennial family firms we will explore in Chapter 13. The fifth- and sixth-generation leaders of these centennial family companies tell us that *the only disagreement worth having in the family business is one over the strategy of the firm and its adaptive capacity.* They consider fights over dividends, salaries, perks, even the presidency, nothing but zero-sum dynamics that end with everyone losing. As the family grows, they remind us, only business growth that provides career opportunities for family and nonfamily employees promotes the positive-sum dynamic required for continuity. These presidents and CEOs emphasize that the second part of the successful continuity story is about commitment by shareholders to govern themselves on behalf of the goal of continued ownership and control.

Communication, information, and engagement that promote family unity and a positive family–business interaction are central to shareholder commitment and the resources of low debt/equity and patient family capital that allow family companies to deploy unique strategies based on unique competitive advantages. When communication and engagement alone cannot bridge the gaps across family branches or between those who are active in the family business and those who are not, different classes of stock and buy–sell agreements need to be exercised in order to prune the equity structure and promote this continued positive family–business interaction among the family members that remain.

The centennial family companies featured in the next chapter have learned how to change in order to continue to realize the value of their unique competitive advantages and to govern the family–business interaction through:

- Nonfamily employees in top management
- Influential boards with outsiders
- Strategic planning processes
- Family meetings and family councils
- An equity structure appropriate to continued control by family members

SUMMARY

1 Next-generation leaders have to be both leaders of change and growth and stewards of culture and values.

2 Leaders of a culture change must: (a) create dissatisfaction with the status quo, (b) have an external (customer/competition) perspective, (c) have the capacity to forge a new direction, and (d) be able to generate a sense of urgency.

3 New leaders must not assume that the transfer of power implicit in being anointed as the successor also confers the authority to lead; such authority can only be earned.

4 The three states involved in the change process are the present, transition, and future states.

5 Commitment planning requires identifying all key individuals in both the organization and the family and then assessing these individuals' current positions on the change, where the leader needs each individual to be with regard to the change, and how the leader can move each individual to where he or she must be for the change to be successful.

6 Two governance bodies that are uniquely qualified to institutionalize the evolutionary process and provide continued governance in family–business relationships are: (a) frequent family meetings, or an ongoing family council and (b) a board with independent outsiders.

7 It often takes a bold vision, crafted out of a sense of urgency by the next generation, to spur rapid action toward change.

8 Younger family members often offer the complementary skills and perspectives needed by the family business to update itself and continue to create value for its customers.

9 Competition today is based on procuring and deploying new products and new product/ service combinations in new supply-chain channels, including the Internet.

10 Through the use of new digital technologies, family companies can deepen their traditionally strong relationships with customers, restructure channel dynamics, take on strategic partners in the value chain, and get closer to the end customer.

11 Intangible assets, such as brand equity, caring and skilled employees, and committed ownership, are difficult to replicate and thus offer family companies a greater probability of creating sustainable competitive advantages over time.

12 Interpreneurship, or intergenerational entrepreneurial activity, is often driven by new products, product line extensions, new markets for existing products, exports, joint ventures, or strategic alliances with other members of the value chain.

13 Putting a product that creates little value for customers in a new distribution channel only glorifies an undifferentiated product; it does nothing to improve its competitive fitness. A growth opportunity needs to be supported by competitive and economic factors that combine to create the most value for customers.

14 Family companies have often been reluctant to grow internationally because of a conservative approach to fiscal management and a propensity for risk avoidance. But the risk/ reward ratio in global commerce has shifted dramatically in the past several years. Global family businesses are poised to take advantage of significant growth opportunities that exploit the comparative advantages of different countries.

BOOK RESOURCE: A Succession Plan Guided by the Three Leadership Imperatives and Five Best Practices for Family-Business Continuity[13]

Michael and Paul Cook drafted this preliminary succession plan in order to synthesize their learning from this textbook and create a platform for action in Vue Systems, Inc., their family-owned business. In addition to drafting the plan, Mike and Paul, with their father's support, scheduled a midsummer family meeting to discuss the plan. It is important to mention that prior to beginning the process of writing this plan, neither Mike nor Paul felt confident that they could lead Vue Systems successfully. They had little agreement as to the future organizational structure of the corporation and their individual roles in it. As a result, Michael Cook, Sr., president and chief executive officer, also lacked confidence in the succession and continuity process. His understandable decision was to delay the transfer of power in the corporation to his two sons.

---

[13]The names of both the company and the owning family have been changed to ensure their privacy.

The Plan for the Future of Vue Systems

Next Generation's Vision

Our goal in 5 years is to see Vue Systems sustain the growth and profitability experienced since 1996—a compounded 15 percent annual growth rate. This growth and profitability will come from an expanded product offering and more effective management styles, but with the same core mission:

To become the leader in providing rubber extrusions for the architectural and other targeted custom markets, while furnishing unsurpassed service and response time. To do so for an appropriate profit and in a unified, focused, and fulfilling work environment.

In order to achieve this mission, Vue Systems will have to have qualities and competencies that span the successful integration of several different functions. Our vision is one that has and always should have an external focus on the customer.

We, as the leaders of Vue Systems in the future, will have to continue raising questions of what we have yet to improve. When employees and managers stop challenging each other and the status quo, the competitive advantage of our highly performing management team will quickly fade. It is important to maintain a culture of continuous improvement through employee training, team building, and continued education programs.

Building more business in our core market is the key to successfully achieving our mission. In order to reduce the risk of committing all our resources to one market, we should always look for opportunities and profit pools in other markets that complement our strengths and competencies. Our current effort to expand into plastic technology is to give our current customers more choices in architectural sealing applications.

Information on our external environment—competitive forces and the changes in our major supply chains—needs to be updated and kept in front of the management team constantly. We need to continue to add more to our current reporting capabilities to give management the necessary information to make decisions. Growth in the markets we participate in is becoming more difficult; the key to future growth is understanding that growth by itself is not healthy for Vue Systems. We need to promote growth that will increase our cash flow and profit going forward.

The last important aspect of what Vue Systems will be like in 5 years is our human resource strategy. The competencies we look for today and in the future should be teamwork, communications, responsiveness, and pride. Those qualities are very important for the leadership of the company. To meet the goal of creating a unified, focused, and fulfilling work environment, all of our employees will be striving to excel in these key competencies going forward. Fair base compensation, coupled with variable pay on the basis of company profitability for family and nonfamily employees, will remain a high priority within our human resource strategy. Promoting and compensating based on individual performance and companywide profitability is the key to a successful human resource strategy in the future.

To now forecast what our sales and product offerings will look like in 5 years would be in direct conflict with our need to stay in touch with the external environment as it changes. We have keys to improving every sector of our business strategy. Five years from now, we will have doubled our revenue, maintained a consistent net income of approximately 7 percent, while meeting ownership expectations of return on equity and dividends.

Our Family Council

Vue Systems has a history of bringing the family together to keep everyone in and outside the business informed on ownership issues that need to be understood at all levels of the family. We still have to bring many family business issues to future family meetings. It is clear that communications in the past several years have not been effective in regard to the family business and other issues a family council should be addressing. The need for a family council, for frequent family council and ownership meetings, is critical. We recently received feedback from a family business survey that perceptions among family members vary greatly in all aspects of business, ownership, and family issues. Perhaps this is the result of not having held the meetings for over 2 years.

Our family will find that being on the same page and sharing a vision of what the family and the company stand for will make family members more confident with the investment they're holding. We will find that the ambiguity that the last few years have fostered will be happily left behind when information starts flowing again. These renewed efforts to start routinely meeting as a family will help prepare the family for the challenges the transition into the new generation may bring.

We view this as an opportunity to improve the family, ownership, and business aspects of our family business. We cannot change the past, but have the opportunity to make a good family business even better and more prepared to deal with the ever-changing and increasingly complex issues that we will face in the future. Our next family council meeting will be attended by the founder and CEO, all of the children, and all of their spouses. Grandchildren will be going as well, but will not be attending the meetings until they reach the age of 16.

Family Meeting Agenda

(12 hours over 3 days of meetings)

1. Goals for the meeting and review of agenda
2. Business-school case on the rise and fall of families in business for discussion
3. Present summary of best management and governance practices
4. Overview of finances and the overall health of the business
5. Family-council logistics

   a. Purpose
   b. Plan for continuation
   c. Family strategy and vision
   d. Family issues
   e. How to get involved

6. Discussion: Goals of the owners of Vue Systems; develop a vision
7. Discussion: Ownership transfer
8. Succession and continuity plan
9. Board of Directors: Education
10. Discussion: Family employment policy; opportunity to get involved
11. Discussion: Life insurance, buy–sell agreement, irrevocable trust

The priority goal of the family council is to promote communication among family members and shareholders on a consistent basis. The issues that we will be communicating to one another may change, but the communication and education efforts must remain constant and effective.

This meeting was the beginning of a tradition in this family business, because we believe in the value that it provides our family, the ownership group, and the business. We also intend to continue having a great deal of fun together in these meetings, as well as engaging nonactive family members in activities that involve the administration of the family council, as well as becoming more in tune with the business matters of Vue Systems. We are excited about the impact this will have on improved communication and ownership continuity.

Estate Planning and Ownership Transfer with Business Agility in Mind

The estate plan has been developed and driven by Michael Cook, father and CEO. He has made all the wealth and ownership-transfer decisions, with the advice of accountants and lawyers, and has kept the entire family and shareholders well informed. He is currently working with a financial planning and insurance company to come up with a comprehensive wealth/ownership-transfer plan that will satisfy his retirement needs when he chooses to become less active in the company. He will first exit his day-to-day role as president and eventually relinquish his role as CEO to become the chairman of the future advisory board. He will transfer more ownership at that time, giving his voting shares to those family members active in the business, yet keeping the total number of shares evenly distributed among all of the children.

Michael Cook has structured a buy–sell agreement that controls the future transfer of ownership. It gives the current owners and the company the right of first refusal if a bona fide offer for the company is made by a third party. It allows gifting and transfer of ownership only to the owners' children, leaving the spouses with other assets that the [owners'] will specifies, funded with life insurance, of which the company is the beneficiary. Each owner has a policy that will give the company the required funds to pay for the shares without crippling Vue Systems. A sale of Vue Systems, Inc. would have to be evaluated and agreed upon by the entire ownership group.

Next-Generation Leadership Development

Both of us, Mike Jr. and Paul, have worked hard to achieve our individual development goals. We have both received bachelor's degrees and master's degrees from reputable universities. We both graduated from a graduate program for next-generation leaders of family enterprises and now have the necessary knowledge and skills to successfully lead our organization and family through the transition.

The challenge we have now is preparing ourselves as a team to effectively lead this organization together. Understanding the strengths and weaknesses we have individually is a key to honest and open communications—being willing to listen and support the other's position, while making effective and prompt decisions. Mike Cook, Jr., is now the president of the organization. Paul is now the chief financial officer, and in that capacity reports to Mike Jr. in the organizational chart. But Paul works together with Mike in leading and managing the organization daily. We see the success or failure of the organization with one president as a win–win or a lose–lose for both of us. As long as we communicate and continue to work on developing our team leadership strategy, we will be improving our ability to successfully lead the extended family and the organization.

Paul's Development Plan

Individually, I have aspirations of improving the quality and quantity of communications with all my siblings and their spouses. Becoming a more effective leader will require learning everything I can from my father before he transitions away from Vue Systems; measuring my development and progress in leadership and self-management competencies through peer and family reports; becoming more active in customer relations with our major accounts and potential accounts; understanding our product application and being prepared to evaluate the market and the customers we serve. All of these developmental goals are important, but as CFO I must maintain the integrity and availability of the accounting and information systems at Vue Systems as well. I must also provide oversight and challenge others based on what the financial information is communicating. All of these efforts will be necessary to make my brother and myself successful in leading our generation to the success we are seeking to accomplish together.

Mike Jr.'s Development Plan

My individual development goals are complementary to Paul's. According to many of the self-assessment tools we used in the next generation leadership program, as well as my knowledge of myself, there are several key areas to improve on:

- Improve goal setting and monitoring of progress.
- Improve my ability to use and analyze objective financial and numeric indicators of progress of self, others, and business.
- Improve reliability by following through with things I say I will do.

In most respects, my weaknesses are Paul's strengths. I believe Paul's statements about the importance of us working together as a team to lead this generation of the business are rooted in this reality. We can only truly be successful if that is the case. That means that both Paul and I must also always work on our teamwork and communication skills. They will be important for our leadership ability, and they will be critical for our interaction with one another.

I also believe both Paul and I need to work in the near term on continuing to expose ourselves to both our internal and our external customers. We must work harder at being seen and heard within our company and within our industry, without acting or being perceived as anything but what we are: intelligent, educated, prepared, grounded leaders of Vue Systems for the next generation—leaders with a respect and dedication to the past, but ideas for improvement in the future, committed to continue building a company that lasts.

Leadership by the CEO and the Chief Trust Officer

Up until about 5 years ago, if you had asked us how difficult it would be for Mike Cook, Sr., to begin transitioning leadership of Vue Systems to the next generation, we both would have had doubts that it would be a smooth process. Vue Systems is his creation—some would say his fifth child. But just as he raised his own children and then let them go and watched them grow into adults, we believe his dream for Vue Systems includes letting it go to the next generation.

We are certain that Mike Sr. will transition out of power as an ambassador for Vue Systems. [See Chapter 5 for a definition of the ambassador exit strategy and the other five strategies.] He will continue to nurture internal and external relationships with employees and customers. He will take them fishing and golfing, he will drop in on a mock up or a job site to provide technical expertise and create and enhance his relationship with others in the industry, and he will coach employees within Vue Systems. Most importantly, he will continue to be a mentor and a resource for the next-generation leaders of Vue Systems.

Just as letting go of his kids couldn't have been easy, it will likely not be easy to transition out of the leadership position at Vue Systems. There will be tests for the next generation of leaders at Vue Systems. There will be economic downturns that will impact our company. There will be mistakes made by Paul and Mike Jr. These times will define the ultimate exit strategy of Mike Cook, Sr. There will be times when he may instinctually become "the old general" who feels the company is going in the wrong direction in the absence of his guidance. Though these times will be trying for him, he will ultimately keep these feelings in check and contribute in a positive manner as ambassador and mentor for Vue Systems and for the next-generation leaders.

The chief trust officer, Barb Cook, our mother, has held many roles at Vue Systems over the years. She has always been Mike Sr.'s partner and confidante. She held a position in the HR department during the first 10 years of the company's existence. Over the past 5 years, she has become less involved with the business aspect of our family business and become more of the glue that keeps the family together, listening when members are troubled and keeping things in perspective.

Over the next several years, her role may change again. There may be times that she will need to be sensitive to the difficulty and emotions that Michael Sr. will inevitably face, particularly early on.

Both of our spouses seem to take the same approach to Vue Systems. They view it as a good job and an excellent opportunity for a career for their respective husbands. They respect the complexities of a family business, but neither of them believes that at this point they have a compelling responsibility or role within the family business. But we hope that as we assume the lead role in the family and the business, they will understand that their roles can be very important. And that, hopefully, their skills in those roles will be as complementary as our skills are to one another.

The Contribution of Key Nonfamily Executives

Our mission/vision and values statement states, "Most of all we will recognize and reward achievements based on merit for those who create and innovate and also those who continually support the day-to-day business requirements." The key to this statement is "based on merit." Clearly, the two of us have been "given" an opportunity at Vue Systems due to our relationship with the founder. But it is just as clear that we have taken the opportunity and run with it. We have prepared ourselves for leadership through formal education and our experiences. Our results can be objectively measured by the results we have had in our jobs. In many respects, our stripes were more difficult to earn than if our last name had been something other than Cook. We recognize that this is O.K., and serves to assure others that nepotism for nepotism's sake is not a practice that Vue Systems condones. The family business survey that we participated in confirmed that the company rewards based on merit. Key nonfamily executives were confident that the succession plan would promote leaders that were prepared, regardless of family ties.

We fully realize that key nonfamily executives have played, and will continue to play, a very important role in Vue Systems' growth and success. Paul is talented in the finance side of the business. Mike Jr. has substantial experience in operations as well as skill in leading people. But there are critical contributions that are uniquely made by key nonfamily members. Mike Scanlon has and will continue to play an important role in sales and marketing. The same is true with Smith McKee in production, Eugene Gormley in engineering, and Stacy Friedman in human resources. And as the organization continues to grow, there will be more areas that need to be led by talented individuals.

As with everything, perception is often reality. We need to be sensitive to the fact that we cannot fill all the top positions at Vue Systems with relatives for two primary reasons. First, we don't have the talent in our family to run a top-notch organization without nonfamily members bringing skills, experience, and a different way of looking at an issue. Second, if the top of the organization were full of people from our family, a reasonable person would assume that there was a cap to their ability to rise to or near the top if they are not part of the Cook family. Our organization's success to date is a result of good leadership and followership at all levels of the organization, and our success will only have a chance of continuing if we commit to recognize and reward achievements based on merit.

Accountability to an Advisory Board

To date, Vue Systems has not realized the potential value of an advisory board and the positive impact it could have on our company. Through our education at the next-generation leadership program, we, along with Mike Cook, Sr., are convinced that an advisory board, will add a great deal of value. As seen on the agenda for the family meeting, we will attempt to educate the family on the need for and role of an advisory board. We will also begin to discuss potential board members.

Mike Cook, Sr., will head up the project of establishing a board of advisors. He will ultimately determine the members of the board; however, we are confident that he will consult us on our thoughts and ideas on members and logistics of Vue Systems's board of advisors. Our goal is to have quarterly board meetings starting in the second quarter of 2005. Mike Cook, Sr., will likely remain chairman of the board of the company for the next 3 to 5 years. We realize that the value the board offers will be contingent on the decisions we make in choosing its members. The board will aid in the transition of power in many ways. From Mike Sr.'s perspective, he will have the opportunity to put a board together that creates accountability and provides insight to the next generation as they assume the leadership role. From our point of view, the board will help Mike Sr. work through the issues that surface in the process of exiting the business as the leader. This can be very valuable assistance. This, along with financial performance review and strategy review, will help Vue Systems continue its success through the next generation.

Conclusion

We must remember that the learning doesn't stop with this plan. We will continue to learn through our experiences. We must continue to study other successes and failures of family businesses. We will learn from teaching other family members. We will continue to learn from our mentor, Mike Sr., for our job is to understand and appreciate the factors that have created success so far and to make changes that are required to fine-tune the organization and adapt us to the changing environment. We intend to follow up on the three leadership imperatives and five best practices, build wealth in our generation, and pass on to the next generation a business that is in better shape than when we took it over. This is our goal of stewardship and continuity, one worthy of our continued best efforts.

CHAPTER 13

Continuing the Spirit of Enterprise: Lessons from Centennial Family Companies

María L. Ferré, fourth-generation President of the Grupo Ferré Rangel, explained: "Our success with continuity in this generation comes from learning from the failure of the second- and third-generation transitions. My father set out to do it differently, and he approached it very conscientiously, with a lot of discipline, having learned in his generation that a group of entrepreneurially prone individuals without a coherent structure can get into a lot of trouble."

The Grupo Ferré Rangel is a media group operating in Puerto Rico and on the United States mainland. In its fourth generation now, the company has 1600 employees and $300 million in annual revenues. *El Nuevo Día*, the flagship newspaper, enjoys 50 percent market share in the Puerto Rico public relations market and commands 80 percent of the newspaper advertising.

The first-generation business was a foundry. As the business grew, it added paper and cement to the business mix. Over the generations, the company expanded to Florida, Panama, Cuba, and then lost some of those businesses—in some cases for political and economic reasons, in others because the businesses were mismanaged. In the 1960s, the third-generation leader, Luis A. Ferré entered politics and became the governor of Puerto Rico.

Soon thereafter, the company confronted a financial crisis that led to the restructuring of the company. When the business was split up, some of the businesses, then owned by individual third-generation family branches, survived, but others did not.

One of Luis A. Ferré's sons, Antonio L. Ferré became the CEO of the Ferré family–controlled but NYSE-listed Puerto Rican Cement. He also bought for $400,000 a little daily newspaper in Ponce, the southernmost city in Puerto Rico, from his father. The purchase of *El Día*, as it was named then, took place at a time when the northern and most populous city, San Juan, was controlled by two other newspapers, *El Mundo* and *El Imparcial*. *El Nuevo Día* ended up taking 80 percent market share in the most important market on the island, all in one generation. Antonio L. Ferré was clearly a third-generation leader with a mission.

Antonio L. Ferré in collaboration with fourth-generation members of the family continued to grow the company by, among other things, launching a new newspaper in 1997. The paper, *Primera Hora*, is a *USA Today*-style newspaper. These two major papers plus a couple of smaller city newspapers, a Hispanic newspaper in Orlando, FL, a printing company, an Internet company, a direct marketing company, and a recycling company now make up the Grupo Ferré Rangel.

To what does the next generation attribute the success that this family in business has had in preserving the company across four generations? The fourth generation, composed of three daughters and two sons is entrepreneurial. With that recognition, fourth-generation siblings have dedicated themselves to building a coherent structure that will not stifle entrepreneurship but that will effectively govern the relationships between them. María Luisa also credits her father and her mother, Luisa Rangel, with promoting strong family unity coupled with unusual support for individual differences in this fourth generation. Perhaps because of the journalistic culture that runs in the family, the opinions of the individual children, however different, were constantly sought and appreciated as they grew up.

María Luisa continued, "as a fourth generation, we also fundamentally bought into the idea that we have to grow, experiment, create new business plans or we would end up becoming our own worst enemies." Zero-sum dynamics, the fourth generation recognizes, represent a powerful social field, particularly among naturally entrepreneurial and competitive siblings. And when the zero-sum dynamic is played across family branches, gender, generation, and those active and inactive in management, continuity is threatened. (*Zero-sum dynamics* refers to a win–lose outcome between two or more parties that nets out to a zero gain. In no-growth contexts, the initial win–lose outcome degenerates into self-reinforcing cycles of lose–lose outcomes. When a union and management fight over contract issues to the point at which both employment and firm survival are put at risk, as we saw happen in both the steel and automotive industries in the United States in the 1980s, you can argue that a zero-sum dynamic has taken hold. The same can happen between branches of an extended family, between heirs of different genders, or between family members who are and are not employed in the family business.)

María L. Ferré adds: "Our success in continuing the entrepreneurial spirit is a result of five professionals who know they complement, they need each other, to be successful. We respect each other and our differences. The siblings have selected me to lead them. So the major distinction between us and the previous generation is the sense of confidence that comes from knowing that we now have a coherent structure to govern the relation between people who are naturally entrepreneurial in nature."

LESSONS IN ADAPTABILITY AND CONTINUITY FROM CENTENNIAL FAMILY COMPANIES

Global economic activity has accelerated to record speeds in the past decade. Similarly, the speed at which fundamental changes have stormed through the global economy, whether the catalyst was technology, the financial and capital markets, customers, global competition, or a combination of these, is unparalleled in human history. This means that more companies are requiring new products/services and growth opportunities, more often, in order to stay alive.

Perhaps then, it should not be a surprise to find that the life cycle of the corporation is shortening, too. Worldwide, corporate sustainability and continuity are much more challenging objectives today. Because of hypercompetition in a global marketplace that includes China, South Korea, and Eastern Europe; because of increasing commoditization; because of Wal-Mart, Metro AG, Carrefour, and Reliance Industries' new grocery-store concept in India; and because of rapidly changing technology and supply chains businesses face declining profit margins and shorter profitable product life cycles. According to a study by Bain & Co., the average life expectancy of a corporation (not just family companies) in the United States has fallen to an extraordinary 14 years. While this phenomenon may be of marginal interest to CEOs of management-controlled firms (whose average tenure has been recently estimated at only 3 years), it is of critical importance to CEOs of family-owned and family-controlled corporations. Why? Because one of the key differences between family firms and their counterparts is the intention, if not outright commitment, to continue across generations of owners or owner-managers.

The inquiry that has resulted in the lessons from centennial family companies was initiated in 2001. I set out to investigate the question of resiliency and continuity among family-owned and family-controlled corporations by interviewing fourth-, fifth-, and sixth-generation leaders of companies that were at least 100 years old. All chairpersons, presidents, and CEOs interviewed are members of the founding family. In a world where entrepreneurship is becoming more important and corporations seem unable to last, what are these longer-lasting family businesses, these centennial family companies, doing to survive and even thrive? Are they promoting a continuing spirit of entrepreneurship, are they relying on serial entrepreneurship (a continuing series of entrepreneurial ventures), or do they have elements in their cultures that enable them to reinvent themselves with every generation? The conclusions are preliminary, because the sample is limited to 16 companies to date. Their annual revenues range from $18 million to $5 billion dollars, and they operate in a variety of industries: newspapers, textbook distribution, brick and tiles, food and beverage, wine, steel and bearings, insurance, bakery and baked goods retailing, farm equipment distribution, auto retailing, and leather accessories. The companies are headquartered in the United States, Latin America, and Europe. I was particularly interested in developing an understanding of the nature of the change efforts to promote continuity these fourth-, fifth-, and sixth-generation leaders had engaged in and in discerning the level of appreciation they had for what their predecessors had done while in leadership positions. Related investigations have been carried out in Spain and England.[1] Because the family-firm leaders I interviewed came from successful centennial companies, we cannot say with certainty that some of these same practices will not be found in companies that have not lasted a century or have been unsuccessful in their continuity efforts. Still, the research provides valuable insights into the actions that leaders of successful centennial family companies consider most critical to their ability to build great companies that last. What follows in this chapter is organized around the major

---

[1]Gallo, M., & Amat, J., *Los Secretos de las Empresas Familiares Centenarias.* Barcelona: Deusto, 2003. Also see, Leach, P., & Bogod, T., *Across the Generations: Insights from 100 Year-Old Family Businesses.* London: BDO Stoy Hayward, 2005.

themes discovered, followed by some of the evidence from the interviews supporting that theme. I also sought additional information from company websites, business cases, public records, books, electronic databases, and trade publications. I hope that drawing a preliminary sketch of successful long-run companies, rooted in the real-life experiences of next-generation CEOs, will assist readers in creating their own visions or dreams of continuity–that is, that the long-range aspirations for your entrepreneurial business become clearer as a result of reading this chapter.

FAMILY CULTURE, ORGANIZATIONAL CULTURE, AND CULTURAL BLUR IN FAMILY FIRMS

Edgar Schein[2] defines *organizational culture* as a set of values, beliefs, and assumptions that influence the practices and behaviors of organizational members. An organization's culture largely reflects what has proven successful, over time, for an organization. This proven way of thinking becomes, over time, the organization's culture. It becomes so matter of fact, Schein argues, that the culture and its values and beliefs drop out of awareness—that is, until the culture is found wanting or there are new challenges to the established culture. At that moment, a reexamination process may make the existing culture more explicit. The culture's set of values, beliefs, assumptions, practices, and behaviors may then be targeted for change in the interest of adaptation. The literature on organizational culture remains rather pessimistic about the capacity to change organizational cultures. Even when it concedes the possibility of doing so through great effort, the literature remains rather skeptical on the ability to do so with speed and a sense of urgency.[3]

The concept of culture is particularly useful in the context of family firms because these tend to exhibit strong cultures[4] and a form of cultural blur—that is, there is little differentiation between assumptions that go into decision making depending on whether the issue is a family, ownership, or business-management issue. And family values and rules often influence decision-making and behavior in the business—as when family members are not held accountable because they are dearly loved relatives. Or just as easily, business values and rules may influence behavior in the context of the family—as when members of the family that have been terminated from employment in the firm appear exiled from the family circle. Cultural blur generally enables families in business to avoid the conflict inherent in the sometimes different goals of the family and the organization they operate. But by minimizing conflict or differences, cultural blur may also undermine the ability of a family in business to address problems in creative ways and to find new solutions to old problems. (See Table 13.1.)

Cultural blur may, on the other hand, endow a business with invisible crossovers, or what the strategic planning literature calls "intangible assets," that can be converted into unique competitive advantages. Love in the family may be the source of a strong commitment to quality and customer service in the organization. Strong ownership commitment may also lead to the patient capital effect ascribed to family firms,

---

[2]Schein, E., *Organizational Culture and Leadership*, 2nd ed. San Francisco: Jossey-Bass, 1992.

[3]Kotter, J., *Leading Change*. Boston: Harvard Business School Press, 1996.

[4]Dyer., W. G., *Cultural Change in Family Firms: Anticipating and Managing Business and Family Transitions*. San Francisco: Jossey-Bass, 1986.

table **13.1**	**Cultural Blur**

- Little differentiation of the assumptions that go into decision making on the basis of it being a family, an ownership, or a management issue.

- Family values and rules are used in the business.

- Business values and rules are used in the family.

- Cultural blur may enable families in business to avoid conflict and the anxiety it provokes.

- By minimizing differences that sometimes lead to conflict, problem-solving ability is diminished.

  But cultural blur may endow the business with "invisible crossovers" that provide it with what the strategy literature refers to as "intangible assets" that can be turned into competitive advantages. For example:

- Love becomes quality and caring customer service in the business.

- Commitment is translated into patient capital and transfer of business knowledge across generations.

- Independence is manifested as a financial principle requiring a low debt/equity ratio for the company.

- Work ethic becomes part of the organizational culture and is evident as a strong commitment to higher productivity.

- Creativity is exercised through continuing entrepreneurship and innovation in the firm.

meaning that they have a longer time horizon on their expectations about return on capital. This form of owner commitment is also credited in the social-capital- and the resource-based-view literature with the transfer of knowledge advantage[5] that is so evident in the sports world by the success of young athletes like Tiger Woods, Serena and Venus Williams, and Dale Earnhardt, Jr. These young successful people were all mentored and coached by their respective parents.

A family value of independence may be translated into a risk-management principle in the corporation. A low debt/equity ratio, for instance, may become a corporate goal, as it has for the Timken Company, discussed later in this chapter. A strong work ethic, an individual value of a founder or successor, may become part of the corporate culture and be evident as a companywide commitment to high productivity. And creativity, which some of the CEOs interviewed acknowledged as a contributing quality of their predecessor CEOs, is evidenced in the context of continuing entrepreneurship and innovation at the corporate level.[6]

Cultural blurring, then, can be the source of competitive advantage and sustainability in a family business. Fisk Johnson, President of SC Johnson, quotes his father

---

[5]Cabrera-Suarez, K, De Saa-Perez, P., & Garcia Almeida, D., The Succession Process from a Resource and Knowledge-Based View of the Firm, _Family Business Review_, _14_(1), 2001, pp. 37–47.

[6]Schein, E., The Role of the Founder in Creating Organizational Culture. _Family Business Review_, _8_(3), 1995, pp. 221–238.

and fourth-generation CEO as saying: "We call our values 'Family values…. World class results.' They are not radically different from the values you hear from major Fortune 500 companies, but I think we are better able to practice those values as a family-owned business. People care about making quality products, really care about the family, each other and the success of the company. I believe this caring attitude translates into the success of the company." He proceeded to elaborate on the advantage that this cultural feature represents for SC Johnson, "when we do a new product launch or a change in our line, we don't have to do all the motivation, resistance to change training and public relations campaigns to convince the employees of the wisdom of bringing about this change." Then he added: "When we decided to take CFC propellants out of our entire product line, we did it in 5 working days and 8 years before the government required us to do so. It was an incredible advantage vis-á-vis our competition. We were able to do it because our employees understood that customers made a connection between high quality products and environmentally friendly products."[7] Because SC Johnson products often occupy that high relative quality position in the marketplace, protecting the brands' position and doing the right thing for the environment represented a compelling win–win situation.

THE TIMKEN COMPANY AND LONG-TERM CONTINUITY THROUGH PRODUCTS AND VALUES

The Timken Company of Canton, Ohio, was founded in 1899. Timken is a publicly traded S&P 500 company that operates in 29 countries, had $5 billion in annual revenues in 2008, and 26,000 employees. (See http://www.timken.com.) The Timken family retains a controlling share in the company. A member of the Timken family has been active in top management in every generation. Tim Timken, a member of the fifth generation, is currently chairman of the board of directors. He commented on the reasons for Timken's outstanding record of continuity:

First of all, we make the best products in the world. We are the leader in bearings. We are the leader in alloy steel. We also recently made a significant acquisition which broadens our product line consistent with the core of the business. So from a product point of view and a service point of view, we believe we are the best at what we do.

Behind the product, there are consistent values. The Timken Company has always believed that our four values: ethics and integrity, quality, innovation, and independence are central. We have been consistent with them for over 109 years. These values go back to our founders, my great-great grandfather, who believed passionately in them, and to this day we hold those in everything that we do. So those are the two primary drivers of our continuity.

I think, finally, that the company was formed on innovation. My great-great grandfather invented the tapered roller bearing as a solution to friction problems in carriages at the time. So going back 109 years, the company has been dedicated to creating value for our customers through innovation. That is still true today, whether it is in our automotive business, our industrial business or our steel business. Unless we can find a way to create value through innovation we are just a commodity player and that's not a position we feel we can win with.

---

[7]Author's personal conversation with Fisk Johnson.

Curious about his own role in preserving and adapting the culture, I asked him what role he had played and foresaw playing in the future regarding the values at the core of Timken's success. He replied:

My belief is that as a family member, and chairman of the board, my role is to make sure we don't lose sight of them. Fortunately, the professional management that we have in place has experienced these core values first hand in the field, and so their commitment to them is there. My role, I guess, is more as the conscience; to make sure those values don't slip away from us. Today, as an example of our commitment to innovation, we spend 50 to 60 million dollars a year on research and development. We've got dedicated facilities all around the world—one here in Ohio, one in Romania, one in France, and one in India–and we run a global network for research and development. If you look at the products that we make today, the core concepts are the same but they look very, very different, and that is the result of the investment that we have made in innovation. [For additional historical data on the Timken Company and Timken's commitment to quality and innovation, see Pruitt.][8]

And regarding our value of independence—our belief is that as a company, we need to control our own destiny. That influences the type of alliances and rela-tionships we enter into; whether it's joint ventures, investments around the world, or labor policy, we believe we are better suited to run our business than anyone else, and as a result we keep our debt to equity capital ratio low. We don't want bankers running our business. Over the years we have enjoyed the flexibility to make sig-nificant investments when we need to.[9]

THE J. M. SMUCKER COMPANY: A PROUD BRAND AND A PROFESSIONALLY MANAGED CORPORATION

J. M. Smucker is the number 1 U.S. producer of jams, jellies, and preserves. Smucker's also makes dessert toppings, juices, and specialty fruit spreads. The J.M. Smucker Company was established in 1897. At the time, Richard Smucker's great grandfather sold apple butter out of the back of a wagon. Richard Smucker is fourth-generation President and co-CEO with his brother, Tim, of the Orville, Ohio, company that employs 3000, operates in 45 countries, and had revenues of over $2 billion in fiscal 2008. When I asked him about the drivers of continuity for the 111-year-old company, he confidently said: "A family with the same religious values, a board of directors with independent outsiders, and a deep appreciation that the consumer is king so we have to continue to improve and innovate. He also highlighted the exemplary role that his father and CEO (Paul Smucker) played by not hanging-on but instead becoming a statesman for the company in 1981 when Tim and Richard succeeded him, and the tremendous influence of his mother, a strong matriarch."[10]

Just as significant though, Richard Smucker pointed out that the last two gen-erations have made very different contributions to the competitive adaptation of the

---

[8]Pruitt, B. H., *Timken: From Missouri to Mars—A Century of Leadership in Manufacturing.* Boston: Harvard Business School Press, 1999.

[9]Author's personal conversation with Tim Timken.

[10]Author's personal conversation with Richard Smucker.

J. M. Smucker Company. In the third generation, Paul turned away from making private label products for supermarket chains that continually insisted on cost reductions and were responsible for margin erosion. Paul Smucker took the considerable risk of abandoning a significant portion of total company sales to turn Smucker's into a branded-products-only company. And in so doing, committed the family to creating one of the truly great brands in America.

Fourth-generation members Tim and Richard, both graduates of the Wharton School, have taken the company to the next level by professionalizing management and modernizing the management of the firm. They brought with them strategic-planning processes, the latest financial concepts and methods along with a cadre of key nonfamily management that was every bit their peer in age and managerial education. That renewed managerial competency is in evidence in the strategy deployed by the firm in the past decade, including the recent acquisition of other powerful brands that are now part of Smucker's: Jif peanut butter, Crisco cooking oil, and Pillsbury baking products. And in its consistent recognition, since the 1998 inception of *Fortune*'s annual survey of the 100 Best Companies to Work For, as one of the top 25 companies to work for in the United States.

With five members of the fifth generation already working in the company, Richard Smucker appeared quite confident that the J. M. Smucker Company would be strategically adapted again by this next generation in the process of providing for continuity across generations of owner-managers.

A SYSTEMS THEORY PERSPECTIVE ON CONTINUITY RESULTING FROM GENERATIONAL CONFLICT AND CULTURE CHANGE

Research on organizational culture postulates that strong cultures are a business asset and that cultures that fit the strategy and are strong are even better. But because the competitive environment is changing all the time, unless the culture is also flexible and agile (think new-age composite as opposed to steel), the organization could get into trouble by failing to adapt appropriately.[11]

General systems theory suggests that organizations need to be both stable and flexible. Its theory of requisite variety suggests that as turbulence and variance increase, systems achieve adaptive capacity by increasing their internal requisite variety. In other words, to the extent that leaders bring more variety inside a system, the organization will have more resources to deal with the increasing variety outside the system. Hiring new people with new skills, implementing new information technology, adding independent outsiders to a board, adopting team structures (in which multiple skills are brought to bear on a given task), and adding redundancy or slack resources all increase requisite variety.[12]

General systems theory also postulates that there is a hierarchy of system levels in which higher-order systems provide more leverage for change than lower-order systems.[13] The individual is the first level of the system. The family around that individual

---

[11]Kotter, J., op. cit.

[12] Von Bertalanffy, L., *General System Theory*, rev. ed. New York: George Braziller, 1975.

[13] Ibid.

is a higher-order system than the individual. The fields of psychology and psycho-therapy, especially among practitioners rooted in a systems perspective, have moved toward working with couples and whole families rather than just the symptomatic individual, in an attempt to produce more and lasting change. The organization, in this case the family business, is a system of yet a higher order. As such it offers still greater opportunities for creating fundamental and longer-lasting change in itself, the family, and the individuals that make up the family.

From this perspective, and moving beyond conflict, two generations can add value in surprising ways. In fact, I would argue (on the evidence of the research[14] and my 28 years of experience as an advisor to family businesses) that the conflict that is inherent across generations is actually one of the keys to the survival of the family business. Other businesses, which cannot count on the emotional component of passionate disagreements about strategic direction, may not get the kind of wake-up call that they need to reinvent themselves as conditions change.

In terms of continuity, then, the proposition is that the business is well served by a disagreement between the generations of owner-managers on the strategy of the entrepreneurial or family-controlled company. The older generation actively represents what has worked well in the past and brings to bear the confidence and wisdom distilled from that success. The new generation challenges that wisdom because its time horizon, which is naturally different from that of the previous generations, alerts next-generation members to new opportunities and new challenges that will surface within that longer time horizon.

THE DISCREDITED NOTION OF REQUIRED CULTURAL REVOLUTIONS

Because of the rather strong organizational cultures observed in many family compa-nies,[15] I interviewed these CEOs with the premise that revolutions and revolutionaries may sometimes be needed to provide these firms and their owning families with the requisite variety needed to adapt and be future-ready across generations of owners.

Ignacio Osborne, sixth-generation CEO of Osborne, a Spanish wine company founded in 1772, disagreed with the premise. According to Ignacio: "It was not a revolution. Even though my family has been in the south of Spain for more than 230 years, the British calm is still in the veins of most of the family. It was not easy, it was complicated, but there were no big conflicts or disagreements with the fundamental change process that my generation was leading. There were many meetings, many sessions, I had only been with the company for 3 years. It was hard, we listened to the disagreements and comments, but there was no conflict or revolution."[16]

Ignacio joined the company in 1993, helping the managing director for a 2½-year transition period. His father and uncle had led Osborne in the fifth generation. Now as the sixth generation took over (Tomas, Ignacio's cousin is the Chairman of the company), competitive conditions had changed. Casa Osborne may not have needed a

---

[14] See, for example: Kellermans, F., & Eddleston, K., Feuding Families: When Conflict Does a Family Firm Good. *Entrepreneurship Theory and Practice*, 2004(Spring), pp. 209–227; Poza, E., *Family Business*. Mason, OH: Thomson South-Western, 2004.

[15] Dyer, W. G., op. cit.

[16] Author's personal conversation with Ignacio Osborne.

revolution, but it certainly needed to change its culture and its strategy to respond to its increasingly successful competitors.

The wake-up call for the change was quite intimate for the family. As Ignacio Osborne revealed, "Up until the fifth generation, at least some of the Osborne family members could live from the dividends generated by the company. In the sixth generation, none of us could live from the dividends. I know this is not very romantic or very family-business oriented, but in practical terms, this was very important. What we did to create the needed fundamental change was to present very early in our leadership of the company a series of alternatives to the board and described eloquently what the challenged situation of the company was. The contrast between our vision and the current situation set the task out for the board and the company. We also described to the board how our generation thought the company had to be managed in order for it to have a future."

The inability of a family company to generate sufficient dividend income to maintain the living standards of a family that generally grows with each generation has issued a wake-up call for other families in business. For example, the McIlhenny family, of Tabasco sauce fame in the United States, did not gun the engines of growth through new products as a result of a grand strategic planning exercise led by McKinsey and Bain Management or the Boston Consulting Group. Instead, it adopted a new strategy and promoted growth opportunities as a result of its CEO putting the choice to family shareholders during a family retreat on Avery Island. The choice: invest in growth so as to expand the profit-generating capacity of the firm or invest in social worker and psychologist fees through a family assistance program aimed at helping family members adjust to their new, less affluent, reality. The family wisely chose to move the challenge to the higher system level, the organization, to try to find a resolution to their quandary, and supported reinvestment in growth. New products and product-line extensions were created. The company grew successfully and the shareholders benefited.

THE EROSION OF THE ENTREPRENEURIAL CULTURE

Multigenerational businesses that are in later stages of development may be experiencing the interaction between family and business as a cost rather than as a resource. The entrepreneurial stage is widely recognized as one that endows the organization with the capacity to be nimble, largely because at that formative stage owners know that the essence of being successful is getting the customers' dollars to move from their bank accounts to the entrepreneur's. In other words, making the sale is the basis of success.

But it does not seem to take long anymore for companies to be asked by their customers to be ISO 9001 certified, to be asked by their lenders to apply standard accounting principles that promote greater transparency (and paperwork), and to have to meet a growing list of industry and government-initiated requirements. So increased regulation and the growing needs for coordination create the need for meetings and more meetings and memos and more e-mailed memos that make the business naturally become more bureaucratic. Collectively, these multiplying requirements may contribute to the business experiencing time delays it never experienced during its entrepreneurial phase.

More important to this discussion is the possibility that the family itself will become an important source of inward-focused time-wasters, in which case, the family begins to represent a cost to the firm rather than the resource represented by a family member in a combined owner-manager role during the entrepreneurial stage.[17] Speed is one of the competitive advantages often inherent in entrepreneurial firms resulting from the invisible crossovers between ownership and management. But in later generations, the family–business interaction, which in earlier periods represented an intangible asset that could be converted into the strategic advantage of speed and agility, can become a cost: the loss of agility in the face of change. A family that is paralyzed because of conflicting views across generations or across branches of the extended family can become inward-looking and become fertile ground for turf wars and feelings of entitlement. In the process, it can forget its most basic comparative advantage in relation to often larger, more bureaucratic corporations–its nimbleness. And, more importantly, by focusing inside, it can lose the ability to keep an eye on new competitive dynamics and the ever-changing marketplace.

Ignacio Osborne, reflecting on this very development, commented: "The biggest source of resistance to any change may have been that the family name is on every product label. So we had to try to explain to family members who have been managing the company that in business today you have to focus on the customer and you have to forget a little bit about the vineyards, the countryside and the craftsmanship in production and look more into the market and what is going on in the world. I think that was the biggest resistance. After all the company has been very successful with the original business model for many years, so why change?"[18]

FAMILY UNITY AND A POSITIVE FAMILY–BUSINESS INTERACTION AS A RESOURCE IN THE CREATION OF INIMITABLE COMPETITIVE ADVANTAGES

Competitive advantages that are more likely available to the family firm are highlighted by the resource-based view of organizations.[19] From this theoretical perspective, the firm is considered to have specific, but often complex and intangible, resources that are unique to it. These resources, often referred to as organizational competencies, include internal processes (e.g., lean processes that result in speed of execution), human resources (e.g., knowledge and skills that result in higher-quality service and support), or other intangible assets (such as brand and reputation). The unique resources are credited to a combination of family unity and career opportunities created by the family firm and can provide the firm with a competitive advantage in certain circumstances.[20] One of these resources in a family firm would be the overlapping owner and manager (agent) relationship, which could lead to advantages from owners monitoring both the

---

[17]Zahra, S., Hayton, J., & Salvato, C., Entrepreneurship in Family vs. Non-Family Firms: A Resource-Based Analysis of the Effect of Organizational Culture. *Entrepreneurship Theory and Practice*, Summer 2004, pp. 363–381.

[18] Author's personal conversation with Ignacio Osborne.

[19]Cabrera-Suarez, et al., op. cit.

[20]Poza, E., Hanlon, S., & Kishida, R., Does the Family Business Interaction Factor Represent a Resource or a Cost? *Family Business Review*, *17*(2), 2004, pp. 99–118.

operations and the operators of the business. The advantages could include reduced overall costs, such as reduced financial reporting, regulatory compliance, and administrative costs. Faster decision making and longer time horizons for increased efficiency in investment activity could represent another advantage. Another resource unique to some family firms is the creation of value for the customer through an organizational culture rooted in close interpersonal relationships with customers and suppliers. This resource is converted by some family firms into a competitive advantage through high quality and high customer service strategies. Marriott and its Ritz-Carlton brand are good examples of capitalizing on this resource.

Similarly, the details and nuances that make execution an important element of any strategy can be transferred from one generation to the next in ways that are simply not available to nonfamily management. The advantage resulting from this transfer of knowledge and of a social network of influential contacts is evident in family-controlled media companies. Donald Graham, Chairman and CEO of The Washington Post Companies, has been eloquent on this "gift," part of the legacy built by his mother and previous CEO, Katherine Graham.

A CUSTOMER-CENTRIC PARADIGM, CONTINUOUS EVOLUTION, AND FAMILY-BUSINESS CONTINUITY

Family firms are particularly prone to becoming inward-focused and losing sight of the customer and relevant competitive shifts as generations transition and wealth and the number of family branches increase. The significant power that the family's emotional life wields on the ownership group often makes the business lose the obsessive customer orientation that defined it during its early entrepreneurial stage.

For Tim Timken, chairman of the board of directors of the Timken Company and fifth-generation leader, keeping the customer first is very important in promoting continuing adaptation. His perspective mirrors that of Ignacio Osborne, of Osborne Wines in Spain, as to the healthy effect of a customer orientation on a successful family ownership group, one that by nature of its success is vulnerable to hubris. "At the end of the day it all starts with the customer," Timken explained. "We as a company believe that unless we have a firm grasp on what the customers need, we're not going to be able to provide value for them. So I spend about 50 percent of my time in the field working with my customers, understanding the directions they are headed in, and understanding how we apply our core competencies to create value for them. That's the start of it all. Then, we need to step back occasionally and ask, okay how we are doing against that standard? Are there other things that we should be doing to create that kind of value?"[21]

Because of this overriding customer-centric paradigm,[22]

the overall vision for the company has evolved over time. We started as the world's best maker of tapered roller bearings, period. And back in 1917, we got into the steel business to support that vision. In recent times, we've expanded it though, and certainly the group that we have on the operating committee right now helps set that

---

[21]Author's personal conversation with Tim Timken.

[22]Von Hippel, E., Thomke, S., & Sonnack, M., Creating Breakthroughs at 3M. *Harvard Business Review*, 77(5), 1999, pp. 47–55.

direction. Back in 1998, when the currency crisis hit and took the economy down with it, it caused us to look in the mirror and say, what are we really trying to do with this business? So we charted the path that said, this is going to be a company that is built around a core set of competencies that really come out of our history as a bearing and steel maker. So we began to push the envelope and say there's a service package that you can wrap around this product. That core product, which used to be a single roller bearing now becomes a package or assembly for the wheel end of a light truck or SUV. It's that kind of constant evolution versus revolution that we've pursued over time. It has worked out very well for us. If you go back in our history, it has been that way. We continue to do that. And we bring professional management in to help us shape that vision. Family members will play a very prominent role in setting the course but this isn't my show. The head of automotive is a very, very qualified woman out of the automotive industry. The head of my industrial business grew up inside our company and has seen every aspect of it. These are people who understand what it takes to compete in the industries that we are in. So I find myself as a part of that team, versus the guy who's always charging out in front. That's just not the role that family members have taken over time. We want to be there with a hand on the steering wheel, wanting to help chart the path but it's not a solo exercise.[23]

At Casa Osborne, Ignacio Osborne observed: "It used to be that the taste of Osborne family members, sophisticated as it was, determined the taste of our products and defined what quality in wines meant. Not anymore. Now we conduct market research, do focus groups, pay attention to trends and changing consumer tastes." He added: "One of the successes we had is we went very quickly. A new business plan for the company was drafted, discussed by the board until we reached some consensus for the future of the company. It was just business and company (not family) and then we managed the communication with the rest of the shareholders to let them know what we were trying to do and why."[24]

So, from what these third-, fourth-, and fifth-generation family business leaders have stated: A new shared vision emerges as a response to customers' needs through product, service, and innovation. This reenergized vision drives the strategic regeneration process. Family management and family shareholders are both a part of that process. Family shareholders are kept in the information loop even if they do not work in the company or regularly attend family meetings. Extensive acknowledgment of family interest in the family council or family meetings are linked to the family's board agenda through at-large representation of the family on the board. This means that current-generation CEOs have to address the issue of corporate control and shareholder liquidity, because as Jim Collins says in *Good to Great*,[25] who is on the bus is ultimately very important. The Deere farm implement distributor in the sample of centennial firms just celebrated their 105th anniversary with $102 million in annual revenues. Third- to fourth-generation CEO Ray Koenig suggested that their recent change in the corporation's code of regulations was an attempt to provide for both a nice retirement for members of the third generation and an orderly transfer of control to next-generation members active in the business.

---

[23]Author's personal conversation with Tim Timken.

[24] Personal conversation with Ignacio Osborne.

[25]Collins, J., *Good to Great: Why Some Companies Make the Leap ... and Others Don't.* New York: HarperBusiness, 2001.

In family businesses, who is on the shareholder bus is extremely important to the long-run commitment and the patient capital required. Unless company leaders provide exit opportunities, the bus ride may become quite unpleasant, its trajectory quite unpredictable, and its destination truly regrettable. But the family need not do this work alone. The board, as Ignacio Osborne, CEO of Osborne Wine Company tells us next, "ends up doing a lot of the lead work in this process of adapting the corporation to its new competitive reality."

THE ROLE OF THE BOARD, FAMILY COUNCIL, SHAREHOLDERS, AND NONFAMILY MANAGEMENT IN ENSURING CONTINUITY

The role of the board is prominent in the governance of the relationship between a family and its business when the family–business interaction is preserved as a positive-sum dynamic. Because of the board's importance, these next-generation leaders frequently undertake a critical review, and often restructuring, of their board. They all come back to the idea that because of the family's legacy on the board, a lot of communication and education needs to take place beyond what is deemed traditional board work and strategic-planning processes. The family's identity remains attached to the company's, so if the company is going to change in order to adapt and grow, the board composition has to change. Ignacio Osborne confessed that "in the span of two years, I took 12 years out of the average age of our board."

The textbook distributor in the study sample received its wake-up call from fifth-generation members of the family. Much more concerned than was the older top-management team, and feeling a sense of urgency about the implications that e-commerce had for the more traditional textbook distribution and retail model, the fifth generation spearheaded approval of a multimillion-dollar unbudgeted capital expense aimed at the sudden and accelerated onslaught of Internet-based booksellers with investments in new technology. The company successfully repelled the incursions from new entrants and protected their business model by expanding their brick-and-mortar retail channels to include business-to-business, business-to-education, and business-to-consumer electronic commerce.

Wake-up calls are often needed when a strong record of success conspires against the minimum level of dissatisfaction with the status quo that is generally essential to being receptive to change. Koenig Equipment's CEO considers the need to create a sense of urgency in the midst of the success that the family has enjoyed in the business to be his biggest challenge as leader of the transition to the next generation. After all, since 1999 the company has grown from four to six locations, more than doubled its sales to $102 million, entered a metropolitan area market with Deere lawn care equipment, and taken on an additional brand in another market. For a family steeped in values of humility and frugality, that is accelerated growth and significant success.

At the Grupo Ferré Rangel, family council meetings took place on a monthly basis in the early years–the readiness-to-change stage. Then there were family retreats, two of them a year, that included the next-generation spouses. In the second stage of a 10-year succession and regeneration process, the Ferré family reconnected with the legacy and its core values, sponsored education in family and business topics, and made it possible for the leadership transition to gain traction. Next-generation members began to assume positions with profit-and-loss responsibility, and this is when the viability of the new vision was really tested. Did next-generation members have what it takes, and did they want to do what it takes to be successful as business leaders of the next generation? Ultimately, the transfer of power and ownership began to take place at a family retreat at which family members decided on the concept of a holding company and creating new and more responsible leadership positions for next-generation family members and key nonfamily executives. This new structure created the opportunity to make key nonfamily employees winners in the succession process too. Family members had noticed that key nonfamily executives who had been great when the successors were younger were now less forthcoming and engaged. As next-generation family members assumed more responsible positions involving profit and loss, competition for the top-level jobs understandably began to develop. But after creating the holding company and reorganizing to a flatter structure made up of several operating-companies, there was more opportunity for everybody, family and nonfamily, to achieve career advancement.

NEXT-GENERATION LEADERSHIP: PARTNERSHIPS AND A FOCUS ON THE FUTURE

When asked about his own trajectory at The Timken Company, Tim Timken replied:

> *I'm having a ball. I walked into my first steel mill probably when I was 9 or 10, and for anybody who has ever been in a steel-making facility, it gets under your skin. So there are mornings when it's a little tough to get out of bed, but I'll tell you I wouldn't want to do anything else. I spent a couple of years at the business school at the University of Virginia and I was one of two manufacturing people. That was back in the early 90s, when everyone was writing off manufacturing in the United States and saying that we are going to be a high-tech economy and a service economy, and manufacturing is dead. It's terrible, what are we going to do, let it all go to China? We are very active in the National Association of Manufacturers and the American Iron and Steel Institute, we are believers and in the process we're able to create shareholder value, we're able to maintain employment of 26,000 people around the world and that's what we do and I believe that we do it well. So to be a part of that, boy I'll tell you, I am having fun.[26]*

Ignacio Osborne also thrives in his role as fifth-generation CEO. But he adds: "An important part of our success comes from having quickly set the new goals and having quickly shown shareholders positive results against those goals. You cannot come to every board or shareholder meeting and announce what you are going to be achieving next year. You have to show them what you achieved this year or people start not trusting you."[27]

Successful next-generation leaders in family firms that are successful in the long term are very aware that their motto is partnership. (See Table 13.2.) They are cognizant of the fact that they serve the company and the family and may provide the spark for a

---

[26] Author's personal conversation with Tim Timken.

[27] Author's personal conversation with Ignacio Osborne.

table **13.2**	**Next-Generation Leadership**

The next generation:

- Provides the customer-driven vision that promotes innovation and regenerates the company
- Creates a partnership with:
  - Other family members through the family council, family meetings, shareholder meetings and hundreds of informal conversations that inform and educate
  - Key nonfamily management through top management team, operating committees, etc.
  - Boards of directors
  - New members of the ever-changing supply chain
- Engages in a lifelong journey of preparation for leadership rather than "rushing to the Presidency," and then act as stewards of the family and its wealth; they serve the company and family members through the successes they work hard to achieve.

renewed but collective effort on behalf of the business and the family. Tim Timken, for example, served as director of strategic planning for the Timken Company, "so that I provided the spark for some important conversations about strategy yes, but the vision is customer driven–it wasn't about me, it was about the customer. And in order to make it successful I have to share leadership with or create a partnership with other family members through the family council, family meetings, and shareholder meetings. And build a partnership with key nonfamily management, through the top management team, the operating committee, the board of directors."[28]

INCUMBENT-GENERATION LEADERSHIP: GOVERNANCE AND RESOLUTION OF THE PAST

The current generation, on the other hand, builds institutions that will effectively govern the relationship between family, management, and ownership through a strong board, family meetings, the appointment of professional nonfamily employees in top management, equity structures that facilitate control, and buy–sell agreements. Incumbent CEOs, in effect, clean house for the next generation before transferring power. (See Table 13.3 for incumbent-generation CEO leadership initiatives.)

This then allows the next generation to focus on the future rather than the past. Here is an eloquent statement from Ignacio Osborne on the important role of the preceding generation:

Something that is very important, and perhaps I had not mentioned it earlier because we were lucky enough to have it, is a previous generation that always worked for the transition. So once I got the responsibility for the company, I only had to think of the business and of the next generation. They anticipated a lot of problems. When the next generation gets into the company and for the first 2 or 3 years of their term

---

[28] Author's personal conversation with Tim Timken.

table **13.3**	Incumbent-Generation CEO Leadership

- Builds the institutions that will effectively govern the family–business interaction: strong board, family meetings, key nonfamily employees in top management, buy–sell agreements, and equity structure that facilitates control

- In effect "cleans house for the next generation" before …

- Transferring power (with customers, suppliers, employees) while in full command of the corporation.

all they are doing is trying to repair conflicts and problems that they have inherited from the previous generation, then a lot of time is wasted. When we started working, we worked on the present and the future, the past had all been settled.[29]

When this responsibility is not carried out by the incumbent generation, the next generation has to perform it before being able to dedicate itself to building the future. Viena Capellanes, a premium bakery and baked goods chain based in Madrid, Spain, was founded in 1873. It relied on a family council formed by four cousin-members of the fourth generation to bring the company back from near catastrophe. The incumbent CEO died unexpectedly, without as much as having considered succession. The four cousins, concerned about the state of the company and the widespread dispersion of the estate, pruned the family tree and set about turning the company around. All that was left was a very strong reputation and tremendous brand equity for its products. That great reputation for premium baked goods coupled with hard work and a future orientation by the four highly committed cousins has brought life back to Viena Capellanes, which currently serves customers through a much larger retail chain of bakeries and cafés. The cousins unanimously declared that they would rather have had the incumbent CEO resolve family issues left over from the past and create a blueprint for governance.

TEN LESSONS FROM THE JOURNEY THROUGH THE CENTURIES

1. Being a family does not guarantee unity or good relations, but disagreements may be the creative spark needed for adaptation and continuity.
2. If the family is not doing well, the business is hurt.
3. Family unity is the ultimate resource.
4. Spouses are critical, and their engagement is necessary.
5. Planning by the current generation for the benefit of the next is of the essence.
6. Without a new vision by the next generation that pulls the company into the future, there is no commitment to continuity.
7. World-class key nonfamily managers are essential to the process.
8. External assistance by consultants and board members may also be essential.

---

[29] Author's personal conversation with Ignacio Osborne.

9. The incumbent generation needs to build the governance infrastructure for a positive family–business interaction. It also has to be generous in the transfer of power.

10. The next generation is well served by being appreciative of the previous generation's efforts and struggles in the process while it advocates a renewed and revitalized strategic vision for the enterprise.

FAMILY FIRM RESOURCES FOR THE FUTURE

Family Business Programs

According to Boston's Family Firm Institute (FFI; see http://www.ffi.org), a leading professional association that keeps tabs on the field of family business, there has been significant growth in university-based family-business programs in the past few years. The current estimate is that more than 100 family-business centers and programs offer seminars and/or standard curriculum courses at the undergraduate and graduate level. *Family Business* (see http://www.familybusinessmagazine.com) has a directory of these programs throughout the United States. For a listing of programs in Europe, Asia, and Latin America, consult FFI at http://www.ffi.org, the Family Business Network at http://www.fbn-i.org, or your local university.

Family-Business Consultants

Because of the unique nature of the family–management–ownership system, professionals called "family-business consultants" are now available to family-owned and family-controlled corporations. The profession is a highly interdisciplinary one. It draws practitioners from areas such as law, psychology, management, finance, and academia. Again, the Family Firm Institute (see http://www.ffi.org) currently lists over 1200 members worldwide.

Family-business consultants can provide subject-matter expertise and an objective detachment from the family in business. They often work with family enterprises to address management and ownership issues, including the transfer of management responsibilities and ownership (stock and control) to the next generation in a sound and tax-efficient manner. Family-business consultants often help with succession and succession planning, tasks that are experienced maybe once in a CEO's lifetime. Other tasks that family-business consultants are called to perform may include a strategic review or planning process, a review of compensation plans that cover siblings or cousins with very different responsibilities, a survey of the perceptions of family and nonfamily management resulting in feedback for improvement planning, managing sibling rivalries in the top-management team, the launching of a new board of directors or advisory board with independent outsiders in it, and the creation of a family council (see Chapter 11), the body that acts as a board for family matters.

Family-business consultants, like other professional advisors, deserve careful scrutiny in the selection process. Gather information, check references, and find out how long they have been doing this work and how many companies they have already assisted in similar processes. Have several members of management and the ownership group interview the prospective advisors; inquire about their professional fees and any referral fees they may collect on the basis of the project or the sale of products. Be explicit about outcomes expected and have them put all of this in writing.

Family-business consultants can remove barriers, promote momentum, and provide the discipline for continued action that multiyear processes such as succession and the transfer of power require. While the company's board can perform some of these tasks (see Chapter 10), they can often be of greater assistance in these when teamed up with competent outside family-business advisors.

Family Firm Research

Most of the published work on the subject of family firms prior to 1995 was highly anecdotal. Theory development and empirical studies have begun to predominate only in the past several years. Some of this research has appeared in mainstream academic journals in management, such as the *Academy of Management Journal*, the *Journal of Finance*, and *Administrative Science Quarterly*. The most predictable outlets for the latest findings of studies involving family firms are the *Family Business Review, Entrepreneurship Theory and Practice*, the *Journal of Business Venturing*, and for the smaller family firms, the *Small Business Management Journal*. For the student of family firms, whether as a professional service provider to family firms (a lawyer, accountant, financial planner, etc.) or as a traditional student enrolled in an MBA program, a doctoral program in management, or a family-business program, these are the best sources of new knowledge. For business owners, *Family Business Magazine, Fortune Small Business*, and *Business Week Small Biz* can provide an alternative source of family-company profiles, stories, and sometimes the findings from recent research studies.

SUMMARY

1 The first part of the longevity story is all about competitiveness and adaptation. In fact, it may not be much of an overstatement to suggest that the only disagreement worth having in a family business is a disagreement about strategy. When the disagreements are about pay, perks, and the presidency, the path of least resistance often leads to win–lose situations and zero-sum dynamics. And families cannot support zero-sum dynamics because the losers will eventually get their chance to harm the winners, even if it means the destruction of the company and the family.

2 Keeping the business growing through a customer-centric paradigm and providing career opportunities for family and nonfamily employees is at the heart of that positive-sum dynamic and the capacity to have that virtuous cycle working for the owning family.

3 Commitment by shareholders to govern their relationships for a higher purpose on behalf of continued ownership and control is necessary. Communication, information, and engagement that promote family unity are as important to the success of these centennial companies as managing strategically to remain competitive. The primary asset in creating competitive advantage is embedded in the family through the invisible crossovers from the family's culture: the intangible assets, the patient capital, the thrift principle, a strong work ethic, the commitment to excellent quality, the commitment to the long term, and the commitment to financial independence.

4 Centennial family companies have also learned to govern the family–business interaction and mitigate shareholder disunity (two great vulnerabilities of family businesses postulated by agency theory) through more formal structures and processes such as:

- Hiring and retaining professional nonfamily employees in top management
- Influential, independent boards
- Business planning and strategic planning processes
- Extensive communication using family councils and frequent family meetings
- A lean equity structure that promotes continued control by family members while ensuring that the company remains nimble.

5 Finally, centennial family companies have learned to change in order to continue to realize, across generations, the value of their traditional or new, but nevertheless idiosyncratic, competitive advantages. These advantages are often rooted in the unique family and family-business culture. Next-generation family-business leaders recognize that their cultural foundation is not easy to change, notwithstanding what may be the urgent need to do so in response to significant changes in their competitive environment. In partnership, the incumbent and next generations assume the responsibility for leading the change effort. In the best of cases, the incumbent generation focuses its efforts on pruning from the family business unnecessary legacy effects (e.g., highly compensated family members who are no longer adding value to the business and old agreements and policies that no longer make sense) so that the next generation can focus on the present and the future.

PRIVATECO BUSINESS VALUATION REPORT

MARKET VALUATION
of
PrivateCo
prepared by
Robert T. Slee, CBA
Certified Business Appraiser
Valuation Date: June 30, 2008
Date of Report: July 22, 2008
ROBERTSON & FOLEY
6201 FAIRVIEW PARK ROAD
CHARLOTTE, N C
ROBERT T. SLEE
MANAGING DIRECTOR
July 22, 2008
PERSONAL & CONFIDENTIAL
Mr. Bob Mainstreet
1234 Oak Avenue
Anytown, USA 28819

Re: Market Valuation of PrivateCo
Dear Mr. Mainstreet:

I will use this letter to determine the market value of 100 percent of PrivateCo (the "Company"). The purpose of this appraisal is to determine a likely selling price for your shares.

For these purposes, market value is defined as the highest cash purchase price available in the marketplace for the stock of the Company. This letter will use the following format:

I. Discuss the recent operating and financial results of the Company.

II. Establish the concept of market value and describe the valuation process.

III. Derive the market value of 100 percent of the Company.

Since you founded and oversee the management of the Company, there is no reason for us to retell the entire PrivateCo story, or to recount all of the details concerning operating the Company. Therefore, we will summarize these issues next.

I. THE COMPANY

PrivateCo Corporation was founded in 1980 as a manufacturer of laminated panel products primarily supporting the commercial aerospace industry. PrivateCo is a worldwide supplier of laminated products, using lightweight structural materials designed and manufactured to meet its customers' cost and performance requirements.

The Company has assembled over 50 years of manufacturing, engineering, marketing, and product development experience to provide customers with quality products and service. PrivateCo is continuously developing new panels and products, giving it the opportunity to expand from the aerospace industry into the architectural, computer, high-speed rail, marine, medical, space, and tooling industries.

In need of expansion, in May 2000 the Company opened a new 32,000-square foot building to support future demands. The facility houses a new manufacturing computer network which gives PrivateCo the ability to better monitor orders, processes, and costs more efficiently. Quality, service, and delivery are keys to its continued growth and success.

PrivateCo manufactures a standard line of laminated panels used throughout the aerospace, clean room, construction, computer, marine, medical, tooling, rail, and space industries. The products are typically manufactured with strong lightweight honeycomb using fiberglass, aluminum, and carbon skin materials.

PrivateCo has 10 customers that buy more than $100,000 in a given year. These top 10 customers represent about 45 percent of total sales. No single customer comprises more than 15 percent of total sales. About 65 percent of the Company's sales are to aviation-related customers.

The Company uses a work-order system to manage its plant and measure shop costs. Costs are analyzed for every job. Because of the importance of its panels on the customer's part, there is complete material traceability at PrivateCo.

Some PrivateCo panels require certification. These include some FAA (Federal Aviation Administration) panels and several aircraft floor panels.

The Company is an S corporation.

FINANCIAL RESULTS

Table F shows summarized income statement results for the Company since 2005.

Recast EBITDA reflects the amount of adjusted operating cash flow that the Company generates on a pretax and nonleveraged basis. Thus, some owner discretionary expenses and other one-time expenses have been added back. Only shareholder compensation above $150,000 per year is shown in that row.

The mid-2008 results show a substantial increase in recast EBITDA over prior years' levels. On an annualized basis, the 2008 recast EBITDA equals more than $1.2 million. The big question is: What level of recast EBITDA would buyers use to value PrivateCo? On the one hand, the future is quite bright for the Company. I have every reason to believe that PrivateCo will continue to grow, in terms of sales and profits. On the other hand, the Company may not realize recast EBITDA of $1.2 million in 2008.

| *table* **F** | **PrivateCo Corporation** | | | |

Recast EBITDA

Item	6 Months Ending 6/30/08	Year Ending 2007	Year Ending 2006	Year Ending 2005
Sales	$3,142,246	$5,471,823	$4,151,537	$4,569,512
Pretax profits	454,255	445,000	114,721	123,050
Adjustments				
Depreciation				
Amortization	24,566	64,000	58,200	79,000
Owner compensation*	26,628	53,300	53,300	53,300
Country club dues	46,000	132,000	57,000	0
SHH auto expense	2,721	7,300	3,000	1,300
SHH entertainment and travel	5,139	15,700	11,400	12,000
SHH life insurance	14,964	37,500	18,800	22,400
SHH insurance	5,588	5,300	5,000	10,400
Interest expense	4,270	8,000	7,400	4,000
Contributions	10,623	30,800	45,700	66,000
Professional fees	0	1,100	2,900	3,900
Retirement plan	5,911	11,000	10,500	39,000
(discretionary)	0	1,000	450	3,900
Seitz (former partner) payments	40,000	80,000	80,000	80,000
Recast EBITDA	**$641,000**	**$892,000**	**$468,000**	**$498,000**

*Owner compensation in excess of $150,000 per year
SHH = Owner and Majority Shareholder

It is plausible that financial investors would formulate their offer based on a recast EBITDA of about $1 million. Strategic buyers, on the other hand, might view the EBITDA as a higher number, as the following section indicates.

II. MARKET VALUE

We are determining the market value of the Company. The concept of market value requires some explanation.

Private securities do not enjoy access to an active trading market, and therefore must rely on point-in-time valuation or transactional pricing. This means that either a private valuation must be undertaken, or a transaction must occur to determine the value of a private security *for some reason* at *some point in time*. A private appraisal might be needed for many reasons, and these reasons can lead to dramatically different value conclusions.

Every private company has a number of different values at the same time, depending on the reasons for the valuations. Private business valuation is a *range* concept.

Market value is defined as:

> *The highest cash purchase price available in the marketplace for the selected assets or stock of the subject company.*

This definition assumes that the assets or stock of the subject company are valued on a debt-free basis, which means that all interest-bearing debt of the subject must be deducted from the derived market value. Most market valuations are also done on a cash-free basis, meaning that the seller keeps the cash and marketable securities in the company at the closing.

Every company has at least three market values at the same time. This is why market value, much like all business valuation, is a *range* concept. Each market value step, called "a tier," represents the most likely selling price based on the most likely buyer type. The tiers are: Asset, Financial, and Strategic.

The Asset Tier reflects what the subject would be worth if the most likely selling price is based on net asset value, because the most likely buyer is not basing the purchase on the subject's earnings stream, but rather on the subject's assets. In the Asset Tier the buyer is not giving credit to the Seller for goodwill beyond the possible write-up of the assets (that is, no value for the operations of the subject). For these purposes, goodwill is the intangible asset that arises as a result of name, reputation, customer patronage, and similar factors that result in some economic benefit that a buyer is willing to pay beyond the subject's asset value.

The Financial Tier reflects what an individual or nonstrategic buyer would pay for the business. With either buyer type, the valuation is based only on the company's financial statements.

The Strategic Tier is the market value of the company when synergies from a possible acquisition are considered. Synergy is the increase in performance of the combined firm over what the two firms are already expected or required to accomplish as independent companies.

CALCULATING MARKET VALUE

To determine value at the Asset Tier one simply derives the fair market value of the assets of the company and then subtracts the liabilities. Asset appraisals are generally required to establish value of the left side of the balance sheet; whereas, the face value of the liabilities is usually sufficient to determine the right side.

Calculating Financial and Strategic market value is a more interesting exercise. At these levels, an income stream, normally EBITDA, is multiplied by an acquisition multiple. Basically three levels of EBITDA can be used, as follows:

Reported EBITDA (per the income statement—without modification)

Recast EBITDA (Reported EBITDA plus seller discretionary expenses plus one-time expenses)

"Synergized" Recast EBITDA (Recast EBITDA plus the amount of synergies credited to the seller)

Every buyer would like to acquire using reported EBITDA as the main element of cash flow; every seller would like to use "synergized" recast EBITDA as the base. In reality, only the most sought-after companies receive credit for synergies from the buyer. The reason: Synergies are realized during the watch of the buyer. Buyers generally don't want to share these potential future earnings with the seller.

Asset buyers do not rely on earnings to value a company. Financial buyers' value companies using recast EBITDA as the earnings metric; whereas, strategic buyers use synergized recast EBITDA.

Acquisition multiples reflect the risk (from the buyer's view) of achieving the income stream. For instance, a "5" acquisition multiple means that the buyer believes

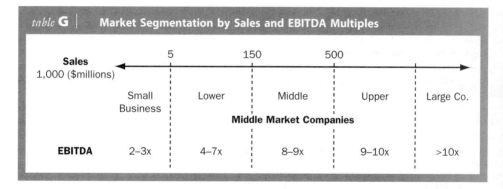

table **G** | **Market Segmentation by Sales and EBITDA Multiples**

the risk of the deal is 20 percent (the reciprocal of 5 is 20 percent). Acquisition multiples tend to group themselves within market segments. Table G shows how the capital markets are segmented, with resulting multiples.

Small businesses typically sell for two to three times EBITDA, whereas large companies usually sell for more than 10 times EBITDA. Lower-middle-market companies (like PrivateCo) usually sell for four to seven times EBITDA. It is quite possible that a company will be viewed by investors as more or less risky than its peer group. Example traits of being viewed as more risky include the lack of management structure, high customer concentrations, and poor financial systems. Companies that have institutionalized their processes and that have sustainable niches will be viewed at the high end of the multiple range, and possibly even outside of the range.

The market value tiers with the corresponding buyer profiles are shown below:

The Tiers of Market Value

Tier	Comments
Strategic	Synergies can result from a variety of acquisition scenarios. Perhaps the most quantifiable group of synergies emanate from horizontal integration. A horizontal integrator can realize substantial synergies by cutting duplicate overhead and other expenses. Some of these savings *may* be shared with the seller. Vertical integration can also create substantial synergies. These tend to be strategic, in that the target helps the acquirer achieve some business goal. Synergies also can result from the different financial structures of the parties. For instance, the target may realize interest expense savings due to adopting the cheaper borrowing costs of the acquirer.
Financial	Most individual buyers are financial buyers. Any institutional buyer that does not currently participate in the subject's industry or cannot leverage the subject's business is probably also a financial buyer. Financial buyers do not bring synergies to a deal, therefore, goodwill is limited.
Asset	When the subject has no current or future earnings prospects, or it is in an industry that does not give credit for *operating* goodwill, its asset value may be the highest value it can achieve or expect. A company in the same industry may buy and deploy the asset base, without pricing in goodwill.

In determining market value, it is important for the appraiser to correctly determine the most suitable value tier. The following guidelines can be used to determine whether a subject's highest value is the Asset Tier.

CHARACTERISTICS THAT DETERMINE WHETHER USING THE ASSET MARKET VALUE TIER IS APPROPRIATE

a. The subject has no earnings history, and future earnings expectations cannot be reliably estimated. In this context, "earnings" are defined as recast earnings before interest, taxes, depreciation, and amortization (EBITDA). EBITDA is recast for one-time expenses and discretionary expenses of the owner. This lack of an earnings base prohibits the buyer from using the subject's earnings as the basis for the valuation.

b. The subject depends heavily on competitive contract bids, and there is no consistent, predictable customer base.

c. The subject has little or no value from labor or intangible assets.

d. A significant portion of the subject's assets are composed of liquid assets or other investments, holding companies.

e. It is relatively easy to enter the industry; or

f. The strong possibility of losing key personnel could have a substantial negative effect on the subject; or

g. The subject participates in an industry that does not typically price a goodwill component into the deal structure. This can be the case in certain custom businesses, such as sawmills, or in smaller distributors, such as building materials suppliers.

If the statements are all true, then the Asset Tier of market value is the appropriate valuation tier for the subject. Typically, however, a subject may exhibit some of the characteristics above, but not all. In these cases, the appraising party should do the following:

1. Use judgment as to which characteristics are most important in this context. For instance, the subject's lack of recast EBITDA and industry segment are more important considerations than barriers to entry.

2. Consider the nature of transactions in the particular industry. For example, if nearly all the transactions involving small private companies in an industry are asset sales without goodwill, this should influence the decision as to the appropriate value tier.

Discussion Question 1: Should PrivateCo be valued at the Asset Tier level? Why or why not? Please discuss the reasons for your determination.

CHARACTERISTICS THAT DETERMINE WHETHER USING THE FINANCIAL MARKET VALUE TIER IS APPROPRIATE

Most individual buyers are financial buyers. The following characteristics can be used to correctly determine whether a seller's highest value is the Financial Tier.

a. The subject exhibits enough recast EBITDA that earnings can be determined by the acquirer as the basis for the valuation. By definition, however, no synergies are available in the Financial Tier.

b. The subject is unlikely to attract a synergistic buyer, either because the likely acquirer is an individual, who cannot bring synergies to a deal, or the buyer is a nonstrategic institution, which does not bring synergies to the acquisition.

Individual buyers tend to acquire companies in transactions of less than $2 million, while nonstrategic institutions (e.g., private equity groups) do not have a financial constraint.

c. The subject's owner-manager will not entertain a synergistic sale since it would result in company relocation, payroll cuts and other expense consolidation. Many owners are concerned for the posttransaction well-being of the people in their organization and will not sell to a consolidator, even if it means foregoing a higher selling price.

Discussion Question 2: Should PrivateCo be valued at the Financial Tier level? Why or why not? Please discuss the reasons for your determination.

CHARACTERISTICS THAT DETERMINE WHETHER USING THE STRATEGIC MARKET VALUE TIER IS APPROPRIATE

The Strategic Tier is mainly concerned with strategic or synergistic combinations, such as horizontal and vertical integrations, or any other combination with which the acquirer can leverage the subject's capabilities. Synergies can result from a variety of acquisition scenarios. Perhaps the most quantifiable group of synergies emanate from horizontal integrations. A horizontal integrator can realize substantial synergies by cutting duplicate overhead and other expenses. Some of these savings *may* be shared with the seller. Vertical integrations also can create substantial synergies. These tend to be strategic, in that the target helps the acquirer achieve some business goal. Synergies also can result from the different financial structures of the parties. For instance, the target may realize interest expense savings due to adopting the cheaper borrowing costs of the acquirer.

The following guidelines can be used to determine whether a subject's highest value is the Strategic Tier.

a. The subject participates in an industry that is being vertically or horizontally integrated, or it can be determined that another buyer type can synergistically leverage the subject's capabilities.

b. Synergies can be quantified with some level of certainty prior to a transaction.

c. Some of the following strategic motivations exist between the subject and prospective acquirers:

1. The subject possesses technology, patents, or a process that is difficult or impossible to duplicate;
2. The subject employs a management team that is considered exceptional;
3. The subject has a strong market position that enjoys monopolistic attributes;
4. The subject uses business practices that are dramatically more efficient than its counterparts;
5. The subject has developed a unique business model that is transferable to an acquirer;
6. The subject has access to worldwide markets that enable it to purchase and sell more effectively than the competition.

If all the statements are true, then the Strategic Tier of market value is the appropriate valuation tier for PrivateCo. Research can be done in the subject's industry to see if vertical or horizontal integrations or other strategic/synergistic acquisitions have been taking place.

Discussion Question 3: Should PrivateCo be valued at the Strategic Tier level? Why or why not? Please discuss the reasons for your determination.

III. DERIVING THE MARKET VALUE OF THE COMPANY

We established several things above that will help us derive the market value of the Company. First, we established the value tiers at which PrivateCo's market value will be determined. We then recast EBITDA for the tier or tiers selected. Finally, any synergies likely to be realized need to be reflected in the recast EBITDA calculation.

The amounts of enjoyed synergies are the estimated synergies credited to, or kept by, a party in a deal. First, the total expected synergies in a deal are forecast. Then, an estimate of the enjoyed synergies credited to each party is made. Usually the buyer is responsible for creating synergies. Buyers do not readily give the value of synergies away since the realization of the synergies happens only while they own the business. A high level of realism and significant experience are necessary when quantifying enjoyed synergies.

The following synergy types may be available to the parties in a transaction.

Synergies with Quantifiable Certainty

1. Cost savings
2. Revenue enhancements
3. Gross margin enhancements
4. Strategic combinations

Each strategic buyer will experience unique levels of synergies with a seller. Strategic buyers may or may not share synergies with the seller as well. In large part, identification and sharing of synergies decides which strategic buyer ultimately wins a deal.

A strategic buyer would most likely move PrivateCo's operations into their own, thereby saving some operating costs. These savings probably range from $300,000 to more than $1 million per year. We would need to study each interested strategic buyer to determine the amount of total synergies available. Then we would estimate how much of the synergy pool they would share. From conversations with several strategic buyers, we assume that total synergies equal $600,000 per year, and that the buyer will share (give credit to the seller) 40 percent of these. This adds $240,000 to the seller's cash flow ($600,000 times 40 percent). This makes the "synergized" recast EBITDA $_____ ($_____recast EBITDA plus $240,000 synergy sharing).

Discussion Question 4: Derive an estimate of the recast EBITDA. Make your assumptions explicit and display your calculations.

The Multiple

Acquisition multiples tend to group by market segment. We can determine a suitable acquisition multiple for the Company by several methods, including (1) Industry-Specific multiples, (2) General Industry multiples, and (3) General Private Equity Group multiples.

INDUSTRY-SPECIFIC MULTIPLES

A number of databases now exist that contain completed transactions for private companies. We have access to several of these, namely, the Institute of Business Appraisers Transaction database, Bizcomps, and Pratt's Stats. We looked for transactions in the Company's industry that were of similar size, specifically:

- with annual sales in the year of the sale between $5 million and $15 million
- with ratios of EBITDA to sales of at least 10 percent

Unfortunately, we found no qualifying transactions in the past 4 years. We do not believe that older transactions would be useful for our purposes here, because acquisition multiples were depressed during the 2001–2004 period.

GENERAL INDUSTRY MULTIPLES—IMAP SURVEYS

A group of international private investment bankers, called the International Network of M&A Partners (IMAP), surveys its members each year about completed transactions. Most of these involve companies with annual sales of $5–100 million. For 2004, there were a total of 94 transactions in the survey, with a total value of more than $2 billion. The survey has not been updated, so we will use these figures only as a guide.

Table H shows a comparison of multiples of earnings before interest and taxes (EBIT) for a variety of companies in the 2002–2004 period. EBIT itself must be defined for meaningful comparison. EBIT is calculated as trailing 12-month earnings before interest and taxes, adjusting for nonrecurring expenses and owners' discretionary expenses, together with salary in excess of fair market rates. Seller notes, etc. are discounted to present value. To compute the multiple, one simply divides the purchase price plus the assumption of any interest-bearing debt by the adjusted EBIT figure.

table **H** | **General Industry Multiples**

	SALES OF COMPANIES		
	Median multiple*		
By product or type:	**2002**	**2003**	**2004**
Nonproprietary Manufacturers[†]	4.7	5.4	6.3
Proprietary consumer mfg.	5.6	5.7	5.1
Proprietary industrial mfg.	5.3	6.0	6.9
Distribution	4.8	5.0	6.3
High-tech, nonproprietary mfg.	7.2	5.5	8.7
High-tech, proprietary mfg.	4.4	8.0	6.3
Service, infotech[‡]	—	7.0	7.6
Service, non-infotech	—	4.6	6.2

*Multiples used were within the middle 50 percent of completed transactions.
[†]Nonproprietary companies include contract manufacturers (e.g., stampers, molders, production fabricators).
[‡]Information technology (IT) consulting, integration, software development, IT staffing. Service company transactions were not surveyed until 2003.

The survey reported 65 percent more buyers in 2004 than 2003, and 59 percent more sellers over the prior period. This seems to confirm that deal inflation continued in 2004, partly explaining the increase in multiples. About 35 percent of IMAP members reported that it was easier to access bank financing in 2004, and most expected this to continue in 2005. Since bank financing has tightened in 2008, a moderating influence on both the number of transactions and their multiples can be expected vis-à-vis 2008–2009. This appears to be confirmed by recent financial data and financial news in general.

PrivateCo probably falls in the category of "Nonproprietary manufacturer." The median EBIT multiples for this category are 6.3 and 5.4 in 2004 and 2003, respectively.

One quick note: the IMAP survey uses recast EBIT, not recast EBITDA, as the income stream. The assumption here is that depreciation and capital expenditures cancel each other out. Most intermediaries use EBITDA without adjusting for normalized capital expenditures. PrivateCo's depreciation and amortization amounted to roughly 8 percent of its cash flow in 2004. When we adjust the EBIT of 6.3 in 2007 for this percentage, we get an equivalent EBITDA multiple of 5.8 (6.3 multiple less 8 percent).

GENERAL PRIVATE EQUITY GROUP MULTIPLES

"Private equity group" refers to the various organizations that provide equity capital to private companies. In the past 20 years, equity providers to companies with revenues in the $5 million to $150 million range have emerged as an industry. Currently, thousands of private equity groups offer more than $100 billion in capital annually to private companies.

Several organizations track average EBITDA multiples paid by private equity groups acquiring private companies. One such newsletter is *CapitalEyes*, which is published every month by Bank of America. Recent issues showed that average EBITDA multiple paid for smaller transactions (like PrivateCo) was 7.0.

DISCUSSION QUESTIONS

1. What market segment would PrivateCo most likely fit? Thus, as a starting point, what multiple of EBITDA would investors be willing to pay for the stock of the Company based on recent multiples?

2. What is the market value or market value range you would assign to PrivateCo? Make your assumptions explicit and consider a range that would reflect both what a financial buyer is likely to pay and what a strategic buyer is likely to offer for PrivateCo based on the multiples from recent transactions?

3. How would the valuation method used and the values determined change if the purpose of the valuation was not a 100 percent sale of the stock of the company, but rather a buy-sell between shareholders or a transfer across generations of family members?

This is an authentic report. PrivateCo, the company, is a small ($5 million to $6 million in annual revenues) family business. The names and some of the figures have been changed both to protect the privacy of the firm and family involved and to make the exercise more student-learning friendly.

RELIANCE INDUSTRIES (PART A)

More inches of newsprint have been dedicated to telling the story of the Ambani family and Reliance Industries than perhaps any other story in Indian business history. Dhirubhai Ambani, a poor schoolteacher's son from the Indian state of Gujarat, built India's largest industrial empire. Along the way, he rewrote the practices of Indian enterprise. At the time of his death, the conglomerate he founded (the Reliance Group), was so large that it alone accounted for more than 3 percent of India's total gross domestic product (GDP) and 10 percent of the country's indirect tax revenue.

The Ambani family's shares in these companies were owned by a web of investment firms. These, in turn, were controlled by over 1000 entities, including offshore trusts in tax-haven countries. This complex structure enabled the family to avoid onerous taxes and still retain family control.

Dhirubhai Ambani died suddenly at age 69 without a will or a succession plan, leaving two sons in executive positions within the business. But under Hindu tradition and succession laws, the eldest son becomes the successor. Soon after Dhirubhai's death, his sons, Mukesh and Anil, began arguing about management and ownership issues and later accused each other of business improprieties. Politicians and financiers, concerned by the instability that this family squabble was having on the financial markets, tried unsuccessfully to broker an agreement between the sons. In the end, the sons would listen only to their mother. A settlement has just been announced. What were the reasons for the conflict? How did Mukesh and Anil resolve it? What would the founder, Dhirubhai have to say about the settlement?

ACHIEVEMENT IS HISTORY. LOOK AHEAD.[1]

Dhirajlal Ambani was born on December 29, 1932, into the Modh Bania, a Hindu commercial caste based in the arid Saurashtra peninsula of India's western Gujarat state. Dhirubhai, as he was known, left home at 16 to work as a gas-station attendant for Shell Petroleum in Yemen. Within a few years he rose to the position of sales manager.

A successful employee, Dhirubhai had an entrepreneur's ability to identify and take advantage of opportunities not observed by others. While in Yemen, Dhirubhai realized that the local currency (the riyal) was worth more for its silver content than for its purchasing power. With this insight, he began to melt the coins into silver ingots at a small profit.

---

[1]Dhirubhai was well-known for mantras about management. This adage reflects his belief that success comes from building on achievement and that achievement becomes history the moment it is achieved.

Dhirubhai returned to India in 1958 with his pregnant wife and infant son to start his own business. He founded Reliance Commercial Corporation with US$100 in his pocket and approximately US$275 in borrowed capital. The company began as a trading company, exporting spices, nuts, and other commodities to the duty-free Yemeni port of Aden. In Aden, Dhirubhai used his many contacts to help develop this market.

By 1965, Dhirubhai shifted Reliance's focus from trading to textiles to take advantage of another opportunity—government programs designed to promote the export of rayon, which was plentiful in India. Reliance exported rayon at a loss because doing so enabled the company to import nylon, which it sold at a premium. By 1966 the Indian economy was growing, and the demand for better clothing was taking hold. Reliance Corporation opened its first textile mill to take advantage of this new market.

In 1978, Reliance began focusing on India's domestic Indian market, after its successful initial public offering (IPO) and the end of the government-sponsored rayon promotion. The Indian wholesale textile market was crowded and extremely competitive. To gain market share and to bypass the competitive wholesale market, Dhirubhai adopted a competitor's idea and opened company stores. He then expanded the idea by traveling throughout India franchising the store concept and promising advertising support to any outlet that would sell Reliance textiles. In this way he built a national customer base that included previously untapped nonmetropolitan markets. By 1980, Reliance fabrics could be found across India in 2100 retail stores and franchised outlets. During this period Reliance established the Vimal textile brand (named for Dhirubhai's eldest nephew). Dhirubhai worked to create a strong brand image and was so successful that it took many years for Reliance to have better name recognition than Vimal.

One of Dhirubhai's mantras stated: "Growth has no limit—keep revising your vision." Dhirubhai did just that after earning his first million in textiles. He began to "backwardly integrate" from fabric weaving to establishing plants to make polyester filament yarn in 1981. His philosophy of entrepreneurial growth was evident when he built a factory at Patalganga (a small village outside of Mumbai, formerly Bombay) that could produce 4000 more tons of polyester yarn than the Indian market required. Soon after the factory was completed, the government issued legislation that limited the use of polyester filament yarn to small textile businesses. To increase demand for Reliance's yarn, Dhirubhai arranged to sell yarn to these small looms and then to buy the fabric that they produced, finishing it and selling it under the Vimal name. Two years later, in 1983, he again moved backward in the supply chain and gained the license to manufacture purified terephthalic acid, one of the chemicals that can produce polyester filament fiber.

From the production of yarn and fiber, Reliance integrated horizontally, and began producing products including high- and low-density polyethylenes used by plastics processors. Reliance slowly began the manufacture of petrochemical intermediaries, including monoethylene glycol and n-paraffin. Reliance achieved domination in these industries soon after its entry, becoming the world's second-largest producer of polyester fiber and filament yarn, the third-largest producer of paraxylene, and the fourth-largest producer of purified terephthalic acid.

From chemicals, Reliance entered the oil and gas exploration business and built refineries through Reliance Petroleum Limited, fulfilling a dream Dhirubhai had cherished since he had worked for Shell Petroleum in Yemen. Reliance Petroleum went public in 1993 in what was, at the time, India's largest public offering.

Reliance Industries fully entered the world industrial stage by building Asia's biggest chemical complex in 1991. The Hazira facility, the world's largest single-feed ethylene cracker[2] was built in Dhirubhai's home state of Gujarat. Building the facility exhausted the local Gujarati resources and required Dhirubhai to create his own infrastructure to support the plant. Reliance Petroleum went public in 1993 in India's largest to-date public stock offering. Other financial firsts include being the first Indian corporation to raise funds through overseas capital markets and being the first private company in India to be rated by international credit agencies. The ability to finance growth enabled Reliance to enter high-growth sectors outside the petroleum and petrochemicals business. The Reliance corporate family also includes financial services and insurance, power, telecommunication, and digital communication initiatives. (See Tables I and J for additional information about Reliance companies and products.)

A second world-class facility, and the world's largest refinery, was then built in Gujarat at the cost of US$6 billion. This facility, known as the Jamnagar plant, extends over 31 square kilometers (the size of Manhattan south of Central Park) and represents the single largest investment ever made at a single location in India. Jamnagar is one of only a few refineries in the world that can take thick high-sulfur highly acid grades of crude oil and turn them into pure low-polluting gasoline and diesel fuel. Like the Hazira plant, building Jamnagar required the creation of infrastructure, including a 350-megawatt power plant, two chemical plants, 105 miles of road, housing for 3000 families, a seawater desalination plant, and an information technology (IT) network that connects 50 servers and 2500 terminals with 200 km of fiber optic cables.

The decision to build Jamnagar illustrates Reliance's innovative business approach. In 1996, when the project was launched, refineries had a historic return on capital of 6 to 8 percent, while the cost of capital was 12 percent. To get adequate returns, Reliance focused on developing efficiencies both in constructing and running the facility. According to a family story, Dhirubhai traveled to Jamnagar during construction to check on the progress. He went for a walk at night and found that work had ended for the day. He asked his eldest son Mukesh, who was managing the project, why work had stopped and observed that there was no reason why they could not run three shifts. Mukesh called in the contractors the following day and made arrangements for them to receive bonuses for meeting or exceeding project deadlines and, in turn, to give bonuses to their employees for meeting or exceeding the deadlines. The Jamnagar complex was completed within 36 months and the refinery's total cost was reduced to the point that it operates at a 30 to 50 percent lower cost than similar refineries in Asia. This was the first significant business achievement by Mukesh after leaving the business school at Stanford and joining the family enterprise at Dhirubhai's request.

While most refineries specialize in a small number of products, the Jamnagar refinery can produce a wide range of petrochemicals. This flexibility enables it to take advantage of market fluctuations and consistently focus on producing high-profit products. Jamnagar is able to change its product mix in response to market demand, which enables it to refine the product with the best profit margin at any given time. From exploration to production to pipelines, Reliance owns a piece of the entire oil and gas value chain, except for gas stations, which, in India, have traditionally been owned by the government.

---

[2]"Cracking" is the name of the process that ethane (a naturally occurring gas) goes through to become ethylene. Ethane is heated to approximately 800 degrees Celsius in a reactor called a "cracker."

table **I** | **Reliance Industries Product Listing by Brand Name and Type**

Polymers, Chemicals, Fibers, and Fiber Intermediates
Location: Hazira, Gujarat state
Repol
- Polypropylene
- Purified terephthalic acid
- Ethylene oxide
- Monoethylene glycol
- Diethylene glycol
- Triethylene glycol
- Ethylene
- Propylene
- Benzene
- Toluene
- Xylene
- Carbon black feed stock
- Vinyl chloride monomer

Reon
- Polyvinyl chloride
Recalir
- Linear low-density polyethylene
Relene
- High-density polyethylene
Recron
- Recron stable fiber
- Recron filament yarn
- Recron fiber fill
Relpet
- Polyethylene terephthalate

Refinery Products, Polymers, and Fiber Intermediates
Location: Jamnagar, Gujarat state
Refinery
- Liquefied petroleum gas
- Propylene
- Naphtha
- Reormate
- Motor spirit
- Middle distillate pool
- Sulfur
- Coke

R Petrochemicals
- Paraxylene
- Polypropylene
Port and terminals
- Power

Textiles
Location: Naroda, Gujarat state
Vimal
- Suitings and shirtings
- Dress materials and sarees
Harmony
- Furnishing fabrics
- Day curtains
- Automotive upholstery
Slumberel
- Fiber-filled pillows

Recron
- Texturized yarn
- Twisted/dyed yarns
Ruerel
- Suitings
Reance
- Shirts
- Trousers
- Jackets

Oil and gas
Location: Panna & Mukta, off Bombay High
Tapti—Northwest of Mumbai
- Crude oil
- Natural Gas
- Exploration & Production
Other Initiatives
- Telecommunications—Reliance Telecom
- Financial services—Reliance Capital
- Engineering, procurement, construction
- Infrastructure—Reliance Industrial Infrastructure
- Infocomm—Reliance Infocomm
- Insurance—Reliance General Insurance

Power generation
Facilities:
- Dahanu Thermal Power Station
- Jogimatti Wind Farm Project
- BSES Kerla Combined Cycle Station
- Goa Power Station

table **J** | **The Reliance Family of Companies**

Reliance Industries Ltd.	In 2002, Reliance Industries and Reliance Petroleum merged into Reliance Industries, India's largest petrochemical firm, second largest company, and largest exporter. Polyesters and polymers account for most of the Reliance Group's sales. The company's leading products are used widely in agriculture, clothing, consumer goods, and electronics. Petrochemical products, including benzene, polypropylene, and polyvinyl chloride are used in packaging, kitchenware, and furniture.
Reliance Capital Ltd.	Reliance Capital is one of India's leading nongovernment-sponsored financial services companies. It focuses on infrastructure projects that offer opportunities for enormous growth and significant tax benefits.
Reliance Energy (formerly BSES Energy)	Reliance Energy generates transmits and distributes electricity to more than 5 million customers in portions of India. Its service area covers more than a million square kilometers and includes the cities of Mumbai and Delhi.
Reliance General Insurance	Reliance General Insurance is one of the few companies in the nongovernmental sector to provide a complete insurance solution. It is also one of the first nonlife insurance products companies to be licensed to operate.
Reliance Industrial Infrastructure	The company was incorporated in 1988 to serve the Patalganga Plant. It transports petroleum products through product pipelines and raw water through water pipelines. The company boasts that there have been no failures or leakage of the petroleum during the past 11 years of operation.
Reliance Infocomm Ltd.	Reliance Infocomm is India's largest mobile service provider, with over 7 million customers. Launched in 2003, it has established a pan-India high-capacity integrated and divergent digital network and offers services for enterprises and individuals, applications, and consulting.
Reliance Mutual Fund	Reliance Mutual Fund was established as a Trust in 1995 with Reliance Capital Asset Management Ltd. It is among the fastest-growing mutual fund companies in India. The company's vision is to be India's largest and most trusted wealth creator.
Reliance Telecom	Reliance Telecom provides cellular services in 10 Indian states. It recently introduced international roaming services throughout India.
Reliance Life Science	Established in 2001, Reliance Life Services is a new initiative of the Reliance Group. The company is developing business opportunities in medical, plant, and industrial biotechnology. It also conducts contract research and clinical trials.

SOURCE: *The Economic Times*, November, 23, 2004, and http://www.hoovers.com.

FINANCING GROWTH

Finding sufficient capital is a challenge faced by most enterprises. In India in the 1970s, the challenge was magnified by a government-controlled financial system. The leading sources of capital were slow-moving state-owned financial institutions that were not always willing lenders and frequently charged high rates of interest. In 1977 Reliance solved its funding challenge in a unique way. It launched the first IPO of company shares in Indian business history. This advance is recorded on the Reliance website as, "Dhirubhai Ambani introduced equity cult in India, a new model of business leadership from a base of the broadest public shareholding."

table **K** | **Ambani Family and Reliance Industries Milestones**

- Dhirubhai Ambani starts Reliance Commercial Corporation in Mumbai. (1958)
- Reliance enters the textile industry and sets up a mill Naroda, Ahmedabad. (1966)
- World Bank team visits mill and declares that it is as modern and well-managed as those in developed countries. (1975)
- Reliance goes public with India's first IPO. (1977)
- Dhirubhai calls Mukesh home from Stanford University's School of Business after 1 year of study toward his MBA. Mukesh begins working at Reliance and later completes his MBA degree. (1981)
- Anil earns his MBA from the University of Pennsylvania's Wharton School and begins working at Reliance. (1983)
- Mukesh Ambani marries Nita. (1985)
- Reliance total assets: $227 million. (1985)
- Reliance Capital, a merchant bank, is created. (1986)
- Dhirubhai suffers his first stroke. He returns as chairman. Mukesh and Anil take on additional responsibilities as co–managing directors of Reliance. (1986)
- Reliance Industrial Infrastructure, a petroleum pipeline provider, comes on line. (1988)
- Reliance sales exceed $404 million. (1988)
- Hazira petrochemical plant commissioned. (1991)
- Anil Ambani marries Tina Munim. (1991)
- Reliance is the first Indian corporation to raise capital from international markets through Global Depository Receipts offering, and sets a record with a Reliance issue that received over 1 million investor applications. (1992)
- Reliance Petroleum goes public in India's largest public offering to date. Sales exceed $909 million, making Reliance Petroleum India's largest publicly traded company. Also Reliance offers the first Euro Convertible bond issue. (1993)
- Awarded Companion Membership of the Textile Institute (UK). Award is limited to 50 members who have substantially advanced the fiber industry. (1994)
- Offers the second Euro issue of Global Depository Receipts. (1994)
- Reliance net profit exceeds $242 million. (1995)
- Reliance Mutual Funds, an asset management and mutual fund provider, is launched. (1995)
- Reliance is first corporation in Asia to issue 50- and 100-year bonds in the United States. (1997)
- World's largest multifeed cracker commissioned in Hazira. (1997)
- Reliance revenue tops $3 billion and total assets approach $8 billion. (1998)
- World's largest petroleum refinery complex commissioned at Jamnagar. (1999)
- Reliance Infocomm, a mobile service provider, is launched. (1999)
- Reliance revenues exceed $4 billion, and total assets are $11.8 billion. (2000)
- Reliance Industries Ltd. and Reliance Petroleum Ltd. merge into Reliance Industries (2002). The new firm is named to the *Forbes Global 500* in 2003, entering at position 306.
- Dhirubhai Ambani dies on July 6. (2002)

Conversion rate: 1 Indian Rupee = 0.022727 U.S. dollar.

SOURCES: www.ril.com and www.indiapublicsector.com.

By selling shares to the public in small lots, Dhirubhai introduced ordinary people who had never owned shares to the financial markets while financing Reliance's growth. In a short time, so many individuals owned shares that Reliance was forced to rent football (soccer) stadiums each year to provide a venue large enough for the annual meeting.

Some entities, such as Reliance Infrastructure and Reliance Capital, were formed primarily to support Reliance Industries. Other units, such as Reliance Telecomm and Reliance Life Science were created to propel Reliance into new technologies and to take advantage of the opportunities presented by the growing Indian economy. (See Table K for additional details.)

THE NEXT GENERATION

Dhirubhai and Kokilaben Ambani had four children: Mukesh, Anil, Nina, and Dipti (Figure Q). In the early years, Dhirubhai, Kokilaben, Mukesh, Anil, and Dhirubhai's mother, uncle, and brother lived together in a one-bedroom house in a lower-middle-class neighborhood in Mumbai. As Reliance flourished, the family moved to more spacious accommodations and most recently to Sea Wind, the family estate. Nina and Dipti moved from Mumbai when each married.

Mukesh, Anil, and their families also resided at Sea Wind. While each family had its own living quarters, the extended family usually had dinner together. Dhirubhai was known for quizzing his grandchildren about current events, a practice he began when his own children were young.

Siblings raised together can be as different in their personalities as people from different families. Mukesh and Anil Ambani are no exception. Each had an especially close relationship with one parent. Mukesh was reportedly his father's favorite. It was Mukesh whom Dhirubhai consulted first about business matters, before asking Anil his opinion. As a child, Anil was closest to his mother, and their special relationship has continued over time. To the public eye, Mukesh and Anil were groomed for careers with Reliance and got along well. Disputes were settled in the privacy of the family compound. When mediation failed, Dhirubhai would reprimand Mukesh and Anil and impose a solution. Dhirubhai's goal was to see Reliance succeed and to prove to the world that India was the place to invest. Family disputes were not going to get in the way of these goals; Mukesh and Anil were expected to work together successfully for the benefit of Reliance and all of India.

In 1997, when Mukesh and Anil were jointly honored as "Businessmen of the Year," they commented that they felt like they had built the company with their father, rather than simply benefiting from his efforts. In their official corporate biographies both brothers take credit for bringing about financial innovation to the Indian capital market through the introduction of international offerings of Global Depository Receipts, convertible issues, and bonds. Their efforts are credited with raising US$2 billion in the past 12 years to fund Reliance's aggressive growth.

MUKESH AMBANI

Mukesh, the eldest, was born in Yemen in 1957. He is described as analytical and detail-oriented; he is known for taking detailed notes during meetings and conversations. Mukesh is a private person who rarely speaks publicly.

figure **Q** | **Ambani Family Tree**

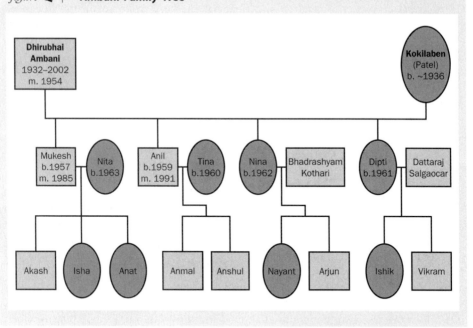

Mukesh earned a Bachelor of Chemical Engineering at the University of Mumbai and continued his graduate studies at Stanford University. After his first year in the MBA program, Dhirubhai called Mukesh home. He was 24 years old. Mukesh recalls that "my father told me you will take this over and I will give you one other person from Reliance. Everyone else has to be new."

The task he was given was to oversee the construction of the petrochemical plant at Patalganga. The technology they selected for the plant came from DuPont. To get DuPont to sell their technology, Dhirubhai sold everything but equity. He later explained, "Technology is available for the asking in the international bazaar. Why should I make a foreign company my partner and give them 51 percent?" The plant was completed in 14 months, ahead of a competitor who had started building before Reliance. Being first to market gave Reliance a significant advantage in the marketplace.

After the success at Patalganga, Mukesh quickly gained a reputation for building new mega-plants under budget and ahead of schedule. He has since directed the creation of over 60 new, world-class manufacturing facilities.

Mukesh happily entered into an arranged marriage at age 28. His mother reportedly saw his future wife, Nita, at a recital and came home and told Dhirubhai that she had found the right match for Mukesh. Dhirubhai interviewed Nita, and the match was made. From the start, Nita was a family insider, taking responsibility for family philanthropy. A former teacher, she is responsible for the creation of the Dhirubhai International School, a premiere K–12 private school that opened in 2003. Nita Ambani serves as the school's chairperson.

ANIL AMBANI

Anil joined Reliance in 1982, a day after he graduated from Wharton with an MBA. Dhirubhai greeted him saying, "You have got an American MBA, now you must get an Indian MBA," meaning that the American degree provided good theory but could not be applied to Indian realities. Anil's first experience with Reliance was in the textile business, where he stayed for 4 years.

After Dhirubhai's first stroke in 1986, Anil assumed new responsibilities. He handled corporate finances and became Reliance's spokesperson. Anil is considered aggressive and has strong financial and networking skills. Anil likes the limelight. Newspaper accounts about Anil and his family are common—he is frequently featured attending social events or advocating physical fitness. Anil was voted Youth Icon in 2003 in an MTV-sponsored survey, and he has his own website.

Anil married the former "Miss India" and film star, Tina Munim. Tina and Anil are said to have met at a party, where Anil was immediately smitten. When the two decided to marry, Dhirubhai opposed the marriage and tried his best to break the alliance. He went so far as to encourage government foreign currency investigations into Tina's accounts. After the marriage, Tina was reportedly given the cold shoulder in the Ambani household.

THE END OF AN ERA

India bade an emotional farewell to Ambani, who passed away on July 6, 2002, two weeks after he suffered a massive stroke. Thousands of mourners, both famous and common, lined the streets the day of his funeral. One day after carrying Dhirubhai Ambani's body to the pyre, his sons were back at work.

One of Dhirubhai's last major decisions was to merge Reliance Industries and Reliance Petrochemicals into Reliance Industries Limited. The merger proclaimed Dhirubhai's desire to keep the company, his legacy, together. He did not want Reliance Industries Limited (RIL) to suffer the fate of other Indian firms that were broken into pieces to satisfy the next generation, only to find individuals in that generation fighting each other in the market and destroying the value created by the founder. The merger also created a business that was large enough to be recognized in the *Forbes Global 500* listing of the world's largest companies. Reliance Industries was selected for the list in 2003, a year after the merger. It was the first Indian business to qualify for the listing and was ranked the 306th largest business in the world.

At the time of Dhirubhai's death, Reliance Group was India's largest private-sector business, with total revenues of US$22.6 billion, exports of US$3.6 billion, and net profits of US$1.4 billion. Reliance exported its products to more than 100 countries around the world. The companies of the Reliance Group included oil and gas exploration and production, petrochemicals, textiles, financial services, and insurance.

Reliance Group's revenue is equivalent to approximately 3.5 percent of India's total GDP. It contributes nearly 10 percent of India's indirect tax revenues and over 6 percent of the country's exports. As one of the first private firms to offer shares to the public, it had 3.1 million shareholders; enjoying the largest participation by investors of any company in India. Today, one in every four Indians holds shares in Reliance.

At the time of Dhirubhai's death, the Ambani family directly or indirectly owned 46 percent of Reliance Industries, including 5 percent held by the family in the names of individual family members. Additional shares were held by a web of companies controlled by RIL's chairman. Three months after Dhirubhai's death, the four Ambani children relinquished their share of their father's assets and signed those assets over to their mother. This was likely done to take advantage of the Hindu Undivided Family Unit, a tax status that permits families, especially those with family businesses, to pay tax as a single entity.

THE STRUGGLE FOR CONTROL

Mukesh became chairman of RIL after his father's death, gaining management control and moving into a position to review and approve or veto major investments and changes in Reliance's businesses. In the beginning, questions arose about the cohesiveness of Reliance's top leadership. The brothers denied any difficulties, saying that differences of opinion are "constructive tension" of the type that their father encouraged as a way to look at an issue from all angles.

But a series of events in 2003 precipitated a struggle for control. Mukesh had taken an interest-free loan from Reliance Industries Ltd. to finance the nascent Reliance Telecomm. Anil questioned this financing arrangement, though the practice of making interest-free loans was common. Mukesh, in turn, was annoyed because Anil, as head of Reliance Energy, had made a US$10 billion capital investment without consulting Mukesh or the RIL board.

The brothers' mutual dissatisfaction continued until a July board meeting. At the meeting, the Reliance board passed a resolution giving Mukesh the authority to "vary or revoke" managing director Anil's duties. Anil maintained that the resolution had been introduced in a sneaky way and sent an e-mail expressing his dissatisfaction to Mukesh. This e-mail was published by a local paper. Anil's dissatisfaction with Mukesh's actions was ironic, given that it was Anil who originally performed the ceremonial role of proposing that Mukesh be elevated to the role of chairman. Mukesh in turn had supported Anil for vice chairman and managing director.

In November 2004, Mukesh Ambani sent an e-mail to Reliance's 80,000 employees stating, "There is no ambiguity in his [Dhirubhai Ambani's] legacy that the Chairman and Managing Director is the final authority on all matters concerning Reliance." He then announced to the press that his father had settled all ownership issues pertaining to Reliance within his lifetime. Anil and other family members responded to the news by asking Mukesh to provide "appropriate details" of the steps taken to settle ownership. In a conciliatory move, Anil also said that he would agree to any settlement that his mother proposed.

For the next 7 months, the brothers' disagreements were played out in the media. Confidential e-mail messages and internal boardroom documents were regularly leaked to journalists. The press suggested that there was a lack of camaraderie between Mukesh's wife, Nita, and Anil's wife, Tina, which contributed to the disagreement. Anil ran a sustained campaign against Mukesh and his associates, accusing them of misleading the public. As the discord continued, it became clear that a formal split between the two brothers would call for a very complex settlement. The interrelationships between the companies that made up RIL were significant. Reliance Industries, for example, owned portions of gas fields that powered Reliance Energy's electricity production.

Mukesh asserted that his father had intended for him to become the managing chairman. He stated that he was also concerned by Anil's lifestyle. Anil's friendships with film stars and his intention to run as a Member of Parliament made the family uncomfortable. Mukesh believed that Anil's political involvement had the potential to harm Reliance. Aligning with one political party was against the practices of Dhirubhai, who had worked to befriend all politicians and bureaucrats at all levels of government.

From Anil's perspective, he and Mukesh had worked as equals for many years and, during that time, he had run his own businesses independently. Anil did not believe that his father had intended for that arrangement to change. He did not find primogeniture compelling and felt that he was more capable of leading Reliance than Mukesh was. He also commented at the time that his political activities were not his brother's business.

KOKILABEN AMBANI INTERVENES

For most of her adult life, Kokilaben Ambani stayed out of the limelight, quietly supporting her husband and raising her family. Kokilaben is described in the press as being quiet, poised, and deeply religious. While not formally educated, she learned conversational English along with her children when her husband hired a tutor for them. With English skills, Kokilaben was able to participate more easily in their frequent business dinners. The Ambani children hold their mother in great esteem, and the family is frequently together, especially during religious holidays.

When the disagreement between Mukesh and Anil first became public, Kokilaben stated that she did not want to mediate because she did not know enough about the business. She did observe that both brothers were made managing director in Dhirubhai's lifetime, a decision that did not seem to suggest to her that Anil should be denied a say in running the business.

As the months passed without resolution, Kokilaben ultimately did intervene, but did so with the help of a family friend and respected banker, K.V. Kamath. In March, Mr. Kamath performed a valuation of the company and drafted a suggested settlement. In the months that followed, and at Kokilaben's request, Mr. Kamath continued to broker the settlement while she held almost daily individual meetings with each of her sons. Together, they were able to fashion a settlement that was ultimately agreeable to both Mukesh and Anil. Throughout the process, Kokilaben appeared to the outside world as graceful, even-handed, and mindful of her late husband's legacy.

THE SETTLEMENT

Peace was declared on June 18, 2005, almost exactly 7 months after Anil Ambani's public questioning of Mukesh Ambani's authority. Peace came with a brief e-mail announcement from Kokilaben Ambani invoking her late husband and the name of the Hindu god Krishna and announcing that she had negotiated a settlement between her sons. Her announcement read:

With the blessings of Srinathji,[3] I have today amicably resolved the issues between my two sons, Mukesh and Anil, keeping in mind the proud legacy of my husband Dhirubhai Ambani.

I am confident that both Mukesh and Anil will resolutely uphold the values of their father and work towards protecting and enhancing value for over 3 million shareholders of the

---

[3]A reference to the Hindu god Krishna.

Reliance Group, which has been the foundational principle on which my husband built India's largest private sector enterprise.

Mukesh will have responsibility for Reliance Industries and Indian Petrochemicals, while Anil will have responsibility for Reliance Infocomm, Reliance Energy and Reliance Capital.

My husband's foresight and vision and the values he stood for combined with my blessings will guide them to scale new heights.

The following day, June 19, 2005, Anil Ambani announced his own plans for the businesses he would be leading—Reliance Energy, Reliance Capital, and Reliance Infocomm—to a gathering of journalists and analysts.

The industrial group's complexity was attacked by financial experts, who restructured the Reliance Group and consolidated units into two separate companies operating in very different industries. A simple formula was then used to split the family's 34 percent ownership in Reliance Group's companies. Kokilaben retained 30 percent, her daughters Nina Kothari and Dipti Salgocar each received 5 percent, and Mukesh and Anil each got 30 percent. The brothers resigned from each other's boards and signed a 10-year no-compete agreement. Both could use the Reliance logo and brand, but Anil's companies would carry the tag line "A Dhirubhai Ambani Enterprise." This vested Anil's companies with his father's reputation, an important corporate asset in Indian business.

		Sales[*]	Profits[*]
MUKESH AMBANI			
Reliance Industries	Petrochemicals, textiles	$16.7 billion	$1.7 billion
Indian Petrochemicals	Petrochemicals	$2.1 billion	$180 million
ANIL AMBANI			
Reliance Energy	Power	$1 billion	$119 million
Reliance Capital	Finance	$67 million[*]	$24 million
Reliance Infocomm	Cellular	$1.2 billion	$11.7 million

[*]For the year ending March 2005; in U.S. dollars

Under the terms of the agreement, Mukesh kept the flagship petrochemical business, Reliance Industries Ltd., and the smaller Indian Petrochemicals. Anil assumed full control of a power company, a telecom and broadband provider, and a finance company. The brothers agreed to swap shares in each others' companies so that neither owned shares in the others' business and Anil received an additional payment (estimated at between US$2 billion and US$3 billion) to equalize the value of the divided assets. While Anil's companies are much smaller, they are in industries with much greater growth prospects.

While a divided RIL was not the vision of Dhirubhai Ambani, his legacy may well be sustained. In dividing RIL into logical pieces along industry lines there is no reason to suspect that the parts will not grow to become greater than the original whole.

"THINK BIG, THINK FAST, AND THINK AHEAD."

"Think big, think fast, and think ahead" was a favorite expression of Dhirubhai Ambani, who brought those words to life during his entrepreneurial career. Mukesh and Anil Ambani moved quickly after the settlement to focus on developing their businesses and go on with their lives. The price of Reliance Industry's stock has regained the value it lost during the Ambani brothers' dispute and moved even higher. Mukesh recently terminated Reliance Infocomm's service of Reliance Industries and awarded Reliance Industries' telecommunications contract to one of Infocomm's competitors. Mukesh and his family have moved from the family estate to a residence of their own.

Anil, while keeping the Reliance name, is actively rebranding each of the companies he received in the settlement. And even though his sons are still very young, Anil has already written a succession plan for his business.

The companies that Mukesh and Anil lead today have both thrived since the settlement between the siblings. Share values in both companies have more than doubled in the past 12 months.

REFERENCES

Anonymous, *Reliance Industries: The Dispute Between Mukseh and Anil Ambani (Part-A)*. Hyderabad, India: ICAFI Center for Management Research, 2005.

Aparna, Y., *Dhirubhai Ambani and Reliance* (No. LDE011). Hyderabad, India: ICFAI Center for Management Research, 2003.

McDonald, H., *The Polyester Prince*. St. Leonards, Australia: Allen & Unwin, 1998.

Piramal, G., *Business Maharajas*. New Delhi, India: Penguin Books, 1996.

Research Associate Tracey Eira Messer prepared this case under the supervision of Professor Ernesto J. Poza. The case was compiled from published sources and is intended to be used as the basis for class discussion rather than to illustrate the effective or ineffective handling of an administrative situation.

SMALL FAMILY BUSINESS | CASE **15**

THE SON-IN-LAW

Jim Martin walked into his father's office and threw his resignation on the desk. Age 34 and general manager of the retail division of his family's furniture business, Jim has been with the company for 10 years. Before that, he had worked in the banking industry for 3 years and had earned his MBA. In his early years at Martin's Inc., he had been energetic, ambitious, and effective. But now he is burned out. He thinks his future looks grim. He feels unrewarded and unacknowledged.

Eric, Jim's brother-in-law, is sales manager of Jim's division. Eric, a high-school graduate who has also been with Martin's for 10 years, has an informal style. Highly sociable, he tends to take long lunch hours and work 9 to 5, in contrast to Jim's 12-hour days. Although sales have remained steady, Jim resents Eric's abbreviated hours and easygoing ways. The fact that his father, CEO Ed Martin, will not make it clear who is to succeed him also gnaws at Jim.

Ed has adopted a hands-off approach, hoping the successor will emerge or that Eric and Jim will work it out between them. To make matters worse, Ed has just announced he intends to divide the company stock equally—as his father had done before him—between his two children, Jim and daughter Sarah. Never invited into the business herself, Sarah pushed for her husband, Eric, to be involved. According to Ed's plan, Eric and Jim will continue to receive identical compensation packages.

Jim just cannot accept the idea that his hard work and better education will not be rewarded with what he considers appropriate remuneration and ownership.

SMALL FAMILY BUSINESS | CASE **16**

THE NEW MBA

It all began to fall apart, thought Rudy Schmitz, right after he returned to the family firm as assistant controller with his new, prestigious MBA. Ever since he was 15, when his father, Will, had started Schmitz Sand and Gravel, Rudy had been fascinated by the company. He worked there part-time through high school, then full-time after getting his undergraduate degree in math.

In addition to Rudy and Will, Rudy's younger brother, Chuck, works in the company in a blue-collar job. Chuck, who barely finished high school, has been with Schmitz for 3 years. He is foreman of the gravel pit and the workers see him as "one of the guys." Also on board is Duke Ferrara, an aggressive, hearty type who, in 5 years with the firm, has risen to general manager. Duke brags openly to the crew about being "superior" to Will. He has pushed unceasingly for stock options, and Rudy is surprised that his father has not asserted himself with Duke.

Rudy finds his excellent relationship with his father now threatened because Will has reneged on a promise to pay Rudy commensurate with his education. In fact, Chuck makes more than Rudy and has resisted Rudy's overtaking him or having clear-cut authority over him. Rudy, whose real love is accounting, wonders how one short management course during his graduate studies could possibly have prepared him for this.

If that were not enough, Rudy has also noticed that Duke has been on a spending spree. In addition to making some expensive purchases, Duke has been paying Schmitz employees much more than the employees of its competitors. Rudy had just begun to fear the company was headed for real trouble when, by coincidence or otherwise, Duke proposed a buyout offer that appears quite low to Rudy.

| CASE **17**

REAL ESTATE DEVELOPMENT PARTNERS, INC.

In late 1948, Dick Randall, president and CEO of Real Estate Development Partners, Inc., arrived in Pennsylvania after serving in World War II. He had saved a little money, and together he and his father bought a piece of property and developed it into a golf course. Eventually, Dick decided to build a golf course and real-estate-development business. His father wanted to limit his personal involvement, so he eventually sold all his interest in the property to Dick. Thus, none of Dick's brothers or sisters were ever part of the family-owned business. The company grew at a rate of approximately 9 percent annually and enjoyed annual revenues of approximately $28 million in 2002. It also saw the value of its assets—mostly undeveloped land—skyrocket.

Over this same period, several national measures of economic activity in the industry indicated considerably lower growth rates in both revenues and asset values of other companies. In fact, Real Estate Development Partners seemed to be growing at twice the rate achieved by the average performers in the industry.

Although he was very pleased with the company's record, Dick felt that he had two major unresolved issues. First, he questioned whether, given the size of his estate and his age, he could do enough to avoid extraordinarily high estate taxes. Second, he was uncertain as to whether his five sons and daughters would get along well enough to allow the family-owned business to continue to a third generation (Figure R). He felt strongly about keeping the business together. Because of the expertise and economies of scale that he had been able to build into the business, he was disinclined to divide it into smaller business units that the sons and daughters could separately own and manage.

Al, the eldest son, had worked in the business since he was 8 years old. Along with his two brothers, Tom and Ken, Al had learned the business from the bottom up by doing mostly odd jobs, especially during the summer months. They mowed lawns, dug ditches, picked up trash, and repaired clubhouses. The three sons were busy in "the house that Dick built." Their sisters, Deb and Amy, on the other hand, always seemed to be protected from toil in the male-dominated industry in which Real Estate Development Partners operated.

Notwithstanding their early experiences in the business, not all the boys went into the family-owned business. One decided to work for a *Fortune 500* company after graduating from college, and developed his career there for over a decade. He had recently returned to the family-owned business, citing a desire to be closer to his family and also to work in a more caring corporate culture. Amy and Deb also went to work for other companies. Amy had returned recently and assumed responsibilities in the marketing department. Thus, four of the five siblings (all except Deb) were now working in the firm. They had very different positions and, as managers, limited interdependence. Most of the need for communication and coordination seemed to emerge around strategic and ownership issues, not the day-to-day running of the business.

figure **R** | **Randall Family Tree**

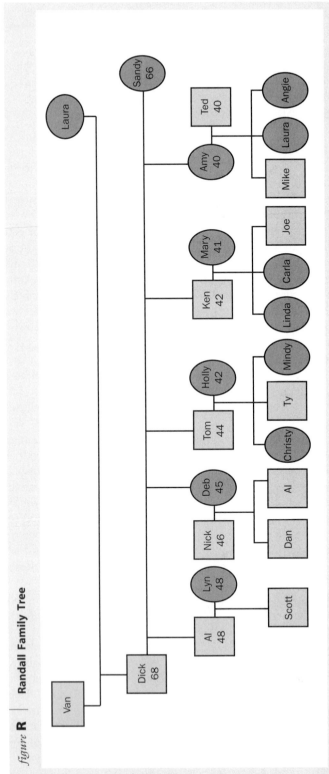

table **L**	**Action Research Results for Real Estate Development Partners**

Family-Business Survey Results

1 The CEO is very satisfied with the company's current results and its track record and believes he has only two major issues in front of him: estate planning and planning for succession.

2 There is a large gap between family managers and nonfamily managers in the extent to which they perceive the organization to be operating with a reasonable plan for where it is going and how it will get there. Nonfamily managers are much less satisfied than family managers in this regard.

3 Family managers, in particular, do not see themselves as having regular reviews of their performance on the job.

4 Neither family nor nonfamily managers know the length of time the present owner-manager will continue as CEO.

5 Family and nonfamily managers agree that those who would be involved do not know the standards and processes through which succession will occur.

6 Family managers do not perceive the company as having an effective board of directors or advisors.

7 Nonfamily managers do not perceive the CEO as delegating authority and responsibility and letting people do their jobs.

8 Both family and nonfamily managers agree the company is market-driven in its activities.

9 Both family and nonfamily managers consider it important that this company remain a family business.

10 Unlike nonfamily managers, family managers do not believe that career paths to senior positions are equally available to men and women.

11 Nonfamily managers feel that they are compensated fairly and equitably and have career paths to senior positions.

12 Nonfamily managers do not perceive that family members working in the company are maintaining helpful and cooperative relationships.

Family Survey Result

1 Family members (both active and inactive in management) agree that the family does not hold family meetings on a regular basis. (But there was a wide range of answers, indicating some in- and out-of-the-loop dynamics at work. More than likely, family members who work at Real Estate Development Partners meet more often and therefore feel more in-the-loop than family members who do not.)

2 Family members do not agree that the standards and processes through which employment in the family firm occurs have been established. The firm has never had an employment policy with requirements to be met by family members seeking to work in the firm.

3 Family members do not agree that how ownership of the family firm will be transferred between generations of the family has been established.

4 Family members differed significantly in the extent to which they agreed with the statement "Family differences are addressed in a constructive way."

5 Family members disagreed about whether the standards and processes through which CEO succession will occur are known to them.

6 Family members strongly agreed that they are free to seek their own careers.

7 Family members agreed that they need to have better communication and meet as a family more frequently to discuss issues and resolve problems.

Dick thought that there were three major ways the company might grow in the future. First, the company could begin operations in Florida, where it already had developed some expertise with smaller real-estate investments. Second, it could convert several of its golf club properties into more lucrative commercial developments. Population growth surrounding several of the company's older properties was pushing office complexes and retail shopping centers right up to the 18th hole. Finally, the company could grow in the property-management area, effectively providing management of properties for other owners and investor groups. In their industry, the service contract side of the business was growing significantly.

AN ACTION RESEARCH CONSULTING PROJECT AND THE RANDALL FAMILY

Because of Dick Randall's concerns regarding the future of the family-owned business, he agreed to participate in an action research effort to discover just how ready he and his family were to transition the business across generations of owner-managers. Given his dream of continuity, he had to prioritize the issues to be addressed.

A family-business consultant visited the offices of Real Estate Development Partners and met with and distributed copies of a family business survey to family members active in the business, several key nonfamily managers, and several family members who were spouses or direct-line descendants and shareholders but did not work in the business. The data-collection meeting ended on a positive note, with all participants expressing their desire to receive the feedback and begin to take constructive steps. Participants were reminded that individual responses would be kept confidential and that feedback would come in the form of averages and ranges of responses, without ever identifying who said what.

Several weeks after this meeting, when the family and family-business survey data had been analyzed, the two-person consulting team met with family members and key nonfamily management to discuss the results. (See Table L for a summary of the findings.) There was concern about the impact that sharing some of these findings might have on individual Randall family members. But, ultimately, the consultants decided to provide the family-business survey results to both the family and the nonfamily managers who had participated. The family survey results were then presented to the family members in the second phase of the meeting, after nonfamily managers had been excused.

This case was prepared by Professor Ernesto J. Poza as the basis for class discussion rather than to illustrate the effective or ineffective handling of a family-business management situation. This case was revised in July 2008.

SMALL FAMILY BUSINESS | CASE **18**

GLASSKING DISTRIBUTOR COMPANY

"Those honchos at headquarters keep coming up with rosy sales projections and glowing strategic plans," lamented Marilyn Green. "Don't they know our entire distribution effort is in the hands of family businesses?" As director of dealer development for GlassKing, a major supplier, Marilyn seems to be spending more time coping with family infighting than she does on new product launches or gaining market share.

Each year, the concerns of her distributors—most of them independently owned family firms—grow more complex and alarming. Succession planning, sibling rivalry, and partnership squabbles have replaced sales growth as a priority. A particularly devastating blow came when Marilyn's West Coast representative called with the news that the head of GlassKing's top dealership, an $80-million company, is involved in a bitter divorce that is consuming virtually all of his energy. Sales have been dropping like a rock. "I'll bet the corporate strategists didn't put this one in the five-year plan!" muttered Marilyn.

Lately, the consequences of unresolved family problems have hit GlassKing's bottom line harder than in the past. Marilyn first noticed a complacency among dealers at an annual sales meeting 5 years ago. They were a little grayer, a little heavier, and clearly less enthusiastic about rapid growth. "They've peaked," she recalls thinking, "and where are all the young people?"

Marilyn remembers when these owners were the best in the business. Now, faced with weekly reports from sales reps about family quarrels and about owners "who think they will live forever," Marilyn is asking: "How did we get into this mess? And how do we get out?"

This case study of a family-business dilemma is part of a series by the Family Firm Institute edited by Ernesto J. Poza. The cases are real, but identities have been changed to protect the privacy of the individuals involved. Copyright © 1990 by the Family Firm Institute, Boston, MA.

NEW WAY DISTRIBUTING | CASE **19**

In 1921, "PaPa" Steve Smith began delivering newspapers by bicycle. He discovered that some of his wealthier customers would pay him to pick up groceries and deliver them along with the newspapers. So he founded New Way Distributing, Inc. and within 15 years, he had 25 trucks and a small warehouse. New Way is a national distributor of specialty food products to grocery stores and restaurants. It specializes in high-end products bought directly from producers and sold to restaurants and, as a retailer would, directly to consumers too.

PaPa died in 1960, survived by two sons who continued to expand the business, in substantial part by establishing small- and mid-size grocery stores in ethnic neighborhoods. The approach involved identifying capable individuals who wanted to start grocery stores, guaranteeing building leases, financing fixtures and inventory, and providing business support services. New Way sells groceries to these new retailers. Its margins are significantly higher than the industry norm, but it periodically loses significant capital when one of these small retailers fails.

Because of the retailers' ever-increasing financing needs, the family left most profits in the business and lived frugally. However, by the early 1990s, New Way's annual sales exceeded $2 billion and the company was generating substantial profits. Compensation to the two brothers increased significantly.

Beginning with PaPa, the family had a history of transferring small blocks of New Way stock to descendents annually. Consequently, while Big Joe (eldest brother) and the younger Peter had voting control, their children and grandchildren owned significant numbers of shares.

Three of Big Joe's six children work in the business today. One of Peter's four children had worked in the business for years, but she recently adopted a baby and is on maternity leave. It is unclear whether she will return to the business or become a stay-at-home mother.

A few years ago, the family's trusted advisor recommended beginning to pay dividends to shareholders, both for tax reasons and to provide cash flow for inactive shareholders. As a result, most family members have accumulated significant funds, a major portion of which they have left "on account" at New Way. The company pays a higher rate of interest on these amounts than is available to family members through the bank. At the same time, the funds constitute cheaper, more stable financing than is otherwise available to New Way.

New Way's CFO spends a fair bit of time, along with another full-time New Way employee, handling financial matters for family members, including preparing tax returns and numerous nonbusiness-related tasks. They also coordinate the employment of outside lawyers and accountants. With the help of an investment consultant, New Way's CFO (a CPA who has spent her entire career involved with operating businesses) also oversees the family's modest investments held outside the business. Other New Way employees also help working family members with personal matters, like performing repairs on cars and homes.

Big Joe died last year. Peter is struggling through succession issues with Big Joe's widow and the active fourth-generation family members. The issues generally involve concerns about whether the two family branches have equal influence over the company and whether compensation for members of the two branches are fair and equal. These issues have strained relationships. There also are serious questions about the ability of any family member to lead the company if Peter becomes disabled or dies.

Last year, the family had its first shareholder meeting, which was led by Peter. Key management personnel made presentations about the company. The family shareholders not working in the business (and their spouses) seemed interested and asked good questions. The family members who do work in the business thought the meeting was successful, but Peter is uncertain about whether to hold another such meeting next year, in part because he doesn't have any ideas as to what else should be covered.

DISCUSSION QUESTIONS

1. If you were Peter, would you hold another shareholder meeting next year? List issues that you think the family should address in next year's meeting.
2. List any other actions that you believe Peter should be taking as part of his current approach to handling the family's financial affairs.

3. Do you think family members are well-advised to leave their money "on account" at New Way? Why or why not?

4. Would a family office be appropriate for this family? List pros and cons.

Reprinted by permission, Ross W. Nager, Senior Managing Director and Principal, Sentinel Trust Company, Houston, Texas; www.SentinelTrust.com.

THE RELIANCE GROUP (PART B)

CASE **20**

Dhirubhai Ambani, the founding entrepreneur of Reliance Industries, died suddenly at the age of 69 without a will or succession plan. He left two sons in executive positions within the business. Under Hindu tradition, the eldest son becomes the successor. But dissatisfied with this traditional legacy, Anil Ambani challenged his older brother Mukesh and began arguing about management and ownership issues. In the end, the brothers listened to their mother, Kokilaben Ambani, and a settlement of their differences was announced on June 18, 2005—7 months after the disagreements started.

THE SETTLEMENT

The Ambani family owned 34 percent of the shares of Reliance Group, a publicly traded but family-controlled corporation. The settlement included Mukesh and Anil each getting 30 percent of the family's ownership stake, Kokilaben retaining 30 percent, and each of her two daughters, Nina and Dipti, who did not work in the business, getting 5 percent of the stock. (See family tree in Figure S.) The brothers signed a 10-year no-compete agreement and resigned from each other's boards. Under terms of the agreement, Mukesh kept the flagship petrochemical business (that enjoyed extraordinary profits in both 2007 and 2008), while Anil assumed full control of an electrical power company, a telecommunications and broadband provider, and a finance company. The brothers swapped shares in each others' companies so that neither owned shares in the others' business, and Anil received an additional payment (estimated at between US$2 billion to $3 billion) to equalize the value of the divided assets.

THE SIBLINGS AND THEIR BUSINESSES AFTER THE 2005 SETTLEMENT

For the next 3 years, both siblings achieved a multitude of successes and multiplied the value of the stock of their respective companies severalfold. But warning shots in the sibling relationship were also fired during this time. Mukesh terminated Reliance Communication's service of Reliance Industries and awarded that contract to a competitor. Mukesh also raised the price of the gas it sold to Anil's electric power company (albeit, in the midst of significantly higher global energy prices) and outbid his brother in a prime-real-estate deal in Mumbai. Anil's company, in turn, took the Maharashtra state government to court after it awarded a bridge-building contract to one of Mukesh's companies.[1]

---

[1]Range, J., Bellman, E., & Cimilluca, D., Feud Clouds MTN-Reliance Talks; Fraternal Dispute 'May Derail Deal'; Early-July Target, *The Wall Street Journal*, June 27, 2008, p. B5.

figure **S** | **Ambani Family Tree**

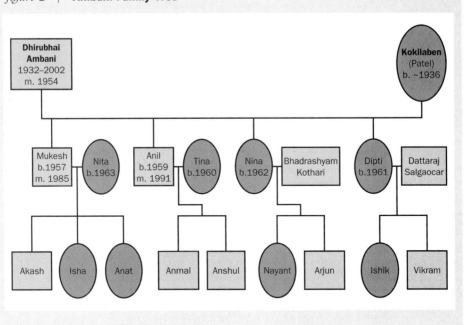

In late May 2008, Reliance Communications, controlled by Anil Ambani, entered exclusive talks with MTN Group of South Africa over a possible combination of the companies that would create a telecommunications juggernaut with more than 100 million mobile customers in Africa, the Middle East, and India.

On Thursday, June 12, just as the talks were progressing and the due diligence work was being done, Reliance Industries, controlled by Mukesh Ambani, sent a letter to MTN stating that Reliance Industries had the right of first refusal on any deal involving the sale of Reliance Communication. Talks were focusing on Anil Ambani selling his 66 percent share in Reliance Communication to MTN in a share swap that would make him the largest shareholder of MTN but make Reliance Communication a subsidiary of MTN. At the time Reliance Communication was valued at approximately US $26 billion while MTN Group was valued at US$30.7 billion. A key motivator for the deal for Anil Ambani, according to a person close to him, was to become a larger business figure than his brother.[2]

Reliance Communications' response to the Reliance Industries' letter was to call it a bad-faith effort to disrupt the talks and to claim that its alleged right of first refusal on the controlling stake in Reliance Communications was invalid because it had only been signed by Reliance Industries executives.[3]

---

[2]Paris, C., & Venkat, P.R., MTN, Reliance Close to Deal; Legal Obstacles Surround Dispute with R-Com Head, *The Wall Street Journal*, July 3, 2008, p. B4.
[3]Range, J., & Cimilluca, D., Feud between Brothers in India Complicates Big Cellphone Deal, *The Wall Street Journal*, June 14, 2008, p. A4.

The disagreement escalated on Wednesday, June 18, exactly 3 years after the sibling settlement brokered by Kokilaben Ambani. Reliance Industries said that Reliance ADA Group, the Anil Ambani company that is parent of Reliance Communications, relied on the same contractual agreement to support its own positions in negotiating about 15 separate matters with Reliance Industries; therefore the agreement must be deemed valid. Reliance Communications responded by stating that the company would consider all options, including launching criminal proceedings against Reliance Industries executives who had signed the agreement. Reliance Industries then countered by issuing a statement to the media claiming that "there is no criminality attached to the signing of the agreement. . . . If any proceedings are adopted, we will not only defend them but will also consider our options for such a malicious action."[4]

RELIANCE COMMUNICATIONS' GLOBAL GROWTH THREATENED

By early July, with Reliance Communications' shares down about 20 percent and the talks with MTN Group seemingly stalled, efforts were being made to restructure the transaction in a way that MTN would be taken over by Reliance Communications. This was an obvious attempt by Anil to address Mukesh Ambani's objections to the deal. Unfortunately, political issues in South Africa raised by the possible takeover of one of its most important companies by a foreign entity, made this approach unlikely to succeed.[5]

On Monday, July 7, the two sibling-led companies again traded accusations. Reliance Communications said Reliance Industries rebuffed its offer to meet to clarify any doubts that Reliance Industries (Mukesh Ambani's company) might have about the talks with MTN. Then Reliance Industries released a statement saying that Reliance Communications officials had failed to show up for a conciliation meeting scheduled earlier that day. Later, Reliance Communications countered by saying that "Reliance Industries' sole objective is to derail the talks with MTN and frustrate a possible combination."[6]

MTN Group and Reliance Communications ended their merger talks on Friday, July 18, claiming that legal and regulatory issues prevented the parties from completing the transaction. To the world it seemed that two brothers, unable to overcome the sibling rivalry evident since their father's death 6 years earlier, had destroyed an opportunity for global expansion. The brothers have continuously wanted to best each other in the highest echelons of Indian business, according to a friend of the family.

A deal between MTN and Reliance Communications would have created a company with a stock market value of about US$50 billion and 110 million customers. But not to be deterred by this setback, Anil's media company, Reliance Big Entertainment launched talks to invest more than $500 million in a joint venture with director Steven

---

[4]Range, J., Family Feud Imperils Deal; The Spat Escalates between 2 Brothers Over Reliance-MTN, *The Wall Street Journal*, June 19, 2008, p. B4.
[5]Cimilluca, D., & Sharma, A., MTN-Reliance Talks Likely to be Extended, *The Wall Street Journal*, July 7, 2008, p. B4.
[6]Paris, C., Guha, R., & Venkat, P.R., Reliance Firms Trade New Barbs; Negotiation Period or Deal with MTN Set to End Tuesday, *The Wall Street Journal*, July 8, 2008, p. B4.

Spielberg. It has also earmarked about a billion dollars to make films with the movie production houses owned by Brad Pitt, Jim Carrey, and others.[7]

But the MTN deal would have been the largest involving an Indian company in an overseas transaction and would have likely placed Anil Ambani at the forefront of India's global expansion. The inability to close on the transaction casts a dark cloud on both brothers' efforts to line up potential partners abroad for global growth opportunities.

WHAT LIES AHEAD

Should Kokilaben Ambani intervene again, as she did in 2005? What would she do if she did intervene? What might be done next in this family-business situation to both protect the growth and health of the Ambani companies and hopefully preserve some form of family unity?

---

[7]Range, J., Bellman, E., & Cimilluca, D., Sibling Rivalry Scuttles Telecom Deal Talks, *The Wall Street Journal*, July 19, 2008, p. A1.

INDEX

A

accounting for family businesses. *See also* financial management
  balance sheet, 202–205
  business valuation adjustments, 215
  business worth assessment, 210–211
  differences from traditional accounting, 210
  income statement, 205–206
  language barrier in, 202
accounts receivable, 206–207
action research, 369–372
Adams Funeral Home case study, 139–141
adaptation
  centennial firms as example of, 326–328
  family-business advisory board and, 262–263
  innovation and, 293–294
Adelphia Communication case study, 251–252
advisors
  communication management using, 276–278
  for family meetings, 277–278
agency costs
  competitive advantage of family businesses and, 15–19
  governance structure and, 250–252
agency theory, family businesses, 13–14
agility
  change management and, 308–309
  competitive advantage of family businesses and, 19
Agnelli family, 85
alienation, conflict management and, 45–46
Ambani, Anil, 355–367, 375–378
Ambani, Dhirubhai, 187, 355–367, 375–378
Ambani, Kokilaben, 365–367, 375–378
Ambani, Mukesh, 355–367, 375–378
ambassador exit style, 114
Anheuser-Busch, 86
annual shareholders' meeting, governance and, 268
appreciative-inquiry processes, change management and, 305–306
appropriate return estimation, 220–221
Arias, Antonio, 157

Arthur Andersen Company, 265
assessment process, succession development and, 88–89
asset protection
  fixed asset turnover, 206–207
  generation-skipping restrictive trusts and, 44–45
  shareholder demand for, 52
  total-asset turnover, 207
AT&T, 101
attributes of next generation, characteristics of, 93–94
auction strategy model, 54

B

Bacardí, Adolfo Comas, 157
balance sheet, examples of, 202–205, 211, 217–218
Bancroft family, 284–285
Bares, Jack, 115
Bean, Leon, 86
Berkshire Hathaway, 57–59, 62
best practices
  CEO governance and, 107–109
  succession planning imperatives, 317–323
Bingham, Barry Jr., 67–69
Bingham, Barry Sr., 29–30, 67–69
Bingham, Eleanor, 67–69
Bingham, Jonathan, 67–69
Bingham, Judge, 67–69
Bingham, Mary, 29–30, 67–69, 117
Bingham, Sally, 67–69
Bingham, Worth, 67–69
Bingham family
  case study, 67–69
  estate planning problems of, 192–193
  family culture in, 29–30, 267
  transfer of power and, 109–110
Blanchard, Al, 160–165
Blanchard, Arnold, 161
Blanchard, Bill, 163–165
Blanchard, George, 160–161
Blanchard, Germaine, 161, 164–165

Blanchard, Mary, 162–165
Blanchard, Molly, 161
Blanchard, Morris, 160–165
Blanchard, Sarah, 161–165
Blanchard family case study, 160–165
Blethen family, family culture in, 30–31
blurred system boundaries
    of centennial firms, 328–330
    in family businesses, 11
BMW Corporation, 85
board of directors
    Adelphia Communication case study, 251–252
    at centennial firms, 338–339
    estate planning and role of, 198–199
    family council boundaries with, 266–268
    financial performance and, 250–252
    governance role of, 55–57, 248–252
    organization role of, 55–57
    succession development and, 89
board service polity, guidelines for, 41–42
Bork, D., 277
borrowing for expansion, case study, 138–139
brand equity, value creation and, 173–176
bridging executives, nonfamily managers as, 238–243
British Sky Broadcasting Group, 285
Brooke, Mark, 85
Brooke, Massimo, 85
Brubeck, Dave, 184
Busch, August, 86
Busch, August A. III, 86
business development, stages of, 179–182
business models, value creation and, 173–174
business partner role of CEO spouse, 119
business rejuvenation matrix, 309
business valuation
    discounted cash flow, 215–224
    estate planning and, 193–194
    family accounting adjustments, 215
    guideline public company method, 224–226
    guidelines for, 211, 213–215
    guideline transaction method, 226–227
    methods for, 215–229
    nonfinancial returns and costs, 229–230
    sample valuation report, 345–354
    underlying factors, 213
Business Week 1000 survey, 201
business worth, evaluation of, 210–211, 213
buy-sell agreements
    estate planning and, 193
    ownership structure and, 60

C

Cabelvision Systems, 265, 310
Cabrera, Carlos, 71
Cadbury, Sir Arthur, 261, 263, 283
Cadbury Schweppes company, 260–261, 263, 283

Caperton, Mary, 29–30, 67–69
capital-asset pricing model (CAPM), 221–222
capital expenditures (CAPEX)
    on balance sheet, 204–205
    future cash flow estimation and, 219
career planning
    for next-generation family members, 96–97
    nonfamily management, 235
Cargill Corporation, 266, 268
Cargill-MacMillan family, 266
Carlock, Randy, 179
Casa Osborne/Osborne Wines, 52, 333–334, 336–338
    board of directors, 56–57
case studies, 69–84, 127–165
cash flow
    business valuation, discounted cash flow, 215–224
    discounted cash flow, 215–224
    future cash flow estimations, 215–219
    future cash flow timing, 220
    as shareholder priority, 51–52
Castañeda, Carlos, 157
Cemex Corporation, 308, 311–312
centennial family firms
    adaptability and continuity lessons from, 326–328
    cultural revolution myth concerning, 333–334
    customer-centric paradigm of, 336–338
    entrepreneurial cultural erosion, 334–335
    family culture, organizational culture, and cultural blur in, 328–330
    family unity and family-business interactions, 335–336
    future resources, 342–343
    Grupo Ferré Rangel example of, 325–326
    incumbent-generation leadership governance, 340–341
    J. B. Smucker Company case study, 331–332
    management structure at, 338–339
    next-generation leadership development, 339–340
    positive-sum dynamics and, 316
    systems theory perspective on, 332–333
    ten lessons from, 341–342
    Timken Company case study, 330–331
Chafee, Andy, 162–165
Chafee, Edward, 163–165
Chafee, Sam, 161
change management
    agility in face of, 308–309
    commitment planning and, 306
    competition and value creation and, 309
    formula for, 297–298
    group consultations, family and shareholders, 304
    institutionalization of change, 306–307
    intergroup consultations, family and nonfamily management, 304–305
    interpersonal skills development in, next-generation family members, 305

next-generation family members involvement in, 309–311

organizational culture and, 293–295

organization development approach to, 303–306

whole-family forums and appreciative-inquiry processes, 305–306

Chapter 11 company model, 55

Charan, Ram, 170

Chief Executive Officer (CEO)

ambivalence in, case study, 137–138

of centennial firms, 327–328

change management and, 297–298, 303–304

dyadic consultations with, 304

estate planning and, 187–188

exit styles of, 112–117

family-business advisory board and, 256–260

family council and, 279

as governance architect, 107–109

governance structure and, 247–252

incumbent-generation leadership by, 340–341

nonfamily management and, 234, 238–243

ownership structure and, 49–50

perceptions of, 107–109

spouse of, role in transfer of power, 117–123

succession planning and continuity planning by, 110–112, 185

transfer of power by, 109–110

chief trust officer, spouse as, 120

Chinese junk strategy model, 54

cigarette boat strategy model, 54

classes of stock

estate planning and, 193–194

ownership structure and, 60

"clicks and bricks" strategy, 307–308

coaching and mentoring, successor-development process and, 88–89

Collins, Jim, 61, 337

Comcast Corporation, 101

commitment to family business

change management and planning for, 306

conflict management and, 45–46

family-business interaction factor, 38–39

family culture and, case studies of, 29–31

family emotional intelligence and, 37–38

family meetings as tool for, 39–40

family systems perspective on, 32–34

family unity and continuity and, 40–41

genograms and family messages and, 34–37

guidelines for building, 27–46

planning and policy making guidelines, 41–44

trusts, legal agreements and personal responsibility and, 44–45

zero-sum dynamics and family culture, 31–32

communication

case studies and examples, 284–285

estate planning and importance of, 197

facilitators and advisors for, 276–278

family constitution, 280–282

family council and, 278–279

family meetings, 271–276

family office and, 282–284

guidelines for family businesses, 271–285

organizational structure and role of, 57–59

ownership and policy making, 279–280

compensation and benefits

family-business advisory board, 260

in family-first businesses, 10

nonfamily management, 235–237

competitive advantage

family unity and family-business interactions and, 335–336

survival through, 311–312

Competitive Advantage, 169–170

competitive advantages

career opportunities, 235

company success through, 311–312

core competencies as, 182–183

family business case study, 133

five forces of, 169–170

value creation and, 309

competitive challenges

resource-based perspective on, 15–19

strategic perspective on, 14

conflict management

disagreements and succession planning and, 101–103

trust building and, 45–46

conservative succession, in family-owned business, 7

continuity

centennial firms as example of, 326–328, 330–331, 338–339

CEO as architect of, 110–112

change and, 294–295

customer-oriented paradigm and, 336–338

estate planning and, 197

evolution and, 296–297

family-business advisory board and, 263–264

family-management-ownership structure, 302–303

in family-owned business, 6–7

generational conflict and cultural change, 332–333

organizational culture and, 293–294

survival of family business and, 308–309

continuous evolution, centennial companies and, 336–338

controlled liquidation model, 54

controlling interests

business valuation discounts for lack of, 228–229

Reliance Industries case study, 362–367

Conway, Bill, 154

Conway, Gerry, 141–155

Conway, Kevin, 150–153

Conway, Marty, 141, 151–152, 154–155

Conway, Neil, 151

Conway, Paul, 151, 153–154

Cool, K., 90

coparcenary division, next-generation family members and challenge of, 91
core competencies
  as competitive advantages, 182–183
  family business case study, 133
Corning Corporation, 240
corporate productivity
  competitive advantage of family businesses and, 18–19
  ownership structure and, 49–50
corporate strategy meeting, Grupo Ferré case study, 158–159
corporate structure, estate planning and, 193–194
cousins
  case study of, 160–165
  next-generation family members as, 98–99
Cox Communications, 265
cultural blur, 328–330
cultural revolutions, discredited concept of, 333–334
customer-oriented company
  centennial companies and, 336–338
  strategic planning and, 182–183
customer-supplier integration
  competitive advantage of family businesses and, 15–19
  strategic planning and, 177
customization capability, competitive advantage of family businesses and, 19

D

Davis, J. A., 104–105
day sales outstanding, 206
  return on equity and improvement of, 209–210
debt ratio, 207
debt utilization, DuPont return on equity and, 208–210
decision making, planning and policy making guidelines, 41–44
depreciation, on balance sheet, 204
Dierickx, I., 90
Dillard's, 311
disagreements, succession planning and management of, 101–103
discounted cash flow
  business valuation and, 215–224
  valuation of, 222–223
discount rates
  appropriate return estimation and, 221–222
  for lack of control, 228–229
Discovery Action Research study
  family-business advisory board, 264
  family-business relationship, 177–178
  family unity and continuity, 40–41
  next-generation leadership research, 103–105
  nonfamily managers, 232
dividend policy, guidelines for, 42

Dolan, Charles, 310
Dolan, James, 310
Dolan family, 265, 310
Dow Jones & Co., 284–285
dual-path trajectory, parallel strategic planning, 180–182
Dumas, Colette, 104
DuPont return on equity calculation, 208–210, 212
durability of family businesses, 7
dyadic consultation, change management and, 304
Dyer, W. Gibb, 232, 277

E

earning before interest, taxes, depreciation, and amortization (EBITDA), 205–206
  financial performance of family business and, 250–252
  future cash flow estimation, 218–219
  guideline public company method, 225–226
  guideline transaction method, family business valuation, 226–227
earnings before interest and taxes (EBIT), 206
Economic Growth and Tax Relief Reconciliation Act, 189
eFollett.com, 307–308
El Caballo, 58
El Imparcial newspaper, 71–72, 325
El Mundo newspaper, 71–72, 325
El Nuevo Día (ENDI) newspaper case study, 70–72, 156–160, 325–326
Emotional Competence Inventory-University Edition (ECI-U), 37–38
emotional intelligence, in family systems, 37–38
employee stock ownership plans (ESOPs), 196
employment policy
  example of, 42–43
  guidelines for, 41
enterprise value (EV)
  estimation methods, 227
  family business valuation and, 226
entrepreneurial culture, erosion of, 334–335
equality
  conflict management and, 45–46
  estate planning and, 197
equity
  business valuation and, 224
  estate planning and value of, 191, 195–196
  shareholder demand for returns on, 52
equity multiplier, return on equity and, 208–210
estate planning
  board of directors and, 198–199
  corporate structure and classes of stock, 193–194
  employee stock ownership plans, 196
  equity and nonfamily employees, 191, 195–197
  FFr case study, 152

guidelines for, 187–199
information and communication to shareholders about, 59
ownership transfer and estate planning inventory, 63–65
pitfalls in, 196–197
speed and agility preservation and, 190–191
trust designations and, 195
estate taxes, 189–199
ethics
Adelphia Communication case study, 251–252
of family businesses, 21
evolution of businesses
future state, 298–300
leadership role in, 295–297
present state, 301–302
states of, 298–302
excess cash, family business accounting and, 210
exit styles of CEOs, 112–117
ambassador exit styles, 114, 124
general exit style, 113–114, 124
governor exit style, 115, 123, 124
inventor exit style, 115–116, 124
monarch exit style, 112–113, 124
transfer of power and succession planning, 124–125
transition czar, 116–117
extended business family, case studies, 157–158

F

facilitators
communication management using, 276–278
policy making using, 44
failure rate for family-owned businesses, 1–6
Fair Market Value, 213–214
fairness principles
conflict management and, 45–46
estate planning and, 197
family assembly
change management and, 305–306
governance and, 268
family bank strategy model, 54
family-business advisory board
case studies, 256–257, 259–260
change management and, 303–304
compensation and motivation, 260
cross-generation adaptations, 262–263
governance role of, 253–264
independent consultants vs., 253–255
members of, 255
recruitment and selection criteria, 256–260
research on, 264
staggered terms for, 258
strategic planning and, 260–262
succession and continuity planning, 263–264
family-business consultants, 243–244, 342–343

family-business interactions, competitive advantages of, 335–336
Family Business Magazine, 85
family business programs, 342
family-business relationship
strategic planning and, 177–178
value creation through, 38–39
Family Business Review, 22, 112
family constitution
guidelines for, 42, 280–282
sample constitution, 286–291
family council
board of directors' boundaries with, 266–268
at centennial firms, 338–339
communication guidelines for, 278–279
governance and, 266
Grupo Ferré case study, 75
guidelines for, 275
organizational structure and role of, 56–57
planning and policy making guidelines for, 41–44
service policy guidelines, 42
Valle family (pseud.) case study, 79–84
family culture
Adelphia Communications case study, 252
case studies of, 29–31, 147–148
of centennial firms, 328–330
examples of, 284–285
nonfamily managers and, 237–238
trust and commitment building tied to, 27–29
zero-sum dynamics and, 31–32
Family Firm Institute, 277, 342
family-first businesses, 9–10
family limited partnership, estate planning and, 193–194
family-management-ownership structure, continuity and, 302–303
Family Matters Project, 47
family meetings
benefits of, 39–40, 273
case studies of, 272
conflict management and, 45–46
facilitators and consultants for, 276–278
FFr case study, 151–152
goal-oriented approach to, 274
Grupo Ferré case study, 158–159
guidelines for, 271–276
organizational structure and role of, 56–57
ownership and policy making at, 279–280
planning and policy making guidelines, 41–44
family messages, trust and commitment building and, 34–37
family office
communication guidelines for, 282–284
governance and, 268–269

family-owned businesses
  agency theory perspective, 13–14
  blurred system boundaries, 11
  characteristics of, 1–6
  defined, 5–6
  durability of, 7
  ethics and social responsibility, 21
  family-first businesses, 9–10
  joint optimization, 12–13
  management-first businesses, 10
  ownership-first businesses, 11
  research on, 21–24
  resource-based view of competitive advantage, 15–19
  statistics on, 3
  stewardship perspective, 20–21
  strategic perspective and competitive challenges, 14
  succession and continuity in, 6–7
  systems theory perspective on, 7–9
family relations
  FFr case study, 150–151
  of next-generation family members, 97–98
family systems perspective
  genograms and family messages, 34–37
  trust and commitment building and, 32–34
family unity and continuity
  competitive advantages of, 335–336
  positive-sum dynamics and, 315–316
  shareholders' priorities and, 51–52
  strategic planning and, 178
  trust and commitment and, 40–41
Family Unity index, development of, 39
Fasteners for Retail (FFr) case study, 141–155
"FBN survey: Families' Importance to economies," 201
Ferré, Antonio Luis, 70, 73–77, 115, 156–160, 325–326
Ferré, Loren, 156–160
Ferré, Luis Alberto, 73, 156–157, 325
Ferré, María Eugenia, 156–157
Ferré, María L., 156–160, 326
Ferré, Tonio, 156–160
Ferré Media Group case study, 69–72, 156–160
Ferré Rangel family case study, 73–77, 338–339
Fiat Corporation, 85
Fidelity Investments, 86
Financial Executives International, 265
financial management. *See also* accounting for family businesses
  balance sheet, 202–205
  business valuation, 211–229
  business worth assessment, 210–211
  DuPont approach to return on equity, 208–210
  financial statement analysis, 206–207
  income statement, 205–206
  nonfinancial returns and costs, 229–230
  valuation of family business and, 201–230
  value creation and, 173–175

financial performance of family-owned businesses, 1–6
  board of directors and, 250–252
  case study, 133–134
  competitive advantage of, 16–19
  next-generation attributes and, 92–93
  trust and commitment building tied to, 29
Financial Times of London, 231
fixed-asset turnover, 206–207
Follett Corporation, 307–308, 310
Foote, Cone & Belding, 294
Ford, William Clay, 85
Ford Motor Company, 85–86, 240
Franklin, Peter, 162–165
free agent, CEO spouse as, 121–122
future cash flow
  estimations, 215–219
  timing of, 220
future planning practices, nonfamily management and, 234
future resources for family firms, 342–343
future state of business, 298–300

G

Gallo, Gina, 88
Gallo, Julio, 88
Gallo of Sonoma premium wines, 88
Gallo Wines, 88
Gander Mounty company, 219
Gannett Company, 68–69
Gardarian, Kathy, 111
Gardarian, Leo, 111
General Electric, 115
general exit style, characteristics of, 113–114, 124
generational conflict, systems theory perspective, 332–333
generation-skipping restrictive trusts
  estate planning and, 195
  failure of, 44–45
genograms
  Ambani family tree, 362, 376
  Conway family tree, 151
  Grupo Ferré case study, 74
  guidelines for constructing, 34–37
  Randall family, 370
  Valle family (pseud.) case study, 80
Gerstner, Lou, 295
global opportunities
  company growth and, 314–315
  Reliance Communications case study, 377–378
goal-oriented family meetings, 274–275
Goleman-Boyatzis Emotional Competencies Inventory, 88–90
González, Luis, 158
Good to Great, 61, 337
Gorman, Leon, 86

governance
    Adelphia Communication case study, 251–252
    annual shareholders' meeting, 268
    board-family council boundaries and, 266–268
    board of directors role in, 55–57, 248–252
    CEO as architect of, 107–109
    defined, 247–248
    estate planning and, 193–194
    family assembly and, 268
    of family business, 23–24, 247–248
    family-business advisory board role in, 253–264
    family council and, 266
    family office and, 268–269
    guidelines for, 247–269
    nonfamily managers and, 233–234
    Sarbanes-Oxley regulations and, 264–266
    shareholder-firm relationships, 55–57
    top-management team and, 269
governor exit style, 115
Graham, Don, 87, 176
Graham, Katharine, 87, 120–121, 167, 176, 231
Grandview Industries case study, 160–165
grantor-retained annuity trust (GRAT), 152, 195
gross margin, 207
group management consultants, 276–278
    family/shareholder groups, 304
growth management
    business valuation and, 214–215
    FFr case study, 148–150
    financing for, 210
    global opportunities and, 314–315
    intergenerational growth and, 313
    Reliance Industries case study, 359–367
Grupo Ferré Rangel case study, 70–77, 115, 156–160
    centennial firm status of, 325–326, 338–339
guideline public company method, business
    valuation, 224–226
guideline transaction method, family business
    valuation and, 226–227

H

Hagedorn, James, 86
Harvard Business Review, 311
Harvey-Jones, Sir John, 262
Hewlett, Bill, 52, 294–295
Hewlett-Packard (HP), 52, 294–295
Hilbert-Davis, J., 277
Hill, Crawford, 284–285
Hubler, Thomas, 179
Huebel, Franz (Dr.), 112

I

Ibbotson, R. G., 221
IBM, 295
Imperial Chemical Industries, 262

InBev Corporation, 86
income statement, examples of, 205–206, 212,
    217–218
incumbent-generation leadership, 340–341
independent advisors/consultants, board of
    directors and, 253–254
industry peers, family business valuation
    and, 225–226
information resources
    business valuation, 214–215
    on family businesses, 21–24
    organizational structure and role of, 57–59
Initial public offerings (IPOs), 265
institutionalization of change, 306–307
intentionally-defective grantor trust (IDGT), estate
    planning, 195
interdependent teams, of next-generation family
    members, 99–100
interest expenses, return on equity and, 208–209
interests of next-generation family members,
    94–95
intergenerational growth, intrepreneurship and, 313
intergroup consultations, family/nonfamily
    management, change and, 304–305
interim CEOs, spouse as, 123
intrepreneurship, 313
inventor exit style, 115–116, 124
IRS Revenue Ruling 59-60, 213–214

J

J. M. Smucker case study, 256–257, 331–332
James, Michael, 252
jealousy, of CEO spouse, 122–123
John Brooke & Sons, 85
Johnson, Abigail, 86
Johnson, Edward C. III, 86
Johnson, Fisk, 41
Johnson, Herbert Fisk, 110
Johnson, Herbert Fisk Jr., 110–111, 311
Johnson, Samuel Curtis III, 103, 110–112, 116, 311
joint optimization
    competitive advantage of family businesses and,
        16–19
    in family businesses, 12–13
    lifecycle of family business and, 179–182

K

Kamath, K. V., 365–367
key ratios, family business accounting, 210, 212
Kimmel, Don, 153
Koenig, Ray, 61, 337
Koenig Equipment, 338–339
Kongo, Masakzu, 85
Kongo, Toshitaka, 85
Kongo Guni, 85

L

lack of control, business valuation discounts for, 228–229
language barriers of accounting, 202
leadership qualities and attributes
  at centennial firms, 339–340
  changing organizational culture and, 294–295
  evolution of change and, 295–297
  incumbent-generation leadership, 340–341
  next-generation family members, 92–97, 103–105
  positive-sum dynamics and, 315–316
  raw materials for change and, 297–298
  succession planning imperatives, 317–323
  successors' capacity for, 191–192
  transfer of power and, 116
  traps and pitfalls for new leaders, 296
legacy building, estate planning and, 197
legal agreements, guidelines for constructing, 44–45
Level 5 leaders, succession planning and continuity, 110–112
leverage effect, return on equity and, 208–210
Levi Strauss, 311
lifecycle of family business
  centennial firms examples of, 326–328
  parallel strategic planning and, 178–182
limited liability company, estate planning and, 193–194
liquidity policy
  appropriate return estimation, 221
  conflict management and, 46
  guidelines for, 42
Litzsinger, Mark, 307–308
L.L. Bean, 86
long-term perspective, competitive advantage of family businesses and, 19
Louisville Courier-Journal
  case study, 67–69
  family culture at, 29–30, 267
  transfer of power at, 109–110, 117, 192–193
Louisville Times, 68–69

M

Madco Company, 177
management-first businesses, 10
management structure
  business valuation and, 214–215
  competitive advantage of family businesses and, 16–19
  family-business advisory board and, 255
  family ownership and, case study, 134–137
  governance and, 247–248
  managers *vs.* owners and, 50–51
  nonfamily management guidelines, 231–244
  Reliance Industries case study, 362–367
  Valle family (pseud.) case study, 79–84

managerial worthiness, in next-generation family members, 96–97
manufacturing businesses, case studies of, 132
marketability discounts, business valuation and, 228–229
market value, sample valuation report, 347–354
marriage choices, next-generation family members and, 98
Marriott, Bill, 241
Marriott, John, 241
Marriott, Richard, 241
Marriott International, 241
Mars, Inc., 174
MBA programs, successor-development process and, 88
McIlhenny Company, 172, 334
Meritool, 115
Microsoft, 175
Milbar Corporation, 115
Milliken Corporation, 311
minority position, business valuation and, 228–229
mission statement, guidelines for, 44
monarch exit style, characteristics of, 112–113, 124
money management, for next-generation family members, 96
Monticelli, Marcello, 88
Morita, Akio, 312
motivation of nonfamily managers, 238
  family-business advisory board, 260
Mulally, Alan, 85
multiyear succession process, 87–88
Murdoch, James, 285
Murdoch, Rupert, 285

N

Nazario, Miguel, 157
negative free cash flow, 219
net present value, business valuation and, 222–224
net working capital investment, 203–204, 219–220
News Corp., 285
newspapers, family ownership of, 87, 120–121
New York Times, 87
next-generation family members
  career planning for, 96–97
  at centennial firms, 339–340
  challenges for, 91–92
  change management and, 309–311
  desirable attributes of, 93–94
  disagreements with, 101–103
  estate planning and role of, 192–193, 198
  family relations and, 97–98
  Ferré Media Group case study, 156–160
  interdependence of team members, 99–100
  interests of, 94–95
  interpersonal skills development in, 305

leadership qualities and attributes, 92–97, 103–105
managerial worthiness in, 96–97
money management for, 96
nonfamily managers and, 232–233
personalities of, 99
positive-sum dynamics and, 315–316
Reliance Industries case study, 361–367
rewards for, 90–91
sibling and cousin teams, 98–99
strategic planning, 168
transfer of power to, 109–110
next-generation members of family businesses
characteristics of successful succors, 89
competitive challenges for, 14
qualifications of, 87–89
succession planning and, 86–87
niche focusing, competitive advantage of family businesses and, 18–19
Nido, Carlos, 158
nonfamily management
beneficial environment for, 239–243
as bridging president/CEO, 238–243
career planning for, 235
case studies, 157–158
at centennial firms, 338–339
change management and intergroup consultation, 304–305
compensation and benefits, 235–237
estate planning and equity of, 195–196
family-business consultants, 243–244
family culture and, 237–238
governance practices, 233–234
guidelines for, 231–244
motivation and retention of, 238
next-generation family members and, 232–233
performance feedback, 237
sample letter by, 242
succession planning and, 234
nonfinancial returns and costs, business valuation and, 229–230
Nordstrom, Blake, 86

O

organic competencies, future survival and, 312–313
organizational competencies
future survival and, 312–313
resource-based perspective of competitive advantage, 15–19
value creation and, 173–174, 176
organizational culture
of centennial firms, 328–330
change in, 294–295
commitment planning, 306–307
continuity and, 293–294
development approaches to change, 303–306
evolution of, 296–302
institutionalization of change, 307–308
raw materials for, 297–298
systems theory perspective, 332–333
Organizational Dynamics journal, 22
organization development approach to change, 303–306
Osborne, Ignacio, 52, 56, 333–334, 336–340
Osborne, Tomas, 52, 333–334
Osborne family, 52, 333–334, 336–338
outcome goals, guidelines for, 44
owner-managers, performance feedback and, 237
ownership control
case study, 135
communication and policy making, 279–280
competitive advantage of family businesses and, 18–19
defined, 5
ownership-first businesses, 11
ownership structures
board of directors role, 55–57
buy-sell agreements, 60
classes of stock and, 60
defined, 49
design and execution of, 59–60
information, communication, and education for shareholders, 57–59
managers *vs.* owners, 50–51
overview of, 49–50
shareholder-firm relationship, governance of, 55
shareholder priorities, 51–52
shareholder responsibilities, 52–55
ownership transfer and estate planning inventory, 63–65
pitfalls of, 196–198
ownership-transfer policies, organizational design and, 59–60

P

Packard, David, 52, 294–295
parallel strategic planning, lifecycle of family business and, 178–182
parent-child relationships, of next-generation family members, 97–98
parsimony, in family business, 23–24
participation, defined, 5
particularism, in family business, 23–24
Partnership for Family Business, 107
patient capital
competitive advantage of family businesses and, 19
ownership-first businesses and, 11
ownership structure and, 50
value creation and, 173–174
Perdue, Frank, 86
Perdue, Jim, 86
Perdue Farms, 86

performance feedback
  nonfamily management, 237
  value creation and, 175
per-share value, business valuation and, 224
personalism, in family business, 23–24
personality traits, next-generation family members,
  99
personal responsibility, trust and commitment and,
  44–45
Peugeot Corporation, 85
phantom stock, ownership structure and, 60
physical assets, value creation and, 173–175
Pinedo, José, 58
planning guidelines, trust and commitment
  and, 41–44
point-of-purchase industry, case study, 142–144
policy making
  conflict management and, 46
  at family meetings, 279–280
  guidelines for, 44
  trust and commitment and, 41–44
Porter, Michael, 169–170
positive-sum dynamics, family and enterprise
  leadership and, 315–316
Precista Tools, 112
pricing strategies, value creation and, 175
Primera Hora newspaper, 71–72, 156–159, 326
primogeniture, next-generation family members and
  challenge of, 91
prioritization, shareholders' responsibility for, 53–54
procrastination, estate planning and, 196–197
product line development
  case studies of, 129, 144–147
  by centennial firms, 330–331
  organic competencies and, 312–313
  price and performance value, 175
  value creation and, 173–175
profitability measurements
  business valuation and, 214–215
  gross margin and profit margin, 207
  shareholders' understanding of, 58–59
profit margin
  defined, 207
  DuPont return on equity and, 208–210
promotion practices, family employment
  policy, 42–43
public companies
  family business valuation compared with, 224–226
  Sarbanes-Oxley regulations and, 264–266
Puerto Rican Cement, 70, 156, 157, 159, 325–326

Q

Qualis International, 111
quality control, competitive advantage of family
  businesses and, 18–19
Quandt family, 85

R

Randall, Dick, 369–372
Randall family, 369–372
RANFE (Rangel Ferré), 158–160
Rangel, Luisa, 73
Real Estate Development Partners, Inc. case study,
  277, 369–372
real estate investment trust (REIT), 241
rebellious succession, in family-owned
  business, 7
recapitalization of stock, estate planning
  and, 193–194
recruitment and selection criteria, family-business
  advisory board, 256–260
reinvestment strategies, competitive advantage of
  family businesses and, 16–19
relay race analogy, next-generation family members
  and challenge of, 92
Reliance Industries case study, 187, 355–367,
  375–378
research methodology, on family businesses, 21–24,
  343
resource-based perspective
  competitive advantage of family business
    and, 15–19
  lifecycle of family business and, 179–182
retail businesses, case study, 141–155
retention of nonfamily managers, 238
return. *See* appropriate return estimation
return on assets (ROA)
  financial performance of family business
    and, 250–252
  return on equity and, 208–210
return on equity (ROE), DuPont calculation of,
  208–210, 212
return on investment, competitive advantage of
  family businesses and, 18–19
Rigas, Gus, 252
Rigas, John, 251–252
Rigas, Timothy, 251–252
risk analysis
  appropriate return estimation, 221
  business valuation and, 214–215
Roberts, Brian, 101
Roberts, Ralph, 101
Rockefeller's Room 56, 268
Royal Dutch/Shell Group, 184–185

S

sales and distribution
  family business case study, 132–133
  financial statement analysis, 206–207
sales growth rate, business valuation and,
  225–226
Sánchez, Fernando, 157
Sanders, Harlan, 114

Sarbanes-Oxley Act of 2002, family-business advisory board and, 264–266
Schein, Edgar, 328
SC Johnson: A Family Company, 41, 103, 110, 116, 294, 311
Scotts Company, 86
Seattle Times Company, family culture in, 30–31
self-awareness, evolutionary change and, 296–297
self differentiation, family systems perspective and, 33–34
self-management
   evolutionary change and, 296–297
   policy making and, 44
selling, general, and administrative (SG&A) expenses
   gross margin and profit margin, 207
   income statement and, 205–206
senior advisor, spouse as, 120–121
service orientation, case study of, 147
shareholders
   annual shareholders' meeting, 268
   appropriate return estimation and effect of, 221
   at centennial firms, 338–339
   change management and, 304
   disagreements among, 50
   estate planning and role of, 191–192
   information, communication and education for, 57–59
   managers and, 51
   meetings of, 50, 56–57
   priorities of, 51–52
   responsibilities of, 52–55
   returns on equity or invested assets, responsibility for, 52
   shareholder-firm relationship, governance characteristics, 55–57
   strategic planning and, 53–54, 167–168
   Valle family (pseud.) case study, 79–84
   values and principles development by, 53
Shipflat literature holder, development of, 144–145
sibling relationships
   case study, 160–165
   of next-generation family members, 97–98
   team-building and, 98–99
Sidney Printing Works, 101, 310
Sinquefield, R. A., 221
six sigma process, 190
small family business, case studies, 139–141, 367–368, 373–375
Smart Growth: Critical Choices for Family Business Continuity, 313
Smucker, Paul, 331–332
Smucker, Richard, 256–257, 330–331
Smucker, Tim, 256–257, 330–331
social responsibility, of family businesses, 21

Sonnenfeld, Jeffrey, 112
Sony Corporation, 312
Soros, George, 114
Soros Fund Management, 114
speed and agility, estate planning and preservation of, 191–192
speed to market data, competitive advantage of family businesses and, 18–19
Spence, P. L., 112
spouse of CEO
   as business partner, 119
   as chief trust officer, 120
   as free agent, 121–122
   as "interim CEO," 123
   as jealous spouse, 122–123
   role types, 119–123
   as senior advisor/keeper of family values, 120–121
   succession planning and, 124–125
   transfer of power and role of, 117–125
SpringDot, Inc., 101
stakeholders
   family unity and continuity and, 40–41
   lifecycle of family business and, 179–182
   nonfamily CEO credibility with, 241
state inheritance taxes, 189
stewardship perspective, on family businesses, 20–21
stock-keeping units (SKUs), 311
Stocks, Bonds, Bills and Inflation, 221
Stokes, Patrick, 86
strategic planning
   brand equity, 175–176
   case study, 184
   competitive challenges and, 14
   customer-oriented company, 182–183
   customer-supplier integration, 177
   defined, 5
   disciplined execution, 183–185
   family-business advisory board, 260–262
   in family businesses, 169–186
   financial resources, 174–175
   firm lifecycle and, 178–182
   Grupo Ferré case study, 157–160
   guidelines for, 167–186
   organizational capabilities, 176
   physical assets, 175
   product price and performance, 175
   shareholders' development of, 53–54
   value creation and unique business models, 173–174
   vision of family-controlled companies and, 185–186
   zero-sum family dynamic and, 171–172
strengths, weaknesses, opportunities, and threats (SWOT) analysis, strategic planning and, 170–171
subcontractor policy, guidelines for, 41

succession planning. *See also* next-generation family
    members
  case studies, 111, 127–155
  CEO as architect of, 110–112
  CEO governance, 107–109
  change management and, 303–304
  continuity and, 110–112
  disagreements and, 101–103
  dyadic consultation and, 304
  exit styles, 112–117
  family-business advisory board, 263–264
  in family-owned business, 6–7
  FFr case study, 152–155
  fictional example of, 317–323
  Grupo Ferré case study, 73–77
  guidelines for, 85–105
  latter-generation family members, rewards and
    challenges, 90–92
  leadership capacity and, 191–192
  nonfamily management and, 234
  respecting the past and focusing on the future
    and, 103
  spouse of CEO, role of, 117–123
  transfer of power, 109–110, 124–125
  trust building among family members, 117
  vision statement and, 100–101
successor-development process, 88
SuperGrip sign holder, development of, 145–146
survival statistics for family business, 179–182
  change management and, 307–308
  competitive advantage and, 311–312
  organic competencies and, 312–313
systems theory
  centennial firms and, 332–333
  family business model, 7–9
  lifecycle of family business and, 179–182
  strategic planning and disciplined execution,
    183–185

T

Tagiuri, R., 104–105
task competency, nonfamily managers, 232–233
taxation, estate taxes, 189–199
tax exemptions
  estate planning and, 188–189
  pitfalls of, 197
team-building consultants, 276–278
third-generation family members, succession
    development and, 88
Thomas, Dave, 114
time compression diseconomies, latter-generation
    family members and, 90–91
time lags, business growth and, 168–169
Timken, Tim, 330–331, 336, 339–340

Timken Company, 330–331, 336, 339–340
Tobin's Q, financial performance of family business
    and, 250–252
tolerance, family-business interaction factor
    and, 38–39
top-management team, governance and, 269
total asset turnover, 207
  DuPont return on equity and, 208–210
total costs, competitive advantage of family
    businesses and, 19
total-value formula, nonfinancial returns and costs,
    229–230
toy boat strategy model, 54
Toyoda, Akio, 85
Toyoda family, 85
Toyota Corporation, 85
transfer of power
  CEO exit styles and, 112–117
  succession planning and, 109–110
  trust building and, 117
transfer-of-wealth approaches, estate planning and,
    190–191
transition czar exit style, 116–117, 124
transition state of business evolution, 301–302
  family-management-ownership structure and,
    302–303
triangulation, family systems perspective and, 33–34
trust in family businesses
  conflict management and, 45–46
  family-business interaction factor, 38–39
  family culture, case studies of, 29–31
  family emotional intelligence and, 37–38
  family meetings as tool for, 39–40
  family systems perspective, 32–34
  family unity and continuity, and 40–41
  genograms and family messages and, 34–37
  guidelines for building, 27–46
  information and communication and, 58–59
  planning and policy making guidelines, 41–44
  transfer power and, 117
  trusts, legal agreements and personal
    responsibility and, 44–45
  zero-sum dynamics and family culture, 31–32
trusts
  estate planning and role of, 195
  guidelines for constructing, 44–45
Tyson, Don, 86
Tyson, John, 86
Tyson Foods, 86

U

U. S. Steel, 175
unified credit exemption, 189
unused assets, cost of, 206–207

V

vacation policies, nonfamily management, 236–237
value. *See also* business valuation
 brand equity and, 173–176
 competitive advantages and creation of, 309
 customer-supplier integration and, 177
 estate planning and, 193–194
 family-business interaction factor and addition of, 38–39
 financial resources and creation of, 173–175
 organizational competency and creation of, 173–174, 176
 physical assets and creation of, 173–175
 product price and performance and, 173–175
 sources of, 173–174
 strategic planning and creation of, 167–168
 unique business models and creation of, 173–174
values and principles
 of centennial firms, 330–331
 FFr case study, 147–148
 nonfamily management and, 234
 shareholders' development of, 53
 spouse as keeper of, 120–121
Venetis, Peter, 252
Viena Capellanes, 341
Virtual, Inc., 158
vision statement
 of centennial firms, 337–338
 Grupo Ferré case study, 76–77
 next-generation family members and, 100–101
 strategic planning and, 185–186
Voom Company, 310

W

Wall Street Journal, 87, 284–285
Washington Post Company, 87, 120–121, 176
wavering succession, in family-owned business, 7
Welch, Jack, 109, 115, 190, 295
Wemco, Inc., 247
WHAS radio, 68–69
whole-family forums, change management and, 305–306
wills
 estate planning and role of, 188–189
 succession planning and role of, 110–112
Wm. Wrigley Jr. Company, 174
Work-Out innovation, 190
Wright, Frank Lloyd, 111

Z

zero-sum dynamics. *See also* positive-sum dynamics
 centennial firms and, 326
 conflict management and, 45–46
 family culture and, 31–32
 family meetings as alternative to, 39–40
 strategic planning and, 171–172
Zildjian, Craigie, 85
Zildjian, Debbie, 85
Zildjian Cymbal Company, 85